Data Analysis for Research Designs

A Series of Books in Psychology

EDITORS:

Richard C. Atkinson
Gardner Lindzey
Richard F. Thompson

Data Analysis for Research Designs

Analysis of Variance and
Multiple Regression/Correlation Approaches

. . .

GEOFFREY KEPPEL
SHELDON ZEDECK
University of California at Berkeley

W. H. FREEMAN AND COMPANY
NEW YORK

Library of Congress Cataloging-in-Publication Data

Keppel, Geoffrey.
    Data analysis for research designs: analysis of variance and multiple regression/correlation
approaches/Geoffrey Keppel, Sheldon Zedeck.
      p.   cm. — (A Series of books in psychology)
    Bibliography: p.
    Includes index.
    ISBN 0-7167-1991-6.
    1. Social sciences—Statistical methods. 2. Correlation (Statistics) 3. Regression
analysis. 4. Analysis of variance.
I. Zedeck, Sheldon. II. Title. III. Series.
HA29.K435   1989
300'.1'5195—dc19
                                                  88-32222
                                                   CIP

Printed in the United States of America

  4 5 6 7 8 9 0 VB 9 9 8 7 6 5 4

Contents in Brief

· · ·

Contents

. . .

Preface

. . .

This book brings together two seemingly independent methods of data analysis, the analysis of variance (ANOVA) and multiple regression and correlation (MRC). Historically, ANOVA and MRC were developed for use with different classes of designs—ANOVA for the analysis of experiments and MRC for the analysis of nonexperimental designs and correlational data. Thus, researchers would choose ANOVA when the data to be analyzed came from *experiments* and MRC when the data came from *correlational studies*. Actually, both analytical approaches are based on the same statistical model and, under certain circumstances, produce *identical* statistical results. We hope that an increased familiarity with both procedures will be associated with the introduction of correlational research, generally requiring the use of MRC, into areas of research in which *experiments* are the rule and with an increased use of sophisticated experimental designs and analyses in areas in which *correlational designs* are more common. We also believe that an understanding of both approaches leads to a better understanding of either one.

For example, the analysis of covariance is more easily understood from the perspective of MRC; knowing this removes a great deal of the mystery that usually surrounds the analysis when it is viewed through the perspective of ANOVA. By the same token, the strong emphasis on planned comparisons generally associated

with the analysis of experimental designs and ANOVA can be profitibly applied
to the MRC analysis of field data and correlational designs, as we show in the later
chapters of the book. Finally, we believe that students and researchers should be
sufficiently comfortable with *both* approaches so that they can move freely from
one to the other when such an interchange is appropriate and can select the correct one when it is not. Facility with both ANOVA and MRC will contribute to
flexibility and creativity in analyzing a set of data, regardless of whether the data
are derived from an experiment or from a correlational design.

The subject matter of this book is relevant to a broad audience of students
and researchers. Since our goal is to familiarize experimenters with MRC and correlationalists with ANOVA, researchers in relatively diverse fields may find our
approach challenging and appealing. Thus, the book is appropriate for students
in psychology, sociology, social welfare, public policy, business administration, or
any field that deals with research and experiments in the behavioral and social
sciences.

The Organization of the Book

Our intent is revealed by the order in which we consider various topics in this
book. In general, we begin with the analysis of experiments, in which both ANOVA
and MRC are appropriate, and then turn to the analysis of nonexperimental or
correlational designs, in which only MRC is usually appropriate. The progression
is gradual, allowing the reader to understand the inner workings of the two procedures in relatively simple settings. The first nine chapters, for example, are devoted
to background discussions leading to the analysis of the completely randomized,
single-factor design (Chaps. 9 to 12). We then discuss the analysis of more complicated designs—factorial designs and within-subjects designs (designs with
repeated measures)—by building on the principles established for the earlier and
simpler analysis procedures. We give equal weight to ANOVA and MRC in all
relevant discussions. As the reader masters any given chapter, he or she should
become equally familiar with ANOVA and MRC and competent in applying either
or both (when appropriate, of course) to the analysis of an experiment.

We consider first the general nature of research (Chap. 1) and then the
special qualities of experimental and correlational designs (Chap. 2). Following
these introductory chapters, we present—as a review for most readers—the basic
statistical concepts that underlie ANOVA and MRC (Chaps. 3 to 5). We then develop ANOVA in the context of a simple, two-group experiment (Chap. 6) and
immediately apply MRC, in the form of the product-moment correlation, to the
analysis of the same design (Chap. 7). We present hypothesis testing for the two
procedures in Chap. 8. Both ANOVA and MRC are expanded to include the analysis
of experiments in which a single independent variable consists of any number of
levels or treatment conditions (Chaps. 9 and 10). It is at this point that we first
introduce MRC in its own right. An important theme is underscored in Chap. 11,
where we emphasize the use of planned, focused comparisons between selected

treatment means in the thoughtful analysis of an experiment. This approach to data analysis is easily conducted with either analysis procedure. We complete our discussion of the single-factor design with an examination of the consequences of including two or more statistical tests in the analysis of a single experiment (Chap. 12). We consider in the next three chapters (Chaps. 13 to 15) the analysis of *factorial experiments*, in which two independent variables are manipulated simultaneously in the same study. Again, we focus on the use of analytical comparisons in the detailed examination of the results of such designs (Chaps. 14 and 15). In Chaps. 16 to 18, we turn to the analysis of more complicated designs in which subjects serve in some or even all the treatment conditions—designs which are extremely popular in the behavioral sciences. We summarize and extend the analysis of experiments to multifactor designs in general (Chap. 19), outlining how we can extend the analyses of simpler designs to those that are more complicated.

Up to this point, ANOVA and MRC are *totally interchangeable* in the sense that the statistical results, and consequently the conclusions from the experiments, are identical. We discuss correlational and other nonexperimental designs in Chaps. 20 and 21; generally, designs of these sorts are appropriately analyzed only by MRC. Chapter 20 describes three major uses of MRC—explaining behavior (simultaneous analysis), predicting behavior (stepwise analysis), and testing theories and causal models (hierarchical analysis). Chapter 21 considers several important applications of the hierarchical analysis to correlational research: exerting statistical control over variables (partial and semipartial correlation), studying the interaction of variables, and analyzing the results of pretest-posttest studies.

We conclude our coverage of research designs by considering a number of issues that relate both to experiments and to correlational studies. Chapter 22, for example, discusses an additional control procedure—analysis of covariance—which is frequently used in the analysis of experimental and nonexperimental studies, while Chap. 23 offers an examination of trend analysis, which may be applied to data obtained from experiments and correlational designs. Finally, we examine the analysis of experiments with unequal sample sizes (Chap. 24) in which MRC offers a statistically elegant solution to the complications created when factorial designs become "unbalanced" through the inadvertent loss of subjects during the course of the study. An epilogue (Chap. 25), in which we offer a comparison of the relative advantages of ANOVA and MRC when they are applied to the analysis of different types of experimental designs, concludes the book.

Distinctive Features of the Book

We now mention several distinctive features of this book that may be of interest to an instructor.

Equal Treatment of ANOVA and MRC. We have already noted that we treat ANOVA and MRC equally in our discussions of the analysis of experimental designs. Our experience in the classroom convinces us that MRC is more easily learned when it is introduced *gradually* side-by-side with the arithmetically simpler

ANOVA, which gains its simplicity by the use of designs in which the independent (or manipulated) variables are *independent* of one another—a condition that rarely happens in nonexperimental and correlational research. By the time we turn to the analysis of these latter designs, the student is able to quickly grasp the additional complications created when the variables of interest are intercorrelated rather than independent.

Simple Numerical Examples. We have chosen our numerical examples of the analysis of experiments so that it is possible (and reasonable) to perform the calculations for both ANOVA and MRC by hand with the assistance of a relatively inexpensive electronic calculator (under $30) that is programmed to calculate product-moment correlations (r) and the usual statistical by-products (means, standard deviations, and regression equations). This permits students to acquire a "hands-on" understanding of how ANOVA and MRC work. After students experiment with the alternative formulas for the product-moment correlation that we provide in Chap. 5, calculating r with deviation scores, means and standard deviations, and actual raw scores, they can then use the specialized calculators to ease the computational burden, to follow the examples, and to complete most of the exercises in the text. We believe that computer analysis, which will become necessary in some of the later chapters, is better introduced *after* students have an intuitive and quantitative grasp of the analysis techniques. Not only will they be able to check computer analyses by hand, which is always a good idea, but they will be able to conduct additional analyses—again by hand—when it is inconvenient to return to the computer for this same information.

We use a single experimental context in which to illustrate all the experimental designs we consider in this book. This contributes to the natural progression from one type of design—for example, the single-factor—to designs of greater complexity—factorial designs and designs with repeated measures. Instructors may wish to introduce additional examples, perhaps more complicated, in their classes to round out their coverage of these designs.

Emphasis on Planned Comparisons. Most research in the behavioral sciences is theoretically motivated. Research is not created in a vacuum, but as an attempt to evaluate theoretical explanations and to add new knowledge to the existing data base in a given field of study. We emphasize the use of analytical procedures that help researchers evaluate the specific research hypotheses that lead to the design of their studies and to illuminate the findings they obtain. Planned comparisons are discussed throughout our treatment of experimental designs and extended to the analysis of nonexperimental and correlational designs in the chapters that follow.

Exercises. Relatively simple exercises appear at the end of most chapters. In order to encourage students to "test" their newly acquired knowledge, we have provided relatively detailed answers to these problems in an appendix. As with our continuing experimental example, we provide continuity in the exercises by adapting the problems introduced earlier in the text to illustrate the more complex experimental designs.

Using this Book in the Classroom

This book was written for the advanced undergraduate or first-year graduate student in the behavioral sciences. Students have a heterogeneous background in statistics. Most have had a beginning undergraduate course in statistics, which, for many, was taken two to three years prior to this course, at the start of their academic training in college. Our early chapters are designed to bring students to approximately the same level of competence by the time they are exposed to the analysis of the single-factor design, beginning in Chap. 6. Many instructors will prefer to integrate their lectures and our book with assignments using computers from the very beginning, although we believe that the computer is better introduced in the context of Chap. 16, where we introduce within-subjects designs and where the computer and relevant software programs become a necessity. Before this occurs, we generally illustrate the analyses of completely randomized designs (Chaps. 10 to 15) in our own lectures with multilevel problems that *have* been analyzed by computer, providing students with examples of the coding strategies we recommend for the different analyses and printouts from actual computer analyses *before* they learn how to use the computer and the programs themselves. By delaying students' exposure to the computer until it is necessary, we are able to focus on the logic of the designs and analyses, which often is obscured when students learn to rely on statistical software packages too early in their training.

It would be difficult to cover the entire book in one quarter or one semester. What instructors choose to omit depends, of course, on their goals and emphases. A "minimum" course would include the analysis of the more common experimental designs (Chaps. 1 to 17) and the more common uses of MRC in the analysis of nonexperimental and correlational data (Chaps. 20 and 21). The remaining chapters (Chaps. 18 and 19 and 22 to 24) are included for advanced students and for researchers who must deal with the complexities discussed in them. Chapter 25, the epilogue, should be read by students whether the course extends over one or two quarters or semesters.

This book covers the *essence* of the designs most frequently represented in the literature, namely, between- and within-subjects designs with one or two independent variables. Those students who would like a more comprehensive discussion of only experimental designs may want to consult Keppel's *Design and Analysis* (1982), which provides more detail on simple experimental designs and more systematic coverage of complex designs. *Design and Analysis*, however, does not emphasize the equivalence of ANOVA and MRC in the analysis of designs, nor does it cover such topics as the analysis of correlational studies and nonexperimental designs. In order to facilitate your switching between these two books, we have provided appropriate page references to *Design and Analysis*, and we have adopted a similar notational system for this book.

Acknowledgments

We wish to thank the American Statistical Association, *Biometrics*, and the *Biometrika* Trustees for their permission to reproduce statistical tables in this book.

We are indebted to a number of individuals who provided advice and assistance in the preparation of this book. We should mention first the useful comments we have received over the years from students in our classes, who suffered through draft chapters in varying degrees of development. We received helpful suggestions from Scott E. Maxwell, University of Notre Dame, and John Schuck, Bowling Green State University. We wish to mention the assistance of others in the production of this book, including Sheila Keppel who helped proofread the statistical tables. We also thank W. Hayward Rogers of W. H. Freeman for his early enthusiasm and interest in this project; his successor, Jonathan Cobb, for his continued support; Richard K. Mickey for his expert and constructive editing of the manuscript; and the production staff of W. H. Freeman—the project editor, Stephen Wagley; the designer, Lynn Pieroni; and the production coordinator, Julia DeRosa—for their careful attention to details. Finally, we wish to express our appreciation to our wives and families (Sheila, Melissa, and Peter Keppel; Marti, Cindy, Jason, and Tracy Zedeck) who cheerfully (usually) tolerated our preoccupation with the book.

Each of us wants to acknowledge the contribution of the other to our advancement and development in design and data analysis. This book had its origins when the experimentalist (GK) audited a data analysis course taught by the correlationalist (SZ); a year later, the roles of student and teacher were reversed. Since that time, we have jointly offered a data analysis course in which we not only taught our students, but each other as well. We debated the different approaches to data analysis and the philosophies (and biases) associated with them in and out of class. We learned from each other, and we compromised on what is the "best" way to analyze data. Both of us believe we are better off because of this collaboration and we are pleased to see this text as a product of the collaboration. We wish to note that the order of the authors is arbitrarily alphabetical. Though many have commented on our book during its development, we take equal responsibility for the end result.

Geoffrey Keppel
Sheldon Zedeck

Data Analysis for Research Designs

1

Introduction

. . .

Although this is a textbook about data analysis, we will start by drawing your attention to a seemingly different subject. A key point, one that we will return to again and again, is that data analysis alone does not enable researchers to achieve their main goal, namely, to answer questions. To reach that goal, researchers must concentrate on their design: it must be as sound as possible, and it must be appropriate for the questions they want answered. In this first chapter, we are going to concentrate on the purposes of research, the role of statistics and data analysis in research, and the steps required to conduct research. In exploring these issues, we will present alternative designs and introduce concepts and terms. Some of the terms we will not fully define in this chapter; we introduce them here, however, because they apply to particular points we are using to illustrate the content of the text. Also, in this chapter, we will put forth our own views on the subject of data analysis. In particular, we will identify some of the issues we would consider in choosing between two strategies for data analysis: analysis of variance (ANOVA) and multiple regression and correlation (MRC).

1.1 PURPOSES OF RESEARCH

The primary objective of a research project is to answer questions in such a way that the results, conclusions, and inferences drawn from the study can be offered with confidence and integrity. To accomplish this objective, one needs to be successful in *asking* (posing) the questions, *designing* procedures by which information (data) can be collected and gathered, *analyzing* the data, and *interpreting* the results. Performing these tasks in a systematic way allows researchers to pursue the fundamental goals of any science: to understand, explain, and predict phenomena.

Asking Questions

In the behavioral sciences, many kinds of questions can be asked. Consider the following. At what stage in infancy does the neonate begin to distinguish shapes and forms? Do people attribute successful performance on a task to internal or to external factors? Does learning take place in the subcortex? Is job stress greater for male or for female executives? What are the characteristics of sensory memory? Is psychoanalysis effective? Do known political assassins have a particular psychological profile? Will use of home computers facilitate creative thinking? Are the Democrats viewed as the party of the working class? Are Hispanics different from other cultures in their way of dealing with social inequality?

Several characteristics of the above questions illustrate important points made in this book. First, the questions represent several disciplines within the behavioral sciences: psychology, sociology, and educational psychology. We have deliberately chosen such examples to make the point that the material and content presented in this text are not unique to a particular specialty, but can be used by educational psychologists, cognitive experimental psychologists, industrial/organizational psychologists, biological psychologists, sociologists, political scientists, and many others.

Second, most of the questions are reasonably unambiguous and specific, focussing on only a small area of the body of research. In general, they can ultimately be posed as a dichotomy—yes or no, more or less, larger or smaller. The significant aspect, and one that will be emphasized throughout this text, is that the questions asked can be answered by straightforward analytical comparisons that can ultimately be reduced to a contrast between two entities, groups, or combinations of groups. We will refer to such questions or analytical comparisons as **single-*df* comparisons** (single–degree-of-freedom comparisons—here is the first example of a term that we now merely introduce but will discuss more fully in subsequent chapters).

Third, all the questions contain critical factors that are potential objects of investigation; such factors are referred to as **variables**. Basically, a variable is a property, characteristic, or quality in which individuals, animals, or objects differ among themselves. In some cases a variable is defined *qualitatively*; for example, the gender of executives can be of two kinds—male and female. In other cases it is defined *quantitatively*; for example, the number of days it takes before an infant can differentiate among a number of shapes is a quantitative variable. The specific measurement and operationalization of quantitative and qualitative variables will be an important consideration in this book.

Fourth, some questions appear to make the group the focus of interest whereas others focus on the individual. The distinction between a group focus and an individual focus is reflected in a traditional view of research in which psychology is divided into two subdisciplines. The division was clearly enunciated by Cronbach (1957), who believed that two historic schools of method and thought existed in psychology—the experimental and the correlational. Experimental psychology has traditionally focused on differences among *average levels* of performance obtained from groups of subjects receiving different treatment and has essentially ignored the performance of individuals making up each group. In fact, researchers working in this tradition have viewed any deviation from the average performance within a group as uncontrolled variability, or "error." In contrast, correlational psychology focuses on exactly this variability, treating the variation among individuals as the object of study; thus, it is the study of *individual differences*. As will be emphasized throughout this book, however, this distinction is unnecessary from the point of view of data analysis. We intend to demonstrate that whether the researcher is interested in group differences as reflected by group means or in the particular individual differences within groups, either the traditional ANOVA or MRC technique of data analysis might be appropriate; the choice depends on the design used to collect the data.

To further elaborate, the traditional distinction between experimental psychology and correlational psychology has focused on the point of interest for the researcher—the typical group member as defined by the average level of the group or the variation among group members on one variable relative to the treatment received. Unfortunately, this distinction of purpose has carried over to distinctions of design and analysis. We maintain that whereas it is useful to speak in terms of experimental and correlational *designs*, it is unnecessary to maintain the distinction between experimental and correlational *statistics* (ANOVA and MRC, respectively), since the results are statistically identical. This latter point will be repeatedly stated and demonstrated throughout this book.

Related to the above is a fifth characteristic, namely, that questions can be posed specifically either to explore *differences* between two or more treatment groups on a particular performance variable or to explore *relationships* among variables (in this case, the correlation between variation in group membership and variation in performance). Another major purpose of this text is to convince you that finding differences among groups is *logically equivalent* to looking for relationships among variables. The apparent dissimilarity between an emphasis on differences and an emphasis on relationships, as indicated above, corresponds to the traditional division of psychology into the two subdisciplines recognized by Cronbach (1957). Our goal in this book is to eliminate the schism between advocates of the two analytical approaches by demonstration and by appeal to intuitive logic and sense.

Comment.   When you ask a research question, you raise several issues, and you have to address these issues in the course of your research. The solutions for the various issues are not unique. Concern for and response to the issues, however, will influence the type of analysis you perform on the information you have collected. Consequently, if you examine the list of issues we have raised up to this point, what you should grasp is that you have choices in the "*how*" of asking questions, taking measurements, analyzing results, and placing emphasis. We anticipate that by the time you have gone through this book, you will understand that some choices are better than others.

Reasons for Research

Another factor—besides the kind of question asked—that influences the type of analysis, and, perhaps even more important, the whole of research, is the reason for the research. In other words, why has the researcher asked the question? What is the goal in designing research to answer the particular question? The answers to these questions are crucial, since often the design of research depends on the particular purpose that the research is intended to serve. The experimentalist and the correlationalist may differ in their orientation toward research design, but they do research for similar reasons, and the framing of their questions is essentially equivalent. In this section, we will briefly consider the most common purposes of research: (1) exploration, (2) description, (3) explanation, and (4) prediction. These purposes are not mutually exclusive. Research is often undertaken to accomplish more than one purpose. However, for now, they can be considered to be useful ways of categorizing the reasons for conducting research.

Exploration. Research is often undertaken to explore a topic of interest. Students often do exploratory research in order to determine whether they are interested in a subject or will enjoy doing more extensive research in it. Exploratory studies are often done to satisfy curiosity, to test the feasibility of undertaking a more detailed and precise study, and to try out ideas and methods for future research. Results from such studies provide insights into a phenomenon and suggest ways for more rigid testing. In many regards, such research is undertaken as a *pilot study* to determine whether subsequent research is likely to be fruitful.

We do not mean to suggest that exploratory research is loose or haphazard. Rather, it serves as a preliminary step in the development of more systematic and programmatic research.

Description. Many researchers are interested in precisely describing or classifying situations, events, and people (or groups). Descriptive statistics are often gathered for the purpose of summarizing data, or, more precisely, for showing typical or representative values of the variable studied. For example, we often want to know characteristics of various populations or subgroups. We might be interested in the average starting salary for new MBAs, or the ethnic breakdown of those who voted for a candidate in the last election, or the Scholastic Aptitude Test (SAT) scores for those who are enrolled in college preparatory courses. Descriptive research will give us answers to such questions. Do not assume, however, that descriptive research is the simplest. You will need to consider sampling and measurement issues such as reliability and validity—issues that are discussed in texts such as the one by Ghiselli, Campbell, and Zedeck (1981).

Explanation. Reporting *what* someone has done is description; studying *why* something is done is explanation. The crucial component of any explanatory study is examining variables or concepts in tandem to determine the associative relationships or cause-and-effect relationships. We want to learn whether the X variable is "causing" the Y variable, Y is causing X, or a third variable Z is influencing X

and Y. Explanatory studies usually involve a large network of results from which the reasons for the occurrence of the behavior can be deduced.

Prediction.   As we have said, researchers often wish to establish relationships between at least two variables. Research is often undertaken for the purpose of using information on one variable to predict something about an individual subject on the second variable. Formal prediction studies are the basis of personnel psychology, where relationships between test scores and subsequent on-the-job performance obtained from one group of individuals are used to predict the performance of new applicants on the basis of *their* test scores.

1.2   MYTHS ABOUT DATA ANALYSIS

There are many myths about data analysis and its relationship to research. Of particular concern for this book are several myths associated with the differences between analysis of variance (ANOVA) and multiple regression and correlation (MRC), which we will now consider in some detail.

Our primary purpose in this book is to demonstrate that ANOVA and MRC— although they are different tools for data analysis—are equivalent in terms of the conclusions that can be drawn from their application to a set of data. The design under which the data are collected, however, may determine which strategy for analysis is appropriate: MRC and ANOVA are both appropriate for experimental designs, but only MRC is appropriate for most nonexperimental designs. (The distinction between the two kinds of designs and the appropriateness of the two strategies will be elaborated in later sections.) We have several reasons for wanting to demonstrate the statistical equivalence of the two methods. First, until relatively recently (Cohen, 1968), ANOVA and MRC have been treated as two distinct analytical approaches. It is often assumed that ANOVA is appropriate for data collected in an experiment conducted in a laboratory whereas MRC is most appropriate for data collected in nonexperimental designs, in a field setting, or via surveys. Second, it has also been assumed that ANOVA concentrates on statistical significance levels, *t* ratios, *F* ratios, and the like, and that, in contrast, MRC concentrates on indices of strengths of relationships and correlational coefficients such as *r* and *R*. Third, tradition has it that only ANOVA can be used to find cause-and-effect relationships whereas MRC is restricted to demonstrations of relationships among variables, that is, to showing that variables covary.

We could easily dispel these myths by showing the equivalence of ANOVA and MRC by algebraic procedures. Both techniques are based on general linear models in which the basic observation (the raw data describing an event) can be decomposed into effects and error components. In fact, it is easy to demonstrate that ANOVA is a special case of MRC. We prefer, however, to demonstrate this equivalence by applying both techniques to the *same* set of data collected in a design for which both techniques are appropriate, namely, an *experiment*, and showing that they yield the *same* statistical results from which we can then draw conclusions and inferences. We do this instead of a proof so as not to perpetuate a new myth that seems to be emerging—that is, that MRC and ANOVA are totally *interchangeable* under *all* circumstances.

Our categorization of the last statement as a myth is not contradictory to our earlier statement that it is a myth to assume that MRC and ANOVA are distinct. The two approaches *are* algebraically equivalent—but which should be applied is dependent on the *design* used to collect the data. Also, demonstrating equivalence by application should illustrate the advantages and disadvantages of each.

A more basic point now needs to be emphasized. Today, in most cases, data are analyzed by means of a computer, but the computer does not "know" how the data have been collected or which research paradigm has been used. It is the design that allows one to make either causal or relational conclusions, and not whether the data have been analyzed by ANOVA or MRC. Cause-and-effect statements can be made if the research design is set up to demonstrate causality. In essence, then, we intend to emphasize the design as the key to interpretations and conclusions to be drawn and to show that the analytical technique is in fact a tool for researchers that permits them to test the reliability or confidence of the conclusion. In some cases, ANOVA and MRC can be applied interchangeably; in other cases, MRC may be more appropriate (recall that MRC is the more general model whereas ANOVA is a special case). It is because of these "other cases" that we will go through the demonstration of equivalence and, in addition, indicate the conditions in which one strategy is preferable to or more appropriate than the other. The key aspects of these "other cases" are the issues we raised when we discussed the art of asking questions. For example, gender of the subject in a stress study may require an MRC analysis. In particular, the types of variables and the foci of the researcher's interest play a role in choosing the strategy for data analysis. What that role is will be elaborated upon throughout the book.

1.3 CONDUCTING RESEARCH PROJECTS: AN OVERVIEW

Your instructor has most likely informed you by this time that one of the requirements of the course is to conduct your own piece of research. What follows should help you get started and, perhaps of most importance, show you how *we* undertake a research project.

Posing a Question

Your first reaction to your instructor's requirement is likely to be, What am I going to study? Do not feel discouraged; this is a normal reaction. At the outset of this chapter we indicated that the objective of research is to answer questions. No doubt, you have questions about the findings and the theory within your discipline of interest. The starting point in your research is to take your interests or ideas and put them into a question.

Earlier, we presented a number of questions; now we will try some more. For example: Is a satisfied employee a better performer? Can people's prejudice be alleviated by getting them involved with members of other races? Does immediate feedback on an exam improve learning? Does enrichment of the environment yield changes in the brain? Questions like these can be derived from one or more of the following sources:

1. The scientific literature
2. Social issues
3. Your general interest in the discipline
4. Ideas suggested by others
5. Elaboration or extension of your previous research
6. Daily observations that have stimulated your curiosity
7. Your own "theory"

These sources are obvious and varied, and you can undoubtedly think of others. Nevertheless, once your question is posed, you have begun research. Now the research process is a matter of formalizing and structuring the question and its components into something that can be tested.

Conceptualizing the Question

Each of the above questions contains at least two basic units, variables, or concepts—for example, satisfaction and performance, prejudice and involvement, feedback and learning, and enrichment and brain development. These concepts, however, are relatively abstract and consequently need some elaboration, specification, and precision. For example, what does satisfaction mean? Is it a belief, a state of happiness, an affective reaction, or something entirely different? Satisfaction toward what object? The job? the task? the salary? Is performance a general behavior? an output? a specific domain such as quality of work? Does "changes in the brain" mean structural change or chemical change?

Specifying precisely what the terms mean *and* linking the concepts by a statement of relationship are the essential steps in formulating a *theory*. A theory deals with the logical deductions or assumptions that are used to describe relationships. Research offers a means for seeing whether these relationships actually exist as we believe them to exist.

A theory contains at least two theoretical units that are connected by an indication of the systematic relationship between them. For example, we can propose the following theoretical statements for the questions above:

1. Assembly-line workers who have positive feelings toward their tasks will produce more units per hour than those with negative feelings.
2. Willingness to hire a minority person will be greater after the employer has written a 10-page document supporting equal employment opportunity.
3. Correcting and instructing a student on his or her mistakes immediately after a test will result in better performance on the next test.
4. Living in a stimulating and challenging environment is associated with increased enzyme activity in the cortex.

Tests of the theory or parts of the theory are begun by using the deductions to formulate **research hypotheses**. The examples of theory given above are, in essence, research hypotheses. Research hypotheses are proposed answers to the questions you hope to resolve conclusively by means of your research project. Notice that we have made the questions more specific and refined so that it is now possible to operationalize the concepts.

Each of the above statements involves only two specific units. Usually, however, a theory is a general and more or less comprehensive set of relationships that deal with a particular phenomenon. Hypotheses may also take the form of deductions from a much more elaborate theoretical formulation. For example, Piaget (1965) proposed a theoretical model that suggests that there are three main stages of mental growth or cognitive development; within each of these stages, there are substages. A specific research question that can be posed on the basis of the broader theory is, What is the relationship between extent of cognitive development in the first stage and facility of language development?

You may have been exposed to the concept of a **null hypothesis** in an earlier course. Research hypotheses are not the same as null hypotheses, however. Whereas the former are statements of the relationship between units, the latter are *statistical* expressions of the relationship between the units. In particular, null hypotheses state that there is *no* difference between groups or *no* relationship between the concepts. (In Chap. 8 we will consider null hypotheses in more detail.)

Operationalizing the Concepts

Once you have isolated the concepts from your original question, you need to further refine them to the point where you can specify the steps, operations, or procedures needed to measure them. The task of operationalizing terms is equivalent to asking the question, How do you know it when you see it? Satisfaction, for example, conceptualized as a positive feeling toward a task, can be operationalized as a 10-item questionnaire to which respondents indicate, say, their degree of liking (on a 5-point scale) for each of 10 aspects of a task such as autonomy, challenge, interest, or sense of accomplishment. An alternative operationalization is to assess the degree of pleasure one appears to be having while doing a task; this assessment can be made by independent judges or observers. The point, for now, is that a concept can have alternative operationalizations.

To turn to another area of interest, an enriched environment can be operationalized as an environment that contains five objects to manipulate, three paths to explore, and six problems to solve, as opposed to an impoverished environment in which there are no objects, paths, or problems. Or environmental enrichment can be determined by assessing the wealth in a community.

Appropriate description of the operationalization of concepts is crucial to our assessment of the appropriateness of the conclusions as well as to attempts to replicate a study. If you wish to retest a hypothesis that has been studied by someone else, then you need to know the exact details of the earlier researcher's procedures, stimuli, instruments, measures, instructions, and other factors that formed the basis for his or her conclusions.

Methodology

A methodology is a process by which data are collected. Behavioral scientists have generally used four types of methodology to collect data: (1) case studies; (2) content analysis; (3) experiments; and (4) nonexperiments such as field studies, survey research, and correlational, naturally occurring designs. We will consider each type briefly in this overview and return to the discussion of experiments and nonexperiments in Chap. 2.

Case Studies.   The **case study** is an in-depth, detailed analysis and examination of a small number of subjects, or of a single subject (case), group, or event. Often the researcher is an *observer, participant,* or *interviewer* and the data are collected in a relatively unsystematic fashion. Many details are collected and gathered, with no requirement that the subject or groups studied be compared with any other subject or group. Data are basically collected for descriptive purposes. Thus, as you can see, the major value of a case study is to suggest reasonable hypotheses that can be tested in a more formal manner. Perhaps the best examples of case studies can be drawn from the clinical literature. Data collected from in-depth interviews may be used to describe a client, patient, or unit. These data are then put into narrative descriptions of the case. Psychoanalytic theory first evolved from Freud's case studies of individual patients.

Content Analysis. An examination of spoken or written material for the purpose of classifying or coding the information is the primary ingredient of **content analysis**. The researcher (analyst) often counts particular *kinds* of information or the *amount* of time or number of words devoted to a particular topic or theme. Rules for counting and classifying the information are stated before the data are examined and are based on theoretical notions adopted by the analyst. One example of such an analysis is a test of the hypothesis that the cognitive complexity of speeches increases as people become more enmeshed in a crisis situation. This hypothesis can be studied by examining the speeches of United Nation delegates in the course of a discussion on resolutions designed to bring about a cease-fire in some part of the world. The fruitfulness of such analyses depends on the rules for classifying words, phrases, or statements according to cognitive complexity, or, in other words, on the operationalization of the concept.

Comment. We introduce the two procedures above for the purpose of acquainting you with techniques for data gathering that need not involve many subjects. They *are* means by which research hypotheses can be studied, but you must understand that there are limitations to the conclusions that can be made. For example, is it wise to *generalize* from a single case? Would you conclude that all, most, or some of the population at large is similar to the case studied? The answer to both of these questions is likely to be no. Would you infer that impending crises *cause* people to become more "cognitively complex" in their speeches? The answer should again be no, since there is no way to be certain whether the complexity is an antecedent or a consequence of the crisis, and there is no control of the situation (e.g., over the amount of information provided, the content of the speeches, the severity of the crisis, and other important determiners of complexity and crisis).

Experiments. **Experiments**, as defined here, are special procedures designed to permit inferences about causes and effects. Four basic elements are typically viewed as critical to an experimental design: *random selection* of subjects, *random assignment* of subjects to the different treatment conditions, *experimenter manipulation* of the treatments, and *experimenter control* over the conduct of the experiment.

The presence of all these elements provides us with more confidence that our causal conclusions and inferences are sound than any other procedure we have available in the behavioral sciences. We discuss these elements in Chap. 2.

Nonexperimental Designs.   In an experiment, as implied above, the researcher has control over almost the entire experimental environment. There are many situations, however, in which this sort of control is either not possible or even not desirable. We will refer to studies that are conducted in such situations as **nonexperimental designs**; they include quasi-experimental designs, naturally occurring designs, survey research, and field studies. We elaborate further on nonexperimental designs in Chap. 2.

Collecting Data

Once you have established and implemented the design, your next step is to collect data. You should take every precaution to prevent the data collection procedures from contaminating your results. In particular, data collectors should be unaware of or blind to the conditions for which they are collecting the data. Such a precaution prevents self-fulfilling prophecies whereby the experimenter emits cues to the respondent that are in line with the hypothesis. A good source on such biases is Rosenthal and Rosnow (1969).

Analyzing the Data

We have devoted a considerable amount of space in this chapter to methodology and only a minor amount to the central topic of the book, data analysis. The emphasis has been deliberate. Though there are numerous techniques of data analysis, no technique, regardless of its elegance, sophistication, and power, can save the research when the design is poor, improper, confounded, or misguided. As we have stated, and will state again and again, sound inferences and generalizations from a piece of research are a function of design and not statistical analysis.

By giving analysis as one of the last steps in this section we do not mean to imply that no consideration is given this topic until after the data have been collected. In fact, the sequence of steps in planning research is not immutable. But we strongly advise against seeking a research topic merely to fit an available technique of data analysis. We also strongly advise, however, that you not delay consideration of data analysis until all the data are collected; you may find that violations of assumptions, restrictions in range of data, and similar concerns will prevent the data from being analyzed by any technique. For example, if your data do not conform to the shape of the distribution required by the analytical technique, your choice of technique may be inappropriate.

Publishing the Results

Once you have analyzed the data, the final step is to present the results in a meaningful way (usually by summarizing the data and the results of the statistical analyses in tables), discuss them, interpret them, and suggest future research. You will usually do all of this in your research report. To facilitate communication with your discipline, we suggest that you consult guides such as the publication manual of the American Psychological Association (1983).

1.4 SUMMARY

In this chapter we have introduced the primary reasons for conducting research: (1) exploration, (2) description, (3) explanation, and (4) prediction. For the purpose of data analysis, either ANOVA or MRC can be applied to the data collected in many situations for any of these purposes.

We have also introduced the steps one goes through in conducting research: identifying the question to be studied, conceptualizing the variables, operationalizing them, selecting a method to collect data on the variables, and analyzing and interpreting the results.

In the course of introducing the issues of research design, we have also introduced the essence of this book, namely, that there are two strategies of statistical analysis that can be applied to the data—ANOVA and MRC. Our main theme is that when they are appropriately applied, the two strategies are equivalent in the statistical conclusions that they yield. We noted that for some designs, the two strategies can be interchangeable, whereas in other situations, such as in non-experimental designs, only MRC is appropriate. Furthermore, the type of variable studied (a point elaborated upon in subsequent chapters), as well as whether the focus of interest is in group differences or individual differences, may favor a particular choice of strategy.

Another point we have emphasized is that the nature of the design determines how the results are *interpreted*, whereas the statistical strategy is a means of describing, summarizing and presenting the findings. Chapter 2 focuses on the principles of research design.

2

Principles of
Research Design

. . .

Chapter 1 offered a broad overview of types of research commonly found in the behavioral sciences. Chapter 2 focuses on two that are the main concern of this book, namely, experimental and nonexperimental designs.

2.1 PRINCIPLES OF EXPERIMENTAL DESIGNS

As we stated in Chap. 1, experiments are special procedures designed to permit inferences about causes and effects. We briefly mentioned that the four basic ingre-- dients of random selection, random assignment, experimenter manipulation, and experimenter control constitute what is typically referred to as an **experimental design**. We will now discuss these ingredients in more detail.

Random Selection

The first requirement of an experimental design is that subjects be selected in an appropriate manner to participate in the study. Ideally, subjects would be **randomly selected** from some larger population of interest. A primary advantage of random selection is the increased generalizability of the findings to the larger population. Public opinion polls (e.g., the Gallup poll) and various government surveys depend heavily on certain forms of random selection so that results can be extended to very large groups of individuals (e.g., the citizens of the United States).

Random selection rarely occurs in psychological experiments, however. Instead, researchers usually include anyone who shows up in response to a notice for subjects on a bulletin board, a direct classroom request for participation, and so on, just so long as the subjects satisfy certain criteria of the research. Although failure to randomly sample limits the degree to which researchers can generalize their results to the larger population, other ways have been found to accomplish the same goal. A common method, for example, is to repeat the experiment with a new set of subjects; the more frequently the same outcome is observed in replications, as they are called, the more confidence researchers can place in the generality of the results.

Random Assignment

The second requirement of an experimental design is that subjects be **randomly assigned** to the different conditions of the experiment. Usually, tables of random numbers are used to determine which subject is placed in which treatment condition. Random assignment is critical to the assumption that the groups formed prior to the introduction of the experimental treatments are equal (equal in the probabilistic sense, or in the "long run"). If subjects can be considered equal at the outset, then any differences that occur after introduction of a treatment can be attributed to the experimenter's intervention. We will spend a great deal of time in future chapters discussing various statistical procedures that help ensure that such a conclusion is valid.

Researchers do use other procedures to help make certain that groups of subjects are equated before the start of the experiment. In some cases, subjects are *matched* in ability and then assigned randomly to the different treatment conditions. A more common procedure is to use the *same subject* in all of the treatment conditions. Designs in which subjects serve in more than one of the treatment conditions are called **within-subjects designs**. Although within-subjects designs may seem an ideal solution to the problem of equating groups before the administration of the different treatment conditions, they are not, as you will see when we consider these designs in later chapters (Chaps. 16, 17, and 18).

Experimenter Manipulation

The third requirement is **experimenter manipulation**. Experiments, as previously stated, are undertaken for the specific purpose of testing cause-and-effect relationships. To directly test causality, the experimenter needs to have control of the variable that is presumed to have the causal impact. To have control means to manipulate or intervene. Suppose you wanted to study whether having prior information about applicants for admission to graduate school influences interviewers' final evaluation of them. You could control the experiment by creating two groups of subjects, one made up of interviewers who are given prior information and the other, of interviewers who are not. We will now use this simple experiment—in which prior information is offered as a cause and influence on evaluation as the effect—to illustrate several aspects of experiments in general and to introduce several of the terms commonly used in describing experiments.

Independent Variables. As we indicated in the first chapter, the basic concepts to be investigated in an experiment or in any type of research design, for that matter, are referred to as **variables**. One variable in the sample experiment is the information the subjects have on applicants for admission to graduate school prior to an interview. It is a variable because some subjects will be in the "information" condition and others will not; those who are in the "information" condition will, for example, be told the applicant's undergraduate record and be given the applicant's statement of purpose while the other group of subjects are given only the statement of purpose. Thus, the two groups of subjects will *differ* in amount of information—some or none (or, strictly speaking, more or less). "Amount of information" is thus, referred to as the **treatment variable**, and the different states of the variable are known as the **treatment conditions** or **levels** of the treatment variable. Another, more familiar term for "amount of information" is **manipulated variable**, so called because the experimenter has control of the condition to which subjects are randomly assigned. Perhaps the most common term for "amount of information" is **independent variable**. In an experiment, the independent variable is the variable whose effect is being studied. The values or levels of the independent variable that the experimenter chooses to use define the treatment conditions. Thus, there must be at least two values of the independent variable in order to demonstrate that the independent variable is having an effect. If there is only one value, then it is impossible to determine whether the results have anything to do with the presence of the independent variable.

Independent variables, regardless of the term used to describe them, have been classified into three types: (1) social manipulations, (2) environmental treatments, and (3) instructional treatments (Crano & Brewer, 1973). Social manipulations are those obtained by the planned actions of another person associated with the research project who is introduced into the experimental situation by the experimenter. Such a person is referred to as an *accomplice*, a *confederate*, or a *stooge*. Typically, a confederate, whose exact role and function is specified at the outset of the experiment, is paired with a naive subject. For example, in a study of conformity, the confederate might consistently evaluate a colored stimulus as red when in fact it is blue. The purpose of the experiment is to determine whether and when the naive subject forms the same evaluation as the confederate—that is, when the subject concludes that the stimulus is red.

Environmental treatments involve the control and manipulation of the experimental setting and stimuli. For example, in research concerned with the legibility of letters displayed on a computer CRT screen, the experimenter can vary a number of physical characteristics of the stimulus, such as size of letters, brightness of letters, size of screen, and the duration of display. Manipulations of stimuli are often used in human and animal research. In the example we are using in this section, some subjects receive background information on the applicant and others do not; thus, there are two different stimulus conditions.

Instructional manipulations are achieved by varying the instructions given to subjects. One or two words, one or two sentences, or a paragraph will be changed as the instructions are given to different treatment groups, so that different meanings, perspectives, views, positions, and the like are conveyed to the subjects. For example, the experimenter can manipulate subjects' level of anxiety by telling one group that an upcoming exam will be used to select students for a special, highly desired program while telling another group that the exam is being studied for research purposes and will have no impact on selection. (We use this example only to illustrate instructional manipulation; you should be aware that ethical concerns have to be considered in such a manipulation.)

Subject Variables. In addition to studying independent variables, researchers often study the effects of subjects' intrinsic characteristics. For example, they might want to know whether there are differences in performance between genders, racial groups, age groups, and the like. These types of variables have been termed **subject variables**, **classification variables**, and **individual-difference variables**. Such variables have been employed in experiments and analyzed as if they were independent variables. Strictly speaking, however, they are not independent variables, since the experimenter does not control or manipulate who is male or old or Asian. The experimenter may randomly select subjects from larger populations, but he or she does not administer the treatment (sex, race, or age). There is no manipulation, but rather a measurement of a characteristic that already exists. Since there is no manipulation of "treatments," there is no way to state unequivocally that such variables cause differences in performance.

Subject variables can be introduced into experimental designs, although it will always be difficult to interpret the meaning of differences observed between groups. Subject variables can be used to increase the sensitivity of an experimental design. We will discuss one such use in Chap. 22.

Dependent Variables. The second concept or unit of a theoretical statement is the **dependent variable**. It is the measurable response that the subject gives or the behavior observed by the experimenter in conjunction with changes in the manipulated variable. The response or behavior is dependent on the condition in which the subject finds him- or herself. Any behavior capable of being measured or quantified can be a dependent variable—for example, the speed of completing a task; the number of errors made; or ratings or evaluations, such as those that the subjects might give in our experiment on the evaluation of graduate school applicants.

Qualitative and Quantitative Variables. We have just shown how variables can be classified as independent or dependent. There are further classifications of variables, however, one of which is based on how they are measured. We briefly mentioned a classification of independent variables into **qualitative** and **quantitative** variables (Ghiselli et al., 1981). When the independent variable is qualitative, treatment conditions differ in kind; when it is quantitative, they differ in frequency, amount or degree and consequently can be ordered. The independent variable in our sample experiment is a dichotomized quantitative variable: "more" and "less" prior information about the applicants. An example of a qualitative variable would be the type of program applied to—medical school versus a Ph.D. program in biology; the two programs are different in kind and are not regarded as different in amount, frequency, or degree.

The nature of the variable is important because it influences the strategy used for statistical analysis. As you will see, it can affect the choice between ANOVA and MRC as well as the choice of particular techniques within ANOVA or MRC. The nature of the dependent variable is also relevant for analysis considerations. Typically, the dependent variable is quantitative. If the dependent variable is qualitative, then a procedure such as discriminant analysis (one not discussed in this text) may be the most appropriate.

Experimenter Control

The fourth ingredient of an experiment is **experimenter control**. This is more than control of the manipulation. It involves control of all other variables or conditions that might have an impact on the response measure. Control is achieved, in part, by **standardization**. The experimenter has control over the "when," "how," and "to whom" aspects of the project; that is, all subjects are exposed to the same general instructions, environment, and procedures apart from that which defines the relevant treatment condition. In other words, the only difference in the conditions to which the subjects are exposed is in the manipulated variable; all else is kept constant or is assumed to be equivalent as a result of random assignment or control.

Control applies to several aspects of experimental design. The situation in which an experiment is being conducted needs to be controlled. The stimuli, the procedure, the "when," and the "whom" of measurement are all managed by the researcher. Consequently, irrelevant, extraneous forces are not likely to influence the conclusions.

Control can also be obtained by statistical means. As will be shown in Chaps. 20, 21, and 22, it is possible in assigning subjects to groups to compensate for certain factors such as age, experience, and ability so that differences observed between treatment groups can be attributed to the experimental manipulation and not to these other factors.

2.2   PRINCIPLES OF NONEXPERIMENTAL DESIGNS

As we pointed out in the last section, in experimental designs the researcher has control over almost the entire experimental environment. He or she decides, for example, who will receive what treatment and when the critical behavior will be measured. However, in many **nonexperimental designs**, as we will call them, the researcher may lack some part of this control—particularly the *random assignment* of individuals to different treatment groups. Without random assignment to spread all otherwise uncontrolled factors equally over the treatment groups, nonexperimental research designs usually do not allow the inference of cause and effect, at least not as forcefully as do the experimental designs we discussed in Sec. 2.1. In varying degrees, all nonexperimental designs share this particular difficulty.

Experimental designs rule out all differences among the treatment conditions except those specifically associated with the independent variable, either eliminating them by controls exerted on the experimental situation or minimizing them by random assignment of subjects to conditions. As a consequence, any differences observed on the dependent variable are assumed to be caused by the independent variable. Nonexperimental designs, on the other hand, generally fail in exactly this regard; that is, they fail either to hold differences constant or to minimize differences through randomization. There are many ways to classify nonexperimental designs. We will consider two types, **quasi-experimental designs** and **correlational designs**.

Quasi-Experimental Designs

Quasi-experimental designs often resemble experiments. For example, suppose an educational psychologist wants to compare two reading programs for relative effectiveness. The researcher selects one third-grade class to receive one program and another to receive the other program. The teachers in the two classes are given training in carrying out the program, which is introduced during the school year. The average scores of the two classes on a standardized reading test are compared at the end of the school year. Superficially this design seems to qualify as an experiment, but is the researcher justified in attributing any difference observed on the reading test to the two programs? The answer is no, for a number of reasons, the most important of which is the real possibility that the two third-grade classes differed in reading ability *before* the beginning of the term. (We will ignore other obvious differences in this discussion, such as differences in the teaching ability of the two teachers, the effects of other subjects taught in the two classes, the amount of time devoted to the reading instruction, and so on.) What is obviously missing is the *random assignment* of children to the two classes, which is one of the ways in which important differences in an experiment, such as reading ability, in this example, are "equated," or neutralized, before the start of the experiment.

Something often included in quasi-experimental designs like this one is a test or assessment given *before* the differential treatment is introduced. In the present example, the researcher might administer a reading test on the first day of class and compare the *gains* the two classes exhibit on the test given at the end of the school year. Unfortunately, the results from such designs are still difficult to interpret, particularly if the two classes differ on the first test. This type of design is aptly called a **pretest-posttest design** and is widely used in the social sciences. We will discuss the analysis of such designs and the interpretation problems associated with them in Chap. 21.

Another common type of quasi-experimental design is a study in which the independent variable, or treatment, is naturally occurring. For example, suppose we were interested in studying the effects of a particular training course on the performance of firefighters. We would have a problem in controlling who is exposed to the treatment, the training. Let us suppose that for economic, attitudinal, ethical, and political reasons, a training class cannot be divided into a treatment group that receives the special training and a control group that does not. A control group is needed, however, in order to assess the unique effects of the particular training course. What is usually done is to find some other *existing* group to serve as a control or reference group. One possibility is to use a group of firefighters in another city who are receiving a different type of training at the same time or a group in the same city that will receive a different type of training after the current training program is completed. Again, note that because subjects are not randomly assigned to the two groups, serious limitations are placed on any interpretation of the final outcome. The two groups cannot be assumed to be equivalent prior to the experiment. Rather, the groups are intact and may already be formed before the researcher becomes interested in them as groups to study. The experimenter may or may not have control over which group is exposed to the treatment. Differences in performance between nonequivalent groups may depend on factors other than the relevant treatment.

Quasi-experiments such as the two we have illustrated are legitimate designs, provided that the researcher can rule out or deal with challenges to the causal inferences. For a detailed discussion of quasi-experimental designs, see the now-classic monograph by Campbell and Stanley (1966) and the more recent extension of their work by Cook and Campbell (1979). We will return to quasi-experimental designs in Chap. 20.

Correlational Designs

The other type of nonexperimental design we will consider is correlational design. Usually, but not necessarily, all measures are obtained at the same time: levels of both the *presumed effects* and the exposure to *presumed causes* are measured as they occur naturally. The subject is generally measured on two (or more) attributes and the association between the sets of attributes is determined. A correlational study of the relationship between performance and participation in training would focus on an existing group of firefighters. It would consist of examining their records to measure their performance and to determine whether or not they had participated in the training program.

Both correlational designs and their terminology have their roots in the area of tests and measurements. Basically, a group of subjects are measured on one or more *predictor* variables—for example, general intelligence, social or ethnic background, or personality characteristics—and often simultaneously measured on some *criterion*, such as a performance task. A researcher might test the hypothesis, for example, that possession of greater intelligence leads to or causes better performance on the criterion. Usually, a *correlational statistic*, such as Pearson's correlation coefficient, is used to analyze the data obtained.

We need to highlight several aspects of the above example in order to distinguish between experimental and correlational designs. To start, there are similarities in the terminologies used by "experimentalists" and "correlationalists." An experimenter manipulates and controls subjects' exposure to his or her independent variable. The key feature of experimental design is that the treatment differences represented by the independent variable cause or directly affect the subject's response (the dependent variable). In correlational research, the predictor variable often has the same *implied status* as an independent variable; that is, it is the variable whose influence one is studying. The basic difference is in whether causality can be inferred—in this case, whether intelligence has caused the differences on the criterion. In correlational designs, it is acceptable to conclude that responses on the predictor variable are *associated with*, or *covary with* the obtained responses on the criterion variable. As an example, one might draw the following conclusion using one typical correlational design: High scores on one variable are correlated with (are associated with, covary with, or are related to) high scores on the second variable.

Even if time elapses between measurement of the predictor variable and measurement of the criterion as it would if high school grades were used to predict college grade-point averages, the researcher cannot make unequivocal causal statements. High school grades may *predict* college performance, but they do not necessarily *cause* a certain kind of performance. It is quite feasible that a third variable (or a set of other variables) *causes* people to perform at a certain level in high school and also causes them to perform at a similar level in college. Such variables can be of genetic or environmental origin. Without careful control and careful development of the theory, researchers usually have to infer causality in correlational designs with a much lower degree of confidence (if any) than they have in experimental designs. But we should note that with some types of correlational analyses, such as **cross-lagged correlations** and **path analysis**, statements may be made with a reasonable degree of confidence.[1]

Independent variables and predictor variables are treated equivalently from a statistical point of view. We want to know how each affects the dependent variable or criterion. In an experiment, we are interested in *causal* impact, whereas in correlational design, we are interested in *associative* impact.

Certain design requirements are also similar, although different terms are frequently used. Experimentalists, for example, are concerned with manipulation checks, internal validity, and external validity. Correlationalists are concerned with reliability and validity. These terms describe essential ingredients of any research. We will discuss them in the context of the following example.

Suppose you are interested in the influence of anxiety on performance. If you are an experimentalist, you might expose half of the subjects to an anxiety-provoking situation while exposing the other half to a non-anxiety-provoking situation (the latter, a form of control or reference condition); you then measure how well subjects perform a task, perhaps a problem-solving task of some sort. In contrast, if you are a correlationalist, you might choose to measure, usually with a pencil-and-paper test, the level of anxiety that subjects express just before they begin to work on the task. A key question in either approach is, How do we know that subjects in the "anxiety" condition are indeed experiencing anxiety? The experimentalist attempts to answer this question by conducting a *pilot test* before the formal experiment is begun or by introducing *manipulation checks* after each subject completes the task.

Pilot tests are a form of pretesting in which trial subjects are probed and questioned regarding their perceptions and feelings toward the manipulation. Alternatively, a number of subjects might be given the manipulation and then tested to determine whether their reaction correlates with some state or response that would logically seem to indicate the presence of the intended independent variable. You might ask, for example, are physiological measures indicative of anxiety or arousal greater for subjects in the anxiety condition than for those in the control group? Manipulation tests are a form of posttesting in which subjects are asked *after* serving in the main experiment how they perceived the treatment. You might ask them whether the situation or instruction was anxiety-provoking, frightening, or perspiration-inducing. You can use either procedure to demonstrate that it is

---

[1] Cross-lagged correlations and path analysis are beyond the scope of this book, but they are treated by Kenny (1979). A useful discussion can also be found in Pedhazur (1983, pp. 580–614).

the anxiety condition that has produced the desired changes in the subjects' perceptions of the task.

Similarly, if you used the correlational approach, you would need to know whether your pencil-and-paper measure does in fact reflect anxiety. This step generally involves such issues as reliability and construct validity (see Ghiselli et al., 1981) to determine whether the underlying concept—anxiety—is measured in a consistent, reliable fashion.

Regarding the dependent variable, or criterion, both the experimentalist and the correlationalist *should* be interested in demonstrating that the concept, problem-solving performance, can be accurately and reliably measured. Here, again, we are concerned with measurement issues such as reliability and construct validity. Once we are confident that our measures and manipulations are good ones, we then proceed to the following questions. For the experimentalist: Has the experimental manipulation in fact made a difference? For the correlationalist: To what degree does the predictor variable explain or predict the criterion? The experimentalist's question is one of internal validity. If the results show differences between the treatment groups on the dependent measure, then the inference can be made that the treatment was the causal factor—provided that there was randomization and appropriate controls were present. The correlationalist's question is whether the predictor has *criterion-related validity*, or, as previously stated, whether the two variables covary. The degree to which the two variables are related is assessed statistically by using a measure that represents the degree or amount of association.

Both experimentalists and correlationalists are concerned with external validity or generalizability. These issues deal with whether the obtained results can be generalized to populations, settings, and levels of variables other than those used in the sample studied. Formal statistical analysis will provide an index of the confidence in the obtained results, but whether the results are generalizable is a function of the diversity of the sample, the way in which the sample has been selected, and the measures studied.

At this point, you may be wondering which method is better—experimental or correlational designs. We will list the advantages and disadvantages of each, but we leave the question of "best" up to you. First, an experiment has the advantage of providing unequivocal evidence about causation; this results from the randomization process, which rules out all unwanted factors. Second, since all factors are under the control of the experimenter, an experiment provides better control over extraneous variables and reduces their potential impact on the study and its results. Third, an experiment allows you to examine the phenomenon of interest thoroughly, since you have control over which levels of the independent varible to introduce and study. The experimenter has the ability to vary the independent variable systematically and thus to allow for isolation and precise specification of the values on the dependent variable that correspond to the levels on the independent variable.

On the other hand, there are also advantages to the correlational design. First, some variables cannot be studied in an experiment. As previously pointed out, the researcher cannot manipulate variables such as sex, race, age, social class, and personality style—the subject variables. Thus, the correlational design is called for if one of these must serve as the variable of interest. Second, some processes are long-term or evolve over time, and it would be impossible (or unethical, or both) to restrict the subject to a laboratory for the duration of the study. For example, studies of therapies, treatment programs, developmental phenomena, and the like are not suitable for study in the controlled environment of the laboratory. Finally, the correlational design is used to clarify, suggest, refine, or amplify experimental findings.

Please understand that the above is a brief description of some forms of non-experimental research. Chapters 20 and 21 present the techniques necessary for analyzing data from such situations.

Comment.   An essential distinction must be made between *correlational designs* and *correlational statistics* (or correlational techniques of data analysis). Designs are concerned with *how* and *when* data are collected and *by what means*. In correlational designs, as we have pointed out, data are generally collected simultaneously on predictor and criterion variables, often from existing or naturally occurring groups. Correlational statistics, on the other hand, are techniques that can be used on almost any set of data to analyze and determine the degree to which two or more variables are related, or the degree to which they covary. *Designs* permit statements of causation; *statistics* merely tell us whether a reliable relationship exists between the variables and how great its strength is. In both experimental and correlational research, we are interested in determining whether certain variables (the independent or predictor variables) covary with others (the dependent or criterion variables). One design—the experimental design—because it involves manipulation and randomization, permits statements of causality. To state it another way: It is *not* because of the statistics used to analyze the data that causal inferences can be made. The basic point of this text is that the statistics calculated from analysis of variance and from the multiple regression and correlation are both part of the same general linear model. The crucial difference between experimental designs and nonexperimental designs is in how the variables, independent and predictor, are implemented and whether subjects are randomly assigned to treatments.

In a sense, we are saying that you can ignore the traditional remark that correlation does not always mean causation—a remark found in many statistics texts and elsewhere. It is true. But it is also true that application of ANOVA does not necessarily mean causation. What does permit the inference of causation is the research design and the presence of randomization, manipulation, and control.

Experimentalists are mainly interested in the variability they create through manipulation, control, and standardization. Rigorous tests of hypotheses are undertaken, and confident statements about causation are the hallmarks of experimental designs. In contrast, correlational designs have traditionally been used to study correlations present and existing in nature. The correlationalist is particularly interested in observing, organizing, and describing the data from nature's "experiments." Furthermore, correlational research is used to study exactly those phenomena that the experimenter has not learned to control or can never hope to control.

As we indicated earlier, we have subsumed quasi-experiments, field research, surveys, and other correlational studies under the heading of nonexperiments. We stressed the distinction between experimental and correlational research above to illustrate traditional thinking, and, of greater import, traditional confusion about the differences between designs, on the one hand, and the statistics chosen to analyze them, on the other. To avoid future confusion, we will refer to research paradigms as experimental or nonexperimental. To repeat, the primary differences are that the former involve randomization, experimenter manipulation, and control, whereas the latter cannot achieve all of these.

2.3   ANALYTICAL COMPARISONS

As should be obvious at this point, a primary objective of this book is to acquaint you with the analytical techniques of ANOVA and MRC and to demonstrate their appropriateness for both experimental and nonexperimental designs. Though the remaining chapters concentrate on data analysis and statistics, we cannot overemphasize the attention that you should give to issues of design when you begin planning a research project. Recall that the nature of your design dictates what kinds of inferences you can make, particularly whether you can make causal as opposed to associative inferences. Data analysis and statistics are merely the tools the investigator uses to provide some confidence in the interpretation of the research.

Another objective of this book is to emphasize the use of what we will call **analytical comparisons**—analyses that focus on specific portions of the overall research design. We make this point because we prefer that students take a "hammer-and-chisel" approach rather than resort to more general, overall, global analyses. For example, a researcher will often conduct an overall test to determine whether there is any difference in the effects produced among the several levels of the independent variable. Overall tests like this are referred to as **omnibus tests**, and their purpose is to establish the presence of *some* difference among many treatment groups. This strategy is acceptable, but we believe that the most interesting questions can be reduced to simple, focused analytical comparisons that involve only two groups (two actual groups, or two combinations of several of the groups). Ideally, this approach should be part of the overall research plan formulated before the study is initiated. There are researchers, however, who prefer to determine whether there is an omnibus effect before refining their analyses and searching for where the differences actually lie. We suggest that these researchers concentrate their efforts on answering the specific questions they have in mind when they originally design their studies and that they continue with this approach of "chipping away" at the omnibus finding in a multilevel design to determine where, among the several levels of the study, the actual differences exist.

As an example, suppose we want to study whether home computers are the best means for improving performance of trainees interested in learning a skill. One way to design the study is to randomly assign subjects to different methods of instruction such as home computer instruction, programmed instruction text, traditional lecture, and self-teaching (no formal instruction). The design has four treatments, but we are not as interested in whether there are differences *somewhere* among the four methods (as an omnibus test would reveal) as we are in whether there is a difference between home computers and all the other methods (the combination of the three non-computer methods) or between home computers and programmed text *or* lecture *or* self-teaching. Each of these comparisons involves the difference between two groups or combinations of groups, and each provides a different glimpse of the outcome of the study. Because they are usually specified at the outset of the research, the comparisons are referred to as **planned comparisons**.

There will be times, however, when we will not be certain about the specific differences we might expect or should be studying; this usually occurs when we are involved in more exploratory research. Consequently, we create many levels (treatments) and analyze the data with an omnibus test. Nevertheless, the end product of analysis should still be analytical comparisons. For example, suppose we were interested in studying whether food deprivation causes decay in motor performance. We set up a design in which rats are randomly assigned to one of several deprived levels: 2 hours, 4 hours, 6 hours, and 8 hours. After exposing the rats to their appropriate level of deprivation, we test the rats' reaction time on some apparatus. Suppose that an omnibus analysis indicates a significant difference in performance among the different groups of rats. Is there a difference between 2 hours and 4 hours? between 2 hours and 6 hours? Is there a difference shown by other, similar comparisons? Comparisons of this sort, which are conducted after the omnibus test, are called **post hoc comparisons** and represent the method of chipping away we believe ought to be part of a data analyst's repertoire.[2]

Most of the hypothetical experiments cited in this chapter represent the kind of research found in the experimental literature. Typically, such research has been analyzed by ANOVA and by planned and post hoc procedures. We hope that it will become apparent to you that such experiments can also be analyzed from the correlational point of view, or by MRC. However, the traditional MRC analyst, too, who deals with correlational data, has tended to focus on omnibus analyses as well. But correlationalists, too, have ways of making analytical comparisons that are equivalent to planned or post hoc analyses. Their analytical comparisons are accomplished by conducting **hierarchical analyses**, which we will consider in Chap. 20 and 21 of this book.

The point is that both ANOVA and MRC should be used to study the *specific* questions of research. Finding a difference *somewhere* is not as informative as finding a difference between two specific groups. The goal of this book is to illustrate how MRC and ANOVA can be used to make analytical comparisons for several different types of research designs.

2.4 SUMMARY

In this chapter we have reviewed the essential ingredients of experimental and nonexperimental designs and pointed out their similarities and differences in procedure, terminology, and permissible interpretations. A key distinction is that experimental design involves random assignment of subjects to conditions or treatment groups, thus creating equivalence among groups prior to the introduction of the experimental treatments. In contrast, nonexperimental designs lack random assignment; they involve the study of existing, naturally occurring groups.

From the perspective of data analysis, ANOVA and MRC are appropriate for analyzing experimental designs, but MRC is the preferred strategy for analyzing nonexperimental designs. The reason for this position is developed in the remainder of this book.

---

[2] An alternative to this approach is trend analysis which we consider in Chap. 23.

3

Overview of
Design and Analysis

. . .

In Chapter 2 we presented some of the basic principles and issues in design and analysis. The purpose of Chapter 3 is (1) to illustrate the application of those principles, (2) to provide a bridge between conceptual terms and analysis, and (3) to offer a capsule view of data analysis in which you can see how ANOVA and MRC are equivalent. Most of you have probably read a research article in your field of interest and have studied and tried to interpret the statistics in the article. This brief chapter will present the fundamental statistics—the common end products of data analysis. We are presenting them at this point in the book to give students who are not very familiar with data analysis a glimpse into the process of analysis and to show them how statistics are extracted from a set of data. Those students who have had some passing contact with ANOVA or MRC should still review the material, since in this chapter we give our first concrete illustration of the similarities between ANOVA and MRC that we stress in this book. By examining the statistics derived from each analytical strategy, you will discover that the statistical test of significance—the final product of most analyses—is identical for both strategies. We do not derive, present, or discuss formulas in this chapter; you will need to trust that we are using appropriate formulas and using them correctly.

3.1   THE STEPS IN EXPERIMENTAL ANALYSIS

Suppose that we wish to determine whether the medium in which a sales promotion is presented influences consumer's attitudes toward a product. Suppose, further, that we have engaged two data analysts as consultants to advise us on what statistics to use and how to interpret them. In selecting our consultants, we choose one analyst trained in the ANOVA strategy and one trained in the traditional correlational strategy. How will each of them go about setting up the experiment, analyzing it, and interpreting the results?

1. Posing a Question

The question will be the same whether it is phrased by the ANOVA analyst or the MRC analyst: Do different media for presenting sales messages lead to different attitudes toward a product among consumers?

2. Conceptualizing the Question

The question we have formulated suggests that we are interested in two phenomena in this research: (1) the medium of presentation and (2) the attitudes of consumers.

The question, as posed above, is the basis for the research hypothesis. The way the research hypothesis is *expressed*, however, will differ between the two consultants. That is, the ANOVA analyst would propose that there is a *difference* in attitudes that is a function of the medium of presentation, whereas the MRC analyst would propose that there is a *relationship* between medium and attitude. The *null hypothesis* corresponding to the ANOVA analyst's hypothesis is that there is *no difference* between the two conditions, and the MRC analyst's null hypothesis is that the *correlation is zero* between the medium of presentation and attitudes of consumers.

3. Operationalizing the Concepts

Let us suppose that the sales message consists of a 10-minute film that promotes a book on data analysis, claiming that its use will lead to better grades in a course on undergraduate statistics. Two forms of the film will be used—one in color and one in black and white. A questionnaire will be used to assess the attitudes expressed by subjects after observing and listening to the presentation. *Operationalizations* of these variables can be the same whether your data-analytic orientation is ANOVA or MRC. The independent variable is the medium of presentation, operationalized as a 10-minute film in color and in black and white; and the dependent variable is subjects' attitude, operationalized by a questionnaire with, let us say, two questions.

4. Methodology and Collecting Data

Suppose now that both analysts choose to study the basic research question with an *experiment*. This decision is made in order to control extraneous factors and to permit drawing a causal link between medium and attitude. A film is produced (professionally) that is designed to promote the book. As we have indicated already, the variable "medium of presentation" has two conditions: a color version of the film and a black-and-white version. This is the only aspect that differs; actors, script, and the rest are identical. Thus, we have an *independent variable*, the medium, which varies in kind—color or black and white—and which is manipulated by the experimenter. Attitudes, which constitute the *dependent variable*, are measured by summing the responses of subjects to the following two questions:

1. Is the book likely to be well received by consumers?
2. Is the book likely to be sold as a result of the promotion?

Each question has a 5-point response scale that ranges from "strongly disagree" (1 point) to "strongly agree" (5 points).

The methodology is such that 20 student volunteers from an introductory psychology class are *randomly assigned* to either the color or the black-and-white condition. After viewing the appropriate version of the film, they complete the two-item questionnaire. The lowest possible score is 2, which indicates that the subject holds a negative attitude toward the book; and the highest possible score is 10, which indicates that the subject has a positive attitude toward the book.

5. Analyzing the Data

Data analysis begins with scoring the simple questionnaire and combining the responses to each of the two items for each subject. Table 3-1 shows the "scores" for the 10 subjects in each condition.

The basic statistics derived from an ANOVA performed on the data collected in this experiment are as follows:

> *Mean* assessment (attitude) for the color condition = 6.80; *standard deviation* = 2.04.
>
> *Mean* assessment for the black-and-white condition = 3.20; *standard deviation* = 1.48.
>
> F ratio = 20.38; $df = 1$, 18; $p < .01$.

These are the statistics of greatest interest to the ANOVA data analyst. In addition, however, most computer programs will provide other valuable information such as *sums of squares (SS)* and *mean squares (MS)* for *between-groups* and

Table 3-1
Data Layout for an Analysis of Variance

Subject	Color	Subject	Black and White
1	4	11	2
2	6	12	3
3	5	13	4
4	7	14	2
5	10	15	2
6	8	16	2
7	6	17	5
8	5	18	6
9	7	19	2
10	10	20	4

within-group sources. (We do not expect you to understand these terms at this point, although many of you will remember having seen some of them in research publications and in introductory classes in statistics and experimental design.) The typical layout is as follows:

Source	SS	df	MS	F
Between	64.80	1	64.80	20.38
Within	57.20	18	3.18	
Total	122.00	19		

Given this information, most researchers will concentrate on the F ratio of 20.38. Since this value has been determined to be statistically significant ($p < .01$), the experimenter concludes that the difference between the two groups (i.e., the difference between the mean of 6.80 and the mean of 3.20) is a significant one that would occur by chance less than 1 time out of 100 (the latter is indicated by the expression $p < .01$). In essence, the experimenter concludes that there is support for the research hypothesis that the medium of presentation makes a difference in consumers' attitudes. All the subsequent discussion in a research report is likely to be based on the finding of this significant F ratio.

Now let us look at what the MRC analyst will do with the same data. In order to analyze the data via MRC, you need two numerical values for each subject. One numerical value is needed for the dependent variable (Y); this is the opinion expressed on the questionnaire. The other numerical value is chosen to represent the version of the sales message (X) to which the subject is exposed. Since there are two ways in which the promotion is presented—color and black and white—we will choose the value $+1$ to represent exposure to color and -1 to represent exposure to black and white. The format for the data layout is present in Table 3-2.

Examination of the data layout shows that subjects 1 to 10 all have a condition, or X, value of $+1$, and that subjects 11 to 20 all have corresponding values of -1. (Why we have chosen these values of $+1$ and -1 is irrelevant at this stage; the important point is to note that the two conditions are assigned different values and that everyone in the "color" condition has the value $+1$ and everyone in the "black-and white" condition has the value -1.)

Analysis of the 20 pairs of data points by MRC would typically yield the following output:

r (correlation) $= +.73$ F ratio $= 20.38$ $df = 1, 18$ $p < .01$

Table 3-2
Data Layout for an MRC Analysis

Subject	Condition (X)	Response (Y)	Subject	Condition (X)	Response (Y)
1	1	4	11	−1	2
2	1	6	12	−1	3
3	1	5	13	−1	4
4	1	7	14	−1	2
5	1	10	15	−1	2
6	1	8	16	−1	2
7	1	6	17	−1	5
8	1	5	18	−1	6
9	1	7	19	−1	2
10	1	10	20	−1	4

In addition, most computer printouts will also provide SS information in the following format:

Source	SS	df	r	r^2	F
Regression	64.80	1	.73	.53	20.38
Residual	57.20	18			
Total	122.00	19			

Given this information, most researchers would concentrate on the r result of $+.73$ and its F ratio of 20.38. Since this value of F has been determined to be statistically significant, the researcher would conclude that the relationship between the responses made by the subjects and the medium to which they have been exposed (reflected by the statistic $r = +.73$) is a significant one that would occur by chance less than 1 time out of 100 (that is, $p < .01$). The positive sign of the correlation means that higher scores on X (the quantity, $+1$ for subjects who have been exposed to the color version) correspond to higher scores on the attitude questionnaire while lower scores on X (the quantity -1, for those exposed to the black-and-white version) correspond to lower scores on the attitude questionnaire.

Note that the conclusions drawn by the ANOVA and MRC analysts are identical. The ANOVA analyst states that there is a *significant difference* in opinions expressed between those exposed to the color version and those exposed to the black-and-white version and the difference is in favor of the former (the means are 6.80 and 3.20, respectively). The MRC analyst concludes that there is a *significant relationship* that shows that those exposed to a black-and-white message tend to hold lower opinions than those exposed to a color message.

The common points of emphasis for the two analysts are the SS's and the F ratio (see Table 3-3). Since the F value is significant, both analysts conclude that there is an effect—that there is a difference between means (as shown by ANOVA) or that there is a relationship (according to MRC). The important point for now is that a single set of data, whether set up in the typical ANOVA format or in the MRC format, has yielded *identical F* ratios, with identical *df's*, and thus identical *p* values. Consequently, both analysts arrive at the identical conclusion— that the type of presentation affects the opinion of the subjects. You should also note that some other values are identical, though they have different terms attached to them. For example, the SS between groups equals the regression SS (with the value 64.80), and the SS within groups equals the residual SS (with the value 57.20). The reason for these equalities will be explained in subsequent chapters.

Table 3-3
Comparison of ANOVA and MRC Statistical Outcomes

	ANOVA		MRC	
	Color	Black and White		
Descriptive statistics				
Mean	6.80	3.20	Correlation	+.73
Standard deviation	2.04	1.48		
F ratio	20.38			20.38
df	1, 18			1, 18
p value	<.01			<.01
SS				
Between groups	64.80		Regression	64.80
Within groups	57.20		Residual	57.20
Total	122.00			

3.2 NONEXPERIMENTAL ANALYSIS

How would the question posed in our example be studied in a nonexperimental design? One approach would be to go to a convention attended by statistics instructors and set up two booths in the book exhibit hall. In one booth, the color film would be shown, and in the other, the black-and-white film. As people left the booths they would be asked to fill out the questionnaire. Let us assume that 10 different instructors fill out questionnaires in each of the two booths and that the data obtained are identical to those already listed in Tables 3-1 and 3-2. As we have already argued, ANOVA and MRC will produce the same value of F and support the same statistical conclusion—in this case, significance at $p < .01$. There is an important difference between the experimental example and this nonexperimental example. While the experimental example allowed us to conclude that the type of message influences opinions about the book, the nonexperimental design does not. The reason for this important difference lies in the fact that subjects are *not* randomly assigned to the two conditions in the nonexperimental example as they were in the experimental example. Consequently, there is no simple way to avoid the very real possibility that the differences in opinion exist *prior* to data collection and that the presentation of the two versions of the promotion has no differential influence on the ratings. For example, a certain type of person might be attracted to booths where color sales films are playing. This might be a type of person who is positive about many things in the world. We cannot be certain that the promotion is *causing* the responses to the questionnaire. Thus, even though ANOVA and MRC produce the same statistical outcomes in this second example, our inference of cause and effect is subtantially weakened, since subjects have not been randomly assigned to the two different conditions.

3.3 SUMMARY

As we have said repeatedly, a major purpose of this book is to show that we arrive at the same conclusion whether we analyze the data from an experiment by ANOVA or by MRC. Another major purpose of this book is to encourage all researchers to look at data from as many perspectives as are meaningful, and to look for both differences *and* relationships. The two hypothetical analysts we have described have different perspectives, but their analyses of the data are based on the same underlying statistical model (the general linear model). The main difference at *this* point between ANOVA and MRC, except for the statistics used, is the way in which the research hypothesis is phrased. Whereas the traditional ANOVA analyst would be concerned with whether there are *differences* in opinions as a function of medium (and therefore would concentrate on differences between means), the MRC analyst would be concerned with whether there is a *relationship* between the medium of presentation and the responses on the questionnaire. Table 3-3 summarizes the two perspectives and shows how they converge.

In addition, we have shown in this chapter that a question of interest can be posed so that it lends itself equally to study in the laboratory as an experimental design and to study in the field as a nonexperimental design. In the latter case, MRC is the preferred analysis, for reasons which will be presented in Chap. 20.

4

Basic Concepts
in
Statistical Analysis

. . .

41

This chapter deals with several fundamental statistical indices that you will find important in the analysis of data, regardless of whether you are using ANOVA or MRC. These indices form the basis of formulas that are used in both of these two analysis strategies. Portions of this chapter may cover material you have studied previously; we encourage you to go through the entire chapter nevertheless, in part as a review, and in part as an introduction to our own approach to the topics. We will be considering measures of central tendency and variability, giving special attention to the concept of a sum of squares, which is a key statistic involved in most of the statistical techniques we discuss in this book.

4.1   MEASURING CENTRAL TENDENCY

A measure of central tendency is a single value that is considered to be representative of an entire set of scores or observations. While alternative measures are available, the **arithmetic mean** (or **mean**, for short) is the most useful measure of central tendency in the statistical analysis of data. The mean is calculated by dividing the sum of the observations by the number of observations in the set. This operation is summarized by the following formula:

$$\text{mean } (\bar{Y}) = \frac{\Sigma\, Y}{N} \tag{4-1}$$

where $\bar{Y}$ is the mean of values of the variable denoted as Y, Y represents the individual scores in the set, Σ (uppercase Greek sigma) stands for the instruction "take the sum of," and N indicates the total number of scores or observations in the set.

As an example of this calculation, consider the data appearing in Table 4-1. There are 24 observations for Y. When it is necessary to specify a particular score, we will add a numerical subscript to designate its ordinal position in the set; for example, Y_2 would represent the second score in the set, namely, 49. To illustrate

Table 4-1
A Set of N = 24 Observations

53	44	47	13
49	48	42	16
47	35	39	16
42	18	37	10
51	32	42	11
34	27	33	6

the calculation of the mean,

$$\bar{Y} = \frac{\Sigma Y}{N}$$

$$= \frac{Y_1 + Y_2 + \cdots + Y_{23} + Y_{24}}{N}$$

$$= \frac{53 + 49 + \cdots + 11 + 6}{24} = \frac{792}{24}$$

$$= 33.00$$

This value, 33.00, is taken as the single value that best describes the entire set of 24 scores.

One property of the mean that is frequently mentioned is that its value represents an algebraic balancing point of a set of scores—that is, the mean is that point from which the deviation of the scores *below* exactly matches the corresponding deviation of the scores *above*. Figure 4-1 illustrates this important property. As you

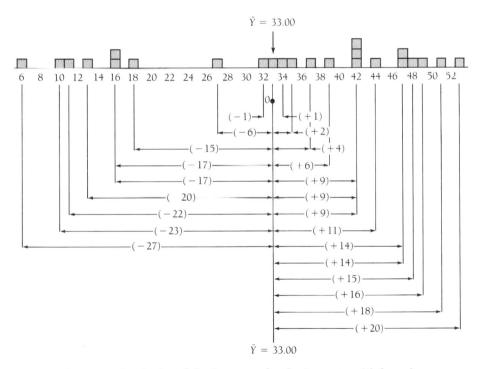

Figure 4-1 Graphic display of the deviation of each observation (Y) from the mean of the observations (Ȳ). Note that the sum of the negative deviations (Y scores falling below the mean) equals the sum of the positive deviations (Y scores falling above the mean).

can see, each of the scores from Table 4-1 is represented by a box plotted at the appropriate position on a number line. The extent to which each score deviates above or below the mean ($\bar{Y} = 33.00$) is indicated directly underneath the number line. There are 9 scores with values less than the mean, 1 with a value equal to the mean, and 14 with values greater than the mean. The sum of the 9 negative deviations (-148) exactly equals—except for sign—the sum of the 14 positive deviations ($+148$); the deviations from the mean are in algebraic balance. Expressing this property in symbols, we have

$$\sum (Y - \bar{Y}) = 0 \qquad\qquad (4\text{-}2)$$

As you will see next, the mean serves as a reference point against which we can express another important characteristic of a set of scores, the degree to which the numbers vary.

4.2   MEASURING VARIABILITY

The concept of variability is central to an understanding of data analysis. By *variability*, we mean the degree to which people differ in response measures when measured under seemingly identical circumstances. There are two primary reasons for variability. First, people differ from each other in the degree to which they respond to situations or circumstances. Measurement theorists treat variability between subjects as "individual differences." Second, responses and observations will vary as a result of measurement error, unsystematic influences, or unreliability of the measuring device. In general, the concept of variability can be used to represent the degree of agreement or similarity in responses or observations; the less the variability, the more alike the values. The cause of the variability is important in interpreting the data.

Variability as a statistical concept is expressed in terms of **deviations from the mean**, since the mean is the score that represents the "typical" observation in a distribution. We want to know the degree to which the scores in the set deviate from the "typical" score. A set of tightly grouped scores will have smaller deviations than a set of less tightly grouped scores. Consider again the data plotted in Fig. 4-1. Suppose the scores took on only the values 32, 33, and 34. Assuming that the mean is again 33, the deviations will be either -1, 0, or $+1$. In contrast, the deviations in Fig. 4-1 range from -27 to $+20$, or a 47-point spread. If the scores exhibited absolutely no variability—that is, all 24 scores were 33—there would be no scatter or dispersion around the mean, and the value of all 24 deviations would be 0.

A natural index of variability would be the average deviation from the mean, that is,

$$\frac{\Sigma\ (Y-\bar{Y})}{N}$$

But this index is not useful, because of the property of deviations expressed in Eq. (4-2), namely, that $\Sigma\ (Y-\bar{Y}) = 0$. What this means, then, is that the numerator in the above formula would always be 0 and that the index would be the same (0) for *all* sets of scores, regardless of the variability present.

Sum of Squares

We can obtain a nonzero numerator by averaging instead the *squared* deviations from the mean. Since squared deviations can take on only positive values, there is no canceling of positive and negative numbers when they are summed. The sum of the squared deviations from the mean—called the **sum of squares** (SS)— then also takes on values that reflect variability: 0 when variability is absent, and positive values when variability is present. For the 24 scores appearing in Table 4-1 (and depicted in Fig. 4-1),

$$SS = \Sigma\ (Y-\bar{Y})^2 \tag{4-3}$$
$$= (53-33)^2 + (49-33)^2 + \cdots + (11-33)^2 + (6-33)^2$$
$$= (20)^2 + (16)^2 + \cdots + (-22)^2 + (-27)^2$$
$$= 400 + 256 + \cdots + 484 + 729 = 5000$$

Another computational formula for SS involves two sums, the sum of the actual, or "raw," scores $(\Sigma\ Y)$ and the sum of the *squared* raw scores $(\Sigma\ Y^2)$. More specifically,

$$SS = \Sigma\ Y^2 - \frac{(\Sigma\ Y)^2}{N} \tag{4-4}$$

From Table 4-1,

$$\Sigma\ Y = 53 + 49 + \cdots + 11 + 6 = 792$$
$$\Sigma\ Y^2 = 53^2 + 49^2 + \cdots + 11^2 + 6^2 = 31,136$$

and

$$SS = 31,136 - \frac{(792)^2}{24}$$

$$= 31,136 - \frac{627,264}{24} = 31,136 - 26,136$$

$$= 5000$$

which is identical to the value obtained from Eq. (4-3). As you will see, sums of squares lie behind most of the analyses we will consider in this book.

A key point to recognize is that use of the mean as the point from which the deviations are calculated results in the smallest possible value of the *SS*. That is, if any value other than 33 were used in Eq. (4-3) to determine the sum of squares, the result would be *greater* than 5000. This point is important when we consider the concept of least squares in Chap. 5.

The Variance

The **variance** is the result of dividing the sum of squares either by (1) the total number of scores N or by (2) a related quantity, the **degrees of freedom** (*df*). The distinction revolves around the concepts of a sample and a population. A **population** is the set of all members of a specified group—for example, all eligible voters—while a **sample** is a *subset* whose scores are used to provide estimates of characteristics of the population from which it is drawn. The first method of calculation defines what is called the *descriptive* version of the variance, which is used when the actual data set is in fact that for the population itself, for example, the test grades of all the students in your class. The second method defines the *inferential* version of the variance, which is used when one is interested in making inferences about a larger population and thus about individuals who are *not* included in the data set. Not all statistical indices come in two versions, as the variance does. The mean, for example, has only one version, which is used in either situation. In most applications with which we will be concerned, we will use the second, or inferential, version of the variance.

The general rule for computing the *df* is:

$$df = \begin{pmatrix} \text{number of} \\ \text{independent} \\ \text{observations} \end{pmatrix} - \begin{pmatrix} \text{number of} \\ \text{restraints} \end{pmatrix} \tag{4-5}$$

The phrase *number of restraints* is used to indicate that in computing some statistics used to describe samples, there are restrictions placed on the "freedom" with which the observations may vary. If we have an estimate of the mean of the distribution—for example, $\bar{Y} = 6.0$—and there are five scores entering into the calculation of this mean, then only four scores in the sample are free to take on any value. This happens because the fifth score must be the particular value that will result in a mean of 6.0, which is calculated on the entire set. For the present case, where only a single set of scores is involved,

$$df = \text{number of scores} - 1 = N - 1 \tag{4-6}$$

$$= 24 - 1 = 23$$

The variance, then, is calculated as follows:

$$\text{variance } (\hat{\sigma}^2) = \frac{SS}{df} \tag{4-7}$$

$$= \frac{5000}{23} = 217.39$$

(The caret, or "hat," above the symbol for the variance is used to indicate that the computational result is a variance *estimate*.) The descriptive version of the variance, which divides the SS by N rather than by $N - 1$, is slightly smaller in value ($5000/24 = 208.33$).

The reason for dividing the sum of squares by the degrees of freedom is statistical in nature. In statistical estimation, the data of a sample are used to estimate characteristics of the population. The descriptive variance calculated from a single data set, which divides SS by N, slightly underestimates the population variance, while the estimated variance ($\hat{\sigma}^2$), for which SS is divided by $N - 1$, removes this small bias present in the descriptive variance.

The Standard Deviation

Another common measure of variability is the **standard deviation**, which is simply the square root of the variance; that is,

$$\text{standard deviation } (\hat{\sigma}) - \sqrt{\text{variance}} \tag{4-8}$$

For the present example,

$$\hat{\sigma} = \sqrt{217.39} = 14.74$$

The standard deviation is usually reported in research papers rather than the variance. One reason is that the standard deviation represents variability in "un-squared" units that can be related to the original scale of measurement. If the distribution of numbers reflects measurement in feet, for example, then the standard deviation is also in feet; that is, in the present example, one standard deviation is 14.74 feet. We cannot interpret the variance (217.39) in units of feet.

Aside from being used to describe distributions, the standard deviation is also used for constructing the confidence interval for the mean (i.e., the range within which the population mean falls with a specified degree of confidence) and for defining **standard scores**, which permit the comparison of scores between groups that have different means and variabilities. On the other hand, the variance is used for testing hypotheses in the analysis of experiments.

4.3   SUMMARY

This chapter has covered the statistical indices that are at the root of most data analyses used in the behavioral sciences. The mean and the deviations from the mean have a central role in all the analyses we will consider in this book. The arithmetic mean offers a measure of central tendency; and the variance, which is based on the sum of squared deviations from the mean, provides a measure of variability, as does the standard deviation.

4.4   EXERCISES

1. To illustrate basic statistical procedures, an instructor collected the heights (measured in centimeters) and weights (measured in kilograms) of the 15 male students in her section. The values were as follows:

Student	Height (cm)	Weight (kg)	Student	Height (cm)	Weight (kg)
1	149	54	9	172	55
2	153	52	10	178	73
3	167	53	11	173	78
4	161	57	12	164	58
5	151	47	13	181	73
6	154	62	14	182	68
7	177	69	15	159	58
8	162	60			

a. Calculate the average height and weight of the 15 students.
b. Find the deviations from the mean for the two sets of scores and verify that the sum (within rounding error) of each set of deviations is zero.
c. Calculate the sums of squares for the two sets of scores in two ways, with Eq. (4-3), which is based on deviations from the mean, and the other with Eq. (4-4), which is based on the actual scores.
d. Complete the analysis by calculating the variances and standard deviations for the two sets of scores.

NOTE: Save your calculations for the exercises in Chap. 5.

5

Basic Statistical Concepts
in Correlation
and Regression

. . .

In this chapter we introduce the basic statistical concepts in correlational and regression analysis. We will present two measures that are used to show the relationship between variables—the correlation ratio and the Pearson correlation coefficient—as well as the regression equation, which is a useful summary of the relationship.

5.1   MEASURES OF CORRELATION: AN OVERVIEW

Chapter 4 focused on data sets in which each subject provides an observation, or score, on a *single* variable Y. Our emphasis was on *describing* the properties of such data sets. To elaborate, we demonstrated that data sets on a single variable could be described and summarized by statistics such as measures of central tendency and variability.

As we pointed out in Chap. 1, however, researchers are also interested in explaining or predicting behavior. Thus, when they observe variability in the data taken on a variable, they want to understand the "why" of the variability. To do so, they seek out information on at least one more variable that *may* be related to their first variable. They examine the data on both variables to determine whether there is a "link" between the variables—that is, whether data on their original variable (the *predicted* variable) vary as a function of changes in their second variable (the *predictor*). In this chapter, we examine statistical measures for determining the relationship or degree of linkage between variables.

In survey work, for example, the "scores" might represent some characteristic of individual subjects (e.g., a personality characteristic such as compulsiveness), or they might represent an expression of their belief or opinion on some topic. If we collect data on both the "characteristic" and the "opinion," we can examine the relationship between the two. The mean and the variance (or standard deviation) can be used to summarize and describe the information contained within *each* data set. Researchers who want to go beyond the description of each data set and look for relationships have traditionally used measures of correlation and regression.

5.2   THE CORRELATION RATIO

The **correlation ratio or eta squared** (η^2) is a general measure of association that reflects or indicates any relationship present between two variables. Eta *can* be used to analyze experimental data, but we will show how it is used in nonexperimental designs to illustrate its basic concepts and how they underlie other correlational statistics that are relevant to MRC. All that is necessary to appreciate eta is an understanding of the mean and the variance, topics we discussed in Chap. 4.

The Formula

To make matters simple, we will begin by stating that the formula for eta (as a descriptive statistic) is based on a ratio of two variances. One of these is the total variance in Y (σ_Y^2), and the other is the variance in Y that can be explained by taking into account information provided by a second variable, X. This latter variance is represented as $\sigma_{Y'}^2$ and is referred to as the variance in Y that is *common* to the variance in X. The formula for eta,

$$\eta = \sqrt{\frac{\sigma_{Y'}^2}{\sigma_Y^2}} \tag{5-1}$$

yields an index that indicates the degree of relationship between X and Y. The square of eta, which is more relevant to the present discussion, is interpreted as a *proportion of variance*. That is,

$$\eta^2 = \frac{\sigma_{Y'}^2}{\sigma_Y^2} \tag{5-2}$$

represents the proportion or percentage of total Y variability that is explainable or predictable from a knowledge of X. Correlational results are often described in these terms or by similar phrases such as *percentage of common variance, percentage of variance explained*, or *percentage of variance accounted for*.

Though Eq. (5-2) shows eta squared to be a ratio of two variances, it may be understood by viewing it from the perspective of the relationship or association between two variables, X and Y. We can make the leap from variances to percentages and from percentages to associations because of the way in which variances are calculated. When we make the statement that a statistical association between X and Y exists, we are saying that variability in one variable leads to (affects, causes, or overlaps with) variability in the second variable. If a relationship exists between X and Y, the two variables covary and are assumed to share something in common. As a consequence of their commonality, one of the variables can be used to explain some portion of the variability of the other.

Another way of finding whether an association exists is to determine whether having information on one variable results in reduction in the variability of the other. We will demonstrate how this might occur with a set of hypothetical data. This time, instead of basing our argument on variances, we will make the same point more simply by using the ranges of scores. (Eta and its relationship to the reduction of variability are fully developed in Ghiselli et al., 1981.)

A Comparison of Ranges

Assume that we have 16 subjects ($N = 16$) and that each supplies us with two scores, an X score and a Y score. These scores are displayed in Table 5-1. Suppose our primary interest lies in predicting or explaining the variation observed in the distribution of Y scores. If we were asked to estimate the Y value a subject might have and we knew nothing else about that subject, then the best estimate we could give would be the mean of the entire distribution; in this case, application of Eq. (4-1) gives us $\bar{Y} = 14.00$.

An examination of the set of Y scores shows that they exhibit considerable variability, however, ranging in value from a high of 23 for subject 16 to a low of 7 for subject 1. Using the range of these scores as a crude estimate of this variability, then, we can say that the variability in Y is $23 - 7 = 16$ points. Since our best estimate of any particular subject's Y score is the mean (14.00) but an *actual* score can fall anywhere from 7 through 23, a degree of uncertainty or error surrounds this particular estimate.

On the other hand, if a relationship exists between X and Y, we can use information available on X to reduce this uncertainty in estimating Y. Let us see how this may be accomplished. The simplest way to use our information about X is to

Table 5-1
Two Sets of Scores Obtained from the Same $N = 16$ Subjects

Subject	X	Y
1	1	7
2	2	9
3	3	13
4	4	15
5	1	8
6	2	11
7	3	14
8	4	19
9	1	9
10	2	14
11	3	17
12	4	20
13	1	11
14	2	15
15	3	19
16	4	23

group the Y scores according to their X values and then use the mean of the Y scores for each X group rather than the overall mean of the Y scores to estimate Y. We have illustrated the process in Fig. 5-1 by plotting the Y scores grouped according to the values of X. The Y means are 8.75, 12.25, 15.75, and 19.25 for subjects with X values $= 1, 2, 3,$ and 4, respectively. Now, if we are asked to estimate Y, we first find out the subject's X score (group number) and then use the appropriate group mean as the estimate. That is, if $X = 1$, the Y estimate is 8.75; if $X = 2$, the Y estimate is 12.25; and so on.

An examination of Fig. 5-1 shows that the uncertainty associated with these particular Y estimates is markedly less than the uncertainty associated with Y when there are no X data. More specifically, the Y scores for subjects who have a value of 1 on X vary from 7 through 11—a range of 4 points. Those with a value of 2 on X have a range of 6 points $(15 - 9)$; those with values of 3 and 4 on X have ranges of 6 and 8, respectively. These four ranges, which collectively reflect the uncertainty that remains in the estimate of Y even when information about X is taken into account, are all much less than the range of the ungrouped Y scores, which reflects the uncertainty present when information about X is either not available or disregarded. In terms of numbers, we are comparing an average range of $(4 + 6 + 6 + 8)/4 = 6.0$ for the four subgroups with a range of 16 for the total distribution (a range which ignores X information). Even when we use X information, there is still a certain amount of variability left over (an average of 6 points

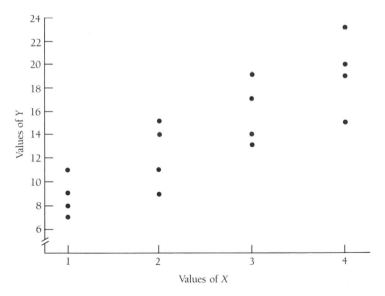

Figure 5-1   Plot of the data of Table 5-1.

in this example). If the variability in Y is 16 points, and if we use X and find that 6 points of variability is not attributable to X, then 10 points (16 − 6) must be attributable to X; this latter amount is explainable Y variability. In short, we are able to reduce the amount of variability by an average of 10 points (16 − 6) when we take X into consideration in this example.

You will recall that we stated that eta squared consists of a ratio of a variance that reflects the commonality between X and Y to a second variance, the total Y variance. Using ranges as approximations of variances in the formula yields us information on the average reduction in range. We divide the average range resulting from the use of X information (as a substitute for the common variance) by the overall range in Y (in place of the total variance). Using the numbers we have just derived, we have 10/16 = .63. (The actual value of eta square calculated with variances instead of ranges is .74.)

The eta squared value reflects the proportion of Y variability associated with X. The remaining amount .37 (that is, 1 − .63), reflects the proportion of Y variability that is *independent* of X. Stated another way, any variability observed within the four X subgroups, after taking into account X information (i.e., holding X constant), cannot be due to variations in the X variable. This remaining, or *residual*, variability represents variation in the Y variable that cannot be related to, explained by, or caused by X. In the present case, the residual variability is 6 points.

In fact, we can determine eta squared directly by calculating the residual variance. The above indicates that the proportion of Y variability that is predictable from X, or $\sigma^2_{Y'}$, is $\sigma^2_Y - \sigma^2_{residual}$. Substituting into Eq. (5-2) yields

$$\eta^2 = \frac{\sigma^2_{Y'}}{\sigma^2_Y} = \frac{\sigma^2_Y - \sigma^2_{res.}}{\sigma^2_Y} = 1 - \frac{\sigma^2_{res.}}{\sigma^2_Y} \tag{5-3}$$

Comment

We have discussed the correlation ratio because it directly expresses the proportion of explainable variation—variability that is common between X and Y—which is the concept we wish to demonstrate. We will not do more with the formula here, because the statistic has certain limitations. For example, eta (or eta squared) does not indicate the *form* of the relationship between two variables (such as linearity); in this sense, the index is too general to be used to analyze research questions in nonexperimental situations. In addition, the index usually yields different values from the same data set, depending on whether one is interested in explaining variability in Y or variability in X. The measure is useful, however, in a demonstration of the link between ANOVA and MRC, the two approaches to the analysis of data that are the subject of this book. We will consider next a correlational index that overcomes the limitations associated with the correlation ratio.

5.3   THE PEARSON CORRELATION COEFFICIENT

The correlation ratio (eta squared) reflects the degree to which two variables X and Y covary in any form, linear or nonlinear. The **Pearson correlation coefficient** (r), on the other hand, detects one particular relationship between the variables, namely, the *linear* relationship between X and Y, or the relationship that can be described by a straight line. Although this property may appear to be overly restrictive, there are distinct advantages to the index, in analyzing both experimental and nonexperimental data. These will become apparent to you as you progress through the book.

Two important pieces of information are provided by r. The first is the *direction* of the relationship between the two variables. A positive coefficient indicates that X and Y vary in the *same direction* (as X increases, Y increases; or as X decreases, Y decreases), while a negative coefficient indicates that they vary in *opposite directions* (as X increases, Y decreases; or as X decreases, Y increases). The direction of the relationship can be seen easily from a scatterplot, which is a graph in which the subjects are located with reference to their X and Y scores. The data in Fig. 5-1 reflect a positive relationship between the two variables.

The second piece of information is the *strength* of the relationship between the X and Y variables. One way of expressing the strength is by the squared Pearson correlation coefficient (r^2). You will recall from Sec. 5.2 that eta squared offered a similar index. The difference is that r^2 represents the proportion of Y variability accounted for by a knowledge of the *linear* relationship between X and Y, while eta squared includes both the linear relationship and more complex relationships between the two variables. This difference between the two statistics is reflected in the fact that a regression equation (elaborated upon in Sec. 5.4) accompanies r and allows us to predict a Y from X. For eta, we know there is a relationship, but there is no regression equation to allow us to predict one variable from the other. We cannot predict because eta is independent of the form of the relationship.

There are several formulas for the Pearson coefficient. One formula, which we will use to gain an intuitive understanding of correlation and its relationship to ANOVA, deals entirely with scores in deviation form and does not use sample size (N) directly:

$$r = \frac{\Sigma\,[(X - \bar{X})\,(Y - \bar{Y})]}{\sqrt{\Sigma\,(X - \bar{X})^2\,\Sigma\,(Y - \bar{Y})^2}} \qquad (5\text{-}4)$$

where

$\Sigma\,(X - \bar{X})^2$ is the sum of the squared deviations of the X scores from their mean

$\Sigma\,(Y - \bar{Y})^2$ is the sum of the squared deviations of the Y scores from their mean

$\Sigma [(X - \bar{X})(Y - \bar{Y})]$ is the sum of the products of the X and Y deviations for the individual subjects

We will illustrate the use of this formula momentarily.

If the data are in raw-score form, two alternative formulas may be more appropriate. The first is to be used if you have already calculated the means and standard deviations for the X and Y scores. Under these circumstances,

$$r = \frac{\Sigma XY - N\bar{X}\bar{Y}}{(N - 1)\hat{\sigma}_X\hat{\sigma}_Y} \tag{5-5}$$

where

N represents the number of paired observations (sample size)

$\bar{X}$ and $\bar{Y}$ are the means of the X and Y scores, respectively

$\hat{\sigma}_X$ and $\hat{\sigma}_Y$ are the corresponding estimates of the standard deviations

ΣXY specifies the sum of the products of the pairs of scores

The second formula uses only X's and Y's and avoids the accumulation of rounding error that occurs with formulas using the means:

$$r^2 = \frac{[N \Sigma XY - (\Sigma X)(\Sigma Y)]^2}{[N \Sigma X^2 - (\Sigma X)^2][N \Sigma Y^2 - (\Sigma Y)^2]} \tag{5-6}$$

where

N is the sample size

ΣX and ΣY specify the sums of the X and Y scores, respectively

ΣX^2 and ΣY^2 specify the sums of the squared X and Y scores, respectively

ΣXY specifies the sum of the products of the pairs of scores

The value of r is simply the square root of r^2. The *direction* of the relationship in Eq. (5-6) is indicated by the bracketed quantity in the numerator. That is, if the quantity within the brackets is positive, r is positive, and if the quantity is negative, r is negative.

We will calculate r for a hypothetical example, using Eq. (5-4), the formula expressed in terms of deviations, although the r value will be the same regardless of whether the formula is written in raw-score form or in deviation units. For convenience, the data from Table 5-1 are presented again in columns 1 and 2 of Table 5-2. For each subject, the deviation of the X score from $\bar{X}$ is presented in column 3 and the deviation of the Y score from $\bar{Y}$ is presented in column 5. The numerator of Eq. (5-4) requires the multiplication of the two deviations for each subject; the products are listed in column 7. The denominator requires the squared deviations of both variables, and these are given in columns 4 and 6. The three sums specified

Table 5-2
Numerical Example of the Pearson Correlation r

Subject	(1) X	(2) Y	(3) $(X - \bar{X})$	(4) $(X - \bar{X})^2$	(5) $(Y - \bar{Y})$	(6) $(Y - \bar{Y})^2$	(7) $(X - \bar{X})(Y - \bar{Y})$
1	1	7	-1.50	2.25	-7.00	49.00	10.50
2	2	9	-0.50	.25	-5.00	25.00	2.50
3	3	13	0.50	.25	-1.00	1.00	$-.50$
4	4	15	1.50	2.25	1.00	1.00	1.50
5	1	8	-1.50	2.25	-6.00	36.00	9.00
6	2	11	-0.50	.25	-3.00	9.00	1.50
7	3	14	0.50	.25	0.00	0.00	0.00
8	4	19	1.50	2.25	5.00	25.00	7.50
9	1	9	-1.50	2.25	-5.00	25.00	7.50
10	2	14	-0.50	.25	0.00	0.00	0.00
11	3	17	0.50	.25	3.00	9.00	1.50
12	4	20	1.50	2.25	6.00	36.00	9.00
13	1	11	-1.50	2.25	-3.00	9.00	4.50
14	2	15	-0.50	.25	1.00	1.00	$-.50$
15	3	19	0.50	.25	5.00	25.00	2.50
16	4	23	1.50	2.25	9.00	81.00	13.50
Sum	40	224	0.00	20.00	0.00	332.00	70.00

by the formula are also presented in the table. Substituting in Eq. (5-4), we find

$$r = \frac{70.00}{\sqrt{(20.00)(332.00)}}$$

$$= \frac{70.00}{\sqrt{6640.00}} = \frac{70.00}{81.49} = .86$$

This result would also be obtained if Eq. (5-5) or (5-6) were used to calculate r. The r^2 for these data is .74.

5.4   THE LINEAR REGRESSION EQUATION

Whereas r and r^2 provide information about the strength of a relationship, additional information is available from the same set of X and Y scores, namely, a prediction formula, referred to as a **regression equation**. The regression equation is typically used to make predictions about one variable from information that is known about the other variable; this is the classic utilization of a regression equation, and its logic is consistent with the logic we used to describe eta. A less frequent but equally plausible use is to test hypotheses pertaining to group differences obtained in experiments. We will discuss such uses when we are farther along, but for now let us focus on the equation and its components.

A regression equation that is used to describe the linear relationship between two variables X and Y is:

$$Y' = a + bX \qquad\qquad (5\text{-}7)$$

where

Y' is the estimated or predicted Y score (the value of Y that will be predicted given particular X values)

a and b are constants calculated from the set of X and Y scores

X is the particular value of the predictor variable to be entered into the regression equation

This equation will allow us to estimate Y values given known X values.[1]

The constant b is referred to as a **regression coefficient**. It represents the slope of the so-called best-fitting line that describes the relationship between X and Y. If we are interested in predicting Y from X, then the b value is

$$b = \frac{\Sigma\,[(X - \bar{X})\,(Y - \bar{Y})]}{\Sigma\,(X - \bar{X})^2} \qquad\qquad (5\text{-}8)$$

(There is a corresponding formula for predicting X from Y, which is not of interest to us at this time.)

To illustrate the calculations, we will enter the relevant values from Table 5-2. More specifically,

$$b = \frac{70.00}{20.00} = 3.50$$

This value of 3.50 for the slope gives us two pieces of information. First, the positive sign indicates that the slope is positive, or that Y increases as X increases; this you can see in Fig. 5-1. Second, the value indicates the amount of change in Y associated with a change of 1 unit in X. For example, a change from 1 to

---

[1] At this point, you might wonder why we would want to estimate or predict Y values when, in fact, we already know them. The reason for doing this is to fulfill a classic purpose of regression statistics; that is, to predict scores on a *new* sample based on results from data collected in an original similar sample.

2 on the X variable (a 1-unit change) will produce a change of 3.50 in the Y variable. Another way of looking at this is that there is a difference of 3.50 points on Y between subjects with an X value of 1 and subjects with an X value of 2.

The other constant, a, is referred to as the **intercept**. From the point of view of classical measurement, a is the value of Y' when X is zero. As you will see, the intercept provides more interesting information when it is used to interpret results of experimental data. One way of determining a is by the following equation:

$$a = \bar{Y} - b\bar{X} \qquad\qquad (5\text{-}9)$$

Using the information from Table 5-2 and previous calculations, we find that

$$a = 14.00 - (3.50)(2.50) = 14.00 - 8.75 = 5.25$$

We can now write the regression equation by substituting the values for a and b in Eq. (5-7):

$$Y' = a + bX$$
$$= 5.25 + 3.50X$$

Using this equation, we can calculate Y' for any value of X. We will illustrate this process in Sec. 5.6. Figure 5-2 shows this regression line obtained by calculating a Y' for each X and then connecting the points (X, Y').

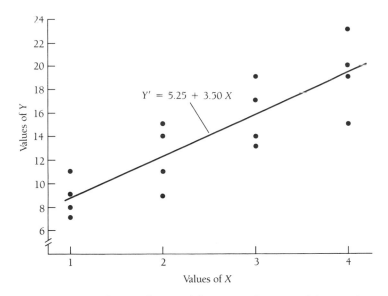

Figure 5-2   Regression line predicting Y' from X on the basis of the data from Table 5-1.

The regression coefficient represents what is known as a **least squares esti-mate**. You will recall that we mentioned the method of least squares when we were discussing the mean. That is, the mean is a least squares estimate because the sum of the squared deviations from the mean is smaller than the sum of those from any other value. Similarly, the regression coefficient is a least squares estimate because the sum of the squared deviations of the Y scores from the *regression line* is smaller than from any other line that would be used to depict the relationship.

5.5   THE RELATION BETWEEN REGRESSION AND CORRELATION

Regression and correlation are directly linked. In Sec. 5.4, we indicated that the regression equation may be used to make predictions. But predictions can be made and are most precise when there is correlation. We saw this when we presented the correlation ratio in Sec. 5.2. In that section, we showed that the best predic-tion of Y without X information is $\bar{Y}$. However, if X and Y are related, the best prediction of a Y with a particular value of X is the mean of all Y scores with that value of X.

When we restrict ourselves to linear correlation, we not only compute an index of correlation r_{XY}, but at the same time develop a regression equation to yield predicted Y values, $Y' = a + bX$. Thus, in the calculation of correlation and regression, we involve three kinds of information for each subject: the obtained X, the obtained Y, and the predicted score Y'.

An important link between correlation and regression is that the correlation between X and Y is identical to the correlation between Y and the value predicted by X, which is labeled Y' and is derived from the regression equation, Eq. (5-7). That is,

$$r_{XY} = r_{YY'} \tag{5-10}$$

Also, it can be shown that

$$r_{XY}^2 = \frac{\Sigma (Y' - \bar{Y})^2}{\Sigma (Y - \bar{Y})^2} \tag{5-11}$$

Thus, we see that the correlation between X and Y is based on the deviations of predicted scores Y' from $\bar{Y}$ relative to the deviations of actual obtained Y scores from $\bar{Y}$. Stated another way, r_{XY}^2 represents the proportion of variability in Y that is predictable from the information on X used to obtain Y'. We will illustrate the use of this equation in Sec. 5.6.

The importance of this link between correlation and regression is twofold. First, it indicates that when we speak of correlation, we are also speaking about prediction. Second, and of perhaps greater importance when we turn to multiple correlation and multiple regression, is that we will be able to interpret the relationship between one Y score and a set of X scores in the same way as we interpret the relationship between one Y score and one X score.

5.6   DECOMPOSITION OF AN OBSERVED SCORE

Now that we have indicated that there are links between X, Y, and Y', we can take any observed Y and decompose it into a set of meaningful components. We do this to illustrate fundamental properties of correlation and regression and to eventually establish the link between ANOVA and MRC. We start with three kinds of information: (1) the observed score Y, (2) the predicted score Y', and (3) the group mean $\bar{Y}$. It is possible to put this information into an equation that shows an observed score Y to be made up of the following components:

$$Y = \bar{Y} + (Y' - \bar{Y}) + (Y - Y') \qquad (5\text{-}12)$$

$$\quad\;\; [1] \qquad\quad [2] \qquad\qquad [3]$$

where

[1] is the mean of the Y scores

[2] is the deviation of the predicted score from the mean

[3] is the deviation of the observed score from the predicted score

You can verify the correctness of this decomposition by adding together the quantities on the right of the equal sign. What you will find is that $\bar{Y}$ is canceled by $-\bar{Y}$ and that Y' is canceled by $-Y'$, leaving Y on both sides of the equation.

But let us go one step further and subtract $\bar{Y}$ from both sides of the equal sign, which does not disturb the equality established in Eq. (5-12). What this yields is an equation that is expressed entirely in deviations:

$$Y - \bar{Y} = (Y' - \bar{Y}) + (Y - Y') \qquad (5\text{-}13)$$

In words, the deviation of a Y score from the mean $(Y - \bar{Y})$ is made up of two component deviations: the deviation of the predicted Y score from the mean $(Y' - \bar{Y})$ and the deviation of the original, obtained Y score from the predicted value $(Y - Y')$.

The relationships expressed in Eqs. (5-12) and (5-13) are represented geo-metrically in Fig. 5-3. We start with a pair of scores X_i and Y_i and locate the pair in a scatterplot. This pair is located at the intersection of two lines, one extending perpendicularly from X_i on the X axis (the unbroken vertical line in the figure) and the other extending perpendicularly from Y_i on the Y axis (the uppermost dashed horizontal line in the figure). The point of intersection (X_i, Y_i) is indicated by an unfilled circle. Next consider the regression line—the diagonal line in the figure—and the point at which the line drawn from X_i intersects the regression line. This point is indicated by a filled circle. The dashed line drawn from the point of intersection to the vertical axis locates Y_i', the Y score predicted from X_i and the regression line. Finally, the bottommost dashed line indicates the position of the mean of the Y scores $(\bar{Y})$ on the vertical axis.

We can now illustrate the meaning of the two equations by examining certain vertical differences represented in Fig. 5-3. Equation (5-12) is represented by the three parts into which the vertical line running from X_i to Y_i is divided. That is, you can easily see that Y_i, which is represented by the full extent of the vertical line, is made up of three components, namely, the mean of the Y scores (the seg-ment running from 0 to $\bar{Y}$), the deviation of the predicted score Y_i' from $\bar{Y}$ (the middle segment), and the deviation of the actual score Y_i from Y_i' (the top segment).

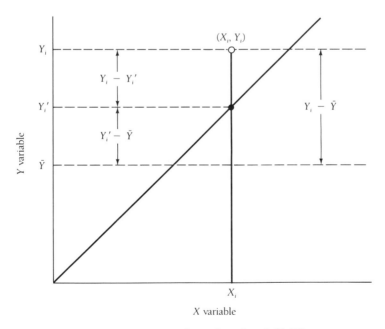

Figure 5-3   Geometric representation of Eqs. (5-12) and (5-13).

Equation (5-13), on the other hand, is represented by the vertical distances between the three dashed lines in the figure. As you can see, the deviation of Y_i from $\bar{Y}$, which is represented by the distance between the top and bottom lines, is obviously made up of two component parts, the deviation of Y'_i from $\bar{Y}$ (the distance between the middle and bottom lines) and the deviation of Y_i from Y'_i (the distance between the top and middle lines).

The value of subdividing the total deviation $Y_i - \bar{Y}$ into two component deviations is seen when they are transformed into *component sums of squares*. This may be accomplished by determining the component deviations for all of the observations, squaring them, and then summing the squares. The result of these operations produces the following useful equation:

$$\Sigma \, (Y - \bar{Y})^2 = \Sigma \, (Y' - \bar{Y})^2 + \Sigma \, (Y - Y')^2 \qquad (5\text{-}14)$$

$$\quad [1] \qquad\qquad\qquad [2] \qquad\qquad\quad [3]$$

In words, the sum of squares of the Y scores [1] is composed of two component sums of squares, one based on differences between the predicted Y score and the Y mean [2] and one based on differences between the actual and predicted Y scores [3].

Let us examine Eq. (5-14) and the relationship between these three sums of squares more closely. As we have noted already, the term on the left of the equal sign, [1], is the sum of squares based on the deviations of the Y scores from their mean. For any set of data, this value is fixed, with the constraint that the terms labeled [2] and [3] sum to it; see Eq. (5-14). What this constraint means is that any change in one of the components must produce a corresponding change in the opposite direction for the other. We will examine the two components separately to see why they are affected oppositely by the presence of correlation between the X and Y variables.

The sum of squares labeled [2] represents the extent to which a predicted score Y', which is derived from the linear relationship between X and Y given in Eq. (5-7), differs from the Y mean. You will recall from Sec. 5-2 that we could use $\bar{Y}$ to predict a Y score in the absence of any information about the X variable (or when there is no systematic relationship between X and Y). In other words, [2] represents the extent to which a Y score *is* predictable from X. If there were a zero relationship or a small relationship between the two variables, then Y' would be equal to $\bar{Y}$ or close to it, and consequently, the squared differences would be small and, correspondingly, [3] would be large. If there were a strong relationship, such as that depicted in Fig. 5-1, the predicted value Y' would tend to be quite different from $\bar{Y}$. The result in this case would be a large value for [2] relative to [3]. Because [2] increases as the relationship between X and Y increases, we will label this quantity as the sum of squares due to *prediction*, or more commonly, the **sum of squares due to regression**, symbolized as $SS_{reg.}$.

The sum of squares labeled [3] represents the degree to which the predicted Y value Y' approaches the actual Y value. Let us see how this quantity is affected by the presence of a linear relationship between X and Y. With a relatively weak relationship between the two variables, the difference between Y and Y' will tend to be great, creating a large value for [3] relative to [2]. With a stronger relationship, these differences will be smaller, and consequently, there will be a smaller value for [3] relative to [2]. Since this sum of squares is the deviation of an actual Y score from a predicted Y score, it represents *error in prediction*, and we refer to it as the **residual sum of squares** or $SS_{res.}$.

The purpose of this discussion is to underscore the relationship between linear regression and correlation and to show how to express the Pearson correlation coefficient in terms of sums of squares. In Eq. (5-11), we indicated that

$$r_{XY}^2 = \frac{\Sigma \, (Y' - \bar{Y})^2}{\Sigma \, (Y - \bar{Y})^2}$$

Using our terminology for the terms in Eq. (5-14), we may express this ratio as

$$r_{XY}^2 = \frac{SS_{reg.}}{SS_Y}. \tag{5-15}$$

This formula clearly indicates that r_{XY}^2 reflects the proportion of Y variability that is associated with variation in the X variable. The logic underlying its interpretation is equivalent to that used for eta squared as represented by Eq. (5-3).

It is useful at this point to return to the numerical example. Table 5-3 presents again the X and Y scores for each of the 16 subjects, in columns 1 and 2, respectively. To obtain the predicted scores Y', we substitute the X score for each subject in the obtained regression equation and solve for Y'; the Y' scores are provided in column 3. Let us see how they are obtained. In previous calculations, we found the regression equation to be

$$Y' = 5.25 + 3.50X$$

To illustrate the use of this equation for the third subject, we find that

$$Y_3 = 5.25 + (3.50)(3) = 5.25 + 10.50 = 15.75$$

The three relevant deviations specified in Eq. (5-13), $(Y - \bar{Y})$, $(Y' - \bar{Y})$, and $(Y - Y')$, are listed in columns 4, 5, and 6, respectively. With this information, you can verify that the relationship expressed in Eq. (5-13) holds for each of the

Table 5-3
Component Deviations Underlying Linear Regression

	(1)	(2)	(3)	(4)	(5)	(6)
Subject	X	Y	Y'	$(Y - \bar{Y})$	$= (Y' - \bar{Y}) +$	$(Y - Y')$
1	1	7	8.75	−7.00	−5.25	−1.75
2	2	9	12.25	−5.00	−1.75	−3.25
3	3	13	15.75	−1.00	1.75	−2.75
4	4	15	19.25	1.00	5.25	−4.25
5	1	8	8.75	−6.00	−5.25	−0.75
6	2	11	12.25	−3.00	−1.75	−1.25
7	3	14	15.75	0.00	1.75	−1.75
8	4	19	19.25	5.00	5.25	−0.25
9	1	9	8.75	−5.00	−5.25	0.25
10	2	14	12.25	0.00	−1.75	1.75
11	3	17	15.75	3.00	1.75	1.25
12	4	20	19.25	6.00	5.25	0.75
13	1	11	8.75	−3.00	−5.25	2.25
14	2	15	12.25	1.00	−1.75	2.75
15	3	19	15.75	5.00	1.75	3.25
16	4	23	19.25	9.00	5.25	3.75

subjects. For the third subject, for example,

$$(Y_3 - \bar{Y}) = (Y'_3 - \bar{Y}) + (Y_3 - Y'_3)$$
$$(13 - 14.00) = (15.75 - 14.00) + (13 - 15.75)$$
$$-1.00 = 1.75 + (-2.75) = -1.00$$

When all 16 of the deviations are squared and summed, we obtain

$$\Sigma (Y - \bar{Y})^2 = (-7.00)^2 + (-5.00)^2 + \cdots + (5.00)^2 + (9.00)^2$$
$$= 332.00$$
$$\Sigma (Y' - \bar{Y})^2 = (-5.25)^2 + (-1.75)^2 + \cdots + (1.75)^2 + (5.25)^2$$
$$= 245.00$$

and

$$\Sigma (Y - Y')^2 = (-1.75)^2 + (-3.25)^2 + \cdots + (3.25)^2 + (3.75)^2$$
$$= 87.00$$

We can verify Eq. (5-14) by showing that the sum of the two component sums of squares equals the total variation in Y. That is,

$$\Sigma \, (Y' - \bar{Y})^2 + \Sigma \, (Y - Y')^2 = 245.00 + 87.00 = 332.00$$
$$= \Sigma \, (Y - \bar{Y})^2$$

We can now substitute in Eq. (5-11) as follows:

$$r_{XY}^2 = \frac{\Sigma \, (Y' - \bar{Y})^2}{\Sigma \, (Y - \bar{Y})^2}$$
$$= \frac{245.00}{332.00} = .74$$

We obtained the same value, of course, simply by squaring the Pearson coefficient calculated with Eq. (5-4). That is,

$$r^2 = (.86)^2 = .74$$

A final analysis you should undertake is that of the correlation between Y and Y' (we leave the calculations to you; use columns 2 and 3 in Table 5-3). Correlation of these data yields an r^2 of .74, which is identical to the value derived in the preceding paragraph. This analysis is crucial to your understanding of correlation. Again, the correlation obtained between X and Y is *identical* to the correlation obtained between Y and corresponding values predicted by the regression equation based on the same data set. In essence, Y' embodies exactly that aspect of X that is correlated with Y. This fact will be noted again when we discuss multiple correlation.

5.7   SUMMARY

The association between two variables, usually indicated as Y and X, is reflected in two statistical measures, eta and the Pearson correlation coefficient. Eta indicates the general relationship between X and Y; we have presented eta squared to show how the relationship can be expressed as the percentage of variance explained. The Pearson coefficient, which concentrates on linear relationships, is the one that will be emphasized when we analyze experiments. The Pearson coefficient squared represents the proportion of Y variability that is associated with (or accounts for) variations in the X variable.

Along with the Pearson correlational index, there is a regression equation, or formula for predicting Y from X. Regression equations express the relationship in terms of the values of Y that are predicted from values of X (or Y′); the regression coefficient b, which is a component of the regression equation, expresses the relationship between the two variables in terms of changes in Y associated with changes in X.

There is a definite link between correlation and regression (prediction), conceptually and statistically. From a conceptual perspective, if there is a relationship between two variables X and Y, then we can predict one from the other. Statistically, $r^2_{XY} = r^2_{YY'}$. This latter relationship is important for concepts developed later in the text.

Finally, if there is a relationship between Y and X scores, the Y scores can be decomposed into concepts that reflect SS due to regression and SS due to error. In Chap. 7 we will relate these concepts to ANOVA concepts to illustrate the equivalence of MRC and ANOVA.

5.8   EXERCISES

1. In the exercises for Chap. 4, you were asked to calculate the means and standard deviations for measures of height and weight obtained from 15 male students. Since measures of height and weight are available for all the students, it is possible to determine the relationship between the two sets of scores. For the purpose of this analysis, let height be the X variable and weight be the Y variable.

a. Calculate the Pearson correlation coefficient from these two sets of scores, using Eq. (5-4), which is based on deviations of the X and Y scores from their respective means. (You have already obtained most of the information you need for this analysis from your answers to Problem 1 at the end of Chap. 4.)

b. Calculate r by means of the two alternative formulas—Eq. (5-5) and Eq. (5-6)—that are based on the X and Y scores rather than on deviations. (When you use Eq. (5-5), be sure to use the inferential version of $\hat{\sigma}_X$ and $\hat{\sigma}_Y$, and when you use Eq. (5-6), be sure to note the direction of the relationship, which is indicated by the sign of the bracketed quantity in the numerator.)

2. Calculate the regression equation for predicting a student's weight (Y′) from a knowledge of his height.

a. What exactly does the value of b tell us about the relationship between height and weight for these students?

b. What weight do you predict for a student who is 151 cm tall?

   c. What weight do you predict for a student whose height is equal to the mean of the set of 15 scores? Explain.

   3. Although r is usually expressed in terms of the relationship between X and Y, the statistic may also be defined in terms of the relationship between Y and Y', the value of Y predicted from a knowledge of X. With the values appearing in columns 2 and 3 of Table 5-3, show that the resulting $r_{YY'}^2$ is identical to the value of .74 that we calculated with Eq. (5-4).

6

Basic Statistical Concepts
in ANOVA

. . .

The previous chapters laid the foundation for the basic statistical concepts in research and statistics. Now it is time to relate specific analytical statistics to research design. This chapter deals with the analysis of the simplest experimental design, one in which two groups of individuals are treated differently and the effects of the differential treatment are assessed. We will show how the results of this simple experimental design are analyzed by means of the analysis of variance (ANOVA). In Chap. 7 we will consider the corresponding analysis with MRC procedures.

6.1   SUBDIVIDING THE TOTAL SUM OF SQUARES

Suppose we examined the data from an experiment in which two groups received different treatments but we did not take this fact into consideration in our analysis. Although we could calculate a mean and a standard deviation to describe the *total* data set, they would not be particularly useful, since this summary would obscure any effects that the two different treatments might have. Of course, these effects are precisely what we are most interested in. The analysis of variance does start, however, with a sum of squares based on the total data set. This *SS* is subdivided (or partitioned) into a number of separate parts, each of which provides different information useful for the statistical analysis of the experiment.

Notation and Labels

Let us consider the outcome of a hypothetical experiment in which fifth-grade students are introduced to a set of vocabulary words presented in the context either of a lecture on physical science or of one on social science. A vocabulary test, with 60 words, follows the lecture. The purpose of the experiment is to determine which of the two lectures produces better performance on the vocabulary test. The researcher begins with a total of 24 subjects and randomly assigns them so that each will fall into one of the two lecture conditions; equal numbers of subjects (12) are assigned to each group. We will use s to represent the treatment group sample size and N to represent the total number of subjects in the experiment. In this example, then, group sample size is $s = 12$, and $N = 12 + 12 = 24$. (We will assume equal sample sizes for most of the experimental designs we consider in this book; Chap. 24 deals with unequal sample sizes.)

We will call the independent variable **factor** *A*. The specific treatment conditions (or "treatments," for short) will be referred to as the **levels** of the independent variable, symbolized as *level* a_1 and *level* a_2. A lowercase *a* without a subscript designates the number of levels constituting factor *A*. In this example, there are $a = 2$

levels: level a_1 (physical science) and level a_2 (social science). The total number of subjects N is specified by multiplying the number of treatment levels or conditions by the number of subjects per level—that is, $N = (a)(s) = (2)(12) = 24$.

The results of the experiment are presented in Table 6-1. The individual scores Y on the vocabulary test can range from 0 to 60. You will note that the notational system has been expanded in order to specify precisely the treatment membership of any given score. The symbol for the individual observations remains the same (Y), with subscripts added so that we can refer to specific scores. Generally, we will use subscripts only when necessary to avoid confusion.

The sums or totals of the scores for the two different treatment groups are specified by the notation A_1 and A_2; thus, A_1 is the sum of the Y scores for the 12 children assigned to level a_1 (physical science) and A_2 is the corresponding sum for the 12 children assigned to level a_2 (social science). The grand total of the scores (or sum of all the scores) is symbolized by T. Applying this notation to the present example, we have

$$A_1 = 53 + 49 + \cdots + 32 + 27 = 480$$
$$A_2 = 47 + 42 + \cdots + 11 + 6 = 312$$
$$T = A_1 + A_2 = 480 + 312 = 792$$

Table 6-1
Numerical Example

Physical Science (a_1)	Social Science (a_2)
$Y_1 = 53$	$Y_{13} = 47$
$Y_2 = 49$	$Y_{14} = 42$
$Y_3 = 47$	$Y_{15} = 39$
$Y_4 = 42$	$Y_{16} = 37$
$Y_5 = 51$	$Y_{17} = 42$
$Y_6 = 34$	$Y_{18} = 33$
$Y_7 = 44$	$Y_{19} = 13$
$Y_8 = 48$	$Y_{20} = 16$
$Y_9 = 35$	$Y_{21} = 16$
$Y_{10} = 18$	$Y_{22} = 10$
$Y_{11} = 32$	$Y_{23} = 11$
$Y_{12} = 27$	$Y_{24} = 6$
Sum: $A_1 = 480$	$A_2 = 312$
Mean: $\bar{Y}_{A_1} = 40.00$	$\bar{Y}_{A_2} = 26.00$

The symbols for the two treatment means are $\bar{Y}_{A_1}$ and $\bar{Y}_{A_2}$. Each is based on $s = 12$ observations in this example. The grand mean of all the scores is designated $\bar{Y}_T$ and is based on $N = (a)(s) = (2)(12) = 24$ observations. For these data,

$$\bar{Y}_{A_1} = \frac{A_1}{s} = \frac{480}{12} = 40.00$$

$$\bar{Y}_{A_2} = \frac{A_2}{s} = \frac{312}{12} = 26.00$$

$$\bar{Y}_T = \frac{T}{(a)(s)} = \frac{792}{24} = 33.00$$

The Deviations

We have plotted the data from Table 6-1 in Fig. 6-1, using filled rectangles for the scores from level a_1 and unfilled rectangles for the scores from level a_2. Consider the final score listed for a_2 in Table 6-1, namely, $Y_{24} = 6$. The deviation of this score from the grand mean, $Y_{24} - \bar{Y}_T$, is indicated at the bottom of Fig. 6-1. We will call this deviation the **total deviation**. It is readily apparent that the total deviation is made up of two parts, namely, the deviation of the individual score from its group mean, or $Y_{24} - \bar{Y}_{A_2}$, and the deviation of the group mean from the grand mean, $\bar{Y}_{A_2} - \bar{Y}_T$. We will call these deviations the **within-group deviation** and the **between-groups deviation**, respectively. Thus, we see that a single score can be viewed in terms of how it differs from the total sample, how it differs from other scores in its group, and, indirectly, how its group differs from the total sample. The deviations of Y_{24} are expressed in numbers as follows:

$$Y_{24} - \bar{Y}_T \quad = \quad (Y_{24} - \bar{Y}_{A_2}) \quad + \quad (\bar{Y}_{A_2} - \bar{Y}_T)$$

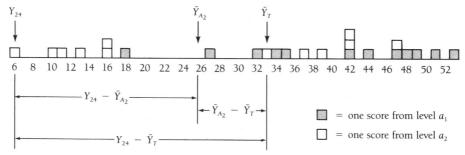

Figure 6-1   A systematic arrangement of scores from Table 6-1. The components of deviation for a single score (Y_{24}) from the grand mean $(\bar{Y}_T)$ are shown beneath the baseline.

Total deviation = within-group deviation + between-groups deviation

$$6 - 33 \quad = \quad (6 - 26) \quad + \quad (26 - 33)$$
$$-27 \quad = \quad (-20) \quad + \quad (-7)$$
$$-27 \quad = \quad -27$$

These two component deviations provide useful information concerning the outcome of an experiment. The within-group deviations, for example, represent the variability of subjects treated alike, that is, how subjects still differ even though they are in the same treatment condition. Because subjects in a particular treatment group are all given the same treatment—either a lecture on physical science or one on social science—any remaining variability in Y scores among the subjects within a group must be due to factors other than the differences between the two treatments. We will refer to any such differences as *uncontrolled variability*. An alternative way of describing these same differences is to characterize them as reflecting variability on the dependent variable Y that is *not attributable* to or "explained" by the manipulation of the treatment.

The between-groups deviations, on the other hand, represent that part of the total deviation that *is* associated with the two treatment conditions. You should realize that differences between groups will nearly always be present even if the independent variable is *completely ineffective*. This is due in large part to the fact that subjects are assigned *randomly* to the different conditions, creating differences between the group means that result entirely from chance. There is no satisfactory way of avoiding this problem. For this reason, then, the between-groups deviation is assumed to reflect the *joint presence* of two factors, chance differences as well as the possible differential effects of the treatments themselves.

6.2   SUMS OF SQUARES: COMPUTATIONAL FORMULAS

The partitioning presented in Sec. 6.1 can be applied to all the scores in an experiment. The three sets of deviations, when squared and summed, will produce three corresponding sums of squares, namely,

SS_T: the sum of squares based on the total deviations (that is, $Y - \bar{Y}_T$), where the subscript T refers to the total variability

$SS_{S/A}$: the sum of squares based on the within-group deviations (that is, $Y - \bar{Y}_A$), where the subscript S/A stands for the variability of subjects (S) within each of the levels of factor A (A)

SS_A: the sum of squares based on the between-groups deviations $(\bar{Y}_A - \bar{Y}_T)$, where the subscript A refers to variation associated with the independent variable, factor A

In addition, you should note that the two component sums of squares $SS_{S/A}$ and SS_A combine to equal the total sum of squares SS_T. That is,

$$SS_T = SS_{S/A} + SS_A \qquad (6\text{-}1)$$

These three sums of squares are the basic components of ANOVA. When you are computing sums of squares with a calculator, you will find it much easier to use computational formulas than to deal with the three sets of deviations for each subject. We will consider the appropriate computational formulas next.

Basic Ratios

Computational formulas for any sum of squares can be expressed in terms of what we will call **basic ratios**. Because all basic ratios involve the same set of simple arithmetic operations, you should take note of these consistent operations, since they will be found in all standard analyses of variance. The present design requires three such ratios, one based on the Y scores, another based on the A treatment sums, and a third based on the grand sum T. Each set of terms contributes to the numerator of a different basic ratio. More specifically, all members of a given set of quantities—the Y's, the A's, and T—are first *squared* and then *summed*. (In the case of T, where there is only one quantity, just the first operation is performed.) Using the data from Table 6-1, we obtain

$$\Sigma\, Y^2 = 53^2 + 49^2 + \cdots + 11^2 + 6^2 = 31{,}136$$
$$\Sigma\, A^2 = 480^2 + 312^2 = 230{,}400 + 97{,}344 = 327{,}744$$
$$T^2 = 792^2 = 627{,}264$$

Each of these numerators is divided by a different number, which is found by applying a simple rule that involves the term appearing in the numerator:

Whatever the term—that is, Y, A, or T—we divide by the number of scores that contribute to that term.

For Y this number is 1, because each Y score is based on a *single* observation; this is equivalent, of course, to not dividing at all. For A this number is s, because this is the number of scores that are summed to produce any one of the treatment sums, while for T this number is $(a)\,(s)$, or N, because this is the number of scores that are actually summed to produce the grand sum.

For convenience, each basic ratio is given a special symbol consisting of a pair of brackets enclosing the letter code used to designate terms in the numerator. The formulas for the three basic ratios are

$$[Y] = \Sigma\, Y^2 \tag{6-2}$$

$$[A] = \frac{\Sigma\, A^2}{s} \tag{6-3}$$

$$[T] = \frac{T^2}{(a)\,(s)} \tag{6-4}$$

Applying these formulas to the partial answers we have already calculated, we find

$$[Y] = 31{,}136$$

$$[A] = \frac{327{,}744}{12} = 27{,}312.00$$

$$[T] = \frac{627{,}264}{(2)\,(12)} = 26{,}136.00$$

Sums of Squares

The three sums of squares are easily calculated by combining the basic ratios in different patterns. These patterns are specified by the deviations themselves. You will recall that the total sum of squares is based on the following deviation:

$$Y - \bar{Y}_T$$

The computational formula combines the two ratios identified by this deviation as follows:

$$SS_T = [Y] - [T] \tag{6-5}$$

where $[Y]$ is the basic ratio based on the individual Y scores or observations and $[T]$ is the basic ratio based on the grand sum T.

The within-groups sum of squares is based on the deviation of individual observations from the relevant treatment mean, that is,

$$Y - \bar{Y}_A$$

The computational formula combines the two ratios identified by these deviations as follows:

$$SS_{S/A} = [Y] - [A] \tag{6-6}$$

where $[Y]$ is the basic ratio based on the individual Y scores and $[A]$ is the basic ratio based on the two treatment sums.

Finally, the between-groups sum of squares is based on the deviation of the treatment means from the grand mean:

$$\bar{Y}_A - \bar{Y}_T$$

The computational formula combines the two ratios identified by these deviations as follows:

$$SS_A = [A] - [T] \qquad (6\text{-}7)$$

where $[A]$ is the basic ratio based on the treatment sums and $[T]$ is the basic ratio based on the grand sum.

We will now calculate these sums of squares by substituting in these three formulas the quantities we calculated in the last section:

$$SS_T = [Y] - [T] = 31{,}136 - 26{,}136.00 = 5000.00$$

$$SS_{S/A} = [Y] - [A] = 31{,}136 - 27{,}312.00 = 3824.00$$

$$SS_A = [A] - [T] = 27{,}312.00 - 26{,}136.00 = 1176.00$$

As a computational check and as a demonstration of the relationship among these three sums of squares, we will apply Eq. (6-1) to these calculations:

$$SS_{S/A} + SS_A = 3824.00 + 1176.00 = 5000.00 = SS_T$$

Comment.   There is an alternative way of computing the within-groups sum of squares that illustrates some of the logic underlying the analysis of variance. The $SS_{S/A}$ is actually a *composite* based on the individual sum of squares for each of the treatment groups. That is,

$$SS_{S/A} = SS_{S/A_1} + SS_{S/A_2} + \cdots \qquad (6\text{-}8)$$

In the present case, there are two within-group sums of squares, one for a_1 and one for a_2. Using the data from Table 6-1, we find

$$SS_{S/A_1} = (53^2 + 49^2 + \cdots + 32^2 + 27^2) - \frac{480^2}{12}$$

$$= 20{,}482 - 19{,}200.00 = 1282.00$$

$$SS_{S/A_2} = (47^2 + 42^2 + \cdots + 11^2 + 6^2) - \frac{312^2}{12}$$

$$= 10{,}654 - 8112.00 = 2542.00$$

Completing the operations specified in Eq. (6-8), we find that

$$SS_{S/A_1} + SS_{S/A_2} = 1282.00 + 2542.00 = 3824.00 = SS_{S/A}$$

6.3 MEAN SQUARES AND THE *F* RATIO

We are now ready for the final steps in the analysis: calculating variances and forming the statistic to test for the presence of treatment effects, the *F* ratio. When variances are employed in ANOVA, they are called **mean squares**; the *F* statistic is simply a ratio of two mean squares. A mean square is essentially an "average" sum of squares—not a strict arithmetic average, however, but one based on degrees of freedom rather than on the number of observations.

Degrees of Freedom

As indicated in Chap. 4, the general rule for computing the degrees of freedom (*df*) associated with any sum of squares is

$$df = \begin{pmatrix} \text{number of} \\ \text{independent} \\ \text{observations} \end{pmatrix} - \begin{pmatrix} \text{number of} \\ \text{restraints} \end{pmatrix} \tag{6-9}$$

Consider the *df* associated with SS_T. The number of independent observations is $(a)(s)$. There is one restraint placed on this sum of squares, namely, that the sum of the deviations is zero. Thus, $df_T = (a)(s) - 1$.

Consider next the SS_A. In this case, there are *a* independent observations, one for each of the *a* treatment means. The same restraint placed on SS_T is also placed on this sum of squares: the sum of the deviations of the treatment means from the grand mean must equal zero. As a consequence, $df_A = a - 1$, one less than the number of treatment means.

The determination of the *df* associated with the within-groups sum of squares $SS_{S/A}$ is a bit more complicated, but follows the general rule specified by Eq. (6-9). You will recall from Eq. (6-8) that this sum of squares represents a pooling of separate *SS*'s obtained from the different treatment groups. The *df* are obtained the same way. That is, the number of *independent observations* associated with any treatment group is *s* and the *df* for the corresponding *SS* is $s - 1$; the restraint is that the sum of the within-group deviations must sum to zero for *each of the groups*. The $df_{S/A}$ is calculated by combining the separate *df*'s for the different groups:

$$df_{S/A} = df_{S/A_1} + df_{S/A_2} + \cdots$$

Since the *df* for each group is $s - 1$ and there are *a* different groups, we can express the formula as

$$df_{S/A} = (a)(s - 1)$$

Mean Squares

The variance estimates required in ANOVA are given by the formula

$$MS = \frac{SS}{df} \tag{6-10}$$

As applied to the two component sources of variance,

$$MS_A = \frac{SS_A}{df_A} \quad \text{and} \quad MS_{S/A} = \frac{SS_{S/A}}{df_{S/A}}$$

The mean square on the left is influenced by two factors, the presence of treatment effects and uncontrolled variation, while the mean square on the right is influenced by uncontrolled variation alone. That is, the MS_A represents the deviation of the treatment groups from the grand mean, which in essence is due to the effects of the independent variable as well as the chance differences that occur in any experiment; the $MS_{S/A}$ represents the deviation of scores within the treatment groups, and since all members of each group are treated alike, it reflects uncontrolled or random variability.

The F Ratio

The final step in the calculations is the formation of the F ratio, which is used to test for significance (see Chap. 8). For the present type of design, the ratio consists simply of the treatment mean square MS_A divided by the within-groups mean square $MS_{S/A}$:

$$F = \frac{MS_A}{MS_{S/A}} \tag{6-11}$$

The result of this division, the F statistic, will be used to evaluate the effectiveness of the treatment conditions against the background of uncontrolled, chance factors that are always present and contribute to group differences.

Summary of the Analysis

The computational formulas for the completely randomized single-factor ANOVA are presented in Table 6-2. The first column lists the sources of variance usually extracted from the analysis. Column 2 gives the three basic ratios that are combined in different patterns to produce the sums of squares. These patterns are indicated in column 3. The formulas for the degrees of freedom, mean squares, and F ratio are entered in the remaining columns of Table 6-2.

Table 6-2
Summary of the Analysis of Variance

Source	Basic Ratio	SS	df	MS	F
A	$[A] = \dfrac{\Sigma A^2}{s}$	$[A] - [T]$	$a - 1$	$\dfrac{SS_A}{df_A}$	$\dfrac{MS_A}{MS_{S/A}}$
S/A	$[Y] = \Sigma Y^2$	$[Y] - [A]$	$(a)(s - 1)$	$\dfrac{SS_{S/A}}{df_{S/A}}$	
Total	$[T] = \dfrac{T^2}{(a)(s)}$	$[Y] - [T]$	$(a)(s) - 1$		

The results of the numerical example are summarized in Table 6-3. The SS's were calculated previously and are entered without comment in the table. The df for the three sources are found by substituting in the formulas provided in Table 6-2. To be more explicit,

$$df_A = a - 1 = 2 - 1 = 1$$
$$df_{S/A} = (a)(s - 1) = (2)(12 - 1) = (2)(11) = 22$$
$$df_T = (a)(s) - 1 = (2)(12) - 1 = 24 - 1 = 23$$

As a computational check, we can verify that the df for the two component sums of squares equals the df for the SS_T. That is,

$$df_A + df_{S/A} = 1 + 22 = 23 = df_T$$

The two mean squares are calculated next by dividing each SS by the appropriate df. For this example,

$$MS_A = \frac{1176.00}{1} = 1176.00 \quad \text{and} \quad MS_{S/A} = \frac{3824.00}{22} = 173.82$$

These numbers are entered in the appropriate column of Table 6-3. The F ratio is found to be

$$F = \frac{MS_A}{MS_{S/A}} = \frac{1176.00}{173.82} = 6.77$$

The meaning and usefulness of this statistic will be considered in Chap. 8. For now, we will simply note that the ratio of the numerator to the denominator is a rather large value that is not likely to occur when only chance factors are present.

Table 6-3
Summary of the Analysis

Source	SS	df	MS	F
A	1176.00	1	1176.00	6.77
S/A	3824.00	22	173.82	
Total	5000.00	23		

6.4   SUMMARY

We have shown how a simple two-group experiment may be analyzed by means of ANOVA. With ANOVA the focus is on differences and deviations. Two sources of variation are critical for the analysis of this design: variation that is attributed to the difference between the two treatments and variation that is not and is uncontrollable. These sources are represented by the sums of squared deviations from means. The SS_A reflects the deviation of the two treatment means from the grand mean. For the within-groups source, the $SS_{S/A}$ reflects the variability of subjects given the same treatment condition. The next step consists of calculating mean squares, which is accomplished by dividing the sums of squares by their appropriate numbers of degrees of freedom. Finally, we calculate the F statistic by dividing the treatment mean square MS_A by the within-groups mean square $MS_{S/A}$. This statistic is used to decide whether the results of the experiment reflect at all the effects of the independent variable. The details of this last step will be discussed in Chap. 8.

6.5   EXERCISES

1. In Sec. 6.1, we showed how the deviation of a particular score (Y_{24}) from the grand mean $(\bar{Y}_T)$ may be divided into two components, the deviation of the score from its group mean $(Y_{24} - \bar{Y}_{A_2})$ and the deviation of the group mean from the grand mean $(\bar{Y}_{A_2} - \bar{Y}_T)$. These deviations form the basis for the analysis of the results of a single-factor experiment.

   a. Calculate the same deviations for *all* the scores in Table 6-1, verifying in each case that the sum of the two component deviations equals the deviation from $\bar{Y}_T$.

b. Square all the deviations for all the subjects and then sum each set of squared deviations over all the subjects. Verify that the three sums are identical to those obtained with the computational formulas in Sec. 6.2 (see Table 6-3).

2. A psychologist decides to determine the effectiveness of a new drug on the ability of rats to learn a difficult maze. The design consists of two conditions, one in which the drug is administered by injection 2 hr before testing and another in which an inert substance (e.g., a saline solution) is substituted for the drug. Each group is represented by $s = 9$ subjects randomly assigned to the conditions. The response measure is the number of trials required to learn the maze according to a criterion of errorless performance. The following data are obtained:

Drug	No Drug
30	36
26	35
31	27
30	32
24	29
28	41
25	36
33	28
31	30

a. Calculate the means and standard deviations for the two treatment groups.
b. Calculate the basic ratios.
c. Find the sums of squares for A, S/A, and T.
d. Determine the degrees of freedom and calculate the mean squares.
e. Construct a summary table and calculate F. (Save this information for Problem 1 at the end of Chap. 8.)

7

The Correlational Analysis of Experimental Data

. . .

In Chap. 6, where we discussed the basic concepts in ANOVA, we did so from the perspective of a two-group design. In Chap. 7, we will analyze the same experiment from the perspective of MRC. Before we begin, we wish to offer some preliminary remarks that will help to prepare you for the main topic of this chapter.

First, you will recall from Chap. 5 that two scores, measures, or observations are needed for each subject in order to compute correlational and regression statistics. It is important to note that this same constraint, namely, the need for a *pair of scores* for each subject, also holds when data from experiments—where subjects in different groups provide *single Y* scores—are analyzed by means of correlational procedures. As mentioned briefly in Chap. 3, we create scores for the X variable by using convenient numerical values as labels to distinguish between subjects in the different treatment conditions. We then use those values for the treatment conditions of the X variable, in conjunction with scores on the Y variable (the dependent variable), to calculate correlational and regression statistics. Such labeling is referred to as **coding**. The point for now is that by using a coding system to differentiate subjects receiving different treatments, we are able to obtain values for the X variable and, consequently, now have two values for each subject, an X value and a Y value.

Second, you may be puzzled by the meaning of the *sign* of the correlational index—that is, whether it is positive or negative—when MRC is applied to the analysis of experimental data. Essentially, with experimental data, the + or − for the MRC result will be used to identify the nature of differences between two treatment groups—that is, which group has the "higher" mean value. The crucial point for the analysis of experimental data (or data from any design), however, is that a +.45 correlation between two variables and a −.45 correlation represent equally strong (or weak) relationships.

Finally, as we have pointed out previously, you may find yourself confused by the different emphases; correlational analysis focuses on *relationships of certain strength between variables*, whereas the traditional analysis of experiments (ANOVA) focuses on *differences between means*. As you will see, however, finding a difference between the means of the two groups on a vocabulary test, for example, is equivalent to finding a relationship between vocabulary test scores and the numerical coding of group membership.

7.1   APPLICATION OF THE PEARSON COEFFICIENT TO EXPERIMENTAL DATA

We considered two measures of the association between the X and Y variables in Chap. 5: the correlation ratio (eta squared) and the Pearson correlation coefficient (r). We will concentrate on the Pearson coefficient because of its value in understanding the correlational analysis of a two-group experiment and its use in conducting specific treatment comparisons in experiments with more than two treatment conditions.

The Arrangement of the Data

Before we examine in detail the application of the Pearson correlation coefficient to experimental data, we will first illustrate how such data are set up for analysis. We have already noted that two values are needed for each subject in order to establish a correlation. One of these, of course, is a subject's score on the dependent variable (or Y variable). The other value consists of a numerical code designed to designate group membership; the code numbers will constitute the values of the X variable. The key to the entire operation, then, is the creation of this numerical code. We will discuss the general principles behind the coding of the treatment conditions, as well as different methods of coding, in Chap. 9. For the moment, we will consider the correlational analysis of the example from Sec. 6.1, an experiment comparing the relative effectiveness of two different science lectures in helping students prepare for a vocabulary test.

The data for this example originally appeared in Table 6-1. Recall that these data consist of vocabulary scores (Y values) for fifth-grade children who were exposed either to a lecture on physical science (a_1) or to one on social science (a_2); the total number of subjects is $N = 24$. Also, recall that this is an experiment in which subjects have been randomly assigned to the treatment conditions. Though we will be applying correlational statistics, it is the nature of the design that will allow us to interpret the data from a causal perspective. Evidence of correlation in an experimental design (i.e., a design with random assignment to treatments) indicates that variability in one variable—the independent variable—causes variability in the dependent variable.

For the analysis of variance, we arranged the data into two columns of Y values, one for each treatment condition. For correlational analysis, in general, we create two columns, one for the X values and the other for the Y values. Consider now the layout of Table 7-1. The first thing to notice is that the subjects are listed in one long column, subjects 1 to 12 representing the participants receiving the lecture on physical science (a_1) and subjects 13 to 24 representing those receiving the lecture on social science (a_2). The first two entries for each subject provide the basic information needed for the calculation of the correlation coefficient, namely, values for the X variable (column 1) and for the Y variable (column 2).

The Y values are the individual scores on the vocabulary test (the dependent variable). The X values (the independent variable) represent the information that will distinguish between the two treatment conditions. For this example, we have accomplished this by assigning a value of $+1$ to all subjects in a_1 and a value of

Table 7-1
Correlational Analysis of Experimental Data

Subject	(1) X	(2) Y	(3) $(X - \bar{X})$	(4) $(X - \bar{X})^2$	(5) $(Y - \bar{Y})$	(6) $(Y - \bar{Y})^2$	(7) $(X - \bar{X})(Y - \bar{Y})$
1	1	53	1	1	20	400	20
2	1	49	1	1	16	256	16
3	1	47	1	1	14	196	14
4	1	42	1	1	9	81	9
5	1	51	1	1	18	324	18
6	1	34	1	1	1	1	1
7	1	44	1	1	11	121	11
8	1	48	1	1	15	225	15
9	1	35	1	1	2	4	2
10	1	18	1	1	-15	225	-15
11	1	32	1	1	-1	1	-1
12	1	27	1	1	-6	36	-6
13	-1	47	-1	1	14	196	-14
14	-1	42	-1	1	9	81	-9
15	-1	39	-1	1	6	36	-6
16	-1	37	-1	1	4	16	-4
17	-1	42	-1	1	9	81	-9
18	-1	33	-1	1	0	0	0
19	-1	13	-1	1	-20	400	20
20	-1	16	-1	1	-17	289	17
21	-1	16	-1	1	-17	289	17
22	-1	10	-1	1	-23	529	23
23	-1	11	-1	1	-22	484	22
24	-1	6	-1	1	-27	729	27
Sum:	0	792	0	24	0	5000	168

-1 to all subjects in a_2. This form of coding, in which one group is specifically and directly compared with another group, is called **contrast coding** and will be used frequently throughout this book. Actually, we could have used any two values or numbers for the X variable just so long as the two numbers are different and one number is assigned to all the subjects receiving one of the treatments and the other is assigned to all the subjects receiving the other treatment. We will discuss the general principles of coding in Chap. 9.

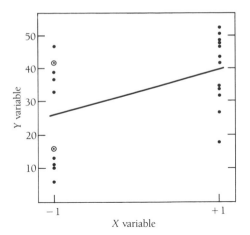

F i g u r e 7-1 Scatterplot of the data appearing in Table 7-1. The X variable consists of two values (−1 and +1) chosen to represent the two levels of the independent variable, and the Y variable consists of scores on the dependent variable. Data points surrounded by a circle represent two subjects with the same value of Y.

Figure 7-1 presents a scatterplot of the data appearing in Table 7-1. There are only two values of the X variable, +1 and −1, but this does not prevent the data from being plotted. We have also calculated and drawn the regression line for these data. The fact that the regression line is not parallel to the baseline—that is, has nonzero slope—suggests that there is a relationship or correlation between the two variables. As you will soon see, the interpretation of this *relationship* between X and Y leads to an exactly equivalent interpretation regarding the *difference* between the two treatment means.

The Calculations

Let us now calculate the Pearson correlation coefficient with this set of data. Application of any of the correlational formulas we presented in Chap. 5 can be used to determine the correlation. We will use Eq. (5-4), which bases the calculations on the deviations of X and Y from their respective means. That is,

$$r = \frac{\Sigma \left[(X - \bar{X})(Y - \bar{Y}) \right]}{\sqrt{\Sigma (X - \bar{X})^2 \, \Sigma (Y - \bar{Y})^2}}$$

The remaining columns in Table 7-1 provide the information required by this formula. More specifically, the deviations for X and Y are given in columns 3 and 5, respectively. The corresponding squares of these deviations are found in columns 4 and 6. The products of the two deviations for each subject are entered in column

7. The sums specified by Eq. (5-4) are listed at the bottom of the table. Substituting in the formula, we find

$$r = \frac{168.00}{\sqrt{(24)(5000.00)}} = \frac{168.00}{346.41} = .4850$$

The value of r^2 is $(.4850)^2 = .2352$.

How do we interpret this finding? The fact that r is not equal to 0.00 suggests that there is a *relationship* between X and Y in this sample, which thus implies that there is a *difference* between the treatments in the average number of words learned. Second, we can also state that because r may take on values between 0.00 and plus or minus 1.00, the obtained relationship of .4850 is moderate to strong, depending on one's frame of reference. Of more interpretive value, however, is the statement that approximately 24 percent ($r^2 = .2352$) of the observed variability in vocabulary scores is due to the differential effectiveness of the two treatments— physical science versus social science lectures. However, since the correlation is not perfect, we cannot say that all of the variability in performance on the test (Y scores) among the 24 subjects is due to the treatment they have received. In fact, 76 percent of the vocabulary score variance is *not* explained by the treatments ($1 - r^2 = .7648$). In subsequent chapters, we will deal with more complex designs that attempt to reduce this unaccounted for variance.

The *F* Ratio

Just as the final step in ANOVA is the calculation of an F ratio to test for the significance of the results, we also test in MRC for the significance of r (or r^2). This is necessary because the correlation obtained in the data set could possibly reflect merely chance factors. Thus, we want to see whether the obtained r is sufficiently different from zero to indicate that the population correlation is nonzero. For r's, we use the following formula:

$$F = \frac{r^2/df_{reg.}}{(1 - r^2)/df_{res.}} \tag{7-1}$$

The result of Eq. (7-1) is used to evaluate the strength of the observed relationship. We will consider tests of significance in Chap. 8.

In the present example, $r^2 = .2352$; therefore, $1 - r^2$ is $1 - .2352 = .7648$. The *df* for the numerator are, as in ANOVA, based on the number of treatments minus 1, or $a - 1$; the *df* for the denominator are the number of subjects in the experiment minus 2 (the *df* for the denominator will be calculated differently in experiments with more than two treatment groups). Thus, application of Eq. (7-1) yields the following:

$$F = \frac{.2352/1}{.7648/22} = \frac{.2352}{.0348} = 6.76$$

Summary of the Analysis

The results of the analysis for the data in Table 7-1 are presented in Table 7-2. The meaningfulness of the F ratio will be discussed in Chap. 8.

Table 7-2
Summary of the Correlational Analysis

Source	Effect	df	F
Regression	.2352	1	6.76
Residual	.7648	22	

ANOVA and Correlational Analysis Compared

Let us now examine some of the parallels between this correlational analysis and the initial steps in the analysis of variance we conducted in Sec. 6.1. Both analyses may be viewed in terms of sums of squares and deviations. For ANOVA, sums of squares are expressed in terms of total, between-groups, and within-group deviations. For correlational analysis, the sums of squares are based, in part, on individual predicted scores. We developed this idea in Chap. 5, but we will repeat the points here.

First, consider the total variation in the Y variable. From the correlational calculations summarized in Table 7-1 (column 6),

$$SS_Y = \Sigma (Y - \bar{Y})^2 = 5000.00$$

and from the ANOVA calculations summarized in Table 6-3,

$$SS_T = [Y] - [T] = 5000.00$$

The total sums of squares from the two analytical techniques are arithmetically and conceptually the same.

Second, there is a parallel between the between-groups sum of squares in ANOVA and the regression sum of squares in linear correlation. You will recall from Chap. 5 that the regression sum of squares $SS_{reg.}$ is based on the deviation of each predicted Y score (Y') from the overall mean of the Y scores ($\bar{Y}$)—that is, $Y' - \bar{Y}$. This sum of squares may be calculated from quantities already available, simply by rearranging the terms in Eq. (5-11). More specifically, starting with Eq. (5-11),

$$r^2 = \frac{\Sigma\,(Y' - \bar{Y})^2}{\Sigma\,(Y - \bar{Y})^2}$$

we obtain

$$\Sigma\,(Y' - \bar{Y})^2 = (r^2)\,\Sigma\,(Y - \bar{Y})^2 \tag{7-2}$$

Thus, the regression sum of squares $\Sigma\,(Y' - \bar{Y})^2$ is equal to the product of r^2 and the total variability in Y, $\Sigma\,(Y - \bar{Y})^2$. Substituting in Eq. (7-2), we find

$$SS_{reg.} = (.2352)\,(5000.00) = 1176.00$$

For the analysis of variance (as shown in Table 6-3),

$$SS_A = [A] - [T] = 1176.00$$

Again, the two sums of squares are identical. Let us see why.

In ANOVA, the SS_A is determined by subtracting the grand mean $\bar{Y}_T$ from the treatment mean $\bar{Y}_A$ for each subject; in correlation and regression, the $SS_{reg.}$ is found by subtracting the grand mean $\bar{Y}_T$ from the predicted value (Y') for each subject. These operations are identical, since the *best* predicted Y values for the two treatments are the two treatment means—that is, Y' for a subject in group a_i is $\bar{Y}_{A_i}$. You can verify this by using the regression line in Fig. 7-1 to find the value of Y when $X = +1$ and -1. That is, if we applied the regression equation associated with the data in Table 7-1 and substituted the value of $+1$ in the equation, the Y' would be the mean value of a_1 (which is labeled $+1$); likewise, substituting -1 yields the mean value of a_2. Thus, both sums of squares are based on exactly the same types of deviations.

Finally, we have the within-groups sum of squares from ANOVA and the residual sum of squares from correlational analysis. The former ($SS_{S/A}$) reflects the uncontrolled variability of subjects treated alike (or $Y - \bar{Y}_A$), and the latter ($SS_{res.}$) reflects variation in Y that is not predicted from a knowledge of X (or $Y - Y'$). Both sums of squares may be calculated by subtraction. In ANOVA, manipulation of Eq. (6-1) shows that

$$SS_{S/A} = SS_T - SS_A$$

or

$$SS_{S/A} = [Y] - [A] = 3824.00$$

For the correlational approach,

$$SS_{res.} = SS_Y - SS_{reg.} \tag{7-3}$$
$$= 5000.00 - 1176.00 = 3824.00$$

Alternatively, the same quantity may be calculated by using the following formula:

$$SS_{res.} = (1 - r^2)(SS_Y) \tag{7-4}$$
$$= (1 - .2352)(5000.00) = (.7648)(5000.00)$$
$$= 3824.00$$

Although the terminology is different—the $SS_{S/A}$ forming the basis for the so-called error term in ANOVA and the $SS_{res.}$ reflecting "uncontrolled" or "unpredicted" variability in correlation-regression—the quantities are the same.

At this point, you may be thinking about the practical implication of this equivalence, namely, that you can use either ANOVA or correlational analysis to calculate the same value of F and arrive at the same statistical conclusions. Which procedure should you use, and why bother learning about an equivalent technique? The procedures you will eventually use in analyzing the results of experimental data are a matter of taste and preference. Our purpose in emphasizing the equivalence of ANOVA and correlational procedures is to establish their *interchangeability* and to make people who have been trained in one approach more aware of the procedures and techniques of the other. We also believe that more complicated correlational procedures—for example, MRC—can be better learned and understood when presented in the context of standard experimental designs. You will better appreciate this advantage when we consider the analysis of nonexperimental designs, in which MRC, in effect, comes into its own and ANOVA is usually not appropriate.

7.2   THE REGRESSION EQUATION

As we have noted previously, the classical use of the regression equation is to predict Y from X. Although such a function would appear to make little sense in the context of an experiment, there is still useful information to be derived from the regression equation. If you have performed your analyses with a computer rather than by hand, you can "ask" the program to include the regression equation in the printout of the analyses. Let us see what the equation can tell us about the analysis.

The formula for the regression equation is given by Eq. (5-7):

$$Y' = a + bX$$

where a is the Y intercept and b is the slope, or regression coefficient. We can calculate both constants with the information provided in Table 7-1. Using Eq. (5-8) and substituting from Table 7-1, we find

$$b = \frac{\Sigma\,[(X - \bar{X})\,(Y - \bar{Y})]}{\Sigma\,(X - \bar{X})^2}$$

$$= \frac{168.00}{24.00} = 7.00$$

Substituting in Eq. (5-9),

$$a = \bar{Y} - b\bar{X} = 33.00 - (7.00)\,(0) = 33.00$$

With these two values, the regression equation becomes

$$Y' = 33.00 + (7.00)\,(X)$$

As we indicated in Sec. 7.1, the regression equation can be used to find the mean associated with each of the two values of X, $+1$ and -1. For $X = +1$,

$$Y' = 33.00 + (7.00)\,(1) = 40.00$$

and for $X = -1$,

$$Y' = 33.00 + (7.00)\,(-1) = 26.00$$

If you calculated the two means $\bar{Y}_{A_1}$ and $\bar{Y}_{A_2}$ independently, you would obtain exactly the same values.

The two constants of the regression equation have special meaning in contrast coding. Specifically, the a value represents the grand mean. Consequently, we find that $\bar{Y}$ for the set of data is $a = 33.00$, which is what we found for $\bar{Y}_T$ in Chap. 6 (p. 72). The b value can be used to calculate the *difference* between the two means associated with the $+1$ and -1 values. That is, by multiplying the b value by each code ($+1$ and -1) and taking the difference between the two products, we obtain the difference between the means for the two groups. In the present case, where $b = 7.00$, we have $(7)\,(1) - (7)\,(-1) = 14$. The difference between the actual means calculated above is $40.00 - 26.00 = 14.00$.

7.3   SUMMARY

In this chapter, we have indicated how the Pearson correlation coefficient r can be used to extract the same information from a two-group experiment that is usually obtained from the analysis of variance. The key to the analysis is the creation of values for the X variable that represent group membership. Once we have accomplished this, the correlation between the X variable and the dependent variable Y reflects the relationship between the experimental manipulation (the independent variable) and the dependent variable. More technically, r^2 represents the proportion of variation in Y associated with the two treatment conditions, and the quantity $1 - r^2$ represents the proportion of variation in Y not associated with the treatments.

In the analysis of a two-group experiment, r^2 and the between-groups sum of squares serve the same function in the sense that both quantities reflect variation associated with the two treatment conditions. Similarly, $1 - r^2$ and the within-groups sum of squares serve the same function in the sense that both quantities reflect variation not associated with the treatments. In Chap. 8, we will show that ANOVA and correlational analysis, which employ different calculations and produce different intermediate quantities (SS's and r^2, respectively), converge in the final steps of the analysis—formation of the F ratio and the test of significance—to produce identical results and conclusions.

The exact correspondence between ANOVA and correlational analysis may be revealed by using the two component sums of squares produced by ANOVA. This correspondence is summarized in Table 7-3. For both procedures, the deviations on which each sum of squares is based are presented first; they are followed by the sums of squares themselves. As indicated in the table, the between-groups sum

Table 7-3
A Comparison of ANOVA and Correlational Analysis

Analysis of Variance		
Source	Deviation	Sum of Squares
Between-Groups	$\bar{Y}_A - \bar{Y}_T$	$SS_A = [A] - [T]$
Within-Groups	$Y - \bar{Y}_A$	$SS_{S/A} = [Y] - [A]$
Total	$Y - \bar{Y}_T$	$SS_T = [Y] - [T]$

Correlational Analysis		
Source	Deviation	Sum of Squares
Regression	$Y' - \bar{Y}$	$SS_{reg.} = (r^2)(SS_Y)$
Residual	$Y - Y'$	$SS_{res.} = (1 - r^2)(SS_Y)$
Total	$Y - \bar{Y}$	$SS_Y = \Sigma (Y - \bar{Y})^2$

of squares SS_A and the within-groups sum of squares $SS_{S/A}$ from ANOVA are equal to the regression sum of squares $SS_{reg.}$ and the residual sum of squares $SS_{res.}$, respectively, from the corresponding correlational analysis. The total sums of squares (SS_T and SS_Y) are identical, of course.

7.4   EXERCISES

1. In Problem 2 of Chap. 6, we considered an experiment in which the effect of a drug on maze learning was studied.

    a. With these data, calculate the Pearson correlation coefficient r using contrast coding to define the X variable.

    b. Calculate the regression equation. What does this equation tell you about the outcome of the experiment?

Significance and Hypothesis Testing

. . .

Once we have formulated a researchable hypothesis, then collected data to test that hypothesis, and, finally, calculated statistics to describe and summarize the results, we need to determine whether the difference observed between the two treatment means (or the relationship found between the two variables) is due to the independent variable or whether it is due entirely to chance. To answer this question, we turn to a formal statistical procedure called **hypothesis testing**. We will examine this procedure first within the context of ANOVA and then turn our attention to the significance of correlational statistics. As you will see, both statistical tests result in the same conclusion concerning the outcome of a two-group experiment.

8.1 THE STATISTICAL HYPOTHESES

With ANOVA, we use the F statistic to evaluate the reasonableness of a statistical hypothesis known as the **null hypothesis**, usually symbolized as H_0. The null hypothesis is quite distinct from a research hypothesis, which usually asserts that the treatment conditions will actually produce true differences in performance. In contrast, the null hypothesis usually states that the independent variable in the experiment is completely *ineffective* and that the means associated with the two treatment *populations* (symbolized as μ_1 and μ_2) are *equal*—that is,

$$H_0: \quad \mu_1 = \mu_2$$

If the difference between the two sample treatment means is too large to be reasonably due to chance factors (and what we mean by "reasonably" we will explain below), the null hypothesis is rejected in favor of a second statistical hypothesis, called the **alternative hypothesis** (H_1). This hypothesis states that the two population treatment means are *not* equal:

$$H_1: \quad \mu_1 \neq \mu_2$$

A rejection of H_0 leads to the acceptance of H_1, which in effect implies support of our original *research* hypothesis. Failing to reject H_0, on the other hand, can be viewed as a failure of the experiment to support the research hypothesis.

The Logic of the F Ratio

In Chap. 6, we indicated that the F ratio (Eq. 6-11) is written as

$$F = \frac{MS_A}{MS_{S/A}}$$

The denominator of the F ratio, $MS_{S/A}$, provides an estimate of error variance regardless of the status of the null hypothesis, and for this reason it is often called the **error term**. To elaborate, you will recall that $MS_{S/A}$ is based on the variability of subjects who are *treated alike*, which means that differences between the two treatment groups do not enter into its determination. As a result, $MS_{S/A}$ simply reflects uncontrolled variability—otherwise known as **error variance**—regardless of whether H_0 is true or not.

In contrast, the numerator of the F ratio, MS_A, is based on the difference between the two means and is sensitive to the presence of any treatment effects. Suppose for the moment that the null hypothesis is true. Under these circumstances, any difference observed between the two treatment means must be due to chance factors that result from the random assignment of subjects to groups and other unsystematic factors. This means, then, that MS_A reflects only error variance. On the other hand, when the null hypothesis is *false*, MS_A reflects the *joint operation* of two factors: error variance and treatment effects.

What are the implications of these considerations for the F ratio? First, if the null hypothesis is *true*, the F ratio consists of one estimate of chance factors, based on the chance difference between the two groups, divided by another estimate of chance factors, based entirely on within-group differences. That is, both the numerator and the denominator of the F ratio would contain estimates of experimental error, and we would have

$$\frac{\text{Experimental error}}{\text{Experimental error}}$$

If such an experiment were conducted a large number of times and F ratios were determined for each experimental result, we would expect the average of these F ratios to be approximately 1.0.

On the other hand, if the null hypothesis is *false*, the numerator of the F ratio will be systematically larger than the denominator—on account of the additional presence of treatment effects—and the average F will be *greater* than 1.0. More explicitly, the ratio will become

$$\frac{\text{Treatment effects} + \text{experimental error}}{\text{Experimental error}}$$

Unfortunately, the fact that *average* values of F will be different when H_0 holds and when H_1 holds does not really help us in deciding between the two hypotheses in a specific experiment. That is, we must realize that a small F ratio does not guarantee that the null hypothesis is true (and the alternative is false), since chance factors may be counteracting any true difference in the population. By the same token, a large F ratio does not necessarily imply that the null hypothesis is false (and the alternative is true), since large differences between the two groups can occur entirely on the basis of chance. What this means is that we simply cannot be certain of avoiding incorrect decisions under these circumstances—that is, when chance factors are operating in an experiment. The best we can do is to adopt a course of action that minimizes incorrect decisions.

The Sampling Distribution of F

Let us see *how* we can minimize the occurrence of incorrect decisions. Suppose we have programmed a computer to draw two samples of scores randomly from a large population and then to compute the F statistic. As we have described the situation, the null hypothesis is true, since the two "treatment" means are drawn from the same underlying population. The scores are then "returned" to the population and the procedure is repeated a large number of times. From what we said in the last section, we would expect the mean of the F's to be close to 1.0.[1] A frequency distribution of these F's would provide a picture of the values F will take when H_0 is true. Such a distribution is called the **sampling distribution** of the F statistic.

Instead of using a computer to generate a sampling distribution of F, we can draw the distribution from formulas provided by statistical theory. Consider the sampling distribution of F that is presented in Fig. 8-1. This is the theoretical sampling distribution of F appropriate for the numerical example we introduced in Chap. 6, namely, two lecture treatment groups with 12 subjects in each group.

As you can see from the figure, extreme values of F occur fairly infrequently. Since it is relatively unlikely that large values of F will occur when H_0 is true, we adopt the strategy of rejecting the null hypothesis whenever this happens in an actual experiment. All we need is to decide on a definition of "extreme" values of F. Once this is done, we can establish a rule to reject H_0 when the F from an experiment falls within the region of extreme values, and not to reject H_0 the rest of the time.

Most researchers in the behavioral sciences have adopted a region known as the **5 percent level of significance**. This is an interval that begins with some value of F, extends to infinity, and contains the *upper 5 percent* of the distribution. We refer to this value as the **critical value of F**. In the present example, the critical

---

[1] Technically, the *median* of the F distribution equals 1. Actually, the mean is slightly larger than 1, since it is defined as

$$\frac{df_{denom.}}{df_{denom.} - 2}$$

This fact does not materially affect the thrust of the argument, however.

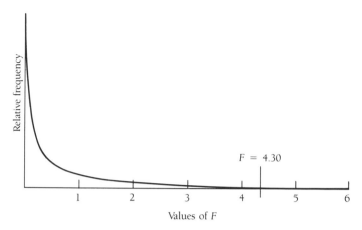

F i g u r e 8-1 Sampling distribution of F when there are $a = 2$ groups of $s = 12$ subjects each.

value of F that divides these extreme values from the rest is $F = 4.30$. That is, 95 percent of the F's have values less than 4.30, while 5 percent have values equal to or greater than 4.30. If we follow the decision rule described in the last paragraph, we would reject H_0 if $F \geq 4.30$ (read "F is greater than or equal to 4.30") and not reject H_0 when $F < 4.30$ (read "F is less than 4.30"). Stated more formally, the decision rule becomes

Reject H_0 when $F_{observed} \geq 4.30$; otherwise, do not reject H_0.

The F distribution is in reality a family of curves; the one appropriate for any experiment is determined jointly by the df associated with the numerator and with the denominator terms of the F ratio. Since the theoretical sampling distributions are continuous functions, we express the significance level in terms of probability, which is based on the proportion of the total area under the curve associated with the rejection region. The Greek letter α (alpha) is used to symbolize this probability. The 5 percent level of significance is specified by the notation

$$\alpha = .05$$

The F Table

The information necessary to determine the critical value of F, namely, the beginning of the rejection region, is found in Table A-1 of the Appendix. To use the F table, we will need to know three factors: the df for the numerator of the F ratio, the df for the denominator of the F ratio, and the significance level we have adopted.

In our numerical example presented in Chaps. 6 and 7,

$$df_{num.} = df_A = 1 \quad \text{and} \quad df_{denom.} = df_{S/A} = 22$$

We coordinate these two numbers (the column labeled 1 and the row labeled 22) and find critical values of F in Table A-1 for six different significance levels ($\alpha = .25$, .10, .05, .025, .01, and .001). Since we are interested in establishing the rejection region for the 5 percent level of significance, we will use the value listed for $\alpha = .05$, namely, $F = 4.30$. Our decision rule, which we introduced earlier in this section, becomes

Reject H_0 when $F_{observed} \geq 4.30$; otherwise, do not reject H_0.

From Table 6-3, we see that our calculations produced an F of 6.77, which exceeds the critical value of F specified by the decision rule. Consequently, we reject H_0, accept H_1, and conclude that there is a real difference between the two groups such that children receiving the physical science lecture learn more vocabulary words than do children receiving the social science lecture.

We could state this conclusion in other ways. We could say, for example, that the difference between the two groups is significant, or that significantly more vocabulary words are learned when the words are introduced in the context of a physical science lecture than in a social science lecture. The term *significant* is not synonymous with *important*, however. It simply is a shorthand way of stating that the difference observed between the two groups is sufficiently large not to be reasonably attributed to chance factors.

You may have noticed that the *df* values listed in Table A-1 are incomplete. The intervals between successive columns and rows increase with the larger numerator and denominator *df*'s. Fine gradations are not needed for the larger *df* values, however, since the numerical values of F do not change greatly from interval to interval. When the critical value of F falls between two rows or two columns of the table, most researchers follow the practice of choosing the row or column with the *smaller* number of *df*.

Other Significance Levels.   Although $\alpha = .05$ is commonly used as the significance level by most researchers, occasionally you will see other probabilities reported in the research literature. As we have already noted, Table A-1 provides F values for six significance levels. In most cases when researchers indicate a probability other than $\alpha = .05$, they are simply providing additional information for readers who may wish to use a different significance level. If you return to the F table (Table A-1), you will see that the calculated F of 6.77 exceeds the critical value of F at $\alpha = .025$ ($F = 5.79$). We could have reported our results as significant at $p < .025$, where p stands for *probability*. This means that the null hypothesis would be rejected by anyone adopting a significance level as small as $\alpha = .025$.

It is important to note that reporting a significance level other than .05 permits *no* inference concerning the strength or magnitude of the effects. We point this out because some researchers have assumed that results that are significant at $p < .025$, for example, are better or stronger than results that are significant at $p < .05$. Comparisons of strength are more appropriately made by obtaining some measure of *effect magnitude*, which we will discuss in some detail in Chap. 10.

Analyses conducted with computers usually state the **exact probability** of the obtained F statistic. This probability refers to the proportion of the sampling distribution of the F statistic falling at or *above* the F obtained in an experiment. In the present case, for example, $F = 6.77$ has an exact probability of $p = .0163$. Knowing this, a reader can simply apply his or her chosen significance level—for example, $\alpha = .05$—and reject H_0 if the exact probability is smaller (which it is in this example) or not reject H_0 if it is larger. In fact, the decision rule can be stated quite simply, without specific reference to F; that is,

If $p \leq .05$, reject H_0; otherwise, do not reject H_0.

In whatever manner the statistical test is reported, however, we must not forget that *our* significance level is decided upon *before* the start of an experiment and alternative ways of reporting probabilities do not change this fundamental point.

8.2 TESTING THE SIGNIFICANCE OF A CORRELATION

As you have seen, the final step in an analysis of variance is to evaluate the significance of the F statistic. What is evaluated is the null hypothesis, which states that the population treatment means are equal. If the $F_{observed}$ falls within the rejection region, we conclude that treatment effects are present—that is, that the population treatment means are not the same. We evaluate the statistical significance of the r statistic in a similar fashion. In this case, the null hypothesis states that there is no relationship between X and Y in the population. In symbols,

$$H_0: \quad \rho = 0$$

where ρ (Greek letter rho) represents the correlation between X and Y in the population. If this hypothesis is rejected, by applying procedures we will describe in the next paragraph, we accept the alternative hypothesis,

$$H_1: \quad \rho \neq 0$$

and conclude that there is a nonzero relationship between the two variables. In the context of the present example, we would conclude that there is a significant association between the type of lecture (the X variable) and vocabulary test scores (the

Y variable). As we have stated before, this conclusion—that there is a *relationship*—is identical to the conclusion that there is a *difference* between the treatments in the number of words learned.

As already pointed out in Chap. 7, an appropriate F ratio is given by Eq. (7-1):

$$F = \frac{r^2/df_{reg.}}{(1 - r^2)/df_{res.}}$$

The *df* in the numerator ($df_{reg.}$) is equal to 1, reflecting the fact that the *df* for a two-treatment experiment is 1. The *df* in the denominator ($df_{res.}$) is equal to $N - 2$, for reasons we will discuss in a moment. For convenience, we can rewrite Eq. (7-1) as follows:

$$F = \frac{r^2}{(1 - r^2)/(N - 2)} \qquad (8\text{-}1)$$

Entering the appropriate data into this equation, we find

$$F = \frac{(.4850)^2}{[1 - (.4850)^2]/(24 - 2)}$$

$$= \frac{.2352}{(.7648)/22} = \frac{.2352}{.0348} = 6.76.$$

This *F* is evaluated in the usual manner with

$$df_{num.} = 1 \quad \text{and} \quad df_{denom.} = N - 2 = 24 - 2 = 22$$

Since the $F_{observed}$ is greater than 4.30 (the critical value for $\alpha = .05$, when $df = 1$, 22), we can declare that the correlation between the type of lecture and vocabulary scores is significant. You should note that the value of $F_{observed}$ is identical within rounding to that calculated with ANOVA (6.77).

Comparison with ANOVA

In order to gain further insight into the parallels between ANOVA and MRC, we can explore and dissect the two F ratios used in the statistical evaluation of the corresponding null hypotheses. Suppose we express Eq. (8-1) in terms of sums of squares. This is easily accomplished by recalling from Eq. (5-15) that

$$r^2 = \frac{SS_{reg.}}{SS_Y}$$

and from our discussion in Chap. 5 that

$$1 - r^2 = \frac{SS_{res.}}{SS_Y}$$

and then substituting this information in Eq. (8-1). The final result of substitution is

$$F = \frac{SS_{reg.}}{SS_{res.}/(N-2)} \qquad (8\text{-}2)$$

What do the components in Eq. (8-2) represent? Let us begin with the denominator, $SS_{res.}/(N-2)$. Of particular relevance is the term $N-2$, which reflects the number of independent observations (the total number of subjects) and the value 2. This value 2 represents the two restraints or restrictions placed on the calculations. These result from the process of obtaining the predicted Y values (Y') from the regression equation, which uses two pieces of information in order to estimate the slope b and the intercept a of the regression line from the N pairs of observations available. From the ANOVA framework, the corresponding sum of squares is $SS_{S/A}$, where the restrictions result from estimating the two group means $\bar{Y}_{A_1}$ and $\bar{Y}_{A_2}$ upon which the deviations of the two sets of Y scores are based. The degrees of freedom in this latter case are indicated as $df_{S/A} = (a)(s-1)$, where a is the number of treatment groups and s is the number of subjects assigned to each treatment group.

Both of these sources of variance have the same number of degrees of freedom. That is,

$$df_{res.} = N - 2 = 24 - 2 = 22$$
$$df_{S/A} = (a)(s-1) = (2)(12-1) = 22$$

In other words, the quantity $N-2$ represents the degrees of freedom associated with $SS_{res.}$, and thus, the denominator of Eq. (8-2) is a mean square—in this case, a mean square for the residual deviations found with linear regression ($MS_{res.}$). That is,

$$\frac{SS_{res.}}{N-2} = \frac{SS_{res.}}{df_{res.}} = MS_{res.}$$

Though we indicated that the equation for the F ratio will be different for experiments in which there are more than two treatments, the conceptual underpinnings are the same. That is, the error term in the denominator will include the df for the error term in the experiment.

Now let us look at the numerator of Eq. (8-2). The df associated with $SS_{reg.}$ is 1; this sole df represents the deviation of the slope constant b from zero. Thus, the numerator could have been written as

$$\frac{SS_{reg.}}{1} = \frac{SS_{reg.}}{df_{reg.}} = MS_{reg.}$$

In sum, the F value obtained to test the significance of a correlation coefficient is a ratio of the $MS_{reg.}/MS_{res.}$, with $df_{num.} = 1$ and $df_{denom.} = N - 2$. This is equivalent to the F ratio of ANOVA for a two-treatment condition, which is $F = MS_A/MS_{S/A}$. In correlational analysis, the denominator reflects an error term against which the effect, $MS_{reg.}$, in the numerator is tested; similarly, in ANOVA, the denominator reflects experimental error and the numerator reflects a combination of treatment effect and experimental error.

8.3   TESTING THE SIGNIFICANCE OF b IN THE REGRESSION EQUATION

How does the b value relate to r in terms of testing a specific hypothesis in a two-group design? Since we have shown in Sec. 7.2 that the regression coefficient based on contrast coding represents information about the difference between the two means, it makes sense to ask whether the value is significantly different from zero. An F test for assessing the significance of the regression coefficient is given by[2]

$$F = \frac{b^2}{MS_{res.}/\Sigma\ (X - \bar{X})^2} \tag{8-3}$$

For the data in Table 7-1, we previously calculated the following quantities:

$$b = 7.00 \qquad S_{res.} = 3824.00 \qquad \Sigma\ (X - \bar{X})^2 = 24.00$$

Thus,

$$MS_{res.} = \frac{SS_{res.}}{df_{res.}} = \frac{3824.00}{22} = 173.82$$

Applying Eq. (8-3) yields:

$$F = \frac{7.00^2}{173.82/24.00} = \frac{49.00}{7.24} = 6.77$$

which is equal to the F we obtained when we conducted the test of significance of r. In other words, a test of b, which *reflects* the relationship between X and Y, is identical to a test of r, which is the index of the relationship between X and Y. Furthermore, these tests equal the ANOVA test of the difference between the two means for the two levels of X.

---

[2] This test is usually expressed as a t test (see Edwards, 1976, p. 106; and McNemar, 1969, p. 160). In this form, the denominator is the standard error of the regression coefficient.

8.4 SOME THEORETICAL CONSIDERATIONS

In this section, we will first consider some problems that are inherently associated with testing hypotheses regardless of whether the context is ANOVA or MRC. Next, we will discuss a related topic, the sensitivity of a statistical test in detecting differences in the population. We will conclude with a brief consideration of the statistical models underlying ANOVA and MRC.

Errors of Statistical Inference

It must be realized at the outset that conclusions drawn from *any* statistical test may be in error. We must make this dismal pronouncement because we have no way of determining the exact situation existing in the treatment populations. All that we have are the data from an experiment, which are assumed to consist of random samples drawn from the different treatment populations. Consequently, any conclusion we may extract from our data represents what is in effect an educated guess about these unknown treatment populations.

What this means, therefore, is that we have no sure way of avoiding errors of statistical inference and, moreover, that we will never know when we are committing them! Realistically, all that we can do is to take steps to *minimize* the occurrence of such errors. We represent our calculated risk taking in terms of probabilities, but in speaking of probabilities we emphasize the susceptibility to error of all conclusions based on sample data. We will consider two types of error: an error we may commit whenever we reject the null hypothesis, and another we may commit whenever we do not reject the null hypothesis. These are known as **type I error** and **type II error**, respectively.

Type I Error. As we have implied, we make a type I error whenever we falsely reject the null hypothesis—whenever we conclude that differences exist among the population treatment means or that the correlation is greater than zero when in fact such is not the case. We directly control the probability of this error in our choice of *significance level*. The probability specified by $\alpha = .05$, for example, refers to the proportion of F's that theoretically occur beyond a particular point on the F distribution—in this case, the value of F marking off the 95th percentile ($F_{.95}$). Under the null hypothesis, values of F falling within this area will occur by chance 5 percent of the time. If we accept $\alpha = .05$ and obtain an F that equals or exceeds the value of $F_{.95}$, we assume that this is *not* one of the extreme F's expected to occur by chance and conclude instead that the null hypothesis is false. But note that we are making an assumption—that the F has not occurred by chance—and that is the very reason why type I errors are committed. This also explains why we set α at .05 or smaller: to keep the probability of our committing this type of error at a reasonably low level. If we set $\alpha = .05$, then, we agree in principle to make a type I error 5 percent of the time when the null hypothesis is true.

Type II Error.   In the preceding section we focused on the possibility of rejecting the null hypothesis, when in reality the treatment means are *equal* or the correlation is *zero*. What about the more interesting situation when the means are *not* the same or the correlation *is* different from zero but we make the error of failing to reject the null hypothesis? When this happens, we commit a type II error. The probability associated with this error is represented by the Greek letter β (beta). Unfortunately, we will never know the exact probability of this error, even though we have a Greek letter reserved for it! This is because we must possess certain details about the theoretical treatment populations—the means and standard deviations or correlation—in order to determine this probability. The best we can do is to make certain assumptions about these parameters and take steps that are known to keep β at a reasonably low value. We will discuss these steps in a moment.

Comment.   We always face the possibility of making an error whenever we draw conclusions from a set of data. The type of error depends on the nature of the conclusion drawn from the results. If the population treatment means really are the same, we will make an error if we conclude that a difference exists between them; this is known as a type I error. The probability of a type I error is specified by our choice of significance level. On the other hand, if in fact a difference exists between the two treatment populations, we will make an error if we fail to reject the null hypothesis; this is known as a type II error.

You should note that we can make only one of these errors in any given statistical test—not both. This is because each error is exclusively associated with a *different conclusion*: a type I error is associated with *rejecting* the null hypothesis, and a type II error with *not rejecting* the null hypothesis. Since the decision rule forces us to choose one of these two conclusions, we will be susceptible only to the error associated with the particular conclusion we make.

Power of a Statistical Test

Power is a statistical concept that refers to the probability of *correctly* rejecting the null hypothesis. It is related to the probability of a type II error as follows:

$$\text{Power} = 1 - \beta \qquad (8\text{-}4)$$

If the probability of making a type II error is .30, for example, power is $1 - .30 = .70$. What this means is that if we repeated the same experiment over and over, we would reject the null hypothesis 70 percent of the time; 30 percent of the time we would commit a type II error.

In contrast with type I error, which is controlled directly by our choice of α, type II error (or power) is controlled indirectly. Several factors are known to increase power, but the most common way is to increase sample size s. There is a practical limit to the use of this strategy, however, since experiments with already large sample sizes require quite sizable increases in sample size to achieve the same gain in power that one would obtain by adding subjects to a less ambitious experiment. An experiment with a sample size of $s = 5$, for example, will benefit more by the addition of another 5 observations per group than will an experiment with $s = 10$ or $s = 20$.

Another way of increasing power consists of bringing under closer control any unsystematic sources of variability that may be operating in an experiment. Most commonly, this involves reducing subject variability through the use of a more homogeneous pool of subjects. Alternatively, more sensitive experimental designs might be chosen, such as designs which use either subjects who are matched on some relevant ability or factor or subjects who serve in *all* the treatment conditions instead of only one. Both of these alternative designs can result in a sizable increase in power, but require a type of statistical analysis other than we have considered so far. A final method, called the **analysis of covariance**, provides a *statistical* solution whereby information about the subjects is collected before the start of the experiment and then used to reduce the influence of chance factors in the experiment. We will consider these alternative designs and the analysis of covariance in later chapters.

Most experiments in the behavioral sciences are designed without consideration of power and, often, are seriously lacking in their ability to detect differences among treatment means when they are present in the population. Cohen (1962) and Brewer (1972) have observed astonishingly low levels of power for experiments reported in the psychological literature. What this means is that findings associated with lower power stand a poor chance of being duplicated by others who wish to repeat or to extend these studies. For this reason, then, we feel it is reckless not to obtain power estimates in the planning stage of an experiment. It is at this point that something can still be done to increase power if it is too low, either by increasing sample size, by attempting to reduce error variance, or by choosing a potentially more sensitive experimental design or statistical procedure. Power determinations are not difficult to obtain, and they often provide useful insight into the nature of the phenomenon under study. Cohen devotes an entire book (1977) to the discussion of power in a variety of different research settings. Other, less comprehensive presentations are also available; see for example, Keppel (1982, Chap. 4), Myers (1979, pp. 86–88), and Winer (1971, pp. 220–228). We suggest that you consult these references for further discussion of the topic.

Statistical Models and Assumptions

The theoretical justification of the inferential procedures we have outlined in this chapter is dependent on a set of assumptions and complex statistical proofs. We will highlight some of these arguments here.

The Analysis of Variance.   Underlying ANOVA is a model—known as the **linear model**—that expresses the score of a subject in any treatment condition as the sum of certain parameters of the population. Three assumptions underlie the use of the F distribution for evaluating the null hypothesis. Briefly, we assume that the treatment populations are *normally distributed*, that they have *equal variances*, and that the individual observations are *independent* of (i.e., uninfluenced by) any other observations, either within the same treatment population or between treatment populations.

Research over the last two decades has shown that even sizable violations of the first two assumptions do not appear to distort the distribution of the F statistic seriously.[3] The assumption of independence is usually satisfied by assigning subjects randomly to the treatment conditions and administering the treatments individually to the different subjects. In short, the F statistic is amazingly insensitive to even flagrant violations of the assumptions of normality and of the homogeneity of variances. The main requirement is that subjects be randomly assigned to the treatments.

Multiple Regression and Correlation.   The model underlying the MRC analysis is algebraically equivalent to the one underlying ANOVA. The difference is in the way the linear model is expressed. The assumptions underlying the use of the F distribution in evaluating the null hypothesis are identical to those summarized for ANOVA. That is, it is assumed that the treatment populations are normally distributed and have equal variances and that all individual observations are independent of one another.

8.5   SUMMARY

The final step in the statistical analysis of an experiment is the significance test. Significance testing begins with the formulation of a *null hypothesis* (H_0), which will be evaluated with the statistical evidence generated by the study. This hypoth-

---

[3] The F statistic *is* sensitive to concurrent or simultaneous violations of the assumptions of normality and homogeneity. See Myers (1979, pp. 66–72) for an excellent discussion of these problems.

esis generally consists of a statement proposing that there are *no treatment effects* or that there is *no relationship between the variables*. With ANOVA, for example, the null hypothesis states that the two population treatment means are the same; that is,

$$H_0: \quad \mu_1 = \mu_2$$

With correlational analysis, the corresponding null hypothesis states that the correlation between the independent variable X and the dependent variable Y in the population is zero. In symbols,

$$H_0: \rho = 0$$

(An alternative approach is to test the significance of the regression coefficient; in this case, the null hypothesis would state that the slope of the regression line relating X and Y in the population is zero.) A second statistical hypothesis, which is called the *alternative hypothesis* (H_1), is also formulated at this time. This hypothesis essentially states that the null hypothesis is *false*, implying that there *is* a difference between the population treatment means or a correlation in the population between X and Y. Our task now is to decide which of these two statistical hypotheses is more likely to be correct, given the outcome of the experiment we have just completed.

At this point, we return to the experiment and, depending on the statistical approach we have followed, examine either the observed difference between the two means (for ANOVA) or the correlation between X and Y (for MRC). Because of the operation of chance factors, which stem largely from the random assignment of subjects to conditions, we fully expect to find some difference between the two means or a nonzero value for the product-moment correlation even if the null hypothesis is true. To deal with this problem, we calculate an F ratio which relates *systematic variation* (variation associated with the experimental manipulation) to *unsystematic variation* (chance or random variation). Systematic variation, which is reflected by MS_A in ANOVA and by r^2 in MRC, is influenced by two sources, chance effects and potential treatment effects; while unsystematic variation, which is reflected by $MS_{S/A}$ in ANOVA and by $(1 - r^2)/(N - 2)$ in MRC, is influenced by chance factors alone.

We now compare the value of F obtained in the experiment with the so-called *critical value* of F, which is based on the theoretical sampling distribution of F and is found in a statistical table. This value sets the lower boundary of the range of F's within which we will reject the null hypothesis. If the observed F falls within this range—if it is equal to or greater than the critical value of F—we reject the null hypothesis and conclude that treatment effects are present in the population. If the observed F is smaller than the critical value, we do not reject the null hypothesis.

We discussed in detail the errors of statistical inference that may occur through hypothesis testing. A type I error occurs when a null hypothesis is rejected falsely; we keep the probability of such errors at a low value through our choice of significance level. A type II error occurs when treatment effects are present in the population but the null hypothesis is not rejected; we control the probability of such errors indirectly through our choice of sample size and of experimental design. Power, which is defined in terms of type II error, refers to the sensitivity of a statistical test. A consideration of the statistical models underlying ANOVA and MRC reveals that the F test is relatively insensitive to violations of the assumptions of normality and of homogeneous treatment variances.

8.6   EXERCISES

1. Consider again the experiment presented in Problem 2 of Chap. 6, which you analyzed with analysis of variance.

a. State the decision rule for rejecting the null hypothesis, using $\alpha = .05$. Is the F obtained from ANOVA significant?
b. What is the decision rule if instead you use $\alpha = .10$? Is the F significant?

2. In Problem 1, Chap. 7, you calculated an r based on this same set of data.

a. Complete the correlational analysis by calculating the F ratio.
b. State the decision rule for evaluating the null hypothesis at $\alpha = .05$. Is the F significant?
c. Verify that the F from ANOVA and that from the correlational analysis are the same.

9

General Coding of Experiments for MRC Analysis

. . .

111

You saw in Chap. 7 that you could use correlational techniques to analyze a single-factor experiment with two independent treatment groups. You could accomplish this by coding each subject in such a way that group distinction is reflected directly in the correlational statistics. In Chap. 9 we will discuss the general rules for coding and provide an overview of the different kinds of coding strategies, in anticipation of our discussion of the analysis of multigroup designs, which begins in Chap. 10. We will consider first a general rule for coding treatment conditions and then describe briefly three methods in common use.

9.1   THE CODING OF TREATMENT CONDITIONS

A General Rule for Coding

Coding implies assigning a numerical value for the purpose of identifying subjects with regard to the treatment condition they receive. A general rule for coding of a simple experimental design is:

> **The codes assigned to subjects can be any value provided that they (1) differ between treatment conditions and (2) are identical for all subjects receiving the same treatment.**

This rule states that we can assign any value to subjects in a_1, such as 1096, and any *different* value to those in a_2, such as 7.59. However, each subject in a_1 would then be coded with an X value of 1096, and each subject in a_2 would be coded with an X value of 7.59. These particular values may appear to be nonsensical and arbitrary—and, in fact, they are! But the analysis can proceed, nevertheless, since the essential purpose of coding is to provide a numerical value that can be arithmetically manipulated—that is, multiplied, divided, subtracted, or added.

To be more specific, the formula for r corrects for the specific coded values chosen by *standardizing* the X and Y distributions (changing the X and Y distributions so that they have equal means and standard deviations). In Chap. 5, we presented several formulas for computing r; see Eqs. (5-4), (5-5), and (5-6). Another formula, which uses data already presented in standardized form, is:

$$r = \frac{\Sigma\, z_X z_Y}{N} \tag{9-1}$$

In Eq. (9-1), z_X refers to the distribution of X scores that has been standardized to have a mean of 0.00 and a standard deviation of 1.00. Similarly, z_Y refers to the distribution of Y scores that has been standardized to have a mean of 0.00 and a standard deviation of 1.00. Note that a standard score is obtained by subtracting the mean of the distribution from each raw score and dividing the difference by the standard deviation of that distribution; thus, $z_X = (X - \bar{X})/SD_X$.

Given a set of data, Eq. (9-1) yields the same value as Eqs. (5-4), (5-5), and (5-6). In essence, the correlational formula converts the distributions of the X and Y variables to standardized distributions with equal means and standard deviations. Consequently, it does not make a difference what values are used for X, since the distributions are effectively transformed to have a mean of 0.00 and a standard deviation of 1.00.

We do not advocate a nonsensical coding, however, but mention it to highlight the purpose of coding, which, to repeat, is merely the creation of numerical values for X that distinguish between the two treatment groups. There are some coding systems that are more meaningful, however, and we will present three—contrast coding (sometimes called *orthogonal coding*), dummy coding, and effect coding. While we will predominantly use contrast coding, we present the three systems because there are times when the others are more informative or easier to use in calculations.

Three Types of Coding

Contrast Coding. We introduced **contrast coding** in Chap. 7. In general, contrast coding involves identification of specific comparisons of interest and assigning values that enable the treatments to be directly compared. In a two-group design, in which the only possible comparison is between the means of the two treatment groups, this was accomplished by assigning the value $+1$ to one group and the value -1 to the other group. When applied to the analysis of an experiment with more than two treatment conditions, this coding system provides us with the most useful information of all the coding methods. Since you will more fully appreciate its value when we consider more elaborate designs, we will describe it only briefly here.

The primary value of contrast coding is, as previously indicated, that its use results in a comparison that is expressed as the difference between two means. Contrast coding requires that the sum of the coded values across all subjects equal zero.[1] In the present case, since we have two groups, a_1 and a_2, we assign the value $+1$ to all subjects in a_1 and the value -1 to all subjects in a_2. You may wish to reexamine Table 7-1 (p. 86), which lays out the data from a two-condition experiment in a form that is suitable for correlational analysis with contrast coding. Since the *same* number of subjects (12) are placed in each condition, the sum of all the $+1$s and -1s equals zero, thereby fulfilling the requirement. Keep in mind,

---

[1] This discussion assumes treatment groups with equal sample sizes. We consider the coding and analysis of experiments with unequal sample sizes in Chap. 24

however, that this example of contrast coding is a special case resulting when $a = 2$. As we turn to experiments with more complicated designs, we will expand our treatment of contrast coding and its specific requirements.

Dummy Coding.   Another coding method is referred to as **dummy coding**. This type of coding merely requires that the first group be assigned the value of 1 and the second group the value of 0. Table 9-1 illustrates the coding. Note that the only difference between Tables 7-1 and 9-1 is in the X column; in contrast coding, $+1$ and -1 were used to provide X values for the subjects, while in dummy coding, 1 and 0 are used.

Table 9-1

An Example of Dummy Coding

Subject	X	Y	$(X - \bar{X})$	$(X - \bar{X})^2$	$(Y - \bar{Y})$	$(Y - \bar{Y})^2$	$(X - \bar{X})(Y - \bar{Y})$
1	1	53	.50	.25	20	400	10.00
2	1	49	.50	.25	16	256	8.00
3	1	47	.50	.25	14	196	7.00
4	1	42	.50	.25	9	81	4.50
5	1	51	.50	.25	18	324	9.00
6	1	34	.50	.25	1	1	.50
7	1	44	.50	.25	11	121	5.50
8	1	48	.50	.25	15	225	7.50
9	1	35	.50	.25	2	4	1.00
10	1	18	.50	.25	-15	225	-7.50
11	1	32	.50	.25	-1	1	$-.50$
12	1	27	.50	.25	-6	36	-3.00
13	0	47	$-.50$	.25	14	196	-7.00
14	0	42	$-.50$	.25	9	81	-4.50
15	0	39	$-.50$	.25	6	36	-3.00
16	0	37	$-.50$	.25	4	16	-2.00
17	0	42	$-.50$	.25	9	81	-4.50
18	0	33	$-.50$	.25	0	0	.00
19	0	13	$-.50$	.25	-20	400	10.00
20	0	16	$-.50$	.25	-17	289	8.50
21	0	16	$-.50$	.25	-17	289	8.50
22	0	10	$-.50$	.25	-23	529	11.50
23	0	11	$-.50$	.25	-22	484	11.00
24	0	6	$-.50$	.25	-27	729	13.50
Sum	12	792	0.00	6.00	0	5000	84.00

Again, any of the equations for r—Eq. (5-4), (5-5), or (5-6)—can be used. Substituting the values from the last row of Table 9-1 in Eq. (5-4), we obtain:

$$r = \frac{\Sigma\,[(X - \bar{X})(Y - \bar{Y})]}{\sqrt{\Sigma\,(X - \bar{X})^2\,\Sigma\,(Y - \bar{Y})^2}}$$

$$= \frac{84.00}{\sqrt{(6.00)(5000.00)}} = \frac{84.00}{173.21} = .4850$$

The value of r^2 is $(.4850)^2 = .2352$. This outcome obtained with dummy coding is identical to that obtained with contrast coding. (Obviously, the outcome of the F test will be the same as well.)

This result should serve as a demonstration that the particular coding values do not influence the obtained correlation. This is true provided that the general coding rules are followed. That rule, again, states that all subjects within a treatment condition must receive the same value and that a different value must be used for the two conditions.

While the conclusions supported by the correlational statistics are the same regardless of the coding system used, the information contained within the corresponding regression equations is not. Recall from Chap. 7 that when contrast coding is used, the a constant in the equation represents the grand mean $\bar{Y}_T$; the b value is used to assess the *difference* between the two treatment means.

Without showing the calculations, we give the regression equation for the dummy-coded data:

$$Y' = 26.00 + (14.00)(X)$$

Here, again, in the two-treatment situation, the a and b values have special meaning. The a value of 26.00 represents the mean Y value of the group assigned the X value 0, in this case, a_2. The b value directly reflects the difference between $\bar{Y}_{A1}$ and $\bar{Y}_{A2}$, or $40.00 - 26.00 = 14.00$.

We will not use dummy coding for calculating F ratios in the analysis of experiments, because its interpretive output is limited, particularly when compared with contrast coding. We have illustrated it for two reasons, however: first, it is an easy coding system to apply; and second, we want to show that different coding schemes produce identical values for the squared correlation coefficients and for the F tests and to indicate that there is a regression equation which—like that for contrast coding—is both systematic and meaningful.[2]

---

[2] Dummy coding is sometimes recommended when a researcher is interested in comparing one of the treatment means in a multigroup experiment with *all* of the remaining treatment means; this frequently occurs in an experiment in which several experimental conditions are to be compared with one control or reference condition. We will not discuss this method, however, because the same information can also be obtained by an appropriately chosen set of contrast codes, which we consider in detail in Chap. 11.

Effect Coding.   A third type of coding is **effect coding** (sometimes called *effects coding*). In a two-treatment situation, effect coding is the same as contrast coding; once we have more than two treatments, it takes on special meaning. We only mention effect coding here in order to be complete in our presentation. In effect coding, as in contrast coding, the *a* value in the regression equation shows the grand mean $\bar{Y}_T$. The *b* values for effect coding will be explained when we turn to experiments with more than two treatment conditions; in these situations, the *b* values represent differences between a treatment mean and the grand mean, such as $\bar{Y}_{A_1} - \bar{Y}_T$.

In summary, for a given set of data, each coding system yields the identical r^2. The differences are in the information provided by the regression equation. For now, we will simply list them in the following table:

Code	a	b
Contrast	$\bar{Y}_T$	Used to calculate difference between conditions compared
Dummy	$\bar{Y}$ of condition assigned all 0s	Indicates difference between conditions
Effect	$\bar{Y}_T$	Indicates difference between $\bar{Y}_A$ and $\bar{Y}_T$

9.2   THE CODE MATRIX

The simplest way to plan and lay out a coding scheme, regardless of specific coding strategy, is to construct a *code matrix*. A code matrix is a cellular layout of the experiment. In the two-group experiment, there are two cells, a_1 and a_2. To illustrate, each row in the following table is a code matrix for a two-group experiment; the three rows each indicate one of the three types of codes we have discussed in this chapter:

	a_1	a_2
Contrast	+1	−1
Dummy	1	0
Effect	+1	−1

Thus, to determine how to assign codes to subjects in an experiment so that the data can be analyzed by MRC, we simply represent the experiment in cellular fashion and fill in code values that conform to the coding rules. For the two-group experiment, we start with the empty code matrix

and then insert the appropriate codes into the cells. (Again, because of the statistical operations, all three types of coding produce the same value of r^2; and in two-group experiment, the distinction between contrast coding and effect coding is not apparent.)

9.3 SUMMARY

In order to adapt correlational techniques to the analysis of experiments, we must first distinguish the treatment conditions from one another. We accomplish this by a process called *coding*. For the two-group experiment, coding is relatively uncomplicated—we simply assign one numerical value to all the subjects receiving one of the treatment conditions and a different numerical value to all the subjects receiving the other treatment condition. No matter what numbers we choose to represent the two treatment conditions, we will obtain the same value for r^2. Thus, $SS_{reg.}$, $SS_{res.}$, and the F ratio remain constant regardless of what values are used in coding; the regression coefficient b and the intercept a, however, change with different coding schemes.

Three methods of coding are commonly used in correlational analysis. Contrast coding, which concentrates on the difference between two means, is most useful for the analysis of experiments. Dummy coding and effect coding are useful in certain restricted situations, which we will note in subsequent discussions. Chapter 10 will show how contrast coding can be extended to the analysis of experiments with more than two treatment conditions.

9.4 EXERCISES

1. Suppose you conduct a "goal-setting" experiment in which one group of subjects is instructed to "do your best" on a 1-hr proofreading task while a second group is instructed to "proof at least 40 pages in an hour." In your experiment

you wish to determine whether specific goals yield better results than general, "do-your-best" goals. Ten subjects are randomly assigned to each condition and the numbers of errors each subject located are given below:

Do Your Best		Specific Goal	
24	41	33	29
29	40	28	19
33	29	44	40
19	25	47	37
32	34	39	35

a. Set up a code matrix for contrast coding and one for dummy coding.
b. Calculate r^2 using each code system.
c. Calculate the F ratio obtained with each code system.
d. Calculate the regression equation using each code system.
e. Compare and contrast the information obtained from the two regression equations.

10

Overall Analysis of the Single-Factor Design

. . .

In Chaps. 6 through 9, we illustrated the analysis of an experiment consisting of only two treatment conditions. With this simplest of experimental designs, we were able to introduce you to the general principles of hypothesis testing and to show you the equivalence between an analysis of variance and a correlational analysis conducted on the same set of experimental data. As you are undoubtedly aware, however, most experiments in the behavioral sciences contain more than two treatment conditions, and the reason is obvious: an increase in the number of treatments or levels of treatments provides us with the opportunity to obtain more specific information about the nature of the relationship between the independent and dependent variables. Fortunately, the parallel between ANOVA and correlational analysis is essentially unaffected by the number of treatment conditions included in the design, as you will see later in this chapter.

10.1   THE OVERALL ANALYSIS: THE ANOVA APPROACH

The ANOVA approach to the overall analysis of a single-factor experiment is identical to that presented in Sec. 6.1. Although we developed our computational formulas in that chapter in the context of a two-group experiment, they are general and applicable to any single-factor experiment in which equal numbers of subjects (s) are assigned randomly to any number of treatment conditions (a). (Unequal sample sizes are discussed in Chap. 24.) To illustrate, we have expanded the example from Chap. 6, in which vocabulary words were introduced through lectures dealing with either physical science or social science, to include a third condition, one in which the words are introduced through a lecture on *history*. The experiment now consists of $a = 3$ conditions, and we now have 12 more subjects, who are exposed to the history lecture. The data for all three conditions are presented in Table 10-1. (Notice that the data for the first two conditions come from the original example.) Table 10-1 also provides the treatment sum and mean at the bottom of each column of scores.

The steps in the analysis are summarized in Table 10-2. The upper half of the table details the operations for calculating the three basic ratios—[Y], [A], and [T]—while the lower half of the table presents the ANOVA summary table. (See Secs. 6.2 and 6.3 if you need to refresh your understanding of these different steps.) The null hypothesis assessed in this analysis,

$$H_0: \quad \mu_1 = \mu_2 = \mu_3$$

specifies that the three population treatment means are equal. It is important to note that any and all true differences among the means will contribute to the

Table 10-1

Vocabulary Scores Following Three Different Lectures

Physical Science (a_1)	Social Science (a_2)	History (a_3)
53	47	45
49	42	41
47	39	38
42	37	36
51	42	35
34	33	33
44	13	46
48	16	40
35	16	29
18	10	21
32	11	30
27	6	20
Sum: 480	312	414
Mean: 40.00	26.00	34.50

Table 10-2

Numerical Example

Basic Ratios

$$[Y] = \Sigma\, Y^2 = 53^2 + 49^2 + \cdots + 30^2 + 20^2 = 46,194$$

$$[A] = \frac{\Sigma\, A^2}{s} = \frac{480^2 + 312^2 + 414^2}{12} = \frac{499,140}{12} = 41,595.00$$

$$[T] = \frac{T^2}{(a)(s)} = \frac{1206^2}{(3)(12)} = \frac{1,454,436}{36} = 40,401.00$$

Summary of the Analysis

Source	SS	df	MS	F
A	$[A] - [T] = 1194.00$	2	597.00	4.28
S/A	$[Y] - [A] = 4599.00$	33	139.36	
Total	$[Y] - [T] = 5793.00$	35		

possible rejection of the null hypothesis. This point is emphasized by the corresponding alternative hypothesis,

$$H_1: \quad \text{Not all the } \mu_i\text{'s are equal.}$$

In other words, it is *not* necessary that *all* μ_i's be different for H_0 to be false, but only that there be differences among some of the μ_i's.

The F test, summarized in Table 10-2, is known as the **omnibus** or **overall F test**, because it evaluates the significance of what in effect is the *average variability* among the entire set of treatment means. The F of 4.28 exceeds the critical value listed in Table A-1 of Appendix A ($F = 3.32$, for $df_{num.} = 2$ and $df_{denom.} = 33$ at $p < .05$). The omnibus null hypothesis is rejected, and we conclude that it was not by chance that the three lectures differed in their success in teaching vocabulary words to the students. We will now turn to correlational statistics to see how they reach this same conclusion.

10.2 THE OVERALL ANALYSIS: THE MRC APPROACH

The Pearson correlation coefficient r was designed to represent the relationship between a dependent variable Y and a second variable X, usually referred to as a predictor variable. It is possible to extend the correlational logic in this situation to one in which there continues to be one dependent variable but there is *more than one* predictor variable—**multiple regression and correlation (MRC)**.

The multiple correlation coefficient R is an index of the relationship between Y and a *set* of X variables. Traditionally, multiple correlational analysis was undertaken to determine the amount of variability in Y that can be explained by a number of X variables. For an example, consider a study in educational research in which we want to know how much of the variability in college grade-point average (GPA) can be explained by three *different* predictor variables such as high school grades (X_1), aptitude test scores (X_2), and achievement test scores (X_3). Each of these measures represents an X variable that can be used separately or with the others to predict college performance (the Y variable). We could, of course, use the Pearson coefficient r to represent the relationship between college GPA and any one of these X variables. For instance, the relationship between college GPA and high school GPA might produce an r^2 of .15 (that is, $r = .39$). On the other hand, the MRC procedure allows additional information, e.g., the aptitude and achievement test scores, to be included in the analysis, with the hope of increasing the percentage of college GPA variability that can be explained to a level appreciably above the 15 percent associated with high school GPA alone. In other words, the more information (variables) we include in our data set, the greater the percentage of variability in the dependent variable we are likely to explain.

How does this apply to the analysis of an experiment? You have seen that we can represent the treatment effects in a two-group experiment with an appropriately chosen coding system to represent the X variable. In our example we coded the two levels of the variable by $+1$ and -1. In order to represent the additional information available when more than two treatment conditions are included in the experimental design, we use a strategy whereby more X "variables" are added to distinguish among the different treatments that make up the independent variable and, in that way, to capture the *overall* effect of the independent variable on the dependent variable. The key to applying MRC to experimental data, then, is the establishment of a coding system, reflected by a set of X "variables," that will represent all the variability associated with the independent variable. The point here is that though we talk of X "variables" in the experiment at hand, there is only one independent variable, but we will represent its different levels as if we had several X variables.

Before we go on with the application of MRC to experimental data, we need to present MRC in further detail, and to do so we will use the nonexperimental design of our example of predicting GPA. Although MRC can be viewed as an extension of analysis of the correlation between two variables, the arithmetic can become sufficiently complex that calculation by hand is unreasonable—even with an electronic calculator—and so a computer is usually used instead. Fortunately, the basic logic can be illustrated relatively simply with only two different X variables, for which the calculations *can* be accomplished by hand. What is important, then, is to understand fully the concepts, statistics, and analyses for the two-variable case, since these are readily extended to more complex cases involving any number of different X variables. With the help of a computer, this consists of setting up the analysis properly and then extracting the critical information from the computer printout and entering the appropriate values into the general formulas we will provide.

Multiple Correlation

The formula for determining the relationship between one dependent variable Y and two predictor variables X_1 and X_2 is:

$$R_{Y.1,2} = \sqrt{\frac{r_{Y1}^2 + r_{Y2}^2 - 2r_{Y1}r_{Y2}r_{12}}{1 - r_{12}^2}} \qquad (10\text{-}1)$$

or

$$R^2_{Y.1,2} = \frac{r^2_{Y1} + r^2_{Y2} - 2r_{Y1}r_{Y2}r_{12}}{1 - r^2_{12}} \tag{10-2}$$

where the subscripts 1 and 2 in the above equations represent the two different X variables, X_1 and X_2, respectively. The capital R is used to indicate that we are dealing with *multiple* correlation or multiple X variables. Equation (10-1) gives the *multiple correlation coefficient*, and Eq. (10-2) gives what is referred to as the *squared multiple correlation coefficient*.

The amount of Y variability that can be explained by a set of different X variables is a function of two types of relationships:

1. The relationship between Y and *each* X variable *and*
2. The relationship between the X variables themselves

(We will refer to the correlation between any two variables as either a *Pearson* or a *simple* or a *zero-order* correlation. They all refer to the same statistic, *r*.) In Eq. (10-2),

$R^2_{Y.1,2}$ = the squared multiple correlation coefficient representing the correlation between Y and the two X variables
r_{Y1} = the simple correlation coefficient between Y and the first X variable
r_{Y2} = the simple correlation coefficient between Y and the second X variable
r_{12} = the simple correlation coefficient between the two X variables themselves

(The squared multiple correlation coefficient is also known as the **coefficient of multiple determination**, and the correlation between the X variables themselves is usually referred to as an **intercorrelation**.)

The squared multiple correlation coefficient R^2 is the concept that we will most often use for analysis of both experimental and nonexperimental designs. Its interpretation is the same as that given r^2 (see Chap. 5, pages 61–66); that is, R^2 represents the proportion of variability in Y that is predictable or explainable from information or knowledge gained from a set of X variables. The reason we can interpret R^2 in this way will become apparent as we discuss the other concept associated with correlation, and that is regression. But first, it is useful to explore and illustrate further what is taking place when we assess multiple correlation.

Schematic Representation of Multiple Correlation

The squared multiple correlation coefficient represents the degree to which a set of X variables predicts or explains variation in Y. In the present context, the set refers to two variables, X_1 and X_2 (in our example, high school grades and aptitude scores, respectively). The computational formula for $R^2_{Y.1,2}$, Eq. (10-2), takes into consideration any redundancy of information represented separately by the two variables. When there is an intercorrelation between the two variables, for example, $r_{12} = +.50$, there is an overlap of information, a redundancy, between them. This is why we cannot calculate $R^2_{Y.1,2}$ simply by adding together the separate squared correlations between Y and the two X variable—they both capture some of the same variation in Y.

There is only one circumstance under which we can calculate $R^2_{Y.1,2}$ in this manner, namely, when $r_{12} = .00$. To see how this happens, we will substitute $r_{12} = .00$ in Eq. (10-2) and simplify the equation:

$$R^2_{Y.1,2} = \frac{r^2_{Y1} + r^2_{Y2} - (2)(r_{Y1})(r_{Y2})(r_{12})}{1 - r^2_{12}}$$

$$= \frac{r^2_{Y1} + r^2_{Y2} - (2)(r_{Y1})(r_{Y2})(.00)}{1 - .00}$$

$$= r^2_{Y1} + r^2_{Y2} \qquad (10\text{-}3)$$

In all other situations, $R^2_{Y.1,2}$ will not exactly equal the sum of the separate squared correlations. In short, then, Eq. (10-2) takes into consideration the fact that variables 1 and 2 capture some of the same information and provides an estimate of the amount of Y variability that can be explained by the set of variables that is not biased by this overlap.

This situation can be represented by what is known as a **Venn diagram**, as in Fig. 10-1. In this diagram, the circle labeled Y represents the total variation of Y, while the circles labeled X_1 and X_2 represent the total variation of X_1 and X_2,

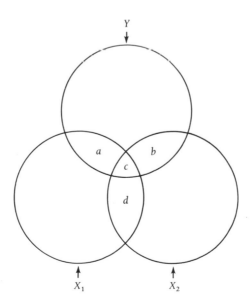

F i g u r e 10-1   Venn diagram representation of multiple correlation.

respectively. The areas of overlap between the circles represent the percentages of variability shared by the three variables. The overlap of the X_1 circle and the Y circle represents the percentage of Y variability shared with X_1, that is, r_{Y1}^2. Similarly, the overlap of the X_2 and Y circles designates the percentage of Y variability shared with X_2, namely, r_{Y2}^2. Finally, the overlap of the X_1 and X_2 circles represents the percentage of either X_1 variability shared with X_2 or of X_2 variability shared with X_1—the intercorrelations may be expressed either way.

You will note that we have used letters to designate the specific portions of overlap among the three circles. The overlap of X_1 and Y consists of the sum of two areas, a and c; the overlap of X_2 and Y consists of the sum of b and c; and the overlap of X_1 and X_2 consists of the sum of c and d. There are two important points to note in this diagram: (1) that the presence of intercorrelation or overlap between X_1 and X_2 indicates that r_{Y1}^2 and r_{Y2}^2 are explaining some of the *same* Y variability (area c) and (2) that the total Y variability explained by the two X variables combined (the sum of a, c, and b) is less than the sum of the Y variabilities explained by the two variables separately—that is, $(a + c) + (c + b)$ is greater than $a + c + b$. Area c, then, represents the redundancy that must be removed from the sum of the separate squared correlations to represent the Y variability *uniquely* predicted by the combination of the two variables. This redundancy is removed statistically by Eq. (10-1) or Eq. (10-2).

If there were more than two X variables present, formulas that extend Eqs. (10-1) and (10-2) would be used to calculate the relationship between Y and the entire set of variables. These formulas are complex, however, and as we have mentioned already, calculations are typically conducted by computers. Nevertheless, these formulas would operate on the same principles illustrated with two variables and the Venn diagram: the individual relationships between Y and the separate variables, and the removal of redundant information represented by the intercorrelations among the variables.

Multiple Regression

Just as there was a regression equation to accompany r, a **multiple regression equation** can be developed to represent the combined relationship of the set of X variables with Y. We will examine the interrelationship between multiple correlation and multiple regression and show that R^2 can be expressed as a ratio of the regression sum of squares—this time based on the deviation of Y values predicted by the multiple regression equation from the overall Y mean (i.e., $Y' - \bar{Y}$)—to the total variation in Y.

The multiple regression equation for two variables is:

$$Y' = a + b_1 X_1 + b_2 X_2 \qquad (10\text{-}4)$$

where Y' = the predicted or estimated Y based on an application of the multiple regression equation

a = a constant, analogous to the Y intercept described in Sec. 5.4

b_1, b_2 = the regression coefficients—also constants—associated with the two variables

X_1, X_2 = the values of the two variables for any given subject

As with the regression equation for a single variable, the constants in the multiple regression equation are determined mathematically by the method of least squares, which produces values of a, b_1, and b_2 that keep the discrepancy between the predicted and actual Y values $(Y - Y')$ to a minimum.

With more than two variables, the regression equation is expanded to include a regression coefficient b for each variable. The general multiple regression equation for k variables is:

$$Y' = a + b_1X_1 + b_2X_2 + \cdots + b_kX_k \qquad (10\text{-}5)$$

The computational formula for any of these constants is not crucial to know (see Ghiselli et al., 1981, Chap. 11, for formulas). It is sufficient to point out, however, that the b values for the X's are determined by consideration of the correlations between each X and Y, the intercorrelations among the variables, and residual variances. The advantage of the multiple regression equation is that each regression coefficient b can be interpreted as the amount by which Y changes *exclusively* with a change in the relevant X, with the influence of all the other variables held constant mathematically. This becomes more meaningful in the use of regression for nonexperimental data, but for now, keep in mind that each of the b's provides information about the relationship between a specific X and the Y.

There are also formulas to determine R^2 directly from the regression coefficients and simple correlation coefficients (see Ghiselli et al., 1981, Chap. 11). But the key for our present purposes is to recall the properties of the Pearson coefficient, namely, that the correlation between X and Y *equals* the correlation between Y and Y' (see pages 60–61) and that the regression sum of squares is equal to the sum of the squared deviations of Y' from $\bar{Y}$; that is, $\Sigma\ (Y' - \bar{Y})^2$. Thus, if we determine the multiple regression equation for a set of data, the combination of the variables, the b's, and the a will yield a Y' which, when correlated with the actual obtained Y scores, indicates the strength of relationship between the set of X's and Y. In symbols,

$$R^2_{Y.1,2\ldots k} = r^2_{YY'} \qquad (10\text{-}6)$$

If multiple correlation is, in effect, a simple correlation between the actual Y values and the corresponding values of Y predicted from the multiple regression equation, the partitioning logic for correlation developed in Sec. 5.6 can be extended to the present situation. Consequently,

$$R^2 = \frac{\Sigma (Y' - \bar{Y})^2}{\Sigma (Y - \bar{Y})^2} = \frac{SS_{reg.}}{SS_Y}$$

That is, if we have a set of data with two X variables and a Y for each subject, we can compute $R^2_{Y.1,2}$ and determine $Y' = a + b_1 X_1 + b_2 X_2$. If we then look at each subject's two X scores and insert them into the regression equation, we will obtain a predicted Y' for each subject. (Recall that we did this in Sec. 5.6 when we had only one X variable.) As a result, we have a Y' for each subject to go along with his or her Y, X_1, and X_2 scores or values. In Eq. (5-11), we indicated that

$$r^2 = \frac{\Sigma (Y' - \bar{Y})^2}{\Sigma (Y - \bar{Y})^2}$$

Thus, we can insert each subject's Y' value and show that

$$r^2 = \frac{\Sigma (Y' - \bar{Y})^2}{\Sigma (Y - \bar{Y})^2} = r^2_{YY'} = R^2_{Y.1,2}$$

The reason for the above identity is that Y' has the same meaning when calculated from Eq. (5-7) for one variable as when calculated with more than one X variable [see Eq. (10-4)]. Given the above identity, we interpret R^2 in the same fashion as r^2, and that is—again—as the proportion of Y variability that is explainable by information obtained from a set of two or more X variables.

MRC for Experimental Data

Given the above formulas and logic of multiple correlation and regression, how can we use MRC to analyze experimental data? The answer is simple and straight-forward: by creating a set of X "variables" that together distinguish among the different levels of the independent variable and by then using the numerical values for these variables to calculate R^2. That is, each of these X "variables" will provide information about differences between some of the treatments. In the two-level experiment, we used one X variable and designated the levels $+1$ and -1. We used only one X variable because all we needed to distinguish was one level from one other level. In a three-group experiment, we need more X "variables" to represent the three levels of the independent variable being manipulated. We create these "variables" by coding the different treatment conditions according to rules that are an extension of the rules we presented in Chap. 9.

We will call X variables that are used to represent the differences among the levels of an independent variable **vectors**, a term that is commonly used in other texts. As you will see, a vector consists of a column of N numbers in which all subjects are represented or classified in some fashion to identify the specific treatment to which they have been exposed. We emphasize this point because MRC analysts in nonexperimental research frequently use the term *independent variable* to refer to an X variable used in a regression equation to predict Y. Confusion is possible if this terminology is carried over to the analysis of experimental data, where the term *independent variable* refers specifically to a *manipulated* variable. To avoid this confusion, therefore, we will use the term *predictor variable* to refer to X variables as they are traditionally used in nonexperimental research and *vector* to refer to X variables used in the MRC analysis of experimental data.

Coding Treatment Conditions

In an experiment in which there are more than two treatment conditions, the coding rule given in Sec. 9.1 is extended as follows:

> **The number of X vectors needed to represent the effects of the independent variable is *one less* than the number of treatment conditions, or $a - 1$.**

This is a rule to be applied to all codings of experimental data. Stated another way, the number of X vectors is equal to the degrees of freedom associated with the particular independent variable, or df_A. In essence, we are going to create a set of X vectors to represent the independent variable of interest; if there are four levels of the variable, we will need $a - 1$, or three, X vectors to represent the information.

The between-groups variability in our original two-group example was represented by values of $+1$ and -1 assigned to subjects in the physical science and the social science conditions, respectively. The same between-groups variability in the present three-group example is represented by assigning a $+1$ to physical science, a -1 to social science, and a 0 to history. However, once we have determined the between groups variability for our original two groups, we need to make only one more comparison to incorporate the information provided by the history condition: we need only compare history *either* with physical science *or* with social science. In the first case, we would use the contrast code $+1$ for physical science, 0 for social science, and -1 for history; and in the second case, we would use 0, $+1$, and -1, respectively. We do not need both of these comparisons, since if both were included in an analysis, there would be *total* redundancy of information that would make calculations impossible. This problem will be elaborated upon below. While there may be more elegant or more useful ways of representing the effect of this independent variable—which we will discuss in Chap. 11—this is all there is to it! In a moment, we will see how two X vectors are used to calculate the multiple correlation coefficient.

Numerical Example.   We are now in a position to return to our numerical example and show how MRC may be used to produce the same information provided by ANOVA. Table 10-3 presents the data from the numerical example in a form appropriate for correlational analysis. You will note that the subject designations (1 to 36) are listed one after another in a single column. To the right of these numbers, we have placed a column that gives each subject's score on the dependent variable Y; and to the right of this, two columns of vector codes. The numbers in the first vector column represent a comparison between physical science and social science, while the numbers in the second vector column represent a comparison between social science and history. How did we decide on the values to use in these vectors? The answer is based on our rules for coding and establishing vectors. Specifically, we created a code matrix that represents the experiment in cellular fashion. The following is the code matrix for the present experiment:

	a_1	a_2	a_3
Vector 1			
Vector 2			

This arrangement shows that the number of vectors needed is equal to 1 less than the number of treatments for the independent variable, or $a - 1$. To determine which values are to be placed in each vector, we adhered to our coding rule (see page 112) and decided that vector 1 would provide an indication of the differences between those subjects in a_1 and those in a_2. Thus, all subjects in a_1 would receive a $+1$, all subjects in a_2 would receive a -1, and all subjects in a_3 would receive a 0. For vector 2, we decided to distinguish between a_2 and a_3; thus, all subjects in a_1 received a 0, all subjects in a_2 received a $+1$, and all subjects in a_3 received a -1. This coding resulted in the following code matrix:

	a_1	a_2	a_3
Vector 1	$+1$	-1	0
Vector 2	0	$+1$	-1

We then used the values listed in the code matrix to obtain the values found in Table 10-3.

Table 10-3
An Example of Contrast Coding

	Subject	Dependent Variable Y	X Variables (Vectors) (1)	X Variables (Vectors) (2)
a_1	1	53	1	0
	2	49	1	0
	3	47	1	0
	4	42	1	0
	5	51	1	0
	6	34	1	0
	7	44	1	0
	8	48	1	0
	9	35	1	0
	10	18	1	0
	11	32	1	0
	12	27	1	0
a_2	13	47	−1	1
	14	42	−1	1
	15	39	−1	1
	16	37	−1	1
	17	42	−1	1
	18	33	−1	1
	19	13	−1	1
	20	16	−1	1
	21	16	−1	1
	22	10	−1	1
	23	11	−1	1
	24	6	−1	1
a_3	25	45	0	−1
	26	41	0	−1
	27	38	0	−1
	28	36	0	−1
	29	35	0	−1
	30	33	0	−1
	31	46	0	−1
	32	40	0	−1
	33	29	0	−1
	34	21	0	−1
	35	30	0	−1
	36	20	0	−1

We wish to emphasize another important point about these vectors. More specifically, the numerical values for the subjects, when taken in pairs, also allow us to distinguish among the treatment groups. You can verify this point yourself by examining the numbers listed in each of the *columns in the code matrix*. The code matrix shows how the three levels of the independent variable are represented. A subject exposed to the physical science treatment (a_1) is represented by the values of $+1$ and 0 in vectors 1 and 2, respectively; a subject in the social science condition (a_2) is represented by -1 and $+1$; and finally, a subject in the history condition (a_3) is represented by 0 and -1. Thus, two vectors for each subject are sufficient to distinguish among the three conditions because each of the three treatments can be represented by a different pair of numbers (codes).

The above code matrix satisfies our rules for coding. First, the values assigned to subjects distinguish among the treatment conditions. Second, as seen in Table 10-3, all subjects in a given treatment condition receive the same set of values. Finally, our new rule, that *only a — 1* vectors are needed to represent these conditions, can be seen in the following. Suppose we created a vector to compare history with physical science. This would yield a third vector as illustrated in the following code matrix:

	a_1	a_2	a_3
Vector 1	$+1$	-1	0
Vector 2	0	$+1$	-1
Vector 3	$+1$	0	-1

Now, the subjects in the treatments would be represented by

$$+1, 0, +1; \qquad -1, +1, 0; \qquad 0, -1, -1$$

But the *same* distinction among treatment conditions is achieved with only *two* vectors, and—more important—if by using Eq. (10-1), we correlated vector 3 (where Y represents vector 3) with the *set* of remaining vectors (1 and 2), we would obtain a multiple correlation coefficient of 1.00, which means that vector 3 provides totally redundant information with respect to this set and is not needed for the omnibus analysis. Moreover, including this redundant vector will often play havoc with computer programs used in MRC analysis. Thus, we must adhere to the $a - 1$ rule and be certain that our coding within each vector is not totally redundant with or does not duplicate other vectors.

We are now ready to calculate the multiple correlation coefficient for our numerical example. From Table 10-3, we find the following relationships:

Correlation coefficient between Y and vector 1: $r_{Y1} = .4506$

Correlation coefficient between Y and vector 2: $r_{Y2} = -.2736$

Intercorrelation coefficient between the two vectors: $r_{12} = -.5000$

By squaring these values and applying Eq. (10-2), we find:

$$R_{Y.1,2}^2 = \frac{(.4506)^2 + (-.2736)^2 - (2)(.4506)(-.2736)(-.5000)}{1 - (-.5000)^2}$$

$$= \frac{.2030 + .0749 - .1233}{1 - .2500} = \frac{.1546}{.7500}$$

$$= .2061$$

and

$$R_{Y.1,2} = \sqrt{.2061} = .4540$$

The value of $R_{Y.1,2}^2$ indicates that approximately 21 percent of the Y variability is due to variation in the independent variable represented by the two vectors.

Analysis of Larger Experiments. We have focused on the analysis of a three-group experiment because by doing so we are able to show how multiple correlation "works" without resorting to more complicated arguments and higher mathematics. The analysis of larger single-factor designs follows the same general procedure of defining $a - 1$ vectors, although the calculations will generally have to be conducted by a computer. It is possible to calculate the overall R^2 by hand, but this is easy only if all the intercorrelation coefficients between pairs of vectors—r_{12}, r_{13}, r_{14}, etc.—are equal to *zero*. If the intercorrelation coefficients are zero, the squared multiple correlation coefficient may be calculated simply by summing the squared zero-order correlation coefficients between Y and all the vectors. In symbols,

$$R_{Y.1,2,\ldots,k}^2 = r_{Y1}^2 + r_{Y2}^2 + \cdots + r_{Yk}^2 \tag{10-7}$$

This is simply an extension of Eq. (10-3). However, when at least one pair of vectors are nonorthogonal or partially correlated with each other, then

$$R_{Y.1,2,\ldots,k}^2 \neq r_{Y1}^2 + r_{Y2}^2 + \cdots + r_{Yk}^2$$

Testing the Significance of Multiple Correlation

The test for significance of R^2 is similar to the tests presented in Chap. 8 for the Pearson coefficient (see pages 101–102). The formula we will present is for an independent variable consisting of any number of groups or conditions (a). The R^2 reflecting the overall effects of factor A will be designated $R^2_{Y.max.}$. The "max." in the subscript indicates that the maximum number of vectors required to represent the overall treatment effects—$k = a - 1$ (or df_A)—are included in the analysis. Under these circumstances,

$$F = \frac{R^2_{Y.max.}/k}{(1 - R^2_{Y.max.})/(N - k - 1)} \tag{10-8}$$

where $R^2_{Y.max.}$ = the squared multiple correlation coefficient between Y and a "maximum" set of vectors needed to represent the effects of the independent variable fully (df_A)

k = this maximum number of vectors

N = the total number of subjects in the experiment or study

This formula is an extension of Eq. (7-1). The numerator of Eq. (10-8), $R^2_{Y.max.}/k$, is analogous to the regression mean square $MS_{reg.}$—that is, the numerator is the proportion of Y variability explained by the vectors, divided by the number of vectors (k), which in this case is equal to the degrees of freedom for the variable, $df_A = a - 1$. Similarly, the denominator of Eq. (10-8) is analogous to the denominator of Eq. (7-1), since $(1 - R^2_{Y.max.})$—the proportion of Y variability *not* explained by the vectors—is divided by a quantity that equals $df_{res.}$: $df_{S/A} = (a)(s - 1)$. That is,

$$df_{res.} = N - k - 1$$
$$= (a)(s) - (a - 1) - 1$$
$$= (a)(s) - a + 1 - 1$$
$$= (a)(s) - a = (a)(s - 1)$$
$$= df_{S/A}$$

Under the null hypothesis that the population multiple correlation coefficient is zero, the F statistic is distributed as F with $df_{num.} = k$ and $df_{denom.} = N - k - 1$. To illustrate with our example,

$$F = \frac{.2061/2}{(1 - .2061)/(36 - 2 - 1)}$$
$$= \frac{.1031}{.7939/33} = \frac{.1031}{.0241} = 4.28$$

which is significant at $p < .05$. We can conclude, then, that there is an association between group membership, as represented by the two vectors, and the dependent variable. This, of course, is the correlational analysis way of saying that treatment differences are present. You will recall that the same conclusion was reached by the ANOVA we conducted in Sec. 10.1. In fact, the value of F and the numerator and denominator degrees of freedom are exactly the same as those reported here (see Table 10-2).

Comment. We have now shown that the equivalency of MRC and ANOVA extends to the analysis of any single-factor experiment. In spite of the vast differences in data arrangements, required formulas, and actual calculations, we reach exactly the same statistical conclusions whether the data of a single-factor experiment are analyzed by ANOVA or by MRC.

For the sake of completeness, we will demonstrate that applying other coding systems to the data in Table 10-3 will yield the same R^2 we obtained with the contrast coding found in our code matrix on page 130. To illustrate, suppose we used dummy coding in our code matrix. Dummy coding assigns a 1 to one of the conditions in a vector and a 0 to all others, with a different condition being assigned the 1 in each of the vectors. Since there are $a - 1$ vectors, one of the conditions—usually the last one in the data matrix—will be assigned 0 in all vectors. In the present example, the code matrix would be as follows:

	a_1	a_2	a_3
Vector 1	1	0	0
Vector 2	0	1	0

In this matrix, for a given subject, the three treatments are designated by the three sets of values 1, 0 for physical science; 0, 1 for social science; and 0, 0 for history.

This example also allows us to illustrate effect coding, which was impossible in Chap. 9 because effect coding and contrast coding are identical in experiments with only two treatment conditions. Effect coding is essentially a variation of dummy coding in which the condition assigned a 0 in *all* vectors—usually the last condition—is assigned a -1 instead. Thus, the code matrix for effect coding for our example would be as follows:

	a_1	a_2	a_3
Vector 1	$+1$	0	-1
Vector 2	0	$+1$	-1

In this case, the subjects in each of the three treatment conditions are designated by three different sets of values, namely, $+1, 0$ for physical science; $0, +1$ for social science; and $-1, -1$ for history.

The results for $R^2_{Y.max.}$ will be identical regardless of which of the three code matrices is used. What will change is the regression equation and the information provided by the regression constants (see Chap. 9, pages 113–116 for a description of these differences).

Calculating the Treatment Means

At some stage in the MRC analysis, we will want to calculate the treatment means. With ANOVA, the means are calculated from the treatment subtotals used to calculate sums of squares and are produced by most computer programs. With MRC, the means are not provided directly, but must be calculated from information found in the multiple regression equation; computation is built into most computer programs. We will show how this is accomplished with two different regression equations—the first, one obtained from the analysis we have just completed; and the second, from an analysis based on dummy coding.

Using Contrast Coding.   You will recall that the regression equation with two X vectors is

$$Y' = a + b_1 X_1 + b_2 X_2$$

A computer analysis based on the data matrix in Table 10-3 produced the following regression equation:

$$Y' = 33.50 + (6.50)(X_1) + (-1.00)(X_2)$$

All we need to do now is to substitute the appropriate values of X_1 and X_2 for each of the treatment conditions and calculate the corresponding treatment mean. Consider again the code matrix for this analysis:

	a_1	a_2	a_3
Vector 1	$+1$	-1	0
Vector 2	0	$+1$	-1

This matrix conveniently specifies the pairs of values associated with the treatment conditions $(+1, 0; -1, +1;$ and $0, -1)$ that are to be substituted in the multiple regression equation for levels a_1, a_2, and a_3, respectively. To illustrate, the three

$\bar{Y}_A$ treatment means are calculated as follows:

$$\bar{Y}_{A1} = 33.50 + (6.50)(+1) + (-1.00)(0)$$
$$= 33.50 + 6.50 + 0.00 = 40.00$$

$$\bar{Y}_{A2} = 33.50 + (6.50)(-1) + (-1.00)(+1)$$
$$= 33.50 - 6.50 - 1.00 = 26.00$$

$$\bar{Y}_{A3} = 33.50 + (6.50)(0) + (-1.00)(-1)$$
$$= 33.50 + 0.00 + 1.00 = 34.50$$

Thus, the three treatment means are 40.00, 26.00, and 34.50.

Using Dummy Coding.   We will now calculate the treatment means using the regression equation obtained with dummy coding. Without showing the calculations, the regression equation produced by dummy coding is

$$Y' = 34.50 + (5.50)(X_1) - (8.50)(X_2)$$

With this information and the values from the code matrix, we find

$$\bar{Y}_{A_1} = 34.50 + (5.50)(1) - (8.50)(0)$$
$$= 34.50 + 5.50 = 40.00$$

$$\bar{Y}_{A_2} = 34.50 + (5.50)(0) - (8.50)(1)$$
$$= 34.50 - 8.50 = 26.00$$

$$\bar{Y}_{A_3} = 34.50 + (5.50)(0) - (8.50)(0)$$
$$= 34.50$$

The means obtained above are identical to the ones obtained with contrast coding.

Recall what the a value represents in each equation. In Chap. 9, we indicated that the a value in contrast coding represents $\bar{Y}_T$, whereas in dummy coding the a value represents the $\bar{Y}$ of the treatment condition assigned all 0s. The two a values, 33.50 and 34.50, for the contrast-coded and dummy-coded equations, bear out these assertions. That is, the grand mean is $\bar{Y}_T = (40.00 + 26.00 + 34.50)/3 = 33.50$, and the mean for the history condition is $\bar{Y}_{A_3} = 34.50$.

10.3   MEASURES OF TREATMENT MAGNITUDE

The basic statistic we have emphasized in our application of MRC to experimental data has been the squared correlation coefficient r^2 or R^2, which provides a measure of the strength of association between Y and X (or a set of X variables). As developed in Chap. 5, r^2 is simply the ratio of a regression sum of squares $SS_{reg.}$, reflecting the differential effects of the treatment conditions, to the sum of squares representing total variation in Y (SS_Y). We have emphasized this statistic because we consider it a meaningful one in that it provides an index of the magnitude of the treatment effects.

This index is useful in comparing related experiments, assuming one also takes into account the context and specifics of the studies involved. That is, in experiments, the experimenter has control over the explicit definition of the independent variable and thus, in many regards, has considerable control over the size of the strength index through his or her choice of X. On the other hand, a strength index often provides insights into the phenomenon studied and can be useful in applied situations when decisions regarding implementation need to be made. In sum, though there are limitations, we nevertheless recommend that a measure of association be determined and interpreted for all experiments. If we analyze experimental data by MRC, we have a direct estimate of the strength of association (r^2 or R^2). If we use ANOVA to analyze these data, then we have several options, to be considered below.

We previously indicated that experimentalists have focused on the F test and whether or not $F_{observed}$ is significant. However, we also pointed out that the F ratio is influenced by the size of the treatment effects *as well as* the sample sizes. Thus, a large F may imply that treatment effects are large, or that sample size is large, or that both factors are contributing to the observed value of F. We will now consider several measures of treatment magnitude.[1]

The Correlation Ratio

In Sec. 7.1 we indicated that the sums of squares normally extracted in ANOVA, namely, SS_A, $SS_{S/A}$, and SS_T, have direct counterparts in MRC. More specifically, when the two procedures are used to analyze the same set of experimental data, we showed that:

$$SS_A = SS_{reg.} \qquad SS_{S/A} = SS_{res.} \qquad SS_T = SS_Y$$

You will recall that we defined $R^2_{Y.max.}$ as the R^2 reflecting the overall effects of factor A. That is, $R^2_{Y.max.}$ consists of the proportion of total Y variability that is associated with the independent variable X, which, in turn, is represented by a set of $a - 1$ vectors. Since $R^2_{Y.max.} = SS_{reg.}/SS_Y$, we can express this quantity in terms of sums of squares from ANOVA:

---

[1] See Keppel (1982, pp. 93–95) for a discussion of certain limitations of measures of treatment magnitude obtained in the context of experiments.

$$R^2_{Y.max.} = \frac{SS_{reg.}}{SS_Y} = \frac{SS_A}{SS_T} \tag{10-9}$$

Thus, $R^2_{Y.max.}$, which can be calculated directly from an ANOVA summary table, represents the proportion of the total sum of squares SS_T contained in the sum of squares for the treatment conditions (SS_A). To illustrate with the numerical example, the ratio SS_A/SS_T as found in Table 10-2, $1194.00/5793.00 = .2061$, is identical to the value obtained for $R^2_{Y.1,2}$ (that is, $R^2_{Y.max.}$) from the MRC analysis we presented on page 133.

In Sec. 5.2, we introduced an equivalent statistic, the correlation ratio η^2,

$$\eta^2 = \frac{\sigma^2_{Y'}}{\sigma^2_Y}$$

which is the proportion of the total Y variability that is known or predictable from a knowledge of X. We will not go through the derivation, but it can be shown that the correlation ratio (eta squared) is conceptually equivalent to components typically calculated in the analysis of variance. That is,

$$\eta^2 = R^2_{Y.max.} = \frac{SS_A}{SS_T}$$

The point is that $R^2_{Y.X_k}$ provides a strength measure that is applicable to situations in which the designs are either correlational or experimental in nature.

Other Measures

Though measures of treatment magnitude have tended to be ignored by experimentalists, several measures, in addition to r^2 and R^2, are available that are useful to the researcher for interpretive purposes. Perhaps the most popular one is **omega squared** (ω^2). This statistic can also be calculated by using the information already available in a summary table of an ANOVA. The computational formula used to give the estimated omega squared ($\hat{\omega}^2$) is:

$$\hat{\omega}^2_A = \frac{SS_A - (a - 1)(MS_{S/A})}{SS_T + MS_{S/A}} \tag{10-10}$$

From the ANOVA summarized in Table 10-2,

$$\hat{\omega}^2_A = \frac{1194.00 - (3 - 1)(139.36)}{5793.00 + 139.36}$$

$$= \frac{1194.00 - 278.72}{5932.36} = .1543$$

This value is interpreted to mean that approximately 15 percent of the total variability observed in the experiment is accounted for by the variations in treatments. Note that this value is less than the R^2 value of .2061 we calculated previously; such differences between omega squared and R^2 are likely to occur when sample sizes are relatively small.

Maxwell, Camp, and Arvey (1981) provide a clear and useful comparison of R^2 and $\hat{\omega}_A^2$, as well as a third index of strength of association, **estimated epilson squared** ($\hat{\epsilon}_A^2$). This third index, commonly called the *adjusted R^2* by many MRC computer programs, is preferable to R^2 (η^2) as an *inferential* statistic. Estimated epsilon squared is defined as follows:

$$\hat{\epsilon}_A^2 = 1 - \frac{(1 - R_{Y.max.}^2)(N - 1)}{N - k - 1} \tag{10-11}$$

As applied to the present example,

$$\hat{\epsilon}_A^2 = 1 - \frac{(1 - .2061)(36 - 1)}{36 - 2 - 1}$$

$$= 1 - \frac{(.7939)(35)}{33} = 1 - .8420$$

$$= .1580$$

You will notice that $\hat{\epsilon}_A^2$ is closer to $\hat{\omega}_A^2$ (.1543) than to R^2 (.2061). In general, R^2 tends to give the largest value, estimated epilson squared the next largest, and estimated omega squared the smallest, with $\hat{\epsilon}_A^2$ much closer to $\hat{\omega}_A^2$ than to R^2. The differences among these three indices tend to decrease as sample size increases.

In sum, we recommend that *some* statistic be used to provide a measure of association for experimental studies. Experimentalists prefer $\hat{\omega}_A^2$ because the index has been adapted to a wide variety of experimental designs and the formulas specify quantities that are readily available from a standard analysis of variance.[2] Moreover, as Dooling and Danks (1975) have shown, $\hat{\omega}_A^2$ is essentially *uninfluenced* by sample size, which means that the index provides a useful supplement to any conclusions drawn from the omnibus F test. For data from nonexperimental designs, we should report either R^2 or $\hat{\epsilon}_A^2$. The important point, however, is that measures of association—$\hat{\omega}_A^2$, $\hat{\epsilon}_A^2$, and R^2—provide useful information about the degree to which an independent variable influences behavior and also an important

---

[2] Because of certain problems and limitations, however, all measures of treatment magnitude should be interpreted with a certain degree of caution. We recommend that students read other discussions of these measures to acquire a better feel for their intent and limitations; see in particular, Maxwell et al. (1981), Dwyer (1974), Vaughan and Corballis (1969), and Keppel (1982, pp. 89–96).

link between the analyses applied to experimental data and those applied to non-experimental data.

10.4   SUMMARY

In this chapter, we demonstrated how the principles of ANOVA that we introduced in earlier chapters can be expanded to apply to a design with any number of treatment conditions. The overall analysis of the single-factor design permits a statistical evaluation of the omnibus null hypothesis, which states that all the population treatment means are equal (ANOVA) or that the population multiple correlation coefficient is zero (MRC). The two versions of the null hypothesis are equivalent. We demonstrated that the F ratios and the conclusions obtained were identical under the two procedures.

Table 10-4 summarizes the points at which ANOVA and MRC are conceptually related. In the first two rows, we show that the treatment effects (between-groups variation) and unsystematic variability (within-group variation) are represented by a mean square in ANOVA and by an average proportion in MRC. In the last row, the two approaches converge to produce the same F ratio.

In the remainder of the chapter, we dealt with measures of treatment magnitude. We argued that measures of treatment magnitude supplement any conclusions drawn from the omnibus F test. One such measure is the squared multiple correlation coefficient (R^2); MRC provides it directly, while in ANOVA, R^2 is calculated from the sums of squares. Other measures of treatment magnitude, such as estimated omega squared and estimated epsilon squared, are viewed as better

Table 10-4

Comparison of ANOVA and MRC

	ANOVA	MRC
Between-groups variation (A)	$\dfrac{SS_A}{a-1}$	$\dfrac{R^2_{Y.max.}}{k}$
Within-groups variation (S/A)	$\dfrac{SS_{S/A}}{(a)(s-1)}$	$\dfrac{1-R^2_{Y.max.}}{N-k-1}$
F ratio	$\dfrac{MS_A}{MS_{S/A}}$	$\dfrac{R^2_{Y.max.}/k}{(1-R^2_{Y.max.})/(N-k-1)}$

indices of the variability explained by treatment manipulations than R^2, which tends to be influenced by sample size (but less so than is the F ratio). Our main point, however, is to encourage you to use measures of treatment magnitude as an aid in interpreting the outcome of an experiment.

10.5 EXERCISES

1. A student was interested in determining the effects of two kinds of verbal reinforcement on children's performance on a simple motor-coordination task. Children were assigned randomly to one of three treatment conditions in which subjects received either praise for correct responses, reproof for mistakes, or no verbal comment at all. The response measure was the number of errors made during the course of testing. The following data were obtained:

Praise	Reproof	None
4	7	7
7	6	3
5	9	7
3	7	5
6	8	7
4	6	8
6	7	5

a. Calculate the mean and standard deviation for each of the groups.
b. Analyze the data with ANOVA and determine whether the independent variable has had an effect. (Save your calculations for the problems at the end of Chaps. 11 and 12.)
c. To complete the analysis, use estimated omega squared ($\hat{\omega}^2$) to estimate the magnitude of the treatment effects.
d. For a comparison with the MRC analysis in Problem 2, calculate $R^2_{Y.max.}$ from the results obtained with ANOVA.

2. With the data provided in Problem 1:

a. Analyze the data with MRC and determine whether the independent variable has had an effect. Use as the two X vectors a comparison between "praise" and "none" $(+1, 0, -1)$ and a comparison between "reproof" and "none" $(0, +1, -1)$. (Save your calculations for the problems at the end of Chaps. 11 and 12.)

b. If you are using a computer, verify that the multiple regression equation is

$$Y' = 6.0476 - (1.0476)(X_1) + (1.0952)(X_2)$$

c. Use the multiple regression equation given in part b to calculate the group means.

d. Redo the overall MRC analysis using effect coding for the data.

3. Use dummy coding to represent the independent variable for the data presented in Table 10-1. Perform an MRC analysis on the data matrix, including a test of the significance of $R^2_{Y.max.}$. Verify that the final outcome is identical to that obtained with contrast coding (Table 10-3) and reported in the text.

11

Detailed Analysis of the Single-Factor Design

. . .

You have seen how the analysis of a single-factor experiment by either ANOVA or MRC is easily extended to any number of treatment conditions. Up to this point, we have considered only one statistical test—the evaluation of the omnibus null hypothesis (indicated by the F ratio for MS_A or for $R^2_{Y.max.}$)—which in most cases is *not* of primary interest to the researcher. This is because the rejection of this null hypothesis simply tells us that it is reasonable to conclude that there is a relationship (MRC) or that differences between treatment conditions are present (ANOVA), but the rejection does not tell us *which* treatments are different. As a consequence, researchers usually plan an experiment around a limited number of focused comparisons that *will* indicate exactly which aspects of the independent variable are producing significant differences and which are not.

The nature of the analyses we might consider for any experiment generally depends on the *research hypotheses* that guided us in the selection of the treatment conditions to be included in the study. Quite naturally, the statistical analysis consists of comparisons created by grouping different subsets of treatment means that in turn provide answers to these questions. If our independent variable consists of *qualitative* manipulations, the analysis will usually take the form of comparisons between pairs of means. On the other hand, if it consists of a *quantitative* manipulation, the analysis will probably focus on an attempt to identify the underlying *trend* or *shape* of the relationship between the independent and dependent variables. This chapter deals with the analysis of qualitative independent variables, which are frequently called **categorical** or **nominal independent variables**. In Chap. 23 we examine the analysis of trend.

11.1   PLANNED COMPARISONS

Planned comparisons are analyses that are planned *before* the start of the experiment. They are frequently obtained by translating research hypotheses into comparisons between means from selected treatments. Usually, these comparisons are tested directly *without* any preliminary assessment of the omnibus F test. As you will see, planned comparisons offer an analytically powerful approach to the analysis of an experiment.

Types of Planned Comparisons

In an experiment with more than two treatment conditions, the most common planned comparison consists simply of the difference between two means. Typically, this difference will be based on a comparison of the mean of one treatment group with the mean of another treatment group. Such a comparison is often called a *pairwise comparison* because it is based on a difference between a pair of treatment means. Less commonly, researchers use *complex* comparisons in which one or even both of the two means being compared are themselves averages of two or more treatment means. We will consider examples of both types of comparisons—pairwise and complex—in a moment.

Either type of comparison is often called a **single-*df* comparison**, in reference to the single degree of freedom associated with a difference between two means. Viewed another way, a single-*df* comparison is equivalent to the treatment source of variation (factor *A*) obtained from an experiment containing $a = 2$ treatment groups, in which the *df* for the treatment source is 1.

As an illustration of planned comparisons, let us return to our continuing example in which vocabulary words were introduced through lectures dealing with physical science, social science, or history. Consider the information provided by this particular experiment. There are three differences between pairs of means—pairwise comparisons—that we might examine, namely, physical science versus social science, physical science versus history, and social science versus history. The original two-group experiment, which we considered first in Chap. 6, yielded only the first difference.

In addition, we might examine at least one complex comparison, the difference between an average of the two science lectures and the history lecture. Two other complex comparisons that are possible with this design, an average of physical science and history versus social science and an average of social science and history versus physical science, do not provide as sharp a comparison as the first and probably would not be of interest to a researcher. In general, the quality of a complex comparison depends on the *logical* basis for averaging treatment conditions. In the first case, taking the average of the physical and social sciences and comparing it with the history condition is based on commonalities between the two sciences not shared with history; in the other two cases, the basis for the comparison is less obvious.

One other type of comparison is common in the behavioral sciences. This occurs when there is a subset of logically similar treatment conditions included as part of a larger study. Suppose we included a fourth condition—a lesson on biological science—in our growing vocabulary experiment. In addition to a variety of new meaningful single-*df* comparisons afforded by this expanded design, it is also possible to consider the differences between means within the subset of *science conditions* (physical, social, and biological sciences). The degrees of freedom for this subset are 1 less than the number of means being examined; that is, $df_{A_{set}} = 3 - 1 = 2$. Common examples of this type of analysis are also found in experiments containing a control group and several experimental groups. In these cases, researchers typically assess the differences within the set of experimental groups, as well as a number of interesting single-*df* comparisons.[1]

The Omnibus *F* Test

The *F* test we considered in Secs. 10.1 and 10.2—the omnibus *F* test—was a single statistical test assessing either significance of the differences among *all* the treatment means or the overall association between type of lecture and vocabulary words learned. This test does not tell us, however, which of these differences are significant and which are not. The omnibus *F* test evaluates what in effect is an *average* of all possible pairwise comparisons.

When we plan specific comparisons, we are not generally interested in the outcome of the omnibus test. Indeed, there is no logical need to conduct the test at all! With planned comparisons, our interest is in certain comparisons and *not* in an average of all pairwise differences. On the other hand, without specific comparisons (or research hypotheses) to guide the analysis—and specific comparisons may be lacking in certain exploratory work—we would probably conduct the omnibus test *first* and let the outcome of the test determine whether we examine the data in more detail.

Such a situation might occur, for example, if we were comparing a number of alternative procedures or products with the goal of identifying the best (or the worst) from the entire set. Under these circumstances, then, the omnibus test tells us whether it is reasonable to conclude that the population treatment means are not all the same. If there is insufficient evidence to reject the omnibus null hypothesis, we conclude that the differences among the treatment means are most likely the result of chance factors that are present in any experiment. On the other hand, if we reject the null hypothesis, we conclude that the means are not all the same and follow the omnibus test with a systematic examination of the data in order to locate the specific differences between the treatment means that are responsible for the significant omnibus *F*. Again, we must stress that rejecting the overall null hypothesis does not identify which means are the same and which are different. Additional analyses are necessary to obtain that important information.

Most experiments in the behavioral sciences are designed to test specific hypotheses, however, and, in our opinion, should be evaluated directly, without reference to the omnibus test. We emphasize this point because one frequently encounters experiments in the research literature that report the result of the omnibus test first, followed by what are in effect *planned comparisons*. We suspect

---

[1] See Keppel (1982, pp. 123–124) for a more detailed discussion of this type of analysis.

that in most cases the inclusion of the omnibus test is a habit the experimenter acquired when this two-step procedure was in common use.

Post Hoc Comparisons

Post hoc comparisons refer to comparisons conducted *after* the data have been assessed by an omnibus *F*. Post hoc comparisons are *unplanned* in the sense that they are suggested by the outcome of the experiment and are not specifically anticipated during the planning stage of the research project. In most cases, they consist of comparisons following up the results of the major analyses. Such comparisons should possess the same qualities associated with planned comparisons: they should be analytical, and they should make sense.

Post hoc comparisons are sometimes called **multiple comparisons**, a somewhat derogatory term that generally refers to the indiscriminate examination of *all possible comparisons*—usually pairwise differences—in an attempt to locate significant effects. There are special procedures available for dealing with multiple comparisons. We believe, however, that most researchers should restrain themselves and focus their attention only on those comparisons that are meaningful and relevant to the original questions guiding the investigation. We will elaborate this point in the next chapter.

11.2   SINGLE-*df* COMPARISONS: THE ANOVA APPROACH

Planned comparisons permit researchers to ask highly focused questions of a set of data. Generally, such questions are expressed as differences between two means, and take the form of single-*df* comparisons. The two means can be means from specific treatment conditions or means formed by combining treatment conditions. We will start by demonstrating how to calculate a "weighted" difference between means and then show how easily the statistical test can be performed.

Single-*df* comparisons are conducted in two steps: first, calculating the difference between the two means of interest; and, second, evaluating the significance of the difference. While you should have no difficulty in calculating the difference, you probably have no clear idea how to translate this difference into a form that then can be used to form an *F* ratio. To facilitate this latter calculation, we will introduce a procedure which at first will appear to obscure the process of calculating the desired difference, but which will simplify the calculation of the quantities needed for the statistical test.

Expressing a Difference as a Sum of Weighted Means

It is useful to express a single-*df* comparison as the *sum* of all the means taken after each has been multiplied by a special weight (or **coefficient**, as it is called). Consider the following expression:

$$\hat{\psi} = (c_1)(\bar{Y}_{A_1}) + (c_2)(\bar{Y}_{A_2}) + (c_3)(\bar{Y}_{A_3}) + \cdots \qquad (11\text{-}1)$$

where $\hat{\psi}$ (Greek psi) = the difference obtained from a given comparison

$\quad\quad c_1, c_2, c_3$ = the coefficients (or weights) assigned to the treatment
$\quad\quad\quad\quad\quad$ means in the experiment

$\quad \bar{Y}_{A_1}, \bar{Y}_{A_2}, \bar{Y}_{A_3}$ = the corresponding treatment means

A compact way of expressing Eq. (11-1) is as follows:

$$\hat{\psi} = \Sigma \, (c_i)(\bar{Y}_{A_i}) \qquad (11\text{-}2)$$

The critical ingredient in these two formulas is the coefficients, which we create to represent a particular comparison.

Let us see how this procedure works. Suppose we wanted to compare the means of the two science conditions. We accomplish this without using coefficients simply by subtracting one mean from the other, that is, taking $\bar{Y}_{A_1} - \bar{Y}_{A_2}$ (or $\bar{Y}_{A_2} - \bar{Y}_{A_1}$; the two differences have the same value except for the sign). We may express this difference using Eq. (11-1), by assigning the coefficient $c_1 = +1$ to physical science, $c_2 = -1$ to social science, and $c_3 = 0$ to history. Entering these coefficients in Eq. (11-1), we find

$$\begin{aligned} \hat{\psi} &= (+1)(\bar{Y}_{A_1}) + (-1)(\bar{Y}_{A_2}) + (0)(\bar{Y}_{A_3}) \\ &= \bar{Y}_{A_1} - \bar{Y}_{A_2} + 0 \\ &= \bar{Y}_{A_1} - \bar{Y}_{A_2} \end{aligned}$$

As you will soon see, the advantage of expressing this difference between the two science conditions as a sum of weighted means is that this difference ($\hat{\psi}$) and the three coefficients ($+1, -1, 0$) provide all the information we need to translate the difference into a sum of squares and then into a mean square and an F ratio.

For comparisons between pairs of treatment means, the coefficients are simple to express:

$\quad +1$ and -1 for the two means being compared
$\quad 0$ for all other treatment means in the experiment

For more complex comparisons, which involve means based on combinations of treatment conditions, the coefficients must be created individually for each comparison, a process we will consider next.

In general, the coefficients may be derived from a specification of the actual difference under consideration. To illustrate, suppose we performed an experiment with $a = 6$ treatment conditions and wanted to compare the average of the means for groups 1 and 2 with the average of the means for groups 3, 4, and 5. This comparison, expressed as a difference between two means, becomes

$$\hat{\psi} = \frac{\bar{Y}_{A_1} + \bar{Y}_{A_2}}{2} - \frac{\bar{Y}_{A_3} + \bar{Y}_{A_4} + \bar{Y}_{A_5}}{3}$$

Rewriting this expression slightly, we have

$$\hat{\psi} = (+\tfrac{1}{2})(\bar{Y}_{A_1} + \bar{Y}_{A_2}) + (-\tfrac{1}{3})(\bar{Y}_{A_3} + \bar{Y}_{A_4} + \bar{Y}_{A_5})$$
$$= (+\tfrac{1}{2})(\bar{Y}_{A_1}) + (+\tfrac{1}{2})(\bar{Y}_{A_2}) + (-\tfrac{1}{3})(\bar{Y}_{A_3}) + (-\tfrac{1}{3})(\bar{Y}_{A_4}) + (-\tfrac{1}{3})(\bar{Y}_{A_5})$$

From the original expression of the difference between two means, we easily determine that the coefficient is $+\tfrac{1}{2}$ for the two groups contributing to the first average (groups 1 and 2), $-\tfrac{1}{3}$ for the three groups contributing to the second average (groups 3, 4, and 5), and 0 for the one group not entering into the comparison (group 6). Thus, the set of coefficients—

$$+\tfrac{1}{2}, \quad +\tfrac{1}{2}, \quad -\tfrac{1}{3}, \quad -\tfrac{1}{3}, \quad -\tfrac{1}{3}, \quad \text{and} \quad 0$$

—which will be used in subsequent calculations, can be obtained directly from the original mathematical expression representing a specific difference between two sets of means.

To illustrate further, suppose we had the following treatment means: 15, 20, and 30. If we wanted to examine a pairwise comparison between condition 1 and condition 3, the difference would be $\bar{Y}_{A_1} - \bar{Y}_{A_3} = 15 - 30 = -15$. A set of coefficients representing this difference is $+1, 0,$ and -1, which when substituted in Eq. (11-1) produces

$$\hat{\psi} = (+1)(\bar{Y}_{A_1}) + (0)(\bar{Y}_{A_2}) + (-1)(\bar{Y}_{A_3})$$
$$= (+1)(15) + (0)(20) + (-1)(30)$$
$$= 15 - 30 = -15$$

or the same value we obtained by subtracting the third mean ($\bar{Y}_{A_3}$) from the first mean ($\bar{Y}_{A_1}$). As another example, suppose we wanted to contrast condition 1 with the average of conditions 2 and 3. In this case,

$$\hat{\psi} = \bar{Y}_{A_1} - \frac{\bar{Y}_{A_2} + \bar{Y}_{A_3}}{2}$$
$$= 15 - \frac{20 + 30}{2} = 15 - 25 = -10$$

A set of coefficients representing this difference is $+1$, $-\frac{1}{2}$, and $-\frac{1}{2}$. These coefficients are easier to see if we represent the difference as

$$\hat{\psi} = \frac{\bar{Y}_{A_1}}{1} - \frac{\bar{Y}_{A_2} + \bar{Y}_{A_3}}{2}$$

where the coefficient for $\bar{Y}_{A_1}$ is $\frac{1}{1} = +1$ and the coefficients for $\bar{Y}_{A_2}$ and $\bar{Y}_{A_3}$ are both $-\frac{1}{2}$. Substituting in Eq. (11-1), we find

$$\hat{\psi} = (+1)(15) + (-\tfrac{1}{2})(20) + (-\tfrac{1}{2})(30)$$
$$= 15 - 10 - 15 = -10$$

For any single-*df* comparison, then, each treatment mean has a coefficient chosen to reflect the difference under consideration. For all means entering into the comparison, each coefficient has a numerical value and a sign; for means not entering into the comparison, the coefficient is 0. *An important property of a set of coefficients is that they sum to zero.* That is,

$$\Sigma c_i = 0 \qquad\qquad (11\text{-}3)$$

In the example with the six conditions,

$$\Sigma c_i = (+\tfrac{1}{2}) + (+\tfrac{1}{2}) + (-\tfrac{1}{3}) + (-\tfrac{1}{3}) + (-\tfrac{1}{3}) + (0)$$
$$= (+1) + (-1) = 0$$

Coefficients generated by the method we have just outlined represent what may be called a **standard set** of coefficients. As a matter of fact, equivalent sets can be derived from the standard set simply by multiplying all coefficients in the set by a constant; coefficients obtained this way will produce exactly the same numerical outcome for the statistical test. Researchers often take advantage of this property to transform fractional coefficients into more convenient whole numbers; this is done by multiplying the standard set of coefficients by the lowest common denominator of the set—that is, the smallest value that can be divided by *both* values in the denominator of the coefficients. For example, if we multiplied the coefficients for the complex comparison we derived previously by 6, which is the smallest number divisible by both 2 and 3, we would produce the set $(+3, +3, -2, -2, -2,$ and $0)$. One advantage of standard sets, however, is that the value of the comparison itself $(\hat{\psi})$ is always expressed as a difference between two means, which is useful when a researcher wishes to construct confidence intervals based on single-*df* comparisons (see Myers, 1979, pp. 305–306). Coefficients obtained by multiplying the standard set by a constant cannot be conveniently used for this purpose, because the value of $\hat{\psi}$ will also reflect the multiplication.

Sums of Squares

Computational Formula. A single-*df* comparison can be easily translated into a sum of squares. We start with the observed difference between the two means ($\hat{\psi}$). By combining this difference with two other familiar quantities, namely, the coefficients c_i and the sample size s, we can now calculate the sum of squares corresponding to any single-*df* comparison as follows:

$$SS_{comp.} = \frac{(s)\,(\hat{\psi})^2}{\Sigma\,(c_i)^2} \tag{11-4}$$

Numerical Examples. As a simple illustration of Eq. (11-4), consider the numerical example from Chap. 6 in which only the two science lessons were compared. (We will present a more complex illustration in a moment.) From Table 6-1, we find that the mean for the physical science condition is $\bar{Y}_{A_1} = 40.00$ and the mean for the social science condition is $\bar{Y}_{A_2} = 26.00$; there are $s = 12$ children in each group. The coefficients representing the difference between these two means are $+1$ and -1, respectively. From Eq. (11-1), we find

$$\hat{\psi} = (c_1)\,(\bar{Y}_{A_1}) + (c_2)\,(\bar{Y}_{A_2})$$
$$= (+1)\,(40.00) + (-1)\,(26.00) = 40.00 - 26.00 = 14.00$$

Substituting in Eq. (11-4), we calculate

$$SS_{comp.} = \frac{(s)\,(\hat{\psi})^2}{\Sigma\,(c_i)^2}$$
$$= \frac{(12)\,(14.00)^2}{(+1)^2 + (-1)^2}$$
$$= \frac{(12)\,(196)}{1+1} = \frac{2352.00}{2} = 1176.00$$

You will note that this sum of squares is identical to the SS_A we obtained in Chap. 6 (see Table 6-3). In fact, this is why we chose this example, namely, to demonstrate that Eq. (11-4) and the general formula for calculating the between-groups sum of squares are equivalent when both are applied to an experiment with $a = 2$ treatment conditions.

For a slightly more complex illustration of the use of Eq. (11-4), consider the data presented in Table 10-1, in which the example from Chap. 6 was expanded to include a history lecture as a third condition. Suppose we were interested in conducting all three comparisons between pairs of means. As you know, the coefficients for these pairwise comparisons are $+1$ and -1 for the two critical means and 0 for all others (since they do not enter into the comparison). The three differences are:

Physical science versus social science

$$\hat{\psi}_1 = (+1)(40.00) + (-1)(26.00) + (0)(34.50)$$
$$= 40.00 - 26.00 = 14.00$$

Physical science versus history

$$\hat{\psi}_2 = (+1)(40.00) + (0)(26.00) + (-1)(34.50)$$
$$= 40.00 - 34.50 = 5.50$$

Social science versus history

$$\hat{\psi}_3 = (0)(40.00) + (+1)(26.00) + (-1)(34.50)$$
$$= 26.00 - 34.50 = -8.50$$

We can now substitute the necessary values in Eq. (11-4) to find the sums of squares associated with these differences; that is,

$$SS_{comp.\ 1} = \frac{(12)(14.00)^2}{(+1)^2 + (-1)^2 + (0)^2} = \frac{2352.00}{2} = 1176.00$$

$$SS_{comp.\ 2} = \frac{(12)(5.50)^2}{(+1)^2 + (0)^2 + (-1)^2} = \frac{363.00}{2} = 181.50$$

$$SS_{comp.\ 3} = \frac{(12)(-8.50)^2}{(0)^2 + (+1)^2 + (-1)^2} = \frac{867.00}{2} = 433.50$$

For an example of a complex comparison, consider the contrast between the group receiving the history lecture and the two combined groups receiving the different science lectures. The standard set of coefficients for this comparison consists of $+\frac{1}{2}$, $+\frac{1}{2}$, and -1. The difference between the two means is

$$\hat{\psi}_4 = (+\tfrac{1}{2})(40.00) + (+\tfrac{1}{2})(26.00) + (-1)(34.50)$$
$$= 20.00 + 13.00 - 34.50 = -1.50$$

Substituting in Eq. (11-4), we find

$$SS_{comp.\ 4} = \frac{(12)(-1.50)^2}{(+\tfrac{1}{2})^2 + (+\tfrac{1}{2})^2 + (-1)^2} = \frac{27.00}{1.50} = 18.00$$

Earlier we indicated that fractional coefficients may be transformed into whole numbers to simplify calculations. If we multiply the standard set of coefficients in this example by 2, we obtain $+1$, $+1$, and -2. With these new coefficients,

$$\hat{\psi} = (+1)(40.00) + (+1)(26.00) + (-2)(34.50)$$
$$= 40.00 + 26.00 - 69.00 = -3.00$$

Substituting in Eq. (11-4), we have

$$SS_{comp.\ 4} = \frac{(12)(-3.00)^2}{(+1)^2 + (+1)^2 + (-2)^2} = \frac{108.00}{6} = 18.00$$

You should note that while these transformed coefficients do produce the same value for the sum of squares (18.00), the value of $\hat{\psi}$ (-3.00) does *not* represent the actual difference between the two means (-1.50). As you have seen, however, Eq. (11-4) compensates for this change. Thus, you can calculate $SS_{comp.}$ with any convenient set of coefficients that are derived from the standard set representing the difference under consideration.

Final Steps

The final steps consist of calculating a mean square, forming an F ratio, and evaluating a null hypothesis. A mean square is calculated by dividing a sum of squares by the appropriate number of *df*. Because the *df* associated with a difference between two means is 1—that is, $df_{comp.} = 1$—each comparison sum of squares is also the mean square. More explicitly,

$$MS_{comp.} = \frac{SS_{comp.}}{df_{comp.}} = \frac{SS_{comp.}}{1} = SS_{comp.}$$

An F ratio is formed by dividing each comparison mean square by the error term from the *omnibus* or *overall analysis*—that is, $MS_{S/A}$. More specifically,

$$F_{comp.} = \frac{MS_{comp.}}{MS_{S/A}} \tag{11-5}$$

The statistical hypotheses for a single-*df* comparison may be expressed as follows:

$$H_0: \quad \psi = 0$$
$$H_1: \quad \psi \neq 0$$

where ψ represents the difference expressed in terms of population means. Rejecting the null hypothesis leads to the conclusion that the observed difference between two means ($\hat{\psi}$) is significant. The obtained value of F is evaluated in the usual manner, with $F_{comp.}$ being compared with the critical value of F listed under $df_{num.} = 1$, $df_{denom.} = df_{S/A}$, and α equal to the level you have chosen for planned comparisons (probably $\alpha = .05$).

You should note two important features of the F test: (1) the test evaluates precisely those comparisons you have earmarked for analysis during the planning

Table 11-1
Summary of Comparisons

Source	SS	df	MS	F
Comp. 1 (physical science vs. social science)	1176.00	1	1176.00	8.44*
Comp. 2 (physical science vs. history)	181.50	1	181.50	1.30
Comp. 3 (social science vs. history)	433.50	1	433.50	3.11
Comp. 4 (combined sciences vs. history)	18.00	1	18.00	.13
S/A		33	139.36	

* $p < .05$.

stages of the study, and (2) the df for the error term ($df_{denom.}$) are determined from the omnibus, *overall analysis* ($MS_{S/A}$) and *not* from the within-groups df associated with the particular groups involved in the analysis. That is, though the comparison may be contrasting conditions 1 and 2, the error term is based on information gathered from all the conditions in the experiment. The operation of both of these features means that Eq. (11-5) provides a powerful test of hypotheses generated by planned comparisons.

The analyses of the four comparisons we considered in the last section are summarized and completed in Table 11-1. Each F is formed by dividing the comparison mean square by the error term obtained from the omnibus analysis ($MS_{S/A} = 139.36$). The critical value of F, which is based on $df_{num.} = 1$ and $df_{denom.} = 33$, is approximately 4.17 at $\alpha = .05$.[2] Only the comparison between the two science lectures (physical science versus social science) is significant.

Orthogonal Comparisons

Central to an understanding of ANOVA and MRC is the fact that a sum of squares can be subdivided into separate and independent components. In ANOVA, we have seen that SS_T may be divided into two useful components, namely, the between-groups sum of squares SS_A and the within-groups sum of squares $SS_{S/A}$. In MRC, the equivalent breakdown consists of dividing the total variability in the dependent variable (SS_Y) into two sums of squares, one representing the variability associated with group membership ($SS_{reg.}$) and the other a residual sum of squares—the variability in Y (the dependent variable) not accounted for by group membership ($SS_{res.}$).

[2] We have used $F(1, 30)$ for the critical value, which is a slightly larger value than required and yields an actual significance level that is somewhat smaller than .05.

It is generally the case that *any* sum of squares with more than 1 *df* can be divided into two or more independent sums of squares, and that the maximum number of such subdivisions is equal to the number of degrees of freedom associated with the sum of squares being subdivided. For the overall analysis, however, we are interested only in the between-groups and within-groups sums of squares. For planned comparisons (or single-*df* comparisons conducted following the omnibus test), we are obviously interested in what we might call *comparison* sums of squares—usually single-*df* comparisons—that contribute to the overall between-groups variability.

The statement that any sum of squares can be divided into two or more independent sums of squares holds only for what are known as **orthogonal comparisons**. Two single-*df* comparisons are said to be orthogonal if they reflect *independent* or completely *nonoverlapping* pieces of information. What this means is that the outcome of one comparison gives no indication whatsoever about the outcome of the other comparison. If all comparisons are orthogonal to one another, we refer to them as a set of **mutually orthogonal comparisons**. Thus, we can say that the SS_A can be broken down into a set of $df_A = a - 1$ mutually orthogonal single-*df* comparisons. In symbols,

$$SS_A = SS_{comp.\ 1} + SS_{comp.\ 2} + \cdots + SS_{comp.\ a-1} \qquad (11\text{-}6)$$

where the $a - 1$ comparisons are mutually orthogonal.

The orthogonality of any two single-*df* comparisons is easily determined by comparing the coefficients defining the two comparisons. Let us call the coefficients for one comparison c_i and the coefficients for the other comparison c_i'. The two comparisons are orthogonal if

$$(c_1)(c_1') + (c_2)(c_2') + (c_3)(c_3') + \cdots = 0$$

or, more compactly,

$$\Sigma\ (c_i c_i') = 0 \qquad (11\text{-}7)$$

To illustrate, suppose in our three-condition experiment we were concerned with a comparison of a_1 and a_3; the coefficient would be $+1$ for a_1, 0 for a_2, and -1 for a_3. Now suppose that another comparison of interest was the average of a_1 and a_3 versus a_2; here the coefficients would be $+\frac{1}{2}$ for a_1, -1 for a_2, and $+\frac{1}{2}$ for a_3. Application of Eq. (11-7) yields the following:

$$(+1)(+\tfrac{1}{2}) + (0)(-1) + (-1)(+\tfrac{1}{2}) = \tfrac{1}{2} + 0 - \tfrac{1}{2} = 0$$

Given this result, our two comparisons are orthogonal and are not providing redundant information. Thus, orthogonality is verified simply by multiplying corresponding pairs of coefficients—one pair for each level of factor *A*—and determining

Table 11-2
Coefficients for Single-*df* Comparisons

	Physical Science	Social Science	History
Comparison 1	$+1$	-1	0
Comparison 2	$+1$	0	-1
Comparison 3	0	$+1$	-1
Comparison 4	$+\frac{1}{2}$	$+\frac{1}{2}$	-1

that the sum of the products equals zero. Any value other than zero indicates that the two comparisons are *not* orthogonal.

In Table 11-1, we tested the significance of the difference between each pair of group means, as well as the difference between the mean for the two combined science groups and the mean for the history group. The coefficients for these comparisons are presented in Table 11-2. From Eq. (11-6), we know that the SS_A can be subdivided into a total of two orthogonal comparisons ($a - 1 = 3 - 1 = 2$). As surprising as it may be, only *one* set of orthogonal comparisons can be formed with the comparisons in Table 11-2. What about the first two comparisons? If we substitute the coefficients for these two comparisons in Eq. (11-7), we find

$$(+1)(+1) + (-1)(0) + (0)(-1) = 1 + 0 + 0 = 1$$

Since the sum is not zero, the two comparisons are not orthogonal. In fact, no set containing any two of the pairwise comparisons is orthogonal. (You may wish to verify this statement for yourself.) The only remaining possibility is a set that contains the fourth comparison and one of the pairwise comparisons. Applying the test to comparisons 1 and 4, we find that this is the orthogonal set:

$$(+1)(+\tfrac{1}{2}) + (-1)(+\tfrac{1}{2}) + (0)(-1) = \tfrac{1}{2} - \tfrac{1}{2} + 0 = 0$$

Earlier in this section, we indicated that a complete set of mutually orthogonal comparisons fully accounts for the original sum of squares. We can illustrate this property by adding together the sums of squares for comparisons 1 and 4 to show that they sum to SS_A. From Table 11-1, we see that

$$SS_{comp.\ 1} + SS_{comp.\ 4} = 1176.00 + 18.00 = 1194.00$$

From our earlier calculations (see Table 10-2). we find that this sum is exactly equal to the SS_A. What about other sets of comparisons? For comparisons 1 and

2, for example, the sum is

$$SS_{comp.\ 1} + SS_{comp.\ 2} = 1176.00 + 181.50 = 1357.50$$

which does not equal SS_A. If you try any other set of comparisons, you will find that none sums exactly to the value of SS_A (1194.00).

What implications does orthogonality have for a researcher? Some authorities suggest that all planned comparisons should be mutually orthogonal. One reason commonly given for this recommendation is that orthogonal comparisons represent an efficient use of an experimental design—a division of between-groups variability into a tidy set of nonoverlapping sources of variability. Most authors of statistics texts for behavioral scientists disagree with this recommendation, however. They argue that orthogonality should not be a *requirement* of planned comparisons. Instead, they feel that the overriding considerations in selecting a set of planned comparisons are the following:

1. The set should be an integral part of the experimental design.
2. The comparisons should represent the primary purpose of the experiment.
3. The comparisons should constitute meaningful and direct tests of the research hypotheses.

The entire set of comparisons we conducted on the data from the vocabulary experiment (see Table 11-1) seems to satisfy these criteria, even though the comparisons are not mutually orthogonal. *All four* comparisons provide useful information concerning the outcome of the experiment.

11.3 SINGLE-*df* COMPARISONS: THE MRC APPROACH

You may recall that in Chap. 10 we demonstrated the equivalency of MRC and ANOVA by using *contrast coding* to represent the levels of the independent variable and by using the R^2 to evaluate the omnibus null hypothesis. The purpose of this section is to show how contrast-coded vectors can be used to conduct the same sorts of single-*df* comparisons we considered with ANOVA in Sec. 11.2.

Contrast Coding

Contrast coding, you will remember, involves the assignment of values to the subjects so that different comparisons between groups are represented by each vector. For the overall analysis, the coding principle requires us to establish $a - 1$, or two, vectors in our current example, to permit the calculation of the omnibus R^2.

Consider again the comparisons listed in Table 11-2. Look at comparisons 1 and 3 and note their coefficients. You should recognize that the coefficients are identical to the codes used in the MRC analysis. The point of this is twofold: (1) the co-efficients used in planned comparisons in ANOVA can serve as the codes used in MRC, and (2) we can substitute the word *vectors* for *comparisons* in tables such as Table 11-2 and, in effect, have a code matrix.

To calculate $R^2_{Y.max.}$, however, our rule is that $a - 1$ vectors (or comparisons) are needed. Thus, any two of the comparisons in Table 11-2 could have been used to calculate $R^2_{Y.max.}$. Although we chose comparisons 1 and 3 for our analysis in Chap. 10, we could have used any set of two to provide a unique numerical representation of the three conditions.

To emphasize this point of correspondence between single-df comparisons and contrast coding of vectors, we will rewrite Table 11-2 into the following code matrix:

	Physical Science	Social Science	History
Vector 1	1	-1	0
Vector 2	1	0	-1
Vector 3	0	1	-1
Vector 4	1	1	-2

The contrast-coded vectors in the table are identical to the coefficients for the four single-df comparisons presented in Table 11-2 for analysis by ANOVA. (Vector 4 represents the same difference of means as comparison 4 in Table 11-2. All that we have done is to multiply the coefficients for that comparison, that is, $+\frac{1}{2}$, $+\frac{1}{2}$, and -1, by 2 to eliminate the fractions.) We will now show how these vectors can be used to assess the significance of these single-df comparisons.

Table 11-3 presents the data layout for this analysis. As usual, the subjects and their scores on the dependent variable (Y) are listed by treatment condition in one long column. The four vectors corresponding to the four single-df comparisons appear in the columns to the right of the Y scores. You should note how the values in the code matrix are assigned to the subjects in the table. Vector 1, for example, which corresponds to comparison 1 in the analysis of variance of Sec. 11.2 (physical science versus social science), consists of $+1$s assigned to subjects 1 to 12 (physical science), -1s assigned to subjects 13 to 24 (social science), and 0s assigned to subjects 25 to 36 (history). This vector will capture any variability associated with the comparison between physical science and social science. The other three vectors are created and interpreted in the same fashion.

Table 11-3
Contrast Coding of Single-df Comparisons

	Subject	Dependent Variable Y	Vectors			
			(1)	(2)	(3)	(4)
a_1	1	53	1	1	0	1
	2	49	1	1	0	1
	3	47	1	1	0	1
	4	42	1	1	0	1
	5	51	1	1	0	1
	6	34	1	1	0	1
	7	44	1	1	0	1
	8	48	1	1	0	1
	9	35	1	1	0	1
	10	18	1	1	0	1
	11	32	1	1	0	1
	12	27	1	1	0	1
a_2	13	47	-1	0	1	1
	14	42	-1	0	1	1
	15	39	-1	0	1	1
	16	37	-1	0	1	1
	17	42	-1	0	1	1
	18	33	-1	0	1	1
	19	13	-1	0	1	1
	20	16	-1	0	1	1
	21	16	-1	0	1	1
	22	10	-1	0	1	1
	23	11	-1	0	1	1
	24	6	-1	0	1	1
a_3	25	45	0	-1	-1	-2
	26	41	0	-1	-1	-2
	27	38	0	-1	-1	-2
	28	36	0	-1	-1	-2
	29	35	0	-1	-1	-2
	30	33	0	-1	-1	-2
	31	46	0	-1	-1	-2
	32	40	0	-1	-1	-2
	33	29	0	-1	-1	-2
	34	21	0	-1	-1	-2
	35	30	0	-1	-1	-2
	36	20	0	-1	-1	-2
		$r_{comp.}$:	.4506	.1770	$-.2736$	$-.0557$

The zero-order correlations between Y and the four vectors are presented at the bottom of the table. Each correlation between a vector and Y reflects the relationship between Y and the comparison represented by the vector. When squared, the correlations represent the proportion of Y variability associated with the individual vectors. In other words, the r^2's are yielding the same information as the $SS_{comp.}$'s in ANOVA obtained with the corresponding coefficients. Consequently, we will refer to them as $r^2_{comp.}$'s. Moreover, we can express the interrelationship between ANOVA and MRC by using the sums of squares from ANOVA to calculate the zero-order correlations $r^2_{comp.}$. Specifically,

$$r^2_{comp.} = \frac{SS_{A comp.}}{SS_T} \tag{11-8}$$

which symbolizes exactly what the $r^2_{comp.}$ represents, namely, the proportion of total variability in Y explained by (or associated with) a particular comparison (or corresponding vector). To illustrate with comparison 1, in which $SS_{comp.\,1}$ is 1176.00, and the total sum of squares SS_T, which is 5793.00,

$$r^2_{comp.} = \frac{1176.00}{5793.00} = .2030$$

which is identical to the square of the zero-order correlation shown in Table 11-3 and which reflects the single-*df* comparison; that is,

$$r^2_{Y1} = (.4506)^2 = .2030$$

The remaining $r^2_{comp.}$'s may be calculated in the same way.

Evaluating Single-*df* Comparisons

You have seen that specific comparisons may be expressed by the zero-order correlations between contrast-coded vectors and the dependent variable. A test of the significance of any $r^2_{comp.}$, then, evaluates the particular difference between two means specified by the coefficients. More explicitly,

A test of r^2_{Y1} evaluates the difference between physical science and social science (comparison 1) or, in other words, the relationship of type of science lecture (physical versus social science) to vocabulary words learned.

A test of r^2_{Y2} evaluates the difference between physical science and history (comparison 2).

A test of r^2_{Y3} evaluates the difference between social science and history (comparison 3).

A test of r^2_{Y4} evaluates the difference between the average of the two science conditions and the history condition (comparison 4).

Table 11-4
Tests of Single-*df* Comparisons

Source	$r^2_{comp.}$	F
Physical science vs. social science	.2030	8.42*
Physical science vs. history	.0313	1.30
Social science vs. history	.0749	3.11
Combined sciences vs. history	.0031	.13

* p < .05.

We can test the significance of these correlations by modifying the equation for the omnibus F test, Eq. (10-8), as follows:

$$F = \frac{r^2_{comp.}}{(1 - R^2_{Y.max.})/(N - k - 1)} \tag{11-9}$$

where the numerator is the squared zero-order correlation based on a vector that reflects a single-*df* comparison and the denominator is the error term from the *overall* analysis.[3] This error term is equivalent to the within-groups mean square $MS_{S/A}$, which you will recall is used in ANOVA to evaluate all single-*df* comparisons. In both cases, then, the appropriate error term takes into account *all the data* we have available for the omnibus analysis and reflects the variation in Y that remains after all effects of the independent variable have been removed.

We can now evaluate the four comparisons by substituting appropriate values from the MRC analysis in Eq. (11-9). As we have indicated, the denominator for all tests is the error term used to evaluate the squared omnibus multiple correlation coefficient, which we calculated in Sec. 10.2; the value of this quantity is .0241. The numerator consists of the squared zero-order correlation for the comparison in question. The resulting F ratios are presented in Table 11-4. To illustrate with the first comparison,

$$F = \frac{(.4506)^2}{.0241} = \frac{.2030}{.0241} = 8.42$$

Within the limits of rounding, this F is identical to that found with ANOVA (see

---

[3] As a reminder, $1 - R^2_{Y.max.}$ is the proportion of Y variability that is *unrelated* to any Y variability associated with the independent variable. This residual proportion is divided by the corresponding "residual" *df*, $N - k - 1$, where N is the total number of subjects in the experiment—$(a)(s)$—and k is the number of vectors required to represent the treatment-group differences completely, namely, df_A or $a - 1$.

Table 11-1). As a result of this test, we can conclude that the two science conditions have differed significantly in their effect on the vocabulary test; or that vocabulary scores are related to the type of science lectures subjects receive. The same
procedures are followed to calculate the F's for the other three comparisons, and
the conclusions they permit are identical to those permitted by ANOVA.

The MRC Analysis with Orthogonal Comparisons

The parallels between ANOVA and MRC are most easily appreciated with orthogonal comparisons. In Sec. 11-2, we showed that the treatment sum of squares
SS_A may be divided into a set of $a - 1$ single-df comparisons ($SS_{comp.}$'s). The only
requirement was that the comparisons be mutually orthogonal. Orthogonality is
verified by showing that

$$\Sigma (c_i c_i') = 0$$

for all pairs of comparisons.

There is an analogous relationship between $R^2_{Y.max.}$, on the one hand, and the
set of squared zero-order correlations between Y and contrast-coded vectors
($r^2_{comp.}$'s), on the other. More specifically, if the contrasts are orthogonal, as derived
from Eq. (10-3), then

$$R^2_{Y.max.} = r^2_{Y1} + r^2_{Y2} + r^2_{Y3} + \cdots$$
$$= \Sigma r^2_{comp.} \tag{11-10}$$

only where the number of $r^2_{comp.}$'s is exactly $a - 1$ and all possible correlations
between pairs of vectors are zero—that is,

$$r_{12} = 0 \qquad r_{13} = 0 \qquad r_{23} = 0$$

and so forth. (This last restriction is equivalent to the requirement of mutual orthogonality in ANOVA.)

As an example, we return to Table 11-3 and the vectors representing the four
single-df comparisons we considered in the last section. Since $a = 3$, only two
$r^2_{comp.}$'s are needed to capture completely the effects of the independent variable.
In Sec. 11-2, we identified comparison 1 (physical science versus social science)
and comparison 4(combined science versus history) as the one orthogonal pair
of comparisons derivable from the total set. This can be easily determined by examining the intercorrelations between pairs of vectors, which are presented in Table
11-5. As you can see, the only intercorrelation equal to zero is r_{14}; all other pairs

Table 11-5
Intercorrelations between Vectors

	Vector 1	Vector 2	Vector 3	Vector 4
Vector 1	—	.5000	−.5000	.0000
Vector 2		—	.5000	.8660
Vector 3			—	.8660

of vectors are correlated. According to Eq. (11-10),

$$R^2_{Y.max.} = r^2_{Y1} + r^2_{Y4}$$
$$= (.4506)^2 + (.0557)^2 = .2030 + .0031 = .2061$$

which is equal to the $R^2_{Y.max.}$ we obtained in Sec. 10-2 with the current set of vectors 1 and 3 (which we called vectors 1 and 2 at that time). Because these latter two vectors are correlated ($r_{13} = -.5000$), we can *not* use them in Eq. (11-10) to calculate $R^2_{Y.max.}$. To illustrate,

$$r^2_{Y1} + r^2_{Y3} = (.4506)^2 + (-.2736)^2 = .2030 + .0748 = .2778$$

which does not equal $R^2_{Y.max.}$ (.2061). To find $R^2_{Y.max.}$ from vectors 1 and 3, we must use Eq, (10-2), which takes into consideration the intercorrelation between the two vectors. (With more than two vectors, we would need a computer, and a program that adjusts for any intercorrelations within the set of vectors.)

It is important to note that an R^2 can always be calculated by means of Eq. (11-10), regardless of the number of treatment conditions. All that is required is that the maximum number of vectors be involved, which is equal to df_A, and that they be mutually orthogonal. We will take advantage of this relationship throughout this book.

To recapitulate, in order to use MRC for single-*df* comparisons of experimental data, several steps need to be followed:

1. Establish a code matrix to represent *all* meaningful comparisons; these comparisons do not need to be orthogonal.
2. Calculate $R^2_{Y.max.}$ by choosing $a - 1$ vectors from the code matrix; these vectors do not need to be orthogonal. If they are orthogonal, $R^2_{Y.max.}$ can be calculated by Eq. (10-7); if they are not orthogonal, use Eq. (10-2) if $a = 3$ or the computer if $a > 3$. The purpose for which $R^2_{Y.max.}$ is needed is to obtain the error term for the F test of the $r^2_{comp.}$.

3. Use the F ratio, Eq. (11-9), to test each $r_{comp.}^2$.
4. If you are interested in group means, you can use the regression equation you obtained when you calculated $R_{Y.max.}^2$ in step 2 above.

11.4   SUMMARY

Most experiments are designed to examine a number of specific research hypotheses, none of which is directly evaluated by the omnibus F test. This is because the omnibus test detects only the *presence* of significant variation among the treatment means, not its locus. Comparisons that focus on differences between two means are known as single-*df* comparisons; they remedy this situation by providing information on the goodness of specific research hypotheses.

Single-*df* comparisons either may be planned and may thus form an integral part of the study or may be unplanned (post hoc) in the sense that they are conducted only after the data have been collected and partially analyzed. Either ANOVA or MRC may be used to test the significance of single-*df* comparisons. As you have seen on a number of occasions, the significance tests for ANOVA and MRC yield identical F's for both the omnibus test and the test of single-*df* comparisons. Table 11-6 summarizes the points of correspondence between the two procedures. In ANOVA, the variation is expressed in terms of sums of squares, while in MRC it is expressed as proportions of Y variability. One point of note is the use in both cases of the error term from the omnibus F ratio as the error term for all the comparison F tests $(F_{comp.})$.

Table 11-6
Points of Correspondence Between ANOVA and MRC

	ANOVA	MRC
Omnibus F	$\dfrac{SS_A/(a-1)}{SS_{S/A}/(a)(s-1)}$	$\dfrac{R_{Y.max.}^2/k}{(1-R_{Y.max.}^2)/(N-k-1)}$
Comparison variation	$SS_{comp.}$	$r_{comp.}^2$
Comparison F ($F_{comp.}$)	$\dfrac{MS_{comp.}}{MS_{S/A}}$	$\dfrac{r_{comp.}^2}{(1-R_{Y.max.}^2)/(N-k-1)}$

11.5 EXERCISES

1. In the problems for Chap. 10, data were presented for an experiment on verbal reinforcement. Using those data, construct three meaningful comparisons and

a. Calculate $SS_{comp.}$ for each comparison.
b. Determine the significance of each comparison.

2. Using the same data as above, calculate the $r^2_{comp.}$'s you have selected and test each for significance.

12

Correction for

Multiple Comparisons

. . .

In Chap. 8 we introduced decision rules that we could use to fix the probability of a type I error at α for the *omnibus* test. If we apply these same rules to single-*df* comparisons (like the comparisons that were the subject of Chap. 11), we in effect fix the type I error at α for *each one of the statistical tests* conducted in the analysis of the experiment. The consequences of applying the rules to several tests at once will be our concern in this chapter.

12.1   PROBLEMS ASSOCIATED WITH ANALYTICAL COMPARISONS

A serious problem exists whenever we perform more than one statistical test in the analysis of any research or experiment: each comparison—whether planned or post hoc—increases our chances of committing a type I error *somewhere* within the entire analysis. In order to talk about this problem, it is convenient to introduce two new terms, *per comparison* and *familywise* type I errors. We will now consider how these two ways of conceptualizing type I error are related.

Per comparison (PC) type I error is the type I error associated with the significance level that we set for any given statistical test. In most cases, a researcher would set the significance level at $\alpha_{PC} = .05$ for all comparisons. What effect does this decision have on type I error? If our focus is on the level of the individual statistical test, we can say that the type I error is .05 for each one of the tests. But suppose we consider a different point of reference, namely, the type I error for the *experiment as a whole*, which includes the entire set of comparisons tested in the analysis. If we do this, the separate per comparison probabilities actually combine to produce a much larger value, which we will call the **familywise (FW) type I error**. This category of error, which has also been called the **experimentwise type I error**, refers to the probability (α_{FW}) that at least one type I error has been committed *somewhere among* the various tests conducted in the analysis. If two tests are conducted, for example, the familywise error will approximately equal the sum of the two *PC* probabilities, namely, .10 (.05 + .05). If there are three tests, α_{FW} will approximately equal .15 (.05 + .05 + .05).

The exact relationship between α_{FW} and the number of statistical tests can be determined by the following formula:

$$\alpha_{FW} = 1 - (1 - \alpha_{PC})^c \tag{12-1}$$

where c represents the number of *orthogonal* comparisons that are conducted. With the *PC* type I error set $\alpha_{PC} = .05$ and with $c = 3$ orthogonal comparisons, for example,

$$\alpha_{FW} = 1 - (1 - .05)^3 = 1 - (.95)^3 = 1 - .857 = .143$$

The same basic relationship between *FW* error, on the one hand, and the number of tests and *PC* error, on the other, holds for nonorthogonal comparisons as well, although the relationship is more complex.

Although researchers have known about the relationship expressed in Eq. (12-1) for some time, they still do not agree on what should be done about it. In reality, each researcher must decide (and justify to others) the steps taken to control *FW* error. What we hope you will extract from the present discussion is an appreciation for the nature of the problem and an understanding of some of the solutions that have been offered. This will better prepare you for determining your own response to the problem of *FW* error.[1]

Possible solutions to the problem of controlling *FW* error are many, but all reduce to the same mechanism, namely, *a decrease in the size of the rejection region* used to evaluate the significance of comparisons. Let us see how this general procedure works. As an example, suppose we planned to conduct five orthogonal comparisons. We know from Eq. (12-1) that if we used $\alpha_{PC} = .05$, the *FW* error would be

$$\alpha_{FW} = 1 - (1 - .05)^5 = 1 - (.95)^5 = 1 - .774 = .226$$

A relatively simple way of reducing *FW* error in this example would be to use a smaller probability for α_{PC}—that is, a higher level of significance for evaluating the *individual comparisons*. More specifically, consider what would happen to *FW* if we use $\alpha_{PC} = .01$ rather than .05 to assess the significance of each of these five comparisons. Turning again to Eq. (12-1), we find the new familywise type I error to be

$$\alpha_{FW} = 1 - (1 - .01)^5 = 1 - (.99)^5 = 1 - .951 = .049$$

which, as you can see, apparently solves the problem of increased *FW* simply and neatly! That is, familywise error is now equivalent to the significance level adopted by most researchers for omnibus statistical tests.

Before you become too complacent with this solution to the problem, you should realize that this control of *FW* error has been accomplished by increasing the probability of another kind of error, namely, *type II error*. This "cost" for controlling *FW* error can also be expressed as a *loss of power*. Let us consider this important point in more detail.

If we use the .01 level of significance rather than the .05 level to evaluate comparison null hypotheses, we are able to reduce familywise error, as you have seen. But as you can also see, this reduction is accomplished by the simple expedient of rejecting *fewer null hypotheses*. We control *FW* error by making it more

---

[1] You will find detailed discussions of the general problem in most advanced statistics texts. For an elaboration of the views set forth in this section, see Keppel (1982, Chap. 8).

difficult to reject null hypotheses; the fewer null hypotheses we reject, the lower our *FW* error. This is exactly what we want to do when the null hypothesis is *true*, of course. But the null hypothesis may also be *false*: some comparisons reflect real differences in the population. Requiring a higher level of significance for these comparisons directly increases type II error, and by definition, decreases power. The problem, then, is to find a way of *balancing* the two kinds of errors.

12.2   PLANNED COMPARISONS

Most recommendations concerning the control of familywise type I error distinguish between planned and post hoc comparisons. Recommendations for planned comparisons usually do not include a correction for familywise error, except perhaps, when the number of the planned comparisons exceeds some reasonable value such as the degrees of freedom for the treatment sum of squares (see Keppel, 1982, pp. 147–150). This disregard for *FW* error is generally defended by the argument that planned comparisons typically constitute the primary purpose of a study, and as such, they should be subjected to the most sensitive statistical test possible. This type of test is one that treats each comparison as if the experiment were specifically designed to focus on it. Any increase in *FW* error resulting from the statistical assessment of planned comparisons is thus accepted as one of the calculated risks of experimentation.

12.3   POST HOC COMPARISONS

Most corrections for familywise error are applied to comparisons conducted after the data have been initially examined and analyzed. Post hoc tests are treated differently from planned comparisons because of their potentially large number and because of their fortuitous, unplanned nature. When one is sifting through a set of data in search of significant differences, considerably more comparisons are examined and assessed than are ever proposed in the planning stage of an experiment. Familywise type I error under these circumstances can be intolerably high.

Recommendations for controlling *FW* error for post hoc comparisons depend on the nature of the pool of differences being examined. We will consider three common situations, in which the pool consists of (1) all possible comparisons, (2) all possible differences between pairs of treatment means, and (3) all possible differences between a control condition and a number of experimental or treatment conditions. The procedures are applicable to all single-factor experiments, regardless of whether the F tests are conducted with ANOVA or MRC. The logic is the same.

All Possible Comparisons

When complex comparisons are included in the total pool of potential comparisons—all the comparisons that one might examine when combing through data—the post hoc pool is often very large indeed, and a severe correction is usually required to keep FW error at a reasonable level. The **Scheffé test** was designed for exactly this type of situation (Scheffé, 1953). The test is simple to perform. All we do is calculate a new critical value of F (F_S) to incorporate into the decision rules, as follows:

$$F_S = (a - 1)F(df_A, df_{S/A}) \qquad (12\text{-}2)$$

where a equals the number of treatment conditions and $F(df_A, df_{S/A})$ is the critical value of F for the *omnibus* F test.[2] This value is found in Table A-1 with $df_{num.} = a - 1$ and $df_{denom.} = df_{S/A}$. (Please note that $df_{num.}$ does *not* equal $df_{comp.}$; the two are often mistakenly equated in applications of the Scheffé test.) One's choice of α at this point determines the maximum value that α_{FW} will ever reach regardless of the number of comparisons actually evaluated. It is this property that makes the Scheffé test particularly attractive to researchers who are poring over large data sets, searching for significant differences.

As an example of the calculations, consider again the four comparisons we analyzed as planned comparisons in Chap. 11. We will treat them now as post hoc comparisons and evaluate them by using the Scheffé test. For Eq. (12-2), we need a ($a = 3$, in this example) and the critical value for the omnibus F test, $F(2, 33) = 3.32$ at $\alpha = .05$. Substituting in the formula, we find

$$F_S = (3 - 1)(3.32) = (2)(3.32) = 6.64$$

We would now use 6.64 as the critical value of F to test the significance of these (and any other) comparisons we conduct, whether with ANOVA or with MRC.

As we have noted already, the Scheffé test guarantees that the FW error will be no greater than the value of α used to enter the F table (.05 in this case), no matter how many comparisons are conducted. An inspection of the $F_{comp.}$'s in either Table 11-1 or Table 11-4 indicates that the comparison between the two

---

[2] In MRC terminology, $df_A = k$ (the number of vectors required for the omnibus R^2) and $df_{S/A} = N - k - 1$ (the degrees of freedom for the residual sum of squares).

science conditions would still be significant under the Scheffé test. You should realize, of course, that only the largest differences will emerge triumphant from an application of the Scheffé test. One way to make this point is to compare the value of F_S (6.64) with the value of the uncorrected F we would use for planned comparisons ($F = 4.17$). Comparisons producing $F_{comp.}$'s that fall between these two critical values would be declared significant if they were planned comparisons and not significant if they were post hoc comparisons subjected to the Scheffé correction.

In summary, the Scheffé test provides protection from FW type I error when a researcher hopes to discover interesting, but still unexpected, differences between treatment conditions and combinations of treatment conditions. Since the total pool of such comparisons is relatively large, so must be the correction required to restore the FW rate to reasonable levels. As we have already noted, however, the "cost" of this protection is a considerable loss in the power to detect real treatment differences. This loss of power may be substantially reduced if something can be done to restrict the size of the comparison pool examined by a researcher. A smaller pool requires a smaller reduction in the α_{PC} to exercise the desired control over FW error. We will next consider two procedures that capitalize on this strategy of restricting one's attention to certain smaller and better-defined subsets of comparisons.

All Possible Differences between Pairs of Means

One obvious way of reducing the pool of post hoc comparisons is to concentrate on the differences between *pairs of treatment means* and simply not consider complex comparisons in the post hoc analysis. To see how this reduces the number of comparisons, let us consider several examples: if $a = 3$, for instance, the total pool contains a combination of 6 pairwise and complex comparisons, while the smaller pool consists of 3 pairwise comparisons; if $a = 4$, the total pool contains 25 comparisons, while the smaller pool contains 6; and finally, if $a = 5$, the total pool contains 90 comparisons, while the smaller pool contains 10. Because of the difference in the size of these two pools, α_{PC} requires a smaller adjustment for pairwise comparisons than it requires when the pool contains both pairwise and complex comparisons. One test that provides control over the smaller pool of differences is called the **Tukey test** (Tukey, 1953).

The Tukey test is most easily performed by calculating the differences between all pairs of means and comparing them against a *minimum*, or *critical*, difference that must be exceeded for an observed difference to be declared significant. This critical value $\bar{d}_T$ is given by the formula

$$\bar{d}_T = \frac{q_T\sqrt{MS_{S/A}}}{\sqrt{s}} \tag{12-3}$$

where q_T = an entry in a special table, called the **studentized range statistic** (Table A-2)

$MS_{S/A}$ = the error term from the overall analysis of variance

s = the sample size of the treatment groups

Using the data from our example to illustrate the Tukey test, we first find the three differences, namely,

$$\bar{Y}_{A_1} - \bar{Y}_{A_2} = 40.00 - 26.00 = 14.00$$
$$\bar{Y}_{A_1} - \bar{Y}_{A_3} = 40.00 - 34.50 = 5.50$$
$$\bar{Y}_{A_2} - \bar{Y}_{A_3} = 26.00 - 34.50 = -8.50$$

Next, we calculate the critical difference $\bar{d}_T$ by using Eq. (12-3). The value for q_T, which is required by the formula, is found by entering Table A-2 and coordinating three quantities, df_{error} (the df associated with the $MS_{S/A}$), k (the number of treatment means—a in this design), and α_{FW} (the FW error rate chosen for the Tukey test). Using $df_{error} = 30$ (since $df_{error} = 33$ does not appear in the table), $k = 3$, and $\alpha_{FW} = .05$, we find $q_T = 3.49$. Substituting this and the other required values ($MS_{S/A} = 139.36$ and $s = 12$) in Eq. (12-3), we find

$$\bar{d}_T = \frac{(3.49)\sqrt{139.36}}{\sqrt{12}} = \frac{41.22}{3.46} = 11.91$$

A comparison of the three observed differences against the new criterion, $\bar{d}_T = 11.91$, indicates that only the difference between the physical science and social science groups (14.00) is significant.

Under some circumstances, you may wish to conduct the Tukey test in the same way we performed the Scheffé test, namely, in conjunction with the F statistic. This method is ideally suited for analysis by MRC, where the computer output for these comparisons is expressed in terms of zero-order correlations from which F ratios can be formed. The new critical value of F required by the Tukey test (F_T) is given by

$$F_T = \frac{(q_T)^2}{2} \tag{12-4}$$

In the present case,

$$F_T = \frac{3.49^2}{2} = 6.09$$

The Tukey test is conducted by using $F_T = 6.09$ as the criterion for evaluating the F_{comp}'s. An inspection of Tables 11-1 and 11-4, where these statistical analyses are

summarized, permits the same conclusion, namely, that only the difference between physical science and social science is significant.

It is instructive to compare the critical values of F for the Scheffé and the
Tukey tests. With this example, the critical value of F was slightly greater for the
Scheffé test (6.64) than that required by the Tukey test (6.09). The difference
between these two critical values increases as the number of treatment conditions
in an experiment increases.

All Possible Comparisons between a Control
and Several Treatment Conditions

A final type of situation involves an even smaller pool of potential comparisons—
an experiment in which one condition, usually a control or baseline condition of
some sort, is compared against a number of experimental or treatment conditions.
As you would suspect, the degree to which this restricted comparison pool is
smaller than the other pools increases directly with the scope of the experiment.
To illustrate, if $a = 3$, then 2 of the 3 pairwise comparisons represent differences
between the control and the two experimental conditions; if $a = 4$, the numbers
are 3 out of 6; and if $a = 5$, they are 4 out of 10. Because the comparisons involved
are fewer than those considered by either the Scheffé test or the Tukey test, the
correction for FW error will not be as severe as that given by either of those tests.
The test developed for this type of situation is known as the **Dunnett test** (Dunnett,
1955).

Like the Tukey test, the Dunnett test is most simply conducted by comparing
the differences between the control and experimental means against a critical difference that must be exceeded to be significant at the chosen α_{FW} level. The formula for calculating this difference $(\bar{d}_D)$ is

$$\bar{d}_D = \frac{q_D \sqrt{2\,MS_{S/A}}}{\sqrt{s}} \tag{12-5}$$

where q_D is an entry in Table A-3 of Appendix A and the other quantities are
familiar to you. The value of q_D is determined by the total number of conditions
(k) involved in the analysis, the degrees of freedom associated with the error term
$(df_{S/A})$, and the value chosen for FW error (α_{FW}).[3]

---

[3] The values of q_D given in the first part of Table A-3 are for situations in which researchers
are interested in the possibility of positive as well as negative differences between the control
and experimental conditions (called *Two-Tailed Comparisons*). A special table is available
for the less common situation in which researchers are concerned only with differences in
"one direction"—that is, either positive or negative differences, not both. This other table
is included in Table A-3 as *One-Tailed Comparisons*.

We will calculate $\bar{d}_D$ using the example from the last section. To find q_D, we look for the entry in Table A-3 at $k = 3$, $df_{error} = 30$, and $\alpha_{FW} = .05$. This value is 2.32. Substituting in Eq. (12-5), we find

$$\bar{d}_D = \frac{(2.32)\sqrt{(2)(139.36)}}{\sqrt{12}} = \frac{38.72}{3.46} = 11.19.$$

As expected, this critical difference is slightly smaller than that required for the Tukey test performed on the same data ($\bar{d}_T = 11.91$).

If you wish to work with the F test, you can use

$$F_D = (q_D)^2 \tag{12-6}$$

as the critical value with which to evaluate $F_{comp.}$. In the present case,

$$F_D = 2.32^2 = 5.38$$

This critical value can be compared with corresponding values for the Scheffé test (6.64) and the Tukey test (6.09) to illustrate the different sensitivities of the three tests.

12.4 THE FISHER TEST

An entirely different approach to the problem of FW type I error is the **protected least significant difference test**, which we will call the **Fisher test** (Fisher, 1949). The test centers on the outcome of the *omnibus* F test; the significance or nonsignificance of this test determines whether additional tests will be conducted at all. If the F is significant, comparisons are evaluated *without* correction for FW error; if the F is not significant, no further tests are conducted.

The Fisher test is most appropriate in situations in which initially, at least, all treatments are given equal consideration, that is, there are no favored treatments or anticipated outcomes—in short, where there are no planned comparisons as we have defined them. An example would be an experiment comparing consumer preferences among alternative ways of packaging a certain product. The object of the study is to discover whether the different package designs make any difference to the potential consumer. This is where the omnibus F test comes into play: it assesses the average differences associated with the treatment conditions. Only if the overall null hypothesis is rejected does the investigator examine the specific differences between conditions to find out which are the best and which are the worst.

Familywise type I error is controlled *indirectly* by the Fisher test. The omnibus *F* test acts as a "filter," which permits additional tests only when the evidence looks "good"—that is, when treatment differences are sufficiently large not to be reasonably attributed to the operation of chance factors. Although it is true that a researcher will sometimes falsely conclude that differences are present in the population when in fact they are not, this does not happen very often (only 5 percent of the time when $\alpha = .05$). Thus, little long-term risk is incurred by following the Fisher procedure. The Fisher test has been studied by statisticians and shown to offer an excellent balancing of type I and type II errors (see Carmer & Swanson, 1973). We do not suggest its use with studies in which planned comparisons are also present, for reasons that have been expressed elsewhere (Keppel, 1982, pp. 158–159).

12.5 RECOMMENDATIONS AND COMMENT

We recommend that planned comparisons be evaluated without undue concern for their effect on familywise type I error. Furthermore, we recommend that planned comparisons be the strategy for research. However, if there is no reason or it is not feasible to conduct planned comparisons, then post hoc comparisons are the alternative. But most researchers become concerned at this point with the greatly increased potential for familywise error associated with post hoc comparisons and adopt some strategy for dealing with it. We have described three techniques which have been developed to correct *FW* error for different pools of possible comparisons. If a mixture of complex comparisons and differences between pairs of means are candidates for post hoc tests, we recommend the Scheffé test. On the other hand, if only pairwise differences are of interest, we recommend the Tukey test. We recommend the Dunnett test when only differences between a control and experimental conditions are involved. The Fisher test seems most appropriate for situations in which planned comparisons are not an integral part of the experimental design.

These recommendations are summarized as a flowchart in Fig. 12-1. We begin at the top with the question "Do you have planned comparisons?" Your answer to this question branches to additional questions and finally to the appropriate set of procedures. If you answer yes, for example, you perform the planned comparisons without undertaking any correction for *FW* error; if you wish to follow these with additional post hoc comparisons, you would select one of the correction procedures we have discussed—Scheffé, Tukey, or Dunnett—depending on the nature of the comparisons you have selected to examine. On the other hand, if you

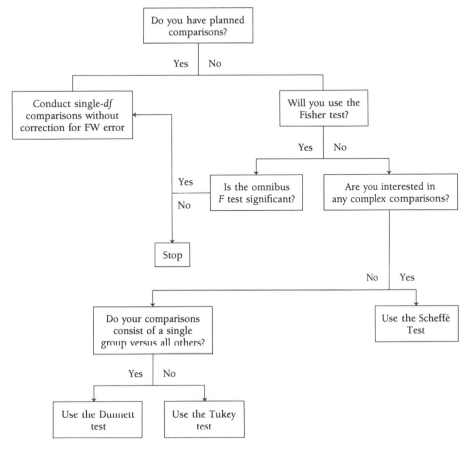

Figure 12-1   Schematic representation of post hoc techniques.

answer no to the initial question, you may perform either the Fisher test or one of the three alternative post hoc tests. These possibilities are presented at the bottom of the flowchart.

Any correction for *FW* error disregards another important concern of researchers, namely, type II error, or the loss of power created whenever an *FW* correction is incorporated into the evaluation process. A constructive suggestion for dealing with this problem is to expand the usual decision rules in which we either reject or do not reject a null hypothesis to include a third course of action, the opportunity to *suspend judgment.* That is, suppose we decided to reject the null hypothesis only when the F_{comp} exceeds the *familywise* criterion but to make *no decision*—that is, to suspend judgment—when an $F_{comp.}$ happens to fall between the criterion for *planned comparisons* and the familywise criterion. To be more explicit, consider the following modified decisions rules:

> If $F_{observed} \geq F_{FW}$, reject H_0,
>
> If $F_{observed} < F_{PC}$, do not reject H_0,
>
> If $F_{observed}$ falls between F_{PC} and F_{FW}, *suspend judgment*.

The first of the decision rules concerns the familywise criterion; an $F_{observed}$ that exceeds this critical value (F_{FW}) will be rejected without question. The second rule concerns the "normal" per comparison criterion applied to uncorrected planned comparisons; an $F_{observed}$ that falls short of this critical value (F_{PC}) will not be rejected. The final rule pertains to our decision when the $F_{observed}$ falls between these two critical values—we suspend judgment. We apply this third rule when we come across an unexpected finding which, if it were the result of a planned comparison, we would have termed significant; we suspend judgment rather than commit a promising finding to potential obscurity by labeling it "not significant" under the more stringent *FW* criterion.[4]

12.6   SUMMARY

One consequence of assessing a number of single-*df* comparisons is an increase in the probability of committing type I errors during the course of the entire analysis. This probability, which is known as *familywise type I error*, increases directly with the number of statistical tests performed, whether they are planned tests or not. Researchers tend to ignore familywise error when doing planned comparisons, however, but usually adopt some way of reducing it with unplanned comparisons. We discussed several techniques that can be used with different types of comparisons. The Scheffé test is used when the pool of possible single-*df* comparisons consists of all pairwise and complex comparisons. The Tukey test is used when the pool consists of all pairwise comparisons. The Dunnett test is used when a single control condition is compared with a number of treatment conditions. The Fisher test, which focuses on the outcome of the omnibus *F* test, is recommended for situations in which there are no planned comparisons motivating the research. Finally, we reiterate that the above concerns are related to the number of comparisons undertaken and *not* to whether the analytical strategy one adopts is ANOVA or MRC.

[4] This suggestion is developed more fully in Keppel (1982, pp. 162–164).

12.7 EXERCISES

1. The experiment described in Problem 1 of Chap. 10 consisted of three conditions, praise for correct responses ("praise"), reproof for mistakes ("reproof"), and no verbal comment at all ("none"). For the questions below, assume that you had no planned comparisons when you designed the experiment. What procedure for controlling *FW* error (Dunnett, Scheffé, or Tukey) is most appropriate under the following circumstances?

   a. All possible comparisons between pairs of means
   b. Comparisons between each of the two "verbal" conditions and the condition receiving no verbal comment
   c. A comparison between "none" and the combined conditions receiving verbal comment of some sort and a comparison of the two verbal conditions

2. Using the data from Problem 1 of Chap. 10,

   a. Conduct a Tukey test.
   b. Conduct a Dunnett test.
   c. What is the critical value for a Scheffé test?

13

Introduction to the Two-Factor Design

. . .

You have seen how a single-factor experiment can be analyzed to yield information concerning a number of research hypotheses. If the manipulation is qualitative in nature, the analysis generally takes the form of assessing miniature two-group "experiments." On the other hand, if the manipulation is quantitative in nature, the analysis usually consists of the examination and assessment of trend components presumed to underlie the relationship between the independent and dependent variables. (We consider trend analysis in Chap. 23.) In either case, the experimental manipulation is conceived as a *single* independent variable—a variation either in the type or in the amount of the independent variable.

We will examine a different kind of design in this chapter, one in which two independent variables (factor *A* and factor *B*) are manipulated *simultaneously* within the context of the same experiment. This type of design, known as the **factorial design**, is quite common in the behavioral sciences, for the important reason that it greatly expands the sorts of questions one can study in an experiment. In this chapter, we will consider the nature of the overall analysis of a two-factor design and show how the analysis is accomplished by ANOVA and MRC. In Chaps. 14 and 15, we will turn our attention to the detailed analysis of the factorial experiment.

13.1   THE OVERALL ANALYSIS

Suppose our experiment comparing the relative merits of teaching vocabulary words in the context of three different types of lectures (factor *A*) is expanded to include a second independent variable, mode of presentation (factor *B*). More specifically, suppose we are comparing computer-assisted instruction with a "standard" method of presentation (a lecture given by a teacher). A factorial design combines the two independent variables in such a way that all possible combinations of the levels of the two variables are represented in the experiment. In the present case, this would mean that different groups of students would receive lectures on physical science, social science, and history, under each of the two methods of presentation, computer or standard, and thus there would be a total of $3 \times 2 = 6$ treatment conditions.

This arrangement is diagramed in Table 13-1, where you can see the exact nature of the design. Each cell represents a different treatment condition of the experiment formed by a unique combination of the levels of the two independent variables. In a completely randomized factorial experiment, which is the kind of experiment we are considering in this chapter, subjects are assigned randomly to the different treatment conditions. Typically, each group is represented by an equal

Table 13-1
An Example of a Two-Factor Design

Method of Presentation (Factor B)	Type of Lecture (Factor A)		
	Physical Science (a_1)	Social Science (a_2)	History (a_3)
Computer (b_1)			
Standard (b_2)			

number of subjects (s). (Factorial experiments with unequal sample sizes are discussed in Chap. 24.)

Factorial experiments are usually described in terms of the number of levels associated with the two independent variables. The present example would be called a *completely randomized 3 × 2* ("three-by-two") *factorial design*, which clearly specifies the fact that two independent variables have been manipulated factorially, one with three levels and the other with two levels, and that the total number of treatment conditions is six. By *completely randomized* we mean that individual subjects are randomly assigned to only one of the treatment combinations; in other types of designs subjects may each receive more than one treatment combination.

Let us now fill in the data for this example. In the upper portion of Table 13-2, we present vocabulary scores for all the sets of s = 6 subjects constituting the different treatment groups. (These data are derived from Table 10-1; the first six scores for each lesson have become the "computed-assisted" scores, and the remaining six scores are the "standard" scores.) The means of the groups are listed in the lower portion of the table in what we will call a *factorial matrix*.

You will notice that the two "margins" of the matrix contain the averages of the means in the individual columns (the column marginal means) and in the individual rows (the row marginal means). The marginal means can be thought of as the results of two "artificial" *single*-factor experiments, one in which the independent variable is the type of lecture (the column marginal means, 40.00, 26.00, and 34.50) and another in which the independent variable is the method of presentation (the row marginal means, 41.33 and 25.67). These average effects are artificial in the sense that they are not the product of an *actual* single-factor design in which only one independent variable is manipulated, but rather are the effects produced by averaging or "collapsing" over the levels of the other independent variable manipulated in the factorial experiment.

Table 13-2
Numerical Example

Vocabulary Scores

	Physical Science		Social Science		History	
	Computer	Standard	Computer	Standard	Computer	Standard
	53	44	47	13	45	46
	49	48	42	16	41	40
	47	35	39	16	38	29
	42	18	37	10	36	21
	51	32	42	11	35	30
	34	27	33	6	33	20
Sum:	276	204	240	72	228	186
Mean:	46.00	34.00	40.00	12.00	38.00	31.00

Matrix of Means

Method of Presentation (Factor B)	Type of Lecture (Factor A)			Average
	Physical Science (a_1)	Social Science (a_2)	History (a_3)	
Computer (b_1)	46.00	40.00	38.00	41.33
Standard (b_2)	34.00	12.00	31.00	25.67
Average	40.00	26.00	34.50	

These two sets of average effects are called the **main effects** of the two variables. The term *main effect* is not to be interpreted to mean "primary" or "important." Whether main effects are of any systematic interest to a researcher depends primarily on the *joint influence* of the two variables, which is revealed by an examination of the means within the body of the factorial matrix.

Consider, for example, the three means in the first row of the matrix (46.00, 40.00, and 38.00). These means reflect the effects of the three lectures for those students receiving the computer presentation. They show that the group receiving the lecture on physical science has surpassed the group receiving the lecture on social science by 6.00 words (46.00 − 40.00) and the group receiving the lecture on history by 8.00 words (46.00 − 38.00), and that social science has surpassed history by 2.00 words (40.00 − 38.00).

What about the corresponding manipulation under the standard presentation? The three means in the second row (34.00, 12.00, and 31.00) show a striking change in the effects of the three types of lecture, namely, a very substantially increased difference between physical science and social science (34.00 − 12.00 = 22.00 words) and a somewhat reduced difference between physical science and history (34.00 − 31.00 = 3.00 words). The difference between social science and history actually shows a reversal for the two methods of presentation, namely, a *marked inferiority* for social science with the standard presentation (a difference of 19.00 words) as opposed to the *small superiority* (2.00 words) found with the computer presentation. It appears, then, that the type of lecture produces different results with the two methods of presentation. It is for this reason, therefore, that the *average* effects of the type of lecture—reflected by the column marginal means—represent a distorted picture of the results of the actual factorial experiment revealed by the two sets of row means within the body of the matrix.

We reach a similar conclusion if we consider the difference between the two methods of presentation. While we find the computer method to be superior when we examine the row marginal means (41.33 − 25.67 = 15.66 words), the *magnitude* of the difference depends on the type of lecture. This is easily seen if we examine the pairs of row means column by column, within the body of the factorial matrix. More specifically, for physical science the difference is 12.00 words (46.00 − 34.00), for social science it is 28.00 words (40.00 − 12.00), and for history it is 7.00 words (38.00 − 31.00). Again, we see that the main effect of an independent variable is not representative of the results of the actual factorial experiment.

This type of situation—in which the effects of one of the independent variables depend on the levels of the other independent variable—is called **interaction**. Stated another way,

> **Interaction is present when the *pattern of differences* associated with either one of the independent variables changes as a function of the levels of the other independent variable.**

When this happens, the main effects do not yield a faithful picture of the results of a factorial experiment. You should note that this definition of interaction is technically correct only for population treatment means. In an actual experiment, which is assumed to be drawn randomly from these populations, the presence or absence of interaction is assessed by an *F* test designed for that purpose. We will discuss this statistical test shortly.

The way in which interactions operate can be seen by examining 2 × 2 designs. For example, suppose we have the following 2 × 2 layout with the cells labeled as shown:

$$A$$

	a_1	a_2
B b_1	μ_1	μ_2
b_2	μ_3	μ_4

Interaction is present when the effects of one independent variable depend on the levels of the other independent variable. Thus, an interaction is present when the difference between cell means μ_1 and μ_2, which represents the effect of factor A at one level of factor B (level b_1), *does not equal* the difference between cell means μ_3 and μ_4, which represents the effect of factor A at the other level of factor B (level b_2). That is,

$$\text{An interaction is present when } \mu_1 - \mu_2 \neq \mu_3 - \mu_4$$

(Again, as a reminder, the issue of "presence" or "absence" will be determined by an appropriate statistical test to account for differences that are due to chance.) Alternatively, we can define interaction in terms of the other independent variable: an interaction is present when the difference between cell means μ_1 and μ_3 (the effect of factor B at level a_1) does not equal the difference between cell means μ_2 and μ_4 (the effect of factor B at level a_2). That is,

$$\text{An interaction is present when } \mu_1 - \mu_3 \neq \mu_2 - \mu_4$$

Finally, another way of considering interaction is to look at the cell means on the *diagonals* of the 2×2 matrix. In this case, interaction is present when the sum of the cell means on one diagonal is not equal to the sum of the cell means on the other diagonal. That is,

$$\text{An interaction is present when } \mu_1 + \mu_4 \neq \mu_2 + \mu_3$$

All three ways of expressing interaction in a 2×2 matrix are equivalent.

Factorial designs and the assessment of interaction are valuable to any scientific enterprise, since they reveal how independent variables *combine* to influence behavior. More complex factorials in which three or more independent variables are manipulated yield extensive information on the interaction of independent variables. Ultimately, factorial designs can be used to provide a comprehensive picture of the behavior under study.

It is instructive to consider an example in which interaction is entirely absent. Consider the matrix of means in Table 13-3. First, you should note that we have chosen numbers for this example to duplicate exactly the two sets of marginal means from Table 13-2. What has changed in this example is the means within the matrix. Consider the pattern of differences revealed by the rows in Table 13-3;

Table 13-3
An Example of No Interaction

Method of Presentation (Factor B)	Type of Lecture (Factor A)			Average
	Physical Science (a_1)	Social Science (a_2)	History (a_3)	
Computer (b_1)	47.83	33.83	42.33	41.33
Standard (b_2)	32.17	18.17	26.67	25.67
Average	40.00	26.00	34.50	

for example, between the means for physical science and social science, *exactly the same difference* is found for the marginal means (40.00 − 26.00 = 14.00 words) as for the computer presentation (47.83 − 33.83 = 14.00) and the standard presentation (32.17 − 18.17 = 14.00). Similarly, the difference between the marginal means for physical science and history (40.00 − 34.50 = 5.50) is identical to the difference found between means for the computer presentation (47.83 − 42.33) and for the standard presentation (32.17 − 26.67). We find the same outcome if we examine the other independent variable. That is, the difference between the marginal means for computer and standard presentations is 41.33 − 25.67 = 15.66, and exactly the same difference is found for all three lectures (47.83 − 32.17, 33.83 − 18.17, and 42.33 − 26.67).

It is obvious in this case that the effects of the two independent variables, as reflected by the actual treatment means, are perfectly reflected in the marginal means, and that there is no interaction. In the case where interaction is absent, then, the influence of either variable is *not* dependent on the levels of the other.

The presence or absence of interaction is also effectively revealed by the kind of pictorial representation of the outcome of an experiment found in Fig. 13-1. The six treatment means from the original example (Table 13-2) are plotted in Fig. 13-1(a), while those from the second example (Table 13-3) are plotted in Fig. 13-1(b).[1] In each part of Fig. 13-1, the means for the levels of factor B are connected by separate lines. In such a graphic representation, interaction will be revealed by the presence of *nonparallel* lines, as in Fig. 13-1(a), while the absence of interaction results in *parallel* lines, as in Fig. 13-1(b). We will now turn to the statistical assessment of interaction (and of main effects), first by ANOVA and then by MRC.

[1] For convenience, we have treated factor A as a continuous independent variable, which of course it is not. This method of plotting data is commonly used by researchers, however, as it reveals the presence (or absence) of interaction quite clearly.

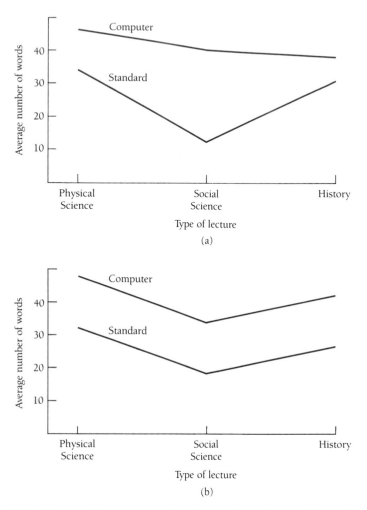

F i g u r e 13-1   Two possible outcomes of the factorial experiment. (a) Graph displaying an interaction between the two independent variables. (b) Graph indicating that there is no interaction.

13.2   THE FACTORIAL ANALYSIS: THE ANOVA APPROACH

The analysis of variance is based on a partitioning of the total sum of squares into a number of component sums of squares, each of which reflects useful sources of variation. We will begin by describing these sources; as in the single-factor design, they may be expressed quite simply as deviations from means.

Sources of Variability

For the single-factor design, the deviation of each observation Y from the grand mean $\bar{Y}_T$ was divided into two portions: the deviation of the observation from the relevant treatment mean $\bar{Y}_A$ and the deviation of that treatment mean from the grand mean. In symbols,

$$Y - \bar{Y}_T = (Y - \bar{Y}_A) + (\bar{Y}_A - \bar{Y}_T)$$

You will recall that the first deviation to the right of the equal sign formed the basis for the within-groups sum of squares, and the second deviation, the basis for the between-groups sum of squares.

We use analogous partitioning of the deviations with the two-factor design. The total deviation may again be divided into the deviation of each observation Y from the relevant treatment mean—in the two-factor design, $\bar{Y}_{AB}$, which represents the mean for a combination of levels of the two independent variables—and the deviation of this treatment mean from the grand mean. In symbols,

$$Y - \bar{Y}_T = (Y - \bar{Y}_{AB}) + (\bar{Y}_{AB} - \bar{Y}_T)$$

As in the single-factor design, these two components form the basis for the within-groups and between-groups sums of squares, respectively. The within-groups sum of squares, which continues to reflect unsystematic variability—the uncontrolled variability of subjects treated alike—will be used to form the error term in the analysis of variance. The between-groups sum of squares, on the other hand, reflects several sources of systematic variability, which we will now isolate by further partitioning.

In Sec. 13.1 we indicated that these sources of variability are the main or average effects of the two independent variables and the effects of interaction between the variables. For the two main effects, the deviations involve the relevant column and row marginal means, namely,

$$\bar{Y}_A - \bar{Y}_T \qquad \text{and} \qquad \bar{Y}_B - \bar{Y}_T$$

for A and B, respectively. The deviation representing interaction is derived from the deviations we have already specified. Interaction may be viewed as the variability between groups that is *not* attributed to either of the two main effects. Thus, the interaction deviation is given by

$$(\bar{Y}_{AB} - \bar{Y}_T) - (\bar{Y}_A - \bar{Y}_T) - (\bar{Y}_B - \bar{Y}_T)$$

which simplifies to

$$\bar{Y}_{AB} - \bar{Y}_A - \bar{Y}_B + \bar{Y}_T$$

when we remove the parentheses and cancel out two of the grand means. To summarize, the deviation of each observation from the grand mean may be divided into four components: a within-groups deviation, and deviations attributed to the main effects of A and B and to the $A \times B$ interaction; in symbols,

$$Y - \bar{Y}_T = (Y - \bar{Y}_{AB}) + (\bar{Y}_A - \bar{Y}_T) + (\bar{Y}_B - \bar{Y}_T) + (\bar{Y}_{AB} - \bar{Y}_A - \bar{Y}_B + \bar{Y}_T) \quad (13\text{-}1)$$

If the partitioning specified in Eq. (13-1) is accomplished for each observation and the deviations are squared and summed, the relationship between the components may be expressed in terms of sums of squares:

$$SS_T = SS_{S/AB} + SS_A + SS_B + SS_{A \times B} \quad (13\text{-}2)$$

Note that the within-groups sum of squares is designated by the subscript S/AB, which clearly specifies the nature of this sum of squares—the variability of subjects within their treatment groups.[2] Our next step is to examine the computational formulas for calculating these sums of squares.

Computational Formulas

You will recall from Chap. 6 that sums of squares based on particular deviations are easily formed by combining certain basic ratios in patterns that reflect the components of those deviations (see Sec. 6.2, under "Basic Ratios"). We will use Eq. (13-1) to perform a similar function for the present design.

Notation.   Lowercase letters are used to designate certain numbers relevant to a specific experiment:

a = the number of levels of factor A.
b = the number of levels of factor B.
s = the sample size (the number of subjects randomly assigned to each of the different combinations of the levels of the two independent variables).

We will refer to specific levels of independent variables and combinations of levels with lowercase letters and numerical subscripts. Levels of factor A will be designated a_1, a_2, etc., while levels of factor B will be designated b_1, b_2, etc. Specific treatment combinations are designated by the appropriate levels of the two variables. For example, a_1b_2 refers to the treatment group receiving level a_1 in conjunction with level b_2, and a_2b_1 to the pairing of levels a_2 and b_1.

---

[2] As in the single-factor design, the $SS_{S/AB}$ consists of the variability of subjects treated alike, pooled over all of the treatment groups. There are six treatment groups in the present example, which means that $SS_{S/AB}$ is the sum of the six within-group sums of squares.

All the necessary calculations involve various sums and subtotals, which we will represent with capital letters:

Y = the individual observation or score.

AB = the subtotal for any one of the treatment groups; when needed, subscripts are used to specify the particular levels of the two factors a given group has received. For example, $(AB)_{1,2}$ = the sum of the scores for subjects receiving the combination of levels a_1 and b_2, and $(AB)_{2,1}$, the sum associated with the combination of levels a_2 and b_1.

A = the sum of all the AB sums for a particular level of factor A. Subscripts, again, may be used to designate specific levels.

B = the analogous sum for factor B.

T = the grand sum of the scores.

The Preliminary Analysis.   The first step in the analysis usually consists of summing the Y scores and their squared values for each of the $(a)(b)$ treatment groups or combinations. The two resulting sets of sums may be used to calculate the usual descriptive statistics, the group means and the standard deviations. In addition, the two sets of sums are used to calculate the basic ratios entering into the calculation of the factorial sums of squares. The first set (the AB sums) are entered into a special matrix used to facilitate the calculation of basic ratios, while the second set (the sum of the squared Y scores) are simply combined to form one of the basic ratios required to calculate $SS_{S/AB}$ and SS_T.

The AB Matrix.   We continue the analysis by entering the AB treatment sums according to the levels of the two independent variables into what we call an **AB matrix**. An AB matrix based on the sums from Table 13-2 is presented in Table 13-4. The column marginal totals (A) are formed by adding the AB sums within the individual columns of the matrix, and the row marginal totals (B) are similarly

Table 13-4

AB Matrix of Sums

	a_1	a_2	a_3	Sum
b_1	276	240	228	744
b_2	204	72	186	462
Sum	480	312	414	1206

Table 13-5

Basic Ratios and Analysis Summary

Basic Ratios

$$[Y] = \Sigma\, Y^2 = 53^2 + 49^2 + \cdots + 30^2 + 20^2 = 46{,}194$$

$$[AB] = \frac{\Sigma\,(AB)^2}{s} = \frac{276^2 + 204^2 + \cdots + 228^2 + 186^2}{6} = \frac{267{,}156}{6} = 44{,}526.00$$

$$[A] = \frac{\Sigma\, A^2}{(b)\,(s)} = \frac{480^2 + 312^2 + 414^2}{(2)\,(6)} = \frac{499{,}140}{12} = 41{,}595.00$$

$$[B] = \frac{\Sigma\, B^2}{(a)\,(s)} = \frac{744^2 + 462^2}{(3)\,(6)} = \frac{766{,}980}{18} = 42{,}610.00$$

$$[T] = \frac{T^2}{(a)\,(b)\,(s)} = \frac{1206^2}{(3)\,(2)\,(6)} = \frac{1{,}454{,}436}{36} = 40{,}401.00$$

Summary of the Analysis

Source	SS	df	MS	F
A	$[A] - [T] = 1194.00$	2	597.00	10.74*
B	$[B] - [T] = 2209.00$	1	2209.00	39.73*
A × B	$[AB] - [A] - [B] + [T] = 722.00$	2	361.00	6.49*
S/AB	$[Y] - [AB] = 1668.00$	30	55.60	
Total	$[Y] - [T] = 5793.00$	35		

*$p < .01$.

formed within the rows. The grand total T is obtained by summing either set of marginal totals. We are now ready to calculate the basic ratios.

Basic Ratios.   Formulas for the five required basic ratios, of which four are based on the sums appearing in the AB matrix and the fifth on the individual Y scores, are presented in the upper portion of Table 13-5. The first basic ratio we will consider is simply the sum of all of the squared scores. The formula for this ratio and the expansion based on the data from Table 13-2 are presented in the first row of the table.

The other basic ratios are based on the different sets of sums appearing in the AB matrix. In all cases, the numerator is formed by squaring the entire set of relevant sums (either AB, A, B, or T) and then summing the squares. In symbols, the numerators are:

$$\Sigma\,(AB)^2, \quad \Sigma\, A^2, \quad \Sigma\, B^2, \quad T^2$$

Each denominator consists of the number of observations contributing to the squared terms in the corresponding numerator:

s for the basic ratio based on the AB sums
$(b)(s)$ for the basic ratio based on the A sums
$(a)(s)$ for the basic ratio based on the B sums
$(a)(b)(s)$ for the basic ratio based on T

(The denominator for the basic ratio, which is based on the individual scores, Y, is 1 and does not need to be specified.)

The completed ratios and relevant calculations performed on the data from the numerical example are found in the remaining rows of the upper portion of Table 13-5. For convenience, each ratio is uniquely coded in order to simplify computational formulas for the different sums of squares.

Sums of Squares.   The computational formulas for the sums of squares, which are presented in the bottom portion of Table 13-5, are specified in terms of the basic ratios. You will note that the patterns of combination are identical to the patterns of the components of the deviations upon which the sums of squares are based; see Eq. (13-1). The results of the operations are given in the column labeled SS. As an arithmetic check, you should verify that the sum of the component sums of squares equals the total sum of squares:

$$SS_T = SS_A + SS_B + SS_{A \times B} + SS_{S/AB}$$
$$= 1194.00 + 2209.00 + 722.00 + 1668.00$$
$$= 5793.00$$

The Analysis of Variance

The final steps in the calculations consist of determining the degrees of freedom for each source, calculating the mean squares, and forming the three F ratios for the effects analyzed. These steps are summarized in the remaining columns of the table.

Degrees of Freedom.   The degrees of freedom for any main effect are simply the number of levels for each factor less 1. In this case,

$$df_A = a - 1 = 3 - 1 = 2$$
$$df_B = b - 1 = 2 - 1 = 1$$

The degrees of freedom for the $A \times B$ interaction are found by multiplying the df's for the two main effects. That is,

$$df_{A \times B} = (df_A)(df_B) = (2)(1) = 2$$

The degrees of freedom for the within-groups source ($df_{S/AB}$) are found by pooling the df's for all the treatment groups. The degrees of freedom for any one group are $s - 1$. Since there are $(a)(b)$ groups,

$$df_{S/AB} = (a)(b)(s - 1)$$
$$= (3)(2)(6 - 1) = (6)(5) = 30$$

Finally, the degrees of freedom for SS_T are 1 less than the total number of observations, $(a)(b)(s)$; in symbols

$$df_T = (a)(b)(s) - 1$$
$$= (3)(2)(6) - 1 = 36 - 1 = 35$$

As a check, df_T should equal the sum of the component df's:

$$df_T = df_A + df_B + df_{A \times B} + df_{S/AB}$$
$$= 2 + 1 + 2 + 30 = 35$$

Mean Squares and F Ratios.   Any mean square is calculated by dividing a sum of squares by its degrees of freedom. The mean squares for the analysis are presented in Table 13-5. The F ratios are found by dividing the mean squares representing the factorial effects of interest by the within-groups mean square:

$$F = \frac{MS_{effect}}{MS_{S/AB}}$$

The F ratios for the two main effects and for the interaction are listed in the last column of the table.

The statistical hypotheses underlying the F tests are pairs of null and alternative hypotheses. For the main effects, the null hypothesis states that the population treatment means corresponding to the separate main effects are the same; the alternative hypothesis states that they are not all equal. For the interaction, the null hypothesis states that interaction effects are completely absent in the population; the alternative hypothesis states that they are not.

The logic behind these F tests is the same as that described for the single-factor design. Each numerator provides a population estimate of one of the three factorial effects *plus* error variance, while the denominator provides an estimate of error variance alone. Under the null hypothesis, both numerator and denominator mean squares reflect error variance and the expected value of each of the three F ratios is approximately 1.0. A significant F indicates that the null hypothesis is untenable and that we should accept the alternative hypothesis that a particular factorial effect—A main effect, B main effect, or interaction—is present.

We evaluate each null hypothesis by comparing the value of F we calculate and the critical value found in Table A-1, which, as usual, is determined by the df's associated with the numerator and denominator terms and the significance level chosen for the statistical tests. At $\alpha = .05$, the critical value for the A main effect and the $A \times B$ interaction is $F(2, 30) = 3.32$ and that for the B main effect is $F(1, 30) = 4.17$. An inspection of values in Table 13-5 indicates that all three factorial effects are significant. This means that:

1. There are differences overall among the three types of lecture.
2. There are differences overall between the two methods of presentation.
3. The differences among the three types of lecture depend on the method of presentation.

13.3   THE FACTORIAL ANALYSIS: THE MRC APPROACH

The identical statistical outcomes found with ANOVA for the two-factor design can be obtained with MRC. The researcher's critical step is in establishing vectors that capture the variation in Y that is of specific interest. The sources of this variation are, of course, the same sources that we normally isolate and study in an analysis of variance. We will consider the coding process first and then show how the factorial effects may be evaluated with MRC.

Coding of Vectors

Contrast coding is easily adapted to the analysis of a factorial experiment. The strategy we will follow is to establish sets of vectors for each of the two main effects and then use these vectors to define the vectors for the interaction.[3]

Coding Main Effects.   We code each main effect by disregarding the levels of the other independent variable (or main effect) and then treating the main effect of interest as if it represented an independent variable in a *single*-factor design. The main effect of factor A, for example, requires two vectors ($df_A = 2$) to capture this variation, since there are three levels and we need $a - 1$ vectors in such a

---

[3] The method we recommend is not the only way to extract information about the main effects and interaction. On the other hand, its advantage, as you will see, is the ease with which the factorial analysis can be accomplished and the fact that it focuses on the sorts of meaningful questions we will consider in subsequent chapters.

situation. One possible code matrix is as follows:

	a_1	a_2	a_3
Vector 1	$+1$	-1	0
Vector 2	$+1$	$+1$	-2

The two sets of coefficients we have chosen consist of two meaningful comparisons, one between physical science and social science $(+1, -1, 0)$ and the other between the two combined science groups and history $(+1, +1, -2)$. These coefficients are assigned to subjects according to the level of factor A they receive, with no consideration given to the levels of the other independent variable (factor B). Thus for the first vector, which we label $A1$,

$+1$ is assigned to all subjects receiving the physical science lecture (subjects in a_1b_1 and a_1b_2).

-1 is assigned to all subjects receiving the social science lecture (a_2b_1 and a_2b_2).

0 is assigned to all subjects receiving the history lecture (a_3b_1 and a_3b_2).

The second A vector ($A2$) is created the same way but with the coefficients $+1$, $+1$, and -2 assigned to all subjects receiving the physical science, the social-science, and the history lecture, respectively.

The assignment is illustrated in the first two vector columns listed in Table 13-6. Again, to reiterate how these coefficients represent information, subject 1 has values of $+1$ and $+1$, subject 13 has values of -1 and $+1$, and subject 25 has values of 0 and -2. These pairs of values for each subject distinguish the three levels of the A variable.

It is important to note that *any* of the coding schemes presented for single-factor designs in Chap. 9 can be used to represent the main effect of factor A. That is, the vectors do not need to be contrast-coded; nor do they need to be orthogonal, as they are in the present instance (see Table 10-3 for an example with nonorthogonal comparisons) or to represent meaningful single-df comparisons (see Sec. 10.2 for an example with dummy coding). The MRC analysis will always provide exactly the same information about the A main effect as long as the coding scheme consists of $a - 1$ vectors that provide unique patterns differentiating the levels of factor A (note that the number of vectors equals the df for the factor). For the vector codes, we prefer to use coefficients that represent meaningful comparisons, because they provide information that will be useful in the detailed analysis of factorial designs to be discussed in Chaps. 14 and 15.

Table 13-6
An Example of the Orthogonal Coding of Factorial Effects

Subject			Dependent Variable Y	(1) A1	(2) A2	(3) B1	(4) A1B1	(5) A2B1
a_1	b_1	1	53	1	1	1	1	1
		2	49	1	1	1	1	1
		3	47	1	1	1	1	1
		4	42	1	1	1	1	1
		5	51	1	1	1	1	1
		6	34	1	1	1	1	1
	b_2	7	44	1	1	-1	-1	-1
		8	48	1	1	-1	-1	-1
		9	35	1	1	-1	-1	-1
		10	18	1	1	-1	-1	-1
		11	32	1	1	-1	-1	-1
		12	27	1	1	-1	-1	-1
a_2	b_1	13	47	-1	1	1	-1	1
		14	42	-1	1	1	-1	1
		15	39	-1	1	1	-1	1
		16	37	-1	1	1	-1	1
		17	42	-1	1	1	-1	1
		18	33	-1	1	1	-1	1
	b_2	19	13	-1	1	-1	1	-1
		20	16	-1	1	-1	1	-1
		21	16	-1	1	-1	1	-1
		22	10	-1	1	-1	1	-1
		23	11	-1	1	-1	1	-1
		24	6	1	1	-1	1	-1
a_3	b_1	25	45	0	-2	1	0	-2
		26	41	0	-2	1	0	-2
		27	38	0	-2	1	0	-2
		28	36	0	-2	1	0	-2
		29	35	0	-2	1	0	-2
		30	33	0	-2	1	0	-2
	b_2	31	46	0	-2	-1	0	2
		32	40	0	-2	-1	0	2
		33	29	0	-2	-1	0	2
		34	21	0	-2	-1	0	2
		35	30	0	-2	-1	0	2
		36	20	0	-2	-1	0	2
		r:		.4506	$-.0557$	.6175	$-.2575$	.2415
		r^2:		.2030	.0031	.3813	.0663	.0583

The main effect of factor B is coded in a similar fashion, but, again, *without* consideration of how the A effect is coded. That is, we construct a code matrix that assigns the same coefficient to *all* subjects receiving a particular level of factor B, disregarding the A treatment they have received. In the present example, only one vector ($B1$) is required, since there are only two levels of B and $df_B = 1$. The code matrix is as follows:

	b_1	b_2
Vector 1	$+1$	-1

For this vector, we use $+1$ and -1 as the coefficients for levels b_1 and b_2, respectively. Specifically,

> $+1$ is assigned to all subjects receiving the computer presentation (subjects in a_1b_1, a_2b_1, and a_3b_1).
> -1 is assigned to all subjects receiving the lecture (a_1b_2, a_2b_2, and a_3b_2).

This assignment of values is illustrated in the third vector column in Table 13-6.

Coding the Interaction.   In order to code the interaction, we need a scheme that together with the vectors representing the two main effects will identify each treatment cell and distinguish it from the others. The easiest way to accomplish this goal is to apply the rule that the number of vectors needed to express an effect is equal to the number of degrees of freedom for that effect. From ANOVA, we know that the degrees of freedom for the $A \times B$ interaction are $df_{A \times B} = (df_A)(df_B)$; and from previous chapters, we know that df are identical for MRC and ANOVA effects. For the numerical example, we know that $df_{A \times B} = 2$ vectors will be needed to represent interaction in this example. An easy way to construct these vectors is by multiplying each vector representing the A main effect by each vector representing the B main effect. In the present case, then, there are two interaction vectors, one formed by multiplying $A1$ and $B1$ ($A1B1$) and the other by multiplying $A2$ and $B1$ ($A2B1$). The results of these two multiplications are presented in the last two vector columns in Table 13-6. If this process is done by a computer, all that is needed to create the interaction vectors is a command to multiply the appropriate codes for the main effects. The computer will carry out the arithmetic operations and create the interaction vectors for the analysis.

Interaction vectors will be important in the remainder of this book, and so we illustrate the process more closely by presenting the codes for subjects 1, 7, 13, 19, 25, and 31 in Table 13-6. These individual subjects represent each of the

Table 13-7
Calculating the Interaction Vectors

Subject Number	Treatment Condition	Vector 4				Vector 5			
		A1	×	B1	= A1B1	A2	×	B1	= A2B1
1	a_1b_1	+1	×	+1	= +1	+1	×	+1	= +1
7	a_1b_2	+1	×	−1	= −1	+1	×	−1	= −1
13	a_2b_1	−1	×	+1	= −1	+1	×	+1	= +1
19	a_2b_2	−1	×	−1	= +1	+1	×	−1	= −1
25	a_3b_1	0	×	+1	= 0	−2	×	+1	= −2
31	a_3b_2	0	×	−1	= 0	−2	×	−1	= +2

six treatment combinations. We have indicated that interaction vector A1B1 (vector 4) is created by multiplying one of the vectors representing the A main effect (A1) by the single vector B1 representing the B main effect. These calculations are presented under "Vector 4" in Table 13-7. Similarly, interaction vector A2B1 (vector 5) is created by multiplying the other vector representing the A main effect (A2) by the vector representing the B main effect. These calculations are found under "Vector 5" in Table 13-7.

We present a final point about interaction codes here, a point that we explore in greater detail in Chap. 15. In previous chapters, we indicated that codes within a vector represent a meaningful comparison. The same is true here. Examine vector 4 in Table 13-6. Subjects in a_1b_1 (subjects 1 through 6) and a_2b_2 (subjects 19 through 24) have the same value (+1); likewise, subjects in a_1b_2 and a_2b_1 have the same value (−1). (We will ignore subjects in a_3b_1 and a_3b_2, since they have 0s in vector 4.) These four treatment conditions and their codes yield the following matrix:

	a_1	a_2
b_1	(1) +1	(2) −1
b_2	(3) −1	(4) +1

By creating this matrix, we are showing that vector 4 represents the comparison of subjects in one diagonal (cells 1 and 4) with subjects in the other diagonal (cells 2 and 3). But this is exactly what an interaction is. Recall from Sec. 13.1

that if the combined means for cells 1 and 4 equal the combined means for cells 2 and 3, then there is *no* interaction. As we indicated there, expressing interaction in terms of the combined diagonal means is equivalent to expressing interaction in terms of the difference between the means for cells 1 and 2 versus the difference between the means for cells 3 and 4. The point of this is that each of the interaction vectors in Table 13-6 (vectors 4 and 5) contains information about some particular interaction comparison.

The MRC Analysis

Forming Sets of Multiple Correlations.   We must introduce one new idea that lies behind the MRC analysis of the two-factor design, namely, the concept of *sets of vectors* and the multiple correlation between Y and the vectors in a set ($R_{Y.set}$). In the present case, we will define a set of vectors for each source of variability that is of interest to us in the overall analysis of our factorial experiment. We will calculate:

> $R_{Y.A}^2$, which is based on the *set* of vectors representing the A main effect ($A1$ and $A2$), or vectors 1 and 2
>
> $R_{Y.B}^2$, which is based on the *set* of vectors representing the B main effect ($B1$), or vector 3
>
> $R_{Y.A \times B}^2$, which is based on the *set* of vectors representing the $A \times B$ interaction ($A1B1$ and $A2B1$), or vectors 4 and 5

One more $R_{Y.set}^2$ is required to conduct the analysis, namely, the multiple correlation between Y and a set consisting of *all* the vectors required to distinguish among the different treatment conditions and combinations. In the two-factor case, the number of vectors in this set is $(a)(b) - 1$, which in the present case represents the five vectors 1 through 5. This squared multiple correlation coefficient for the set of five vectors, which we have referred to as $R_{Y.max.}^2$, is used to calculate the error term, $1 - R_{Y.max.}^2$, or the variation in Y *not* accounted for by group differences—that is, the experimental manipulations. This *residual variation* will form the basis for the error term, just as you would suspect from your knowledge of the analysis of the single-factor design. Since we have a completely randomized factorial design with an equal number of subjects in each condition, the sets of vectors are orthogonal and $R_{Y.max.}^2$ can be obtained by adding the squared multiple correlation coefficients for the three effect sets mentioned above.

The Statistical Analysis.   The next step is to calculate these four $R_{Y.set}^2$'s. If you are using a computer, you could instruct the program to calculate an R^2 for each of the four sets of vectors and then use the results to complete the analysis. In the present example, we can take advantage of the fact that all five vectors in Table 13-6 are *mutually orthogonal*, which greatly simplifies the calculations and permits hand calculation by Eq. (10-7).[4] That is, we can calculate these values simply by summing the relevant zero-order correlation coefficients.

The squared zero-order correlations between Y and the vector values are given in Table 13-6 at the bottom of the vector columns. For simplicity, we will designate these by column number; for example, r_{Y1}^2 refers to the squared zero-order correlation between Y and $A1$, r_{Y2}^2 to the squared correlation between Y and $A2$, and so on. We can now represent the calculations as follows:

$$R_{Y.A}^2 = r_{Y1}^2 + r_{Y2}^2$$
$$= .2030 + .0031 = .2061$$

$$R_{Y.B}^2 = r_{Y3}^2 = .3813$$

$$R_{Y.A \times B}^2 = r_{Y4}^2 + r_{Y5}^2$$
$$= .0663 + .0583 = .1246$$

$$R_{Y.max.}^2 = r_{Y1}^2 + r_{Y2}^2 + r_{Y3}^2 + r_{Y4}^2 + r_{Y5}^2$$
$$= .2030 + .0031 + .3813 + .0663 + .0583 = .7120$$

The first three quantities represent the proportion of variability in Y that is associated with the A main effect, the B main effect, and the $A \times B$ interaction, respectively. The final quantity, which represents the proportion of Y variability associated with *all* treatment variation, is used to calculate the error term. That is,

$$R_{res.}^2 = 1 - R_{Y.max.}^2 = 1 - .7120 = .2880$$

is the proportion of Y variability that represents *residual* variation, variation that is not due to the systematic differences introduced by the experimental manipulations. The four proportions are entered in the second column of Table 13-8.

The remainder of the analysis exactly parallels the analysis of variance. From an MRC perspective, the degrees of freedom are determined by the number of vectors required to specify a particular source of variability. From Table 13-6, we can see that these are 2, 1, and 2 for A, B, and $A \times B$, respectively. The degrees of freedom for the S/AB source are given by the general formula for a residual source of variation,

$$df_{res.} = df_{S/AB} = N - k - 1 \tag{13-3}$$

---

[4] Each vector in Table 13-6 is orthogonal to all of the others, a fact that you might wish to verify by showing that the sum of the cross-products of all pairs of vectors is zero. We will illustrate the calculations when nonorthogonal vectors are used instead of mutually orthogonal ones later in this section.

Table 13-8
Summary of the MRC

Source	R^2	df	Mean R^2	F
A	.2061	2	.1031	10.74*
B	.3813	1	.3813	39.72*
A × B	.1246	2	.0623	6.49*
S/AB	.2880	30	.0096	
Total	1.0000	35		

*$p < .01$.

where N is the total number of observations and k is the number of vectors used to specify the $R^2_{Y.max.}$ upon which the residual source is based. In this design,

$$N = (a)(b)(s) = (3)(2)(6) = 36$$
$$k = (a)(b) - 1 = (3)(2) - 1 = 5$$

Substituting in Eq. (13-3), we find that

$$df_{S/AB} = 36 - 5 - 1 = 30$$

These degrees of freedom are identical to those listed in Table 13-5.

The F ratio for each factorial effect is determined by adapting Eq. (10-8). To test the three effects, we use the following:

$$F_A = \frac{R^2_{Y.A}/df_A}{(1 - R^2_{Y.max.})/(N - k - 1)}$$

$$F_B = \frac{R^2_{Y.B}/df_B}{(1 - R^2_{Y.max.})/(N - k - 1)}$$

$$F_{A \times B} = \frac{R^2_{Y.A \times B}/df_{A \times B}}{(1 - R^2_{Y.max.})/(N - k - 1)}$$

These F's are presented in Table 13-8. Except for slight rounding error, the resulting F's are identical to those found with the corresponding analysis of variance (see Table 13-5).

Comparison with ANOVA. You have already seen that the same statistical outcomes are obtained with ANOVA and MRC. Moreover, we can generate one analysis from the other by applying some simple arithmetic manipulations. More specifically, as indicated in Sec. 10.3, the sums of squares from ANOVA can be transformed into R^2's simply by dividing each sum of squares by the total sum of squares. On the basis of the SS data in Table 13-5, we find the following:

$$R^2_{Y.A} = \frac{SS_A}{SS_T} = \frac{1194.00}{5793.00} = .2061$$

$$R^2_{Y.B} = \frac{SS_B}{SS_T} = \frac{2209.00}{5793.00} = .3813$$

$$R^2_{Y.A \times B} = \frac{SS_{A \times B}}{SS_T} = \frac{722.00}{5793.00} = .1246$$

$$R^2_{Y.S/AB} = \frac{SS_{S/A}}{SS_T} = \frac{1668.00}{5793.00} = .2879$$

Within the bounds of rounding error, these values are the same as those given in Table 13-8.

Likewise, the R^2's from the MRC analysis may be converted to corresponding sums of squares simply by multiplying each R^2 by SS_Y (the total sum of squares):

$$SS_A = (R^2_{Y.A})(SS_Y) = (.2061)(5793.00) = 1193.94$$

$$SS_B = (R^2_{Y.B})(SS_Y) = (.3813)(5793.00) = 2208.87$$

$$SS_{A \times B} = (R^2_{Y.A \times B})(SS_Y) = (.1246)(5793.00) = 721.81$$

$$SS_{S/AB} = (R^2_{Y.S/AB})(SS_Y) = (.2880)(5793.00) = 1668.38$$

Again, except for rounding errors, these values equal those presented in Table 13-5.

An Example with Nonorthogonal Vectors

We illustrated the calculation of the critical $R^2_{Y.set}$'s with mutually orthogonal vector sets so that readers with only hand calculators at their disposal would be able to conduct the analysis. We do not suggest that calculations be done by hand when computers are readily available! We will now demonstrate that the MRC analysis is not dependent on the use of orthogonal vectors. We will use two nonorthogonal comparisons as vectors to define the A main effect. (If df_B were greater than 1, we could represent the B main effect with nonorthogonal vectors as well.) Because interaction vectors are formed by cross-multiplying the A and B vectors, the nonorthogonality of the two A vectors also extends to the interaction vectors. On the other hand, the nature of the factorial design guarantees that the *different* $R^2_{Y.set}$'s (that is, $R^2_{Y.A}$, $R^2_{Y.B}$, and $R^2_{Y.A \times B}$) will remain independent of each other, regardless of the orthogonality of the vectors used to define a main effect. That is, given the nature of the experimental design, there is no relationship between the A, B, and $A \times B$ effects.

To illustrate the analysis, let us use the following code matrix:

	a_1	a_2	a_3
Vector 1	$+1$	-1	0
Vector 2	0	$+1$	-1

The first vector representing the A main effect consists of a comparison between physical science and social science $(+1, -1, 0)$, while the second vector consists of a comparison between social science and history $(0, +1, -1)$. These two comparisons are not orthogonal, because our rule for orthogonality, Eq. (11-7), yields a value other than zero; that is,

$$\Sigma \, (c_i)(c_i') = (+1)(0) + (-1)(+1) + (0)(-1) = -1$$

Also, we can show nonorthogonality because the zero-order correlation coefficient between these two vectors, r_{12}, equals $-.5$. Nevertheless, we will use the above code matrix. The resulting five vectors are shown in Table 13-9. Note that the two interaction vectors are formed by multiplying values for each A vector by corresponding values for the single B vector. These two vectors are presented in the last two columns of Table 13-9. A quick inspection of the values for the two interaction vectors reveals that they are not orthogonal; that is,

$$\begin{aligned}
\Sigma \, (c_i)(c_i') &= (+1)(0) + (-1)(0) + (-1)(+1) + (+1)(-1) \\
&\quad + (0)(-1) + (0)(+1) \\
&= -2
\end{aligned}$$

The zero-order correlation coefficient between these two vectors is $r_{45} = -.5$.

If you were using a computer, you would now instruct the program to calculate the same four R^2's we calculated previously, namely,

$R^2_{Y.A}$ (based on vectors 1 and 2)
$R^2_{Y.B}$ (based on vector 3)
$R^2_{Y \times B}$ (based on vectors 4 and 5)
$R^2_{Y.max.}$ (based on all five vectors)

As you have seen already, these R^2's provide the information needed to complete the two-factor analysis. Since $R^2_{Y.A}$ and $R^2_{Y.A \times B}$ involve two vectors each, we can use Eq. (10-2) to illustrate the calculations. (If more than two vectors were needed to define these sets, we would have to turn to a computer for the calculations.)

TABLE 13-9
Nonorthogonal Coding of Factorial Effects

		Subject	Dependent Variable Y	Vectors				
				(1) $A1$	(2) $A2$	(3) $B1$	(4) $A1B1$	(5) $A2B1$
a_1	b_1	1	53	1	0	1	1	0
		2	49	1	0	1	1	0
		3	47	1	0	1	1	0
		4	42	1	0	1	1	0
		5	51	1	0	1	1	0
		6	34	1	0	1	1	0
	b_2	7	44	1	0	−1	−1	0
		8	48	1	0	−1	−1	0
		9	35	1	0	−1	−1	0
		10	18	1	0	−1	−1	0
		11	32	1	0	−1	−1	0
		12	27	1	0	−1	−1	0
a_2	b_1	13	47	−1	1	1	−1	1
		14	42	−1	1	1	−1	1
		15	39	−1	1	1	−1	1
		16	37	−1	1	1	−1	1
		17	42	−1	1	1	−1	1
		18	33	−1	1	1	−1	1
	b_2	19	13	−1	1	−1	1	−1
		20	16	−1	1	−1	1	1
		21	16	−1	1	−1	1	−1
		22	10	−1	1	−1	1	−1
		23	11	−1	1	−1	1	1
		24	6	−1	1	−1	1	−1
a_3	b_1	25	45	0	−1	1	0	−1
		26	41	0	−1	1	0	−1
		27	38	0	−1	1	0	−1
		28	36	0	−1	1	0	−1
		29	35	0	−1	1	0	−1
		30	33	0	−1	1	0	−1
	b_2	31	46	0	−1	−1	0	1
		32	40	0	−1	−1	0	1
		33	29	0	−1	−1	0	1
		34	21	0	−1	−1	0	1
		35	30	0	−1	−1	0	1
		36	20	0	−1	−1	0	1
			r:	.4506	−.2736	.6175	−.2575	.3379
			r^2:	.2030	.0749	.3813	.0663	.1142

For the A main effect,

$$R_{Y.A}^2 = \frac{r_{Y1}^2 + r_{Y2}^2 - 2r_{Y1}r_{Y2}r_{12}}{1 - r_{12}^2}$$

$$= \frac{(.4506)^2 + (-.2736)^2 - (2)(.4506)(-.2736)(-.5000)}{1 - (-.5000)^2}$$

$$= \frac{.2030 + .0749 - .1233}{1 - .2500} = \frac{.1546}{.7500} = .2061$$

which is identical to the value presented in Table 13-8 based on orthogonal vectors. For the $A \times B$ interaction,

$$R_{Y.A \times B}^2 = \frac{r_{Y4}^2 + r_{Y5}^2 - 2r_{Y4}r_{Y5}r_{45}}{1 - r_{45}^2}$$

$$= \frac{(-.2575)^2 + (.3379)^2 - (2)(-.2575)(.3379)(-.5000)}{1 - (-.5000)^2}$$

$$= \frac{.0663 + .1142 - .0870}{1 - .2500} = \frac{.0935}{.7500} = .1247$$

which is also identical, within rounding error, to the value in Table 13-8.

The same point would be made if the example included more levels of both independent variables, although we would have to use a computer to calculate the respective R^2's rather than bask in the simplicity of Eq. (10-2), which applies only to two vectors. What this shows, again, is that the type of code for a particular variable does *not* change the R^2 for that variable. Whether we use orthogonal or nonorthogonal vectors (or even dummy coding) for the A effects, we will obtain the same result. (Since the R^2's do not change, the F ratios obviously do not change.)

Comment

We emphasize again that your choice of vectors should be based on meaningful single-*df* comparisons, which will provide useful information in subsequent analyses. If you have to add one or more relatively meaningless comparisons to constitute a maximum set of vectors for either the A or the B main effect, there is no problem, since the additional vectors serve their purpose in extracting variation due to the main effects and to the interaction and thus in deriving the error term; they can be ignored in later analyses that *do* focus on meaningful comparisons. (We discuss such analyses in the next two chapters.)

However, it will generally not be the case that the number of meaningful comparisons will be less than the number of vectors needed to calculate $R_{Y.max.}^2$. Rather, the number of meaningful comparisons will most likely be greater than the required number of vectors. Consequently, we suggest that at the outset you establish all your meaningful comparisons for each factor. For example, for the *A* factor in our experiment, we can construct the following code matrix, which contains all the meaningful questions in which we are interested:

	a_1	a_2	a_3
Vector 1	$+1$	-1	0
Vector 2	$+1$	$+1$	-2
Vector 3	$+1$	0	-1
Vector 4	0	$+1$	-1

Once this matrix is established, we choose any two vectors to use in our analysis (to calculate $R^2_{Y.A}$ and to contribute to the calculation of the interaction vectors and $R^2_{Y.max.}$), but at the same time we instruct the computer to calculate $r^2_{comp.}$ for the remaining comparisons (vectors). We will discuss the analysis of single-*df* comparisons for both MRC and ANOVA in Chaps. 14 and 15.

Finally, if we want to determine the mean of any of the treatment conditions, we compute the regression equation associated with the $R^2_{Y.max.}$ and insert into the equation the codes that represent the particular treatment condition. For the present example, as shown in Table 13-6, the regression equation is

$$Y' = a + (b_1)(X_1) + (b_2)(X_2) + (b_3)(X_3) + (b_4)(X_4) + (b_5)(X_5)$$
$$= 33.50 + (7.00)(X_1) + (-.50)(X_2) + (7.83)(X_3)$$
$$+ (-4.00)(X_4) + (2.17)(X_5)$$

More specifically, from Table 13-6, we see that the vector codes yield the following layout for the subjects in the six conditions:

Vectors

Cell	(1)	(2)	(3)	(4)	(5)
a_1b_1	$+1$	$+1$	$+1$	$+1$	$+1$
a_1b_2	$+1$	$+1$	-1	-1	-1
a_2b_1	-1	$+1$	$+1$	-1	$+1$
a_2b_2	-1	$+1$	-1	$+1$	-1
a_3b_1	0	-2	$+1$	0	-2
a_3b_2	0	-2	-1	0	$+2$

That is, subjects in the a_1b_2 condition are represented by the five values $+1$, $+1$, -1, -1, and -1. To illustrate, the calculation for the mean for cell a_1b_2 is as follows:

$$\begin{aligned}
\bar{Y}_{A_1B_2} &= 33.50 + (7.00)(+1) + (-.50)(+1) + (7.83)(-1) \\
&\quad + (-4.00)(-1) + (2.17)(-1) \\
&= 33.50 + 7.00 - .50 - 7.83 + 4.00 - 2.17 = 34.00
\end{aligned}$$

As another example, consider the subjects in cell a_3b_2. Application of the code values in the regression equation given above yields

$$\begin{aligned}
\bar{Y}_{A_3B_2} &= 33.50 + (7.00)(0) + (-.50)(-2) + (7.83)(-1) \\
&\quad + (-4.00)(0) + (2.17)(+2) \\
&= 33.50 + 0.00 + 1.00 - 7.83 + 0.00 + 4.34 = 31.01
\end{aligned}$$

which is within rounding error of 31.00, the treatment mean given in Table 13-2.[5]

13.4 SUMMARY

In this chapter, we introduced the factorial design, a design that permits the simultaneous manipulation of two independent variables. This is accomplished by including all possible combinations of the levels of the two variables in a single experiment. A factorial design can be thought of as a set of single-factor experiments in which the same independent variable is manipulated, but where each single-factor experiment is conducted with different levels of the other independent variable. We use this arrangement to determine whether or not the effects of the first independent variable are the same for all the single-factor experiments. If it appears that the effects are not all the same, an *interaction* is said to be present, and we focus our efforts on analyses designed to identify the sources of the differences. On the other hand, if the effects seem to be roughly the same, no interaction is said to be present, and we shift our attention to an analysis of the *main effects* of the two independent variables—the effects of each of the independent variables averaged over all levels of the other.

   In the overall analysis of the factorial design, we isolate the sources of systematic variation associated with the two independent variables (that is, their main effects and their interaction) and compare the systematic variation with the un-

---

[5] Rounding error can be reduced by carrying out the calculations to four decimal places and rounding the final value.

systematic, or residual, variation that is present in the experiment (as it is in any experiment). With ANOVA, the focus is on sums of squares that are based on different sets of deviations from means. With MRC, the focus is on $R^2_{Y.set}$'s that are based on vectors selected to represent different aspects of the treatment effects. The statistical tests conducted with the two analysis procedures yield identical F's.

13.5 EXERCISES

1. In Chap. 10, Problem 1, we introduced an experiment on the effects of verbal reinforcement on the performance of children on a simple motor-coordination task. Now, we extend that experiment by introducing a second factor B, which consists of a group of children (b_1) versus a group of adults (b_2). The data are as follows:

	Praise (a_1)	Reproof (a_2)	None (a_3)
	4	7	7
	7	6	3
	5	9	7
Children (b_1)	3	7	5
	6	8	7
	4	6	8
	6	7	5
	16	13	18
	15	18	12
	20	14	16
Adult (b_2)	16	12	15
	19	16	17
	16	13	17
	16	15	14

a. Analyze the data with ANOVA.
b. Plot the cell means.
c. Analyze the data with MRC.

14

The Analysis of Main Effects
and Simple Effects

· · ·

213

In Chap. 13, you saw how you could study the influence of two independent variables that were being manipulated simultaneously in the context of a single experimental design. The critical question surrounding the analysis of this joint manipulation is whether the two independent variables *interact* to influence behavior. If they do, you need to examine the influence of each independent variable with the specific levels of the other variable clearly in mind. On the other hand, if they do not interact, you may examine the influence of either variable without reference to the other independent variable. The analyses covered in Chap. 13—the evaluation of the two main effects and that of the interaction—assess overall or *omnibus* effects: they indicate only whether a main effect or an interaction is present, not what is responsible for the significant *F*.

You will recall that we faced a similar problem with the omnibus test in the analysis of the single-factor design. The solution then was to locate meaningful differences between means. We look for the same sort of information with the factorial design, except that the procedures are more complicated, and which procedures we use depends on whether significant interaction is present. If there is a significant interaction, for example, we tend to focus our attention on the *individual treatment means* within the body of the *AB* matrix, our goal being to establish how the effects of one independent variable *change* with the different levels of the other independent variable. Without a significant interaction, we turn instead to the *marginal means*—in effect, treating the design as two separate *single*-factor experiments.

In Sec. 14.1 we will consider significant main effects, not because they are more important, but because the analysis is easily generalized from the single-factor design. The analysis of interaction, which we consider in Secs. 14.2 through 14.4 and in Chap. 15, takes two forms. The first consists of a systematic examination of the data row by row or column by column in the *AB* matrix in an attempt to establish the nature of the interaction. This approach is called **analysis of the simple effects** of an interaction. It involves an examination of the effects of *one* of the independent variables while the other independent variable is held constant. For example, we would look at the differences in vocabulary scores for the different types of lectures, but only under one method of presentation at a time—the computer *or* the standard method. The second approach, which we will consider in Chap. 15, consists of an examination of smaller factorial designs constructed from the larger design in order to express interaction in terms of more focused manipulations. We will call this approach **analysis of interaction comparisons**. In essence, this analysis takes a multilevel factorial design (e.g., a 4 × 3 design) and reduces it ideally to a number of 2 × 2 designs. Both types of analyses are useful, and we need to master both in order to understand fully the wealth of information available from the results of a factorial experiment.

14.1 DETAILED ANALYSIS OF MAIN EFFECTS

If the interaction is not significant, the design becomes for all practical purposes *two* single-factor designs. That is, we examine each factor alone—looking at the differences among the *row marginal means* and the differences among the *column marginal means* separately—without reference to the levels of the other independent variable. Only main effects associated with more than 1 *df* are candidates for further analysis, of course, since a main effect with 1 *df* is already a difference between two marginal means. In our present example, then, the *B* main effect, consisting of two levels and based on 1 *df*, reflects the difference between computer presentation and the standard presentation; no further analysis is possible. The *A* main effect, consisting of three levels and based on 2 *df*, reflects the undifferentiated effects of the three different lectures; additional analyses are necessary to determine which comparisons between treatments are useful and interesting.

The ANOVA Approach

The analysis under ANOVA consists of a simple extension of the procedures described for the single-factor design. We first express the comparison $(\hat{\psi}_A)$, which is usually a difference between two means, in terms of coefficients c_i. That is,

$$\hat{\psi}_A = \Sigma \ (c_i)(\bar{Y}_{A_i}) \tag{14-1}$$

This comparison is then combined with other quantities to calculate the sum of squares associated with it:

$$SS_{A_{comp.}} = \frac{(b)(s)(\hat{\psi}_A)^2}{\Sigma \ (c_i)^2} \tag{14-2}$$

This formula is identical to Eq. (11-4), the formula for the single-factor design, except for the insertion of *b* in the numerator to reflect the number of observations contributing to each mean. More specifically, there were *s* observations associated with each $\bar{Y}_A$ in the single-factor design, and there are $(b)(s)$ observations associated with each of the means contributing to the main effect of factor *A* in the two-factor design. The error term for these single-*df* comparisons is the within-groups error term from the overall analysis, $MS_{S/AB}$. We use this error term because it captures *Y* variability based on the full set of available data.

We will use the data from Chap. 13 for a numerical example. The marginal means are 40.00, 26.00, and 34.50 for the lectures on physical science, social science, and history, respectively. Suppose we wish to compare the average of the means for the two science lectures with the mean for the history lecture. For this comparison, we will use the coefficients $(+\frac{1}{2}, +\frac{1}{2}, -1)$. With these coefficients, we can calculate the difference between the combined science mean and the history mean:

$$\hat{\psi}_A = (+\tfrac{1}{2})(40.00) + (+\tfrac{1}{2})(26.00) + (-1)(34.50)$$
$$= 33.00 - 34.50 = -1.50$$

This value is substituted in Eq. (14-2) to obtain

$$SS_{A_{comp.}} = \frac{(2)(6)(-1.50)^2}{(+\tfrac{1}{2})^2 + (+\tfrac{1}{2})^2 + (-1)^2}$$
$$= \frac{27.00}{1.50} = 18.00$$

Since this sum of squares is based on 1 df, $MS_{A_{comp.}} = 18.00$. The F ratio is:

$$F = \frac{MS_{A_{comp.}}}{MS_{S/AB}}$$

From Table 13-5, we find that $MS_{S/AB} = 55.60$. Completing the operations, we find

$$F = \frac{18.00}{55.60} = .32$$

This difference is not significant. The df's for this F are $df_{num.} = 1$ and $df_{denom.} = df_{S/AB} = 30$. (Be sure to note that the denominator df are those associated with the error term from the omnibus analysis, $df_{S/AB}$.)

Single-df comparisons involving the main effect of factor B (which are not possible in the present example because $df_B = 1$) would be calculated in the same manner. All one needs to do is to modify Eq. (14-2) to reflect the appropriate number of observations contributing to each marginal mean, namely, $(a)(s)$. Thus,

$$SS_{B_{comp.}} = \frac{(a)(s)(\hat{\psi}_B)^2}{\sum (c_j)^2} \tag{14-3}$$

From this point on, we would follow exactly the same steps we outlined above for comparing the A treatment means.

The MRC Approach

The detailed analysis of main effects is easily accomplished with MRC, provided we use meaningful comparisons as vectors. For our example, consider the first two vectors we established for the data set in Chap. 13 (Table 13-6), which we used to capture the A main effect. The first vector ($A1$), based on the coefficients $(+1, -1, 0)$, specifies a comparison between physical science and social science, while the second vector ($A2$), based on the coefficients $(+1, +1, -2)$, specifies a comparison between the combined science conditions and the history condition.

This latter comparison is the same comparison we just considered in the first part of this section, "The ANOVA Approach." All that we have to do now is to locate the appropriate zero-order correlation between Y and $A2$ from the MRC analysis and test its significance.

From Table 13-6, we find $r_{Y2}^2 = .0031$. To test the significance of this r^2, we calculate the F ratio using Eq. (11-9):

$$F = \frac{r_{comp.}^2}{(1 - R_{Y.max.}^2)/(N - k - 1)}$$

where $r_{comp.}^2$ is the squared zero-order correlation coefficient representing the single-df comparison and $R_{Y.max.}^2$ is the squared *omnibus* multiple correlation coefficient, obtained when the required full set of vectors (the vectors for the design—A, B, and $A \times B$, or 5 vectors) is entered into the analysis. The numerator of the F ratio reflects the proportion of Y variability associated with a single vector, which in this case represents a single-df comparison. The denominator contains the quantity $1 - R_{Y.max.}^2$, which is the proportion of Y variability not associated with the combined effects of the experimental treatments. This residual term is divided by the appropriate df, which corresponds, of course, to the df for the within-groups source of variance, $df_{S/AB}$. (In MRC, as you know, these df are represented by $N - k - 1$, where N is the total number of observations and k is the maximum number of vectors required to capture the combined treatment effects.)

All that we need to complete this example is the residual term and the residual df, which may be found in Table 13-8—namely, $1 - R_{Y.max.}^2 = .2880$ and $df_{S/AB} = N - k - 1 = 30$. If we substitute the different quantitites in Eq. (11-9), we obtain

$$F = \frac{.0031}{.2880/30} = \frac{.0031}{.0096} = .32$$

which is identical to the F we obtained with ANOVA for this comparison.

The correspondence between ANOVA and MRC, again, can be demonstrated in other ways as well. The $SS_{A_{comp.}}$ can be obtained from the MRC analysis simply by multiplying the $r_{comp.}^2$ by SS_Y. Thus,

$$SS_{A_{comp.}} = (r_{comp.}^2)(SS_Y) = (.0031)(5793.00) = 17.96$$

which, except for rounding error, is equal to the value of 18.00 obtained with ANOVA. The $r_{comp.}^2$ may also be calculated from ANOVA by dividing the $SS_{A_{comp.}}$ by SS_T. That is,

$$r_{comp.}^2 = \frac{SS_{A_{comp.}}}{SS_T} = \frac{18.00}{5793.00} = .0031$$

which is equal to the squared correlation coefficient obtained with MRC.

Comment

You have seen how differences among the marginal means may be analyzed by either statistical approach. With ANOVA, the focus is on the difference between the means represented by the single-*df* comparison of interest. With MRC, the focus is on the zero-order correlation between Y and the vector reflecting the single-*df* comparison. An obvious strategy in planning the MRC analysis is to represent the main effects of the two independent variables by meaningful comparisons. This way the relevant zero-order correlations are readily available for a detailed analysis of the main effects—if such an analysis is appropriate, of course. If you desire additional comparisons, you can calculate these $r_{comp.}$'s by simply including appropriate vectors when you set up the data for analysis and instructing the computer to include these vectors in the zero-order correlation matrix available from the MRC program.

As we pointed out earlier, systematic interest in differences among the marginal means generally is relevant only when the interaction is not significant. The primary reason has to do with *interpretation*: differences among marginal means are often difficult to interpret when there is a significant interaction—as are the main effects themselves. When interaction is present, any conclusion drawn from an analysis of the marginal means will need to be qualified. Consider the data from our numerical example presented in the upper half of Fig. 13-1. The analysis revealed a signficant main effect of presentation method. Although it would probably be safe to conclude that the computer method was generally superior to the standard method, since the computer method was consistently better for all three lectures, we would still have to take into consideration the fact that the *size* of its superiority depends on the type of lecture presented—large for social science and small for physical science and history—whenever we interpret the results of the experiment.

14.2   USING ANOVA TO ANALYZE SIMPLE EFFECTS

General Considerations

Once a significant interaction has been established, researchers usually turn their attention to an analysis of the means *within* the body of the *AB* matrix; they have little interest in the analysis of the marginal means. One commonly used technique consists of the systematic analysis of the treatment means—either one row at a time or one column at a time.[1] This type of analysis is called the analysis of **simple main effects**, or **simple effects**, for short.

The analysis of simple effects consists of the examination of the effects of *one* of the independent variables with the *other* independent variable *held constant*. In the context of our example, we might examine separately the effects of the different lectures under computer presentation and then their effects under the standard presentation. In each situation, we are holding presentation method constant while permitting only the type of lecture to vary in the analysis.

In essence, then, this is an analysis scheme that views the factorial design as a collection of *separate single-factor experiments*, each involving the same manipulation. Because there is a significant interaction, we can conclude that the outcomes of these "separate experiments" are in fact *not the same*; the analysis of simple effects represents an attempt to determine the ways in which these outcomes differ. It is in this sense that we come to "understand" or "explain" a significant interaction through the analysis of simple effects.

The analysis described above focused on the simple effects of factor *A*, which consisted of the effects of types of lectures for the computer presentation (referred to as the *simple effects of A at level b_1*) and for the standard presentation (referred to as the *simple effects of A at level b_2*). We could just as well have considered the effects of the two methods of presentation (factor *B*) separately at each level of factor *A*. In this case, there would be three "single-factor experiments" all involving the comparison of computer and standard presentation, but with the type of lecture held constant. Specifically, there would be one such "experiment" for the subjects receiving the physical science lecture, one for the subjects receiving the social science lecture, and one for the subjects receiving the history lecture. These analyses would be called the *simple effects of factor B at levels a_1, a_2, and a_3*, respectively.

Analysis of Simple Effects

Since the specification of a simple effect is equivalent to a single-factor experiment, the analysis builds on procedures we have already considered in earlier chapters. We isolate the appropriate column or row in the *AB* matrix and calculate a sum of squares based only on the data in it. We then treat this subset of the data, which represents the comparison of interest, exactly as if it had come from an actual single-factor experiment, rather than from a "slice" or a part of the *AB* matrix.

As an example, the treatment sums for the three lectures (factor *A*) given with the computer presentation (level b_1) are:

---

[1] Occasionally, it is profitable to conduct the analyses both ways, i.e., by rows and by columns.

	a_1	a_2	a_3	Sum
	276	240	228	744

Each sum is based on $s = 6$ observations. If we treat these data as the results from a single-factor experiment, the between-groups sum of squares ("SS_A") is calculated by:

$$SS_{A \text{ at } b_1} = \text{``}SS_A\text{''}$$

$$= \frac{\Sigma \text{``}A\text{''}^2}{s} - \frac{\text{``}T\text{''}^2}{(a)(s)}$$

where "A" and "T" are data drawn from one of the rows of the AB matrix. Substituting in this formula, we find

$$SS_{A \text{ at } b_1} = \frac{276^2 + 240^2 + 228^2}{6} - \frac{744^2}{(3)(6)}$$

$$= \frac{185,760}{6} - \frac{553,536}{18}$$

$$= 30,960.00 - 30,752.00 = 208.00$$

The *df* associated with this sum of squares is 1 less than the number of treatment conditions; that is,

$$df_{A \text{ at } b_1} = a - 1 = 3 - 1 = 2$$

The mean square is formed in the usual manner by dividing the *SS* by the appropriate *df*:

$$MS_{A \text{ at } b_1} = \frac{SS_{A \text{ at } b_1}}{df_{A \text{ at } b_1}}$$

$$= \frac{208.00}{2} = 104.00$$

The *F* is calculated by dividing the mean square representing systematic variance by the *error term from the overall omnibus analysis* (see Table 13-5). For these data,

$$F = \frac{MS_{A \text{ at } b_1}}{MS_{S/AB}}$$

$$= \frac{104.00}{55.60} = 1.87$$

which is not significant. (With $df_{num.} = 2$ and $df_{denom.} = 30$, the critical value of F at $\alpha = .05$ is 3.32.) It appears that the three types of lectures produce roughly equivalent results under the computer presentation.

The corresponding analysis for the standard presentation produces a different conclusion. The treatment sums at level b_2 are:

a_1	a_2	a_3	Sum
204	72	186	462

Following the same steps, we find

$$SS_{A \text{ at } b_2} = \frac{204^2 + 72^2 + 186^2}{6} - \frac{462^2}{(3)(6)}$$

$$= \frac{81,396}{6} - \frac{213,444}{18}$$

$$= 13,566.00 - 11,858.00 = 1708.00$$

$$MS_{A \text{ at } b_2} = \frac{1708.00}{2} = 854.00$$

$$F = \frac{854.00}{55.60} = 15.36$$

where the value of F is significant.

Thus, the analysis shows that the interaction may be characterized as consisting of a nonsignificant effect of lectures under computer presentation and a significant effect of lectures under the standard presentation. As informative as this conclusion may be, we still do not know exactly what differences are responsible for the *significant* simple effect. All that the analysis establishes is that differences exist among the three lectures, not *where* they exist. Additional analysis will be necessary to reveal this important information.

Simple Effects of Factor B

The analysis of the simple effects of factor B is conducted in an analogous fashion. We use the same two-step process of determining which simple effects are significant and—when we locate those that are—of testing specific differences between means. If the simple effects are each associated with 1 *df*, as they are in the numerical example, only the first step is possible. That is, the analysis will consist of comparing the two methods of presentation separately for each of the three lecture conditions, and no further analysis is possible.

Analysis of Simple Comparisons

With the single-factor design, the determination of a significant omnibus *F* is usually followed by a number of additional statistical tests designed to establish the critical factors responsible for the significant *F*. We follow exactly the same logic when we discover a significant simple effect in a factorial experiment. In our example, an examination of the treatment means for the standard presentation suggests that there is a sizable difference in performance between subjects receiving the social science lecture and those receiving the other two lectures. The social science subjects recalled 12.00 vocabulary words, while the physical science subjects recalled 34.00 words and the history subjects recalled 31.00 words. We can test this observation by considering two comparisons: one, between physical science and history, to establish the equivalence of these two conditions; and another, between social science (12.00) and the average of physical science and history (32.50), to establish the discrepancy between social science and the other two groups.

It is important to note at this point that to be of any analytical benefit, single-*df* comparisons should represent meaningful questions. The analysis suggested in the preceding paragraph does not give us much insight into the underlying reasons for the effect. What is the basis for comparing physical science and history? A more revealing comparison is between the two science conditions. We made this point previously when we first introduced single-*df* comparisons in the analysis of the single-factor design. The point is equally valid when we are analyzing significant simple effects.

The analysis of simple comparisons is merely an extension of the analysis of single-*df* comparisons that we applied to the single-factor design. We use coefficients to express the simple comparisons in which we are interested and calculate the sums of squares. As an example, suppose we wanted to compare the two science means. The coefficients for this comparison are (c_i: $+1, -1, 0$), and the corresponding means are 34.00, 12.00, and 31.00 for physical science, social science, and history, respectively. The difference between the two means ($\hat{\psi}$) is

$$\hat{\psi}_{A \text{ at } b_2} = (c_1)(\bar{Y}_{A_1B_2}) + (c_2)(\bar{Y}_{A_2B_2}) + (c_3)(\bar{Y}_{A_3B_2})$$
$$= (+1)(34.00) + (-1)(12.00) + (0)(31.00)$$
$$= 34.00 - 12.00 = 22.00$$

This difference is substituted in an equivalent of Eq. (11-4) as follows:

$$SS_{A_{comp.} \text{ at } b_2} = \frac{(s) \, (\hat{\psi}_{A \text{ at } b_2})^2}{\Sigma \, (c_i)^2}$$

$$= \frac{(6) \, (22.00)^2}{(+1)^2 + (-1)^2 + (0)^2}$$

$$= \frac{2904.00}{2} = 1452.00$$

Since there is 1 df associated with this comparison, $MS_{A_{comp.} \text{ at } b_2} = 1452.00$. The F ratio is formed by dividing the comparison mean square by the error term from the overall analysis ($MS_{S/AB}$) That is,

$$F = \frac{MS_{A_{comp.} \text{ at } b_2}}{MS_{S/AB}}$$

$$= \frac{1452.00}{55.60} = 26.12$$

which, with $df_{num.} = 1$ and $df_{denom.} = 30$, is significant.

14.3   USING MRC TO ANALYZE SIMPLE EFFECTS

You will recall that with MRC the number of vectors required to represent any given source of variability fully is equal to the df associated with that source. For the simple effects of factor A, then, $a - 1$ vectors will be needed for each level of factor B; for the present example, the number of vectors is 2. For simple effects of factor B, $b - 1$ vectors will be needed for each level of factor A; for the present example, the number is 1.

Coding Simple Effects

The method we will use to construct vectors that reflect simple effects is based on the vectors we use to code the relevant *main effect*. This method follows a relatively simple procedure:

1. Construct vectors to define the relevant main effect.
2. Use a coefficient of 0 for all observations *not relevant* to a particular simple effect.

The 0s in the second part of the procedure serve to eliminate data irrelevant to the analysis—in this case, the data contributing to the *other* simple effects—while the coefficients assigned in the first part serve to detect the presence of simple effects within the isolated level. Let us see how this is done.

We will illustrate the construction of vectors with the simple effects of factor A. As we have done before, we set up a code matrix to pinpoint the contrasts of interest; this matrix will be used for assigning X "values" to subjects. If we are interested in the simple effects of factor A, we need to construct vectors that provide information about such effects. If the effects of interest are physical science compared with social science and the combined sciences compared with history, we can start our code matrix by using the entire matrix we constructed in Chap. 13 (page 198), which is

	a_1	a_2	a_3
Vector 1	+1	−1	0
Vector 2	+1	+1	−2

This matrix will be used to represent the contrasts at each level of B, and thus we can use it to test for the simple effects of A. Table 14-1 illustrates how the coding

Table 14-1
Code Matrix for the Analysis of Simple Effects

		Vectors					
		(1) A1	(2) A2	(3) A1 at b_1	(4) A2 at b_1	(5) A1 at b_2	(6) A2 at b_2
b_1	a_1	1	1	1	1	0	0
	a_2	−1	1	−1	1	0	0
	a_3	0	−2	0	−2	0	0
b_2	a_1	1	1	0	0	1	1
	a_2	−1	1	0	0	−1	1
	a_3	0	−2	0	0	0	−2
r:		.4506	−.0557	.1365	.1314	.5006	−.2102
r^2:		.2030	.0031	.0186	.0173	.2506	.0442
		Main effect of factor A		Simple effect of factor A at b_1		Simple effect of factor A at b_2	

matrix is applied to this analysis. (To conserve space, we have omitted listing the Y scores in this table, showing only the assignment of coefficients to the six different treatment groups. In an actual analysis, the Y scores would be added and assigned the set of coefficients appropriate to the relevant treatment group.) Let us see how this procedure works.

We start with the two vectors defining the main effect of factor A. These vectors, which appear in columns 1 and 2, are the ones we used in Chap. 13 to represent the main effect of factor A in the overall statistical analysis. (Vector A1 compares physical science with social science, and vector A2 compares the combined science conditions with history.) Columns 3 and 4, which consist of the two vectors defining the simple effect of A at level b_1 (computer presentation), are derived from vectors A1 and A2. You can see that the coefficients from the code matrix are exactly duplicated for the groups at b_1 and that 0s are assigned to all treatment groups at b_2. The vectors in columns 5 and 6 are constructed the same way. This time, however, the coefficients from the code matrix are duplicated for the groups at b_2 and 0s are assigned to all treatment groups at b_1.

Consider the information provided by these two sets of simple-effects vectors. Collectively, columns 3 and 4 represent the simple effect of A at level b_1, while columns 5 and 6 represent the simple effect of A at level b_2. An $R^2_{Y.set}$ based on each of these sets of vectors will reflect the proportion of Y variability associated with each simple effect. *Individually*, however, each of the vectors represents a different *simple comparison*, namely, physical science versus social science for computer presentation (column 3) and for standard presentation (column 5), and combined science versus history for computer presentation (column 4) and for standard presentation (column 6). As you can see, a careful selection of the comparisons used to code the main effect of an independent variable sets the stage for a potentially useful analysis of simple effects if the A × B interaction is significant. We will have more to say about the selection of vectors after we consider a numerical example.

Numerical Example of Simple Effects

The squared zero-order correlation coefficients obtained with these different vectors are presented at the bottom of Table 14-1. Since we have used orthogonal vectors to define the sets, we can calculate the required R^2's as a sum of the individual squared zero-order correlation coefficients. Substituting from Table 14-1, we find

$$R^2_{Y.A \text{ at } b_1} = r^2_{Y3} + r^2_{Y4}$$
$$= .0186 + .0173 = .0359$$

$$R^2_{Y.A \text{ at } b_2} = r^2_{Y5} + r^2_{Y6}$$
$$= .2506 + .0442 = .2948$$

If the vectors had not been orthogonal, we would have had to calculate an $R^2_{Y.set}$ that takes the intercorrelation of the vectors into consideration. (The same $R^2_{Y.set}$'s would be obtained in any case.)

The F ratio for this analysis is the same one we would use to evaluate any $R^2_{Y.set}$ in the context of this two-factor design. That is, $R^2_{Y.set}$ can refer to a squared multiple correlation between Y and any meaningful set of vectors, such as $R^2_{Y.A}$, $R^2_{Y.B}$, and $R^2_{Y.A \times B}$ from the overall analysis; and $R^2_{Y.A \text{ at } b_1}$ and $R^2_{Y.A \text{ at } b_2}$, from the present analysis. The general form for the F ratios adapted from Eq. (10-8), then is

$$F = \frac{R^2_{Y.set}/df_{set}}{(1 - R^2_{Y.max.})/(N - k - 1)} \tag{14-4}$$

which contains terms that should by now be familiar to you. As with all F ratios, the numerator reflects the presence of systematic variability (and error variability, of course) and the denominator reflects unsystematic, or uncontrolled, variability. For this example,

$$F = \frac{R^2_{Y.A \text{ at } b_1}/df_{A \text{ at } b_1}}{(1 - R^2_{Y.max.})/(N - k - 1)}$$

$$= \frac{.0359/2}{(1 - .7120)/(36 - 5 - 1)}$$

$$= \frac{.0180}{.2880/30} = \frac{.0180}{.0096} = 1.88$$

and

$$F = \frac{R^2_{Y.A \text{ at } b_2}/df_{A \text{ at } b_2}}{(1 - R^2_{Y.max.})/(N - k - 1)}$$

$$= \frac{.2948/2}{(1 - .7120)/(36 - 5 - 1)} = \frac{.1474}{.0096} = 15.35$$

These two F's are identical (within rounding error) to the ones we obtained with ANOVA.

To further emphasize again the correspondence between ANOVA and MRC, we can calculate the sums of squares, which are central in ANOVA, from these two R^2's. More specifically,

$$SS_{A \text{ at } b_1} = (R^2_{Y.A \text{ at } b_1})(SS_Y)$$

$$= (.0359)(5793.00) = 207.97$$

$$SS_{A \text{ at } b_2} = (R^2_{Y.A \text{ at } b_2})(SS_Y)$$

$$= (.2948)(5793.00) = 1707.78$$

Again, these values deviate only slightly, as a result of rounding, from those obtained previously (208.00 and 1708.00, respectively).

Analysis of Simple Comparisons

Any significant simple effect may be analyzed further by conducting a number of single-df comparisons. As we have noted already, you can easily accomplish this with MRC, provided that you have included coefficients in order to represent these comparisons as vectors. Each simple comparison is reflected by a zero-order correlation between Y and the vector defining the appropriate single-df comparison. The F ratio for this analysis is the same one we would use to evaluate any r^2 in the context of this type of design:

$$F = \frac{r^2}{(1 - R^2_{Y.max.})/(N - k - 1)} \tag{14-5}$$

You will recall that the effects of the different lectures given with the standard presentation (simple effects of A at b_2) were significant. The two vectors we constructed for this analysis (see Table 14-1) each capture a different facet of this simple effect, namely, a comparison between physical science and social science (column 5) and a comparison between the combined sciences and history (column 6). The squared zero-order correlation coefficients between these vectors and Y are found at the bottom of Table 14-1. All we need to do now is to substitute these values in Eq. (14-5), the F ratio appropriate for single-df comparisons. We will illustrate the calculations with the first vector (column 5), which consists of the comparison we calculated with ANOVA:

$$F = \frac{r^2_{Y5}}{(1 - R^2_{Y.max.})/(N - k - 1)}$$
$$= \frac{.2506}{.0096} = 26.10$$

Except for rounding error, the value is identical to one obtained with ANOVA.

Practical Considerations

As you have seen, central to the MRC analysis is the choice of vectors to represent sources of variability that are of interest to us. When we considered the MRC analysis of the single-factor design in Chap. 11 (see Sec. 11.3), we suggested how the analysis might be arranged to make maximal use of the MRC approach to analyze the data from an experiment. We will now offer a similar strategy for the analysis of the two-factor design in order to test for simple effects; it can serve as an alternative to the strategy presented in the last section.

Before we begin, however, we should remind you that we assume that you will use a computer for the analysis under this strategy, although hand calculation is often possible, provided that you select orthogonal vectors to represent the treatment effects of interest to you. Whether you decide to use ANOVA or MRC when you are analyzing a two-factor design of your own depends on a number of factors, including your research orientation and personal preferences as well as the availability of a computer and relevant statistical programs. Our purpose here is not to side with one technique or the other; rather, we continue to stress and illustrate the points of equivalence and correspondence between the two techniques. In the discussion that follows, we will first describe a systematic plan for creating the necessary vectors and then indicate how to select the vectors for the actual statistical analysis.

Creating Vectors.   We will describe the process of creating vectors as a series of five steps:

1. Establish a code matrix for one of the independent variables which includes *all* the meaningful comparisons of interest to you; we will choose factor A. If at this point you have fewer vectors than degrees of freedom (that is, fewer than $df_A = a - 1$ vectors), you will need to add vectors so that you can complete the statistical analysis. For the present example, this is not a problem, since there are at least four vectors that are of potential interest:

	a_1	a_2	a_3
Vector 1	$+1$	-1	0
Vector 2	$+1$	$+1$	-2
Vector 3	$+1$	0	-1
Vector 4	0	$+1$	-1

These four vector codes are assigned to the appropriate treatment conditions in Table 14-2. Although we will need only two vectors to represent the A main effect, we have included *all* meaningful comparisons (vectors 1 through 4) in anticipation of a more analytical assessment of the data. For example, these four vectors could be used to examine a significant A main effect following the procedure we described in Sec. 14.1 (assuming that the $A \times B$ interaction is *not* significant).

Table 14-2

A Code Matrix for the Analysis of the Numerical Example

| | | $A_{comp.}$ | | | | $A_{comp.\ at\ b_1}$ | | | | $A_{comp.\ at\ b_2}$ | | | $B_{comp.}$ | $B_{comp.\ at\ a_i}$ | | | Interaction | |
	1	2	3	4	5	6	7	8	9	10	11	12	13	14	15	16	17	18
a_1b_1	1	1	1	0	1	1	1	0	0	0	0	0	1	1	0	0	1	1
a_2b_1	-1	1	0	1	-1	1	1	1	0	0	0	0	1	0	1	0	-1	1
a_3b_1	0	-2	-1	-1	0	-2	-1	-1	0	0	0	0	1	0	0	1	0	-2
a_1b_2	1	1	1	0	0	0	0	0	1	1	1	0	-1	-1	0	0	-1	-1
a_2b_2	-1	1	0	1	0	0	0	0	-1	1	0	1	-1	0	-1	0	1	-1
a_3b_2	0	-2	-1	-1	0	0	0	0	0	-2	-1	-1	-1	0	0	-1	0	2

Vectors

2. Create all necessary vectors that anticipate an analysis of the simple effects of factor *A* (assuming this time that the interaction *is* significant). In the last section, we simply duplicated the code matrix for each level of *B*. Repeating this strategy, we obtain a situation whereby vectors 5 through 8 capture the different aspects of the simple effects of factor *A* at level b_1, while vectors 9 through 12 capture the corresponding aspects of the simple effects of factor *A* at level b_2. Each vector represents a specific meaningful question. For the subjects receiving the computer presentation, for example, vector 5 compares physical science and social science, vector 6 compares the two combined science conditions and history, vector 7 compares physical science and history, and vector 8 compares social science and history. Vectors 9 through 12 represent the same comparisons, but for the subjects receiving the standard presentation.

3. Establish a code matrix to represent all meaningful comparisons for the other independent variable. In our example, only one vector is possible for factor *B*, which we will label as vector 13:

	b_1	b_2
Vector 13	$+1$	-1

This code matrix is used to assign the codes to the treatment conditions, as you can see in Table 14-2.

4. Create vectors that reflect the simple effects of factor *B*, again in anticipation of later analyses. Vectors 14 through 16 in Table 14-2 are the result of this step. Vector 14, for example, compares computer and standard presentations for children receiving the physical science lecture; vector 15 compares the two methods of presentation for children receiving the social science lecture; and vector 16 compares the two methods for children receiving the history lecture. (In essence, each of these vectors is a duplication of vector 13, adjusted for the appropriate level of *A*.)

5. Finally, form a number of interaction vectors—at least as many as there are degrees of freedom for the *A* × *B* interaction. In our example, we need two, which are listed as vectors 17 and 18 in Table 14-2. Vector 17 is formed by multiplying one comparison from the *A* code matrix (vector 1) by the single comparison from the *B* code matrix (vector 13), while vector 18 is formed by multiplying another comparison from the *A* code matrix (vector 2) by vector 13. (This is the traditional way of establishing interaction vectors as presented in Chap. 13.) At this point, we simply need

these two interaction vectors to represent $A \times B$ interaction. The analytical use of interaction vectors will be discussed in Chap. 15.

Specifying Multiple Correlations.   We are now ready to indicate how the analysis might proceed. In this example, we have created a total of 18 vectors. They can be used as follows:

1. Compute $R^2_{Y.A}$ using two of the A vectors (any two from vectors 1 through 4).
2. Compute $R^2_{Y.B}$ using the only vector possible (vector 13), since factor B has only two levels.
3. Compute $R^2_{Y.A \times B}$ by using two interaction vectors (e.g., vectors 17 and 18 in our example), although any set of two interaction vectors constructed from vectors 1 through 4 and vector 13 would produce the same $R^2_{Y.A \times B}$.
4. Compute $R^2_{Y.max.}$ by summing the R^2's obtained in steps 1 to 3—that is $R^2_{Y.max.} = R^2_{Y.A} + R^2_{Y.B} + R^2_{Y.A \times B}$. We can calculate $R^2_{Y.max.}$ this way because the three $R^2_{Y.set}$'s are mutually orthogonal, given the way the factorial design is constructed and the three effects are defined. Alternatively, we can calculate $R^2_{Y.max.}$ using any two vectors from factor A (vectors 1 through 4), one vector from factor B (vector 13), and two interaction vectors (vectors 17 and 18); that is,

$$R^2_{Y.max.} = R^2_{Y.A,B,A \times B}$$

In terms of vectors numbers from Table 14-2, we could have calculated $R^2_{Y.max.}$ as follows:

$$R^2_{Y.max.} = R^2_{Y.1,2,13,17,18}$$

This quantity is used to calculate the error term for all the F tests conducted with this type of design; see Eq. (14-4).

5. Compute zero-order correlation coefficients for each of the vectors not designated in steps 1 to 4; these r's can be used either alone or in combination to examine particular effects, as we have noted previously. Each of these correlation coefficients can be tested for significance by Eq. (11-9).

14.4 COMMENTS ON THE ANALYSIS OF SIMPLE EFFECTS

The analysis of simple effects and simple comparisons constitutes an extremely useful tool for analyzing a significant interaction. Because the analysis is dependent on finding significant effects before additional analyses are conducted, it represents

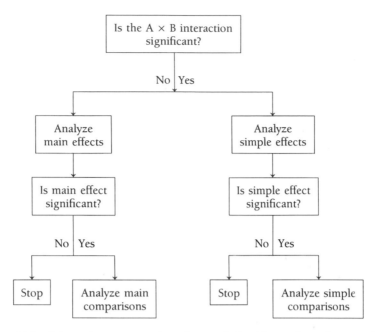

F i g u r e 14-1   Schematic representation of an analysis with no planned comparisons.

a strategy that is ideally suited when a researcher has no planned comparisons clearly in mind.[2] This often happens with factorial designs. In this section, we will summarize the basic characteristics of this particular approach to the analysis of a factorial experiment.

Summary of the Approach

We can think of this analysis strategy as a series of steps. Consider the decision tree presented in Fig. 14-1. At the top, we have listed the first step in the analysis— evaluating the significance of the overall $A \times B$ interaction. You will recall that a significant interaction means that the simple effects of a factor are *not the same* at all levels of the other factor—that is, the simple effects of factor A are not the same at all levels of factor B, and the simple effects of factor B are not the same at all levels of factor A.

[2] Some authors recommend corrections for familywise type I error. In general, we feel that the procedure itself reduces type I error simply by requiring a significant F before additional analyses are undertaken. In this sense, the analysis corresponds to Fisher's least significant difference test, which we discussed in Chap. 12.

This conclusion leads directly to the next step in the analysis, namely, an examination of the effects of one of the independent variables at each level of the other independent variable. This step is indicated at the top of the right-hand "branch" of the decision tree. If a simple effect is significant at this point, the data contributing to that effect may be examined for meaningful single-df comparisons, which also are tested for significance; if the effect is not significant, we stop the analysis of that particular simple effect. These two possibilities are listed at the bottom of the figure. The goal of this approach to the analysis of the overall $A \times B$ interaction, then, is to establish statistically the exact pattern of differences responsible for the significant interaction.

A *nonsignificant* interaction, on the other hand, means that it is safe to interpret the effects of either factor *without reference* to the other factor. This is accomplished by assessing the significance of the two main effects. This step is listed at the top of the left-hand branch of the decision tree. The analysis of the main effects functionally treats the factorial at this point as two separate single-factor experiments: One involves factor A with the data from the different levels of factor B merged or combined for the analysis; the other involves factor B, with the data from the different levels of factor A merged for the analysis. A significant main effect will trigger a search for significant and meaningful comparisons, in the same manner in which a significant omnibus F in an actual single-factor experiment will trigger additional analyses. If a main effect is not significant, we will generally stop our analysis of it. These two options are enumerated at the bottom of the figure.

Variance Sources Contributing to Simple Effects

Although it is not immediately obvious, simple effects reflect two sources of variability—interaction, of course, and the main effect of the independent variable under study. We can easily demonstrate this by showing that the sum of the simple effects of a factor exactly equals the sum of the interaction and the main effect of the factor. That is,

$$\Sigma\, SS_{A \text{ at } b_j} = SS_{A \text{ at } b_1} + SS_{A \text{ at } b_2} + \cdots$$
$$= SS_{A \times B} + SS_A \tag{14-6}$$

$$\Sigma\, SS_{B \text{ at } a_i} = SS_{B \text{ at } a_1} + SS_{B \text{ at } a_2} + \cdots$$
$$= SS_{A \times B} + SS_B \tag{14-7}$$

To illustrate with the simple effects of factor A, we find that the sum of the simple effects,

$$208.00 + 1708.00 = 1916.00$$

equals the sum $SS_{A \times B}$ and SS_A:

$$722.00 + 1194.00 = 1916.00$$

Likewise, we can demonstrate that the R^2's associated with simple effects reflect the sums of R^2's associated with the interaction and the main effect of the factor. By examining the simple-effect r^2's in Table 14-1, and given the $R^2_{Y.A}$ and the $R^2_{Y.A \times B}$ from Table 13-8, we see that

$$\Sigma R^2_{Y.A \text{ at } b_j} = R^2_{Y.A} + R^2_{Y.A \times B}$$

$$R^2_{Y.A \text{ at } b_1} + R^2_{Y.A \text{ at } b_2} = R^2_{Y.A} + R^2_{Y.A \times B}$$

$$(.0186 + .0173) + (.2506 + .0442) = .2061 + .1246$$

$$.3307 = .3307$$

Furthermore, if we go back to our ANOVA results, we can determine the R^2 by dividing the SS for the combined simple effects by the SS for the total; in this case, $1916.00/5793.00 = .3307$, which is identical to the result we have just found.

This demonstration points up one potential limitation of an analysis of simple effects, namely, that the analysis is sensitive both to interaction effects and to main effects. With large main effects present, analyses of simple effects may not be particularly helpful in explaining or interpreting interaction.

Consider, for instance, the simple effects of factor B in the present example, where there was a sizable main effect. If we carried through the calculations, we would find that all three simple effects of factor B are significant. Because of the consistent superiority of the computer presentation, which is reflected in the significant main effect, no pattern of significant and nonsignificant simple effects emerges to help in the interpretation of the interaction. All we can conclude in this case is that the simple effects are not the same—this is what the significant interaction tell us.

The analysis of the simple effects of factor A, on the other hand, is more informative since it shows nonsignificant simple effects under computer presentation (level b_1) and significant simple effects under the standard presentation (level b_2). This finding suggests that the effects of different types of lectures, found with the standard presentation, are greatly diminished with the computer presentation.

14.5   USING A COMPUTER

We have already indicated that the sorts of calculations outlined above would be conducted by a computer rather than by hand. Most of you will have access to a computer and to at least one of the more popular statistical programs, such as the Statistical Package for the Social Sciences (SPSS), the Biomedical Programs (BMDP), and the Statistical Analysis System (SAS) to assist you in your statistical analysis; these programs support both the MRC and ANOVA approaches. In order to use these programs and adapt them to your needs, you will have to construct a set of **program statements**. While the exact nature of these statements will depend on your computer system and the statistical program you select, these statements generally consist of **system statements**, **control statements**, and **procedure statements**, in addition to a listing of the actual data to be analyzed. System statements provide access to the particular statistical program you wish to use, and these statements will vary depending on the type of computer system at your disposal. Control statements provide the computer program with information about the nature and number of your independent and dependent variables. Procedure statements consist of a specification of the actual statistical procedures you want the program to perform.

The ANOVA programs will calculate the means and standard deviations of the treatment groups and calculate the F tests for the two main effects and the interaction. They will also provide you with an exact probability for each F, saving you a trip to an F table. All you need to do is to compare the exact probability p of each F with your chosen significance level α and apply the following decision rule:

if $p \leq \alpha$, reject H_0; otherwise, do not reject H_0.

Depending on the program, you may find it easier (or necessary) to conduct your planned analyses—the sorts of analyses discussed in this chapter and to be covered in the next—by hand. This you can accomplish with the information provided in the computer printout (the table of treatment means and the omnibus error term) and the formulas presented here and in the next chapter.

The MRC programs also require additional work on your part. First, you will need to use the regression equation associated with $R^2_{Y.max.}$ and the relevant vectors to calculate the treatment means. (We illustrated this procedure in Sec. 13.3.) Second, you will have to create your own summary table for the analysis of the main effects and interaction (see Table 13-8 for an example), in which you list the various R^2's you have specified—$R^2_{Y.A.}$, $R^2_{Y.B.}$, and $R^2_{Y.A \times B}$—and the quantity $1 - R^2_{Y.max.}$ (which will serve as the error term), the appropriate degrees of freedom, and then the F ratios. However, the computer printout provides direct results for the additional information needed. If the interaction is significant, the correlations between Y and the vectors created for the analysis of simple effects and simple comparisons (see Table 14-2) are used to conduct these and other analytical statistical tests. If the interaction is not significant, the correlations between Y and the original vectors are used for the analysis of the two main effects.

A number of useful discussions of specific computer programs are available to guide you through a computer analysis. There are, of course, the various program manuals prepared by the developers of the programs, but beginners often find these too general and too brief. A useful introduction to computers is found in a book by Cozby, entitled *Using Computers in the Behavioral Sciences* (1984). A comprehensive and detailed description of SPSS, BMDP, and SAS, including annotated examples of actual computer printouts, has been published by Barcikowski (1983). We should also mention several advanced statistical texts that integrate computer analysis with the discussion of statistical analysis. These include books by Berenson, Levine, and Goldstein (1983); Pedhazur (1982); and Stevens (1986).

14.6 SUMMARY

The outcome of the statistical test of the $A \times B$ interaction materially affects how we go about analyzing a factorial design. If the interaction is significant, the analysis focuses on the specific treatment conditions in an attempt to determine the reasons for the significant interaction. Two types of analyses are useful at this point: the analysis of simple effects, which we considered in this chapter; and the analysis of interaction comparisons, which we consider in Chap. 15. On the other hand, if the interaction is not significant, we examine the combined data in order to study the main or average effects of the two independent variables.

In order to analyze main effects, we transform the factorial design into two single-factor designs, one in which factor A is manipulated and factor B is disregarded, and another in which factor B is manipulated and factor A is disregarded. Generally, when we discover a significant main effect, we conduct a number of single-df comparisons that focus on meaningful contrasts between treatment conditions or combinations of conditions. With either ANOVA or MRC, the analysis of comparisons is similar to the analysis used in an actual single-factor experiment. If we use ANOVA, we examine and work with differences between means, whereas with MRC we express the differences in terms of zero-order correlations between Y and vectors representing meaningful comparisons.

For the analysis of simple effects, we divide the data into a set of related single-factor experiments in which we study the effects of one of the independent variables as we systematically change the levels of the other independent variable from experiment to experiment. In a 3×2 design, for example, we might be concerned with two separate single-factor experiments, each consisting of three levels of factor A but differing with regard to the particular level of factor B; or we might be concerned with three separate single-factor experiments, each consisting of two levels of factor *B* but differing with regard to the level of factor *A*. The researcher's goal in either case is to establish a pattern of significant and nonsignificant differences that will be useful in interpreting a significant interaction. The ANOVA approach obtains this information by treating each of the simple effects exactly as if it *had* been obtained from a separate single-factor experiment. No new procedures are involved. (The only difference is in the use of the error term from the overall factorial design rather than an error term based only on the data involved in the analysis.) The MRC analysis employs special vectors that are sensitive only to a particular simple effect; these are easily constructed by adapting the vectors already used to define the relevant *main* effect.

This particular approach to the analysis of a factorial design is summarized in Fig. 14-1 as a series of decisions determined by the outcome of certain critical statistical tests. The test for interaction, for example, determines whether one examines the simple effects or the main effects. The test of a given simple effect determines whether there is sufficient justification for examining simple comparisons. Similarly, the test of a main effect determines whether there is justification for examining meaningful comparisons involving the average effects of the two independent variables.

14.7 EXERCISES

1. Using the results you obtained in the exercise in Chap. 13, conduct an analysis of simple effects using:
   (a) ANOVA.
   (b) MRC.

15

The Analysis of Interaction Comparisons: The Interaction Contrast

. . .

239

As you saw in Chap. 14, the analysis of simple effects consists of transforming the overall factorial design into a set of single-factor designs which are then treated for analysis purposes as if they were individual single-factor experiments. This analysis technique represents one major approach to the analysis of interaction. There is another major approach to the analysis of interaction, however, that consists of transforming the original factorial into a number of smaller, more analytical *factorial designs*. We will call these smaller factorials **interaction comparisons**. Let us consider two examples.

Factor *A* in our example consists of three different lectures. As we argued in Chap. 11, when we first considered analytical comparisons, the overall manipulation in a single-factor design is more appropriately viewed as a number of single-*df* comparisons—in essence, as a number of minature two-group experiments. This same way of conceptualizing an independent variable can be extended to the factorial design. That is, rather than focus on the 3 × 2 factorial in its entirety, we might concentrate instead on the analysis of several smaller factorials each created out of the larger design.

To illustrate, suppose we view factor *A* as consisting of two comparisons, a comparison between the two science conditions and a comparison between the combined science conditions and the history condition, rather than as an independent variable consisting of three types of lecture, physical science, social science, and history. When we combine the two comparisons with the other independent variable (factor *B*), we create the two miniature factorials that are presented in Table 15-1. Note how these two *component factorials* are constructed: by crossing factor *B* (computer presentation versus standard presentation) with each of the two comparisons derived from factor *A*.

Consider now the sorts of information we can obtain from these two smaller factorials. The component factorial on the left, for example, permits the direct assessment of an interesting interaction, one that compares the two science lectures under two methods of presentation. An examination of the means entered

Table 15-1
Two Interaction Comparisons

	Physical Science	Social Science		Combined Sciences	History
Computer	46.00	40.00	**Computer**	43.00	38.00
Standard	34.00	12.00	**Standard**	23.00	31.00

into the body of this table suggests that the difference in favor of the physical science lecture obtained with the standard presentation (34 versus 12) is greatly reduced with the computer presentation (46 versus 40). The interaction obtained with the original 3×2 design does not reflect this component interaction *directly* because it also includes the effects of the history lecture.

The component factorial on the right provides information on another interesting interaction: the interaction of the difference between the combined science conditions and the history condition with the two different methods of presentation. In this case, we see that the combined science conditions were favored with the computer presentation (43 versus 38) but that this advantage was reversed with the standard presentation (23 versus 31).

The advantages of creating interaction comparisons are particularly evident when we compare their results with those of the analysis of the $A \times B$ interaction from the overall design. In the first place, interaction comparisons focus on particular aspects of the overall interaction, in the same way that single-*df* comparisons focus on particular aspects of an overall, omnibus F test in a single-factor design. The F test of the $A \times B$ interaction *is* an omnibus test and, as such, tells us nothing about the *locus* of the interaction effects; instead, the test simply tells us whether interaction effects are present *somewhere* in the body of the AB matrix. In contrast, then, interaction comparisons are analytically *focused*. In the second place, we can test *planned* interaction comparisons directly, without first testing for omnibus interaction. Since the omnibus interaction is a composite, or *average*, of individual interactions, our chances of finding any particular interaction with the omnibus $A \times B$ test are greatly reduced. In this sense, interaction comparisons provide more sensitive or powerful tests of these component interaction effects. For these two important reasons, then, we recommend that in formulating your research hypotheses you specify one or more interaction comparisons and that you treat these as *planned comparisons*, conducting these tests *instead* of the test of the overall $A \times B$ interaction, which does not provide a direct assessment of these research hypotheses.

In general, interaction comparisons can be profitably undertaken whenever a multilevel independent variable is conceptualized in terms of single-*df* comparisons. In the present case, only factor A can be treated in this manner, because factor B, with only two levels, can be subdivided no further. In larger factorials— a 3×3 design, for example—frequently both independent variables can be transformed into single-*df* comparisons, which means that we can then examine the overall factorial design as if it were a set of 2×2 component factorials; such component factorials are called **interaction contrasts**. Interaction contrasts are particularly useful, since they represent the ultimate refinement of an $A \times B$ interaction. That is, since an interaction contrast has only 1 *df*, the interaction can be subdivided no further. Technically, any interaction formed by a 2×2 arrangement of the independent variables is an interaction contrast, whether the two "levels" of an independent variable are the result of applying a single-*df* comparison to the overall factorial design or they exist because only two levels have been included in the design. The two interaction comparisons presented in Table 15-1 are interaction contrasts. Because of their important analytical properties, we will focus on the analysis of interaction contrasts in this chapter.[1]

15.1   UNDERSTANDING INTERACTION CONTRASTS

You have seen how an interaction contrast is derived from the original factorial design. The main focus of the analysis is the evaluation of the *interaction*, of course. Let us see in a little more detail how interaction contrasts are created.

Creating Interaction Contrasts

Interaction contrasts represent a natural extension of single-*df* comparisons—which we use to analyze the effects of single independent variables—to the analysis of interaction. We illustrated this point in Table 15-1 by presenting two interaction contrasts using comparisons that figured heavily in our analysis of the lecture variable (factor *A*) when it appeared in our numerical example of the single-factor design. As you saw, these interaction contrasts were formed by transforming the levels of factor *A* into more meaningful arrangements. Thus, the 2×2 design defining an interaction contrast was obtained simply by refining factor *A*.

For the sake of completeness, consider for a moment an expanded version of our numerical example in which a movie condition (b_3) is added to the levels of factor *B* to create the 3×3 factorial design presented at the top of Table 15-2. Several single-*df* comparisons involving factor *B* immediately suggest themselves. In addition to the original comparison between the computer and the standard presentation, we could compare the movie condition separately with each of the other two methods of presentation—that is, we could examine computer versus movie and standard presentation versus movie. There might even be an interest in comparing the standard method with the computer and movie methods combined. Each of these single-*df* comparisons made possible by the "new" level of factor *B* may be used to create a set of interaction contrasts simply by crossing

---

[1] For a discussion of other types of interaction comparisons, see Boik (1979) and Keppel (1982, pp. 222–227).

Table 15-2
Examples of Interaction Contrasts

	Physical Science	Social Science	History
Computer			
Standard			
Movie			

	Physical Science	Social Science
Computer		
Standard		

	Combined Sciences	History
Computer		
Standard		

	Physical Science	Social Science
Computer		
Movie		

	Combined Sciences	History
Computer		
Movie		

	Physical Science	Social Science
Standard		
Movie		

	Combined Sciences	History
Standard		
Movie		

	Physical Science	Social Science
Combined		
Standard		

	Combined Sciences	History
Combined		
Standard		

them with each of the two comparisons involving factor *A*. With two comparisons extracted from factor *A* and four from factor *B*, we can form a total of eight interaction contrasts. These are presented as 2×2 designs below the 3×3 design in Table 15-2.

Each of these designs captures a different aspect of the overall $A \times B$ interaction. The four designs on the left all involve a comparison of the two science lectures. Starting from the top, the contrasts address the following basic questions:

Is the difference between the two science lectures the same for the computer presentation as it is for the standard presentation?

Is this difference the same for computer presentation as it is for the movie presentation?

Is this difference the same for the standard presentation as it is for the movie presentation?

Is this difference the same for the standard presentation as it is for the computer and movie presentations combined?

The four designs on the right involve a comparison of the combined science lectures with the history lecture. Here, the basic question is whether the difference between the combined science conditions and the history condition is the same for the computer and the standard presentations, for the computer and the movie presentations, and so on. Each of these very specific questions is assessed by testing the interactions revealed by these component 2×2 designs.

In short, interaction contrasts may be derived from any factorial design just so long as the overall $A \times B$ interaction is associated with more than 1 df. If both independent variables have more than two levels, as in the example in Table 15-2, interaction contrasts are formed by crossing single-df comparisons created from both factors. If only one independent variable has more than two levels, as in the example we have been developing in this book, interaction contrasts are formed by crossing single-df comparisons from that factor with the other independent variable. Finally, if neither independent variable has more than two levels, a "true" 2×2 design already exists and the $A \times B$ interaction becomes an interaction contrast by "default."

The important point about interaction contrasts is that they are analyzed in the same manner whether they are obtained from a 3×3, a 3×2, a 2×3, or a 2×2 factorial design. We will consider the analyses in Secs. 15.2 and 15.3.

Defining Interaction Contrasts

Consider the interaction contrast presented in Table 15-3. This particular 2×2 matrix compares the combined science conditions with the history condition under two methods of presentation (computer and standard). An interaction is present if the effect of one of the factors depends on the levels of the other. You can see that an interaction is present in this case, since the difference between combined sciences and history seems to depend on whether subjects received the computer presentation or the standard presentation. More specifically, under the computer presentation, the combined science subjects surpassed the history subjects by 5

Table 15-3
An Example of an Interaction Contrast

	Combined Sciences	History	Difference
Computer	43	38	5
Standard	23	31	−8
Difference	20	7	

words, while under the standard presentation the science subjects lagged behind the history subjects by 8 words. As we developed in Chap. 13 (pages 187−188), an interaction contrast is defined as the *difference* of these *differences*. In the present case,

$$\hat{\psi}_{A \times B} = (43 - 38) - (23 - 31) = 5 - (-8) = 13$$

This same value is found if the interaction is defined in terms of the other comparison, namely, the differences between the two methods of presentation:

$$\hat{\psi}_{A \times B} = (43 - 23) - (38 - 31) = 20 - 7 = 13$$

Interaction contrasts, then, are based on a direct comparison of *simple effects*—the effects of one factor at the different levels of the other factor. Since each factor is represented by a single-*df* comparison, these simple effects reflect differences between two means. You will generally find it useful to examine these simple effects when the interaction contrast is significant.

15.2   USING ANOVA TO ANALYZE INTERACTION CONTRASTS

In this section, we will show how to assess interaction contrasts—interactions in component 2 × 2 designs—whether the "2" for either factor results because we are making a single-*df* comparison or because the experiment involves only two levels of the factor. The actual calculations are relatively simple; they are based on the value of the interaction contrast ($\hat{\psi}_{A \times B}$) itself and on an adaptation of the general formula for single-*df* comparisons. We will first show how to calculate the interaction contrast and then consider the computational formulas.

Constructing the 2 × 2 Matrix

As you saw in Sec. 15.1, we can obtain an interaction contrast by reducing a factorial design to a 2 × 2 cellular layout. The 2 × 2 layout that defines an interaction contrast is easy to construct when it represents two actual levels of one factor crossed with two actual levels of the other factor—you simply extract the four relevant means from the overall AB matrix and place them in a 2 × 2 layout. The first three 2 × 2's on the left in Table 15-2 are of this sort. When either one or both of the factors in the 2 × 2 layout represent a complex comparison, however, the construction is more complicated. The remaining 2 × 2's in the table are of this sort. The method we will present was designed to avoid errors in this vital step and to facilitate the eventual calculation of the sum of squares for an interaction contrast.

We will illustrate the procedure with the interaction contrast formed by crossing the two complex comparisons that we considered in Table 15-2, namely, the comparison between the combined science conditions and the history condition and the comparison between the standard condition and the combined computer and movie conditions. We start with the overall AB matrix of means, which is presented in the upper left of Table 15-4. (As you can see, we have used the means from our original numerical example and created additional means for the three movie conditions.) The coefficients representing the two comparisons are also shown in the matrix. We will use these coefficients to combine appropriate means and to locate the results in a 2 × 2 matrix.

Table 15-4
Forming an Interaction Contrast

		Physical Science (a_1) $+\frac{1}{2}$	Social Science (a_2) $+\frac{1}{2}$	History (a_3) -1	Combined Sciences (a_+)	History (a_-)
Computer (b_1)	$+\frac{1}{2}$	46	40	38	$(46 + 40)/2 = 43$	$38/1 = 38$
Standard (b_2)	-1	34	12	31	$(34 + 12)/2 = 23$	$31/1 = 31$
Movie (b_3)	$+\frac{1}{2}$	36	38	36	$(36 + 38)/2 = 37$	$36/1 = 36$

	Combined Sciences (a_+)	History (a_-)
Combined (b_+)	$(43 + 37)/2 = 40$	$(38 + 36)/2 = 37$
Standard (b_-)	$23/1 = 23$	$31/1 = 31$

We begin with the coefficients for factor A; these indicate that the means in column a_1 are to be averaged with the corresponding means in column a_2 to form a single column of means while the means in column a_3 are left unchanged. This step is completed in the 2×3 matrix on the right of the original AB matrix. For convenience, we have designated the levels of the "new" factor A as a_+ (the combined sciences) and a_- (history), the subscript plus referring to the "level" created by averaging the means associated with the "positive" coefficients $(+\frac{1}{2})$ and the subscript minus referring to the "level" created by using the means associated with the "negative" coefficient (-1). (We have dropped the plus and minus signs at this point, since they have served their purpose of locating the means in the matrix.)

The coefficients for factor B are now brought into play to transform the 2×3 matrix into the desired 2×2 matrix. More specifically, the coefficients indicate that the means in row b_1 are to be combined with the corresponding means in row b_3 to form a single row of means in the new matrix while the means in row b_2 remain unchanged. This step is completed in the 2×2 matrix in the bottom of Table 15-4. Applying the new subscript notation to these transformed levels of factor B, we use b_+ to refer to the combined computer and movie conditions and b_- to refer to the standard condition.

Calculating the Interaction Contrast

As you saw in Sec. 15.1, the interaction contrast is calculated directly from the 2×2 matrix. The interaction contrast is expressed as the difference between two simple effects, either the difference between the simple effects of $A_{comp.}$ at the two "levels" of the other comparison ($\hat{\psi}_{A \text{ at } b_+}$ and $\hat{\psi}_{A \text{ at } b_-}$) or the difference between the simple effects of $B_{comp.}$ at the two "levels" of the other comparison ($\hat{\psi}_{B \text{ at } a_+}$ and $\hat{\psi}_{B \text{ at } a_-}$)—either difference will work when we are dealing with an interaction contrast. In symbols,

$$\hat{\psi}_{A \times B} = \hat{\psi}_{A \text{ at } b_+} - \hat{\psi}_{A \text{ at } b_-} \qquad (15\text{-}1)$$

or

$$\hat{\psi}_{A \times B} = \hat{\psi}_{B \text{ at } a_+} - \hat{\psi}_{B \text{ at } a_-} \qquad (15\text{-}2)$$

Using the information in the 2×2 matrix in Table 15-4, we find

$$\hat{\psi}_{A \times B} = (40 - 37) - (23 - 31)$$
$$= 3 - (-8) = 11$$

with Eq. (15-1), and

$$\hat{\psi}_{A \times B} = (40 - 23) - (37 - 31)$$
$$= 17 - 6 = 11$$

with Eq. (15-2).

Completing the Analysis

The interaction sum of squares, which we will refer to as $SS_{A_{comp.} \times B_{comp.}}$, uses familiar information:

$$SS_{A_{comp.} \times B_{comp.}} = \frac{(s)(\hat{\psi}_{A \times B})^2}{[\Sigma (c_i)^2][\Sigma (c_j)^2]} \tag{15-3}$$

where s = the number of subjects in each treatment condition

$\hat{\psi}_{A \times B}$ = the interaction contrast

$\Sigma (c_i)^2$ = the sum of the squared coefficients for $A_{comp.}$

$\Sigma (c_j)^2$ = the sum of the squared coefficients for $B_{comp.}$

The df for an interaction contrast is 1; thus, $MS_{A_{comp.} \times B_{comp.}} = SS_{A_{comp.} \times B_{comp.}}$. The F becomes

$$F = \frac{MS_{A_{comp.} \times B_{comp.}}}{MS_{S/AB}} \tag{15-4}$$

The error term in Eq. (15-4) is based on the error term from the overall analysis.

As a numerical example, we will complete the analysis that we began in Table 15-3, in which we contrasted the combined science conditions with the history condition under two methods of presentation, computer and standard. The interaction contrast for this example is $\hat{\psi}_{A \times B} = 13$. The other quantities specified by Eq. (15-3) are

$$s \text{ (sample size)} = 6$$
$$\Sigma (c_i)^2 = (+\tfrac{1}{2})^2 + (+\tfrac{1}{2})^2 + (-1)^2 = 1.5$$
$$\Sigma (c_j)^2 = (+1)^2 + (-1)^2 = 2$$

Substituting in Eq. (15-3), we find

$$SS_{A_{comp.} \times B_{comp.}} = \frac{(6)(13.00)^2}{(1.5)(2)} = \frac{1014.00}{3} = 338.00$$

Since $df = 1$, $MS_{A_{comp.} \times B_{comp.}} = 338.00$; the error term, $MS_{A \times B}$, comes from the overall analysis we reported in Chap. 13 (55.60). The F becomes

$$F = \frac{338.00}{55.60} = 6.08$$

which is significant, $p < .05$.

Simple Effects of an Interaction Contrast

It is often profitable to follow the discovery of significant interaction contrasts with an analysis of the simple effects from which the interaction is derived. The goal, of course, is to attempt to establish statistically the pattern of differences responsible for the significant interaction.

Calculating Simple Comparisons.   We start with one of the comparisons defining the interaction contrast and then test the significance of this difference at both "levels" of the other comparison. In the example we have been considering (see Table 15-3), we could examine separately the simple effect of $A_{comp.}$ (combined sciences versus history) at b_+ (computer presentation) and at b_- (standard presentation). That is, we would evaluate two differences, namely,

$$\hat{\psi}_{A \text{ at } b_+} = 43 - 38 = 5$$
$$\hat{\psi}_{A \text{ at } b_-} = 23 - 31 = -8$$

We have already shown that the difference *between* these differences (the interaction) is significant. What we are interested in now is whether either difference is significant by itself.[2]

Calculating Sums of Squares.   The computational formula for the sums of squares involves familiar operations; specifically,

$$SS_{A_{comp.} \text{ at } b_+} = \frac{(s)(\hat{\psi}_{A \text{ at } b_+})^2}{\Sigma (d)^2 \text{ at } b_+} \tag{15-5}$$

$$SS_{A_{comp.} \text{ at } b_-} = \frac{(s)(\hat{\psi}_{A \text{ at } b_-})^2}{\Sigma (d)^2 \text{ at } b_-} \tag{15-6}$$

The only unfamiliar term, d, represents the set of individual coefficients that underlie the different simple effects, as we explain in what follows.

The d coefficients (or $d_{i,j}$ coefficients; subscripts are used when it is necessary to specify a particular coefficient) are associated with the individual cells in the original AB matrix.[3] Consider the matrix appearing in Table 15-5. Along the upper margin we have listed the three levels of factor A and the coefficients associated with the $A_{comp.}$ we have been evaluating $(+\frac{1}{2}, +\frac{1}{2}, -1)$. Along the left-hand margin of the matrix we have listed the two levels of factor B and the coefficients associated with $B_{comp.}(+1, -1)$. The coefficients within the body of the matrix

---

[2] Alternatively, we could examine the simple effect of $B_{comp.}$ (computer versus standard) at a_+ (combined sciences) and at a_- (history). Translated into numbers,

$$\hat{\psi}_{A \text{ at } b_+} = 43 - 23 = 20$$
$$\hat{\psi}_{A \text{ at } b_-} = 38 - 31 = 7$$

In this case, we would be assessing the significance of each difference separately.

[3] These coefficients can also be used as an alternative way to calculate interaction contrasts (see Keppel, 1982, pp. 230–231).

Table 15-5
Calculating Interaction Coefficients (d)

	a_1 ($\frac{1}{2}$)	a_2 ($\frac{1}{2}$)	a_3 (-1)	$\Sigma\,(d)^2$
b_1 (1)	$\frac{1}{2}$	$\frac{1}{2}$	-1	1.5
b_2 (-1)	$-\frac{1}{2}$	$-\frac{1}{2}$	1	1.5
$\Sigma\,(d)^2$	1		2	

(the d's) are simply the *products* of the pairs of coefficients—one from $A_{comp.}$ and the other from $B_{comp.}$—associated with *the individual cells*. For example, the coefficient for cell a_1b_1 is found by multiplying the coefficient at level a_1 ($+\frac{1}{2}$) by the coefficient at level b_1 ($+1$); that is, $d_{1,1} = (+\frac{1}{2})(+1) = +\frac{1}{2}$. The coefficient at cell a_3b_2 is found by multiplying the coefficient at level a_3 (-1) with the coefficient at level b_2 (-1); in this case, $d_{3,2} = (-1)(-1) = +1$. The remaining coefficients are constructed the same way.

You will notice that we have subdivided the 3×2 matrix with dashed lines to mark off the 2×2 matrix of the interaction contrast. In each margin of this subdivision we have entered the sum of the squared coefficients. The sum for the first column a_+ (combined sciences), is

$$\Sigma\,(d)^2 \text{ at } a_+ = (+\tfrac{1}{2})^2 + (-\tfrac{1}{2})^2 + (+\tfrac{1}{2})^2 + (-\tfrac{1}{2})^2$$
$$= .25 + .25 + .25 + .25 = 1$$

and the sum for the second column, a_- (history), is

$$\Sigma\,(d)^2 \text{ at } a_- = (-1)^2 + (+1)^2 = 1 + 1 = 2$$

The two row sums are calculated in the same manner.

We are now able to complete the calculations. Substituting in Eqs. (15-5) and (15-6), we find

$$SS_{A_{comp.} \text{ at } b_+} = \frac{(6)(5)^2}{1.5} = 100.00$$

$$SS_{A_{comp.} \text{ at } b_-} = \frac{(6)(-8)^2}{1.5} = 256.00$$

These sums of squares are based on 1 *df*. As usual, the *F* ratio is formed by dividing each mean square by the error term from the overall analysis ($MS_{S/AB} = 55.60$). We find that the comparison between the combined sciences and history

($A_{comp.}$) is not significant under computer presentation (level b_+), where $F = 100.00/55.60 = 1.80$, but is significant under the standard presentation (level b_-), where $F = 256.00/55.60 = 4.60$.

The other set of simple effects is easily tested. In Table 15-3 we found the difference between computer and standard presentations ($B_{comp.}$) at level a_+ (combined sciences) to be $\hat{\psi}_{B \text{ at } a_+} = 20$; substituting in Eq. (15-7) gives us

$$SS_{B_{comp.} \text{ at } a_+} = \frac{(s)\,(\hat{\psi}_{B \text{ at } a_+})^2}{\Sigma\,(d)^2 \text{ at } a_+} \tag{15-7}$$

$$= \frac{(6)\,(20)^2}{1} = 2400.00$$

The corresponding difference at level a_- (history), which was found to be $\hat{\psi}_{B \text{ at } a_-} = 7$; substituting in Eq. (15-8) gives us

$$SS_{B_{comp.} \text{ at } a_-} = \frac{(s)\,(\hat{\psi}_{B \text{ at } a_-})^2}{\Sigma\,(d)^2 \text{ at } a_-} \tag{15-8}$$

$$= \frac{(6)\,(7)^2}{2} = 147.00$$

In these tests, we find that the comparison between the computer and standard presentations ($B_{comp.}$) is significant for the combined sciences (level a_+), where $F = 2400.00/55.60 = 43.17$, and not significant for history (level a_-), where $F = 147.00/55.60 = 2.64$.

15.3 USING MRC TO ANALYZE INTERACTION CONTRASTS

We will base the MRC analysis of interaction contrasts on the vectors used in the original analysis, in particular, those designed to capture the variation associated with the $A \times B$ interaction. You will recall how we constructed these vectors. We started by coding each main effect with vectors representing comparisons of potential interest to us. We continued this process until we had constructed $a - 1$ vectors for the A main effect and $b - 1$ vectors for the B main effect. We created interaction vectors by cross-multiplying all possible combinations of the A and B vectors. We will now show how these vectors may be used to extract information about interaction contrasts.

Calculating Interaction Contrasts

Assuming that the two comparisons defining the relevant 2×2 matrix (or interaction contrast) have been included in the overall analysis, all that we need in

Table 15-6
Code Matrix for the Analysis of an Interaction Contrast
(*Abbreviated version of Table 13-6*)

		Vectors				
		(1) $A1$	(2) $A2$	(3) $B1$	(4) $A1B1$	(5) $A2B1$
a_1	b_1	1	1	1	1	1
	b_2	1	1	-1	-1	-1
a_2	b_1	-1	1	1	-1	1
	b_2	-1	1	-1	1	-1
a_3	b_1	0	-2	1	0	-2
	b_2	0	-2	-1	0	2
	r:	.4506	$-.0557$	.6175	$-.2575$	.2415
	r^2:	.2030	.0031	.3813	.0663	.0583

order to calculate an r^2 representing the particular interaction contrast is the interaction vector based on these two comparisons. The example we used with ANOVA involved an $A_{comp.}$ consisting of a comparison between the combined science conditions and the history condition and a $B_{comp.}$ consisting of a comparison between the computer and the standard presentations. For convenience, we have depicted in Table 15-6 the complete set of vectors from the overall analysis as presented in Table 13-6. As you can see, we have omitted the Y scores in this table, showing only the assignment of coefficients to the six different treatment groups. The two comparisons of interest to us at this moment are represented by the vectors in column 2 (vector $A2$) and column 3 (vector $B1$) of the code matrix. What we need for the analysis, however, is the interaction vector created from these two vectors; this vector ($A2B1$) and its associated r^2 are found in column 5.

The contrast represented in vector 5 can be illustrated in a table similar to the one we used in the ANOVA discussion (Table 15-5). Arranging the values of vector 5 in tabular form yields the following:

	a_1	a_2	a_3
b_1	$+1$	$+1$	-2
b_2	-1	-1	$+2$

If we then sum the coefficients for a_1 and a_2 separately for each level of factor B—that is, the two $+1$ values of a_1b_1 and a_2b_1 and the two -1 values of a_1b_2 and a_2b_2—we obtain the following matrix:

	$a_1 + a_2$	a_3
b_1	(1) $+2$	(2) -2
b_2	(3) -2	(4) $+2$

In Chap. 13, we indicated that one way of determining whether an interaction exists was to determine whether the sum of the means of cells (1) and (4) in a matrix like this one equals the sum of the means of cells (2) and (3); if so, there is no interaction. Effectively, then, given our coding, vector 5 has been coded so that it represents the particular interaction contrast in which we are interested, namely, an interaction formed by crossing a comparison between the two science conditions and history with the two levels of factor B. We consider next the statistical evaluation of this interaction contrast.

From Table 15-6, we see that $r_{Y5}^2 = .0583$. The formula for the F ratio for this analysis is the same one we have used before to evaluate r^2 in the context of a factorial design, namely, Eq. (11-9):

$$F = \frac{r^2}{(1 - R_{Y.max.}^2)/(N - k - 1)} \tag{15-9}$$

Substituting in Eq. (15-9), we find

$$F = \frac{.0583}{(1 - .7120)/(36 - 5 - 1)}$$

$$= \frac{.0583}{.2880/30} = \frac{.0583}{.0096} = 6.07$$

which is equal (within rounding error) to the F we obtained with ANOVA ($F = 6.08$). We can further show the equivalence between the two methods by examining the corresponding sum of squares, which is found by multiplying r_{Y5}^2 by the total sum of squares:

$$SS_{A_{comp.} \times B_{comp.}} = (.0583)(5793.00) = 337.73$$

The value we found from ANOVA for the comparison is 338.00.

Simple Effects of an Interaction Contrast

Tests for simple effects conducted within the analysis of an interaction contrast focus on the desired comparison for one factor at each level of the other factor. As we pointed out in Sec. 15.2, "levels" of a factor used for a single-df comparison are not necessarily actual levels of an independent variable. The example we have been considering is the interaction contrast involving the comparison between the combined science conditions and the history condition ($A_{comp.}$) and the comparison between the computer presentation and the standard presentation ($B_{comp.}$). If we examine the simple effects of $A_{comp.}$, these will involve actual levels of factor B; that is b_+ = computer presentation and b_- = standard presentation. On the other hand, if we examine the simple effects of $B_{comp.}$, one of these simple effects involves a *combination of levels*, namely, the combined science conditions (a_+); and the other is an actual level of factor A, the history condition (a_-). We need a way of analyzing both types of situations. Let us see how we conduct an analysis of simple effects, first, when actual levels are involved, and second, when a "level" is actually a combination of levels.

An example of the first situation is an analysis of $A_{comp.}$ at b_+ and b_-. As a point of reference, the means being compared are:

	Combined Sciences	History
Computer	43	38
Standard	23	31

The simple effect for subjects in the computer condition consists of a difference of 5 (43 − 38) in favor of the combined science conditions; the corresponding simple effect for subjects in the standard condition consists of a difference of 8 (23 − 31) in favor of the history condition.

The MRC analysis begins with the vector representing $B_{comp.}$ (B1), which is presented in column 1 of a new code matrix, Table 15-7. (Again, you should note that the code matrix does not include the Y scores but shows only the assignment of coefficients to the six different treatment conditions.) Following a procedure we introduced in Sec. 14.3, we use this vector to differentiate between the "levels" of $B_{comp.}$. One of these levels is represented by the *positive* coefficients in vector B1 (level b_+ = computer presentation), while the other level is represented by the *negative* coefficients (level b_- = standard presentation). (If zeros had appeared in the vector, the levels of the factor represented by the zeros would have been disregarded.) We are now ready to construct the vectors for the two simple effects.

Table 15-7

Code Matrix for Simple Comparisons in an
Interaction Contrast

		Vectors			
		(1) $B1$	(2) $A2B1$	(3) $A2$ at b_+	(4) $A2$ at b_-
$a_1 \begin{cases} b_1 \\ b_2 \end{cases}$	b_1	1	1	1	0
	b_2	-1	-1	0	-1
$a_2 \begin{cases} b_1 \\ b_2 \end{cases}$	b_1	1	1	1	0
	b_2	-1	-1	0	-1
$a_3 \begin{cases} b_1 \\ b_2 \end{cases}$	b_1	1	-2	-2	0
	b_2	-1	2	0	2
r:		.6175	.2415	.1314	.2102
r^2:		.3813	.0583	.0173	.0442

Next, we take the relevant *interaction vector* from Table 15-6 (column 5) and place it in Table 15-7 (column 2). The vector representing the difference between the combined sciences and history at level b_+ (column 3) is created by duplicating the entries from the interaction vector (column 2) for all conditions that have a *positive* entry in column 1 and by entering 0s for all other conditions. We will refer to the simple effect represented by this vector as $A_{comp.}$ at b_+ to emphasize that the level involved is the one represented by positive numbers in column 1. The final vector (column 4), which represents the corresponding difference at level b_-, is formed by repeating the relevant codes from the interaction vector (column 2) for all conditions that have a *negative* entry in column 1 and entering 0s for all other conditions. (We will refer to the simple effect coded in column 4 as $A_{comp.}$ at b_-.) The two r^2's for these two vectors ($r^2_{Y3} = .0173$ and $r^2_{Y4} = .0442$) represent the proportions of total Y variability associated with the two simple effects. All we need to do at this point is to evaluate these two r^2's with Eq. (15-9).

Rather than compute the two F's to show the equivalence of this method and the ANOVA method, we will compare the two sets of sums of squares instead. From ANOVA, the two sums of squares were 100.00 and 256.00 for the two levels of factor B. We obtain identical values (within rounding error) when we multiply the corresponding r^2's by the total sum of squares ($SS_Y = 5793.00$). For level b_+, the value is $(.0173)(5793.00) = 100.22$; and for level b_-, the value is $(.0442)(5793.00) = 256.05$.

As an exmple of the second type of situation for analyzing simple effects, we will perform the corresponding analysis for the other comparison, namely, the effect of $B_{comp.}$ (computer versus standard) at the two "levels" of $A_{comp.}$, a_+ (the combined science conditions) and a_- (the history condition). In terms of the means, the simple effect for subjects in the combined science conditions consists of a difference of 20 ($43 - 23$), while the simple effect for subjects in the history condition consists of a difference of 7 ($38 - 31$). As in the previous analysis, we will use the relevant comparison vector for $A_{comp.}$ (vector $A2$), which is presented in column 1 of Table 15-8, to identify the "levels" of $A_{comp.}$ for the two simple effects a_+ and a_-. More specifically, we use the positive entries to identify subjects receiving a science lecture and the negative entries to identify subjects receiving the history lecture.

Let us go through this procedure again. We start with column 2 in Table 15-8, which contains the vector reflecting the appropriate interaction contrast (vector $A2B1$). We construct the vector representing the comparison between computer presentation and standard presentation for the combined science condition by extracting the relevant codes from the interaction vector (column 2) for all conditions with a *positive* entry in column 1 and assigning 0s to all others; the resulting vector appears in column 3. The vector representing the same comparison for subjects receiving the history lecture is constructed by extracting the entries from the interaction vector (column 2) for all conditions with a *negative* entry in

Table 15-8
Code Matrix for Simple Comparisons in an Interaction Contrast

		Vectors			
		(1) $A2$	(2) $A2B1$	(3) $B1$ at a_+	(4) $B1$ at a_-
a_1	b_1	1	1	1	0
	b_2	1	-1	-1	0
a_2	b_1	1	1	1	0
	b_2	1	-1	-1	0
a_3	b_1	-2	-2	0	-2
	b_2	-2	2	0	2
	r:	$-.0557$	$.2415$	$.6437$	$-.1593$
	r^2:	$.0031$	$.0583$	$.4143$	$.0254$

column 1 and assigning 0s to all others; this vector appears in column 4. The squared zero-order correlation coefficients for these last two vectors represent the proportions of Y variation associated with the two simple effects they reflect; we assess the significance of these correlations by calculating and evaluating the F obtained from Eq. (15-9).

Again, we can show that MRC and ANOVA produce equivalent results. From ANOVA, the two sums of squares were 2400.00 and 147.00. From the MRC, we find $(.4143)(5793.00) = 2400.04$ and $(.0254)(5793.00) = 147.14$, respectively.

Comment

In the MRC analysis above, we used coding that comes directly from an ANOVA perspective, creating vectors by multiplying coefficients for the two main effects. Recall from Chap. 14, however, that vectors can be *directly* created to represent any comparison. This is an easier strategy to implement. All that we need is a row of "labels" to signify all the possible treatment cells, such as the following:

$$a_1 b_1 \quad a_2 b_1 \quad a_3 b_1 \quad a_1 b_2 \quad a_2 b_2 \quad a_3 b_2.$$

Then, depending on which contrast is of interest, we can enter code values (coefficients) to represent the contrast. For example, suppose that in our 3×2 design with cell numbers 1 through 6 we are interested in the interaction contrast involving a_1 and a_2 at the two levels of B. The following shows the six cells in the experiment:

	a_1	a_2	a_3
b_1	1	2	3
b_2	4	5	6

Cells 1, 2, 4, and 5 are the ones of interest. Since we are interested in interactions, and since, as we also indicated in Chap. 13, diagonals of such cell representations reflect interactions, we can code the interaction by placing $+1$s in cells 1 and 5, -1s in cells 2 and 4, and 0s in cells 3 and 6. Thus, the vector for this interaction contrast would be transformed to read as follows:

$$a_1 b_1 \quad a_2 b_1 \quad a_3 b_1 \quad a_1 b_2 \quad a_2 b_2 \quad a_3 b_2$$
$$+1 \quad -1 \quad 0 \quad -1 \quad +1 \quad 0$$

Note that this is the same as vector 17 in Table 14-2, which was constructed to represent an interaction.

As another example, suppose we were interested in comparing the *combined* cells 1 and 2 with cell 3 and the combined cells 4 and 5 with cell 6. We then arrange the six treatment cells to create the following table:

	a_1	a_2	a_3
b_1	1	2	3
b_2	4	5	6

This table has the same tabular form as the representation of this interaction contrast in Table 15-5 (page 250). Again, resorting to our diagonal representation, we code the interaction contrast by placing $+1$s in cells 1 and 2 and a $+2$ in cell 6, while placing -1s in cells 4 and 5 and a -2 in cell 3. The code matrix then becomes:

$$
\begin{array}{cccccc}
a_1b_1 & a_2b_1 & a_3b_1 & a_1b_2 & a_2b_2 & a_3b_2 \\
+1 & +1 & -2 & -1 & -1 & +2
\end{array}
$$

This is the same as vector 18 in Table 14-2.

In essence, our message is that if you understand interactions, all you need to do is to set up the design and directly insert code values that follow the simple rule that the sum of the coefficients in a vector equals 0 and that the coefficients reflect the comparison of interest. In other words, interaction contrasts can be established directly without resorting to multiplying of vectors or relying on vectors created by multiplying main-effect vectors.

15.4 COMMENTS ON THE DETAILED ANALYSIS OF INTERACTION

In this chapter and in Chap. 14, we have covered the major analytical approaches available for intelligently analyzing the results of a two-variable factorial design. Which approach you take depends on whether single-*df* comparisons have entered into the plan of the experiment. If they have not, then the key to the analysis is the omnibus test of the $A \times B$ interaction. As you saw in Chap. 14, this test is followed by an analysis of simple effects if the interaction is significant and by an analysis of main effects if it is not. On the other hand, if single-*df* comparisons have been planned, then the key to the analysis is interaction comparisons. As you saw in this chapter, the test of interaction comparisons is also followed by an analysis of simple effects if the interaction is significant.

There are times when the analysis of the omnibus interaction, as described in Chap. 14, will lead to the subsequent analysis of interaction contrasts. Suppose a researcher has conducted an omnibus analysis and has discovered a pattern of significant and nonsignificant simple comparisons. The researcher might like to conclude that this pattern is sufficient for interpreting the outcome of the experiment, but further analysis may not support this notion. What is needed is a test of interaction in which the relevant comparisons are compared directly, and this, of course, is exactly what the analysis of interaction comparisons provides. We suggest, therefore, that researchers evaluate the significance of the relevant interaction comparison when they wish to make statements concerning differences uncovered in simple comparisons.

Finally, you may have noticed that we have not mentioned corrections for familywise type I error stemming from the analyses discussed in this chapter and in Chap. 14. While most correction techniques can be adapted to the factorial design, there is little agreement among researchers whether or not to correct for familywise error in the detailed analysis of a factorial experiment. One of the reasons for this state of affairs is the relative lack of the sort of indiscriminate hypothesis testing often seen in the analysis of single-factor experiments, which is what has generated most of the discussion of familywise error.[4]

Factorial designs are usually undertaken when something is known about one or both of the independent variables. Such designs are not created in a vacuum. The result is an experiment that is more theoretically motivated than is the typical single-factor design. In our opinion, the analysis of a factorial should emphasize planned comparisons, which will usually take the form of interaction comparisons. Planned comparisons are typically few in number, which should help to moderate any concern for familywise error that a researcher might have. In addition, both ANOVA and MRC lean heavily on the occurrence of a significant F, for either an interaction or a simple effect, to justify further statistical analysis—a procedure that again helps to reduce familywise error. In any case, the current research climate appears to favor hypothesis testing that focuses on specific comparisons without a correction for familywise type I error.

15.5 SUMMARY

In this chapter, we considered a second major way of analyzing interaction in a two-factor design: an analysis of *interaction comparisons*. Interaction comparisons consist of smaller, more highly focused factorials derived from the original design.

[4] See Keppel (1982, pp. 240–242) for a more thorough discussion of this matter.

Single-*df* comparisons form the basis for interaction comparisons, creating miniature 2 × 2 designs when they are applied to both independent variables. The 2 × 2 arrangements are used to represent *interaction contrasts*.

An interaction contrast is defined in terms of differences between two means. For example, an interaction contrast is present when the difference obtained for $A_{comp.}$ at one "level" of $B_{comp.}$ is different from the corresponding difference obtained at the other "level" of $B_{comp.}$. The focus of an interaction contrast is quite specific, particularly in comparison with the omnibus $A \times B$ interaction, which reflects the combined influence of more than one interaction contrast. A significant interaction contrast leads to the assessment of relevant simple effects and a more detailed examination of the factors influencing the interaction.

The analysis of interaction contrasts with ANOVA is based on the interaction contrast itself and a formula related to the one we use to analyze single-*df* comparisons in a single-factor design. The corresponding analysis with MRC takes advantage of zero-order correlation coefficients obtained with interaction vectors that have ideally been included in the overall analysis and are thus readily available for the analysis.

15.6   EXERCISES

1. Using the data in Problem 1 in Chap. 13, construct two meaningful interaction contrasts, one comparing the difference between praise and reproof for children and adults and the other comparing the difference between the two combined reinforcement conditions (praise and reproof) with no verbal reinforcement ("none") for childen and adults. Analyze these results via:

(a) ANOVA.

(b) MRC.

16

The Within-Subjects Single-Factor Design

• • •

All the experimental designs we have considered so far are examples of a particular class of designs in which subjects serve in only *one* of the treatment conditions. Because the assignment of subjects to conditions is random in these designs, they are called **completely randomized designs**. Since all treatment effects are based on differences between independent groups of subjects, these designs are also called **between-subjects designs**.

In another class of designs, one that is quite popular in the behavioral sciences, subjects serve in *several* or even *all* of the treatment conditions. Because different treatment effects observed in the same subjects represent differences *within* rather than *between* subjects, these designs are called **within-subjects designs**. (Such designs are also referred to as designs with **repeated measures**.) In this chapter, we will discuss the simplest within-subjects design, in which all subjects receive all levels of a single independent variable. In Chap. 17, we consider a relatively common factorial design in which only the levels of one of the independent variables are administered to the same group of subjects, while the levels of the other independent variable are administered to different groups of subjects.

16.1   ADVANTAGES AND DISADVANTAGES OF WITHIN-SUBJECTS DESIGNS

Advantages

There are several reasons why researchers choose within-subjects designs. One of these derives from the fact that these designs permit the examination of the effects of all levels of an independent variable at the level of the *individual subject*. Since each subject receives all the treatment conditions, we can study how each level of the independent variable affected each of the participants. All else being equal, researchers usually prefer to observe directly the effects of each level of the independent variable on individual subjects rather than inferring the effects of the levels from differences between groups of subjects receiving different treatments.

The within-subjects design is also ideally suited for studying such phenomena as learning, transfer of training, and practice effects of various sorts. In a learning experiment, for example, subjects are usually given repeated exposures on a particular task, and their performance is assessed following each practice trial. The researcher can then determine how subjects improve over repeated presentations of the task. The independent variable in this case consists of the number of learning trials given all subjects.

The primary reason why researchers choose within-subjects designs, however, is that such designs may help them increase the statistical *sensitivity*, or *power*, of the experiment. Under most circumstances, the error terms used to evaluate the significance of treatment effects in within-subjects designs are considerably *smaller* than those used in corresponding between-subjects designs. With smaller error terms, more treatment effects will be significant, and so the power will be increased. Why are error terms smaller in this type of design? We will consider a simple explanation before turning to the detailed analysis in later sections of this chapter.

Suppose we are comparing three treatment conditions in a between-subjects design. By now you realize that even sizable differences among the means might be entirely due to uncontrolled factors. A major source of uncontrolled variability is the fact that subjects with widely different abilities are randomly assigned to the treatment groups. As you have seen, the pooled within-groups mean square (for example, $MS_{S/A}$, for a single-factor experiment) provides an estimate of the degree to which the differences among the means may be reasonably viewed as only the result of uncontrolled subject differences.

Consider another comparison of three treatment conditions, this time set up as a within-subjects design in which subjects receive all three treatments. How are we now to interpret differences found among the treatment means? Can uncontrolled factors still affect the outcome of the experiment, or are they all eliminated because the same subjects are tested in all the treatment conditions? A moment's reflection should suggest that it is virtually impossible to remove completely the influence of uncontrolled factors in any experiment. There are still differences introduced by our inability to exactly duplicate the treatment conditions for different subjects; things that might vary from test to test include factors inherently associated with the treatments themselves, such as the calibration of any equipment and the exact reading of instructions; and other, external factors, such as room temperature, lighting, and background noises. Moreover, even the same subject will change slightly on repeated testing: variations in motivation, attitude, and other factors can cause inconsistent behavior in subjects. On the other hand, it will usually be true that the collective influence of all of these uncontrolled factors will be less with this design than with randomly formed groups of subjects. The result, then, is a smaller error term with which to evaluate the observed differences among treatment means. Assuming that the treatment effects are the same in the two designs, the within-subjects design will be more sensitive than the corresponding between-subjects design. This is because the *denominator* in the F ratio is smaller and, thus, the F ratio itself is larger.

How can the between-subjects design "compete" with this more sensitive design? First, there are circumstances in which testing subjects more than once is either not possible or not feasible. Any experiment using differential instructional sets to define the different treatments, for example, can probably not be convincingly administered to the same subjects. As another example, there are some experiments in which previously administered treatments continue to influence subjects' behavior under a new treatment condition. Second, there are experiments in which subjects are not willing or able to serve in more than one treatment condition. Human subjects who are serving in an experiment as part of a course requirement, for example, may have only an hour or two to spend; a complete administration of the treatments, on the other hand, may take considerably longer. Third, it is always possible to achieve an increase in power by adding to the sample size, rather than by selecting a within-subjects design. Of course, limits on time, money, and other resources may reduce the effectiveness of this strategy. Finally, between-subjects designs can often be made considerably more sensitive through the use of a statistical procedure called the *analysis of covariance*. (We consider this analysis in Chap. 22.)

Disadvantages

There are several problems associated with repeated measures, namely, practice effects, differential carryover effects, and the potential for violations of certain statistical assumptions. We will consider each briefly.

General Practice Effects.   There is no foolproof way of escaping the fact that the performance of the subjects will change systematically during the course of receiving some or all of the treatments in an experiment. The changes may be either positive or negative. On the positive side, in experiments where familiarity with the experimental procedures increases performance, subjects will usually improve as they gain experience with the general requirements of the experiment. On the negative side, subjects may "deteriorate" on subsequent tests as they become bored or tired during the course of the experiment. We will refer to any such changes that occur during the course of testing as **practice effects**. As conceptualized, practice effects are assumed to be *general* and *not the result of exposure to any particular treatment condition* (or conditions). Since it is unlikely that these positive and negative effects of repeated testing will be in perfect balance, we must take their net effect into consideration when designing an experiment.

One solution is to introduce procedures that are designed to eliminate the general effects of repeated testing. If improvement with repeated trials is a possibility, for example, subjects can be given preliminary training on a relevant task before they receive the independent variable so that the improvement is unlikely to occur during the actual experiment. (This technique is frequently used in psychophysical studies and in experiments with animals.) As for the negative factors, boredom can often be minimized through the use of monetary incentives designed to maintain the same level of motivation during the course of the study, while fatigue can be reduced by introducing rest periods between successive administrations of the treatments.

Rarely will these steps remove all practice effects *completely*, however. For this reason, then, researchers usually employ an additional technique which spreads any remaining practice effects equally over the treatment conditions. To see how this works, consider a within-subjects design consisting of only two treatment conditions. Suppose there is a positive practice effect in this experiment, with subjects showing higher scores on whatever task they receive second. If the treatments are presented in the same order to all subjects—for example, condition 1 and then condition 2—it will not be possible to disentangle any effects produced by the different treatments from the overall improvement due to the practice effects. This is because performance on only one of the conditions (condition 2) will show the benefits from practice. We can avoid this problem quite simply by reversing the order of the two conditions (administering condition 2 and then condition 1) for half of the subjects. This way, scores in both conditions benefit equally from any practice effect, removing it as a potential source of bias.

A common technique for neutralizing the effects of practice is **counterbalancing**, which consists of the systematic variation of the order in which the treatments are presented to different subjects. This procedure, which is discussed in most elementary textbooks on experimental design, guarantees that each treatment condition is presented an equal number of times first, second, third, and so on, in particular sequences of conditions given different subjects.

Differential Carryover Effects. **Differential carryover effects** are lingering effects of one or more earlier treatment conditions that combine with the effects of treatments administered later in the testing order. Since these effects will rarely be the same for all conditions—which is why the word *differential* is used—they cannot be neutralized with counterbalancing. For this reason, therefore, they pose a serious problem for any researcher contemplating a within-subjects design.

Consider, for example, an experiment consisting of a drug condition and a control condition. We can reasonably expect that if subjects experience the drug condition first, its effect will influence how they behave when they subsequently receive the control condition, but that experiencing the control condition first will have little effect on how they respond to the subsequent drug condition. The only circumstance under which counterbalancing will work is when the carryover effects for all conditions and orders are the same. Consequently, counterbalancing will not eliminate carryover effects in this situation.

Problems of this sort can occur whenever the treatment conditions differ dramatically, as do the control condition and the experimental condition we discussed in the preceding paragraph. Similar problems often result when instructions are used to create a new treatment condition and to change a subject's perception of a task performed in a prior treatment condition—a common technique in behavioral research. It may be virtually impossible with instructional independent variables to have subjects completely disregard what they have been told in a previous condition. Greenwald (1976) provides a useful discussion of these sorts of problems, which he refers to as *context effects*.

It is often difficult to distinguish between practice effects and differential carryover effects, since both effects result from subjects' receiving more than one of the treatment conditions. The difference lies in whether changes with successive testing are the same for all conditions. In the drug example, they are not. You can always check for the presence of differential carryover effects by plotting the means for each treatment condition on a graph as a function of when it was administered—overall means for first, second, and third place, and so on—and then comparing the "practice" curves for the different conditions. Practice effects will be revealed if the functions for the different treatments exhibit the *same overall shape*; differential carryover effects will be revealed if the shapes are *different*.

You should always consider carefully the possibility of differential carryover effects whenever you contemplate a within-subjects design. Even if you do not expect differential carryover effects to appear, you should nevertheless always examine the treatment means for them. If they do appear, you can still compare the treatment conditions on the *first test*, of course, since carryover effects cannot appear until after the first test; but any statistical tests on the data will probably lack power because of the small number of subjects assigned to the different conditions.

Statistical Assumptions.   The use of the F test to evaluate the significance of treatment effects is predicated on a number of assumptions. In addition to the assumptions of normality, homogeneity of within-treatment variances, and independence, which underlie the statistical analysis of completely randomized designs (see Sec. 8.4), within-subjects designs operate under an assumption concerning the correlations between the multiple measures obtained from the same subjects: that the correlations between all possible pairs of treatments are equal. With three treatments, the assumption is that the correlations between levels a_1 and a_2, between levels a_1 and a_3, and between levels a_2 and a_3 are equal. For the evaluation of F ratios with completely randomized designs (see Sec. 8.4) only severe violations concerning the nature of the distributions of treatment populations are critical, but such is not the case with within-subjects designs. Even minor violations of the underlying assumption will affect how we evaluate the significance of an F ratio in that the critical values of F obtained from Table A-1 are *too small*—the actual critical values we should be using are larger than those listed in the F table. A relatively simple solution to this problem is to use a slightly more stringent significance level—.025 rather than the standard .05—which will correct the difficulty in most situations.[1] Fortunately, evaluation of single-*df* comparisons seems to be unaffected by these violations, provided that specific error terms are used for these tests (Keppel, 1982, pp. 472–473). We will discuss the use of such error terms in Sec. 16.4.

16.2 THE OVERALL ANALYSIS: THE ANOVA APPROACH

For the overall statistical analysis of the single-factor within-subjects design, we make use of procedures we considered in earlier chapters. Only one point is new: in order to evaluate the significance of the treatment effects, we need to calculate an error term that takes into account that all subjects receive all the treatment conditions.

Design and Notation

The single-factor within-subjects design is defined as an experiment in which all subjects are tested under all the treatment conditions. In fact, the design can be viewed as a type of factorial design in which the independent variable (factor *A*) and *subjects* (factor *S*) are crossed to form all possible combinations of the levels of the two factors. We will refer to this arrangement as an (*A* × *S*) design to emphasize the relationship of this design to an actual factorial. (We use parentheses to designate a within-subjects factor, for reasons that we will explain in Sec. 17.1.)

As an illustration of the (*A* × *S*) design, consider an experiment in which $s - 3$ subjects are each tested under all $a = 3$ treatment conditions. We will assume that some form of counterbalancing is used in order to balance possible practice effects.[2] This design and the notation required are presented on the right-hand side of Table 16-1. For contrast, the corresponding between-subjects design is presented on the left. It is important to note the differences between these two designs. Both designs produce the same quantity of data, namely, three *Y* scores obtained from each of the conditions. The basic difference is that the *same* three subjects are represented under each of the three treatments in the within-subjects design, while three *different* subjects are correspondingly represented in the between-subjects design. Because of this difference, we have one additional piece of information from the (*A* × *S*) design that we lacked with the other design, namely,

---

[1] The nature of these assumptions and the steps that can be taken to reduce the effects of violating them are discussed in most advanced statistical books (see, for example, Keppel, 1982, pp. 467–473; Kirk, 1982, pp. 256–262; Myers, 1979, pp. 171–174; and Winer, 1971, pp. 281–283).

[2] This could be accomplished, for example, by presenting the three conditions in the order 1-2-3 for the first subject, 2-3-1 for the second subject, and 3-1-2 for the third subject.

Table 16-1

Comparison of the Between-Subjects and Within-Subjects Designs

	Between-Subjects Design						Within-Subjects Design			
a_1		a_2		a_3			a_1	a_2	a_3	Sum
s_1	$Y_{1,1}$	s_4	$Y_{2,4}$	s_7	$Y_{3,7}$	s_1	$Y_{1,1}$	$Y_{2,1}$	$Y_{3,1}$	S_1
s_2	$Y_{1,2}$	s_5	$Y_{2,5}$	s_8	$Y_{3,8}$	s_2	$Y_{1,2}$	$Y_{2,2}$	$Y_{3,2}$	S_2
s_3	$Y_{1,3}$	s_6	$Y_{2,6}$	s_9	$Y_{3,9}$	s_3	$Y_{1,3}$	$Y_{2,3}$	$Y_{3,3}$	S_3
Sum	A_1	Sum	A_2	Sum	A_3	Sum	A_1	A_2	A_3	T

an overall sum of the treatment scores for each subject. The sums for individual subjects, which are designated S_1, S_2, and S_3, are represented as row marginal sums in the table. As you will see, we will need these sums when we calculate the new error term.

The Analysis

With the between-subjects design, we divided the total sum of squares SS_T into two component parts, the treatment sum of squares SS_A and the within-groups sum of squares $SS_{S/A}$. This latter quantity, which is based on the pooled variation of subjects treated alike, is used to calculate the error term; it is an estimate of the uncontrolled variability present in an experiment based on a between-subjects design. As we have pointed out already, the $(A \times S)$ design provides a way of reducing this uncontrolled variability; it effectively reduces the contribution of chance factors to the differences among the treatment means. Using each subject for all the treatments allows us to obtain an estimate of the degree to which individual subjects respond consistently across the conditions, or an estimate of the consistency of individual differences. If we can assess this consistency, we have, in effect, explained more of the dependent variable, and thus leave a lower amount of unexplained variability.

Calculating the New Sums of Squares. The key to the analysis, then, is to estimate the degree to which using the same subjects represents a consistent or constant factor in the experiment. Such an estimate is easily calculated from the information provided by the overall sums for the respective subjects. That is, the sum for each subject (S_j) can be transformed into a mean for each subject $(\bar{Y}_{S_j})$, which in turn can be represented as a deviation from the overall mean $\bar{Y}_T$ and, ultimately, as a sum of squares SS_S. Stated another way, we can compute a main effect of subjects (SS_S), which represents the degree to which the subjects behave *consistently* as they shift from treatment to treatment. If we subtract this sum of squares from the pooled "within-groups" sum of squares $SS_{S/A}$, which, you will recall, would represent uncontrolled variation if we ignored the fact that the same subjects are involved, we obtain a new sum of squares that can be used to estimate the degree to which uncontrolled factors are operating in the $(A \times S)$ design. That is,

$$SS_{error\ term} = SS_{S/A} - SS_S$$

We noted in the preceding paragraph that the subject sum of squares is based on the deviation of each subject's average score $\bar{Y}_S$ from the grand mean $\bar{Y}_T$; in symbols,

$$\bar{Y}_S - \bar{Y}_T$$

As you have seen before, we can use this deviation to express the sum of squares in terms of basic ratios. More specifically,

$$SS_S = [S] - [T]$$

where $[S]$ and $[T]$ represent basic ratios based on subject sums S and the grand sum T, respectively. The only new quantity is $[S]$, which is calculated as follows:

$$[S] = \frac{\Sigma S^2}{a}$$

where S = the sum obtained by adding together all the Y scores for each subject

a = the number of treatments given to each subject

The formula for $[T]$ should be familiar to you by now.

As we indicated earlier, the sum of squares for the error term used in the analysis of the $(A \times S)$ design may be obtained by subtraction. Expressing that sum of squares in terms of basic ratios, we find that

$$\begin{aligned}
SS_{error\ term} &= SS_{S/A} - SS_S \\
&= ([Y] - [A]) - ([S] - [T]) \\
&= [Y] - [A] - [S] + [T] \quad\quad\quad\quad (16\text{-}1)
\end{aligned}$$

It is also possible to conceptualize this sum of squares as an *interaction*, which is how we will designate the error term in the remainder of the chapter. We pointed out already that the data matrix for the $(A \times S)$ design in Table 16-1 is in fact a factorial matrix, where the columns represent the levels of the independent variable (factor A) and the rows the "levels" of the subject "factor."[3] From our knowledge

---

[3] The only difference between the matrix in Table 16-1 and those associated with factorial designs we considered previously is that each cell of this matrix contains *one* observation rather than the sum of several.

of factorial designs, we would expect to subdivide the total sum of squares into sums of squares for two main effects (SS_A and SS_S) and an $A \times S$ interaction ($SS_{A \times S}$). There would be no "within-cell" variation, of course, since there is only one observation per cell in this matrix. We can now calculate the interaction sum of squares by subtracting the sums of squares for the two main effects from the total sum of squares:

$$SS_{A \times S} = SS_T - SS_A - SS_S$$
$$= ([Y] - [T]) - ([A] - [T]) - ([S] - [T])$$
$$= [Y] - [A] - [S] + [T]$$

which is identical to Eq. (16-1).

Expressing the error term as an interaction sum of squares provides us with another way of understanding the nature of this new quantity: the $A \times S$ interaction represents the *unique manner* in which the different subjects respond to the treatment conditions. In other words, the error term consists of variability not attributable either to the treatment effects or to consistent individual differences.

Computational Formulas.   The computational formulas for the overall analysis of variance are presented in Table 16-2. We have already discussed the formulas for the sums of squares. The formulas for the degrees of freedom require little comment, except for the error term, which reflects the form usually associated with an interaction. That is, the *df* for an interaction are generally specified as the

Table 16-2
ANOVA: Computational Formulas

Source	Basic Ratio*	df	Sum of Squares	MS	F
A	$[A] = \dfrac{\Sigma A^2}{s}$	$a - 1$	$[A] - [T]$	$\dfrac{SS_A}{df_A}$	$\dfrac{MS_A}{MS_{A \times S}}$
S	$[S] = \dfrac{\Sigma S^2}{a}$	$s - 1$	$[S] - [T]$	$\dfrac{SS_S}{df_S}$	
$A \times S$	$[Y] = \Sigma Y^2$	$(a - 1)(s - 1)$	$[Y] - [A] - [S] + [T]$	$\dfrac{MS_{A \times S}}{df_{A \times S}}$	
Total	$[T] = \dfrac{T^2}{(a)(s)}$	$(a)(s) - 1$	$[Y] - [T]$		

* Bracketed letters represent complete terms in computational formulas; a particular term is identified by the letter(s) appearing in the numerator.

product of the *df*'s associated with the relevant main effects. In the present case,

$$df_{A \times S} = (df_A)(df_S)$$
$$= (a - 1)(s - 1)$$

The remainder of the analysis is relatively straightforward. The treatment effects are assessed by evaluating the significance of an F ratio formed by dividing MS_A by $MS_{A \times S}$.

A Numerical Example

For a numerical example, we return to the data we used to illustrate the analysis of the between-subjects single-factor experiment. In that experiement, subjects were randomly assigned to one of the three treatment conditions; lectures on physical science (a_1), social science (a_2), and history (a_3). Each condition was assigned 12 subjects, for a total of 36 subjects. Suppose instead that the experiment was an $(A \times S)$ design in which we had only 12 subjects and each of the 12 subjects received all three lectures rather than only one. Consider the data presented in Table 16-3. The data matrix of Y scores (the AS matrix) displays the data by treatment and subject and provides all the information necessary to conduct an overall ANOVA.

Table 16-3
Numerical Example: AS Matrix

	Treatments			
	a_1	a_2	a_3	Sum
s_1	53	47	45	145
s_2	49	42	41	132
s_3	47	39	38	124
s_4	42	37	36	115
s_5	51	42	35	128
s_6	34	33	33	100
s_7	44	13	46	103
s_8	48	16	40	104
s_9	35	16	29	80
s_{10}	18	10	21	49
s_{11}	32	11	30	73
s_{12}	27	6	20	53
Sum	480	312	414	1206

Table 16-4
Summary of the Analysis

Source	Basic Ratio	Sum of Squares	df	MS	F
A	$[A] = 41{,}595.00$	$[A] - [T] = 1194.00$	2	597.00	12.30*
S	$[S] = 43{,}932.67$	$[S] - [T] = 3531.67$	11	321.06	
$A \times S$	$[Y] = 46{,}194$	$[Y] - [A] - [S] + [T] = 1067.33$	22	48.52	
Total	$[T] = 40{,}401.00$	$[Y] - [T] = 5793.00$	35		

* $p < .01$.

We will assume that the order in which the lectures were given was systematically varied among the subjects, using some appropriate counterbalancing scheme. In the present case, one could arrange the three lectures in all six possible orders, namely,

1–2–3;   1–3–2;   2–1–3;   2–3–1;   3–1–2;   and   3–2–1

and use each order twice, so that, for example, subjects 1 and 2 would receive order 1-2-3, subjects 3 and 4 would receive order 1-3-2, and so forth. However it is accomplished, the arrangement should guarantee that each lecture is presented equally often as the first, the second, or the third condition subjects encounter, in order to balance practice effects evenly among all three treatment conditions.[4]

Without comment, we will calculate the basic ratios needed for the ANOVA:

$$[T] = \frac{T^2}{(a)(s)} = \frac{1206^2}{(3)(12)} = 40{,}401.00$$

$$[A] = \frac{\Sigma A^2}{s} = \frac{480^2 + 312^2 + 414^2}{12} = 41{,}595.00$$

$$[S] = \frac{\Sigma S^2}{a} = \frac{145^2 + 132^2 + \cdots + 73^2 + 53^2}{3} = 43{,}932.67$$

$$[Y] = \Sigma Y^2 = 53^2 + 49^2 + \cdots + 30^2 + 20^2 = 46{,}194$$

The values of these basic ratios are entered in Table 16-4, where they are combined to produce the required sums of squares. The F of 12.30, which is evaluated with $df_{num.} = 2$ and $df_{denom.} = 22$, is significant at the $p < .01$ level.

[4] This experiment would probably also require the use of three different vocabulary tests. That is, each subject would receive a different vocabulary test following each lecture. Good experimental design would also require that each of the tests be used equally often with each of the three treatment conditions. Otherwise, it would not be possible to separate out the effects of the experimental treatments (lectures) from any differences in test difficulty.

We mentioned in Sec. 16.1 that when certain statistical assumptions are not met by the experimental data, a more conservative method of evaluating the significance of the obtained F may be necessary. One approach we suggested was to adopt a slightly more stringent significance level and to evaluate the F with this new critical value. To illustrate, we might consider setting $\alpha = .025$, for example, rather than equal to the usual .05. The critical value would now become 4.38 rather than the 3.44 normally appropriate when the statistical assumptions are met. In the present example, this new significance level does not change our decision; the F is still significant.[5]

16.3   THE OVERALL ANALYSIS: THE MRC APPROACH

There are several ways to approach the analysis of the $(A \times S)$ design with MRC procedures. As you might suspect, the differences are in the coding used to represent the new critical source of variability. As we did when we discussed previous designs, we will emphasize contrast coding. The coding system needs to take into account the fact that "subjects" constitute a main effect. Thus, for within-subjects designs, the only new coding for us is the coding of "subjects"; otherwise, the coding system for treatment effects is the same as it was in the between-subjects design.

Coding the Main Effects

As we just stated, we will represent the variability of subjects with *contrast coding*. The number of vectors needed for this main effect is the number of subjects minus 1. With contrast coding, we easily construct a set of vectors whereby each vector in essence "compares" a subject systematically with each of the other subjects. The code matrix depicted in Table 16-5 indicates the results of this simple strategy. As you can see, the first subject has been used as the "comparison" subject, who is assigned a +1 in *all* the subject vectors (vectors 1 to 11); the remaining subjects

[5] An alternative approach is to use the so-called Geisser-Greenhouse correction (Geisser & Greenhouse, 1958), which gives us the appropriate critical value for the worst situation in which the assumptions are maximally violated. For this design, the correction consists of using $df_{num.} = 1$, rather than 2, and $df_{denom.} = s - 1 = 11$, rather than 22. The new critical value of F is now 4.84, and again, the observed F is significant. The Geisser-Greenhouse correction is only necessary when assumptions are maximally violated, however; the correction for in-between situations—between maximum violation and no violation—is more complicated (see Keppel, 1982, pp. 470–472).

Table 16-5
Code Matrix for Subjects

Subject	Subject Vectors										
	S1	S2	S3	S4	S5	S6	S7	S8	S9	S10	S11
1	1	1	1	1	1	1	1	1	1	1	1
2	−1	0	0	0	0	0	0	0	0	0	0
3	0	−1	0	0	0	0	0	0	0	0	0
4	0	0	−1	0	0	0	0	0	0	0	0
5	0	0	0	−1	0	0	0	0	0	0	0
6	0	0	0	0	−1	0	0	0	0	0	0
7	0	0	0	0	0	−1	0	0	0	0	0
8	0	0	0	0	0	0	−1	0	0	0	0
9	0	0	0	0	0	0	0	−1	0	0	0
10	0	0	0	0	0	0	0	0	−1	0	0
11	0	0	0	0	0	0	0	0	0	−1	0
12	0	0	0	0	0	0	0	0	0	0	−1

are assigned a −1 when they are "compared" with the first subject and a 0 when they are not. Thus, the first subject vector (S1) in Table 16-5 (which is the first column of the code matrix) has a +1 assigned to the first subject, a −1 assigned to the second subject, and a 0 assigned to all other subjects. The second vector (S2) has a +1 again assigned to the first subject, a −1 to the *third* subject, and a 0 to all others. To continue, the final subject vector (S11) has a +1 assigned to the first subject, a −1 to the twelfth (and last) subject, and a 0 to all others. This systematic method of coding subjects permits us to "capture" the variability due to differences among subjects in this experiment. It is as if we had 12 treatment conditions and the first treatment were compared with every other treatment.[6]

The entire coding scheme and the data for analysis are shown in Table 16-6. We begin by arranging the Y scores from Table 16-3 into a single column of observations, as we have done in column 2 of Table 16-6. Though we have only 12 subjects, we do have 36 rows of data. You should note that the sets of 12 scores—one set for each treatment condition—are arranged so that all subjects occupy the same ordinal positions in the three sets. The first subject is listed first

[6] The vectors created by this coding are not mutually orthogonal. On the other hand, orthogonality within the *set* of vectors is not critical since the $R^2_{Y.S}$ will reflect subject variability regardless of the intercorrelation between the vectors.

Table 16-6
An Example of Coding in the (A × S) Design

	Subject (1)	Y (2)	A1 (3)	A2 (4)	S1 (5)	S2 (6)	S3 (7)	S4 (8)	S5 (9)	S6 (10)	S7 (11)	S8 (12)	S9 (13)	S10 (14)	S11 (15)
										Vectors					
a_1	1	53	1	1	1	1	1	1	1	1	1	1	1	1	1
	2	49	1	1	-1	0	0	0	0	0	0	0	0	0	0
	3	47	1	1	0	-1	0	0	0	0	0	0	0	0	0
	4	42	1	1	0	0	-1	0	0	0	0	0	0	0	0
	5	51	1	1	0	0	0	-1	0	0	0	0	0	0	0
	6	34	1	1	0	0	0	0	-1	0	0	0	0	0	0
	7	44	1	1	0	0	0	0	0	-1	0	0	0	0	0
	8	48	1	1	0	0	0	0	0	0	-1	0	0	0	0
	9	35	1	1	0	0	0	0	0	0	0	-1	0	0	0
	10	18	1	1	0	0	0	0	0	0	0	0	-1	0	0
	11	32	1	1	0	0	0	0	0	0	0	0	0	-1	0
	12	27	1	1	0	0	0	0	0	0	0	0	0	0	-1
a_2	1	47	-1	1	1	1	1	1	1	1	1	1	1	1	1
	2	42	-1	1	-1	0	0	0	0	0	0	0	0	0	0
	3	39	-1	1	0	-1	0	0	0	0	0	0	0	0	0
	4	37	-1	1	0	0	-1	0	0	0	0	0	0	0	0
	5	42	-1	1	0	0	0	-1	0	0	0	0	0	0	0
	6	33	-1	1	0	0	0	0	-1	0	0	0	0	0	0
	7	13	-1	1	0	0	0	0	0	-1	0	0	0	0	0
	8	16	-1	1	0	0	0	0	0	0	-1	0	0	0	0
	9	16	-1	1	0	0	0	0	0	0	0	-1	0	0	0
	10	10	-1	1	0	0	0	0	0	0	0	0	-1	0	0
	11	11	-1	1	0	0	0	0	0	0	0	0	0	-1	0
	12	6	-1	1	0	0	0	0	0	0	0	0	0	0	-1

Table 16-6 Continued

Subject (1)	Y (2)	A1 (3)	A2 (4)	S1 (5)	S2 (6)	S3 (7)	S4 (8)	S5 (9)	S6 (10)	S7 (11)	S8 (12)	S9 (13)	S10 (14)	S11 (15)
								Vectors						
1	45	0	-2	1	1	1	1	1	1	1	1	1	1	1
2	41	0	-2	-1	0	0	0	0	0	0	0	0	0	0
3	38	0	-2	0	-1	0	0	0	0	0	0	0	0	0
4	36	0	-2	0	0	-1	0	0	0	0	0	0	0	0
5	35	0	-2	0	0	0	-1	0	0	0	0	0	0	0
6	33	0	-2	0	0	0	0	-1	0	0	0	0	0	0
7	46	0	-2	0	0	0	0	0	-1	0	0	0	0	0
8	40	0	-2	0	0	0	0	0	0	-1	0	0	0	0
9	29	0	-2	0	0	0	0	0	0	0	-1	0	0	0
10	21	0	-2	0	0	0	0	0	0	0	0	-1	0	0
11	30	0	-2	0	0	0	0	0	0	0	0	0	-1	0
12	20	0	-2	0	0	0	0	0	0	0	0	0	0	-1

a_3

in all three sets, the second subject is listed second in all sets, and so on. Thus, the code matrix (see Table 16-5) is repeated three times. Any other arrangement would cause confusion in assigning numerical values for the different vectors. In Table 16-6, the subjects are identified in the first column, and, as noted above, the corresponding Y scores are listed in the second column. The next two columns contain vectors coding the treatment effects. As in between-subjects designs, we need to identify meaningful comparisons, and here we repeat those of previous chapters:

	a_1	a_2	a_3
Vector $A1$	1	-1	0
Vector $A2$	1	1	-2

Vector $A1$ represents a comparison between physical science and social science (column 3), and vector $A2$ (column 4) represents a comparison between the combined sciences and history. The next 11 columns (5 through 15) present the subject vectors needed for the analysis. As you can see, the code matrix for subjects presented in Table 16-5 is simply repeated in its entirety for each level for factor A. In this manner, the three scores for the first subject (that subject's scores at a_1, a_2, and a_3) are compared systematically with the three scores for each of the other subjects over the 11 vectors (vectors $S1$ through $S11$, columns 5 through 15).

As you know from Sec. 16.2, the standard ANOVA partitions the total Y variability into three sources, namely, A, S, and $A \times S$. By using the vectors presented in Table 16-6, we can calculate $R^2_{Y.set}$'s for the first two ($R^2_{Y.A}$ and $R^2_{Y.S}$) and calculate the remaining $R^2_{Y.A \times S}$ by subtraction. For $R^2_{Y.A \times S}$, then,

$$R^2_{Y.A \times S} = 1 - R^2_{Y.A} - R^2_{Y.S} \qquad (16\text{-}2)$$

What Eq. (16-2) implies is that if we subtract from unity (1) the variability that is explained by the treatments (A) and the variability explained by subjects in the experiment (S), the remaining variability is unexplained or based on uncontrolled factors; this latter quantity, the $A \times S$ interaction, will be used to calculate the error term.

The analysis now proceeds along familiar grounds. We start by using the two A vectors (columns 3 and 4) to calculate $R^2_{Y.A}$, and the eleven S vectors (columns 5 through 15) to calculate $R^2_{Y.S}$. (It should be noted that the A and S effects are orthogonal because of the nature of the design.) We find that

$$R^2_{Y.A} = .2061 \qquad \text{and} \qquad R^2_{Y.S} = .6096$$

Table 16-7
Summary of the MRC Analysis

Source	R^2	df	Mean R^2	F
A	.2061	2	.1031	12.27*
S	.6069	11	.0554	
A × S	.1843	22	.0084	
Total	1.0000	35		

* $p < .01$.

Finally, we obtain $R^2_{Y.A \times S}$—the "residual" source of variability—by substituting the above quantities in Eq. (16-2) and completing the indicated calculations:

$$R^2_{Y.A \times S} = 1 - .2061 - .6096 = .1843$$

This residual source of variability may also be designated by the quantity $1 - R^2_{Y.max.}$, where $R^2_{Y.max.}$ is based on columns 3 through 15 in Table 16-6.

For convenience, we have entered these quantities into a summary table (Table 16-7) for the final steps in the analysis. In an MRC analysis, the df are determined by the number of vectors used to represent any given source: 2 vectors for A and 11 vectors for S. The df for the "residual" source—the A × S interaction—are the number of vectors needed to compute the residual sum of squares; they can be found by substituting in the general formula for a residual source of variability, namely,

$$df_{A \times S} = N - k - 1$$

where N refers to the total number of observations and k refers to the total number of vectors used to calculate the $R^2_{Y.max.}$. In the present case,

$$R^2_{Y.max.} = R^2_{Y.A} + R^2_{Y.S}$$

which is based on 13 vectors, 2 from A and 11 from S. Thus,

$$df_{A \times S} = 36 - 13 - 1 = 22$$

Of course, these df's are the same as those calculated for ANOVA, and except for rounding error, the F's are identical (12.27 versus 12.30).

Comment.   Let us examine what the $R^2_{Y.S}$ represents. In this numerical example, $R^2_{Y.S} = .6096$, which means that there was a fairly high degree of consistency within the subjects; in general, a high performer was high in all conditions (e.g., subjects

1 and 2), whereas a low performer was low in all conditions (e.g., subjects 10 and 12). What would we conclude if $R^2_{Y.S}$ were equal to 1.00? This would mean that the same person was the highest scorer in *all* conditions, another person was the next highest scorer in *all* conditions, all the way down to the last person, who was the lowest performer in all conditions. Furthermore, with $R^2_{Y.S} = 1.00$, there would be no treatment effect, because the squared multiple correlation $R^2_{Y.A}$ would be 0.00. On the other hand, if $R^2_{Y.S}$ were equal to 0.00, the situation would be equivalent to a completely randomized design in which each Y score is independent of the others, since $R^2_{Y.A \times S}$ would equal $1 - R^2_{Y.A}$, which is $R^2_{Y.S/A}$ in the completely randomized design.

In essence, the correlational analysis of the experiment illustrates the manner in which a within-subjects design operates. The design takes advantage of the fact that subjects are consistent in their responses (behavior) and that their consistency can explain some of the variability among the Y scores. Thus, we have increased the power of the experiment and are more likely to find significant treatment effects.

Coding the $A \times S$ Interaction

Although the $A \times S$ interaction is conveniently found by subtraction, $R^2_{Y.A \times S}$ can be calculated directly by means of *interaction vectors*. More specifically, interaction vectors can be created simply by cross-multiplying each of the A vectors with all the S vectors. In the present case, we would have two sets of interaction vectors: one set formed by cross-multiplying the numerical codes constituting vector $A1$ with the corresponding codes constituting the 11 subject vectors ($S1$ through $S11$), and another set formed the same way between $A2$ and the subject vectors. Table 16-8 illustrates the results of this process. Vector $A1S1$, for example, is created by cross-multiplying vectors $A1$ and $S1$ from Table 16-6; vector $A1S2$ is created by cross-multiplying vectors $A1$ and $S2$; and so on. Twenty-two vectors are produced by this process, which is no surprise, since $df_{A \times S} = 22$. Table 16-8 shows the outcome for these and other other selected interaction vectors. An R^2 based on these 22 vectors gives the interaction *directly* without the subtraction process involved in Eq. (16-2). That is, $R^2_{Y.A \times S} = .1842$, which, except for rounding error, is identical to the value we obtained with Eq. (16-2).

Because we can always obtain $R^2_{Y.A \times S}$ by subtracting $R^2_{Y.A}$ and $R^2_{Y.S}$ from 1, interaction vectors are not needed for the omnibus analysis we have just performed. On the other hand, it is frequently useful to include these vectors in setting up any analysis, since the interaction vectors are needed for conducting single-df comparisons in within-subjects designs. (Single-df comparisons in within-subjects designs are discussed in Sec. 16.4.)

Table 16-8
Vectors Representing the $A \times S$ Interaction

Subject		Y	Vectors									
			$A1S1$	$A1S2$	$\cdots$	$A1S10$	$A1S11$	$A2S1$	$A2S2$	$\cdots$	$A2S10$	$A2S11$
a_1	1	53	1	1	$\cdots$	1	1	1	1	$\cdots$	1	1
	2	49	-1	0	$\cdots$	0	0	-1	0	$\cdots$	0	0
	3	47	0	-1	$\cdots$	0	0	0	-1	$\cdots$	0	0
	4	42	0	0	$\cdots$	0	0	0	0	$\cdots$	0	0
	5	51	0	0	$\cdots$	0	0	0	0	$\cdots$	0	0
	6	34	0	0	$\cdots$	0	0	0	0	$\cdots$	0	0
	7	44	0	0	$\cdots$	0	0	0	0	$\cdots$	0	0
	8	48	0	0	$\cdots$	0	0	0	0	$\cdots$	0	0
	9	35	0	0	$\cdots$	0	0	0	0	$\cdots$	0	0
	10	18	0	0	$\cdots$	0	0	0	0	$\cdots$	0	0
	11	32	0	0	$\cdots$	-1	0	0	0	$\cdots$	-1	0
	12	27	0	0	$\cdots$	0	-1	0	0	$\cdots$	0	-1
a_2	1	47	-1	-1	$\cdots$	-1	-1	1	1	$\cdots$	1	1
	2	42	1	0	$\cdots$	0	0	-1	0	$\cdots$	0	0
	3	39	0	1	$\cdots$	0	0	0	-1	$\cdots$	0	0
	4	37	0	0	$\cdots$	0	0	0	0	$\cdots$	0	0
	5	42	0	0	$\cdots$	0	0	0	0	$\cdots$	0	0
	6	33	0	0	$\cdots$	0	0	0	0	$\cdots$	0	0
	7	13	0	0	$\cdots$	0	0	0	0	$\cdots$	0	0
	8	16	0	0	$\cdots$	0	0	0	0	$\cdots$	0	0
	9	16	0	0	$\cdots$	0	0	0	0	$\cdots$	0	0
	10	10	0	0	$\cdots$	0	0	0	0	$\cdots$	0	0
	11	11	0	0	$\cdots$	1	0	0	0	$\cdots$	-1	0
	12	6	0	0	$\cdots$	0	1	0	0	$\cdots$	0	-1
a_3	1	45	0	0	$\cdots$	0	0	-2	-2	$\cdots$	-2	-2
	2	41	0	0	$\cdots$	0	0	2	0	$\cdots$	0	0
	3	38	0	0	$\cdots$	0	0	0	2	$\cdots$	0	0
	4	36	0	0	$\cdots$	0	0	0	0	$\cdots$	0	0
	5	35	0	0	$\cdots$	0	0	0	0	$\cdots$	0	0
	6	33	0	0	$\cdots$	0	0	0	0	$\cdots$	0	0
	7	46	0	0	$\cdots$	0	0	0	0	$\cdots$	0	0
	8	40	0	0	$\cdots$	0	0	0	0	$\cdots$	0	0
	9	29	0	0	$\cdots$	0	0	0	0	$\cdots$	0	0
	10	21	0	0	$\cdots$	0	0	0	0	$\cdots$	0	0
	11	30	0	0	$\cdots$	0	0	0	0	$\cdots$	2	0
	12	20	0	0	$\cdots$	0	0	0	0	$\cdots$	0	2

In essence, the MRC strategy allows us at least two options for determining the error term:[7]

1. To calculate the error term directly by creating interaction vectors based on the vectors established for A and S
2. To calculate the error term indirectly by summing $R^2_{Y.A}$ and $R^2_{Y.S}$ to obtain $R^2_{Y.max.}$ and subtracting this sum from 1, as specified in Eq. (16-2)

16.4 COMPARISONS INVOLVING THE TREATMENT MEANS

As we have stated throughout this book, researchers usually design single-factor experiments with specific comparisons between the treatment conditions in mind. The same analytical procedures available for the analysis of a between-subjects design are available for a within-subjects design. The only complication is the determination of the *error term*. With the completely randomized design, the error term for the omnibus analysis ($MS_{S/A}$) is used as the denominator term of the F ratio for *any* comparison undertaken in the analysis. This procedure was justified by the assumption that population treatment variances are equal, which implies that the overall error term provides a perfectly suitable estimate of error variance present in any comparison conducted on the treatment means.[8]

With the ($A \times S$) design, on the other hand, there is no assurance that the error term from the omnibus analysis ($MS_{A \times S}$) can serve a similar function in the detailed analysis of an experiment. This certainty is lacking because the $A \times S$ interaction is actually an average of a number of *component interactions*, which may or may not be appropriately estimated by the overall error term. In many cases, they are not. The solution to this problem is conceptually simple, namely, to use as error terms $A \times S$ interactions that are each relevant to specific *single comparisons*, which we will call $A_{comp.} \times S$ interactions. As you will see, each of these error

---

[7] A third method of coding is frequently recommended for the analysis of within-subjects designs called *sum coding* or *criterion scaling* (see, for example, Edwards, 1979, pp. 120–123; Pedhazur, 1977). This ingenious method captures the entire source of subject variability with a *single vector*, in that the vector contains the sum of scores across all of the conditions for each subject. Unfortunately, this method of coding is *not* useful for conducting single-*df* comparisons, which, for most researchers, is the primary purpose of an experiment and its analysis.

[8] This statement is correct only when the homogeneity assumption is reasonably met by the data. With heterogeneous variances, special error terms are recommended (see Keppel, 1982, pp. 116–117).

terms is based *only* on the data contributing to the particular comparison under study.

Computational Procedures: ANOVA

A single-*df* comparison $A_{comp.}$ reflects the variability associated with the difference between two means. The error term for the mean square based on this difference reflects the degree to which individual subjects deviate from this average difference. This particular variation is represented by an *interaction*, $A_{comp.} \times S$, which, as we have already noted, is not necessarily estimated by the overall $A \times S$ interaction. We will consider the analysis of two comparisons, one a comparison between two means (physical science and social science) and the other a complex comparison (combined sciences and history).

The Computational Formulas.   We begin with the comparison between physical science and social science. Consider the data arrangement in Table 16-9. The original *AS* matrix of *Y* scores is presented on the left. In the middle are the scores for each subject that will actually enter into this analysis, namely, a score obtained

Table 16-9
Calculation of a Separate Error Term

Subject	AS Matrix			Comparison Matrix		Calculations	
	a_1	a_2	a_3	Physical Science	Social Science	Difference	SS
1	53	47	45	53	47	6	18.00
2	49	42	41	49	42	7	24.50
3	47	39	38	47	39	8	32.00
4	42	37	36	42	37	5	12.50
5	51	42	35	51	42	9	40.50
6	34	33	33	34	33	1	.50
7	44	13	46	44	13	31	480.50
8	48	16	40	48	16	32	512.00
9	35	16	29	35	16	19	180.50
10	18	10	21	18	10	8	32.00
11	32	11	30	32	11	21	220.50
12	27	6	20	27	6	21	220.50
Mean:				40.00	26.00	14.00	

after the physical science lecture and a score obtained after the social science lecture. Consider this *comparison matrix* carefully. What we have is a matrix of scores that could be viewed as the results of a "miniature" $(A \times S)$ design with only *two levels*. If in fact there were only two levels, we could calculate the standard sources of variance—an A, an S, and an $A \times S$ interaction—using the formulas from Sec. 16.2. The F test would consist of dividing the treatment mean square MS_A by the error term, $MS_{A \times S}$. This is exactly what we will accomplish in the analysis, except that the "treatment effect" is really the comparison effect $(MS_{A_{comp.}})$ and the "error term" is an interaction based only on the data involved in the comparison $(MS_{A_{comp.} \times S})$.

There are several ways to calculate the necessary sums of squares. The method we will illustrate focuses on the *difference* score for each subject. The differences are given in the right-hand portion of Table 16-9. For the first subject, the difference is $53 - 47 = 6$; for the second subject, the difference is $49 - 42 = 7$; and so on. The bottom row of the table gives the means for the two treatment conditions and the difference between them; that is,

$$\hat{\psi} = 40.00 - 26.00 = 14.00$$

The first step is to transform these various differences into sums of squares. The sum of squares for any given subject is given by

$$SS_{A_{comp.} \text{ for } s_j} = \frac{(\text{Diff.})^2}{\Sigma (c_i)^2} \tag{16-3}$$

(In a moment, we will eventually combine the sums of squares from all the subjects.) Next, we calculate the comparison sum of squares $SS_{A_{comp.}}$, using the formula originally presented in Chap. 11:

$$SS_{A_{comp}} = \frac{(s)(\hat{\psi})^2}{\Sigma (c_i)^2} \tag{16-4}$$

The interaction sum of squares $SS_{A_{comp.} \times S}$ is obtained by subtracting the comparison sum of squares $SS_{A_{comp.}}$ from the sum of the subject sums of squares. That is,

$$SS_{A_{comp.} \times S} = \Sigma \frac{(\text{Diff.})^2}{\Sigma (c_i)^2} - SS_{A_{comp.}} \tag{16-5}$$

(Although we will not demonstrate it here, this sum of squares is identical to an "$SS_{A \times S}$" obtained by treating the comparison matrix as an actual within-subjects design.)

Before we turn to the numerical example, let us look at the operations specified in Eq. (16-5). Consider the first quantity on the right side of the equation. This is a composite sum of squares that combines the treatment sums of squares for the individual subjects. This quantity reflects the difference between the two treatments and the *unique way* in which each subject responds to the two treatments (the interaction). To make this sum useful as an error term, we must remove the *systematic source* of variability—the treatment difference—from the composite sum of squares. This is precisely what we accomplished by subtracting $SS_{A_{comp.}}$ in Eq. (16-5).

A Numerical Example.   We will illustrate the calculations with the data in Table 16-9. Using Eq. (16-3), we find the comparison sum of squares for the first subject to be:

$$SS_{A_{comp.} \text{ for } s_1} = \frac{(6)^2}{(+1)^2 + (-1)^2 + (0)^2} = 18.00$$

The sums of squares for all 12 subjects are given in the final column of the table. The sum of these individual sums of squares is

$$\Sigma SS_{A_{comp.} \text{ for } s_j} = 18.00 + 24.50 + \cdots + 220.50 + 220.50$$
$$= 1774.00$$

For the comparison sum of squares, we substitute the difference between the two means in Eq. (16-4) and find

$$SS_{A_{comp.}} = \frac{(12)(14.00)^2}{(+1)^2 + (-1)^2 + (0)^2} = 1176.00$$

Finally, from Eq. (16-5), we obtain

$$SS_{A_{comp.} \times S} = 1774.00 - 1176.00 = 598.00$$

The formula for the F is given by Eq. (16-6):

$$F_{comp.} = \frac{MS_{A_{comp.}}}{MS_{A_{comp.} \times S}} \qquad (16\text{-}6)$$

Since there is 1 *df* for the comparison, $MS_{A_{comp}} = 1176.00$. The degrees of freedom associated with the error term are given by Eq. (16-7):

$$df_{A_{comp.} \times S} = (df_{A_{comp}})(df_S)$$
$$= (1)(s-1) = s-1 \qquad (16\text{-}7)$$

For the present example, $df_{A_{comp.} \times S} = 12 - 1 = 11$, and $MS_{A_{comp.} \times S} = 598.00/11 = 54.36$. Substituting in Eq. (16-6), we find

$$F_{comp.} = \frac{1176.00}{54.36} = 21.63$$

which is significant. (As a reminder, this F is evaluated with $df_{num.} = 1$ and $df_{denom.} = 11$.) You should note that the error term for this comparison does *not* equal the error term for the omnibus F test ($MS_{A \times S} = 48.52$).

A Second Numerical Example. For a second example, we will compare the average of the two science conditions with the history condition. Table 16-10 presents the relevant comparison matrix. Entries in the first column consist of each subject's average vocabulary score obtained following the two science lectures; entries in the second column consist of each subject's score obtained following the history lecture. The difference scores and sums of squares based on these differences are found in the last two columns of the table. For the first subject, the average science score is $(53 + 47)/2 = 50.00$ and the history score is 45.00—a difference of 5.00 words. If we translate this difference into a sum of squares, we find

$$SS_{A_{comp.} \text{ for } s_1} = \frac{(5.00)^2}{(+\frac{1}{2})^2 + (+\frac{1}{2})^2 + (-1)^2} = 16.67$$

The sum of the sums of squares for all subjects is:

$$\Sigma SS_{A_{comp.} \text{ for } s_j} = 16.67 + 13.50 + \cdots + 48.17 + 8.17$$
$$= 487.37$$

Table 16-10
Calculation of a Separate Error Term

| Subject | Comparison Matrix | | Calculations | |
	Combined Science	History	Difference	SS
1	50.00	45	5.00	16.67
2	45.50	41	4.50	13.50
3	43.00	38	5.00	16.67
4	39.50	36	3.50	8.17
5	46.50	35	11.50	88.17
6	33.50	33	.50	.17
7	28.50	46	−17.50	204.17
8	32.00	40	−8.00	42.67
9	25.50	29	−3.50	8.17
10	14.00	21	−7.00	32.67
11	21.50	30	−8.50	48.17
12	16.50	20	−3.50	8.17
Mean:	33.00	34.50	−1.50	

Using the data at the bottom of Table 16-10, we find:

$$SS_{A_{comp.}} = \frac{(12)(-1.50)^2}{(+\frac{1}{2})^2 + (+\frac{1}{2})^2 + (-1)^2} = 18.00$$

The sum of squares for the error term is

$$SS_{A_{comp.} \times S} = 487.37 - 18.00 = 469.37$$

Continuing with the calculations, we find $MS_{A_{comp.}} = 18.00$ and $MS_{A_{comp.} \times S} = 469.37/11 = 42.67$. The $F_{comp.}$ is not significant $(18.00/42.67 = .42)$.

Comment.   It is interesting that the two sums of squares we obtained for error terms for the two comparisons add up to the sum of squares for the error term from the overall analysis. That is,

$$598.00 + 469.37 = 1067.37$$

which, except for rounding error, equals $SS_{A \times S}$ (1067.33). This has occurred only because the two comparisons were *orthogonal*, a property that extended to the two error terms, which is why the two sums of squares totaled $SS_{A \times S}$.

    You may have noticed that the two error terms in our hypothetical experiment differed by a relatively small amount (54.36 versus 42.67). In actual experiments, however, sizable differences do occur; and even small differences, such as these, can affect the outcome of a statistical test. For these reasons, we recommend that you use separate error terms for the different comparisons of interest unless there is convincing evidence that such a procedure is not necessary.

Computational Procedures: MRC

The analysis of single-*df* comparisons with MRC is a relatively simple matter and is most easily conducted by adopting a strategy of assuming that an omnibus analysis is necessary (though in fact it is not), coding for comparisons and subjects, and creating vectors for interactions of treatments with subjects. As you know, the variation associated with the comparison itself is reflected in the zero-order correlation between Y and the appropriately coded comparison vector. As we will show, the variation associated with an $A_{comp.} \times S$ interaction is reflected in the subset of the *interaction vectors* formed by cross-multiplying the particular comparison vector with all the individual subject vectors.

    Consider the vectors in Table 16-11. Vector 1 (A1) specifies the comparison between the two science conditions. The vectors in columns 2 through 12 are the interaction vectors found by cross-multiplying the numerical values of vector A1 with corresponding values from all the subject vectors presented in Table 16-6.

Table 16-11
Vectors Representing a Single-df Comparison

	Subject	Y	(1) A1	(2) A1S1	(3) A1S2	(4) A1S3	(5) A1S4	(6) A1S5	(7) A1S6	(8) A1S7	(9) A1S8	(10) A1S9	(11) A1S10	(12) A1S11
									Vectors					
a_1	1	53	1	1	1	1	1	1	1	1	1	1	1	1
	2	49	1	−1	0	0	0	0	0	0	0	0	0	0
	3	47	1	0	−1	0	0	0	0	0	0	0	0	0
	4	42	1	0	0	−1	0	0	0	0	0	0	0	0
	5	51	1	0	0	0	−1	0	0	0	0	0	0	0
	6	34	1	0	0	0	0	−1	0	0	0	0	0	0
	7	44	1	0	0	0	0	0	−1	0	0	0	0	0
	8	48	1	0	0	0	0	0	0	−1	0	0	0	0
	9	35	1	0	0	0	0	0	0	0	−1	0	0	0
	10	18	1	0	0	0	0	0	0	0	0	−1	0	0
	11	32	1	0	0	0	0	0	0	0	0	0	−1	0
	12	27	1	0	0	0	0	0	0	0	0	0	0	−1
a_2	1	47	−1	−1	−1	−1	−1	−1	−1	−1	−1	−1	−1	−1
	2	42	−1	1	0	0	0	0	0	0	0	0	0	0
	3	39	−1	0	1	0	0	0	0	0	0	0	0	0
	4	37	−1	0	0	1	0	0	0	0	0	0	0	0
	5	42	−1	0	0	0	1	0	0	0	0	0	0	0
	6	33	−1	0	0	0	0	1	0	0	0	0	0	0
	7	13	−1	0	0	0	0	0	1	0	0	0	0	0
	8	16	−1	0	0	0	0	0	0	1	0	0	0	0
	9	16	−1	0	0	0	0	0	0	0	1	0	0	0
	10	10	−1	0	0	0	0	0	0	0	0	1	0	0
	11	11	−1	0	0	0	0	0	0	0	0	0	1	0
	12	6	−1	0	0	0	0	0	0	0	0	0	0	1

Table 16-11 Continued

					Vectors								
Subject	Y	(1) A1	(2) A1S1	(3) A1S2	(4) A1S3	(5) A1S4	(6) A1S5	(7) A1S6	(8) A1S7	(9) A1S8	(10) A1S9	(11) A1S10	(12) A1S11
1	45	0	0	0	0	0	0	0	0	0	0	0	0
2	41	0	0	0	0	0	0	0	0	0	0	0	0
3	38	0	0	0	0	0	0	0	0	0	0	0	0
4	36	0	0	0	0	0	0	0	0	0	0	0	0
5	35	0	0	0	0	0	0	0	0	0	0	0	0
6	33	0	0	0	0	0	0	0	0	0	0	0	0
7	46	0	0	0	0	0	0	0	0	0	0	0	0
8	40	0	0	0	0	0	0	0	0	0	0	0	0
9	29	0	0	0	0	0	0	0	0	0	0	0	0
10	21	0	0	0	0	0	0	0	0	0	0	0	0
11	30	0	0	0	0	0	0	0	0	0	0	0	0
12	20	0	0	0	0	0	0	0	0	0	0	0	0

a_3

(These vectors are also the first 11 vectors of the interaction represented in Table 16-8). Note that the 12 coded vectors in Table 16-11 represent only *one* comparison (physical science versus social science) *and* the $A \times S$ vectors created by that comparison; the table is incomplete in that a second comparison vector and its associated $A \times S$ vectors are not shown—this is because, for now, we are interested in only the $A1$ comparison.

Let us see how the analysis proceeds. We need the squared zero-order correlation coefficient reflecting the comparison (r_{Y1}^2) and the squared multiple correlation coefficient reflecting the $A_{comp.} \times S$ interaction. This latter quantity is obtained by computing a squared multiple correlation coefficient based on the 11 interaction vectors listed in Table 16-11. That is,

$$R_{Y.A1S1, \ldots, A1S11}^2 = R_{Y.A1 \times S}^2$$

A computer analysis reveals that $r_{Y1}^2 = .2030$ and $R_{Y.A1 \times S}^2 = .1032$. The squared zero-order correlation is associated with 1 df, while the error term is associated with $s - 1$ df. The F ratio is given by

$$F_{comp.} = \frac{r_{Y1}^2}{(R_{Y.A1 \times S}^2)/(s - 1)} \tag{16-8}$$

With these data,

$$F_{comp.} = \frac{.2030}{(.1032)/(12 - 1)} = \frac{.2030}{.0094} = 21.60$$

The analysis of variance produced an $F_{comp.}$ of 21.63.

If we were interested in another comparison, such as the combined science conditions versus the history condition, we would proceed in a similar manner. We would start with the vector representing this comparison and calculate the interaction vectors associated with it by cross-multiplying this vector with each of the subject vectors. (See Table 16-8 for an illustration of these vectors, which are labeled $A2S1$ through $A2S11$.) A computer analysis reveals that r_{Y2}^2 (the subscript 2 referring to the second comparison vector, column 4 in Table 16-6) is .0031 and $R_{Y.A2 \times S}^2$ is .0810. The F is

$$F_{comp.} = \frac{.0031}{(.0810)/(12 - 1)} = \frac{.0031}{.0074} = .42$$

The $F_{comp.}$ from ANOVA is .42.

Comment. Assuming that you will be testing planned comparisons, we recommend that you arrange your analysis by coding the comparisons, coding subjects, and letting the computer create $A \times S$ vectors. By following this strategy, you would have all the information you needed for analyzing single-*df* comparisons. All that you would need to do is to select the $A \times S$ vectors that are appropriate for the particular single-*df* comparisons of interest and complete the analysis.

16.5   SUMMARY

In this chapter we introduced a new type of experimental design, one in which subjects serve in *all* the treatment conditions representing a single independent variable rather than in only one of them. Such a design is called a *within-subjects design* or a design with *repeated measures*. The primary advantage of within-subjects designs, or $(A \times S)$ designs, as we refer to them, is the increased sensitivity they offer because subject differences are held "constant" from treatment to treatment whereas in completely randomized or so-called *between-subjects designs* they can vary. Potential problems with these more sensitive designs include practice effects, differential carryover effects, and violations of certain statistical assumptions. In spite of these problems, however, within-subjects designs are extremely popular in the behavioral sciences.

   The ANOVA approach treats the overall analysis as if the data were generated from a factorial experiment: the treatment conditions and the subjects are the two "factors," and together they form an $(A \times S)$ design. The error term for this analysis is the $A \times S$ interaction. The MRC approach is based on vectors that reflect the comparisons of interest and the appropriate sources of variability. No new procedures are required for either approach.

   The analysis of single-*df* comparisons introduces a special problem in that a *separate error term* must be calculated for each of the comparisons analyzed in the within-subjects experiment. In ANOVA, this is accomplished by placing the relevant data in a comparison matrix and performing the necessary calculations on difference scores reflecting the comparison of interest for the individual subjects. In MRC, the analysis is performed by identifying the interaction vectors reflecting the desired error term and then using these vectors to calculate the squared multiple regression coefficient needed to complete the analysis.

16.6   EXERCISES

   1. Use the data provided in Problem 1 of Chap. 10, and treat the design as if there were seven subjects, each of whom participated in all three conditions.

(a) Calculate the F ratio for the omnibus effect.
(b) Analyze the single-df comparison for "praise" versus "reproof."
(c) Analyze the single-df comparison for "praise" *and* "reproof" combined versus "none."

2. Using the same data as in Problem 1, above:
(a) Do an MRC analysis to determine the omnibus effect.
(b) Analyze the single-df comparison for "praise" versus "reproof."
(c) Analyze the single-df comparison for "praise" *and* "reproof" combined versus "none."

17

The Mixed
Two-Factor Design

. . .

Within-subjects factorial designs combine the usual advantages of a factorial—the ability to study the effects of several independent variables manipulated simultaneously—with the increased sensitivity achieved when the same subjects are used in some or even all of the treatment conditions. As a consequence, such designs provide flexibility in the kinds of problems that can be studied and the comparisons that can be emphasized.

17.1   DESIGNING WITHIN-SUBJECTS FACTORIALS

Types of Designs

We can classify two-variable factorial designs into three types according to how individual subjects are assigned to the treatment conditions. At one extreme are factorial designs in which particular subjects serve in only *one* of the treatment conditions formed by crossing the two independent variables. At the other extreme are factorials in which all subjects receive *all* the treatment conditions of both variables. Between these two extremes is the so-called **mixed design**, in which independent groups of subjects represent the individual levels of one variable but all groups receive all the conditions of the second variable. That is, each group of subjects receives only the treatment conditions formed by combining all the levels of one independent variable with *one* level of the other independent variable. In our notation we will distinguish between these different designs by placing the within-subjects factor (or repeated factor) within parentheses. Thus, the completely randomized factorial design is referred to as the $A \times B$ design. The design consisting completely of repeated measures is designated $(A \times B \times S)$ to indicate that both factor A and factor B are within-subjects factors; and the mixed design is designated $A \times (B \times S)$ to show that factor B is the within-subjects factor.

　　We have illustrated these three designs in the context of a 2×3 factorial in Table 17-1. At the top is the "pure" within-subjects design, in which each of the $s = 3$ subjects receives *all six of the treatment conditions* created by crossing the two levels of factor A with the three levels of factor B. At the bottom is the "pure" between-subjects design, in which a given set of subjects ($s = 3$) is randomly assigned to *only one* of the six conditions. In the middle is a mixed design in which any given subject receives *only three* of the six treatment conditions. More specifically, one set of randomly assigned subjects (for example, s_1, s_2, and s_3) receives all three levels of factor B but only in combination with the a_1 level of factor A, while a different set of subjects (s_4, s_5, and s_6) receives the three levels of factor B in combination with the a_2 level of factor A.

Table 17-1
Comparison of Two-Factor Designs

$(A \times B \times S)$ Design

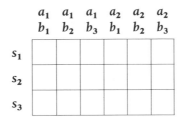

$A \times (B \times S)$ Design

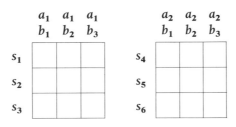

$A \times B$ Design

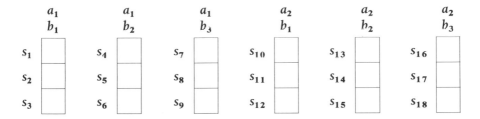

As illustrated in Table 17-1, all three designs involve exactly the same quantity of data, but the within-subjects designs require fewer subjects than the completely randomized design to yield a given number of scores. That is, three observations are made for each treatment condition, but the 18 scores that result are obtained from only *three* different subjects in the $(A \times B \times S)$ design, *six* different subjects in the $A \times (B \times S)$ design, and *18* different subjects in the $A \times B$ design. Thus, within-subjects designs offer the advantage of requiring a smaller total number of subjects. Another reason for selecting a within-subjects factorial design is the greater sensitivity and power it offers over its completely randomized between-subjects counterpart.

Choice of Design

In deciding to use *any* within-subjects design, we have to consider whether it is appropriate or not. We have to convince ourselves that *differential carryover effects*—carryover effects that are *not* solved by counterbalancing—will not present a problem. (We discussed the problem of differential carryover effects in Sec. 16.1.) The issue must be confronted at the start of planning, since it will probably be impossible to solve the problem after the data are collected.

Once you have convinced yourself that a within-subjects manipulation offers an appropriate way to design your experiment, you should then consider whether each group of subjects will receive *all* treatment conditions or just some of them. As you have seen, there are two main options for the two-variable factorial, namely, (1) a design in which both variables are represented as within-subjects manipulations and (2) a design in which one variable is represented as a within-subjects manipulation and the other as a between-subjects manipulation. The first option has the advantage that any increased sensitivity afforded by the use of the same subjects will be extended to the statistical assessment of all factorial effects. On the other hand, you may find it unreasonable to administer all conditions to each subject, when you take into account time contraints, fatigue, or boredom. Under these circumstances, a mixed factorial design will be the answer. In this case, you might choose as the variable for the within-subjects manipulation the one that is most important to you and, hence, the one that you wish to subject to the most sensitive test; or you might choose the one that you expect to produce *smaller* differences, which will be more easily detected with the smaller error term usually associated with a within-subjects manipulation.

For the remainder of this chapter, we will consider the overall analysis of the mixed factorial design. As you will see, the statistical analysis combines elements from the two basic single-factor designs—the completely randomized design and the within-subjects design—both of which are represented in the mixed factorial design. We will discuss the analysis of the $(A \times B \times S)$ design in Chap. 19.

17.2   THE OVERALL ANALYSIS: THE ANOVA APPROACH

Perhaps the most common examples of mixed factorials in the behavioral sciences are experiments designed to study *learning*. In learning experiments, subjects are assigned randomly to single levels of factor *A*, which consists of the different treatments, the between-subjects factor. If the experiment were a completely randomized single-factor design, each subject would provide a single score or observation and the different groups of subjects would be compared on the averages of the single measures. In a learning experiment, however, subjects are given repeated administrations of the same treatment condition and performance is recorded following each of the trials. Learning is inferred from any improvement observed over the course of training. In this experiment, then, "trials" represent the levels of a second independent variable, which in this case is a within-subjects factor. This type of study is a factorial design because all levels of factor A (the different treatment groups) are combined with all levels of factor B (the training trials). The design is a mixed factorial because subjects receive all the training trials under *one* of the levels of factor A.

The value of the learning experiment lies in the information it provides. We can combine the scores for the different subjects, of course, and then compare the different treatment groups using measures of average performance. If we were to do that, the analysis would be exactly equivalent to a completely randomized *single-factor* experiment. But when we take into consideration the within-subjects factor (trials), we are able to study the *course of learning* over the training trials and to compare the *shapes* of the learning curves for the different treatment groups. That is, this type of experiment allows us to determine whether the effects of practice (trials) are the same for the different levels of factor A—which in effect tests whether there is an $A \times B$ interaction (an interaction of factor A with trials). This opportunity to examine the course of learning and to compare the learning curves for the different treatment conditions provides researchers with important and useful information.

An Overview of the Analysis

We have indicated already that the analysis of the mixed factorial combines features of both within-subjects and between-subjects designs. Consider the $A \times (B \times S)$ design illustrated in Table 17-1. At the outset, you should realize that this design yields the same factorial information that any $A \times B$ design provides, namely, two main effects and an $A \times B$ interaction. The primary difference in the analysis is in the nature of the error terms required to assess the significance of these factorial effects. While only one error term is required for the completely randomized factorial, two are necessary for this mixed factorial—one for assessing effects based on independent groups of subjects (the A main effect) and one for assessing effects based on repeated measures (the B main effect and the $A \times B$ interaction).

Let us consider first the between-subjects portion of the analysis, using the design in Table 17-1 as a point of reference. Suppose we were to "eliminate" factor B for the moment, as we can do simply by adding together the three scores for each subject. What we would be left with are three combined scores at level a_1 (one for each of the three subjects) and, correspondingly, three combined scores at level a_2. With this particular information, we could actually analyze these data as a single-factor design in which factor A (with two levels) is a between-subjects factor. Such an analysis would provide us with the treatment mean square MS_A and a within-groups error term $MS_{S/A}$. This is exactly how we will assess the main effect of factor A in the mixed factorial, treating the main effect as if it were the treatment mean square in a *single*-factor design.

Consider next the within-subjects portion of the analysis. For the three subjects assigned to receive level a_1 in conjunction with factor B, this portion of the design may be viewed as a single-factor within-subjects design—technically, a $(B \times S)$ design at level a_1. Similarly, for the three subjects at the other level of factor A, the design may be described as a $(B \times S)$ design at level a_2. The two sets of B treatment means—one at a_1 and one at a_2—provide information for the $A \times B$ interaction and, if combined, information for the B main effect. From the analysis of an actual *single-factor* within-subjects design, which we covered in Chap. 16, we would expect to use an interaction of factor B and subjects $(B \times S)$ to derive the error term for evaluating treatment effects involving factor B. The error term for evaluating the B main effect and the $A \times B$ interaction in the *mixed design* is in fact based on an average or pooling of these $B \times S$ interactions. We will designate this within-subjects error term $MS_{B \times S/A}$, which refers to a $B \times S$ interaction pooled over the levels of factor A.

The contribution of the two single-factor designs to the analysis of the mixed factorial is summarized in Table 17-2; each entry represents the sources of variability we normally identify in these designs. For the completely randomized single-factor design, which appears on the left, two sources are listed, the effects of factor $A(A)$ and the error term $MS_{S/A}$, while for the single-factor within-groups design, which appears on the right, three sources are listed, the effects of factor $B(B)$, the effects of subjects (S), and the error term $MS_{B \times S}$. For the mixed factorial design, which

Table 17-2
A Comparison of the Sources of Variance in
Two Single-Factor Designs with Those in the
Mixed Factorial Design

Between Subjects (Completely Randomized)	Mixed Factorial $A \times (B \times S)$	Within Subjects $(B \times S)$
$A \longrightarrow$	$\rightarrow A$	
	$B \longleftarrow$	$\longrightarrow B$
	$A \times B$	
$S/A \longrightarrow$	$\rightarrow S/A$	S
	$B \times S/A \longleftarrow$	$\longrightarrow B \times S$

appears in the middle, the three factorial effects (A, B, and $A \times B$) are listed first, followed by the two error terms (S/A and $B \times S/A$). An inspection of the table shows how each of the single-factor designs contributes to the analysis of the mixed factorial.

Notational System

The notational system for the mixed factorial is summarized in Table 17-3. With one exception, the representation of the scores and various sums required for the analysis is identical to the one introduced for the $A \times B$ design. That is,

Y = a subject's score on the dependent variable; we have omitted subscripts for the sake of simplicity.

AB = the sum of the Y scores for all subjects receiving a particular combination of the levels of the two independent variables; the first subscript indicates the level of factor A and the second subscript the level of factor B.

A = the sum of the scores for all subjects receiving a particular level of factor A.

B = the sum of the scores for all subjects receiving a particular level of factor B.

T = the sum of all the scores in the experiment.

The one new quantity, AS, designates the sum of the Y scores for each subject; for example, $AS_{1,1}$ is the sum of the three observations obtained for the first subject.

Table 17-3
Notational System: Mixed Factorial Design

	a_1					a_2			
	b_1	b_2	b_3	Sum		b_1	b_2	b_3	Sum
s_1	Y	Y	Y	$AS_{1,1}$	s_4	Y	Y	Y	$AS_{2,4}$
s_2	Y	Y	Y	$AS_{1,2}$	s_5	Y	Y	Y	$AS_{2,5}$
s_3	Y	Y	Y	$AS_{1,3}$	s_6	Y	Y	Y	$AS_{2,6}$
Sum	$AB_{1,1}$	$AB_{1,2}$	$AB_{1,3}$	A_1	Sum	$AB_{2,1}$	$AB_{2,2}$	$AB_{2,3}$	A_2

AB Matrix

	b_1	b_2	b_3	Sum
a_1	$AB_{1,1}$	$AB_{1,2}$	$AB_{1,3}$	A_1
a_2	$AB_{2,1}$	$AB_{2,2}$	$AB_{2,3}$	A_2
Sum	B_1	B_2	B_3	T

(The first subscript identifies the level of factor A, and the second subscript, the particular subject.)

Lowercase letters will continue to refer to the number of levels of an independent variable. That is, a represents the number of levels of factor A, and b, the number of levels of factor B. The number of observations contributing to any given treatment condition is s. The total number of observations is $(a)(b)(s)$; we also use N to represent this number in MRC analysis.

Basic Ratios and Sums of Squares

Each sum of squares is calculated by combining basic ratios, which are based on the different quantities specified in Table 17-3. Since all the basic ratios previously introduced for the analysis of the $A \times B$ design are needed for the analysis of the mixed design, we will not discuss them here (see Sec. 13.2). These ratios are presented again in Table 17-4. The one new ratio is based on the sum of the Y scores for the individual subjects, which we have designated AS. This ratio is formed in the usual manner, namely, by squaring all subject sums and then summing and dividing by b, the number of observations contributing to any AS sum. This ratio is presented in the second row in Table 17-4.

The patterns in which the basic ratios are combined to produce the various sums of squares are presented in the third column of the table. Although we do not do so here, we could show that all the component sums of squares are based on different sets of deviations, all of which combine to equal the so-called total deviation, the sum of the deviations of all individual Y scores from the grand mean.[1]

Degrees of Freedom

The degrees of freedom for the different sources of variance are presented in the fourth column of Table 17-4. The df for the factorial effects and "total" should be familiar and should require no explanation. The df for S/A are defined in the same way as the $df_{S/A}$ are defined in the completely randomized single-factor design. That is, there are $s - 1$ df associated with the s subject means at each level of factor A; pooling these df over all a levels of factor A—that is, forming the product $(a)(s - 1)$—gives us the df for this source of variability. To specify the degrees of freedom for $B \times S/A$, we begin with the df associated with the $B \times S$ interaction at any one of the levels of factor A, namely, $(b - 1)(s - 1)$; pooling these df over the levels of factor A—that is, forming the product $(a)(b - 1)(s - 1)$—gives us the df for this source of variability.

---

[1] It is also possible to derive these patterns from the df statements associated with each source of variance (see Keppel, 1982, pp. 411–412).

Table 17-4
Computational Formulas

Source	Basic Ratio*	Sum of Squares	df	MS	F
A	$[A] = \dfrac{\Sigma A^2}{(b)(s)}$	$[A] - [T]$	$a - 1$	$\dfrac{SS_A}{df_A}$	$\dfrac{MS_A}{MS_{S/A}}$
S/A	$[AS] = \dfrac{\Sigma (AS)^2}{b}$	$[AS] - [A]$	$(a)(s-1)$	$\dfrac{SS_{S/A}}{df_{S/A}}$	
B	$[B] = \dfrac{\Sigma B^2}{(a)(s)}$	$[B] - [T]$	$b - 1$	$\dfrac{SS_B}{df_B}$	$\dfrac{MS_B}{MS_{B \times S/A}}$
$A \times B$	$[AB] = \dfrac{\Sigma (AB)^2}{s}$	$[AB] - [A] - [B] + [T]$	$(a-1)(b-1)$	$\dfrac{SS_{A \times B}}{df_{A \times B}}$	$\dfrac{MS_{A \times B}}{MS_{B \times S/A}}$
$B \times S/A$	$[Y] = \Sigma Y^2$	$[Y] - [AB] - [AS] + [A]$	$(a)(b-1)(s-1)$	$\dfrac{SS_{B \times S/A}}{df_{B \times S/A}}$	
Total	$[T] = \dfrac{T^2}{(a)(b)(s)}$	$[Y] - [T]$	$(a)(b)(s) - 1$		

* Bracketed letters represent complete terms in computational formulas; a particular term is identified by the letter(s) appearing in the numerator.

Mean Squares and F Ratios

The mean squares are calculated by dividing each sum of squares by the appropriate df, as shown in the fifth column of the table. The F ratios for the three factorial effects are presented in the sixth column. As you can see, the error term for the A main effect is $MS_{S/A}$, while the error term for the B main effect and the interaction is $MS_{B \times S/A}$.

A Numerical Example

For the remainder of this chapter, we will be working again with the vocabulary experiment, modified to illustrate the analysis of the mixed factorial design. One of the independent variables (factor A) is the type of lecture (physical science, social science, and history). The other independent variable (factor B) consists of three vocabulary tests administered at *different times* following the end of the lecture. We will assume that each subject is tested immediately after the lecture (level b_1), then 2 weeks later (level b_2), and finally 2 weeks after the second test (level b_3). The introduction of the three tests will allow us to determine the extent to which the vocabulary words are *forgotten* over the 1-month period spanning the first and last vocabulary tests and to compare the amounts of forgetting associated with the three types of lectures. (Mode of presentation is not a factor in this version of the experiment.)

The design, then, is a 3 × 3 mixed factorial in which the *type of lecture* represents a between-subjects manipulation (factor A) and the *time interval* following the lecture represents a within-subjects manipulation (factor B). Four subjects are randomly assigned to each of the three different lectures; at the end of any given lecture, subjects receive three vocabulary tests separated by intervals of 2 weeks. The data for this example are presented in Table 17-5.[2]

All the quantities we need to form the necessary basic ratios are presented in the table. The upper data matrix organizes the individual Y scores—three for each subject—in such a way that the subtotals needed for the analysis are easily calculated. The column marginal totals, for example, provide the AB sums for each of the treatment conditions; these are placed in the AB matrix to facilitate the calculation of the main effects and the interaction. The row marginal totals, on the other hand, provide the combined test scores for each subject, which we have called AS.

We will now calculate the basic ratios without detailed comment, remembering that $a = 3$, $b = 3$, and $s = 4$. Starting with the upper matrix, we find

$$[Y] = \Sigma \, Y^2$$
$$= 53^2 + 49^2 + \cdots + 30^2 + 20^2 = 46{,}194$$

$$[AS] = \frac{\Sigma \, (AS)^2}{b}$$
$$= \frac{139^2 + 101^2 + \cdots + 114^2 + 96^2}{3} = 42{,}386.00$$

Moving next to the AB matrix, we have

$$[A] = \frac{\Sigma \, A^2}{(b)\,(s)}$$
$$= \frac{480^2 + 312^2 + 414^2}{(3)\,(4)} = 41{,}595.00$$

$$[B] = \frac{\Sigma \, B^2}{(a)\,(s)}$$
$$= \frac{516^2 + 435^2 + 255^2}{(3)\,(4)} = 43{,}375.50$$

[2] In an actual experiment, three sets of vocabulary words would be selected and used equally often for each of the tests.

Table 17-5
Numerical Example

a_1

	b_1	b_2	b_3	Sum
s_1	53	51	35	139
s_2	49	34	18	101
s_3	47	44	32	123
s_4	42	48	27	117
Sum	191	177	112	480

a_2

	b_1	b_2	b_3	Sum
s_5	47	42	16	105
s_6	42	33	10	85
s_7	39	13	11	63
s_8	37	16	6	59
Sum	165	104	43	312

a_3

	b_1	b_2	b_3	Sum
s_9	45	35	29	109
s_{10}	41	33	21	95
s_{11}	38	46	30	114
s_{12}	36	40	20	96
Sum	160	154	100	414

AB Matrix

	b_1	b_2	b_3	Sum
a_1	191	177	112	480
a_2	165	104	43	312
a_3	160	154	100	414
Sum	516	435	255	1206

$$[AB] = \frac{\Sigma \, (AB)^2}{s}$$

$$= \frac{191^2 + 165^2 + \cdots + 43^2 + 100^2}{4} = 44{,}890.00$$

$$[T] = \frac{T^2}{(a)\,(b)\,(s)}$$

$$= \frac{1206^2}{(3)\,(3)\,(4)} = 40{,}401.00$$

These quantities are entered in the second column of Table 17-6.

The required sums of squares, which are obtained by combining the basic ratios in different patterns, are found in the third column of Table 17-6. The remainder of the analysis is summarized in the remaining columns of the table. Note that the error term for the between-subjects factor is $MS_{S/A}$ and for the within-subjects factor it is $MS_{B \times S/A}$. Thus, the respective F ratios are

$$F = \frac{MS_A}{MS_{S/A}} = \frac{579.00}{87.89} = 6.79$$

$$F = \frac{MS_B}{MS_{B \times S/A}} = \frac{1487.25}{28.50} = 52.18$$

$$F = \frac{MS_{A \times B}}{MS_{B \times S/A}} = \frac{80.13}{28.50} = 2.81$$

Table 17-6
Summary of the Analysis

Source	Basic Ratio	Sum of Squares	df	MS	F
A	[A] = 41,595.00	[A] − [T] = 1194.00	2	597.00	6.79*
S/A	[AS] = 42,386.00	[AS] − [A] = 791.00	9	87.89	
B	[B] = 43,375.50	[B] − [T] = 2974.50	2	1487.25	52.18**
A × B	[AB] = 44,890.00	[AB] − [A] − [B] + [T] = 320.50	4	80.13	2.81
B × S/A	[Y] = 46,194	[Y] − [AB] − [AS] + [A] = 513.00	18	28.50	
Total	[T] = 40,401.00	[Y] − [T] = 5793.00	35		

* $p < .025.$
** $p < .01.$

As you can see, the two main effects are significant, while the interaction is not. The nonsignificant interaction implies that the two main effects may each be interpreted without consideration of the other independent variable. That is, the significant effect of lectures does not seem to depend on the time separating the lecture from the test, while the significant effect of time—an apparently steady decline over the three tests—does not seem to depend on the type of lecture the subjects receive.

You should also notice the difference in magnitude of the two error terms. For the between-subjects portion of the analysis, the error term is $MS_{S/A} = 87.89$, while for the within-subjects portion, the error term is $MS_{B \times S/A} = 28.50$, showing the differential sensitivity of the two parts of this experimental design. The smaller error term results because we have taken the "subject consistency" component into consideration, treating it as explained variability, and thus we have a smaller amount of uncontrolled variability associated with the factorial effects based on within-subject differences than with those based on between-subjects differences.

Remember that in any analysis of within-subjects designs you must take into consideration the statistical assumptions underlying the *F* tests. If these assumptions are seriously violated, the table values of *F* used to establish rejection regions will be too small. We mentioned a relatively simple strategy of using the value of *F* at $\alpha = .025$ to establish a rejection region that corrects for this problem. In the present example, the new critical value would be 4.56 (rather than 3.55) for evaluating the *B* main effect and 3.61 (rather than 2.93) for evaluating the $A \times B$ interaction. An inspection of the observed values of *F* in Table 17-6 indicates that the new critical values result in no change in the conclusions we would draw from the analysis—the *B* main effect is significant and the $A \times B$ interaction is not.[3] If you were to find that an *F* is significant with the uncorrected value of *F* but not significant with the corrected value, you might want to take the "suspend judgment" position that we discussed in Chap. 12 (Sec. 12.5).

---

[3] The Geisser-Greenhouse correction, which we mentioned in footnote 5 of Chap. 16, is available for any within-subjects design. The correction adjusts the critical value of *F* by reducing the numerator and denominator degrees of freedom. For the present case, the new value of *F* has $df_{num.} = 1$ and $df_{denom.} = (a)(s-1) = (3)(4-1) = 9$ for the *B* main effect and $df_{num.} = a - 1 = 2$ and $df_{denom.} = (a)(s-1) = (3)(4-1) = 9$ for the interaction. Using these new degrees of freedom, we find the critical value of *F* for the *B* main effect is $F(1, 9) = 5.12$ (rather than 3.55) and the *F* for the interaction is $F(2, 9) = 4.26$ (rather than 2.93). These corrections are for the worst-case situation, where the critical assumptions are maximally violated. Less stringent corrections are available, which take into consideration the degree of statistical violation actually present in a given data set. (See Keppel, 1982, pp. 470–472, for a discussion of the Geisser-Greenhouse correction and other correction procedures.)

17.3   THE OVERALL ANALYSIS: THE MRC APPROACH

The MRC approach is easily adapted to the overall analysis of the mixed factorial design. The factorial effects—*A*, *B*, and *A* × *B*—are coded just as they were in the completely randomized factorial design. *Subjects* are coded as they were in the single-factor within-subjects design (Chap. 16).

Coding

In the single-factor within-subjects design, we coded subjects in a convenient way to represent the variability of subjects in the experiment. By combining this variability represented by $R^2_{Y.S}$ with the effect of treatments ($R^2_{Y.A}$), we were able to calculate the squared multiple correlation coefficient for the remaining source of variability, the $A \times S$ interaction ($R^2_{Y.A \times S}$), by subtraction.

We will follow a similar strategy with the $A \times (B \times S)$ design. We will code subjects separately to represent the variability of subjects for each of the *A* treatment conditions. Adding this information (given by $R^2_{Y.S/A}$) to the factorial effects ($R^2_{Y.A}$, $R^2_{Y.B}$, $R^2_{Y.A \times B}$) and subtracting this sum from 1 will produce the within-subjects error term ($R^2_{Y.B \times S/A}$). Let us see how this is accomplished.

Coding the Factorial Effects.   We start with the vectors needed to code the factorial effects. First, we need to code for factor *A*. Since there are three levels of *A*, we can identify two meaningful contrasts, for which we can construct the following code matrix:

	a_1	a_2	a_3
Vector 1	1	−1	0
Vector 2	1	1	−2

Vector 1 compares the physical science lecture with the social science lecture, while vector 2 compares the combined science lectures with the history lecture. Second, we need to code for factor *B*, which consists of three tests separated by intervals of 2 weeks. Since there are three levels of this factor, we need to identify two contrasts; we construct a code matrix as follows:

	b_1	b_2	b_3
Vector 3	1	−1	0
Vector 4	0	1	−1

Vector 3 contrasts the first two tests, while vector 4 contrasts the second and third tests.

We know that the analysis requires vectors for the interaction between A and B, which we may obtain quite simply by cross-multiplying the appropriate A and B vectors to create the necessary interaction vectors. In our example, there would be four interaction vectors created by this process (vectors $1 \times 3, 1 \times 4, 2 \times 3$, and 2×4, which represent respectively $A1B1, A1B2, A2B1$, and $A2B2$). If we have chosen the vectors reflecting the main effects carefully so that they represent meaningful single-df comparisons, many of the interaction vectors will represent meaningful interaction contrasts. (We discuss the analysis of interaction contrasts in Chap. 18.) Table 17-7 shows the complete code matrix made up of the vectors for factors A and B and the interaction vectors produced by multiplying the main-effect vectors. The eight vectors in the table, which reflect different aspects of the the three factorial effects, correspond to the 8 df associated with the two main effects ($df_A = 2$ and $df_B = 2$) and the interaction ($df_{A \times B} = 4$).

To repeat, the first two vectors represent the A main effect: vector $A1$ represents a comparison between physical science and social science, and vector $A2$, a comparison between the combined sciences and history. (As you know from previous discussions, both comparisons are meaningful research hypotheses with this independent variable.) The next two vectors represent the B main effect: vector $B1$ represents a comparison between the immediate test and the test given 2 weeks

Table 17-7
Code Matrix for the Factorial Effects

		Vectors							
		(1) $A1$	(2) $A2$	(3) $B1$	(4) $B2$	(5) $A1B1$	(6) $A1B2$	(7) $A2B1$	(8) $A2B2$
a_1	b_1	1	1	1	0	1	0	1	0
	b_2	1	1	-1	1	-1	1	-1	1
	b_3	1	1	0	-1	0	-1	0	-1
a_2	b_1	-1	1	1	0	-1	0	1	0
	b_2	-1	1	-1	1	1	-1	-1	1
	b_3	-1	1	0	-1	0	1	0	-1
a_3	b_1	0	-2	1	0	0	0	-2	0
	b_2	0	-2	-1	1	0	0	2	-2
	b_3	0	-2	0	-1	0	0	0	2

later, and vector B2, a comparison between the two delayed tests. The first comparison examines whether there is any forgetting during the first 2 weeks following the lecture, while the second comparison examines whether there is any *additional* forgetting over the final 2 weeks of the experiment. The next four vectors (A1B1, A1B2, A2B1, and A2B2) represent the $A \times B$ interaction and are formed by cross-multiplying the vectors created for the two main effects. Up to this point, we have coded the vectors representing the factorial effects in the same manner we would code any two-factor design.[4]

Coding Subject Variability.   We are now ready to discuss the coding of subjects. As you have seen, the mixed design is actually made up of two or more single-factor within-subjects designs—one for each level of factor A. All that we need to do is to code subject variability separately for each of these "single-factor designs," just as we would for a single-factor within-subjects design, and use the coding vectors for the analysis. In the present example, there are four subjects who receive the three vocabulary tests at varying times after the physical science lecture, another four subjects who receive the same tests after the social science lecture, and another four who receive the tests after the history lecture. We will now use contrast coding to represent each of these separate groups of subjects.[5]

   We have three different sets of four subjects each. The easiest way to code is to adopt a code system for one set of subjects and to repeat it for the remaining sets. For example, we can code for the four subjects in level a_1 by the following.

	Subjects			
	1	2	3	4
Vector 9	1	-1	0	0
Vector 10	1	0	-1	0
Vector 11	1	0	0	-1

[4] While not necessary, we recommend coding factorial effects in this manner—main effects as sets of meaningful single-*df* comparisons and the interaction as a set of interaction contrasts (single-*df* comparisons formed by cross-multiplying vectors representing the main effects). This approach emphasizes the analytical nature of the factorial design and sets the stage for a more focused analysis of the outcome of the experiment, such as those considered in the next section.

[5] Other methods of coding may be used to represent subjects in this design, the most common of which is criterion scaling, which we described in footnote 7 in Chap. 16 (p. 281). While criterion scaling greatly reduces the number of vectors needed to represent variation between subjects, the method does not help in the calculation of the separate error terms frequently required for the detailed analysis of the mixed factorial design (see Chap. 18).

(The vectors are numbered 9 to 11 to continue with the listing of the overall analysis begun in Table 17-7.) The above pattern is repeated for the four subjects in level a_2 (vectors 12 to 14) and for the four subjects in level a_3 (vectors 15 to 17). The results of these codings are shown in Table 17-8.

Consider the first three code vectors in Table 17-8. Collectively, these three vectors isolate the variability of subjects receiving the physical science lecture. The first thing to notice is that only the subjects at level a_1 are involved in these vectors, since 0s are assigned to all subjects in the other two lecture groups. Second, you should also notice that the numbers assigned to any given subject are repeated wherever that subject appears in a vector. In vector 9, for example, the first subject receives a 1 at all three points where he or she appears in the Y column for the three b levels; similarly the second subject receives a -1 at all three points where he or she appears in the Y column. In essence, coding for subjects in each condition of factor A has been accomplished by systematically comparing the first subject with each of the other subjects in that particular group. To elaborate, vector 9 compares the first subject with the second, vector 10 compares the first subject with the third, and vector 11 compares the first subject with the fourth.

The variability of subjects in the other two lecture groups is coded in a similar fashion. That is, the next set of three vectors (vectors 12 to 14) isolates the variability of subjects at level a_2, and the final set (vectors 15 to 17) isolates the variability of subjects at level a_3. For each set, you should again verify that the appropriate group of subjects is isolated (that 0s are assigned to all subjects *outside* of the group).

The Statistical Analysis

We can now proceed with the MRC analysis in the usual fashion by determining the squared multiple correlation coefficients for different *sets* of vectors, each corresponding to one of the sources of variance we extracted by ANOVA. The usual way to set up this analysis is to specify the vector sets in the same order in which we normally list the relevant sources of variances, namely, A, S/A *(subjects)*, B, and A × B. The final squared multiple correlation coefficient $(R^2_{Y.max.})$, which reflects all the variability specified in Tables 17-7 and 17-8, is used to calculate the remaining or *residual* variation $(1 - R^2_{Y.max.})$; this variation corresponds to the B × S/A source in the analysis of variance.

Table 17-9 summarizes the results of this analysis. The standard sources of variability for this type of design are listed in column 1. The squared multiple correlation coefficients representing the separate sources of variability are presented in column 2. More explicitly,

$R^2_{Y.A}$ = the squared multiple correlation coefficient representing the set of
    vectors for factor A (vectors 1 and 2).

Table 17-8
Example of Coding of Subjects in the Mixed Factorial

		Subject	Y	Vectors								
				(9)	(10)	(11)	(12)	(13)	(14)	(15)	(16)	(17)
a_1	b_1	1	53	1	1	1	0	0	0	0	0	0
		2	49	−1	0	0	0	0	0	0	0	0
		3	47	0	−1	0	0	0	0	0	0	0
		4	42	0	0	−1	0	0	0	0	0	0
	b_2	1	51	1	1	1	0	0	0	0	0	0
		2	34	−1	0	0	0	0	0	0	0	0
		3	44	0	−1	0	0	0	0	0	0	0
		4	48	0	0	−1	0	0	0	0	0	0
	b_3	1	35	1	1	1	0	0	0	0	0	0
		2	18	−1	0	0	0	0	0	0	0	0
		3	32	0	−1	0	0	0	0	0	0	0
		4	27	0	0	−1	0	0	0	0	0	0
a_2	b_1	5	47	0	0	0	1	1	1	0	0	0
		6	42	0	0	0	−1	0	0	0	0	0
		7	39	0	0	0	0	−1	0	0	0	0
		8	37	0	0	0	0	0	−1	0	0	0
	b_2	5	42	0	0	0	1	1	1	0	0	0
		6	33	0	0	0	−1	0	0	0	0	0
		7	13	0	0	0	0	−1	0	0	0	0
		8	16	0	0	0	0	0	−1	0	0	0
	b_3	5	16	0	0	0	1	1	1	0	0	0
		6	10	0	0	0	−1	0	0	0	0	0
		7	11	0	0	0	0	−1	0	0	0	0
		8	6	0	0	0	0	0	−1	0	0	0
a_3	b_1	9	45	0	0	0	0	0	0	1	1	1
		10	41	0	0	0	0	0	0	−1	0	0
		11	38	0	0	0	0	0	0	0	−1	0
		12	36	0	0	0	0	0	0	0	0	−1
	b_2	9	35	0	0	0	0	0	0	1	1	1
		10	33	0	0	0	0	0	0	−1	0	0
		11	46	0	0	0	0	0	0	0	−1	0
		12	40	0	0	0	0	0	0	0	0	−1
	b_3	9	29	0	0	0	0	0	0	1	1	1
		10	21	0	0	0	0	0	0	−1	0	0
		11	30	0	0	0	0	0	0	0	−1	0
		12	20	0	0	0	0	0	0	0	0	−1

Table 17-9
Summary of the MRC Analysis

(1) Source	(2) R^2	(3) df	(4) Mean R^2	(5) F
A	.2061	2	.1031	6.78*
S/A	.1365	9	.0152	
B	.5135	2	.2568	52.41**
A × B	.0553	4	.0138	2.82
B × S/A	.0886	18	.0049	
Total	1.0000	35		

* $p < .025$.

** $p < .01$.

$R^2_{Y.S/A}$ = the squared multiple correlation coefficient representing the entire set of nine subject vectors (vectors 9 to 17).

$R^2_{Y.B}$ = the squared multiple correlation coefficient representing the set of vectors for factor B (vectors 3 and 4).

$R^2_{Y.A \times B}$ = the squared multiple correlation coefficient representing the set of four vectors for the $A \times B$ interaction (vectors 5 to 8).

In each of the above, we can directly calculate the amount of variance explained by a set of vectors because the A, B, and subject sets of vectors are orthogonal, given the nature of the experimental design. Thus, $R^2_{Y.max.}$ can be found simply by adding the four squared multiple correlation coefficients denoted above *or* by directly computing $R^2_{Y.max.}$ on the basis of the entire set of vectors (vectors 1 to 17). More specifically,

$$R^2_{Y.max.} = R^2_{Y.1,2,\ldots,16,17}$$
$$= R^2_{Y.A} + R^2_{Y.S/A} + R^2_{Y.B} + R^2_{Y.A \times B}$$
$$= .2061 + .1365 + .5135 + .0553$$
$$= .9114$$

As we have noted already, the final source ($B \times S/A$) represents residual variation—variability that is *not* associated with the vectors created for the analysis. The squared multiple correlation coefficient for this source can be obtained by subtracting $R^2_{Y.max.}$ from 1; that is,

$$R^2_{Y.B \times S/A} = 1 - R^2_{Y.max.}$$
$$= 1 - .9114 = .0886$$

The remainder of the analysis is straightforward. Each $R^2_{Y.set}$ in Table 17-9 (column 2) is divided by the appropriate df (column 3) to obtain the corresponding "Mean R^2" (column 4); the F's (column 5) are formed by dividing mean R^2's representing systematic variance by the appropriate mean R^2 representing unsystematic variance. For A, the error term is $R^2_{Y.S/A}$; and for B and $A \times B$, the error term is $R^2_{Y.B \times S/A}$. Application of Eq. (14-4) or its equivalent yields the appropriate F values. As you can see, if you refer to Table 17-6, these F's are identical within the bounds of rounding to the F's reported with ANOVA.

17.4   SUMMARY

The "mixed" two-factor design contains features of a single-factor between-subjects design and a single-factor within-subjects design. Although subjects are each assigned to only one level of one of the independent variables (factor A), they receive all the treatment conditions formed by combining their respective level with all levels of the other independent variable (factor B). A common example of the mixed design is a learning experiment in which independent groups of subjects (factor A) are given a number of trials (factor B) to permit comparing different groups with regard to the course of learning. One primary advantage of the mixed design is its *efficiency*; fewer subjects are needed to complete the experiment than are needed for its completely randomized counterpart. Another important advantage is its greater *sensitivity*, which results from the smaller error term required for the assessment of certain treatment effects.

The mixed factorial design provides information on the two main effects and the $A \times B$ interaction. The only complication is that two error terms are required, one for the F ratio involving only between-subjects differences (the A main effect) and one for the two F ratios involving within-subjects differences (the B main effect and the $A \times B$ interaction). The first error term corresponds to the pooled within-groups error term appropriate for the completely randomized single-factor design (that is, $MS_{S/A}$). The second error term is based on $B \times S$ interactions—one for each level of factor A—which are pooled and averaged over the independent groups (that is, $MS_{B \times S/A}$).

The calculation of these two error terms, whether by ANOVA or by MRC, is based on procedures that were introduced in preceding chapters. For ANOVA, the only new quantity is a basic ratio based on the separate sums of the scores for the subjects; this basic ratio enters into the calculation of both error terms. For MRC, the procedure is identical to that of the single-factor within-subjects design, but you must keep in mind that two error terms are needed for the analysis.

17.5 EXERCISES

1. A researcher was interested in the effects of two drugs (I and II) on speed of learning in nonhuman primates. Subjects in condition a_1 were a control group that received no drug. Those in condition a_2 received a drug (I) that is known to suppress brain activity, while those in condition a_3 received a drug (II) that is known to enhance brain activity. Twelve young chimpanzees were assigned in equal numbers to each of three treatment conditions. The other independent variable (factor B) consisted of four daily testing sessions introduced after the drug had taken effect. On these tests, subjects were presented with three objects, two of which were identical and one was different; subjects were rewarded with a grape if they selected the unique object. Subjects were given 30 tests on each day. No objects were repeated for any of the subjects. The number of correct choices over each set of 30 trials is presented below:

	Control (a_1)					Drug I (a_2)			
Subject	b_1	b_2	b_3	b_4	Subject	b_1	b_2	b_3	b_4
1	3	5	7	9	5	4	5	3	1
2	6	9	9	13	6	7	9	8	4
3	10	15	14	15	7	12	12	13	9
4	10	12	15	18	8	11	10	11	7

	Drug II (a_3)			
Subject	b_1	b_2	b_3	b_4
9	8	7	5	9
10	9	12	8	11
11	12	9	13	12
12	4	8	13	10

(a) Use ANOVA to test the significance of the two main effects and the interaction.

(b) Use MRC to perform the same statistical tests.

Detailed Analysis of the Mixed Factorial Design

. . .

315

Rarely will we wish to restrict ourselves to a standard analysis of the overall design when we study completely randomized factorial designs. The reason is simple: we will usually be less interested in a significant omnibus effect than in determining what factors contribute to it. If we have no specific planned comparisons in mind, we first test the omnibus $A \times B$ interaction, and we then conduct an **analysis of simple effects**, if the interaction is significant, or an analysis of the main effects, if it is not. (In the latter case, we will generally break down significant main effects into a number of meaningful comparisons involving relevant marginal means.) On the other hand, having planned comparisons leads directly to the analysis of miniature factorials created out of the original design. These analyses are called **interaction comparisons** and may be conducted instead of the standard analysis of the overall factorial design. These two basic approaches to the detailed analysis of a factorial design were discussed in detail in Chaps. 14 and 15.

These same two approaches are available for the analysis of the mixed factorial design. In fact, the ANOVA and MRC approaches are identical to those outlined for the $A \times B$ factorial (i.e., the between-subjects design), except—and this is important—for the error terms used to form the F ratios. We will consider the analysis of main effects in Sec. 18.1 and the analysis of simple effects and of interaction comparisons in the sections that follow.

18.1   DETAILED ANALYSIS OF MAIN EFFECTS

The ANOVA Approach

You may recall that our analysis of the numerical example in Chap. 17 revealed that the overall $A \times B$ interaction was not significant. Under these circumstances, we would probably shift our attention to the detailed analysis of the two main effects, both of which are significant in our example. This analysis is easily accomplished; we simply arrange the data to form two single-factor designs, one involving independent measures (the analysis of the main effect of factor A, i.e., lectures) and the other involving repeated measures (the analysis of the main effect of factor B, i.e., time of testing).

Analysis of the Between-Subjects Factor (Factor A).   The between-subjects, or nonrepeated, factor in this example consists of the three types of lectures. Three groups of subjects are randomly assigned to receive a lecture on either physical science, social science, or history. They receive three vocabulary tests separated by 2-week intervals, and the results are combined into a single score for the analysis of the main effect. Since the main effect of this factor is significant, we would probably be interested in examining one or more comparisons involving the three lecture conditions.

From this point on, the analysis is exactly the same as the one described in Chap. 14 for the $A \times B$ design, except that we use $MS_{S/A}$ as the error term in the mixed factorial, rather than $MS_{S/AB}$. That is, coefficients are used to define the comparison, and the familiar formula for single-df comparisons is used to calculate the sum of squares. To illustrate with the data in Table 17-5, suppose we wish to compare the two science conditions. We obtain $\hat{\psi}_A$ by cross-multiplying the three marginal means calculated from the table (40.00, 26.00, and 34.50) with the relevant set of coefficients $(c_i: +1, -1, 0)$ and summing the products:

$$\hat{\psi}_A = (+1)(40.00) + (-1)(26.00) + (0)(34.50) = 14.00$$

Substituting in Eq. (14-2), we find

$$SS_{A_{comp.}} = \frac{(b)(s)(\hat{\psi}_A)}{\Sigma (c_i)^2}$$

$$= \frac{(3)(4)(14.00)^2}{(+1)^2 + (-1)^2 + (0)^2} = \frac{2352.00}{2} = 1176.00$$

Since $df = 1$, $MS_{A_{comp.}} = 1176.00$. The error term, which is found in Table 17-6 ($MS_{S/A} = 87.89$), is based on 9 df. The resulting F, $1176.00/87.89 = 13.38$, is significant, indicating that subjects recalled more vocabulary words after the lecture on physical science than after the lecture on social science.

Analysis of the Within-Subjects Factor (Factor B). You may recall from Chap. 16 that the detailed analysis of the single-factor within-subjects design required a separate error term for each comparison tested. That is, rather than use the overall $A \times S$ interaction for the error term, we used separate $A_{comp.} \times S$ interactions instead. The same sort of specific error term is required for the mixed factorial design. We will not illustrate this process here; we will do so when we consider the analysis of interaction contrasts, which require the same sort of error term. Nevertheless, it is still worthwhile to present an example at this time. What we will do is to illustrate how the analysis is performed and refer you to later discussions for the details surrounding the calculation of the error term.

Suppose we wanted to compare the performance on the immediate test (b_1) with the performance of the same subjects 2 weeks later (b_2). Applying the codes applicable to this comparison (c_j: $+1$, -1, 0) to the means for the three tests (43.00, 36.25, and 21.25, for the tests following immediately, after 2 weeks, and after 4 weeks, respectively), we find a difference in favor of the first test, namely,

$$\hat{\psi}_B = (+1)(43.00) + (-1)(36.25) + (0)(21.25) = 6.75$$

The sum of squares for this comparison, which is specified by Eq. (14-3), is

$$SS_{B_{comp.}} = \frac{(a)\,(s)\,(\hat{\psi}_B)^2}{\Sigma\,(c_j)^2}$$

$$= \frac{(3)\,(4)\,(6.75)^2}{(+1)^2 + (-1)^2 + (0)^2} = \frac{546.75}{2} = 273.38$$

Since this sum of squares is associated with 1 df, $MS_{B_{comp.}} = 273.38$.

The sum of squares for the error term to test the significance of the comparison is based on an interaction of this comparison and subjects (a $B_{comp.} \times S$ interaction); interactions are calculated for the three lecture groups separately and then combined. The sum of the three individual sums of squares is $SS_{B_{comp.} \times S/A} = 376.37$. (We do not show the calculations here; they are discussed in Sec. 18.4.) The df are obtained by pooling the df's associated with the separate interactions. For any one group,

$$df = (df_{B_{comp.}})\,(df_S) = (1)\,(s-1) = s-1$$

For all three groups,

$$df_{B_{comp.} \times S/A} = (a)\,(s-1) = (3)\,(4-1) = 9$$

The mean square, then, is

$$MS_{B_{comp.} \times S/A} = 376.37/9 = 41.82$$

The final F of $273.38/41.82 = 6.54$ is significant, indicating superior recall on the first test.

The MRC Approach

We can easily conduct the corresponding analyses with MRC by taking advantage of information generated when we plan the overall analysis. We are referring, of course, to the vectors we use in the overall analysis to code meaningful single-df comparisons in which we may be interested.

Analysis of the Between-Subjects Factor (Factor *A*).   Like the preceding analysis based on ANOVA, the detailed MRC analysis of the *A* main effect essentially duplicates the procedures we followed with the completely randomized *A* × *B* design. Variability associated with a single-df comparison is reflected in the correlation coefficient between *Y* and the appropriate main-effect vector. The example we used with ANOVA in the first part of Sec. 18.1 consisted of the contrast between the two science conditions. The vector representing this comparison in the overall MRC analysis is *A*1, which appears in column 1 of Table 17-7. That analysis revealed that $r_{Y1}^2 = .2030$; this correlation is based on 1 *df*, of course. The between-subjects error term $(R_{Y.S/A}^2)$ also comes from the original analysis. From Table 17-9, we find,

$$\text{Mean } R_{Y.S/A}^2 = .0152$$

which is based on 9 *df*. The *F* is $.2030/.0152 = 13.36$; the *F* from ANOVA is 13.38.

Analysis of the Within-Subjects Factor (Factor B). The numerical example we considered with ANOVA compared the performance of subjects on two of the three vocabulary tests they received, namely, the immediate test and the 2-week test. The vector corresponding to this comparison in Table 17-7 is B1, which is found in column 3. For this single-*df* comparison, $r_{Y3}^2 = .0472$.

You will recall that the corresponding ANOVA analysis requires a specialized error term that is based on the data actually contributing to the comparison. The MRC analysis extracts this same information through the creation of appropriate vectors in a manner analogous to the procedure we followed for the *single-factor* within-subjects design we considered in Chap. 16. More specifically, we obtain the equivalent of a $B_{comp.} \times S$ interaction first by specifying a set of *interaction vectors*—each formed by cross-multiplying the main-effect vector (B1) with the full set of nine subject vectors (vectors 9 to 17 in Table 17-8)—and then using the nine new vectors to calculate the appropriate R^2. (We will discuss this analysis in more detail in Sec. 18.4.) These calculations reveal that $R_{Y.B1 \times S/A}^2 = .0650$, which is based on 9 *df*. With this information, we can now complete the analysis as follows:

$$F = \frac{r_{Y3}^2}{R_{Y.B1 \times S/A}^2 / df_{Y.B1 \times S/A}}$$
$$= \frac{.0472}{.0650/9} = \frac{.0472}{.0072} = 6.56$$

The corresponding *F* from ANOVA is 6.54.

18.2 USING ANOVA TO ANALYZE SIMPLE EFFECTS

One very useful way to study interaction systematically is to analyze the simple effects of one or even both of the independent variables. This is accomplished by dividing the original factorial design into a set of single-factor designs in which one of the independent variables is permitted to vary while the other is held constant within any given analysis. In the context of the present example, we might look at the effects of the three lectures (factor A) on the "immediate" test (factor B held constant at level b_1), on the 2-week test (factor B held constant at level b_2), and on the 4-week test (factor B held constant at level b_3). Our goal would be to discover different patterns of results on the different tests. We might also look at the degree of forgetting over the three tests (factor B) for the lecture on physical science (factor A held constant at level a_1), for the lecture on social science (factor A held constant at level a_2), and for the lecture on history (factor A held constant at level a_3). Again, the goal is to find different effects for factor B at the different levels of factor A.

When this method is applied to the mixed factorial, the main complication is in finding the correct error term for assessing the simple effects. As you have seen in the overall analysis of this type of design, there are two error terms, one for assessing effects based on independent observations (the A main effect) and the other for assessing effects based on observations obtained on the same subjects (the B main effect and the $A \times B$ interaction). The same dichotomy is present in the analysis of simple effects. As we show later in more detail, in analyzing the simple effects of factor A (the between-subjects factor) we will use an error term that is equivalent to that used to evaluate an actual single-factor design with independent groups of subjects. Similarly, analyzing the simple effects of B (the within-subjects factor) will require an error term that is equivalent to that used to evaluate an actual single-factor within-subjects design. In this section we will consider how the two analyses are conducted with ANOVA, and in the next with MRC.

You will recall from Chap. 14 that we usually examine simple effects when we wish to determine the factors responsible for a significant $A \times B$ interaction. Since a significant interaction indicates that the simple effects are not all the same, it is natural to turn to an analysis that is designed to reveal which of the simple effects are significant and which are not. On the other hand, since a nonsignificant interaction implies that the simple effects are the same, differing only as a result of chance factors, we usually shift our attention to an analysis of the main effects when the interaction is nonsignificant. We mention this point again because we will use the data from the current numerical example to illustrate the analysis of simple effects, even though we have a nonsignificant $A \times B$ interaction and thus such an analysis would probably not be justified.

Simple Effects of Factor A

In the analysis of the simple effects of factor A, all we need to do is divide the overall design into a set of single-factor experiments, one for each level of factor B, and then analyze them separately. We will illustrate the calculations with a numerical example. Consider the overall data matrix from the original experiment (Table 17-5). Suppose we wish to examine the simple effects of factor A at level b_1—the effects of the three different lectures (factor A) on the vocabulary test given immediately after the presentation (level b_1). We have extracted the data from the overall design to create this "component experiment," which is presented in Table 18-1. What we have done is to take the entire column of data for the "immediate" test (level b_1) from each of the lecture groups and to arrange the smaller data set we have extracted exactly the same way we would list the data from an actual single-factor experiment—an experiment consisting of three independent groups of subjects receiving a lecture on either physical science (a_1), social science (a_2), or history (a_3).

Table 18-1
Data Matrix for the Analysis of the Simple Effects of Factor A
for the Immediate Test (Level b_1)

a_1		a_2		a_3	
s_1	53	s_5	47	s_9	45
s_2	49	s_6	42	s_{10}	41
s_3	47	s_7	39	s_{11}	38
s_4	42	s_8	37	s_{12}	36
Sum	191	Sum	165	Sum	160

From this point on, we treat the data just as we would an actual between-subjects single-factor experiment. We first calculate the three basic ratios, ["Y"], ["A"], and ["T"].[1] Specifically,

$$["Y"] = 53^2 + 49^2 + \cdots + 38^2 + 36^2 = 22{,}492$$

$$["A"] = \frac{191^2 + 165^2 + 160^2}{4} = \frac{89{,}306}{4} = 22{,}326.50$$

$$["T"] = \frac{(191 + 165 + 160)^2}{(3)(4)} = \frac{266{,}256}{12} = 22{,}188.00$$

[1] The quotation marks indicate that the data are not drawn from an actual single-factor experiment, but from a portion of the larger factorial design. The use of single-factor notation stresses the point that the analysis of simple effects is equivalent to the analysis of a single-factor design.

Next, we calculate the two sums of squares:

$$SS_{A \text{ at } b_1} = [\text{``}A\text{''}] - [\text{``}T\text{''}]$$
$$= 22,326.50 - 22,188.00 = 138.50$$

$$SS_{S/A \text{ at } b_1} = [\text{``}Y\text{''}] - [\text{``}A\text{''}]$$
$$= 22,492 - 22,326.50 = 165.50$$

The degrees of freedom for the simple effect are

$$df_{A \text{ at } b_1} = a - 1 = 3 - 1 = 2$$

and for the error term they are

$$df_{S/A \text{ at } b_1} = (a)(s - 1) = (3)(4 - 1) = 9$$

The mean squares are calculated by dividing each sum of squares by the appropriate df, and the F ratio is formed by dividing the mean square representing the simple effect by the mean square representing the variability of subjects treated alike.[2] We find that

$$F = \frac{SS_{A \text{ at } b_1}/df_{A \text{ at } b_1}}{SS_{S/A \text{ at } b_1}/df_{S/A \text{ at } b_1}}$$
$$= \frac{138.50/2}{165.50/9} = \frac{69.25}{18.39} = 3.77$$

The critical value of F is determined in the usual manner, with $df_{num.} = 1$ and $df_{denom.} = 9$. The F ratio we have obtained is not significant.

Single-df Comparisons.   If the F ratio had been significant, we would probably consider conducting one or more single-df comparisons, such as a comparison between the two science conditions and one between the two combined science conditions and the history condition. These would follow the same procedure we outlined in Chap. 11 for single-df comparisons. The error term for each single-df comparison would be the same error term used to evaluate that particular simple effect, which, in this case, is $MS_{S/A \text{ at } b_1}$.

---

[2] If it is safe to assume that the variability of subjects within all the treatment conditions in the experiment is the same—a questionable assumption in many experiments—one may use an error term that consists of an average of the individual variances. This error term, which is called the **within-cell error term** ($MS_{w.cell}$), is used to test the significance of any simple effect of factor A, including single-df comparisons. For a discussion of the within-cell mean square, see Kirk (1982, pp. 508–509) and Winer (1971, pp. 529–532).

Table 18-2
Data Matrix for the Analysis of the Simple Effects of Factor B
for the Physical Science Lecture (Level a_1)

	b_1	b_2	b_3	Sum
s_1	53	51	35	139
s_2	49	34	18	101
s_3	47	44	32	123
s_4	42	48	27	117
Sum	191	177	112	480

Simple Effects of Factor B

For the analysis of simple effects involving the within-subjects factor, we segregate the data into a number of $B \times S$ designs, one for each level of factor A. These component experiments are equivalent to separate single-factor within-subjects designs, which means that they may be analyzed in the manner outlined in Chap. 16. More specifically, each of the simple effects is tested against its own error term. In the context of the present example, the simple effects of B at a_1 would be tested with the $B \times S$ interaction at a_1, the simple effects of B at a_2 would be tested with the corresponding interaction at a_2, and so on.

To illustrate, we will evaluate the differences on the three vocabulary tests for the subjects receiving the physical science lecture—the simple effects of B at level a_1. Table 18-2 presents the appropriate portion of the data extracted from Table 17-5. You will note that this data matrix represents a single-factor within-subjects design in which each of $s = 4$ subjects receives the three vocabulary tests (factor B) administered at different times following the presentation of the lecture. We can now calculate the necessary basic ratios—["Y"], ["B"], ["S"], and ["T"]—following the procedures covered in Chap. 16.[3] That is,

$$["Y"] = 53^2 + 49^2 + \cdots + 32^2 + 27^2 = 20{,}482$$

$$["B"] = \frac{191^2 + 177^2 + 112^2}{4} = \frac{80{,}354}{4} = 20{,}088.50$$

$$["S"] = \frac{139^2 + 101^2 + 123^2 + 117^2}{3} = \frac{58{,}340}{3} = 19{,}446.67$$

$$["T"] = \frac{480^2}{(3)(4)} = \frac{230{,}400}{12} = 19{,}200.00$$

---

[3] Again, the quotation marks indicate that the data are not drawn from an actual single-factor experiment, but from a portion of the larger factorial design.

We need only two sums of squares for the statistical test, namely,

$$SS_{B\,at\,a_1} = [\text{``}B\text{''}] - [\text{``}T\text{''}]$$

$$= 20{,}088.50 - 19{,}200.00 = 888.50$$

$$SS_{B\,\times\,S\,at\,a_1} = [\text{``}Y\text{''}] - [\text{``}B\text{''}] - [\text{``}S\text{''}] + [\text{``}T\text{''}]$$

$$= 20{,}482 - 20{,}088.50 - 19{,}446.67 + 19{,}200.00 = 146.83$$

The degrees of freedom are calculated in the normal manner:

$$df_{B\,at\,a_1} = b - 1 = 3 - 1 = 2$$

$$df_{B\,\times\,S\,at\,a_1} = (b - 1)(s - 1) = (3 - 1)(4 - 1) = 6$$

The two mean squares are calculated by dividing each sum of squares by its degrees of freedom. The value of F is

$$F = \frac{SS_{B\,at\,a_1}/df_{B\,at\,a_1}}{SS_{B\,\times\,S\,at\,a_1}/df_{B\,\times\,S\,at\,a_1}}$$

$$= \frac{888.50/2}{146.83/6} = \frac{444.25}{24.47} = 18.15$$

This F, which is significant, is evaluated with $df_{num.} = 2$ and $df_{denom.} = 6$. We would conclude that time interval had an effect on the number of words recalled for subjects in the physical science condition.

Single-df Comparisons.   When there is a significant simple effect, our attention is drawn to an examination of specific differences between treatment means—that is, single-df comparisons. Suppose we wanted to compare scores on the immediate test with scores on the test given 2 weeks later. As you may recall from Chap. 16, we performed analyses of single-df comparisons by constructing a comparison matrix and calculating a new error term designed for the particular analysis. Such a comparison matrix is presented in Table 18-3.

In the first two columns, we have listed the relevant scores for the four subjects. These consist of the scores obtained from the immediate test and the test administered 2 weeks later. (The coefficients for this single-df comparison are (c_j: $+1, -1, 0$), of course.[4]) The next column contains the differences between the two tests for the individual subjects, while the final column lists the individual sums of squares based on these differences, which we will discuss in the next paragraph.

---

[4] If a more complex comparison were involved, such as the immediate test versus an average of the two delayed tests, we would enter the means for the two combined tests and the scores for the immediate test. The coefficients for this single-df comparison would be (c_j: $+1, -\frac{1}{2}, -\frac{1}{2}$).

Table 18-3
Calculation of a Separate Error Term for a Single-*df* Comparison

	Immediate Test	2-Week Test	Difference	SS
s_1	53	51	2	2.00
s_2	49	34	15	112.50
s_3	47	44	3	4.50
s_4	42	48	−6	18.00
Average	47.75	44.25	3.50	

The bottom row of the matrix gives the means for the two tests and the difference between them ($\hat{\psi}_{B\,at\,a_1}$). We are now ready to proceed with the calculations.

As detailed in Chap. 16 (Sec. 16.4), we begin by calculating a comparison sum of squares for each subject based on the differences listed in Table 18-3. Adapting Eq. (16-3) to the present situation, we have

$$SS_{B_{comp.}\,for\,s_k} = \frac{(\text{Diff.})^2}{\Sigma\,(c_j)^2}$$

For the first subject,

$$SS_{B_{comp.}\,for\,s_1} = \frac{2^2}{(+1)^2 + (-1)^2 + (0)^2} = \frac{4}{2} = 2.00$$

The sums of squares for all four subjects, which are calculated in the same way, are given in the final column of Table 18-3.

The sum of squares for the comparison itself is obtained by substituting the difference between the two means, $\hat{\psi}_{B\,at\,a_1}$, in the standard formula for a single-*df* comparison. Adapting Eq. (16-4) to the present analysis, we have

$$SS_{B_{comp.}\,at\,a_1} = \frac{(s)\,(\hat{\psi}_{B\,at\,a_1})^2}{\Sigma\,(c_j)^2}$$

$$= \frac{(4)\,(3.50)^2}{2} = \frac{49.00}{2} = 24.50$$

The error term is calculated by subtracting the sum of squares for the comparison itself from the combined sums of squares obtained for the individual subjects. Using the data from the last column of Table 18-3 and the sums of squares we have just calculated, we find

$$SS_{B_{comp.}\,\times\,S\,at\,a_1} = (2.00 + 112.50 + 4.50 + 18.00) - 24.50$$

$$= 137.00 - 24.50 = 112.50$$

The df for $SS_{B_{comp}. \, at \, a_1}$ is 1, and the df for $SS_{B_{comp}. \times S \, at \, a_1}$ are

$$df_{B_{comp}. \times S \, at \, a_1} = s - 1 = 4 - 1 = 3$$

The F becomes

$$F = \frac{SS_{B_{comp}. \, at \, a_1} / df_{B_{comp}. \, at \, a_1}}{SS_{B_{comp}. \times S \, at \, a_1} / df_{B_{comp}. \times S \, at \, a_1}}$$

$$= \frac{24.50/1}{112.50/3} = \frac{24.50}{37.50} = .65$$

With $df_{num.} = 1$ and $df_{denom.} = 3$, this F is not significant.

Comment

You may have noticed the relatively small number of degrees of freedom associated with the error term in this last example. Although an actual experiment will have more than 3 df, since there will be larger samples sizes than the $s = 4$ in our example, it will still usually be the case that comparisons of this sort will suffer loss of power. If we had not used a separate error term to evaluate the single-df comparison, power would be considerably greater. To illustrate, the critical value of F with the separate error term is $F(1, 3) = 10.1$ at the 5 percent level of significance. If we had used the error term that we used to evaluate the overall simple effect, the critical value would be $F(1, 6) = 5.99$. Extending the argument further, if we had used the within-subjects error term from the overall analysis of variance— $MS_{B \times S/A}$—the critical value would be $F(1, 18) = 4.41$. If all three calculated error terms are the same size, there will be marked differences in the statistical power of these three alternative tests because of these differences in df and critical values.

The choice of error term is determined by the statistical model underlying the analysis, however, and not by a concern for power. If separate error terms for analyzing simple effects and additional comparisons represent the correct approach to the analysis, then we must live with whatever power is associated with the test we conduct. We can take steps to reduce the power loss simply by increasing sample size. Suppose we had designed the example with $s = 8$ subjects assigned to each lecture and kept everything else the same. Under these circumstances, the critical value of F would be $F(1, 42) = 4.08$ if we used the error term from the overall analysis, $F(1, 14) = 4.60$ if we used the error term from the analysis of the simple effect, and $F(1, 7) = 5.59$ if we used the separate error term for a single-df comparison. There are still differences in the critical values, to be sure, but they are greatly reduced.

18.3 USING MRC TO ANALYZE SIMPLE EFFECTS

You have seen in previous chapters that all we have to do to adapt the MRC approach to the analysis of experimental data is devise vectors at the outset of the analysis that represent the desired sources of variability. The analysis of simple effects is no exception. We will start with vectors that were used for the overall analysis and adapt them for use in calculating simple effects. As you will see, this process is not complicated, though attention must be given to how vectors are selected to reflect error terms.

Simple Effects of Factor *A*

Let us consider what vectors we will need to complete this analysis. First, there are the vectors for the simple effects themselves, and then the vectors for the error term. We can obtain both sets of vectors from the overall analysis. We start with the vectors representing the main effect of factor *A* and the vectors representing subjects. Then we transform these vectors into new vectors that will extract information at only one level of the other independent variable, which, in this case, is factor *B*. This is easily accomplished by a coding system that results in assigning 0s to all observations not relevant for the analysis and retaining the original values from the coding matrix—for all observations that *are* relevant for the analysis.

We now illustrate the procedure. In the example for ANOVA, we considered the effects of the three lectures (factor *A*) on the first vocabulary test administered immediately after the lecture (level b_1). To obtain the same analysis by MRC, we turn to the vectors from the overall analysis—where two vectors represent factor *A* (types of lecture) and 9 vectors represent subjects. The main-effect vectors were presented in Table 17-7 (vectors 1 and 2), and the subject vectors in Table 17-8 (vectors 9 to 17). In Table 17-7, vector 1 compared physical science with social science, whereas vector 2 compared the combined sciences with history; but these comparisons involved subjects in *all three levels* of factor *B*. Likewise, in Table 17-8, we created vectors that distinguished among the four subjects in each of the three lecture conditions, but again, these vectors involved data from all three *B* levels. Now, the simple effects we are interested in are those revealed in the above comparisons, but only for the "immediate" test (level b_1). Thus, to convert these 11 vectors from Tables 17-7 and 17-8 into vectors that will reflect the simple effects of factor *A* at b_1, all we need to do is change all entries for levels b_2 and b_3 in these tables to *zero*. We do this because we are interested only in the differences between the lectures in the first test period. The result of this transformation is found in Table 18-4.

Table 18-4
Code Matrix for the Analysis of the Simple Effects of Factor A at b_1

	Subject	Y	(1)	(2)	(3)	(4)	(5)	(6)	(7)	(8)	(9)	(10)	(11)
													Vectors
a_1 b_1	1	53	1	1	1	1	1	0	0	0	0	0	0
	2	49	1	1	−1	0	0	0	0	0	0	0	0
	3	47	1	1	0	−1	0	0	0	0	0	0	0
	4	42	1	1	0	0	−1	0	0	0	0	0	0
b_2	1	51	0	0	0	0	0	0	0	0	0	0	0
	2	34	0	0	0	0	0	0	0	0	0	0	0
	3	44	0	0	0	0	0	0	0	0	0	0	0
	4	48	0	0	0	0	0	0	0	0	0	0	0
b_3	1	35	0	0	0	0	0	0	0	0	0	0	0
	2	18	0	0	0	0	0	0	0	0	0	0	0
	3	32	0	0	0	0	0	0	0	0	0	0	0
	4	27	0	0	0	0	0	0	0	0	0	0	0
a_2 b_1	5	47	−1	1	0	0	0	1	1	1	0	0	0
	6	42	−1	1	0	0	0	−1	0	0	0	0	0
	7	39	−1	1	0	0	0	0	−1	0	0	0	0
	8	37	−1	1	0	0	0	0	0	−1	0	0	0
b_2	5	42	0	0	0	0	0	0	0	0	0	0	0
	6	33	0	0	0	0	0	0	0	0	0	0	0
	7	13	0	0	0	0	0	0	0	0	0	0	0
	8	16	0	0	0	0	0	0	0	0	0	0	0
b_3	5	16	0	0	0	0	0	0	0	0	0	0	0
	6	10	0	0	0	0	0	0	0	0	0	0	0
	7	11	0	0	0	0	0	0	0	0	0	0	0
	8	6	0	0	0	0	0	0	0	0	0	0	0
a_3 b_1	9	45	0	−2	0	0	0	0	0	0	1	1	1
	10	41	0	−2	0	0	0	0	0	0	−1	0	0
	11	38	0	−2	0	0	0	0	0	0	0	−1	0
	12	36	0	−2	0	0	0	0	0	0	0	0	−1
b_2	9	35	0	0	0	0	0	0	0	0	0	0	0
	10	33	0	0	0	0	0	0	0	0	0	0	0
	11	46	0	0	0	0	0	0	0	0	0	0	0
	12	40	0	0	0	0	0	0	0	0	0	0	0
b_3	9	29	0	0	0	0	0	0	0	0	0	0	0
	10	21	0	0	0	0	0	0	0	0	0	0	0
	11	30	0	0	0	0	0	0	0	0	0	0	0
	12	20	0	0	0	0	0	0	0	0	0	0	0

Alternatively, we could have established a code matrix to represent the simple effects *directly* without transforming the vectors used in the overall analysis. To illustrate, we would start with the following code matrix:

	a_1b_1	a_1b_2	a_1b_3	a_2b_1	a_2b_2	a_2b_3	a_3b_1	a_3b_2	a_3b_3
Vector 1	+1	0	0	−1	0	0	0	0	0
Vector 2	+1	0	0	+1	0	0	−2	0	0

Here we see that there are nine conditions, but we are interested only in those involving level b_1. Consequently, any cell with a b_2 or a b_3 receives a zero. The two vectors, 1 and 2, now concentrate on the comparisons of interest for this analysis.

The analysis is now conducted just as if the design were an actual single-factor design, with the squared multiple correlation coefficient between Y and vectors 1 and 2 ($R^2_{Y.A \text{ at } b_1}$) reflecting the simple effect of factor A and the squared multiple correlation coefficient between Y and vectors 3 through 11 ($R^2_{Y.S/A \text{ at } b_1}$) reflecting the pooled variability of subjects treated alike. A computer analysis gives us

$$R^2_{Y.A \text{ at } b_1} = .0239 \quad \text{and} \quad R^2_{Y.S/A \text{ at } b_1} = .0286$$

As usual, the df for these multiple correlations are determined by the number of vectors needed to specify the different sources of variability. That is,

$$df_{Y.A \text{ at } b_1} = 2 \quad \text{and} \quad df_{Y.S/A \text{ at } b_1} = 9$$

The F is

$$F = \frac{R^2_{Y.A \text{ at } b_1}/df_{Y.A \text{ at } b_1}}{R^2_{Y.S/A \text{ at } b_1}/df_{Y.S/A \text{ at } b_1}}$$

$$= \frac{.0239/2}{.0286/9} = \frac{.0120}{.0032} = 3.75$$

which, within rounding error, is equal to the value obtained with ANOVA ($F = 3.77$) and is not significant.

Single-df Comparisons.   If the simple effect had been significant, we probably would have been interested in conducting a number of meaningful single-df comparisons. These analyses would be particularly easy, since we used these particular comparisons to create the vectors defining the simple effect. For example, vector 1 in Table 18-4 codes a comparison of the two science conditions on the first vocabulary test (level b_1), while vector 2 codes the comparison of the combined science conditions with the history condition, also on the first vocabulary test. All we need to do to complete the analysis is to divide the r^2 for each comparison by the error term we calculated in the preceding paragraph.

Simple Effects of Factor B

With ANOVA, we considered the differences on the three vocabulary tests (factor B) administered to the subjects receiving the lecture on physical science (level a_1). To conduct the same analysis with MRC procedures, we need two sets of vectors, one reflecting the simple effect itself and the other reflecting the error term, which in this case is the $B \times S$ interaction associated with the physical science group (level a_1).

The procedure for constructing these vectors is consistent with the system we have described before. One procedure is to plan for the study of meaningful simple effects. Again, we have nine conditions as follows:

$$a_1b_1 \quad a_1b_2 \quad a_1b_3 \quad a_2b_1 \quad a_2b_2 \quad a_2b_3 \quad a_3b_1 \quad a_3b_2 \quad a_3b_3$$

Since our interest is in the differences among the three vocabulary tests (B) for subjects in the physical science lecture only (level a_1), we insert a 0 in all cells with an a_2 or an a_3 and then create two vectors to represent the kinds of comparisons among the three tests that are of interest to us. For example, if we are interested in comparing the immediate test with the 2-week test and the 2-week test with the 4-week test, we generate the following code matrix.

	a_1b_1	a_1b_2	a_1b_3	a_2b_1	a_2b_2	a_2b_3	a_3b_1	a_3b_2	a_3b_3
Vector 1	$+1$	-1	0	0	0	0	0	0	0
Vector 2	0	$+1$	-1	0	0	0	0	0	0

The other procedure is to transform the vectors from the overall analysis into vectors that reflect the simple effect of factor B at a_1: we could turn to Table 17-7 and transform columns 3 and 4 by assigning 0s to all subjects in a_2 and a_3—that is, by assigning 0s to all irrelevant observations. In this case, the irrelevant observations will be the scores from the other two lecture conditions (social science, a_2, and history, a_3). The two vectors of interest, regardless of the procedure used for generating them, are presented in columns 1 and 2 of Table 18-5. As you can see, both vectors deal only with the data from physical science. Vector 1 compares subjects on the immediate and 2-week tests, while vector 2 compares the subjects on the 2-week and 4-week tests.

Table 18-5

Code Matrix for the Analysis of the Simple Effects of Factor B at a_1

	Subject	Y	Vectors							
			(1)	(2)	(3)	(4)	(5)	(6)	(7)	(8)
a_1 b_1	1	53	1	0	1	1	1	0	0	0
	2	49	1	0	−1	0	0	0	0	0
	3	47	1	0	0	−1	0	0	0	0
	4	42	1	0	0	0	−1	0	0	0
b_2	1	51	−1	1	−1	−1	−1	1	1	1
	2	34	−1	1	1	0	0	−1	0	0
	3	44	−1	1	0	1	0	0	−1	0
	4	48	−1	1	0	0	1	0	0	−1
b_3	1	35	0	−1	0	0	0	−1	−1	−1
	2	18	0	−1	0	0	0	1	0	0
	3	32	0	−1	0	0	0	0	1	0
	4	27	0	−1	0	0	0	0	0	1
a_2 b_1	5	47	0	0	0	0	0	0	0	0
	6	42	0	0	0	0	0	0	0	0
	7	39	0	0	0	0	0	0	0	0
	8	37	0	0	0	0	0	0	0	0
b_2	5	42	0	0	0	0	0	0	0	0
	6	33	0	0	0	0	0	0	0	0
	7	13	0	0	0	0	0	0	0	0
	8	16	0	0	0	0	0	0	0	0
b_3	5	16	0	0	0	0	0	0	0	0
	6	10	0	0	0	0	0	0	0	0
	7	11	0	0	0	0	0	0	0	0
	8	6	0	0	0	0	0	0	0	0
a_3 b_1	9	45	0	0	0	0	0	0	0	0
	10	41	0	0	0	0	0	0	0	0
	11	38	0	0	0	0	0	0	0	0
	12	36	0	0	0	0	0	0	0	0
b_2	9	35	0	0	0	0	0	0	0	0
	10	33	0	0	0	0	0	0	0	0
	11	46	0	0	0	0	0	0	0	0
	12	40	0	0	0	0	0	0	0	0
b_3	9	29	0	0	0	0	0	0	0	0
	10	21	0	0	0	0	0	0	0	0
	11	30	0	0	0	0	0	0	0	0
	12	20	0	0	0	0	0	0	0	0

The vectors for the $B \times S$ interaction at level a_1 are easily obtained by cross-multiplying each of the two main-effects vectors (columns 3 and 4 of Table 17-7) with the three subject vectors representing the subjects in the physical science group, which are found in columns 9 to 11 of Table 17-8. These interaction vectors do not need to be transformed for this analysis, since 0s will be automatically assigned to all observations at the other two levels of factor A.[5] The entire set of interaction vectors is presented in columns 3 to 8 in Table 18-5. Vectors in columns 3 to 5 ($B1S1$, $B1S2$, and $B1S3$), reflect the interaction of $B1$ with the three vectors representing the subjects at level a_1, and the vectors in columns 6 to 8 ($B2S1$, $B2S2$, and $B2S3$) reflect the corresponding interaction with $B2$. Collectively, the six vectors represent the desired $B \times S$ interaction.

From this point on, the analysis is straightforward. A computer analysis reveals that the squared multiple correlation coefficient representing the simple effect of B (calculated with the vectors from columns 1 and 2, Table 18-5) is

$$R^2_{Y.B \, at \, a_1} = .1534$$

and that the squared multiple correlation coefficient representing the simple $B \times S$ interaction (calculated with the vectors from columns 3 through 8, Table 18-5) is

$$R^2_{Y.B \times S \, at \, a_1} = .0253$$

There are 2 df associated with the simple effect (vectors 1 and 2) and 6 df associated with the interaction (vectors 3 to 8). The F is calculated as follows:

$$F = \frac{R^2_{Y.B \, at \, a_1}/df_{Y.B \, at \, a_1}}{R^2_{Y.B \times S \, at \, a_1}/df_{Y.B \times S \, at \, a_1}}$$

$$= \frac{.1534/2}{.0253/6} = \frac{.0767}{.0042} = 18.26$$

This value is different from the value of 18.15 we obtained with ANOVA because of rounding error.

Single-df Comparisons.   Single-df comparisons are easily evaluated at this point, especially if the comparison itself has been used as one of the B vectors in the analysis of the simple effects. In the present case, vector $B1$ reflects the comparison between the immediate and 2-week tests, while vector $B2$ represents the comparison between the 2-week and 4-week tests. Suppose we decided to compare

---

[5] The subject vectors, upon which these interaction vectors are based, were constructed for each level of factor A separately. That is, we used coding to identify subjects one level at a time, using 0's to eliminate all other observations. This means, then, that these $B \times S$ interaction vectors are ideally suited for use in the analysis of simple effects.

the means on the first two tests (immediate and 2-week). This comparison is embodied in column 1 of Table 18-5; the zero-order r^2 between Y and this vector $(r_{Y_1}^2)$ will capture this variation. If, on the other hand, we had not originally created a vector that yielded column 1, we could directly construct a new vector to represent the comparison of interest by using our code matrix strategies.

The error term for this comparison consists of an interaction between the comparison and subjects ($B_{comp.} \times S$ at level a_1); the squared multiple correlation coefficient between Y and the three vectors (vectors 3 to 5) representing this particular interaction, $R_{Y.B1 \times S \, at \, a_1}^2$, will capture this variation. The analysis reveals that

$$r_{Y_1}^2 = .0042 \quad \text{and} \quad R_{Y.B1 \times S \, at \, a_1}^2 = .0194$$

The df for the zero-order correlation is 1, of course; the df for the multiple correlation, which is determined by the number of vectors, is 3. The F is

$$F = \frac{.0042/1}{.0194/3} = \frac{.0042}{.0065} = .65$$

which is identical to the value we obtained with ANOVA.

18.4   ANALYSIS OF INTERACTION CONTRASTS

In Chap. 15, we considered the use of planned comparisons in the context of a factorial design. We discussed how a single-df comparison involving one (or both) of the independent variables could be used to create a component factorial design in which the interaction of the comparison becomes the primary focus of attention. We call component factorials like this *interaction comparisons*. These same types of interaction comparisons may be conducted with the mixed design. As in Chap. 15, we will concentrate on a particularly useful type of interaction comparison called the *interaction contrast*—a factorial arrangement of two single-df comparisons which form a 2×2 design.

The ANOVA Approach

An interaction contrast offers a highly refined and focused view of the interaction of two independent variables. The interaction sum of squares $SS_{A_{comp.} \times B_{comp.}}$ is calculated in exactly the same way as in the $A \times B$ design we considered in Chap. 15. As you might suspect from your understanding of within-subjects designs, we will need separate error terms for each interaction contrast evaluated in the analysis. In brief, the error term for an interaction contrast consists of separate $B_{comp.} \times S$

interactions—one for each level of factor *A*—that are pooled and averaged over all levels of factor *A*. What this requires is the construction of a series of comparison matrices from which this information may be derived.

Calculating the Interaction Contrast.   As an example, let us assume that we wish to determine whether the difference between the two science conditions ($A_{comp.}$) depends on whether the vocabulary test is given immediately or after 2 weeks ($B_{comp.}$). This research question is represented by a 2 × 2 factorial consisting of two levels of factor *A* (physical science and social science) crossed with two levels of factor *B* (immediate test and 2-week test). Alternatively, we can express the same interaction contrast in terms of $B_{comp.}$. In this case we would be asking whether the amount of forgetting over the first 2 weeks ($B_{comp.}$) is the same for the two science conditions ($A_{comp.}$). Either way of expressing the interaction contrast produces the same 2 × 2 factorial for the analysis.

We will conduct the analysis in two steps: we will calculate the interaction sum of squares and then the sum of squares for the error term. For the first sum of squares, we need to determine the value of the contrast ($\hat{\psi}_{A \times B}$), which we can obtain from the 2 × 2 arrangement of the relevant means; we then use Eq. (15-3) to complete the calculations. We discussed this calculation in Chap. 15 (pages 247–248).

As a reminder, $\hat{\psi}_{A \times B}$ is defined as the difference between the two simple effects involving either of the two factors. Table 18-6 presents the four means involved in the contrast. Following the notation introduced in Chap. 15, we have designated the two "levels" of each comparison as positive (subscript plus) or negative (subscript minus), depending upon the sign of the coefficients used to weight the means. Expressed in terms of the two vocabulary tests (simple effects of $B_{comp.}$) at the two levels of $A_{comp.}$, we have

$$\hat{\psi}_{A \times B} = (47.75 - 44.25) - (41.25 - 26.00) = 3.50 - 15.25 = -11.75$$

Alternatively, we obtain exactly the same value by comparing the difference between the two science conditions (simple effects of $A_{comp.}$) at the two levels of $B_{comp.}$;

Table 18-6
Calculating the Interaction Contrast

	Immediate Test (b_+)	2-Week Test (b_-)
Physical Science (a_+)	47.75	44.25
Social Science (a_-)	41.25	26.00

that is

$$\hat{\psi}_{A \times B} = (47.75 - 41.25) - (44.25 - 26.00) = 6.50 - 18.25 = -11.75$$

The interaction sum of squares is found by substituting in Eq. (15-3); that is,

$$SS_{A_{comp.} \times B_{comp.}} = \frac{(s)(\hat{\psi}_{A \times B})^2}{[\Sigma (c_i)^2][\Sigma (c_j)^2]}$$

For this example,

$$\Sigma (c_i)^2 = (+1)^2 + (-1)^2 + (0)^2 = 2$$

and

$$\Sigma (c_j)^2 = (+1)^2 + (-1)^2 + (0)^2 = 2$$

Substituting in the formula, we find

$$SS_{A_{comp.} \times B_{comp.}} = \frac{(4)(-11.75)^2}{(2)(2)} = \frac{552.25}{4} = 138.06$$

Calculating the Error Term.   The second major step in the analysis is the calculation of the sum of squares for the error term. We begin by transforming the original data matrix into a comparison matrix in which $B_{comp.}$ replaces the original three levels of factor B. This has been accomplished in Table 18-7. Next, we treat each of the three comparison matrices as if it were a single-factor within-subjects design. From each, we calculate first the sum of squares for each subject, using the formula

$$SS = \frac{(\text{Diff.})^2}{\Sigma (c_j)^2}$$

For the first subject at level a_1, for example,

$$SS = \frac{2^2}{(+1)^2 + (-1)^2 + (0)^2} = \frac{4}{2} = 2.00$$

The sums of squares for all the subjects in each of the three A conditions are presented in the last column of the appropriate comparison matrix.

The next step is to calculate the sum of squares for the comparison at each of the three levels of factor A. For this, we have

$$SS_{B_{comp.} \text{ at } a_i} = \frac{(s)(\hat{\psi}_{B \text{ at } a_i})^2}{\Sigma (c_j)^2} \tag{18-1}$$

Table 18-7
Calculating the Error Term for an Interaction Contrast

	Level a_1			
	Immediate (b_+)	2-Week (b_-)	Difference	SS
s_1	53	51	2	2.00
s_2	49	34	15	112.50
s_3	47	44	3	4.50
s_4	42	48	−6	18.00
Average	47.75	44.25	3.50	

	Level a_2			
	Immediate (b_+)	2-Week (b_-)	Difference	SS
s_5	47	42	5	12.50
s_6	42	33	9	40.50
s_7	39	13	26	338.00
s_8	37	16	21	220.50
Average	41.25	26.00	15.25	

	Level a_3			
	Immediate (b_+)	2-Week (b_-)	Difference	SS
s_9	45	35	10	50.00
s_{10}	41	33	8	32.00
s_{11}	38	46	−8	32.00
s_{12}	36	40	−4	8.00
Average	40.00	38.50	1.50	

The value of $\hat{\psi}_{B \text{ at } a_i}$ is given in the last row of each matrix. For a_1, for example,

$$\hat{\psi}_{B \text{ at } a_1} = 47.75 - 44.25 = 3.50$$

Substituting in Eq. (18-1), we find

$$SS_{B_{comp.} \text{ at } a_1} = \frac{(4)(3.50)^2}{2} = \frac{49.00}{2} = 24.50$$

$$SS_{B_{comp.} \text{ at } a_2} = \frac{(4)(15.25)^2}{2} = \frac{930.25}{2} = 465.13$$

$$SS_{B_{comp.} \text{ at } a_3} = \frac{(4)(1.50)^2}{2} = \frac{9.00}{2} = 4.50$$

We are now ready to calculate the $B_{comp.} \times S$ interaction, one for each of the three levels of factor A. These are obtained by combining the individual sums of squares for the subjects and then subtracting from this sum the $SS_{B_{comp.} \text{ at } a_i}$. To illustrate, using the quantities we have calculated already, we find

$$SS_{B_{comp.} \times S \text{ at } a_1} = (2.00 + 112.50 + 4.50 + 18.00) - 24.50$$
$$= 137.00 - 24.50 = 112.50$$

$$SS_{B_{comp.} \times S \text{ at } a_2} = (12.50 + 40.50 + 338.00 + 220.50) - 465.13$$
$$= 611.50 - 465.13 = 146.37$$

$$SS_{B_{comp.} \times S \text{ at } a_3} = (50.00 + 32.00 + 32.00 + 8.00) - 4.50$$
$$= 122.00 - 4.50 = 117.50$$

The sum of these three sums of squares gives us the quantity we need for the error term. More specifically,

$$SS_{B_{comp.} \times S/A} = \Sigma \, SS_{B_{comp.} \text{ at } a_i}$$
$$= 112.50 + 146.37 + 117.50 = 376.37$$

The Analysis of Variance. We can now complete the statistical analysis. The df for the interaction sum of squares is 1. The degrees of freedom for the error term consist of the df for the $B_{comp.} \times S$ interactions pooled over the levels of factor A. The df for any one of the $B_{comp.} \times S$ interactions is $(df_{B_{comp.}})(df_S) = (1)(s-1) = s - 1$. Since there is one $B_{comp.} \times S$ interaction for each level of factor A,

$$df_{B_{comp.} \times S/A} = (a)(s-1) = (3)(4-1) = 9$$

The F is

$$F = \frac{SS_{A_{comp.} \times B_{comp.}}/df_{A_{comp.} \times B_{comp.}}}{SS_{B_{comp.} \times S/A}/df_{B_{comp.} \times S/A}}$$
$$= \frac{138.06/1}{376.37/9} = \frac{138.06}{41.82} = 3.30$$

This F is not significant.

Analysis of the Simple Effects of an Interaction Contrast. If the F were significant, we might be interested in examining the simple effects of the interaction contrast.

Our analysis could consist of testing the significance of $A_{comp.}$ (the difference between the two science conditions) at the two "levels" of the B comparison (b_+ = the immediate test and b_- = the 2-week test). Alternatively, we could test the significance of $B_{comp.}$ (the difference between the two tests) at the two "levels" of the A comparison (a_+ = physical science and a_- = social science).

The formulas for calculating the sums of squares associated with these simple effects were discussed in Chap. 15 (pages 248–251). The error term for testing the differences involving repeated measurements (the B comparison) is the error term we used to evaluate the contrast itself, namely, $MS_{B_{comp.} \times S/A} = 41.82$, which we have already calculated. The error term for testing the differences involving different groups of subjects (the A comparison) is the error term we discussed in Sec. 18.2 for single-df comparisons conducted on the data drawn from one level of factor B (see pages 319–326).

The MRC Approach

As you saw in Chap. 15, the MRC approach to the analysis of interaction contrasts takes advantage of vectors already available from the overall analysis, provided, of course, that the researcher has anticipated these analyses in choosing the original vectors. An interaction contrast, which is associated with 1 df, is represented in MRC by a single interaction vector created by cross-multiplying the values of the vector corresponding to $A_{comp.}$ with the values of the vector corresponding to $B_{comp.}$. The critical statistic is a squared zero-order r between Y and the interaction vector. The error term is based on vectors that code the same information required by the corresponding ANOVA, namely, the $B_{comp.} \times S/A$ interaction, translated into a squared multiple correlation coefficient.

The vectors required for this analysis are presented in Table 18-8. To elaborate,

> Vector 1 represents $A_{comp.}$, the comparison between the two science conditions.
> Vector 2 represents $B_{comp.}$, the comparison between the vocabulary tests given immediately after and 2 weeks after the lecture.
> Vector 3 is the interaction vector representing the interaction contrast, which is formed by cross-multiplying the two comparison vectors.
> Vectors 4 through 12 are the nine interaction vectors formed by cross-multiplying vector 2 ($B_{comp.}$) with the different subject vectors, which are not shown here but are found in Table 17-8.

Let us consider the nature of the nine interaction vectors in Table 18-8 (vectors 4 through 12) more carefully. The first three interaction vectors (4 to 6) capture the

Table 18-8
Code Matrix for the Interaction Contrast

A	B	Subject	Y	(1)	(2)	(3)	(4)	(5)	(6)	(7)	(8)	(9)	(10)	(11)	(12)
a_1	b_1	1	53	1	1	1	1	1	1	0	0	0	0	0	0
		2	49	1	1	1	-1	0	0	0	0	0	0	0	0
		3	47	1	1	1	0	-1	0	0	0	0	0	0	0
		4	42	1	1	1	0	0	-1	0	0	0	0	0	0
	b_2	1	51	1	-1	-1	-1	-1	-1	0	0	0	0	0	0
		2	34	1	-1	-1	1	0	0	0	0	0	0	0	0
		3	44	1	-1	-1	0	1	0	0	0	0	0	0	0
		4	48	1	-1	-1	0	0	1	0	0	0	0	0	0
	b_3	1	35	1	0	0	0	0	0	0	0	0	0	0	0
		2	18	1	0	0	0	0	0	0	0	0	0	0	0
		3	32	1	0	0	0	0	0	0	0	0	0	0	0
		4	27	1	0	0	0	0	0	0	0	0	0	0	0
a_2	b_1	5	47	-1	1	-1	0	0	0	1	1	1	0	0	0
		6	42	-1	1	-1	0	0	0	-1	0	0	0	0	0
		7	39	-1	1	-1	0	0	0	0	-1	0	0	0	0
		8	37	-1	1	-1	0	0	0	0	0	-1	0	0	0
	b_2	5	42	-1	-1	1	0	0	0	-1	-1	-1	0	0	0
		6	33	-1	-1	1	0	0	0	1	0	0	0	0	0
		7	13	-1	-1	1	0	0	0	0	1	0	0	0	0
		8	16	-1	-1	1	0	0	0	0	0	1	0	0	0
	b_3	5	16	-1	0	0	0	0	0	0	0	0	0	0	0
		6	10	-1	0	0	0	0	0	0	0	0	0	0	0
		7	11	-1	0	0	0	0	0	0	0	0	0	0	0
		8	6	-1	0	0	0	0	0	0	0	0	0	0	0

Vectors (1)–(12)

Table 18-8 Continued

Subject		Y	(1)	(2)	(3)	(4)	(5)	(6)	(7)	(8)	(9)	(10)	(11)	(12)
	9	45	0	1	0	0	0	0	0	0	0	1	1	1
b_1	10	41	0	1	0	0	0	0	0	0	0	−1	0	0
	11	38	0	1	0	0	0	0	0	0	0	0	−1	0
	12	36	0	1	0	0	0	0	0	0	0	0	0	−1
	9	35	0	−1	0	0	0	0	0	0	0	−1	−1	−1
b_2	10	33	0	−1	0	0	0	0	0	0	0	−1	0	0
	11	46	0	−1	0	0	0	0	0	0	0	0	1	0
	12	40	0	−1	0	0	0	0	0	0	0	0	0	1
	9	29	0	0	0	0	0	0	0	0	0	0	0	0
b_3	10	21	0	0	0	0	0	0	0	0	0	0	0	0
	11	30	0	0	0	0	0	0	0	0	0	0	0	0
	12	20	0	0	0	0	0	0	0	0	0	0	0	0

a_3

Vectors

interaction of the single-*df* comparison ($B_{comp.}$) with the four subjects receiving the lecture on physical science (level a_1); the next three vectors (7 to 9) capture the same interaction with the four subjects receiving the lecture on social science (level a_2); and the final three vectors (10 to 12) capture the corresponding interaction for the four receiving the lecture on history (level a_3). Collectively, these nine interaction vectors capture the interaction required for the error term. The R^2's from the MRC analysis are presented in Table 18-9.[6]

Table 18-9
The R^2's from the MRC Analysis

Source	R^2
$A_{comp.}$	$R^2_{Y.1} = .2030$
$B_{comp.}$	$R^2_{Y.2} = .0472$
$A_{comp.} \times B_{comp.}$	$R^2_{Y.3} = .0238$
$B_{comp.} \times S/A$	$R^2_{Y.4,5,\ldots,11,12} = .0650$

The degrees of freedom for the different sources are identical to those appropriate for the corresponding ANOVA, of course. As usual, we arrive at these numbers simply by counting the number of vectors required to specify the variation associated with the desired source of variability. For the two critical terms,

$$df_{A_{comp.} \times B_{comp.}} = 1 \quad \text{(vector 3)}$$
$$df_{B_{comp.} \times S/A} = 9 \quad \text{(vectors 4 through 12)}$$

The *F* is found as follows:

$$F = \frac{r^2_{Y3}}{R^2_{Y.B1 \times S/A}/df_{B_{comp.} \times S/A}}$$
$$= \frac{.0238}{.0650/9} = \frac{.0238}{.0072} = 3.31$$

The *F* obtained with ANOVA was 3.30.

[6] For continuity, we have designated all squared correlations as multiple correlations, although the first three are more appropriately designated as squared zero-order correlations.

As we noted earlier in this section, a significant interaction contrast would usually lead us to analyses of the simple effects. These might consist of the analysis of $A_{comp.}$ (the difference between the two science conditions) at the two "levels" of the B comparison, or of $B_{comp.}$ (the difference between the two tests) at the two "levels" of the A comparison. Depending on the questions of interest to you, either analysis, or even both analyses, may be appropriate. The details of these analyses were discussed in Sec. 18.3, pages 329–330, for simple effects based on independent groups and in pages 332–333, for simple effects based on repeated measures.

18.5   SUMMARY

In this chapter, we considered the detailed analysis of the mixed factorial design. As you have seen in this chapter and preceding chapters, the factorial design offers a rich source of information beyond that provided in the standard, overall analysis. In the absence of explicit planned comparisons, for example, we begin with the test of the overall $A \times B$ interaction. If the interaction is significant, the analysis usually leads us to an examination and a test of the simple effects of one or even both of the independent variables. If the interaction is not significant, we generally shift our attention to the analysis of the two main effects. With planned comparisons, which are usually expressed as single-df comparisons involving one (or both) of the independent variables, we transform the overall factorial design into a number of component factorials in which the interaction comparison becomes the primary focus of attention.

All these analyses were discussed previously in Chaps. 14 and 15, when we considered the detailed analysis of the completely randomized two-factor design. The purpose of this chapter has been to discuss the complications created when these analyses are applied to a mixed factorial design—in particular, the need for special error terms for performing the desired statistical tests.

With ANOVA, the error terms are obtained from subsets of data derived from the original set of data. Most of the necessary calculations are analogous to procedures appropriate for either the completely randomized single-factor design (the analysis of the A main effect and the simple effects of factor A), the single-factor within-subjects design (the analysis of the B main effect and the simple effects of factor B), or the mixed factorial design (the analysis of interaction contrasts). With MRC, the error terms are easily obtained either by using vectors included in the overall analysis (the vectors for the analysis of the two main effects and of interaction contrasts) or by adapting these vectors for a particular analysis (the analysis of the simple effects).

18.6 EXERCISES

1. The analysis of the data presented in Problem 1 at the end of Chap. 17 revealed a significant $A \times B$ interaction. In order to try to understand the interaction, use ANOVA and MRC to determine whether the effects of training (factor B) are significant for each condition of factor A.

2. As an alternative analysis, use ANOVA and MRC to determine whether the differences among the three treatment groups (factor A) are significant for each of the four sessions (factor B).

3. You may have noticed that the subjects in condition a_2 (drug I) show a marked deterioration in performance over the four training sessions, while subjects in the other two conditions (control and drug II) show substantial improvement. Use ANOVA and MRC to analyze the following interaction contrasts formed with the single-df comparisons described:

(a) An interaction contrast formed by crossing the control and the drug I conditions with the first and last sessions
(b) An interaction contrast formed by crossing the control and the drug II conditions with the first and last sessions

19

Higher-Order
Factorial Designs

. . .

This chapter is included to give you a glimpse at the complexity of higher-order factorial designs and an appreciation of their explanatory potential. Some of you may find this material too abstract and too advanced at the present stage in your training.[1] We suggest that you view this chapter as a sample of the capabilities of experimental design, rather than a complete treatment of the subject. Our goal is to indicate how the principles underlying simpler experimental designs covered in the preceding chapters apply to more complex designs. We hope that this chapter will give you a perspective from which you can design more satisfying and ambitious projects in your future research efforts.

Factorial designs are easily expanded to form higher-order factorial designs— designs that incorporate more than two independent variables. The higher-order factorial designs we will discuss in this chapter all have the same defining property: they include all possible combinations of the levels of the factors in the experiment. A $2 \times 3 \times 2$ design, for example, includes a total of $(2)(3)(2) = 12$ treatment conditions formed by crossing the two levels of factor A with the three levels of factor B and then crossing the resulting six combinations with the two levels of factor C. Designs in which we explore all possible combinations are called **completely crossed factorials**.[2]

With an increase in the number of independent variables comes a marked increase in the amount of information that you can obtain. That is, while the overall analysis of higher-order factorials still consists of the examination of main effects and interactions, you will find that they offer more main effects and interactions to study. Moreover, the *complexity* of the interactions increases as well. In a moment, we will consider the nature of the information that higher-order factorial designs provide.

This chapter can only scratch the surface of the topic. As we have indicated already, our intent is to show how the principles we considered in our discussions of the analysis of one- and two-factor designs *generalize* to the analysis of higher-order designs. At some point you will probably have to consult more comprehensive discussions of this material, but at least you will have some appreciation of how the analyses of complex designs are derived from the analyses of simpler ones.

---

[1] Note to instructors: The material in this chapter may be omitted without affecting your students' understanding of the remaining chapters.

[2] Incomplete factorials, in which *not* all possible combinations are included, are relatively uncommon in the behavioral sciences. For a discussion of these designs, see Kirk (1982, pp. 489–710) and Winer (1971, pp. 604–684).

19.1 THE COMPLETELY RANDOMIZED THREE-FACTOR DESIGN

We will consider briefly the design and analysis of the three-factor design. As we have indicated, the three-factor design is made up of all possible combinations of the levels of three independent variables. For this discussion, we are assuming that subjects are randomly assigned, in equal numbers (s), to the $(a)(b)(c)$ different treatment conditions. Although repeated measures can easily be introduced into this design, they complicate the evaluation process considerably, because they call for a variety of error terms to conduct the different statistical tests. In comparison, the evaluation process for the completely randomized three-factor design is relatively simple, since only one error term is needed to conduct these same tests. It is important to note, however, that all three-factor designs supply the same type of information, which means that we can focus on the information provided by these designs without worrying at this time about the complications created when repeated measures are introduced. We discuss within-subjects designs in Sec. 19.3.

The Design

The three-factor design is a natural outgrowth of the two-factor design. To illustrate, we will start with the 3×2 factorial we used to introduce the $A \times B$ design, an experiment consisting of the three types of lectures (physical science, social science, and history) and two methods of presentation (computer and standard). Suppose we add a third independent variable (factor C)—a developmental variable, age—consisting of $c = 2$ levels, fifth-grade and eighth-grade children. This design is presented in Table 19-1. You will note that the original $A \times B$ design is represented *twice* in this three-factor design, once in conjunction with level c_1 (fifth grade) and once with level c_2 (eighth grade). Taken as a whole, the complete design is made up of all possible combinations of the levels of the three independent variables.

The $A \times B \times C$ Interaction

The one new concept we introduced when we first discussed the two-factor design was, of course, the $A \times B$ interaction. No new concepts are introduced with higher-order designs, although the interactions may be of greater complexity. We will illustrate this point with the $A \times B \times C$ interaction.

All interactions may be defined in terms of *simple effects*. As a reminder from the two-factor case,

> **An $A \times B$ interaction is present when the simple effects of one of the independent variables are not the same at all levels of the second independent variable.**

Table 19-1
An Example of a Three-Factor Design

Fifth-Grade Students (c_1)

	Physical Science (a_1)	Social Science (a_2)	History (a_3)
Computer (b_1)			
Standard (b_2)			

Eighth-Grade Students (c_2)

	Physical Science (a_1)	Social Science (a_2)	History (a_3)
Computer (b_1)			
Standard (b_2)			

The $A \times B \times C$ interaction is defined in an analogous fashion except that we focus on simple *interactions* rather than on simple *effects*. A **simple interaction** is the interaction of two of the independent variables with the third variable *held constant*. Translated to the present context, the presence of an $A \times B \times C$ interaction would mean that the interaction of factors A and B for the fifth-grade students (level c_1) is different from the corresponding interaction for the eighth-grade students (level c_2).[3] In words, then,

> An $A \times B \times C$ **interaction is present when the simple interactions between two of the independent variables are not the same at all levels of the third.**

We can often comprehend interactions more easily if we plot the means on a graph. Consider first one possible outcome of this experiment, which is presented in the upper half of Fig. 19-1. Compare the simple interaction on the left (fifth grade) with the simple interaction on the right (eighth grade). Remember that if the two seem to be different, an $A \times B \times C$ interaction may be present, whereas if they appear to be the same, there is probably no interaction present. Of course, we would eventually base our judgment on the outcome of an appropriate statistical test. For the moment, however, let us just examine the data informally, with an eye toward understanding the concept. The graph on the left suggests that there is an interaction between lectures and methods for the fifth-grade children, while the graph on the right reflects no interaction whatsoever. Since the two simple interactions are *not the same*—we find a sizable interaction on the left and no interaction on the right—we would conclude that an $A \times B \times C$ interaction is present. The next step would be a statistical test that assesses this difference.

In contrast, consider the outcome depicted in the lower portion of Fig. 19-1. In this case, apparently, the same interaction found with the fifth-grade students is also found with the eighth-grade students. This suggests that the two simple interactions are roughly alike and that a statistical test would be likely to reveal that an $A \times B \times C$ interaction is not present.

Sources of Variance

The standard analysis of the three-way factorial examines three types of treatment effects. One of these is the $A \times B \times C$ interaction, of course, which is based on all the individual means of the different treatment conditions. The other two represent

---

[3] The $A \times B \times C$ interaction is defined in terms of the simple interactions created by the combination of any two of the three independent variables. We chose the simple $A \times B$ interaction. We could just as easily have chosen the simple $A \times C$ interaction at the two levels of factor B or the simple $B \times C$ interaction at the three levels of factor A.

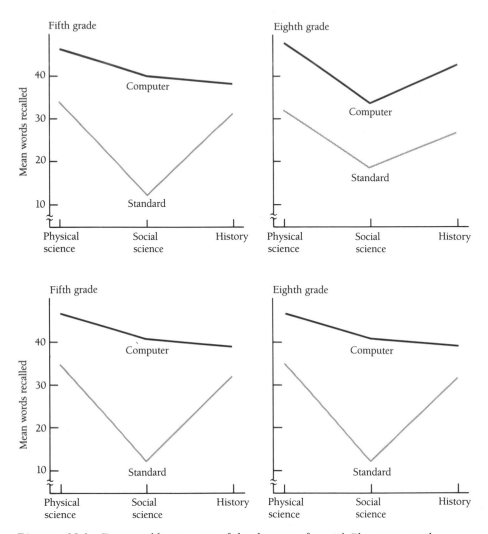

F i g u r e 19-1   Two possible outcomes of the three-way factorial. The upper graph displays an *A* × *B* × *C* interaction, while the lower graph displays no *A* × *B* × *C* interaction.

sources created by averaging or collapsing over some of the treatment conditions. More specifically, we could disregard factor *C* completely by combining the data from the fifth- and eighth-grade students. This would leave us with what amounts to a two-factor design and an *A* × *B* interaction. Alternatively, we could combine the data from the two levels of factor *B* (computer and standard presentation) to create an *A* × *C* design and an *A* × *C* interaction and consequently disregard mode of presentation; or we could combine the data from the three levels of factor *A* (physical science, social science, and history) to create a $B \times C$ design and a $B \times C$ interaction, ignoring type of lecture. Finally, we could examine any of three *main effects*—A, B, and C—by pooling the data over the levels of the other two independent variables. The A main effect, for example, is based on the overall means for the three lectures obtained by averaging the data for all levels of factors B and C.

The interpretation of the results of this analysis generally begins with a test of the $A \times B \times C$ interaction, which we have indicated at the top of Fig. 19-2. A significant three-way interaction means that any effects based on data that are collapsed over the levels of one or two independent variables may provide a distorted picture of the influence of the three factors on the dependent variable. Consequently, the next step is to turn to special analyses that help to identify the sources of the significant interaction. We will discuss these analyses in Sec. 19.2. On the other hand, a nonsignificant interaction indicates that it is "safe" to continue the standard analysis by examining the data with *one* of the factors removed or disregarded. At this point, then, the analysis would focus on all possible interactions between two of the factors—$A \times B$, $A \times C$, and $B \times C$—just as if they had been produced from actual two-factor designs. This step is also shown in Fig. 19-2.

From now on, the analysis should be familiar. We test each of the interactions for significance. If an interaction is significant, we try to discover the differences responsible for it and pay little attention to the main effects. On the other hand, a main effect is of interest for a factor that is not involved in a significant two-way interaction. For example, if only the $A \times B$ interaction is significant, we can safely examine the C main effect because factor C is not involved in an interaction. If

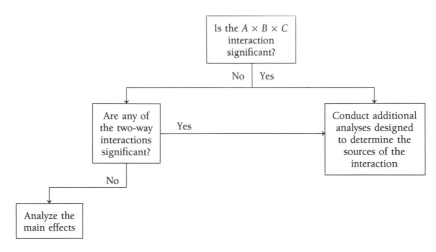

Figure 19-2   Analysis of a three-factor design.

another interaction is also significant, either $A \times C$ or $B \times C$, none of the main effects are left uncontaminated by interaction.[4]

Using ANOVA to Perform the Overall Analysis

The overall analysis represents a simple extension of the operations we followed in the analysis of single-factor and two-factor designs. We calculate sums of squares from basic ratios that are based on the various totals and subtotals we obtain when the data are collapsed over subjects and over the levels of the three independent variables. Degrees of freedom for the three main effects are equal to the number of levels less 1, while the df for interactions are found by multiplying the df's associated with the factors specified by the interaction. The df for the $B \times C$ interaction, for example, are

$$df_{B \times C} = (df_B)(df_C) = (b - 1)(c - 1)$$

while the df for the $A \times B \times C$ interaction are

$$df_{A \times B \times C} = (df_A)(df_B)(df_C) = (a - 1)(b - 1)(c - 1)$$

The mean squares are calculated in the usual fashion by dividing SS's by the appropriate df's. The error term for this analysis is based on the within-group variances obtained for the separate treatment conditions, which are pooled and averaged over all the $(a)(b)(c)$ treatment conditions.

Using MRC to Perform the Overall Analysis

The key to the MRC analysis, as in other designs, is the creation of vectors designed to represent the three main effects. As you know, the number of vectors required is, in essence, specified by the df associated with each source of variability isolated in the analysis. To illustrate, we will start with the main effects. In the present example, we would need two vectors to capture the A main effect ($A1$ and $A2$), one to capture the B main effect ($B1$), and one to capture the C main effect ($C1$). In general, vectors representing interactions are formed by cross-multiplying the vectors of the relevant main effects. For the $A \times C$ interaction, for example, the cross multiplication would involve the two vectors associated with the A main effect and the single vector associated with the C main effect, creating $A1C1$ and $A2C1$. Together, these two vectors capture the variation due to the $A \times C$ interaction. Similarly, we represent the $A \times B$ interaction with two interaction vectors, $A1B1$ and $A2B1$, and the $B \times C$ interaction with one interaction vector, $B1C1$.

---

[4] The logic of this analysis strategy is covered more fully in Keppel (1982, pp. 295–297).

Finally, we represent the $A \times B \times C$ interaction with interaction vectors created by the cross multiplication of all possible combinations of the three main-effects vectors. There are two such interaction vectors in this example,

$$A1B1C1 \qquad \text{and} \qquad A2B1C1$$

(How we multiply these main-effect vectors will be discussed in Sec. 19.2.) The squared multiple correlation coefficients involving the dependent variable Y and the relevant sets of vectors represent the proportions of variability associated with the different factorial effects. The *df* for each correlation are determined by the number of vectors required to define the particular effect. The residual variation is obtained by subtracting $R^2_{Y.max.}$, which is the squared multiple correlation coefficient between Y and all the factorial vectors, from 1. That is,

$$R^2_{Y.max.} = R^2_{Y.A} + R^2_{Y.B} + R^2_{Y.C} + R^2_{Y.A \times B} + R^2_{Y.A \times C} + R^2_{Y.B \times C} + R^2_{Y.A \times B \times C}$$
$$R^2_{residual} = 1 - R^2_{Y.max}$$

19.2   DETAILED ANALYSIS OF THE $A \times B \times C$ INTERACTION

Two general techniques are available for determining the factors responsible for a significant $A \times B \times C$ interaction. These are the *analysis of simple effects* and the *analysis of interaction comparisons*—both variations of the same techniques we used to analyze the $A \times B$ interaction in Chaps. 14 and 15. We are not able to cover these procedures in detail, but we will emphasize their nature and form. A comprehensive discussion of this material may be found in Keppel (1982, Chap. 14).

Analysis of Simple Effects

All interactions may be expressed as differences in simple effects. For the $A \times B$ interaction, for example, the differences of interest to us are in the effects of one of the independent variables at different levels of the other. For the complex or higher-order $A \times B \times C$ interaction, on the other hand, we are interested in the differences in the *interaction* of two of the factors at different levels of the third. Once we detect an interaction, an obvious next step is to examine the simple effects themselves in an attempt to establish its exact nature.

The simple effects of any interaction are revealed by subdividing the original factorial design into a set of less complex designs, each of which defines a different simple effect. You will recall from Chap. 14, for example, that we can uncover the simple effects of the $A \times B$ interaction by analyzing a set of component *single*-factor designs in which we vary one of the independent variables while holding the other constant. We might examine the effects of factor A at level b_1, at level b_2, and so on, or the effects of factor B at level a_1, at a_2, and so on. By transforming a more complex experiment (in this case, the two-factor design) into a set of less complex experiments (component single-factor designs), we are able to discover the ways in which the simple effects differ from one another.

We follow this same general procedure with the three-factor design and the analysis of the $A \times B \times C$ interaction. We transform the more complex experiment (the three-factor design) into a set of less complex experiments, which in this case consist of component *two*-factor designs. These latter designs involve the manipulation of two of the independent variables with the third held constant. There are three possibilities:

> An $A \times B$ design at level c_1, at level c_2, and so on
> An $A \times C$ design at level b_1, at level b_2, and so on
> A $B \times C$ design at level a_1, at level a_2, and so on

A significant $A \times B \times C$ interaction means that the simple interactions are not the same, and this is true for any one of these sets of component factorial designs.

Most researchers have a preferred way of expressing the $A \times B \times C$ interaction and thus will usually examine only the sets in which they are most interested if the interaction proves to be significant. Assuming that the $A \times B \times C$ interaction reflected in the data presented in the upper portion of Fig. 19-1 is significant, we would probably look at the simple interaction of lectures (factor A) and presentation (factor B), first for the fifth-grade students (level c_1—the display on the left)—and then for the eighth-grade students (level c_2—the display on the right). We would choose this alternative because of the way we conceptualized the experiment—the joint manipulation of lectures and presentation at two different age levels.

An analysis of these simple interactions would probably reveal a significant interaction of lectures and presentation for the younger students, but no interaction for the older ones. If this were the case, we would pay little or no attention to the simple interaction for the older students and would concentrate our efforts on analyzing the simple interaction for the younger students. Thus, we would probably consider additional analyses in an attempt to identify the factors contributing to the significant interaction of lectures and methods of presentation for the fifth-grade students. At this point, the analysis exactly resembles the analysis of the simple effects of a significant interaction in an actual *two*-factor design. Thus, we might look at the effects of the three lectures first with the computer presentation and then with the standard presentation. If either of these effects is significant, we could examine meaningful single-df comparisons, such as the difference between the two science conditions and the difference between the combined science conditions and the history condition.

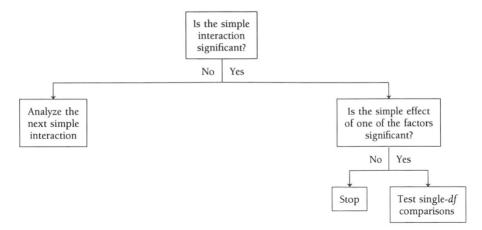

Figure 19-3   Analysis of the three-way interaction.

While this process may sound complicated, it does represent a consistent pattern in which the discovery of a significant higher-order effect is followed by the analysis of a relevant simple effect. As a summary of this approach to the analysis of the three-way interaction, we could say that

A significant $A \times B \times C$ interaction is followed by an analysis of simple interactions, for example, the $A \times B$ interaction for fifth-grade students and for eighth-grade students.

A significant simple $A \times B$ interaction is then followed by the analysis of the simple effects of this interaction, for example, the effects of the different lectures (A) for the fifth-grade students under the two methods of presentation.

A significant simple effect of factor A is then followed by an analysis of meaningful single-df comparisons.

These steps are also diagramed in Fig. 19-3.

The ANOVA Approach.   As you have seen, the simple interaction effects of the $A \times B \times C$ interaction are interactions obtained from component two-factor experiments. What this means is that you may calculate the sums of squares required for the analysis by isolating the data matrix of interest and then applying formulas appropriate for an actual two-factor experiment. From this point on, you will be on familiar ground; you can take advantage of the formulas we covered in Sec. 14.2. The only change is in the error term for the analysis. For all the simple interactions, the error term would come from the overall analysis of the three-factor design and would be $MS_{S/ABC}$, which is based on within-group variability pooled over the $(a)(b)(c)$ treatment groups.

The MRC Approach.   You may easily accomplish the analysis of simple effects with MRC by creating special vectors that reflect the desired simple effects. For the simple $A \times B$ interaction at level c_1, for example, you would start with the vectors defining the $A \times B$ interaction and then modify them for the analysis by assigning 0s to all observations at all levels of factor C not involved in the analysis (level c_2 in this case). You would create the vectors for the $A \times B$ interaction at level c_2 by starting with the same original interaction vectors, but modifying them by assigning 0s to all observations at level c_1. The error term comes from the overall analysis of the entire factorial design, Mean $R^2_{Y.S/ABC}$. For details concerning the analysis of the simple effects, see the discussion in Sec. 14.3.

Analysis of Interaction Comparisons

A second major way of analyzing interaction consists of creating a number of smaller factorial designs by transforming one or more of the independent variables into a form that reflects single-df comparisons. This transformation is possible, of course, only when a factor consists of more than two levels. For the example in Table 19-1, only factor A—with the levels consisting of three different lectures— qualifies as a candidate; the other two factors each consist of two levels.

Table 19-2 illustrates two component factorial designs created from single-df comparisons involving factor A. The analysis in the top half of the table is a three-factor design consisting of a comparison between the two science conditions $(A_{comp.\ 1})$ and the other two factors (method of presentation and grade level). The analysis in the bottom half is a three-factor design consisting of a comparison between the combined science conditions and the history condition $(A_{comp.\ 2})$ and the other two factors. The focus of both of these analyses would be the $A_{comp.} \times B \times C$ interactions.

It is important to appreciate the value of this type of analysis. A significant $A \times B \times C$ interaction found in the overall analysis does not indicate what aspects of factor A are critical. In contrast, the two component factorials provide a more insightful view of the interaction of the three factors. A significant $A_{comp.} \times B \times C$ interaction in the first case would bring attention to the differences between the two science lectures; a nonsignificant interaction would imply that any differences between the two science lectures have little effect on the interaction of the three factors. By the same token, the second case focuses attention on differences between science and history lectures, with no differentiation made between the two science conditions.

Table 19-2
Two Examples of Interaction Contrasts

	Fifth Grade				Eighth Grade	
	Physical Science	Social Science			Physical Science	Social Science
Computer				Computer		
Standard				Standard		

	Fifth Grade				Eighth Grade	
	Combined Science	History			Combined Science	History
Computer				Computer		
Standard				Standard		

Three-factor interaction comparisons associated with a single *df* are called, like their two-factor counterpart, **interaction contrasts**. They are produced from what is conceptually equivalent to a $2 \times 2 \times 2$ design. Such interaction contrasts are valuable because the three-way interaction contrast ($2 \times 2 \times 2$), which is associated with 1 *df*, takes the analysis to the basic level since it cannot be divided into additional component factorials. Both of the examples in Table 19-2 are interaction contrasts.

Other types of interaction comparisons are possible in which some, but not all of the factors are represented by single-*df* comparisons. For example, suppose we have a $3 \times 3 \times 3$ factorial. If only one of the factors (we will choose *A* arbitrarily) lends itself to analytical treatment, the analysis would consist of a number of $2 \times 3 \times 3$ component factorials of the form $A_{comp.} \times B \times C$. If two of the factors (*A* and *B*) are transformed into single-*df* comparisons, the analysis will consist of a number of $2 \times 2 \times 3$ component factorials of the form $A_{comp.} \times B_{comp.} \times C$. These various possibilities are discussed in detail by Keppel (1982, pp. 315–320).

The ANOVA Approach.   We will concentrate our discussion on the analysis of interaction contrasts. The only new operation is the calculation of the contrast itself ($\hat{\psi}_{A \times B \times C}$), which may be obtained directly from a systematic layout of the means. Suppose we were interested in the three-way interaction of the two science conditions, the two methods of presentation, and the two grade levels. We would start by forming a $2 \times 2 \times 2$ matrix corresponding to this interaction contrast. This we have accomplished in Table 19-3, using the data appearing in the upper portion of Fig. 19-1. You will recall that a three-way interaction is defined as the presence of differences in the interaction of two of the independent variables over the levels of the third independent variable. All that we need to do, then, is to compare the simple interaction of two of these factors at the two levels of the third factor.

The 2×2 matrix on the left in Table 19-3 provides information concerning the interaction of the two science lectures with the two methods of presentation for the fifth-grade students, while the matrix on the right provides corresponding information for the eighth-grade students. A value for each of the two interactions may be obtained simply by calculating the difference between the two means in each row and then subtracting the differences for each simple interaction. In this example,

$$\hat{\psi}_{A \times B \text{ at level } c_1} = 6.00 - 22.00 = -16.00$$
$$\hat{\psi}_{A \times B \text{ at level } c_2} = 14.00 - 14.00 = 0.00$$

The value of -16.00 for the interaction at c_1 indicates that there is an interaction between the two lectures and the two methods of presentation for the younger children, while the value of 0.00 indicates the complete absence of such an interaction for the older children. (A value of zero is highly unlikely, of course, because of the inevitable operation of chance factors.) The fact that the two "lecture" $\times$ "method" interactions are different (-16.00 versus 0.00) means that a three-way interaction is present. The value of this interaction contrast is

$$\hat{\psi}_{A \times B \times C} = (\hat{\psi}_{A \times B \text{ at level } c_1}) - (\hat{\psi}_{A \times B \text{ at level } c_2})$$
$$= (-16.00) - (0.00) = -16.00$$

The sum of squares associated with this value is obtained by substituting in a familiar formula, namely,

$$SS_{A_{comp.} \times B_{comp.} \times C_{comp.}} = \frac{(s)(\hat{\psi}_{A \times B \times C})^2}{[\Sigma (c_i)^2][\Sigma (c_j)^2][\Sigma (c_k)^2]}$$

where s = the sample size

$\hat{\psi}_{A \times B \times C}$ = the interaction contrast

$\quad c_i$ = the coefficients associated with factor A $(1, -1, 0)$

$\quad c_j$ = the coefficients associated with factor B $(1, -1)$

$\quad c_k$ = the coefficients associated with factor C $(1, -1)$

This sum of squares is based on 1 df, and the error term comes from the overall analysis.

Table 19-3
Calculating an Interaction Contrast

| | Fifth Grade | | |
	Physical Science	Social Science	Difference
Computer	46.00	40.00	6.00
Standard	34.00	12.00	22.00

| | Eighth Grade | | |
	Physical Science	Social Science	Difference
Computer	47.83	33.83	14.00
Standard	32.17	18.17	14.00

The MRC Approach.   All that is necessary for an analysis of an interaction contrast with MRC is to construct the appropriate interaction vector and then to calculate the zero-order correlation between Y and this vector. The interaction vector is produced by cross-multiplying the relevant main-effect vectors for the three independent variables. In the present example, the vector for factor A would specify the comparison between the two science lectures, while the vectors for factors B and C, which consist of only two levels each, represent the respective main effects. Next, we use the resulting code matrices to create main-effect vectors. Table 19-4 illustrates the process.

The three main-effect vectors—$A1$, $B1$, and $C1$—are listed in columns 1 to 3. The interaction vector, $A1B1C1$, is presented in column 4. The interaction coefficient for each condition is obtained by multiplying coefficients for the three main effects. In the first row, for example, we multiply the coefficient for $A1$ ($+1$) by the coefficient for $B1$ ($+1$) and then multiply the *product* ($+1$) by the coefficient for $C1$ ($+1$), which yields $+1$. Similarly, in the second row, we multiply the coefficient for $A1$ ($+1$) by the coefficient for $B1$ (-1) and then multiply the product (-1) by the coefficient for $C1$ ($+1$), which yields -1. The error term for the analysis is the one from the overall analysis, $R^2_{Y.S/ABC}$.

Table 19-4

Calculating an $A \times B \times C$ Interaction Vector

Conditions			(1) $A1$	$\times$	(2) $B1$	$\times$	(3) $C1$	$=$	(4) $A1B1C1$
c_1	a_1	b_1	1		1		1		1
		b_2	1		-1		1		-1
	a_2	b_1	-1		1		1		-1
		b_2	-1		-1		1		1
	a_3	b_1	0		1		1		0
		b_2	0		-1		1		0
c_2	a_1	b_1	1		1		-1		-1
		b_2	1		-1		-1		1
	a_2	b_1	-1		1		-1		1
		b_2	-1		-1		-1		-1
	a_3	b_1	0		1		-1		0
		b_2	0		-1		-1		0

19.3   HIGHER-ORDER WITHIN-SUBJECTS DESIGNS

In the behavioral sciences, higher-order factorial designs frequently involve re-peated measures—the use of subjects in several or even all of the treatment condi-tions. These designs provide exactly the same information about the effects of the independent variables as do the corresponding completely randomized designs. As you might suspect, however, there is a complication in choosing the error terms with which the various treatment effects are evaluated. In this section, we will discuss a few of the possible within-subjects designs with the purpose of generating some rules that describe the nature of the error terms required to complete the analysis. We will follow this general discussion in Sec. 19.4 with a consideration of how ANOVA and MRC approach the analysis of higher-order within-subjects designs.

A simple approach to understanding the error terms appropriate for any given factorial design is to examine designs that contain only one type of factor—"pure" between-subjects designs (between-*S* designs) and "pure" within-subjects designs (within-*S* designs)—and to discover the principle behind the selection of error terms for these designs. Once this has been accomplished, we can specify the error terms for designs consisting of a "mixture" of between-*S* and within-*S* factors from our knowledge of the "pure" versions of these manipulations.

"Pure" Between-*S* Designs

In "pure" between-*S* designs (commonly called *completely randomized designs*), subjects are assigned randomly to the treatment conditions and each serves in only one of them. No within-*S* factors are present. The error term for all designs of this sort is based on the variability of subjects receiving the same treatment condition. The scores for each treatment condition provide an independent esti-mate of this variability, and the error term for the analysis consists of an average of estimates for the different treatment conditions. This average is often called the *within-groups* error term, because it represents the average variability of subjects within any of the treatment conditions or groups.

To elaborate, the error term in the single-factor design is based on the vari-ability of subjects assigned to level a_1 (S/A_1), level a_2 (S/A_2), and so on, and is symbolized as S/A—the pooled variability of subjects within the levels of factor A. The error term in the $A \times B$ design is based on the pooled variability of subjects assigned to the $(a)(b)$ treatment combinations and is symbolized as S/AB—the variability of subjects within the treatment combinations of factors A and B. The error term in the $A \times B \times C$ design is based on the variability of subjects assigned to the $(a)(b)(c)$ treatment combinations and is symbolized as S/ABC—the vari-ability of subjects within the treatment combinations of factors A, B, and C.

In all completely randomized designs, the within-groups error term is used to assess the significance of all treatment effects extracted in the analysis.[5] As you will see shortly, the same sort of error term will also be appropriate in *mixed* designs when the treatment effects are based entirely on between-*S* differences.

"Pure" Within-*S* Designs

There is a general principle that lies behind the error terms required for "pure" within-*S* designs. This rule may be stated as follows:

> **The error term for evaluating any source of variability in a "pure" within-*S* design is based on the interaction between the factor or factors contained in the source and subjects.**

Let us see how this rule functions in several common examples of "pure" within-*S* designs.

Single-Factor Within-*S* Design.   You have already seen in Chap. 16 how this rule applies to the analysis of the single-factor within-*S* design. As a reminder, the error term for evaluating the overall effects of factor A is based on the interaction between factor A and subjects—the $A \times S$ interaction. You will also recall that the evaluation of single-df comparisons generally requires specialized error terms, unique to each comparison. If we substitute *comparison* for *source*, the rule applies to the analysis of these single-df comparisons as well. That is,

> **The error term for evaluating a single-df comparison is based on the interaction between the comparison and subjects.**

Two-Factor Within-*S* Design. We will now see how the rule generalizes to factorial designs. Let us first look at a factorial design with two within-*S* factors. Space does not permit a formal discussion of the analysis of this particular design, but examples of the design are often found in the research literature. This design is a two-way factorial, symbolized as an $(A \times B \times S)$ design, in which all subjects receive all the $(a)(b)$ treatment conditions. The order of the treatments is usually randomized or varied in some systematic fashion designed to minimize undesired sequence effects.

---

[5] If heterogeneity of within-group variances is present, it may be necessary to use specific error terms to evaluate treatment effects based on *portions* of the data, e.g., simple effects and interaction comparisons. In these cases, a useful procedure is to base the error term on only those observations involved in the calculation of the effect under consideration.

The standard sources of variability examined in the overall analysis of this (or any) two factor design are the two main effects (*A* and *B*) and the $A \times B$ interaction. In the $(A \times B \times S)$ design, these treatment sources are based on different configurations of the within-*S* factors. For example, the levels of factor *B* are totally disregarded in the calculation and assessment of the *A* main effect; for analysis purposes, the configuration of the data is equivalent to a single-factor within-*S* design involving the manipulation of factor *A*. Similarly, the levels of factor *A* are totally disregarded in the calculation and assessment of the *B* main effect; the configuration of the data in this case is equivalent to another single-factor within-*S* design involving the manipulation of factor *B*. Finally, *both* within-*S* factors are involved in the calculation and assessment of the $A \times B$ interaction. Applying the rule to each of these sources produces three different error terms:

The error term for evaluating the *A* main effect is based on the interaction between factor *A* and subjects—the $A \times S$ interaction.

The error term for evaluating the *B* main effect is based on the interaction between factor *B* and subjects—the $B \times S$ interaction.

The error term for evaluating the $A \times B$ interaction is based on the interaction between factors *A* and *B* and subjects—the $A \times B \times S$ interaction.

In each case, then, the error term consists of the interaction of the within-*S* factor (or factors) with subjects. The overall analysis is summarized in Table 19-5.

Three or More Within-*S* Factors.   We are now in a position to describe the analysis of "pure" within-*S* factorials with any number of independent variables. For the overall analysis, all we need to do is to apply the general rule for within-*S* error

Table 19-5
Standard Analysis of the $(A \times B \times S)$ Design

Source	df	Error Term
A	$a - 1$	$A \times S$
B	$b - 1$	$B \times S$
S	$s - 1$	
$A \times B$	$(a - 1)(b - 1)$	$A \times B \times S$
$A \times S$	$(a - 1)(s - 1)$	
$B \times S$	$(b - 1)(s - 1)$	
$A \times B \times S$	$(a - 1)(b - 1)(s - 1)$	

terms to the specific design under consideration. That rule, to repeat, states that

The error term for evaluating any source of variability is based on an interaction between the factor or factors contained in the source and subjects.

To illustrate with the three-factor design,

The error terms for the main effects of A, B, and C are $A \times S$, $B \times S$, and $C \times S$, respectively.

The error terms for the two-way interactions of $A \times B$, $A \times C$, and $B \times C$ are $A \times B \times S$, $A \times C \times S$, and $B \times C \times S$, respectively.

The error term for the $A \times B \times C$ interaction is $A \times B \times C \times S$.

The Mixed Two-Factor Design: A Review

The analysis of mixed factorial designs consists of a blending of a "pure" between-S design and a "pure" within-S design. We discussed this blending of designs in Chap. 17, when we considered the analysis of the mixed two-factor design in which A is the between-S factor and B is the within-S factor. (See Table 17-2, page 298, for a summary.) We will review this analysis here to illustrate how the general principles we have established for "pure" between-S and within-S designs apply to the analysis of the mixed factorial design.

A convenient way to understand the analysis of a mixed factorial is to segregate the treatment sources of variability into two categories, one representing the between-S portion of the analysis and the other the within-S portion. The normal "yield" of treatment effects for a two-factor design—A, B, and $A \times B$—and their error terms are listed in the first and second columns of Table 19-6, respectively.

Table 19-6
Error Terms for the $A \times (B \times S)$ Mixed Factorial Design

Treatment Source	Error Term
Between-Subjects Factor	
A	S/A
Within-Subjects Factor	
B	$B \times S/A$
$A \times B$	$B \times S/A$

You should note that the treatment sources of variability have been segregated into two categories. The first category consists of treatment sources based only on the between-S factor. In this particular design only one treatment source qualifies for membership in this category, namely, the A main effect. The error term for this between-S source is the same error term that would be appropriate if the data were collapsed over the within-S factor, in which case the arrangement would be a completely randomized design—a "pure" between-S design without repeated measures. This operation would produce a single-factor experiment in which S/A, the within-groups source, is the error term.

The second category consists of treatment sources based entirely or in part on the within-S factor in this design (factor B). There are two treatment sources that involve factor B: the B main effect and the $A \times B$ interaction. The error term for either of these within-S sources is essentially the same term that would be appropriate in a corresponding within-S design involving factor B. In the case of a "pure" $(B \times S)$ design, the error term would be the $B \times S$ interaction. In the mixed factorial, there is a different $B \times S$ interaction for each of the independent groups—a $B \times S$ interaction at level a_1 $(B \times S/A_1)$, a $B \times S$ interaction at level a_2 $(B \times S/A_2)$, and so on. These are combined and averaged to form the $MS_{B \times S/A}$ that serves as the error term for both B and $A \times B$ in the mixed factorial design.

Mixed Three-Factor Designs

We will now apply this system to the analysis of mixed three-factor designs. There are two types of mixed designs logically possible with three-factor designs. One of these contains two between-S factors and one within-S factor. If we designate factors A and B as the between-S factors and factor C as the within-S factor, we can refer to the arrangement as an $A \times B \times (C \times S)$ design, the parentheses indicating the portion of the design represented by repeated measures. The other type of mixed design contains one between-S factor and two within-S factors. If we designate factor A as the between-S factor and factors B and C as the within-S factors, we can refer to the arrangement as an $A \times (B \times C \times S)$ design, the parentheses again indicating the portion of the design represented by repeated measures.

Two Between-S Factors and One Within-S Factor. We can create an example of the first type of design by bringing together three of the independent variables we have introduced previously in our fictitious vocabulary experiment. Consider an experiment in which factor A consists of three different lectures (physical science, social science, and history) and factor B consists of two methods of presentation (computer and standard). Subjects are randomly assigned to independent groups receiving $(3)(2) = 6$ different combinations of these two factors. At this point, the experiment is a completely randomized *two*-factor design. In addition, however, each student receives three vocabulary tests (factor *C*), the first immediately following the lecture, the second 2 weeks later, and the third 4 weeks later; thus we have a three-factor design with factor *C* represented as a within-*S* factor.

Table 19-7 indicates the appropriate error term for each of the treatment sources of variability normally extracted from a three-factor design. Again, we have segregated the treatment sources into two categories, one for treatment sources based only on the two between-*S* factors and another for treatment sources based entirely or in part on the one within-*S* factor. In the first category we would place the main effects of *A* and *B* and the *A* × *B* interaction, while in the second category we would place the remaining sources of treatment effects, namely, the main effect of *C*, the *A* × *C* and *B* × *C* interactions, and the *A* × *B* × *C* interaction.

The error term for the between-*S* portion of the analysis is the same error term that would be appropriate if the data were collapsed over the within-*S* factor. Under these circumstances, the design would become a "pure" completely randomized *two-factor design* and $MS_{S/AB}$ would be the error term to evaluate all treatment sources in the first category.

The error term for the within-*S* portion is equivalent to the error term that would be appropriate in a "pure" single-factor within-*S* design in which *C* is the within-*S* factor, namely, a *C* × *S* interaction. In this particular design, there is a different *C* × *S* interaction term for each of the independent groups—a *C* × *S* interaction

Table 19-7
Error Terms for the *A* × *B* × (*C* × *S*) Mixed Factorial Design

Treatment Source	Error Term
Between-Subjects Factors	
A	*S*/*AB*
B	*S*/*AB*
A × *B*	*S*/*AB*
Within-Subjects Factor	
C	*C* × *S*/*AB*
A × *C*	*C* × *S*/*AB*
B × *C*	*C* × *S*/*AB*
A × *B* × *C*	*C* × *S*/*AB*

at a_1b_1 ($C \times S/AB_{1,1}$), a $C \times S$ interaction at a_1b_2 ($C \times S/AB_{1,2}$), and so on. Pooling the interactions over all the $(a)(b)$ groups gives us $MS_{C \times S/AB}$ as the error term for evaluating the remaining treatment sources in the table.

One Between-*S* Factor and Two Within-*S* Factors. As an example of the second type of mixed factorial, suppose that factor *A* (lectures) continues to be a between-*S* factor and that subjects are randomly assigned to different groups destined to receive one of the three lectures. For the within-*S* factors, suppose that half of *each lecture* is presented with the computer method and the other half with the standard method. (We will assume that half of the subjects receive the computer method first and then the standard method, and that the other half receive the standard method first and then the computer method.) Since each subject receives both the computer method and the standard method, method of presentation (factor *B*) is a within-*S* factor. Suppose further that all subjects are tested at all three different time intervals. Again, since each subject receives all three vocabulary tests, this independent variable (factor *C*) is a within-*S* factor as well.

In summary, then, the experiment is a mixed three-factor design in which "lectures" is a between-*S* factor (*A*) while "methods" (*B*) and "tests" (*C*) are within-*S* factors. All subjects receive all six combinations of methods and tests, which together represent a two-factor within-*S* design, but in conjunction with only one of the lectures (levels of factor *A*). In effect, the ($B \times C \times S$) design is represented $a = 3$ times, once with the physical science lecture (level a_1), once with the social science lecture (level a_2), and once with the history lecture (level a_3).

The analysis of this design is summarized in Table 19-8. Again we have segregated the treatment sources in this design into two categories, depending on the presence or absence of repeated measures. In this particular mixed factorial design, the division is simple, since only one treatment source (*A*) is based entirely on a between-*S* factor and the remaining treatment sources involve either one or two within-*S* factors. We will consider the between-*S* portion of the analysis first. If we collapse over the two within-*S* factors, the design becomes a "pure" completely randomized *single*-factor design, which means that $MS_{S/A}$ is the correct error term for this part of the analysis.

We have noted already that the remaining treatment sources are based entirely or in part on within-*S* factors. As discussed earlier in this section, a "pure" two-factor within-*S* design would require *three* error terms, namely,

$MS_{B \times S}$ to evaluate the *B* main effect

$MS_{C \times S}$ to evaluate the *C* main effect

$MS_{B \times C \times S}$ to evaluate the $B \times C$ interaction

Table 19-8

Error Terms for the $A \times (B \times C \times S)$ Mixed Factorial Design

Treatment Source	Error Term
Between-Subjects Factor	
A	S/A
Within-Subjects Factors	
B	$B \times S/A$
$A \times B$	$B \times S/A$
C	$C \times S/A$
$A \times C$	$C \times S/A$
$B \times C$	$B \times C \times S/A$
$A \times B \times C$	$B \times C \times S/A$

In the context of the present mixed factorial design, however, there is a different set of three interactions for each of the lecture groups. That is,

There is a $B \times S$ interaction at level a_1 ($B \times S/A_1$), a $B \times S$ interaction at level a_2 ($B \times S/A_2$), and so on.

Similarly, there is a $C \times S$ interaction at level a_1 ($C \times S/A_1$), a $C \times S$ interaction at level a_2 ($C \times S/A_2$), and so on.

Finally, there is a $B \times C \times S$ interaction at level a_1 ($B \times C \times S/A_1$), a $B \times C \times S$ interaction at level a_2 ($B \times C \times S/A_2$), and so on.

After these three sets of component interactions are pooled and averaged, we have $MS_{B \times S/A}$, $MS_{C \times S/A}$, and $MS_{B \times C \times S/A}$, respectively, as the three within-S error terms for this particular design.

The correct error term for any source based entirely or in part on repeated measures is determined by the within-S factor (or factors) contributing to the source. For example, there are two sources that involve only factor B—the B main effect and the $A \times B$ interaction. As shown in the second column of Table 19-8, the error term for both of these sources is the $B \times S$ interaction pooled over the independent groups $MS_{B \times S/A}$. Similarly, there are two sources that involve only factor C—the C main effect and the $A \times C$ interaction—and the error term for both sources is the $C \times S$ interaction pooled over the independent groups $MS_{C \times S/A}$. The last two sources involve *both* within-S factors (the $B \times C$ and the $A \times B \times C$ interactions). The error term for both sources is the $B \times C \times S$ interaction pooled over the independent groups $MS_{B \times C \times S/A}$.

19.4 USING ANOVA AND MRC TO ANALYZE WITHIN-SUBJECTS DESIGNS

The ANOVA Approach

"Pure" Within-*S* Designs. An easy way to conceptualize the analysis of "pure" within-*S* designs is to think of "subjects" as an additional factor and to analyze the data accordingly. In Chap. 16, for example, you saw that the overall analysis of the *single*-factor within-*S* design resembled the analysis of a *two*-factor design in which factor *A* and "factor *S*" were the two factors. In a similar fashion, the analysis of a two-factor within-*S* design resembles the analysis of a three-factor design in which factor *A*, factor *B*, and "factor *S*" are the three factors. No new or special procedures are involved.[6]

Mixed Factorial Designs. The analysis of mixed factorial designs is more complicated, largely because of the need to deal with pooled sources of interaction in calculating the error terms. You may find it useful to turn to advanced books on experimental design and statistical analysis for further discussion and worked illustrations. Examples of the analysis of mixed three-factor designs are found in a number of different references, including the following:

> The $A \times B \times (C \times S)$ design: Keppel (1982, pp. 475, 606), Kirk (1982, pp. 523–528), Myers (1979, pp. 214–217), and Winer (1971, pp. 563–567)
> The $A \times (B \times C \times S)$ design: Keppel (1982, pp. 476–477, 606–607), Kirk (1982, pp. 535–540), Myers (1979, pp. 220–226), and Winer (1971, pp. 546–550)

The MRC Approach

"Pure" Within-*S* Designs. The MRC analysis of "pure" within-*S* designs—like the corresponding procedure using ANOVA—is relatively easy to generalize to more complex factorials. We start in the usual fashion by establishing a set of vectors for *each of the main effects*, choosing meaningful single-*df* comparisons as vectors when possible. In these designs, *subjects* are also coded as a *main effect*. All we need now are the different sets of interaction vectors—sets reflecting interactions of the independent variables themselves and sets reflecting interactions of the independent variables with subjects. The former provide the $R^2_{Y.set}$'s corresponding to the factorial effects, and the latter provide the $R^2_{Y.set}$'s for the error terms. Once the sets of vectors are identified, the actual analysis should present no problems.

---

[6] The analysis of the $(A \times B \times S)$ design is described in detail by Keppel (1982, pp. 463–467).

We will illustrate this process with the overall analysis of the $(A \times B \times S)$ design. As detailed in Sec. 19.3, this analysis requires different error terms for evaluating the two main effects and the $A \times B$ interaction. These error terms, you may recall, are based on interactions of the effects themselves with *subjects*. More specifically,

> The error term for the A main effect is based on the interaction of factor A with subjects—the $A \times S$ interaction.
>
> The error term for the B main effect is based on the interaction of factor B with subjects—the $B \times S$ interaction.
>
> The error term for the $A \times B$ interaction is based on the interaction of factors A and B with subjects—the $A \times B \times S$ interaction.

Let us see how these quantities are obtained with MRC.

The first step is to code the three main effects. The A main effect requires $a - 1$ vectors, which, ideally, should represent meaningful single-*df* comparisons. (These comparisons do not need to be orthogonal.) Similarly, the B main effect requires $b - 1$ vectors, which would be constructed in the same manner. The third source, the main effect of subjects, requires $s - 1$ vectors; these vectors may be constructed in the manner we described in Chap. 16, simply by comparing the first subject with each of the subjects in the experiment (see pages 273–274). The sources remaining to be specified are all interactions based on A, B, and S. Consequently, the vectors representing these sources are interaction vectors formed by cross-multiplying the relevant sets of main-effect vectors.

Table 19-9 makes these operations explicit. For simplicity, we will assume that the design is a 3×3 factorial with $s = 3$ subjects receiving all $(a)(b) = 9$ of the treatment conditions. This means that the sets of vectors capturing the three main effects consist of two vectors each:

> Vectors $A1$ and $A2$ for the A main effect
> Vectors $B1$ and $B2$ for the B main effect
> Vectors $S1$ and $S2$ for the S main effect

These vector sets are listed in the third column of Table 19-9. The vector sets for the $A \times S$ interaction are obtained by cross-multiplying each of the two A vectors with each of the two S vectors; the four resulting interaction vectors are also enumerated in column 3. The remaining two-way interactions—$B \times S$ and $A \times B$—are obtained the same way. The vectors defining the $A \times B \times S$ interaction are obtained by cross-multiplying three vectors, one from each of the vector sets defining the three main effects. The vector set for the three-way interaction contains all possible combinations of the A, B, and S vectors. The eight resulting interaction vectors are listed in the last row of column 3.

The $R^2_{Y.set}$'s required for the analysis may be obtained directly by specifying the appropriate set of vectors and calculating the squared multiple correlation be-

Table 19-9
Analysis of the $(A \times B \times S)$ Design

(1) Source	(2) df	(3) Vectors	(4) $R^2_{Y.set}$
A	$a - 1$	$A1, A2$	$R^2_{Y.A} = R^2_{Y.A1,A2}$
S	$s - 1$	$S1, S2$	$R^2_{Y.S} = R^2_{Y.S1,S2}$
$A \times S$	$(a-1)(s-1)$	$A1S1, A1S2,$ $A2S1, A2S2$	$R^2_{Y.A \times S} = R^2_{Y.A1S1, \ldots, A2S2}$
B	$b - 1$	$B1, B2$	$R^2_{Y.B} = R^2_{Y.B1,B2}$
$B \times S$	$(b-1)(s-1)$	$B1S1, B1S2,$ $B2S1, B2S2$	$R^2_{Y.B \times S} = R^2_{Y.B1S1, \ldots, B2S2}$
$A \times B$	$(a-1)(b-1)$	$A1B1, A1B2,$ $A2B1, A2B2$	$R^2_{Y.A \times B} = R^2_{Y.A1B1, \ldots, A2B2}$
$A \times B \times S$	$(a-1)(b-1)(s-1)$	$A1B1S1, A1B1S2,$ $A1B2S1, A1B2S2,$ $A2B1S1, A2B1S2,$ $A2B2S1, A2B2S2$	$R^2_{Y.A \times B \times S} = R^2_{Y.A1B1S1, \ldots, A2B2S2}$

tween Y and the set of vectors. That is,

$$R^2_{Y.A} = R^2_{Y.A1,A2}$$
$$R^2_{Y.S} = R^2_{Y.S1,S2}$$
$$R^2_{Y.A \times S} = R^2_{Y.A1S1,A1S2,A2S1,A2S2}$$

and so on. These operations are indicated in the final column of the table. All that remains is to divide the $R^2_{Y.set}$'s by the appropriate degrees of freedom and to calculate the F ratios.[7] (The df for each source are listed in column 2 and are equal, of course, to the number of vectors required to define the given source.)

[7] Alternatively, the last $R^2_{Y.set}$ in the table, $R^2_{Y.A \times B \times S}$, may be obtained by treating the squared multiple correlation as *residual* variation. That is, instead of adding the last set of vectors to the analysis, we simply use the formula, $1 - R^2_{Y.max}$, to calculate the same quantity. More specifically, the combination of the vector sets from A through $A \times B$ in Table 19-9 captures all the Y variability except that associated with the $A \times B \times S$ interaction, namely,

$$R^2_{Y.A \times B \times S} = 1 - R^2_{Y.A1,A2, \ldots, A2B1,A2B2},$$

or in terms of the $R^2_{Y.sets}$,

$$R^2_{Y.A \times B \times S} = 1 - (R^2_{Y.A} + R^2_{Y.S} + R^2_{Y.A \times S} + R^2_{Y.B.} + R^2_{Y.B \times S} + R^2_{Y.A \times B})$$

Mixed Factorial Designs.   The analysis of mixed factorial designs by MRC is quite similar to the analysis of the $(A \times B \times S)$ design we just illustrated. We start by coding each of the main effects associated with the independent variables in the factorial design. There is no main effect of subjects in the mixed factorial designs, because subjects do not receive all the treatment conditions as they do in "pure" within-S designs. Instead, subjects are coded separately for each independent group of subjects, and the vector sets are pooled to form the required sources of variability in a manner similar to that described in Chap. 17 (pages 308–309). After this has been accomplished, the remainder of the analysis is the same as for the "pure" within-S design.

As we have indicated already, subjects in the mixed design are coded separately for each independent group. We accomplish this by using coding to identify the subjects in the group we are interested in and assigning 0s to all others. The $R^2_{Y.set}$ obtained when the subject vectors for all the groups are included in the analysis serves as the error term for the between-S sources. More specifically, the multiple correlation between Y and the subject vectors identifying the subjects in any given group reflects the variability among those particular subjects; the multiple correlation between Y and *all* the sets of subject vectors reflects the combined variability obtained from all the independent groups.

Error terms for the portion of the analysis dealing with repeated measures are based on interactions between within-S factors and subjects pooled over the independent groups. Vectors for these error terms are easily obtained by cross-multiplying the vectors representing treatment sources with the entire collection of subject vectors. The necessary pooling is accomplished by including all the relevant interaction vectors in the analysis.

The $A \times (B \times S)$ Design.   We will first illustrate this procedure with the mixed design we considered in Chap. 17. The standard sources of variability isolated in the analysis of the $A \times (B \times S)$ design are listed in the first column of Table 19-10 in the order in which they are usually reported. Again, we will assume that $a = 3$ and $b = 3$, with different groups of $s = 3$ subjects receiving all levels of factor B in conjunction with the different levels of factor A. Coding begins with the A main effect; this requires two vectors representing single-df comparisons, $A1$ and $A2$. Similarly, two vectors are chosen to code the B main effect, $B1$ and $B2$.

Subjects are coded next, with coding applied *separately* to each of the three independent groups of subjects. The variability of subjects within any one treatment group requires $s - 1$ vectors, which, in the present case, is 2. For level a_1, the vectors are $S1$ and $S2$. The coding we use consists of a set of vectors comparing the first subject with each of the other subjects in the group. Vector $S1$, for example, would have $+1$s assigned to all Y scores produced by the first subject, -1s assigned to

Table 19-10
Analysis of the $A \times (B \times S)$ Design

(1) Source	(2) df	(3) Vectors	(4) $R^2_{Y.set}$
A	$a - 1$	A1, A2	$R^2_{Y.A} = R^2_{Y.A1,A2}$
S/A	$(a)(s - 1)$	S1, S2 S3, S4 S5, S6	$R^2_{Y.S} = R^2_{Y.S1,\ldots,S6}$
B	$b - 1$	B1, B2	$R^2_{Y.B} = R^2_{Y.B1,B2}$
$A \times B$	$(a - 1)(b - 1)$	A1B1, A1B2, A2B1, A2B2	$R^2_{Y.A \times B} = R^2_{Y.A1B1,\ldots,A2B2}$
$B \times S/A$	$(a)(b - 1)(s - 1)$	B1S1, B2S1, B1S2, B2S2 B1S3, B2S3, B1S4, B2S4 B1S5, B2S5, B1S6, B2S6	$R^2_{Y.B \times S/A} = R^2_{Y.B1S1,\ldots,B2S6}$

all Y scores produced by the second subject, and 0s assigned to all others, including *all* subjects receiving other levels of factor A, namely, levels a_2 and a_3. Vector S2 would again have $+1$s assigned to all Y scores produced by the first subject, -1s assigned to the *third* subject, and 0s to all others. Since the third subject is the last one at level a_1, coding at this level is complete. The code matrix for subjects at a_1 is as follows.

	s_1	s_2	s_3
Vector 1	$+1$	-1	0
Vector 2	$+1$	0	-1

For the next level, a_2, the vectors for coding subjects are S3 and S4, and the same process is repeated, except that the focus is on the Y scores produced by the three subjects at level a_2. For the final level, a_3, the subject vectors are S5 and S6, and the focus is on the Y scores produced by the subjects at level a_3. For the overall analysis, we need to pool the separate variability estimates from the three groups. We easily do so with MRC simply by including all six subject vectors in the analysis, as we have done in Table 19-10.

The remaining two sources in the analysis are interactions. We obtain the interaction vectors by simply cross-multiplying relevant vectors. Depending on the particular interaction, these vectors represent either main effects or subjects. The $A \times B$ interaction, for example, is coded by cross-multiplying each of the two A vectors with each of the two B vectors; the combinations are listed in Table 19-10. The $B \times S/A$ interaction, on the other hand, is coded by cross-multiplying each of the two B vectors with all six of the subject vectors; the combinations for this interaction are also specified in the table.

The analysis begins with the calculation of the required $R^2_{Y.set}$'s. We calculate a separate squared multiple correlation coefficient for each of the appropriate sets. The nature of this squared multiple correlation coefficient is indicated in the fourth column of the table.

Higher-Order Mixed Factorial Designs.   Designs of any degree of factorial complexity can be analyzed by MRC in this manner. To repeat, we start with a listing of the sources of variability normally extracted in the analysis. Each main effect is then represented by a complete set of single-*df* comparisons. We use coding to represent the variability of subjects in each of the independent groups. All remaining sources of variability are interactions, which we code simply by cross-multiplying the vectors from the relevant main effects and from subjects. The different sets of vectors are correlated with Y to obtain the appropriate $R^2_{Y.set}$ from the analysis.

19.5   SUMMARY

Previous chapters covered the detailed analysis of single-factor and two-factor designs, both completely randomized designs (between-*S* designs) and designs with repeated measures (within-*S* designs). For this chapter we extended our coverage by offering a broad overview of the analysis of higher-order factorial designs. The intent was to show how the analyses of these more complex factorial designs are based on the analyses of less complex designs.

Factorial designs with three or more independent variables introduce no new principles of analysis. An overall analysis will still consist of the evaluation of main effects and interactions, and a more detailed analysis will consider simple effects and interaction comparisons. The difference is an increase in the *number* and in the *complexity* of these detailed analyses. An $A \times B \times C$ design, for example, provides information about three main effects ($A, B,$ and C), three interactions involving two of the independent variables ($A \times B, A \times C,$ and $B \times C$), and one interaction involving all three independent variables ($A \times B \times C$). The analysis of simple effects begins with the three-way interaction, which, if significant, leads to the examination of interactions involving two of the factors at each of the levels of the third factor (simple interactions). If the three-way interaction is not significant, attention focuses on interactions between two of the factors averaged over the levels of the third factor. From this point on, the analysis is equivalent to three separate two-factor designs. Interaction contrasts consist of a number of component three-factor designs derived from the original design by transforming multilevel independent variables into single-*df* comparisons and forming factorials based on these comparisons. In short, higher-order factorial designs are rich with information about the ways in which independent variables combine to influence behavior.

Higher-order factorial designs also range from the completely randomized designs to designs in which subjects serve in all the treatment conditions. If subjects serve in only one of the treatment conditions, the design is a between-*S* design; if they serve in two or more of the treatment conditions, the design is a within-*S* design. We referred to designs in which subjects receive all the treatment conditions as "pure" within-*S* designs and designs in which subjects receive some of the treatment conditions as "mixed" within-*S* designs.

Between-*S* and within-*S* designs provide the same type of information about the effects of the independent variables, but they differ in the nature of the error terms needed to assess the significance of these effects. A between-*S* design requires a single error term, which is based on the variability of subjects treated alike and averaged over all the treatment conditions. Generally, this error term is used for all analyses. A within-*S* design, on the other hand, usually requires a number of different error terms, the number depending on the nature of the design and on the nature of the analyses. In all cases, the error terms for factorial effects based on repeated measures consist of interactions between subjects and the independent variables involved.

The advantages of within-*S* designs over between-*S* alternatives are economy (fewer subjects are usually required) and sensitivity (the error terms are smaller). The disadvantages are the possibility of differential carryover effects and the complications arising from violations of certain statistical assumptions. Mixed factorial designs represent a partial solution to these problems by reducing the likelihood of carryover effects and the occurrence of statistical violations, while retaining the advantage of smaller error terms for those portions of the analysis that are based on repeated measures.

The analysis of higher-order factorials may be accomplished by either ANOVA or MRC. The ANOVA approach was briefly sketched; we provided references for discussions and examples of the detailed analyses in more advanced textbooks. These analyses are all based on various arrangements of the data designed to facilitate the calculation of sums and subtotals, basic ratios, and, ultimately, sums of squares and *F* ratios. We described the MRC approach in somewhat more detail to illustrate the procedure used in this approach to data analysis: coding main effects for between-*S* designs and coding main effects and subjects for within-*S* designs, and then representing sources of variability with vector sets based on the codes or on interactions between them.

19.6 EXERCISES

NOTE: The following problems deal with the identification of sources of variability that would normally be isolated in an analysis. These sources are those that are needed regardless of whether the data are eventually analyzed by ANOVA or MRC.

1. For each treatment source of variability that can be isolated from a "pure" three-factor within-subjects design $(A \times B \times C \times S)$, indicate the nature of the error term with which you will assess its significance.

2. Consider a factorial design that includes four independent variables *A*, *B*, *C*, and *D* each consisting of two levels, and which is thus a $2 \times 2 \times 2 \times 2$ design.

   a. Construct a diagram of this design showing all the treatment conditions.
   b. List all the treatment effects that may be obtained from this design. (HINT: There are a total of 15 main effects and interactions possible with this design.)

3. Assume that factor *D* in Problem 2 is a within-subjects factor.

   a. What is the nature of the error terms? (HINT: There are two).
   b. Indicate the appropriate error term for each of the main effects and interactions available with this design.

4. Assume that factors *C* and *D* in Problem 2 are within-subjects factors.

   a. What is the nature of the error terms? (HINT: There are four.)
   b. Indicate the appropriate error term for each of the main effects and interactions available with this design.

20

Nonexperimental Research

. . .

377

Up to this point in the book, we have emphasized the use of ANOVA and MRC as two functionally equivalent strategies for the purpose of analyzing research that is consistent with the requirements of experimental design. We have been able to consider them equivalent because of the nature of the designs we have looked at so far—they have been designs in which equal numbers of subjects are randomly assigned to the different conditions. In this chapter, and the next, we will consider the analysis of *nonexperimental designs* for which ANOVA procedures are usually not appropriate. These are designs for which the random assignment of subjects to conditions is not possible and in which the independent variables are often naturally occurring and not under the control of the researcher. It is precisely with such designs that MRC truly comes into its own, since its analysis techniques are not restricted by the conditions of collecting the data, the way in which subjects are assigned, or the nature or type of data collected.

20.1 A COMPARISON OF EXPERIMENTAL AND NONEXPERIMENTAL RESEARCH

As we stressed in Chaps. 1 and 2 and highlighted in the other chapters of this book, laboratory experimentation is defined by a particular set of constraints. In brief, laboratory experiments involve random assignment of subjects to conditions as well as experimenter control of the level and manipulation of the independent variable. The end product of experimental, laboratory research is a confident statement of the cause-and-effect relationship between the independent and dependent variables. The features of experimental design allow the researcher to conclude whether the outcome of the experiment—the performance result—is due to the manipulation. When such a statement can be made, we say that the experiment has **internal validity**.

Some Potential Difficulties with Experimental Research

Experimental research has some limitations, however. Perhaps the most common concern about such research is its limited **external validity**, which refers to the degree to which a researcher can generalize beyond the laboratory and beyond the type of sample used as subjects. It has been argued that experimental research has limited external validity and is an inadequate representation of a real or natural process. The experimental situation can be viewed as artificial or contrived and usually is limited by the nature of the subjects studied (college students or infrahumans).

Though random assignment is a key feature that sets experimental research apart from other kinds of research, we do not want to overemphasize its value. Random assignment should result in equivalence of the treatment groups *prior to presentation of the treatment*, but the equivalence is *probabilistic*; that is, if subjects are randomly assigned to treatment conditions, it is highly likely that all treatment groups will be equivalent prior to the introduction of the manipulation, but their equivalence is not guaranteed. (You will see that experimentalists are aware of this issue and thus resort to ANCOVA—see Chap. 22—in some situations.) In fact, the *likelihood* of equivalence is *lower* when there are small numbers of subjects in the experiment. On the other hand, the statistical tests that we conduct on the data gathered in experiments take this likelihood of equivalence into account, since the significance of differences among treatment groups is, in part, a function of sample size; the larger the sample size, and therefore the greater the likelihood of equivalence prior to treatment, the smaller the differences that are required to be considered statistically significant.

Another concern with equivalence is evident when the experiment continues over a long time period, as might occur when there is more than one session of subject participation (as in the within-subjects, or repeated-measures, designs we discussed in Chaps. 16 through 19). In such a situation, there is again no guarantee that equivalence will be maintained: there may be differential attrition of subjects, and the experimenter will have no control over what subjects are exposed to outside the laboratory setting. The point of these concerns is that although random assignment is a desirable feature—and a necessary requirement of experiment research—it does have its limitations, and researchers need to be aware of them when interpreting the results of their experiments.

Research in Which Random Assignment and Direct Manipulation Are Not Possible

Another limitation of experimental research is the simple fact that it is often not practical to assign subjects at random to different treatments or to manipulate the variable that is of interest. There are many important questions that *cannot* be studied in the laboratory because the manipulations involved are either impractical, or unethical. Let us provide some examples of interesting research questions that are problematic for study with experimental designs in a laboratory setting:

1. *An impractical situation.* Suppose our research question pertains to the influence of type of political campaign on voting behavior. To study this research question, we might decide to contrast two styles of campaigns (the independent variable), each conducted by one of two candidates who are both from the same party; we would then observe how the nature of

the two campaigns influences the voters in an election. This question calls for an analysis of the campaigns, and the campaigns are likely to extend over a relatively long period of time (e.g., three months). We can approximate an *experimental situation* by exposing two randomly formed groups of voters to a specific aspect of the two campaigns (e.g., exposing each group to literature distributed by one of the candidates) and then asking the voters to express their voting *intentions*. It should be apparent that such a measure of the effects of the two campaign strategies, which is the issue of interest, is artificial, constrained, and limited—only minimally related to the actual campaigns that would be conducted. In a *nonexperimental study*, we would not attempt to manipulate the nature of the two campaigns, nor would we control exposure to the materials. Instead, we would simply let the election take its course and find ways to relate various aspects of the two campaigns as they develop over time to the actual votes in the election. In some sense, the nonexperimental situation is most appropriate for studying broader factors and features, whereas the laboratory experiment is appropriate for "teasing out" the details of a particular phenomenon.

2. *An impossible situation.* Oftentimes, we are interested in so-called subject variables such as age, gender, and race, and their relationship to dependent measures such as learning rate, performance, and the like. It is simply not possible to assign subjects randomly to the "levels" of a subject variable, although we can randomly select subjects from groups with certain characteristics to participate in the study. Many questions of a developmental nature also cannot be manipulated. For example, if we wanted to determine at what grade level children begin the process of logical reasoning, we would need to study class and age groups that already exist.

3. *A potentially unethical situation.* Research questions that involve risk, both psychological and physical, would pose ethical concerns if they were studied in an experiment, since it would be unethical to assign some of the subjects to a risk or hazard condition. Hazardous situations, however, can be studied as they occur naturally; the researcher can then study them without exposing subjects to risk or harm. For example, if the question of interest is whether exposure to an earthquake results in increased frequency of nightmares among 5-year-olds, we would not want to create an earthquake intentionally (assuming that we had such powers) and observe who has nightmares. You may argue that we can simulate traumatic events in a laboratory and then study the reaction to such events, but our counterargument is that such designs may be appropriate for studying some behaviors (e.g., increased heart rate), but it may be inappropriate for studying behavior that could be harmful to the subject.

Even if we were able to and wanted to conduct experiments in a natural environment, referred to as the "field," doing so would raise several additional concerns. For example, suppose a corporation has two plants and we decide to use employees in one as a treatment group and those in the other as a control; which is to be which, we will decide randomly. If the question of interest is the degree to which a program (the treatment) improves or changes employees' behavior, is it ethically responsible to *withhold* that treatment from one group, the control group? For example, if we want to introduce a new monetary reward system or a new manufacturing process, the control subjects may wonder why they are not receiving the new rewards or being introduced to the new methods; not being part of the treatment group may mean that subjects will earn less and their loss cannot be recovered. Also, withholding of the new program or process may cause this group to fall behind in its subsequent performance and thereby may create a greater loss in present and future earning power. (Attempts to keep the new program secret from the control group border on the unethical, and besides, the news would spread like wildfire!)

Another concern is that subjects in natural, existing groups are often not as agreeable as, for example, college sophomores with respect to participation in experiments. Subjects may be unwilling to serve in the research, to serve as a control, or to receive a treatment. Refusals will affect the degree of equivalence of groups if, for example, a certain "type" of individual is less likely to be willing to participate. Thus, if we find differences between the treatment and control groups, and different numbers of subjects refused to serve in the two groups, how can we tell whether the differences are due to the actual treatments or to the differential loss of subjects?

Examples of Nonexperimental Research

We will not enter into a debate over whether the benefits of experimental research outweigh its disadvantages or whether experimental research is "better" than nonexperimental research. It is our position, however, that experimental research provides information that furthers our understanding of behavioral processes; it provides this information in a relatively neat and clean fashion. The limits and generalizability of a particular experiment can be assessed by additional and expanded research: the study might be replicated, more subjects—or just different subjects—might be used, and different levels of the independent variable might be introduced.

If our decision is to study research questions outside the laboratory, however, what designs are available to us? One form of nonexperimental research is known as the **quasi-experiment** (Campbell & Stanley, 1966; Cook & Campbell, 1979).

Quasi-experiments are studies in which the researcher observes and collects data on what happens and when it happens. The basic difference between it and experimental research is that the researcher *cannot control* what happens to whom, since there is no random assignment of subjects to conditions. Yet under such circumstances, by gathering data over time and places, and with awareness of the limitations, we can still discuss cause-and-effect relationships. We will consider quasi-experimental designs in Chap. 21.

Another type of nonexperimental research is known as **correlational research**, where we study the degree to which two or more variables covary in an intact, naturally occurring group of subjects. Here we have no interest in controlling the occurrence of a variable (or variables) and make no attempt to do so; rather, the interest is in determining the extent to which variables are related to each other or share a common underlying construct. For example, researchers may be interested in the degree to which certain personality constructs, such as empathy, extroversion, and self-confidence are interrelated. They will collect data on these constructs in a group of subjects and study the relationships.

Yet another form of nonexperimental research is the **observational study**, in which the researcher is either an observer of or a direct participant in a group situation being studied; the researcher thus observes the group's behavior either from within or from without and generates inferences about it. A related research strategy is the **case study**, in which there is an in-depth analysis of a particular situation or subject. These last two particular strategies are usually not amenable to statistical analysis, however, and thus we will not pursue them further in the chapter; we will concentrate on analysis of quasi-experimental and correlational designs. We will present the MRC strategies of data analysis that are necessary to answer specific kinds of research questions and those that are appropriate for specific kinds of field designs.

Comment

We consider it worth repeating that MRC is generally the better strategy for analyzing nonexperimental research. Given your study of the preceding chapters, you might be wondering why ANOVA is not appropriate, particularly since we have demonstrated on many occasions that the two analytic strategies yield identical conclusions. The answer is that in order to use ANOVA, we would probably have to "distort" the nature of the data and the representativeness of the variables as they exist in the setting. ANOVA, as we have described it so far, generally requires orthogonality between the independent variables; orthogonality is achieved by design and by having equal sample sizes per condition. In natural settings, however, it is highly unlikely that the independent variables will be orthogonal or that there will be equal numbers of subjects at the different levels of the independent variable. As a rule, there will be a different number of subjects at each level of the variable of interest. If we constrain or force a nonexperimental situation to arrive at equal sample sizes, we will obtain a distorted picture of the influence of the independent variables on the dependent variable. For example, we know that there are more females than males in the population. Should we conduct our research with an equal number of males and females just because ANOVA is statistically simple and could be applied to the data? Or should we try to represent the variable of interest as it occurs in its natural setting? Similarly, most naturally occurring variables are not orthogonal. Forcing such variables into a factorial design with equal sample sizes will also distort the outcome of the study. MRC can handle unequal sample sizes and nonorthogonality, and in contrast to ANOVA, does not require changing the true nature of the variable and its relationship to other variables; thus MRC is the recommended strategy. (Nonorthogonality can also occur in a factorial experimental design when subjects are lost for various reasons, including equipment failure and experimenter error. We will discuss this sort of problem in Chap. 24.)

Yet another reason for not using ANOVA for nonexperimental designs is that often, in such research, the "independent" variables of interest are continuous or quantitative variables. We frequently measure variables that range along a continuum from low to high, small amount to large amount, and so on. Application of ANOVA procedures to such variables usually requires a division of the continuum in order to create two or three "conditions" or groups. For example, if we have a continuous measure of intelligence where the scores range from 10 to 70, we may trichotomize the distribution and create three groups of "brightness" such that individuals scoring between 10 and 30 are called "dull," while those scoring between 31 and 50 are called "average" and those between 51 and 70 are called "bright."

We question this trichotomization strategy for two reasons. First, by arbitrarily creating groups, we lose potentially important information that we could use in the analysis. More specifically, all subjects scoring within a group are made to look more similar than they actually are, while subjects in different groups are sometimes made to look more different than they are. For example, two subjects who score 30 and 31 (a difference of 1) are classified as different ("dull" and "average," respectively), while two subjects who score 11 and 15 (a difference of 4) are classified as being the same ("dull"). This artificiality will be maintained if we analyze the study as an experiment, and any differences in intelligence among subjects within the same group will contribute to error variance. On the other hand, if we treat the study properly as a nonexperimental design, we will leave the intelligence variable intact and allow the variable to exert its full influence on the other variables included in the study. Such an analysis will usually require the use of MRC and the techniques we will cover in this chapter and the next. Thus, the manipulation of the data to accommodate a paradigm results in artificial and perhaps meaningless distinctions as well as incorrect determination of the statistical contribution of the variable.

Second, the exact nature of the "splits" can also influence the results. Suppose we were to divide the same set of data two different ways—in halves and in thirds. An analysis of these two groupings of subjects will produce different *F* ratios, with the possibility that one will be significant and the other nonsignificant.

In essence, it is not necessary (or even desirable) to transform a variable into a form that attempts to mimic a true experiment. What we advocate is using all the data from nonexperimental research in order to truly represent the relationships among the variables in the population, *not* discarding some data in order to achieve equal sample sizes. As a consequence, our analysis will involve special features of MRC—features with no counterpart in ANOVA—which will provide a clearer picture of the relationships among variables and more power to find those relationships.

20.2   AN EXAMPLE OF THE DIFFERENCES BETWEEN EXPERIMENTAL AND NONEXPERIMENTAL RESEARCH

Experimental research can be conducted in a "true" laboratory (usually, it seems, on the top or bottom floor of the psychology department building), or it can be implemented in a natural setting (i.e., one that already exists and is not created by the experimenter) with all the experimental constraints in place. Nonexperimental research relies on the collection of data that exist in naturally occurring, intact groups. As we pointed out previously, the research question of interest can be studied in one or both of the types of settings. At this point, we want to illustrate how the two types of research designs would *differ* for the same question of interest; we will briefly present the steps undertaken in the two approaches.

The Experimental Design

For example, suppose we are interested in gaining a better understanding of how children learn in particular environments. From an experimental perspective, we have the following scenario:

1. The *research hypothesis* is that *environmental conditions* influence learning performance of children.
2. The components of the hypothesis are operationalized as follows. The *dependent variable* is some measure of learning—for example, a score on

a test that measures how much knowledge a child possesses after having been exposed to a topic; in this case, let us say knowledge of and ability to solve algebraic equations with three unknowns. The *independent variable* consists of the nature of the teacher-child relationship, which is operationalized and manipulated in an environment such that the teacher is either warm, receptive, supportive, and positive in his or her interaction with the children (level a_1), or is cold, distant, withdrawn, and negative (level a_2).

3. The experimental research could be conducted as follows. A group of 30 students from the fifth grade of a local elementary school are selected for the study and randomly assigned in equal numbers to the treatment conditions. One condition, the "warm environment," would consist of a teacher who is trained to be warm, supportive, positive, and reinforcing. The teacher would work with the children in solving algebraic problems, explain the concepts, indicate where there are problems or incorrect solutions and show how to correct them, and provide positive reinforcement. The second condition, the "cold environment," would consist of a teacher who simply explains the concepts, assigns the problems to the children, grades the solutions, indicates only whether the solutions are correct or incorrect, and provides negative comments when the solutions are incorrect. Both groups would meet with their teacher for 4 hours. A "manipulation check" is necessary to confirm that subjects in the respective groups perceived the class environments as "warm" or "cold." That is, after the experiment is completed, the researcher would ascertain, perhaps via questionnaire or interview, whether the subjects indeed perceived the teacher as "warm" or "cold," whether the teacher explained concepts or provided negative feedback, and similar questions. In essence, the check is to determine whether the subjects were sensitive to the manipulation and whether the manipulation has been *perceived* as intended.

The procedure for this experiment requires that the subjects be exposed to 4 hours of one of the treatment conditions. After treatment, subjects are given a 10-item test on equations with three unknowns. The research hypothesis suggests that those who are exposed to the "warm environment" will do better on this test than those exposed to the "cold environment."

The Nonexperimental Design

With a nonexperimental design, we can also gain an understanding of the relationship between learning and classroom environment by carrying out the following procedure. The researcher goes into existing fifth-grade classes in a local elementary school (several classes are used in order to obtain a relatively large sample size and to facilitate finding differences on the variables of interest—classroom environment and knowledge of solutions of equations with three unknowns) and administers a questionnaire on the "climate" of the classroom and a test that requires solutions of equations with three unknowns. This is a viable approach if we can assume that among the different classes there will be variance and individual differences among the students in their *perceptions* of teachers as "warm" or "cold." The question to be answered is whether the variance in perception of the environment is related to performance on a test that measures ability to solve equations with three unknowns. Those students who perceive that they are in a "warm" relationship with the teacher are expected to do better on the test than those who perceive a "cold" relationship.

A Comparison

It is useful to enumerate the critical differences between the two approaches:

Experiment	Nonexperiment
Random assignment of subjects.	Subjects in already existing, naturally occurring classes.
Treatments are manipulated and controlled. Process of random assignment ensures equivalence of two (or more) treatment groups in abilities.	No control over the degree or amount of presence of the "independent" variable. "Actual" levels of environmental variables are a function of the perception of students and of the behavior of different teachers and are likely to be numerous.
Treatment is viewed as a dichotomous variable, "warm" or "cold."	Treatment is viewed as continuous, from "warm" to "cold."
A fixed temporal sequence between exposure to manipulation and assessment on dependent variable.	Measures on independent and dependent variables are essentially obtained simultaneously.

There are obvious variations and elaborations of the above research designs, but the point for now is that both designs give us information on the relationship between classroom environment and learning. The experimental design permits us to make inferences of causality with some degree of confidence; the nonexperimental design permits conclusions about association or relationship. The experimental design, with its control and standardization, allows us to rule out nontrivial alternatives to the explanations suggested by the research; the nonexperimental design leaves room for the possibility that the relationship between climate and learning is due to some third variable, but it is still useful, since it provides explanatory power. A possible third variable is the maturity of the students. That is, those who are more mature may deal with their environment differently and may have different tolerances and different ways of interacting with others. It could be that the more mature students are likely to perceive the same environment as "warmer."[1] Nevertheless, we can determine the degree to which the two variables of interest, environment and learning, are associated. If we know that the two variables are related, we can then use one variable to predict variation in the other; or we can deduce that there is something in common between the two.

Comment

The question to be asked, again, is whether it is appropriate to use either MRC or ANOVA statistical procedures for the above designs. For our example, it is appropriate to use MRC or ANOVA for the experiment, but only MRC for the nonexperimental situation. Again, ANOVA is inappropriate for nonexperimental research because it forces a distortion of the way the variables are represented and distributed in the population. In order to create an arrangement that resembles an experimental design, it would be necessary to assign or categorize children in the nonexperimental situation into a number of categories, even though such a procedure might artificially contrast and distort the findings. Many researchers, however, use ANOVA to analyze nonexperimental research. They do so because the procedures are familiar to them and convenient. As you will see, MRC does not need to create such distinctions; it leaves data as collected for purposes of analysis. As a result, the MRC analysis will almost always be more powerful for nonexperimental research.

A second issue relates to the use of the terms independent variable and dependent variable. In nonexperimental research, the use of the terms is arbitrary and at times incorrect. It is arbitrary in that the concern is often for the relationship between two variables and not the influence of one (the independent variable) on the other (the dependent variable).

In summary, we have stressed that we can have two types of designs (experimental and nonexperimental), and, as we already know, two types of analyses (ANOVA and MRC). While we are clear as to when the MRC or ANOVA strategy

---

[1] A test of this new hypothesis would be undertaken in another experiment in which both environment and maturity of students would be examined for their influence on learning.

is appropriate for experimental or nonexperimental designs, the merits of which design is better can be argued endlessly when both designs are feasible. In reality, however, for some questions there is no alternative to nonexperimental research. The question then becomes how best to analyze the data obtained in a nonexperimental research project. This chapter, and the next one, are devoted to nonexperimental research. In some respects, the following discussions are more concerned with issues of design than analysis, since we will focus on strategies for collecting and analyzing data; the analyses of the data collected in nonexperimental situations are the same as the analyses we have already developed in this book.

20.3   USING MRC TO EXPLAIN BEHAVIOR

Though there are limitations on drawing inferences regarding cause and effect from nonexperimental designs, they are useful for fulfilling other purposes of research mentioned in Chap. 1. In particular, nonexperimental research allows us (1) to increase our understanding of relationships among variables (to fulfill the *explanatory purpose*), (2) to predict a criterion outcome based on predictor information (to fulfill the *predictive purpose*), and (3) to test the contribution made by variables in a theoretical model that is being proposed to explain a phenomenon or behavior (to perform *model testing*). In this section and the next two, we will provide examples of nonexperimental research and the analytical strategies necessary to accomplish the explanatory, predictive, and model-testing purposes of research. We will begin with the explanatory purpose.

In the behavioral sciences, we are often interested in examining the relationship between variables in order to increase our understanding of a particular variable or phenomenon. For example, what personality style distinguishes those who become politicians from those who become members of the clergy? What background and personal characteristics (e.g., age, education level, personal styles, and so on) are associated with those who have been convicted of child abuse? What type of person completes college in 4 years, and what type starts college but never finishes? How do the interests of preschoolers differ from those of adolescents?

In these questions, we see that the main variables of interest are, respectively, occupational choice (politician versus clergy), characteristics of child abusers, characteristics of people who complete college, and developmental differences between age groups. To obtain an understanding of such phenomena, we hypothesize that a set of information (the X variables) might be related to the variable of interest (the Y variable) and then, via analysis, determine the degree to which this set of information explains the variance in the main variable of interest. The outcome of this analysis contributes to an understanding of the behavioral phenomenon. Though we may want to make cause-and-effect statements, most often the best we can do in these situations is to make statements of association.

The Simultaneous Analysis

Let us take a specific example. Suppose we are interested in studying variables that might be related to computer programming proficiency; that is, what are the characteristics that distinguish good programmers from poor? Suppose we hypothesize that computer programming proficiency is related primarily to two variables, logic and personal style. To conduct the research, we might go into an office that employs a large number of computer programmers and administer three tests. Our first test is a set of 10 problems that require programming solutions. Each problem is scored as correctly or incorrectly programmed; the individual scores range from 0 to 10. This score represents programming proficiency, the main variable (concept) of interest, and is labeled Y. Second, to measure logic ability, we administer a test with 20 problems that reflects the subject's ability to analyze problems critically; individual scores can range from 0 to 20. This variable is designated X_1. Finally, we use a personality instrument of 30 items that measures the subject's style of approaching problems; individual scores can range from 0 to 30 and are interpreted as an indication of one's compulsiveness and attention to detail. This variable is designated X_2. Suppose we administer these three instruments to 20 programmers and obtain the data shown in Table 20-1.

Our basic question is, What is the relationship between logic ability (X_1) and personal style (X_2), on the one hand, and computer proficiency (Y), on the other? To answer this question, we undertake an MRC analysis referred to as a **simultaneous analysis**. By *simultaneous,* we mean that we are interested in the *combined* influence or relationship of the two variables X_1 and X_2 on the major variable of interest, Y. We are *not* interested, *at this point*, in questions of whether X_1 or X_2 is related by itself to Y. However, for illustrative purposes, we will use the simple relationships between the separate X variables and Y to determine the overall R^2 involving Y and the two X variables, that is, $R^2_{Y.1,2}$.

To answer the question, we calculate the correlation coefficients for X_1 and Y, X_2 and Y, and X_1 and X_2 for the data in Table 20-1 (the r's appear at the bottom of the table) and then we apply an equation based on Eq. (10-2).[2] We

---

[2] A computer will generally be required with more than two X variables.

Table 20-1
Data on Programming Proficiency, Logic Ability,
and Personal Style

Subject	Y (Proficiency)	X_1 (Logic)	X_2 (Style)
1	4	7	4
2	9	16	12
3	8	17	20
4	10	19	24
5	2	5	9
6	5	10	10
7	1	7	4
8	3	6	12
9	7	14	22
10	8	20	14
11	6	13	15
12	4	12	17
13	8	18	26
14	2	9	8
15	5	7	14
16	7	12	23
17	6	6	16
18	5	10	19
19	2	8	9
20	7	16	21

$$r_{Y1} = .8391 \qquad r_{Y2} = .7428$$
$$r_{12} = .6537$$

obtain the following results:

$$R^2_{Y.1,2} = \frac{r^2_{Y1} + r^2_{Y2} - 2r_{Y1}r_{Y2}r_{12}}{1 - r^2_{12}} \qquad (20\text{-}1)$$

$$= \frac{(.8391)^2 + (.7428)^2 - (2)(.8391)(.7428)(.6537)}{1 - (.6537)^2}$$

$$= \frac{.7041 + .5518 - .8149}{1 - .4273} = \frac{.4410}{.5727} = .7700$$

We interpret the obtained R^2 of .7700 just as we have been interpreting the R^2's, in the preceding chapters. That is, approximately 77 percent of the variability in computer programming proficiency is explainable by the *set* of information collected—logic and personal style characteristics.

The next question is whether the relationship is statistically significant. The specific question is whether the R^2 for the *set* of two X variables, or the omnibus R^2, is significant. To answer this question, we use an equation based on Eq. (10-8):

$$F = \frac{R^2_{Y.1,2}/k}{(1 - R^2_{Y.1,2})/(N - k - 1)} \tag{20-2}$$

where N is the number of subjects in the study and k is the number of predictor variables in the explanatory set. In Chap. 10, k represented the number of vectors needed to represent the different levels of an independent variable; the number of vectors required to code the independent variable is 1 less than the number of levels. In the present case, k refers to the number of X variables in the set. This really is not a conceptual or analytical difference, however, since both X_1 and X_2 are continuous variables and require no special coding; the values for each variable are, in essence, the codes. As in Chap. 10, k and $N - k - 1$ represent the degrees of freedom for the treatment and error terms, respectively.

Application of Eq. (20-2) yields the following:

$$F = \frac{.7700/2}{(1 - .7700)/(20 - 2 - 1)} = \frac{.3850}{.2300/17} = \frac{.3850}{.0135} = 28.52$$

The above F ratio with $df_{num.} = 2$ and $df_{denom.} = 17$ is significant ($p < .01$).

The simultaneous analysis of the variables in a set for explanatory purposes does not typically examine the individual contributions of the components within the set. However, as should be obvious from Eq. (20-1), the components r^2_{Y1} and r^2_{Y2} are available for examination and interpretation. The r^2_{Y1} ($= .7041$) indicates that *without* consideration of information on personal style or knowledge of any other information, logic ability explains 70 percent of the variability in computer programming proficiency. Likewise, the r^2_{Y2} ($= .5518$) indicates that 55 percent of the variability in computer programming proficiency is related to variability in personal style; like the other correlation coefficient this result and interpretation ignore any other information about the subjects.

The first thing to note about this analysis is that the sum $r^2_{Y1} + r^2_{Y2}$ does *not* equal $R^2_{Y.1,2}$. This is a common result in nonexperimental research and occurs because of an intercorrelation between the various X variables. In the present example, the correlation between logic and personal style, $r_{12} = .6537$, indicates that those who have high scores on the logic test also tend to have high scores on the personal style test. Thus, there is considerable redundancy or overlap for this set of variables. Since we are interested in the *set* as a whole and its contribution in explaining variability in computer programming proficiency, we need to be certain

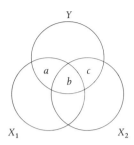

Figure 20-1   Venn diagram to illustrate multiple correlation.

that the obtained result $R^2_{Y.1,2}$ does not give us an estimate that is overly influenced by the intercorrelation between X_1 and X_2.

As in Chap. 10, we will use Venn diagrams to illustrate the way in which the statistics operate. The Venn diagram in Fig. 20-1 illustrates the interplay between the variables. As you can see, r^2_{Y1} is represented by the area labeled $a + b$, and r^2_{Y2} is represented by the area labeled $b + c$. If we add r^2_{Y1} and r^2_{Y2}, we obtain

$$(a + b) + (b + c) = a + c + 2b$$

However, as the diagram shows, $R^2_{Y.1,2}$ is $a + b + c$. Thus, the sum of the individual components has an "extra" b. This "extra" is subtracted out in Eq. (20-1), and thus $R^2_{Y.1,2}$ gives us an estimate of the amount of variance explained by the whole set (X_1 and X_2) that does not include redundant information.[3]

The logic of the above extends to situations in which there are more than two X variables. For example, if we had four X variables, the determination of $R^2_{Y.1,2,3,4}$ would be based on the squared correlation coefficients r^2_{Y1}, r^2_{Y2}, r^2_{Y3}, and r^2_{Y4} as well as the possible intercorrelation coefficients r_{12}, r_{13}, r_{14}, r_{23}, r_{24}, and r_{34}. If any of the intercorrelation coefficients are different from 0.00, then the squared zero-order correlation coefficients involving Y and the four X variables are not directly additive; that is,

$$R^2_{Y.1,2,3,4} \neq r^2_{Y1} + r^2_{Y2} + r^2_{Y3} + r^2_{Y4}$$

There is no simple, single formula to compute the overall R^2 when there are more than two X variables; the results, however, can be obtained by using a multiple correlation computer program.

You should note that we have not made cause-and-effect statements in discussing this example. The *design* is one in which we collected information from

---

[3] If there were no correlation between X_1 and X_2, then $R^2_{Y.1,2}$ would be obtained by adding r^2_{Y1} and r^2_{Y2} as specified in Eq. (10-3). This is analogous to adding components in ANOVA where the variables are independent.

subjects at a single point in time, and so it does not permit us to conclude that personal style or logic ability *causes* someone to become proficient in computer programming. Even if the data were collected over time, with one variable measured before the other, all that we could state is that personal style and logic ability are, together, related or associated with computer proficiency and that together they explain about 77 percent of its variability.

The example in this section involved two variables that are both quantitative and continuous. There is nothing, however, to prevent us from using qualitative or categorical variables, alone or in conjunction with quantitative variables in the same analysis. For example, suppose we had hypothesized that in addition to logic and personal style, a subject's major field of study in college was also relevant in explaining computer proficiency. If we categorize each subject according to whether he or she was a physical science major, a social science major, or a humanities major, we are essentially describing "major" as a variable with three levels. The manner in which we use this additional information is identical to the way in which we used "treatment" information in experimental designs. In essence, we need to code subjects for "major" and include the coded information in the MRC analysis. Our choice of coding is, as in experimental design, from among contrast, effect, and dummy coding, although in experimental designs we stressed contrast coding because of our interest in representing specific comparisons between selected groups or conditions. In the present situation, any coding will accomplish our goal of representing this new information in the analysis. Most typically, researchers use *dummy coding*, since it is simple to create and involves no negative numbers. To include "major" as a variable in this analysis, we need two vectors, labeled X_3 and X_4. A coding matrix such as the following would be used:

	X_3	X_4
Physical science	1	0
Social science	0	1
Humanities	0	0

Table 20-2 shows the new coding as well as scores on X_1 and X_2 for the 20 subjects. Subjects in the physical science major are coded 1 and 0, subjects in the social science major are coded 0 and 1, and subjects in the humanities are coded 0 and 0. In nonexperimental research, the only constraint for coding is that subjects in the same group have the same codes and that the codes be different from group to group; there are no constraints such as those in experimental designs, where we require the sum of the values in the vector to equal zero.

Table 20-2
Data on Programming Proficiency, Logic Ability,
Personal Style, and College Major

Subject	Y (Proficiency)	X_1 (Logic)	X_2 (Style)	Major X_3	X_4
1	4	7	4	1	0
2	9	16	12	0	1
3	8	17	20	1	0
4	10	19	24	0	0
5	2	5	9	0	1
6	5	10	10	0	1
7	1	7	4	1	0
8	3	6	12	0	0
9	7	14	22	0	1
10	8	20	14	1	0
11	6	13	15	0	1
12	4	12	17	0	0
13	8	18	26	0	1
14	2	9	8	0	0
15	5	7	14	1	0
16	7	12	23	0	1
17	6	6	16	0	1
18	5	10	19	1	0
19	2	8	9	0	0
20	7	16	21	0	0

If you examine Table 20-2 carefully, you will note that there are not equal numbers of subjects in all majors. Rather, there are six in the physical sciences, eight in the social sciences, and six in the humanities. We have intentionally chosen unequal sample sizes, since, in the real world, there would not be equal numbers in all majors. To "force" equal numbers would distort the results of the analysis. Furthermore, having unequal numbers gives us the opportunity to demonstrate that calculations of correlations do not depend on the number of subjects at a particular level of the variable. This is one of the ways in which MRC is more flexible than ANOVA—the analysis is easily performed regardless of whether there are equal or unequal numbers of subjects per condition or level. As you will see in Chap. 24, when there are unequal numbers of subjects per condition, the ANOVA calculations needed to arrive at an F ratio are modified from those used in the preceding chapters.

To return to our example and analyze the data in Table 20-2, we again conduct a simultaneous analysis, this time with four X's and one Y variable. Calculations performed on a computer yield an $R^2_{Y.1,2,3,4}$ of .8215. To test for the significance of this entire *set* of information, we use Eq. (20-2) and obtain the following result:

$$F = \frac{R^2_{Y.1,2,3,4}/k}{(1 - R^2_{Y.1,2,3,4})/(N - k - 1)}$$

$$= \frac{.8215/4}{(1 - .8215)/(20 - 4 - 1)} = \frac{.2054}{.1785/15} = \frac{.2054}{.0119} = 17.26$$

With $df_{num.} = 4$ and $df_{denom.} = 15$, the R^2 of .8215 is significant at the .01 level. This result means that 82 percent of the variance in computer proficiency can be explained by this *new set* of variables—logic, personal style, and college major.

Other Useful Analyses

In the examples we have been using in this section, we have so far concentrated on assessing the amount of variance explained by *all* the information we have on the subjects—the nonexperimental version of the omnibus R^2 we presented in the chapters on the analysis of experiments. At first, our information consisted of scores on logic and personal style; in the second example, it consisted of data for logic, personal style, and college major. Since we were interested in how much variance can be explained by *all* the information available, a *simultaneous* (or omnibus) analysis was appropriate.

Variables Considered Separately.   Of course, there are other questions we can ask. One question we previously mentioned is, What is the contribution of each of the types of information *without* consideration of the other information? By "without consideration" we mean this. Suppose you did not know anything about subjects' personal style and college major. Then, asking how much the variation in logic (X_1) contributes to the explanation of the variability of Y is the same as asking what r^2_{Y1} is. Or suppose you had no information on logic or major. Then, if you wanted to know to what degree personal style explains Y, you would simply look at either r_{Y2} or r^2_{Y2}. These correlation coefficients between Y and each X alone are measures of what are referred to as *zero-order* or *simple correlations*. They reflect the degree to which variability in Y is explained by changes in an X variable without taking into account any information other than values of the X variable; they represent the nonexperimental analogue of main effects in the analysis of experiments.

The point of the above discussion is that the explanatory contribution of a particular quantitative variable, such as personal style, when we *ignore* all other information available or known, may be assessed via simple correlation coefficients (or their squares). If we also have categorical data that are represented by two or more vectors, such as subjects' major field of study, we use a *multiple correlation* coefficient to assess the contribution of this variable. To illustrate with the previous example, the squared multiple correlation coefficient $R^2_{Y.3,4}$ indicates the degree to which college major explains variability in programming proficiency, when we disregard all other information available to us.

Incremental Variance.   We could ask other interesting questions besides how individual X variables influence Y. For example, since we know that there are intercorrelations among variables within the entire set, we also know that the r^2's for individual X variables are not directly additive in yielding $R^2_{Y.1,2,3,4}$. The question often asked is, How much additional or **incremental variance** is explained by one variable or set of variables above and beyond the variance that is explained by another variable or another set? That is, how much *more* does X_2 tell us about Y than X_1 already tells us about Y? A related question is, Do we need *all* the information available to explain the variance in the criterion? Does the addition of college major explain a significant amount of variance beyond what is explained by the logic information alone? You may have noticed, for example, that our original analysis with two variables (logic and style) produced an R^2 of .7700, while the analysis with the addition of the third variable (college major) produced an R^2 of .8215. This relatively small gain (.8215 − .7700 = .0515) may result because (1) "major" does not correlate with programming proficiency (Y) or (2) major does highly correlate with either logic or personal style (or, more likely, both) and thus provides no new information. The *significance* of any gain in explanation obtained by adding a variable (or variables) will be discussed in Sec. 20.4.[4]

Yet another useful question is, Which variable is most "important" in explaining the criterion? All these questions of "importance" and "increment" can be analyzed, but by strategies other than simultaneous analysis. These other, interesting analyses will be presented in later sections of this chapter as well as in Chap. 21, but we raise the questions here for two reasons. First, looking at the variance that can be explained by *all* the information or by *parts* or *sets* of information illustrates the richness of research. Looking at the contribution of one or more variables in a set of information in the nonexperimental situation is analogous to conducting single-*df* comparisons in experimental conditions. Second, these questions illustrate that more than one analytical strategy can be used to analyze data and that we select a strategy on the basis of the questions of interest, rather than have the chosen strategy influence the questions we ask.

---

[4] For your information, an F test evaluating this increment is not significant. The formula for this F is given by Eq. (20-4).

Let us elaborate on the second point above. We conduct simultaneous analyses on sets of variables that we have determined—through our understanding of the phenomenon of interest and through our knowledge of the literature—to be potential contributors to the explanation of the dependent measures. Thus, we are not suggesting the "mindless" addition of variables to sets of data in order to determine how high we can boost the ultimate R^2. Our point is that there are usually reasons to include variables in most nonexperimental designs. For simultaneous analysis, however, we have no particular reason for focusing on one set or variable, but we are interested rather in a total set's explanatory power.

20.4   USING MRC TO PREDICT BEHAVIOR

In fields such as educational, industrial, clinical, and personality psychology, we often wish to predict people's behavior on the basis of a set of information we have on them. For reasons of parsimony, efficiency, and economy, we often look for a subset of the total available information that by itself can explain and predict future performance or behavior to a useful degree. Though we may have a "theory" about what is important in the available data set, the question we ask is, Given that there are (for example) five different kinds of information (or data on five variables) on the individuals, how much of that information will we need to explain a significant and sufficient amount of the variability in future performance or behavior? Are all five variables necessary? Would a subset that included four variables predict just as well as the complete set of five variables? Another way of framing the question is, Suppose we have available five variables; if we take into account the "best" variable of the five (i.e., the one with the highest r_{YX}), will prediction improve or increase as we add into our prediction system a second and then a third and then a fourth variable, and so forth? In essense, does the inclusion of more and, perhaps, different information yield a significant increment or change in the amount of Y variance that can be explained? To answer such questions, we can use a **forward stepwise** analytical MRC strategy. This stepwise strategy differs from simultaneous MRC in that the latter is concerned with the amount of variance explained by *all* the available information while the former is concerned with finding an efficient *subset* to predict a criterion.

The Stepwise Strategy

A stepwise strategy is a rather atheoretical, mechanical process that is best performed by a computer program. The atheoretical part of the strategy is the determination of which of the variables should be included in the final subset. There may be a theory when the research program is developed and the variables to be considered for analysis are determined and selected for assessment, but there is little, if any, theory in determining which variables to enter and in what order. The typical computer programs are designed so that the user can evaluate the amount of incremental variance explained as each variable enters into the analysis. Most programs are set up to enable the user to identify the smallest subset needed to yield the final R^2 that explains a significant and large amount of the variance. That is, the goal of the analysis is to add variables to the subset until the addition of a variable no longer results in a significant increment in explanatory power.

An Example.   To illustrate the use of the forward stepwise strategy, we will draw on an example from personnel psychology. Suppose we worked in a company that was interested in developing a selection system for hiring clerical staff. We hypothesize, on the basis of our study of the job and our knowledge of the literature, that the following kinds of information might be predictive of job performance in a clerical position: (1) clerical aptitude, (2) spelling ability, (3) interest in clerical tasks, and (4) interpersonal skills. Each of these knowledges, skills, and abilities is measured by a standardized pencil-and-paper instrument (the specific tests are irrelevant for the purpose of this illustration); in personnel psychology, these variables are referred to as *predictors*.

The validation approach we adopt will be that of **predictive validation.**[5] In general, a predictive validation approach is one in which a test or set of tests is administered to a group of candidates for employment; all candidates are hired, regardless of their scores on the predictors (tests), and then actual job performance is measured a certain amount of time after hire (e.g., 90 days later). The goal of this research is to find a sizable and significant correlation between the predictor scores (one or more of the predictors) and the actual performance on the job (Y) assessed 90 days after hire.

To implement the stepwise analysis for the predictive validation approach, we might recruit 30 applicants to take the test battery (all 4 predictors), hire all 30 applicants without regard to their test scores, place them on the job, and then obtain supervisory ratings of their performance 90 days after placement. For our example, we will assume the following:

1. Supervisory ratings (Y) are based on a 1 to 7 scale, where 1 reflects "very poor" job performance and 7 reflects "excellent" job performance.

---

[5] See Ghiselli et al. (1981, pp. 267–271) for a detailed discussion of this strategy as well as alternative strategies.

2. Scores on each of the four tests can range from 0 to 25, where 0 indicates little knowledge, skill, or ability and 25 indicates a great deal of knowledge, skill, or ability. Table 20-3 shows the obtained ratings and scores on the 4 tests for each of the 30 participants in this study.

The statistical analysis of the predictive validation approach is that of *forward stepwise MRC*. As we indicated, the computer programs typically used for stepwise

Table 20-3
Data on Job Rating, Clerical Aptitude, Spelling, Interest, and Interpersonal Skills

Subject	Y (Job Rating)	X_1 (Aptitude)	X_2 (Spelling)	X_3 (Interest)	X_4 (Interpersonal)
1	3	7	10	6	4
2	7	22	22	19	17
3	4	12	10	4	7
4	2	9	8	8	9
5	1	4	7	4	3
6	5	10	17	16	18
7	6	14	22	22	24
8	6	13	25	21	22
9	7	19	19	24	18
10	4	14	13	11	14
11	1	3	7	8	6
12	3	3	12	12	11
13	2	8	13	14	10
14	5	15	19	22	19
15	6	18	21	20	24
16	6	17	19	19	12
17	7	22	25	18	20
18	5	20	22	19	24
19	2	6	9	7	2
20	3	6	7	13	9
21	1	4	5	5	5
22	2	5	7	11	9
23	3	12	14	18	16
24	7	15	19	16	15
25	4	8	14	10	15
26	3	6	11	12	10
27	2	3	9	10	8
28	4	19	12	13	18
29	3	7	6	10	14
30	5	20	15	18	12

MRC identify the smallest set of variables that are needed to maximize the amount of variance explained (i.e., yields the highest correlation with Y). The program first identifies the single best predictor (i.e., the one with the highest simple correlation with Y) and continues to add variables, one at a time, such that the change (increase) in R^2 is maximized and significant. It is in searching for the second variable, third variable, and so on, that the strategy is atheoretical and mechanical; the amount of gain in R^2 and not a theoretical position determines inclusion into the subset. In essence, the program seeks the next predictor to add, largely on the basis of trial and error. Usually, the researcher instructs the program to continue to add variables until the increment in explained variance is no longer significant at the .05 level. Thus, in the present case, such an analysis could indicate that one, two, three, or four tests are needed to predict Y, or even that none of the predictors that we hypothesized to be predictive of clerical performance does in fact relate to the supervisory ratings (i.e., none of the single zero-order correlations is significant). The point is that the statistical analyses will determine which of the four, if any or if all, are needed.

The Results.   Application of a forward stepwise regression program to the data in Table 20-3 yields the output presented in Table 20-4. You should note two aspects of this summary of the stepwise analysis. First, while the correlation in the first row is a zero-order correlation (r^2_{Y2}) involving Y and a single X variable (X_2), we have expressed it as a multiple correlation ($R^2_{Y.2}$) in order to streamline the presentation. Second, the subscripts indicating the X variables are attached to the R^2's in the order in which the variables are selected; for example, by the time the program completes the second step, it has chosen variable X_2 and then variable X_1, and so the subscripts are not the usual 1-2 order. By adopting this new notation, we can illustrate here that the computer program has selected X_2 as the best single predictor (and has thus entered it first into the analysis) and that the addition of X_1 on the second step has resulted in more of an increase in explained variance than would adding either of the remaining variables, X_3 or X_4.

Table 20-4
Summary of the Forward Stepwise MRC

Step	X Variable Entered	R^2	Increment
1	2	$R^2_{Y.2} = .8075$	—
2	1	$R^2_{Y.2,1} = .8588$	.0513
3	3	$R^2_{Y.2,1,3} = .8601$	.0013
4	4	$R^2_{Y.2,1,3,4} = .8603$	.0002

The results of the forward stepwise analysis indicate that X_2 is the best predictor of performance (it has the highest zero-order correlation), and therefore it is entered into the analysis first. In step 2, X_1 is identified by the analysis as creating the largest gain in R^2 (a gain of .0513). That is, the computer determines that the R^2 for two predictors (X_2 and one other) is highest when X_1 is included as opposed to when X_3 or X_4 is included. The next largest gain in R^2 (for three predictors) is when X_3 is added into the system (a gain of .0013). The final step shows the gain provided by X_4 and the R^2 for the full test battery (a gain of .0002).

The first question to be asked of the results is whether the first squared correlation coefficient, $R^2_{Y.2}$ (or r^2_{Y2}, since the quantity represents a zero-order correlation), is significant. If the answer is yes, then we know that at least one predictor can be used, and we move on to test for the significance of the gains in R^2 that are obtained by adding variables (information) to the calculations. If the answer is no, then the analysis is terminated, since the "best" predictor is not significantly related to the dependent variable. Assuming that the answer to the first question is yes, the next question to be asked in the analysis is which of the increments is statistically significant. That is, with the addition of X_1 (step 2) to the analysis, is the increment of .0513 significant? If so, the next question is whether the increment resulting from the addition of X_3 (step 3), or .0013, is also significant. The final question is whether the increment of .0002 that results from inclusion of X_4 (step 4) is significant.

Statistical Evaluation of the Increments

To test for the significance of the first predictor entered into the analysis, we use the logic we presented for tests of significance with data from experimental designs. The error term we recommend is one that includes *all* the X variables incorporated into the design, not just those extracted in the stepwise analysis. Thus, the error term is based on $R^2_{Y.max.}$, where *max.* refers to *all* the X variables in the design.

For the test for significance of the first predictor, then, we recommend Eq. (10-8), which we adapt as follows:

$$F = \frac{R^2_{Y.X_i}/k_i}{(1 - R^2_{Y.max.})/(N - k - 1)} \tag{20-3}$$

where X_i = the variable selected in the first step in the stepwise analysis

$\qquad k_i$ = the number of vectors associated with the X variable selected

$R^2_{Y.max.}$ = the squared multiple correlation coefficient between Y and all X variables included in the analysis

$\qquad k$ = the number of vectors represented in $R^2_{Y.max.}$

For the tests of the *increments*, we use the following equation:

$$F = \frac{(R^2_{Y.larger\ set\ (l)} - R^2_{Y.smaller\ set\ (s)})/(k_l - k_s)}{(1 - R^2_{Y.max.})/(N - k - 1)} \tag{20-4}$$

where $R^2_{Y.larger\ set}$ = the R^2 for the larger set of X variables (abbreviated $R^2_{Y.X_l}$)

$R^2_{Y.smaller\ set}$ = the R^2 for the smaller set of X variables (abbreviated $R^2_{Y.X_s}$)

$\qquad k_l$ = the number of vectors in the larger set

$\qquad k_s$ = the number of vectors in the smaller set

$\qquad k$ = the *total* number of vectors contributing to $R^2_{Y.max.}$

A simpler version of Eq. (20-4) is as follows:

$$F = \frac{R^2_{increment}/(k_l - k_s)}{(1 - R^2_{Y.max.})/(N - k - 1)}$$

A key aspect of Eq. (20-3) and Eq. (20-4) is that $R^2_{Y.max.}$, or the R^2 associated with *all* possible predictors, is used to determine the error term, and this error term is used for testing the significance of the increments *at each step*. Other error terms have been proposed, the most common of which are based only on those variables entering the analysis. Some have suggested that if only X_1 and X_2 are significant in a stepwise analysis, for example, the error term should be based on $R^2_{Y.1,2}$ rather than on $R^2_{Y.max.}$. In fact, most computer software programs use this restricted R^2 to calculate the error term. This point is controversial, but we feel that our recommendation is most compatible with the original intent of our predictive validation approach, where a certain number of variables were hypothesized, studied, and introduced into the analysis. This approach is also consistent with our previously stated position that the error term should reflect only *residual* variation; residual variation, in our opinion, should be defined by all variables originally thought to be relevant to the study.

In the present example, the F evaluating the significance of the X variable entered first, X_2, which is specified by Eq. (20-3), produces

$$F = \frac{R^2_{Y.X_2}/k_2}{(1 - R^2_{Y.max.})/(N - k - 1)}$$

$$= \frac{.8075/1}{(1 - .8603)/(30 - 4 - 1)} = \frac{.8075}{.1397/25} = \frac{.8075}{.0056} = 144.20$$

which, with $df_{num.} = 1$ and $df_{denom.} = 25$, is significant. Evaluation of the remaining steps requires the use of Eq. (20-4). For the increment associated with step 2, we find

$$F = \frac{(R^2_{Y.X_l} - R^2_{Y.X_s})/(k_l - k_s)}{(1 - R^2_{Y.max.})/(N - k - 1)}$$

$$= \frac{(.8588 - .8075)/(2 - 1)}{(1 - .8603)/(30 - 4 - 1)} = \frac{.0513/1}{.1397/25} = \frac{.0513}{.0056} = 9.16$$

which, with $df_{num.} = 1$ and $df_{denom.} = 25$, is significant. The increments associated with the other two steps are not significant. That is,

$$F = \frac{(.8601 - .8588)/(3 - 2)}{(1 - .8603)/(30 - 4 - 1)} = \frac{.0013/1}{.1397/25} = \frac{.0013}{.0056} = .23$$

and

$$F = \frac{.8603 - .8601)/(4 - 3)}{(1 - .8603)/(30 - 4 - 1)} = \frac{.0002/1}{.1397/25} = \frac{.0002}{.0056} = .04$$

Thus, we conclude that since step 2 is a significant increment and the other two steps yield nonsignificant increments, then the test battery should be composed of only X_1 and X_2, or clerical aptitude and spelling ability.

In summary, all that is needed to explain performance (Y) is the results of the X_2 (spelling ability) and X_1 (clerical aptitude) tests; this combination explains about 86 percent of the performance variance ($R^2_{Y.2,1} = .8588$). Note that if we were interested in how much Y variance is explained by *all* the available information, we would concentrate on a *simultaneous analysis*, which, of course, we performed in order to obtain the error term. The $R^2_{Y.2,1,3,4}$ (equal also to $R^2_{Y.max.}$) of .8603, which produces an F of 38.41 as found in the following:

$$F = \frac{R^2_{Y.max.}/k}{(1 - R^2_{Y.max.})/(N - k - 1)}$$

$$= \frac{.8603/4}{(1 - .8603)/(30 - 4 - 1)} = \frac{.2151}{.1397/25} = \frac{.2151}{.0056} = 38.41$$

With $df_{num.} = 4$ and $df_{denom.} = 25$, the F is significant. On the other hand, the stepwise results indicate that all that is needed to explain approximately the same percentage of the variance is predictors X_1 and X_2. Thus, there is no need for more than X_1 and X_2 to predict future performance. In practice, then, the regression equation associated with X_1 and X_2 would be calculated and used to predict the potential performance of new applicants.

The regression equation for the present data set is

$$Y' = -.0339 + .1164X_1 + .1917X_2$$

To use this equation, we simply administer the two tests to a *new* applicant and enter into the equation that applicant's test score values. For example, if an applicant scored 14 and 10 on X_1 and X_2, respectively, use of the equation would yield the following:

$$Y' = -.0339 + (.1164)(14) + (.1917)(10)$$
$$= -.0339 + 1.6296 + 1.9170 = 3.5127$$

The applicant's predicted performance level would be 3.51. (This value is slightly below the midpoint, 4.0, of the performance scale. The issues to be considered in deciding whether to hire the applicant are beyond the scope of the present book; see Ghiselli et al., 1981, for a discussion of such topics as setting cutoffs, cross-validation, test fairness, and utility, all of which affect the final decision to implement the test battery and use it for decisions to hire or not.)

The Intercorrelation Matrix

Some insights into how the stepwise strategy works can be found by examining the **intercorrelation matrix** associated with the data. An intercorrelation matrix is a convenient way of presenting a set of zero-order correlations. In its simplest form, a full intercorrelation matrix is a square matrix that shows the correlation between each variable and each other variable under consideration. Down the left side of the matrix we list all the variables; we also list all the variables at the top of the matrix. The following shows the layout of a study in which there are four variables:

	X_1	X_2	X_3	X_4
X_1		r_{12}	r_{13}	r_{14}
X_2	r_{21}		r_{23}	r_{24}
X_3	r_{31}	r_{32}		r_{34}
X_4	r_{41}	r_{42}	r_{43}	

Each value in the matrix is the correlation between a row variable and a column variable. For example, the first row shows the correlations between X_1 and X_2, X_3,

Table 20-5
Intercorrelation Matrix

	X_1	X_2	X_3	X_4
Performance (Y)	.8522	.8986	.7996	.7737
Clerical Aptitude (X_1)		.7957	.7206	.7213
Spelling Ability (X_2)			.8507	.8368
Interests (X_3)				.8426
Interpersonal Skills (X_4)				

and X_4, respectively. There are two points to note about such a matrix: (1) the diagonal is blank, since the values it would contain represent the correlations between the variable and itself; and (2) the matrix is symmetrical in that what is *above* the diagonal mirrors the results found *below* the diagonal. This occurs because the correlation between, for example, X_3 (row 3) and X_4 (column 4) is the same as the correlation between X_4 (row 4) and X_3 (column 3); that is, $r_{34} = r_{43}$. Thus, ordinarily, we show only the upper half of the matrix.[6]

Let's return to our specific example, with four tests and a performance variable, and examine Table 20-5, where the simple correlation coefficients are presented. First, note that the variable having the highest correlation with Y is X_2 (i.e., $r_{Y2} = .8986$); this was the first variable entered into the analysis. Approximately 81 percent ($r_{Y2}^2 = .8986^2 = .8075$) of variability in Y can be explained by X_2. Second, given the high intercorrelations among the remaining variables (X_1, X_3, and X_4), which range from .7206 to .8426, it is not surprising that only one additional variable, X_1, which was entered in the second step, was determined to yield a significant increment. The relatively high intercorrelations among the remaining predictors are the very reason why only one additional variable was added to the stepwise analysis. The greater this *redundancy* among these X variables, the less likely that any of these variables will add much predictive power to the analysis. Consequently, not all the X variables are needed. In the present case, statistical analysis indicates that only X_1 is needed beyond X_2.

We recommend that you always obtain a correlation matrix for the data used in a predictive MRC strategy or, for that matter, any MRC strategy. Frequently, a matrix helps explain the MRC results. (In addition, a table of means and variances

---

[6] Some researchers prefer to fill in all the cells, while others prefer to fill in the redundant cells of the matrix with additional information. For example, one could list the correlation coefficients in the upper half and the squared correlation coefficients in the lower half.

for each variable should be calculated. These data, too, can shed light on the obtained MRC results.)

Comment

As indicated, the stepwise strategy is a rather mechanical, atheoretical process. It is atheoretical in the sense that there is no hypothesis regarding what is most important or should be entered first. The results rely on simple correlations and intercorrelations for the specific sample. Slight changes in these correlations could influence the final results so that different variables are entered in the analysis at specific steps. For example, slight changes in intercorrelations could mean that a variable entered on step 2 in the present data set might enter on step 3 or not at all. Consequently, the results should be considered somewhat tenuous and should be viewed cautiously.

For more confidence in the results, the analysis should be based on a relatively large sample size and few X variables. If the results are based on the reverse, that is, relatively few subjects and many X variables, the stability of the values in the prediction equation becomes a problem. One suggestion is to have about 40 subjects for each X variable.[7] Also, it is important to corroborate the results with another sample from the same population, before actually implementing the results and using the regression equation to make future selection decisions. The corroboration process, known as **cross-validation**, is discussed in Ghiselli et al. (1981). In brief, cross-validation determines whether the results generated in one sample are applicable to a second sample from the same population.

There are three aspects of MRC used for predictive purposes that the researcher should be aware of. First, we stressed forward stepwise analysis, which is concerned with the *addition* of variables to the analysis. An alternative procedure is **backward stepwise MRC**, in which all variables are entered on the *first step* and then variables are deleted one at a time to determine the *loss* in R^2 when a given X variable is removed. The variables are eliminated in reverse order, the weakest predictor being removed first, the next weakest second, and so on. The analysis proceeds until the elimination of a variable results in a *significant decrement* in R^2. If there is no significant loss in R^2 when a variable is removed, then the variable is not needed; a significant loss means the variable is useful.

---

[7] This general recommendation does not apply to the analysis of experimental data where the factors are orthogonal. Determination of sample size in an experiment depends largely on concerns for *power*. Ideally, researchers should use a sample size that will offer an acceptable level of statistical power. The number will be affected by the nature of the design, the variability of subjects, and the size of the expected treatment effects.

Use of backward selection can result in our retaining different sets of predictors from those we identify by forward stepwise selection. This is because the logic for the two procedures is different. Forward stepwise selection starts with the premise that we need to build on the best predictor and we can do so quickly by finding the variable that yields the greatest gain. In backward selection, on the other hand, we start with the full set and seek to eliminate at the outset the variable with the smallest contribution to R^2. Our preference is to use forward stepwise selection, since it attempts to build on the explained variance as opposed to reducing the amount of explained variance.

The second point is that our use of $R^2_{Y.max.}$ to determine the error term for assessing the significance of the increment obtained at each step differs from the way in which the error term is calculated by many computer programs for MRC. In general, these programs base the error term on only those X variables currently included in the R^2. To illustrate with our example, the computer's error term—the denominator in Eq. $(11-9)$—to evaluate the first X variable, X_2, would be

$$\frac{1 - R^2_{Y.2}}{N - k - 1} = \frac{1 - .8074}{30 - 1 - 1} = \frac{.1926}{28} = .0069$$

The error term for evaluating the increment obtained when the second variable (X_1) is added would be

$$\frac{1 - R^2_{Y.2,1}}{N - k - 1} = \frac{1 - .8588}{30 - 2 - 1} = \frac{.1412}{27} = .0052$$

Similarly, the error terms for the next two steps, in which X_3 is added and then X_4, are

$$\frac{1 - R^2_{Y.2,1,3}}{N - k - 1} = \frac{1 - .8601}{30 - 3 - 1} = \frac{.1399}{26} = .0054$$

and

$$\frac{1 - R^2_{Y.2,1,3,4}}{N - k - 1} = \frac{1 - .8603}{30 - 4 - 1} = \frac{.1397}{25} = .0056$$

respectively. Our main objection to this approach is that a residual error term may contain significant variability that has not yet been considered because it has not yet entered the analysis. The error term for step 1, for example, might include the significant increment associated with X_1, X_3, or X_4 in addition to actual residual variation.

We stated previously our reasons for using $R^2_{Y.max.}$ to calculate residual variation—that is, why we prefer to make use of all the information available for the analysis. The use of $R^2_{Y.max.}$ to estimate residual variation does not rely on statistical outcomes, such as the process outlined above, or depend on the whims of either the data or the researcher! If you accept our argument, you will need to calculate new *F* ratios for the tests for increments provided by computer printouts; but if you follow Eq. (20-4), the process is simple and straightforward.

Third, in the stepwise analysis illustrated, though only two variables were determined to be needed, the illustration showed all four steps. Most computer printouts will show only the two steps and then indicate that no further gain can be accomplished by the addition of other variables.

20.5 USING MRC TO TEST MODELS

Regression analyses of nonexperimental data can provide insights into and support for theories and, in particular, for **causal models**. That is, MRC can be used to study patterns of correlations among variables and to suggest causal linkages among the variables. Furthermore, if a hypothesis based on your theory proposes that a *particular X* variable has a certain influence on the dependent variable, you can use MRC to test that hypothesis, since MRC will isolate the effect of that variable from the effects of other variables. You will find MRC useful in this way whether the effect of the particular *X* variable on *Y* is (according to your theory) *direct* or *indirect* (i.e., mediated or transmitted by another variable).

Using MRC to test causal models is a complex process.[8] A complete presentation of the issues involved and the approaches for causal model testing are beyond the scope of this book. There are a number of elaborate approaches in statistical analysis that are available for those who wish to study causal models; interested students should consult books on **causal analysis** and **path analysis** (e.g., Asher, 1976; Blalock, 1964; Kenny, 1979), **confirmatory factor analysis**, and **LISREL computer programs** (Jöreskog, 1969; Jöreskog & Sorbom, 1984).

Testing Causal-Priority Models

To illustrate the model-testing uses of MRC, we will describe a simple case in which we wish to establish causal priority among a set of *X* variables in their

---

[8] Usually, the particular strategy chosen to test a model depends on certain assumptions that pertain to the potential for reciprocal or two-way causative effects between independent variables in the system, feedback loops from a dependent variable back to an independent variable, the completeness of the hypothesized model, and the degree to which there may be unmeasured common causes.

explanation of Y. We will assume that the X variables represent a complete set—complete in the sense that there are no other variables that might be reasonably considered. In order to test a causal-priority model or theory with MRC, we first need to postulate a temporal sequence of causes. The model hypothesizes that when the variables act in a certain order, they can influence the impact of other variables. Of course, if theory indicates that some variables should be considered first, then we have an a priori or hypothesized order. The analysis we perform is called a **hierarchical analysis**; we use MRC to assess the increment in accountable variance as the causal order is followed.

With a hierarchical strategy, the theoretical model dictates and the *researcher* specifies the order in which variables are entered into the analysis. The researcher looks at each critical step to see if his or her theory of temporal order is useful. The model is an appropriate description if at each step there is a significant increase in explained variance. Typically, if we are testing a causal-priority model, we assume that no variable entering at a later step in the analysis is a *cause* of a variable that has already been entered. In the following example, we will illustrate hierarchical analysis as a strategy to test a particular causal-priority theory; in Chap. 21, we will use hierarchical analysis as a strategy for *controlling* variables.

An Example of a Hierarchical Analysis

Suppose we were interested in studying the factors that lead to the success of graduates of a university's MBA program. Our measure of success is the level of management to which a graduate advances. One way to study a causal sequence is to examine alumni records and obtain names of graduates of the MBA program. In these records, suppose we find information such as gender, scores on an entrance aptitude exam for business school, and date of entry and graduation. We contact the graduates and ask them what level of management they have attained: low, middle, or upper (assuming that each level is reasonably defined). We code the three levels as 1, 2, and 3, respectively, and treat this index of success as a continuous variable. This variable, which is labeled Y, is the outcome in which we are interested. The reason we choose the three kinds of information from the files is that we hypothesize or expect that each will explain a different aspect of behavior that leads to success in business. For example, given the history of corporations, we would expect males to have a greater likelihood of being successful in climbing the corporate ladder. We also expect those with higher scholastic aptitude to advance farther in the organization. Finally, we expect those who took a shorter amount of time to graduate to be in the higher-level positions. Thus, each variable provides an explanation of success, but some of the variables may be intercorrelated. For example, those who took a shorter time to graduate may have had higher aptitude scores. The point is that we have three variables and we want to see if a particular temporal sequencing of the three variables is meaningful in explaining success in a business career.

We begin the process by constructing a particular theoretical model that will specify the causal order of the variables; we then enter the variables into the analysis in the prescribed order. We have the following list of variables:

X_1 = gender

X_2 = aptitude score determined prior to entry into MBA program

X_3 = years to graduate

Y = management level attained

A logical order for entering the variables is X_1 first, X_2 second, and X_3 last. Gender (X_1) can influence aptitude test scores, but aptitude test scores cannot influence gender; entrance aptitude test score (X_2) can influence how long it takes to graduate (X_3), but years to graduate cannot influence entrance scores. Thus, we have a specified order for examining the variables to determine the degree to which each can explain business success (Y). We then proceed with a hierarchical analysis in which we first correlate X_1 with Y; we then derive the squared multiple correlation coefficient between X_1 and X_2 and Y, or $R^2_{Y.1,2}$; and finally we enter all three variables—X_1, X_2, and X_3—to determine how all the information relates to Y. The key to hierarchical analysis is the *increments in explained variance* as we move from step 1 to step 2 and then to step 3.

Suppose the results were as follows:

Step 1: $R^2_{Y.1} = .25$
Step 2: $R^2_{Y.1,2} = .30$
Step 3: $R^2_{Y.1,2,3} = .32$

How would we interpret them? First, we see in step 1 that the squared correlation coefficient between gender and success explains 25 percent of the Y variance. Assume for this correlation that we have coded males as $+1$ and females as -1; the simple correlation coefficient for Y and X_1 is $+.5$. From this information, we would conclude that a large amount of variance can be explained by knowledge of a subject's gender $(.5^2 = .25)$ and that males generally attain a higher level in management (higher "scores" on X_1—the $+1$s for males—are associated with higher scores on Y). Step 2 indicates that information on gender *and* aptitude scores explains 30 percent of the variance. The increment in explained variance $(R^2_{Y.1,2} - R^2_{Y.1})$ reflects the contribution of aptitude scores in explaining variance *after* gender has already been entered and taken into account. This procedure is similar to the stepwise analysis, where we examined the systematic addition of variables to a multiple correlation and asked whether each added variable was needed to significantly improve the prediction. Here, too, we want to know whether the second variable is needed, but the second variable is one *we* have identified as the second variable; in the stepwise procedure, by contrast, the *computer program* identifies the second variable. The increment tells us that after knowing how well gender can explain Y, we can explain an additional 5 percent by knowing the aptitude score. Finally, step 3 shows us how much incremental variance is explained by knowing the years it took the individuals to graduate. In the present example, we gain an additional 2 percent explained variance. You understand, of course, that we would test the significance of each of the two increments with Eq. (20-4), where the error term for each test is based on $R^2_{Y.max.}$ (or $R^2_{Y.1,2,3}$ in this case).

What we have accomplished in the above is a test of the validity of a model specifying a causal ordering of the variables. If each analysis of the increment shows a significant result, we conclude that each variable is important and necessary. If any variable yields an increment that is *not* significant, then we no longer consider that variable a necessary variable in our model.

The hierarchical analysis we have just described yields different information from what we would obtain using different approaches to analyzing the same set of data. Consider the following possible alternatives:

Alternative 1: Suppose we conducted a hierarchical analysis in which we entered the variables in a different order, namely, X_2 (aptitude test score) first, then X_1 (gender), and then X_3 (time to graduation) and obtained the following results:

Step 1: $R^2_{Y.2} = .29$
Step 2: $R^2_{Y.2,1} = .30$
Step 3: $R^2_{Y.2,1,3} = .32$

As you can see, the final step, in which all three X variables are included, produces the same R^2 of .32 as before, but the *increments* from step to step are not all the same. The results now indicate that when we enter X_2 first, we attribute 29 percent of the Y variance to aptitude scores, whereas the previous analysis attributed only 5 percent additional variance to them. Furthermore, since the R^2 in step 2 is .30, the increment of .01 would lead us to conclude that gender (X_1) has either no influence or minimal influence on business success. Other orders of the variables might lead to still different conclusions. The point is that the order we originally considered was specified by a particular theory, while these others were not. The value of a hierarchical analysis, then, depends on how convincingly the theory predicts the causal sequence.

Alternative 2: Suppose we rejected the hierarchical strategy in favor of an analysis of the simple correlations between Y and the separate X variables. Suppose further that we obtained the following squared simple correlation coefficients:

$$r_{Y1}^2 = .25 \qquad r_{Y2}^2 = .29 \qquad r_{Y3}^2 = .31$$

If we interpreted each of the above relations, we would conclude that all the X variables explain business success about equally and that perhaps all three are needed for a full account of the data. However, the question we ask in a hierarchical analysis of the model is whether each of the variables is necessary when considered in its turn in the logical order specified. In essence, we determine by hierarchical analysis whether the data are a good fit of a model specified a priori.

Alternative 3: Suppose we conducted a stepwise analysis. This analysis would allow a computer program to select the order of entry. In the present example, X_3, or years to graduate, would be entered first, since it has the largest squared simple correlation coefficient, $r_{Y3}^2 = .31$; and we would probably conclude that this variable is all that is needed to explain business success. This would result in our drawing incorrect conclusions about the contribution to explaining Y made by the other two X variables.

In this section we have presented a simple but straightforward example of MRC for one type of model testing. It was presented to illustrate that MRC can be used to test models. Again, see some of the more advanced texts we have cited for a more complete and elaborate discussion of the use of MRC for model testing.

20.6 SUMMARY

In most of this book we are focusing on the analysis of experimental designs by ANOVA and MRC, but there are situations in which only nonexperimental designs are appropriate for studying questions of interest. There are times when we turn to nonexperimental designs because experimental designs lack generalizability or external validity, or because they are contrived or too artificial for the question of interest. On the other hand, it may be impossible, impractical, or unethical to study some questions with experimental designs. If any of these circumstances exist, researchers may use quasi-experimental designs, in which they control what data they will collect and when the data will be collected, but they do not control what happens to whom, since there is no random assignment of subjects to conditions. Yet another possible design is correlational research, in which we study the degree to which two or more variables covary in an intact, naturally occurring group of subjects.

In nonexperimental designs, MRC is usually the only appropriate analysis strategy. It allows the researcher to use the data on continuous "independent" variables as they are collected (i.e., without breaking down the range of scores into categories) and to deal with unequal sample sizes without making any adjustment.

We explored the use of MRC in three of the basic areas of research: (1) explanation, (2) prediction, and (3) model testing. For explanatory purposes, we presented a *simultaneous* MRC strategy whereby all the X variables are studied as a *set* for their relationship to Y.

To predict behavior, MRC can be used in the forward *stepwise* strategy, in which the "best" predictor is entered into the analysis first and additional predictors are added only if they yield significant increments to R^2. This strategy is atheoretical and mechanical—the computer does it for you!

For one form of model testing, MRC is used when the variables are entered into the analysis in an order specified in advance and the order is consistent with logic and theory. The researcher specifies the order of entry and uses MRC in a *hierarchical* fashion, checking on each addition to determine whether increments are significant. The difference between a stepwise analysis and a hierarchical one is that in the former, the *computer program* selects the order in which the variables will be considered; the order is based on the simple correlations, and the goal is to maximize R^2 at each step in the analysis. With a hierarchical strategy, the theoretical model dictates the order in which the variables are entered into the analysis.

20.7 EXERCISES

1. Suppose we wanted to study the influence of several variables on a dependent variable, success as a lawyer. Assume that we were able to study lawyers in a large firm (one that employs 100 lawyers) in which the senior partner in the firm is able to rate each lawyer on a scale from 1 to 7, where 1 represents "poor performance" and 7 represents "excellent performance." The predictors are: (1) bar exam scores (X_1), (2) number of cases won in the last year (X_2), and (3) amount of money (in millions of dollars) brought into the firm (X_3). The data

for 20 lawyers in the firm are as follows:

Lawyer	Y	X_1	X_2	X_3
1	1	450	5	.4
2	6	700	4	1.6
3	7	640	7	1.8
4	4	580	2	.5
5	3	490	4	.5
6	5	550	4	1.2
7	4	440	6	.8
8	3	470	3	.6
9	5	490	4	.9
10	6	500	4	.9
11	3	450	3	.9
12	6	560	5	1.4
13	5	580	2	1.2
14	4	590	1	1.3
15	3	440	7	.6
16	2	430	1	.5
17	6	600	2	1.0
18	5	590	5	1.1
19	4	500	8	.4
20	2	420	1	.4

a. Analyze the above data with a simultaneous MRC analysis. (Computer analyses are necessary for this example.)
b. Analyze the above data with a forward stepwise procedure.
c. Specify a meaningful causal order and conduct a hierarchical analysis.

21

Other Applications of MRC to Nonexperimental Research

. . .

417

In the preceding chapter, we described the use of MRC in nonexperimental situations where the *general* questions of research pertained to explanation, prediction, or model testing. In Chap. 21 we will address *specific* focused questions for which MRC statistics and strategies are appropriate. In particular, we will focus on how to use MRC strategies to obtain statistical control of variables in our data set and how to assess relationships between two variables that may vary as a function of a third variable. Finally, we will use MRC to assess pre- and postmeasure research designs.

21.1   THE NEED FOR STATISTICAL CONTROL

In laboratory research, the experimenter controls all critical aspects of the research situation. Consequently, the experimenter can conclude with relative certainty whether the independent variable has a direct effect on the dependent variable. If all features of the experiment—except for the levels of the independent variable—are either held constant or controlled by other means, then any differences on the dependent variable associated with the different levels of the independent variable must be due to the manipulation (and the inevitable chance factors present in any experiment). In nonexperimental research, however, the researcher often cannot control what happens to whom. Thus, if the relationship between data on X and data on Y obtained in a nonexperimental setting is a strong one, it may be that the observed relationship is due to a third variable that influences both the X variable and the Y variable. That is, the observed relationship could mean that X causes Y, that Y causes X, or that something is influencing both X and Y simultaneously. In other words, in nonexperimental situations, we are often concerned with whether the relationship between X and Y is the relationship we think it is.

To elaborate, suppose that the literature or our conceptual model suggests a number of additional variables that are reasonable correlates of X and Y, the two variables of particular interest to us. If further statistical analyses reveal that these other variables are, in fact, *not* affecting the relationship between X and Y, we can conclude with some confidence that this relationship is a meaningful one—that is, that X has a direct effect on Y. If we cannot rule out the involvement of one or more other variables, we will be forced to accept that the observed relationship between X and Y may be spurious or false. A **spurious correlation** is one whose magnitude is inflated because the variables in the relationship are related to additional variables that are not being considered in the analysis. Calling a correlation spurious does not imply that a relationship does not exist. Instead, the term simply means that the correlation does not reflect a *direct link* between the two variables.

A *non*spurious correlation, then, is what we will call a *meaningful relationship* in which one variable (X) has a direct link with or direct influence or effect on the other (Y). (The influence can also be one of Y upon X.) Our purpose is to determine whether other variables can account for the observed relationship between the two variables of primary interest or whether the two variables are joined by a true causal link.

Let us examine some findings that have been reported in the literature and some questions raised about them. Does a strong correlation between level attained in an organization (X) and salary (Y) mean that there is a relationship between reward and responsibility such that those who are higher in the organization will receive higher salaries? Could it be that *age* is one factor that determines salary so that those who are older are paid more? Or could *length of service* be another factor such that those who have more experience reach higher levels and are paid more? If X is the "level attained" variable and Y is the "salary" variable, a third variable, Z, could be an "age" or "experience" variable.

Statistical analyses can be undertaken to provide insight into whether the relationship between X and Y is spurious and can be explained by inclusion of information on another variable Z, such as age in our example. That is, if we find that $r_{XY}^2 = .30$, then we might be inclined to conclude that 30 percent of the variance in one variable (e.g., Y) is explainable by knowledge of the other variable (X). If we explored another variable in the situation, however, would we find that 30 percent of the Y variance is still attributed *uniquely* to X, or would we find that a large part of this common variance between X and Y is also related to Z?

Other examples of relationships that might be spurious are illustrated in the following research questions. (1) Is the relationship between a personality construct (X) and the likelihood of being a juvenile delinquent (Y) a meaningful one, or could information on socioeconomic status help explain the observed relationship? (2) Does a positive correlation between intelligence of the youngest sibling (Y) and family size (X) suggest that by merely increasing family size, intelligence of the youngest will be enhanced, or should we look at the type of social and intellectual interaction that occurs in families of different sizes to determine whether the quality of interaction influences intellectual development of children? (3) If there is a correlation between high school grades and first-year college grades, can a third variable such as scholastic aptitude explain the relationship? (4) If a test of job knowledge predicts ratings of job performance, is the obtained relationship a meaningful one, or is the relationship due to age or seniority?

All the examples above describe situations in which we might find relationships between two variables but we would need to determine whether these relationships are spurious and can be explained by other variables. In all these situations, we would have no control in assigning subjects to the levels of the X variable and would be unable to make all subjects equivalent on all other potentially relevant variables (as identified by the literature or our conceptualization of the problem). We can resort to certain statistics and statistical strategies to gain some degree of control: analysis of **partial correlations** and **semipartial correlations**. These particular correlational statistics are used as means of statistical control; that is, by using these statistics we can control for differences among subjects on a particular variable and statistically remove the effect of the variability in that variable that is related to one or both of the primary variables of interest. If the two primary variables X and Y still reveal a correlation after we have controlled for, equated for, or removed the effect of the third variable on them, then we have more assurance that our initial variables are directly linked. We will now illustrate the two approaches, partial correlation analysis and semipartial correlation analysis, with examples of questions that often are studied in nonexperimental situations.

21.2 PARTIAL CORRELATION ANALYSIS

Partial correlation analysis is a statistical technique with which we are able to study the extent of the relationship between two variables of interest *after* we have "removed" the influence of a third variable from them. In other words, we are interested in the relationship between two variables that remains after we have controlled for differences in a third. Here, *to control for* implies that the individuals we are studying may differ on this third variable, and that it is the differences on that variable that may be accounting for the observed correlation between the other two variables.

The Logic behind Partial Correlation

To be consistent with the terminology we have used throughout this book, we will designate the variable we wish to explain or predict as Y and the other two variables as X variables.[1] For convenience, we will assume that the primary relationship of interest is between Y and X_1 and that when we study a third variable (X_2) it is in order to remove, or control for, all influences this variable may have on the primary

[1] Many data analysts refer to all variables as X, and a number of authors of statistics books maintain this notation in their presentation of formulas for partial correlation analysis. We prefer to designate one of the variables Y to highlight the fact that most researchers consider one of the variables to be *primary* (the one to be predicted or explained by the others).

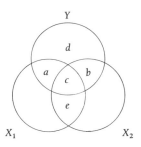

Figure 21-1   Venn diagram.

relationship. Partial correlation analysis, then, focuses on the relationship between two variables while a third variable is held constant; it "removes" the effect of X_2 from *both* Y and X_1.

Let us illustrate the way in which partial correlation analysis operates by using the Venn diagram presented in Fig. 21-1. Consider first the relationship between Y and X_1. As you can see from the diagram, the overlap between the two variables is represented by the area $a + c$. Expressed as a proportion, the squared correlation coefficient between Y and X_1 is represented by the following ratio of areas:

$$r_{Y1}^2 = \frac{a + c}{a + b + c + d}$$

As indicated, partial correlation analysis is concerned with the relationship between Y and X_1 when the effect of X_2 is removed. Consider what happens when we remove the intersection with X_2 from the area common to the two variables. With reference to Fig. 21-1, this process removes areas b and c from Y and areas c and e from X_1. If we now form a new ratio that takes these two subtractions into consideration and that focuses on a reduced baseline, we have

$$r_{Y1.2}^2 = \frac{a}{a + d}$$

where $r_{Y1.2}^2$ represents the partial correlation between Y and X_1, with X_2 held constant[2]

a represents the variability Y and X_1 have in common that is independent of X_2

$a + d$ represents the variability in Y that is independent of X_2

[2] This notation is commonly found in reference books and in the literature. The r^2 stresses the fact that the relationship of interest is between two variables (i.e., it is a squared zero-order correlation) and the "dot" separates the two variables of interest (Y and X_1 here) from the control variable (X_2).

Let us now consider the formula for the squared partial correlation coefficient, but from the perspective of multiple correlation analysis (we can represent partial correlations in terms of multiple correlations, since we are concerned with at least two X variables):

$$r_{Y1.2}^2 = \frac{R_{Y.1,2}^2 - R_{Y.2}^2}{1 - R_{Y.2}^2} \tag{21-1}$$

where $R_{Y.1,2}^2 =$ the squared multiple correlation coefficient between Y and the combination of X_1 and X_2

$R_{Y.2}^2 =$ the squared correlation coefficient between Y and X_2

(This last quantity is a squared zero-order correlation coefficient expressed as a squared multiple correlation coefficient.) With reference to the Venn diagram, examination of Eq. (21-1) shows us the following. The first term in the numerator, the squared multiple correlation coefficient $R_{Y.1,2}^2$, covers the areas $a + b + c$. The second term in the numerator, the squared simple correlation coefficient between Y and X_2, $R_{Y.2}^2$, is represented by $b + c$. Since this second term is subtracted from the first, the result for the numerator is

$$(a + b + c) - (b + c) = a$$

In the denominator, we are subtracting the same squared simple correlation coefficient between Y and X_2 from 1, which may also be expressed as $(a + b + c + d)$; this difference leaves us with $a + d$:

$$1 - (b + c) = (a + b + c + d) - (b + c) = a + d$$

Thus, Eq. (21-1) gives us the same ratio of areas, $a/(a + d)$, we found initially with the Venn diagram.

There is another way of understanding the meaning of a partial correlation, which is a little more statistical in nature. Suppose we correlate X_2 with Y and, from the information we derive, calculate a regression equation predicting a subject's score on Y from his or her score on X_2. Then, if we subtract the predicted Y scores from the actual Y scores, we will have a new set of scores (*residual scores*), which we will call Y_e. Finally, suppose that we now correlate the Y_e scores with the X_2 scores. What we will find is that the two variables are *statistically independent* ($r_{Y_e X_2} = 0$); that is, the new Y_e scores are free from the influence of X_2. Turning our attention now to X_1, we can duplicate the same steps, but this time we predict X_1 from X_2. Use of the resulting regression equation will yield predicted X_1 scores, which, when subtracted from the original X_1 scores, will yield another residual set, which we will call X_e. These new X_e scores, too, are statistically independent of X_2 ($r_{X_e X_2} = 0$). We now have two sets of residual scores, Y_e and X_e, both of which are free from influence of X_2. Now, suppose we correlate these two sets of *residual scores*. The result, $r_{Y_e X_e}$, would be the partial correlation coefficient $r_{Y1.2}$—the correlation between Y and X_1 with the effects of X_2 removed separately from the two variables.

A Numerical Example

Let us now illustrate partial correlations with an example. Suppose we administered a job knowledge test (X_1) that measures knowledge of banking, accounting, and finance to a group of bankers $(N = 90)$ and we then determined the relationship of the test scores to ratings of job performance (Y) provided by supervisors of these bankers. The hypothesis that has prompted us to study this relationship is that knowledge of banking, accounting, and finance facilitates bankers performance and, consequently, results in better ratings of their work. If there is a positive relationship, we may conclude that the greater the knowledge a banker has, the more likely that he or she will be evaluated highly on a rating form. If we found such a relationship, however, we might be concerned that a variable such as experience as a banker (X_2) could explain someone's score on a job knowledge test *and* could influence the supervisor's rating of that banker. That is, a banker's experience may facilitate his or her ability to answer questions; also, senior people might be presumed to be justified in receiving higher ratings.

   Suppose the following data represented the relationships between the three variables:

$$r_{Y1} = .30 \; (r^2_{Y1} = .09) \qquad r_{Y2} = .30 \; (r^2_{Y2} = .09) \qquad r_{12} = .20 \; (r^2_{12} = .04)$$

From this information we can calculate the squared multiple correlation coefficient between Y and the other two variables $(X_1$ and $X_2)$. Using Eq. (10-2), we find

$$R^2_{Y.1,2} = \frac{r^2_{Y1} + r^2_{Y2} - 2r_{Y1}r_{Y2}r_{12}}{1 - r^2_{12}}$$

$$= \frac{.09 + .09 - (2)(.30)(.30)(.20)}{1 - .04} = \frac{.18 - .0360}{.96} = \frac{.1440}{.96} = .1500$$

Application of Eq. (21-1) results in the following:

$$r^2_{Y1.2} = \frac{R^2_{Y.1,2} - R^2_{Y.2}}{1 - R^2_{Y.2}} = \frac{.15 - .09}{1 - .09} = \frac{.06}{.91} = .0659$$

$$r_{Y1.2} = \sqrt{r^2_{Y1.2}} = \sqrt{.0659} = .2567$$

In this example, since the correlation between test scores and performance ratings $(r_{Y_1} = .30)$ is relatively close to the relationship between test scores and performance ratings when the effect of experience is removed from both variables $(r_{Y1.2} = .2567)$, we would conclude that the obtained relationship is *not* being influenced to any real extent by the experience variable. If we postulate that no other variable influences the relationship, this set of data allows us to conclude that performance ratings of a banker can be attributed to job knowledge and that experience is *not* a factor in the relationship.

Suppose, however, we found the following relationships:

$$r_{Y1} = .30 \ (r_{Y1}^2 = .09) \qquad r_{Y2} = .30 \ (r_{Y2}^2 = .09) \qquad r_{12} = .60 \ (r_{12}^2 = .36)$$

From this information, we find by use of Eq. (10-2) that

$$R_{Y.1,2}^2 = \frac{.09 + .09 - (2)(.30)(.30)(.60)}{1 - .36} = \frac{.18 - .1080}{.64} = \frac{.0720}{.64} = .1125$$

Application of Eq. (21-1) yields:

$$r_{Y1.2}^2 = \frac{R_{Y.1,2}^2 - R_{Y.2}^2}{1 - R_{Y.2}^2} = \frac{.1125 - .09}{1 - .09} = \frac{.0225}{.91} = .0247$$

$$r_{Y1.2} = \sqrt{.0247} = .1572$$

In this case we see a large drop from the original correlation coefficient (from .30 to .1572); thus, we conclude that the relationship between test scores and performance ratings is influenced by experience.

Testing the Significance of Partial Correlations

There are several ways to test the significance of a partial correlation. The formula we prefer is based on Eq. (20-4), which is used to test the significance of *incremental variance*. When that formula is adapted to the present situation, the F ratio becomes

$$F = \frac{(R_{Y.1,2}^2 - R_{Y.2}^2)/(k_l - k_s)}{(1 - R_{Y.1,2}^2)/(N - k - 1)} \tag{21-2}$$

where $R_{Y.1,2}^2 =$ the squared multiple correlation coefficient between Y and
the combination of X_1 and X_2

$R_{Y.2}^2 =$ the squared correlation coefficient between Y and X_2

$k_l, k_s =$ the numbers of vectors for $R_{Y.1,2}^2$ and $R_{Y.2}^2$, respectively

$N =$ the sample size

k = the number of vectors associated with the R^2 involved in
    calculating the residual term[3]

The reason for focusing on incremental variance may be found by examining the
formula for the squared partial correlation coefficient, Eq. (21-1):

$$r^2_{Y.1,2} = \frac{R^2_{Y.1,2} - R^2_{Y.2}}{1 - R^2_{Y.2}}$$

As you can see, the numerator in this formula is identical to the incremental variance designated in the numerator of Eq. (21-2), which is why this formula provides a significance test of the partial correlation. That is, if the increment is zero,
the partial correlation is zero also. Applying Eq. (21-2) to the first example, we find

$$F = \frac{(.15 - .09)/(2 - 1)}{(1 - .15)/(90 - 2 - 1)} = \frac{.06/1}{.85/87} = \frac{.06}{.0098} = 6.12$$

which, with $df_{num.} = 1$ and $df_{denom.} = 87$, is significant. In the second example,

$$F = \frac{(.1125 - .09)/(2 - 1)}{(1 - .1125)/(90 - 2 - 1)} = \frac{.0225/1}{.8875/87} = \frac{.0225}{.0102} = 2.21$$

which is not significant.

This significance test is often expressed in terms of the squared partial correlation coefficient itself (see McNemar, 1969, p. 185). That is,

$$F = \frac{r^2_{Y1.2}}{(1 - r^2_{Y1.2})/(N - 3)} \tag{21-3}$$

The reason for subtracting 3 from N in the denominator, rather than the 2 you
would expect with the evaluation of a zero-order correlation, is the loss of an additional degree of freedom occurring because we are holding the third variable, X_2,
constant. Applying this alternative formula to the two examples, we find

$$F = \frac{.0659}{(1 - .0659)/(90 - 3)} = \frac{.0659}{.9341/87} = \frac{.0659}{.0107} = 6.16$$

and

$$F = \frac{.0247}{(1 - .0247)/(90 - 3)} = \frac{.0247}{.9753/87} = \frac{.0247}{.0112} = 2.21$$

---

[3] As you can see, k_l and k are the same values, since they refer to the same squared
multiple correlation coefficient, $R^2_{Y.1,2}$, which appears in both the numerator and the denominator of Eq. (21-2).

Except for rounding errors, both F's are identical to those found with Eq. (21-2). The first F ratio, 6.16, which is significant, means that even with X_2 controlled the relationship between Y and X_1 is a significant relationship; the same conclusion cannot be applied to the second F value, 2.21, which is not significant.

Interpreting Partial Correlations

The interpretation of the partial correlation coefficient is usually in terms of its square, $r^2_{Y1.2}$. In the first example, with the obtained partial correlation coefficient $r_{Y1.2} = .2567$, we would conclude that 6.6 percent ($.2567^2 = .0659$) represents the proportion of variance on the performance variable that is uniquely associated with variance on the test variable, after we have controlled for experience. In the second example, with the obtained partial correlation coefficient $r_{Y1.2} = .1572$, we would conclude that 2.5 percent ($.1572^2 = .0247$) represents the proportion of variance on the performance variable that is associated with test scores after we have held constant, or controlled for, experience.

The essential difference between the two examples is the correlation coefficient r_{12} for job knowledge (X_1) and experience (X_2), since the correlation coefficient for job performance (Y) and experience (X_2) is the same in both examples ($r_{Y2} = .30$). More specifically, r_{12} is relatively low in the first example (.20) and relatively high in the second example (.60). This relatively strong relationship between knowledge and experience in the second example greatly reduces the strength of the relationship that is *uniquely associated* with job knowledge and *performance*.

Another way of determining a partial correlation coefficient is to use an equation that incorporates zero-order or simple correlation coefficients directly, which is an equation that some of you may recognize from an earlier course. The formula for expressing the partial correlation coefficient in terms of zero-order correlations between individual pairs of variables is:

$$r_{Y1.2} = \frac{r_{Y1} - r_{Y2}r_{12}}{\sqrt{1 - r^2_{Y2}}\sqrt{1 - r^2_{12}}} \tag{21-4}$$

This formula shows us that the relationships of X_2 to both Y and X_1 are taken into account in the determination of the partial correlation coefficient. Using the information from the two examples, we find

$$r_{Y1.2} = \frac{.30 - (.30)(.20)}{\sqrt{1 - (.30)^2}\sqrt{1 - (.20)^2}} = \frac{.30 - .06}{\sqrt{1 - .09}\sqrt{1 - .04}}$$

$$= \frac{.24}{\sqrt{.91}\sqrt{.96}} = \frac{.24}{\sqrt{.8736}} = \frac{.24}{.9347} = .2568$$

and

$$r_{Y1.2} = \frac{.30 - (.30)(.60)}{\sqrt{1 - (.30)^2}\sqrt{1 - (.60)^2}} = \frac{.30 - .18}{\sqrt{1 - .09}\sqrt{1 - .36}}$$

$$= \frac{.12}{\sqrt{.91}\sqrt{.64}} = \frac{.12}{\sqrt{.5824}} = \frac{.12}{.7632} = .1572$$

for the first and second examples, respectively. Except for rounding error, both values equal those we obtained with Eq. (21-1).

More Complex Partial Correlations

The basic rationale for using partial correlations, which we have considered in this section, may also apply in the case of more complex studies. For example, it is possible to remove the effects of more than one variable from two variables of interest. To illustrate, suppose we added a fourth variable X_3, age, to our example and that we wanted to "partial out" (or hold constant) both experience (X_2) and age (X_3) from the relationship between knowledge (X_1) and job performance (Y). The formula for the squared partial correlation coefficient we would use is

$$r_{Y1.23}^2 = \frac{R_{Y.1,2,3}^2 - R_{Y.2,3}^2}{1 - R_{Y.2,3}^2} \tag{21-5}$$

where $r_{Y1.23}^2$ = the squared partial correlation coefficient between Y and X_1, with the combined effects of X_2 and X_3 removed

$R_{Y.1,2,3}^2$ = the squared multiple correlation coefficient between Y and the combined effects of all the X variables, X_1, X_2, and X_3

$R_{Y.2,3}^2$ = the squared multiple correlation coefficient between Y and the combined effects of the two control variables, X_2 and X_3

If you compare this formula with Eq. (21-1), you will see that the only change is the addition of X_3 to each of the terms in the formula. The numerator in Eq. (21-5) removes the effects of the two control variables from X_1, while the denominator removes the effects of the two control variables from Y. Thus, $r_{Y1.23}^2$ would reflect the relationship between knowledge and job performance with the effects of *both* age and years of experience held constant and removed from the two variables involved in the correlation. Partial correlations of this sort are known as **higher-order partial correlations**. Most comprehensive computer programs will perform the necessary calculations for these correlations.

Recapitulation

In essence, partial correlations are used to investigate relationships between two or more variables while holding constant or controlling other variables. In experimental research, as we indicated, we obtain control by design and by random assignment of subjects to conditions; as a result, we are able to interpret unambiguously the effect of the independent variable on the dependent variable. In nonexperimental designs, where we cannot achieve the same sort of control, we can still obtain a less ambiguous understanding of the relationship between two variables by statistically controlling for other variables that we presume to have a potential influence on our primary variables of interest.

21.3 SEMIPARTIAL CORRELATION ANALYSIS

Another correlational technique we use to exert statistical control over variables studied in nonexperimental research is the analysis of **semipartial correlation**.[4] This procedure is intimately related to partial correlation analysis, as you will see in a moment. Although we did not refer to it as such, you were introduced to semipartial correlation analysis in Chap. 20, when we discussed the *hierarchical strategy* for MRC and the analysis of *incremental variance*. We will begin with a consideration of the simplest example of semipartial correlation analysis, namely, the introduction of a third variable to refine the analysis of a correlation between two variables of primary interest. The focus of this analysis, however, is on the influence of this third variable on only *one* of the two variables. That is, the literature or conceptual model suggests that the third variable is related to only one of the other variables.

The Logic behind Semipartial Correlation Analysis

As you discovered in Sec. 21.2, the "partialing" procedure in partial correlation analysis removes the influence of the control variable X_2 from *both variables* of primary interest, Y and X_1. The resulting partial correlation coefficient, $r_{Y1.2}$, then, reflects a relationship between Y and X_1 that is uncontaminated by any intercorrelations with X_2—either between Y and X_2 or between X_1 and X_2. In contrast, with the semipartial correlation technique, we limit the control or refinement to the X_1 variable, leaving the Y variable intact. We are interested in doing this for two, somewhat related reasons. First, we might wish to refine the conceptual meaning of X_1 as a variable, removing from it any "contamination" or "natural correlation" that may be produced by other variables, in particular, by X_2. Suppose we constructed a pencil-and-paper test of mechanical aptitude (X_1) that would predict the performance of automobile mechanics (Y). Of course, since the test

---

[4] Semipartial correlation analysis is also called **part correlation** analysis by some authors, but the latter term is not widely used.

relies on written questions and answers, scores on the test (X_1) may reflect skills in reading comprehension as well as mechanical aptitude. By including a test of reading comprehension (X_2) in our analysis, we will be able to remove from our aptitude test any contamination from reading comprehension skills. The resulting correlation between job performance (Y) and our more refined test (X_1) is a semipartial correlation. Second, there are situations in which researchers are interested in the *unique contribution* of one or more variables in predicting or explaining some behavioral measure (Y). For example, suppose we have two different tests that are both correlated with Y. For theoretical reasons, we might want to determine the amount of Y variance each variable explains that is unique or different from the variance explained by the other. We will illustrate both of these uses, but first let us present the formula for the semipartial correlation coefficient.

Consider again the Venn diagram in Fig. 21-1, in which the three circles represent variability in Y, X_1, and X_2 and the overlapping areas represent the degree to which any one variable is correlated with another. Our primary interest is in the extent to which X_1 can explain variability in Y without any contribution from X_2. Inspection of the diagram indicates that X_1 and Y have areas a and c in common, but that only area a is unique to X_1. We can isolate this area by calculating the R^2 between Y and the two X variables combined (area $a + b + c$) and subtracting from this quantity $R^2_{Y.2}$ (area $b + c$), leaving that portion of Y that is unique to X_1, namely, area a. From this geometric representation, we can derive the formula for this semipartial correlation coefficient; more specifically,

$$R^2_{Y(1.2)} = R^2_{Y.1,2} - R^2_{Y.2} \qquad (21\text{-}6)$$

where $R^2_{Y(1.2)} =$ the squared semipartial correlation coefficient for Y and X_1, with the effects of X_2 removed from X_1

$R^2_{Y.1,2} =$ the squared multiple correlation coefficient for Y and the two X variables

$R^2_{Y.2} =$ the squared zero-order correlation coefficient for Y and X_2 (expressed as a multiple correlation coefficient)

The notation designating the semipartial correlation means that the influence of X_2 is removed from X_1 and the residual variation—the "(1.2)" in the subscript—is then correlated with Y. It is instructive to compare Eq. (21-6) with Eq. (21-1), the formula for a squared *partial* correlation coefficient:

$$r^2_{Y1.2} = \frac{R^2_{Y.1,2} - R^2_{Y.2}}{1 - R^2_{Y.2}}$$

You can see that the numerator of the partial correlation is the semipartial correlation. That is, both remove X_2 from X_1 (isolating area a), but as seen in Eq.

(21-1), the denominator of the squared partial correlation coefficient removes X_2 from Y as well. The relationship between the two correlation coefficients may be represented as follows:

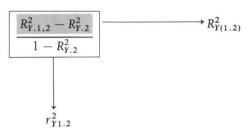

The entire formula within the box defines the squared partial correlation coefficient, while the shaded portion of the numerator defines the squared semipartial correlation coefficient.

A Numerical Example

Let us now illustrate semipartial correlation analysis with an example. Suppose we were interested in the relationship between performance in law school (Y) and the results from the Law School Admissions Test (LSAT). To obtain a clearer understanding of why students succeed or fail in law school, we might hypothesize that there are variables that can explain why people do well on the LSAT, and that if we could control for these variables, we would have a better understanding of the admissions test itself (and its content) and how it relates to performance in law school. For example, we might propose that general cognitive ability, or intelligence, is a major variable that influences performance on the LSAT; that is, that those who do better on the LSAT are those who have greater general intelligence. Our choice of any such alternative variable, or potential explanatory reason for observed relationships, should be based on theory or on an understanding of the research literature pertaining to this subject. For now, let us concentrate on intelligence (X_2) as a potential variable that could elucidate the relationship between law school performance (Y) and the admissions test (X_1).

The specific question we are considering is whether an observed correlation between performance in law school and results on the LSAT is due to or can be explained by differences in intelligence. More specifically, we are postulating that intelligence is related to admissions test results *only*, and, for the sake of argument, we are not interested in whether it relates to performance in law school.

Suppose we obtained from law school records the grade-point average (GPA) and LSAT scores for $N = 100$ graduates of law school. In addition, suppose we also found in the files scores on a general intelligence test for each of these students. Correlational analyses of these data produce the following:

$$r_{Y1} = .50 \ (r_{Y1}^2 = .25) \qquad r_{Y2} = .60 \ (r_{Y2}^2 = .36) \qquad r_{12} = .70 \ (r_{12}^2 = .49)$$

and from this information we find $R_{Y.1,2}^2 = .3725$. Application of Eq. (21-6) yields the following:

$$R_{Y(1.2)}^2 = R_{Y.1,2}^2 - R_{Y.2}^2$$
$$= .3725 - .36 = .0125$$
$$R_{Y(1.2)} = \sqrt{R_{Y(1.2)}^2} = \sqrt{.0125} = .1118$$

With only the GPA and LSAT data, we would have concluded that a moderately strong relationship exists between the two variables ($r_{Y1} = .50$). But when we remove the effect of "intelligence" from the LSAT data, we see that the test now has a lower correlation, $R_{Y(1.2)} = .11$, with GPA. Thus, we can conclude that the LSAT is not as good a predictor of GPA as we may have been led to believe, since a relatively large portion of the relationship seems to be due to the correlation of the LSAT with intelligence. Another way of stating this conclusion is to say that intelligence can explain to some degree how well students do on the LSAT. If we remove the influence of intelligence from the LSAT, can the differences still remaining among the students explain performance in law school? In the current example, the answer is, Not to a great degree.[5]

Testing the Significance of Semipartial Correlations

A more satisfying way to answer the question is to use a statistical test. The *F* test of a semipartial correlation is based on the general formula, introduced in Chap. 20, for the evaluation of incremental variance in a hierarchical analysis, which we also modified in this chapter for the statistical assessment of a partial correlation and called Eq. (21-2). More specifically,

$$F = \frac{(R_{Y.1,2}^2 - R_{Y.2}^2)/(k_l - k_s)}{(1 - R_{Y.1,2}^2)/(N - k - 1)}$$

---

[5] As with the partial correlation, we can express the semipartial correlation entirely in terms of zero-order correlation coefficients. In the present case, the equation for this statistic is

$$r_{Y(1.2)} = \frac{r_{Y1} - r_{Y2}r_{12}}{\sqrt{1 - r_{12}^2}}$$

Inserting the three zero-order correlation coefficients into this formula, we obtain

$$r_{Y(1.2)} = \frac{.50 - (.60)(.70)}{\sqrt{1 - .49}} = \frac{.50 - .42}{\sqrt{.51}} = \frac{.08}{.7141} = .1120$$

which, within rounding error, equals the value we calculated with Eq. (21-6).

Substituting the relevant values in Eq. (21-2), we find

$$F = \frac{(.3725 - .36)/(2 - 1)}{(1 - .3725)/(100 - 2 - 1)} = \frac{.0125/1}{.6275/97} = \frac{.0125}{.0065} = 1.92$$

which, with $df_{num.} = 1$ and $df_{denom.} = 97$, is not significant. This means that the unique contribution of LSAT scores to the prediction of performance in law school is *not* significant.

More General Use of Semipartial Correlations

Semipartial correlation analysis is an example of the more general hierarchical analysis. The procedure addresses the same sort of question we considered in Chap. 20, namely, how much of the variance in Y can be explained by X_1 above and beyond the portion that is explained by X_2, or what the increment in explained Y variance is for X_1 after the Y variance explained by X_2 has been taken into account. Our concern is in the *unique variance* explained by a variable when several variables are potential predictors. As pointed out in Chap. 20, the set of variables that we have as predictors or explanatory constructs in nonexperimental research are not mutually independent. While multiple correlation analysis allows us to determine the extent to which variability in Y is explained by the *total set* of X variables, this information is often not sufficiently analytic, particularly when we want to know the unique contribution of a variable to Y variability, or the contribution that is independent of the other existing variables. We cannot determine the "unique" contribution of a variable in this case by examining its zero-order correlation, since the variable of interest is correlated with other X variables. Thus, hierarchical strategies are used.

Unique Contribution of Single X Variables.   Semipartial correlational strategies or hierarchical analyses can be used to determine the *unique* contribution of single X variables within the context of a larger *set* of variables than we have considered so far. For example, suppose we wanted to predict job performance of managers with a battery of four tests, consisting of a test of reasoning ability (X_1), a management interest inventory (X_2), a test for achievement motivation (X_3), and a test for interpersonal style (X_4). These four tests are chosen because they represent qualitatively different psychological constructs, each of which is expected to explain a somewhat different aspect of job performance (Y). We administer the four tests, obtain measures of job performance, and calculate the correlations among the variables, which are shown in Table 21-1. Suppose a multiple correlation analysis of the full set of predictors yields an $R_{Y.1,2,3,4} = .38$ ($R^2_{Y.1,2,3,4} = .14$). Table 21-1 shows that the best single predictor of performance is X_1, the test of reasoning ability, with a correlation of .31, indicating that about 10 percent ($.31^2 = .0961$) of the performance variance can be explained by the test.

Table 21-1

Pattern of Correlations between Predictors and between Predictors and Job Performance

	Test 1 (X_1)	Test 2 (X_2)	Test 3 (X_3)	Test 4 (X_4)
Job Performance (Y)	.31	.26	.28	.26
Test 1 (X_1)		.43	.40	.33
Test 2 (X_2)			.41	.34
Test 3 (X_3)				.52

If we wanted to know how much variance can be explained by particular tests while other tests are held constant, we can perform a hierarchical analysis in which the order in which the variables are to enter the analysis is specified in advance. For example, we know that 14 percent of the variance is explained by the full battery of four tests, but we may want to know how much variance is explained by X_3 (need for achievement) above and beyond the other X variables. Hierarchical analysis requires that we compute the squared multiple correlation coefficient for Y and the full set of variables ($R^2_{Y.1,2,3,4}$) and then compute the squared multiple correlation coefficient for the *set* of variables that excludes the variable of interest, X_3. This latter quantity is $R^2_{Y.1,2,4}$. Calculation of the difference between these two squared multiple correlation coefficients indicates the amount of variance that is unique to X_3. In symbols,

$$R^2_{Y(3.1,2,4)} = R^2_{Y.1,2,3,4} - R^2_{Y.1,2,4}$$

If the results were $R^2_{Y.1,2,3,4} = .14$ and $R^2_{Y.1,2,4} = .12$, we would conclude that the test of need for achievement explains $.14 - .12 = .02$, or an additional 2 percent of variance beyond what is explained by the other three tests.

Or suppose we wanted to know the unique contribution of X_2. Again, we would use the R^2 for the full set ($R^2_{Y.1,2,3,4}$) and subtract from it the R^2 associated with all the variables except for the variable of interest, X_2—that is, $R^2_{Y.1,3,4}$. If the difference in this case is $.14 - .10 = .04$, for example, we could conclude that X_2 explains 4 percent of job performance variance above the portion that is explained by X_1, X_3, and X_4.

Multiple Semipartial Correlations. We can also look at the unique contributions to explained variance made by *sets* of variables, by conducting a **multiple semi-**

partial correlation analysis. If we calculate $R^2_{Y.1,2}$ and subtract it from $R^2_{Y.1,2,3,4}$, we will have determined the contribution of a set, X_3 and X_4, that is unique and is above and beyond that of another set, X_1 and X_2. This higher-order semipartial correlation is represented by $R^2_{Y(3,4.1,2)}$. That is,

$$R^2_{Y(3,4.1,2)} = R^2_{Y.1,2,3,4} - R^2_{Y.1,2}$$

We would want to look at such *sets* of variables in situations where we have a rather heterogeneous collection of X variables, but there is some conceptual similarity among some of the predictors. For example, suppose we had the following information: X_1 = age, X_2 = gender, X_3 = income, X_4 = a personality measure, X_5 = verbal ability, and X_6 = scores on a deductive reasoning test. If the variable we are interested in explaining is success in college (Y), one obvious analysis is to examine the R^2 for Y and X_1 through X_6, namely $R^2_{Y.1,2,3,4,5,6}$. But we may also want to determine what effect a *set of demographic information* may have on Y, when all other information is held constant. To do this, we treat X_1, X_2, and X_3 (age, gender, and income, respectively) as the "demographic set" and conduct the following analysis:

$$R^2_{Y(1,2,3.4,5,6)} = R^2_{Y.1,2,3,4,5,6} - R^2_{Y.4,5,6}$$

Likewise, we can treat X_5 and X_6 (verbal ability and deductive reasoning, respectively) as "cognitive information" and assess its influence as follows:

$$R^2_{Y(5,6.1,2,3,4)} = R^2_{Y.1,2,3,4,5,6} - R^2_{Y.1,2,3,4}$$

The differences obtained from these analyses reflect variance uniquely explained by the sets of demographic information and cognitive information, respectively.

A point to keep in mind in these analyses is that regardless of whether we use the term *hierarchical* or the term *semipartial*, we can study the unique contribution to the variance made by the variable (or variables) of interest by controlling the order of entry of variables into the analytic strategy.

Summary of the Various Analysis Strategies

Up to this point, we have discussed several types of correlational analyses that you can conduct on the same set of data. Which analysis you conduct depends on the question you want to answer. As a review (refer to Fig. 21-1), consider the following:

1. If you are interested in the amount of variance that can be explained by all the predictors available, use $R^2_{Y.1,2}$; it represents the ratio $(a + b + c)/(a + b + c + d)$.

2. If you are interested in the amount of variance that can be explained by one predictor *without* consideration of the other predictors, conduct a simple correlation analysis (find r_{Y1}^2 and r_{Y2}^2); the simple r^2's represent the ratios $(a + c)/(a + b + c + d)$ and $(b + c)/(a + b + c + d)$, respectively.

3. If you are interested in how much Y variance can be explained by one variable (e.g., X_1) when another variable is removed only from X_1, conduct a semipartial correlation analysis or a hierarchical analysis to find $R_{Y(1.2)}^2$. This analysis indicates the amount of *unique* variance explained by X_1 independent of X_2; the semipartial correlation is represented by the ratio $a/(a + b + c + d)$.

4. If you are interested in how much Y variance can be explained by X_1 when the effect of X_2 is removed from *both* Y and X_1, conduct a partial correlation analysis (find $r_{Y1.2}^2$); the partial correlation is represented by the ratio $a/(a + d)$.

From the above, you should see that the semipartial correlation technique will yield a lower value than the partial correlation technique. This occurs because the base for the analysis differs. Semipartial correlations explain the proportion of the *total* Y variance that is unique to X_1 (or X_2). In contrast, partial correlations focus on the relationship between Y and X_1 that is *not* explained by X_2, and thus, they focus on only the $a + d$ area of the Venn diagram.

Using Semipartial Correlations with Experimental Data

We have not had occasion to mention the use of either semipartial correlations or a hierarchical strategy in the analysis of experiments. One reason is that the designs we considered through Chap. 19 were based on equal sample sizes; designs like these are sometimes called **balanced designs**. By concentrating on balanced designs and using contrast coding throughout in the coding process, we were able to calculate R^2's representing main effects, interactions, and error terms as orthogonal sources of variability and thus did not need to resort to a hierarchical process in the statistical analysis. We will turn to hierarchical strategies, however, in the next three chapters, where we consider certain specialized experimental designs. Chapter 22, for example, deals with a procedure in which information about the subjects is obtained before the start of the experiment and the information is then introduced to refine the statistical analysis of the experimental data. This useful procedure, called **analysis of covariance**, is conducted by means of a hierarchical strategy in MRC and its equivalent in ANOVA. In Chap. 23, we discuss an analysis procedure, called **trend analysis**, developed for use with *quantitative* independent variables. Under certain circumstances, a hierarchical strategy provides a particularly convenient way of performing a trend analysis. Finally,

Chap. 24 considers **unbalanced designs**, in which the sample sizes are not equal in all the treatment conditions of the experiment. One highly recommended way of analyzing such data is a hierarchical MRC analysis.

21.4 STUDY OF INTERACTIONS IN NONEXPERIMENTAL RESEARCH

As you know from our discussion of interaction (see Chap. 13), the presence of an interaction means that the difference between, for example, two levels of factor A depends on the level of factor B; as you also know, when we find interactions in experimental research, we then study simple effects (Chap. 14) and interaction contrasts (Chap. 15). A primary reason for "dissecting" a significant interaction is to determine exactly where differences are occurring and, consequently, to obtain a more precise understanding of the phenomenon under study and its theoretical explanation. In essence, the study of interactions in much of experimental research is for the purpose of *explanation*. The same can be said for nonexperimental research. Researchers attempt to study their hypotheses and theoretical issues in a field situation and attempt to refine their explanatory statements.[6]

In the study of interactions in *either* experimental or nonexperimental explanatory research, the magnitude of the interaction is generally not large. This means that though the interactions we find may be significant, the r^2 (or $\hat{\omega}^2$) may be a rather small value (less than 5 percent). Though the effect may be small, its statistical significance is important from a theoretical, explanatory standpoint.

Let us return to our numerical example in Sec. 21.3 to illustrate the study of interaction in a nonexperimental situation. Originally, we phrased the research question to reflect a particular interest: Is the relationship between scores on the LSAT (X_1) and law school performance (Y) spurious because intelligence (X_2) has an influence on LSAT scores? To answer this question, we used a semipartial correlation analysis to determine the unique contribution of LSAT after we had controlled for intelligence. Another question we could ask in the above situation is whether LSAT scores and intelligence scores *interact* and whether the interaction component explains a significant portion of Y variance (law school performance).

---

[6] An important area in educational research is concerned with the interaction of aptitudes and treatments, which is often studied via the **aptitude by treatment interaction (ATI) design**. For example, a researcher may be interested in whether individual differences among learners interact with the type of instructional method used. Cronbach and Snow (1977) provide a detailed discussion of this type of design.

What does an interaction mean in this case, particularly when the X variables are both quantitative? In experimental research, we indicated that interactions mean that the *differences* in Y among the levels of one variable (e.g., X_A) depend on the levels of the second variable (X_B). Since we know by now that *differences* among means in ANOVA can be expressed in terms of *relationships* between variables, we can therefore express an interaction in such terms. That is, an interaction means that the relationship between, for example, X_A and Y depends on which level of X_B is being considered.

In our present example, the question of the interaction becomes a question of whether the relationship between law school performance and LSAT is constant or whether it varies as a function of intelligence level. To study this question, we proceed as we have in the past, namely, by creating a vector to represent interaction information. We create this vector as we have for other interactions—we multiply the vector(s) of one variable by the vector(s) of the other variable. In this case, we multiply the X_1 vector by the X_2 vector and obtain an X_1X_2 vector (which we will designate by X_3). The analysis of the interaction is as follows:

Step 1: Calculate $R^2_{Y.1,2,3}$, which also is $R^2_{Y.max.}$. This R^2 tells us how much variance in Y can be explained by all three vectors—the vectors for the two variables (X_1 and X_2) and their interaction (X_3).

Step 2: Subtract $R^2_{Y.1,2}$ from $R^2_{Y.1,2,3}$ to find the amount of variance in Y that can be *uniquely* explained by X_3, or the interaction:

$$R^2_{Y.1,2,3} - R^2_{Y.1,2} = R^2_{Y(3.1,2)}$$

The difference between the two R^2's is a hierarchical analysis. If $R^2_{Y(3.1,2)}$ is a significant increment as determined by Eq. (21-2), then the interaction is significant and we have more insight into our variable of interest, law school performance.

To refresh your memory, the reason why we do not merely examine the r^2 associated with X_3 (vector 3) is because there is intercorrelation (or lack of independence) among X_1, X_2, and X_3. Any correlation among the X variables in nonexperimental research calls for a hierarchical strategy if we are to determine the unique contribution of a given variable (and in this example, the "given variable" is the interaction).

As we pointed out above, in our example we need to study the interaction of X variables that are both quantitative. The strategy we have outlined is not limited to quantitative variables. In the simplest case of interaction, a case in which there are only two X variables, either or both of the variables may be quantitative *or* qualitative. For example, in the study of law school performance, we could have chosen to study the undergraduate major of the students instead of intelligence as our X_2 variable. (Both variables could be studied, but for the sake of argument, we now focus on major.) Suppose we had subjects with undergraduate majors in the social sciences, physical sciences, and humanities. When an X variable consists of three categories, or "levels," as it does in this case, we need two vectors to describe the variable. We then use these vectors to create the interaction *set* by multiplying each vector by X_1. The contribution of the interaction is again assessed via a predetermined order in a hierarchical analysis. More specifically, there would be a total of *five* vectors, one for X_1 (LSAT score), two for X_2 (undergraduate major), and two for X_3 (the interaction of LSAT and major). Symbolically,

$$R^2_{Y.interaction} = R^2_{Y.X_1,X_2,X_3} - R^2_{Y.X_1,X_2}$$

or, in terms of the actual vectors ($X_1 = $ vector 1, $X_2 = $ vectors 2 and 3, and $X_3 = $ vectors 4 and 5),

$$R^2_{Y.interaction} = R^2_{Y.1,2,3,4,5} - R^2_{Y.1,2,3}$$

The hierarchical order is such that we first consider X_1 and X_2 and then consider the R^2 for the full set (X_1, X_2, and X_3) and any increment provided by the interaction.

So far in this chapter, we have been concerned with research undertaken for the purpose of explanation, to gain a better understanding of relationships. The hierarchical analysis identifies the contribution of the interaction to the understanding of the phenomenon and suggests whether further analyses are necessary (in experimental designs, for example, we might wish to study simple effects and interaction contrasts). However, as you know from previous chapters, researchers are also interested in prediction, in practical situations. We have presented examples in which knowledge of certain data can predict success—among law students, applicants for clerical jobs, bankers, and others. To further illustrate the study of interactions in nonexperimental designs, we will focus on a current societal problem, namely, determining whether selection tests predict similarly for categories or groups of people differentiated by such factors as gender, ethnicity, and age. We might want to know, for example, whether a test (X_1) should be used in the same way for males and females to predict performance on some criterion (Y). In personnel psychology, this is a question of **test fairness**: Is the use of the test "fair" for the two groups? More specifically, is the relationship between selection test scores (a continuous X variable) and job performance (Y) the same for males and females (where gender is a qualitative, categorical variable)? We will use X_2 to represent gender.[7] We will begin by discussing the various correlations that will be useful in this analysis. Actual data will not be shown, but hypothetical results will be discussed under the assumptions of both significance and nonsignificance.

---

[7] Most data analysts use a form of dummy coding to represent the groups, rather than either contrast or effect coding, either of which is more appropriate for analyzing the results of an experiment. In the present example, we could use the codes 1 for male and 2 for female.

The Required Correlations

Zero-Order Correlations.   The first set of measures consists of the squared zero-order correlation coefficients for test scores (X_1) and performance (Y), for gender (X_2) and performance (Y), and for test scores (X_1) and gender (X_2); these will be designated r_{Y1}^2, r_{Y2}^2, and r_{12}^2, respectively. These basic statistics tell us whether the selection test predicts job performance (r_{Y1}^2), whether males and females differ on the job (r_{Y2}^2), and whether males and females differ on the selection test (r_{12}^2). Though these r^2's are each restricted to two of the three variables, they provide insight into what may be occurring in subsequent steps of the analytical procedure when we consider interaction. That is, each of these zero-order correlations is in essence a "main effect" in that each explores differences or relationships on one variable relative to a second variable with the third variable disregarded for the moment. However, our primary purpose in this research is to determine whether we need separate regression equations for the two genders or only a single, common regression equation to predict performance levels (Y) for males and females from scores on the selection test (X_1). And since we are concerned with test fairness, we will want to know whether the test can explain performance beyond the degree to which it is explained by other variables, such as gender. In order to answer these questions, we need to study the three variables together and to examine the ways X_1 and X_2 jointly contribute to the prediction. This requires correlation statistics that are based on more than one X variable.

Multiple Correlations.   The analysis also requires two squared multiple correlation coefficients. The first is for Y and the two X variables—test scores (X_1) and gender (X_2)—or $R_{Y.1,2}^2$. This R^2 tells us how much Y variance can be explained by the available information, test scores and gender. This result is not too meaningful by itself, but we need it in order to conduct the hierarchical statistical analysis.

The second squared multiple correlation coefficient is the one taken between Y and *three* X variables—test scores (X_1), gender (X_2), and the *cross product* of test scores and gender (X_1X_2)—or $R_{Y.1,2,1 \times 2}^2$. The cross-product values are obtained in exactly the way in which they were created when we constructed interaction vectors in experimental designs—that is, by multiplying each individual's X_1 score by his or her X_2 score. This R^2, too, is not of major concern, but is needed in the hierarchical analysis, which we consider next.[8]

---

[8] Although we have listed the necessary correlations as an implied series of steps, it is not necessary to calculate the values in three separate analyses. Obviously, it is more efficient to program the computer to give you all the desired outputs in one computer run. We present the correlational analysis in this fashion to simplify the analytical concepts.

The Hierarchical Analysis

Given the above squared correlation coefficients, we now enter into a hierarchical analysis. It is hierarchical in the sense that the researcher needs to identify which correlations are to be compared. To illustrate the analysis, suppose we had the following results:

$$r_{Y1}^2 = .15 \qquad r_{Y2}^2 = .10 \qquad r_{12}^2 = .40$$

We will now use these values to examine different aspects of the relationship between Y and the X variables.

Testing the Interaction. The logical first step in the analysis is to determine whether the interaction vector $X_1 X_2$ adds a significant increment to the R^2 based on Y and the combination of X_1 and X_2. This is accomplished by calculating

$$R_{Y.1,2,1 \times 2}^2 - R_{Y.1,2}^2$$

and evaluating the significance of this difference, which, of course, represents the proportion of explained Y variance obtained when the interaction (or product vector $X_1 X_2$) is added to the squared multiple correlation. Suppose $R_{Y.1,2,1 \times 2}^2 = .18$ and $R_{Y.1,2}^2 = .16$ and we then use Eq. (21-2) to test for the significance of the increment. If the increment, $.18 - .16 = .02$, is *not* significant, this would mean that the interaction vector does not add to the portion of Y already explained by X_1 and X_2. We would interpret this finding to mean that the relationship between test scores and job performance is generally the *same* for both gender groups.

If the increment is significant, however, then it means that there is an interaction and that the relationship between the test and performance differs for males and females. Since the test predicts differently, it may be necessary to use two different regression equations for the gender groups, obtained separately for males and females.

In essence, this analysis tells us whether the slopes of the regression lines for the two groups are the same. Figure 21-2 shows different possible interactions. Figure 21-2(a) shows a positive relationship for males but no relationship for females; the other parts of the figure show opposite relationships for the two genders. This method of graphic representation should not be new to you, since we used it in Chap. 13, where we demonstrated that when there is no interaction, the lines are parallel. However, even when the regression lines are parallel (the above increment is not significant), the two groups may still have different *intercepts*. In Fig. 21-3, the slopes of the two lines are the same but the "male" line has a greater intercept value than the "female" line. To test whether the difference in intercepts is significant, we go to the next part of the analysis. (Again, in our example, the increment in "explained" Y variability due to $X_1 X_2$ is not significant.)

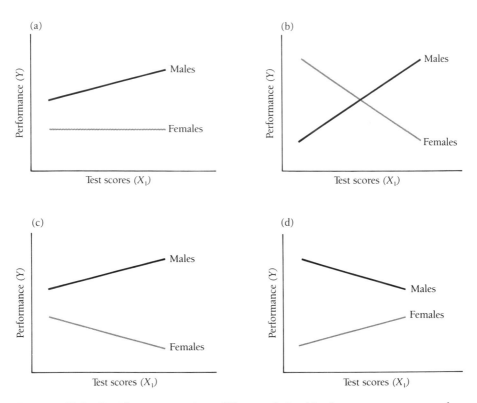

F i g u r e 21-2 Significant interactions: different relationships between test scores and performance as a function of gender.

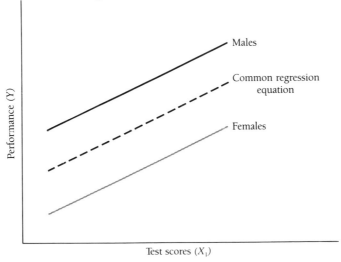

F i g u r e 21-3 Regression lines for a total sample (common regression equation) and for subgroups (males and females).

Testing the Overall Group Differences.   Given the *nonsignificant* interaction, the next step in the test fairness analysis is to determine whether a common regression equation can be used. This is the question of whether males and females differ in performance; it can ordinarily be answered by r_{Y2}^2. But it is also the question of whether performance differences are revealed between the genders after any differences in test scores have been controlled for. Thus, to answer the question, we conduct another hierarchical analysis by calculating

$$R_{Y.1,2}^2 - R_{Y.1}^2$$

and using Eq. (21-2) to evaluate the significance of this difference, which reflects the presence of gender differences on Y beyond the effects of the test scores themselves. In the present case, the increment is $.16 - .15 = .01$ (which we will again assume is *not* significant). If the increment were significant, we would conclude that gender differences are present, and again we might need two separate regression equations for predicting job performance for males and females. If this increment is not significant, then the two gender groups do not differ on Y, and since the interaction is not significant, a *common regression equation* (shown by the dotted line in Fig. 21-3) can be used to predict job performance (Y) from the test (X_1). This common regression equation is

$$Y' = a + (b)(X_1)$$

and is the one associated with r_{Y1}^2. However, before we are justified in using a common regression line to predict job performance, we have to determine whether X_1 is a significant contributor to variance in Y. We turn to the next part of the analysis to answer this question.

Testing the Predictive Power of the Test.   In order to justify the use of a common regression equation, we must demonstrate that a significant amount of Y variance can be explained by test scores above that explained by gender alone. We accomplish this by assessing the significance—by using Eq. (21-2)—of

$$R_{Y.1,2}^2 - R_{Y.2}^2$$

which in the present case is $.16 - .10 = .05$ and *is* assumed to be significant. Since the increment is assumed to be significant, we can conclude that the test is presenting unique information about performance differences and thus we can use it to make decisions. If the increment is not significant, then from a practical standpoint we would conclude that the test tells us no more than we can learn from information on gender alone and thus we would seek new tests as potential predictors.

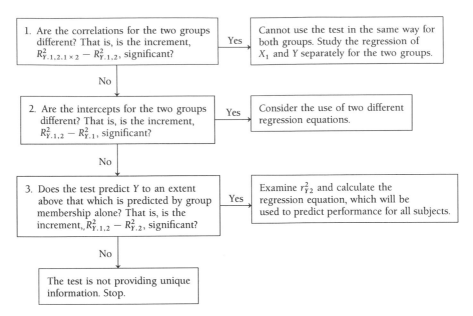

F i g u r e 21-4   Summary of the hierarchical analysis. X_1 = test scores; X_2 = gender; Y = job performance.

Summary

Figure 21-4 summarizes the systematic steps followed in the analysis of interaction for a practical problem in a nonexperimental design. Each of the three boxes on the left side of the figure represents a particular hierarchical analysis: (1) $R^2_{Y.1,2,1\times 2} - R^2_{Y.1,2}$, (2) $R^2_{Y.1,2} - R^2_{Y.1}$, and (3) $R^2_{Y.1,2} - R^2_{Y.2}$, The figure shows you how to proceed when any particular hierarchical analysis is significant or nonsignificant. A test will be considered "fair" when tests for differences in slopes *and* intercepts reveal nonsignificant increments. If either test yields a significant finding, the test is "unfair" for one or more groups.

21.5   PRETEST AND POSTTEST DESIGNS

Another of the common questions in nonexperimental research is whether an intervention such as a sales message, a training program, or a campaign is related to a variable of interest such as purchasing behavior, performance improvement, or voting behavior. In one design frequently used to study the influence of the intervention, the behavior of interest is measured *before* ("pre") and *after* ("post") the intervention; the amount of *change* in the dependent variable is the focus of interest. This type of design is called the **pre-post test design**. Such questions are often studied by examining the amount of change in the dependent variable in the group exposed to the intervention. Though the pre-post test design is common, a number of problems are associated with it; these have been discussed by Campbell and his colleagues (Campbell & Stanley, 1966; Cook & Campbell, 1979), and we will summarize them here.

Single-Group Design

We will begin our discussion of the problems associated with pre-post test designs by considering the simplest kind of example, a study in which a single group is measured before and after all members of the group receive some special treatment (or intervention). We will assume that we are studying the degree to which a stress management program improves employees' job satisfaction. Suppose our subjects are employees in the production department of the ABC Kitchen Appliance Company. In a pretest-posttest single-group nonexperimental research design, we go into the production department and assess the satisfaction level of the employees (we will assume that $N = 50$). The initial assessment provides baseline information; in a case like this, it would usually represent the level of satisfaction that we want to improve upon. After collecting the pretest data, we introduce and conduct a 2-day stress management seminar for the 50 employees, the purpose of which is to teach participants how to reduce stress and to cope with work problems. Four weeks after the intervention program has concluded, when the participants have had an opportunity to try out some of the techniques taught in the seminar, we again assess the same employees' satisfaction by using the same job satisfaction instrument we used for the pretest. Our hypothesis is that there will be a gain in satisfaction. If stress management seminars are useful, the satisfaction levels on the second administration (the posttest) should be higher than the satisfaction levels prior to the intervention (on the pretest). But even if they are higher, can we attribute the increase to the intervention? For the reasons cited below, it is questionable whether we can make any such conclusions. The potential problems are discussed in the Campbell references and are briefly presented here.

1. *History.* Given that there is an interval of time between the two measurements (the pretest and the posttest) and that this is nonexperimental research conducted in an existing organization where control cannot be achieved, other events taking place in the time between the two measurements may be affecting satisfaction. These events can be inside or outside the company. For example, there may be a change in supervisors or an

increase in base salary; or legislation may be enacted to provide rebates for energy-saving appliances, with the result that the demand for appliances increases—a situation that might affect the satisfaction of those responsible for making and selling the appliances. Regardless of the specific reason, the point is that something in the environment, and perhaps outside the plant, may be affecting satisfaction besides the stress management program.

2. *Maturation.* Many characteristics of *people* change over time as a natural consequence of internal events associated with aging. Perhaps with the passage of time, the employees become more satisfied in general and less concerned with problems in the company. With increasing age, one may be more accepting of circumstances. Thus, maturation of the employees could produce a change in satisfaction.

3. *Statistical regression toward the mean.* Because some random fluctuations exist in most measures in the behavioral sciences (due to error of measurement or unreliability of test instruments), it is a statistical fact that subjects whose scores are low in a first assessment will probably show an increase in score toward the grand mean of the satisfaction measure when they are measured on the variable a second time. Likewise, subjects whose scores are high on the first measurement are likely to show a decrease toward the grand mean when they are measured a second time. In general, if there are two measurements on the same variable, low scorers will show an increase in score and high scorers will show a decrease on a second administration. These statistical movements may distort the actual amount of change that takes place, particularly if the group studied happens to score quite low in satisfaction on the pretest, since the posttest will probably show some increase regardless of whether there is an intervention.

4. *Testing.* Exposure to the job satisfaction measure on the pretest may cause people to rethink and reassess their situation, and their change in thinking might in turn produce a change in satisfaction *independent* of the intervention. Thus, it may be that it is not the intervention *per se* that yields the change, but rather the act of testing or measuring, which can cause those serving in the study to perceive their environment differently on the second test, and, most likely, in a more favorable light.

Two-Group Design

The above are some of the reasons for questioning the conclusions drawn by researchers when they have used a pre-posttest design in a nonexperimental situation. A possible solution is to use a two-group design in which one group receives the intervention and the second group, the control group, does not. When a two-group study is conducted as an experiment, subjects are randomly assigned to the two groups. In a nonexperimental design, however, random assignment is usually not possible; instead, each condition is likely to be represented by an already existing or intact group. For example, the intervention could be introduced in plant A of the ABC Company while plant B of the company is not exposed to any intervention; employee satisfaction in both plants would be assessed at the same two times. The design is as follows:

| **Treatment group**: | Pretest | Intervention | Posttest |
| **Control group**: | Pretest | No intervention | Posttest |

But keep in mind that this is a nonexperimental design and subjects are *not* randomly assigned to one group or the other. Are there potential problems with this design? The answer is yes, and the reasons are as follows:

5. *Selection bias.* Because the subjects are *not* randomly assigned to plants, the two groups will probably not be equivalent at the outset. That is, because there is likely to be differential selection of employees for the two plants, it is unreasonable to assume that the two plants are equivalent in all relevant characteristics except for exposure to the intervention. Certain types of people may seek out one plant over another. The plants may be different in construction, organization, geographic location, and other, similar respects, and so different types of employees might seek employment in the two plants. Thus, differences observed between the control group and the experimental group may be due to initial differences in *employees* rather than to the intervention.

6. *Selection-maturation interaction.* Perhaps the subjects in one group (at one plant) are more experienced, have better home lives, are more adaptable, and are therefore less concerned about the influence of work. The subjects in the two groups, in other words, may have different maturation levels. The result is, again, different types of employees in the two plants, and it may be that the existing differences between the groups explain different amounts of change in satisfaction.

7. *Selection-history interaction.* Perhaps the different subjects are exposed to different events because they are in the different plants.

These are not the only problems that can limit our ability to interpret data obtained with the pre-post test design; others are discussed in the Campbell references. But the important point for us is that these problems illustrate (and give us a chance to reiterate) a major theme in this book: the design of the study determines the degree to which we can make statements about cause and effect and the confidence we have in our interpretation of obtained relationships. We have not discussed statistics for the pre-post design, but we have illustrated problems in interpreting results. The solution to such problems generally is not statistical, but rather requires implementing better designs or being able to logically rule out nontrivial alternative explanations for obtained results.

Analysis of Pre-Post Designs

Suppose we use the pre-post design with a treatment group and a control group and we can rule out history, maturation, and the other factors cited above as potential limitations on our interpretation. We can refine our analysis by assessing our subjects and environments on many different kinds of variables (and determining the contribution of these variables to explained variance on the dependent variable), or we can closely control the situation to limit external influences. In truth, of course, we cannot eliminate the problems, but rather, we can only be cognizant of them and take them into account when the results are interpreted. With this caution in mind let us analyze the data.

Change or Difference Scores.   One frequent method of analysis makes use of **change** or **difference scores** for subjects who are exposed to the pretest and the posttest. That is, we would compare the mean of the difference between the pre- and postmeasure scores of the treatment group with the mean difference for the control group and test whether the differences are significantly different. In essence, the measure that would be the unit of analysis is the change or difference score. For the following reasons, we do not recommend the use of change or difference scores:

1. Typically, there is a correlation between the difference score itself and the pre- and postmeasures from which the difference score is obtained. Those who have low *pre*measure scores will show greater difference scores (i.e., gains) than those initially high on the premeasures; also, those with high *post*measure scores will have greater difference scores than those with low postmeasure scores. In essence, the difference score is dependent on or correlated with the premeasure and the postmeasure. Thus, it may be that the difference score does not reflect the influence of the intervention, but instead is confounded by the pre- (or post-) measure. Even if the control group has the *same* average premeasure score as the treatment group, there is still a problem because of the existence of a correlation between the pretest score and the difference score. This correlation indicates that

the influence of the premeasure has not been removed from the postmeasure. As a consequence of these difficulties, any comparison of difference scores between the two groups should be questioned. More specifically, if we use a vector to differentiate a control and a treatment group, any correlation obtained between the difference scores and the vector is in fact spurious and artificial.

2. In almost all measurement situations, we are concerned with the reliability of our measurement or test instruments or variables studied. Briefly, **reliability** is concerned with the consistency with which the variable of interest can be assessed; reliability estimates indicate the stability, internal consistency, and equivalence of the items or parts composing the measurement device.[9] If we use difference scores as the primary dependent variable, we are using values that are formed by two components, a premeasure and a postmeasure, each of which has its own degree of unreliability. Since few measures used in the behavioral sciences are perfectly reliable, use of the difference score compounds the *un*reliability of the two measures. The result is that the difference score is *less* reliable than either of its components. The problem is serious because any decrease in the reliability of a response measure will reduce our chances of finding a significant relationship with an independent variable.

Both of these problems exist because a difference score is derived from the pre- and postmeasures. To repeat, the difference score usually is correlated with the pre- or postmeasures and is less reliable than the original measure. Thus, we are faced with the question, Is there an analytical strategy available to determine the effect of an intervention without using difference scores? The answer is yes, and the strategy is a hierarchical strategy, which we will now examine.

A Hierarchical Strategy. We will demonstrate the use of this hierarchical strategy with our earlier example in which we wished to determine whether a stress management program affects satisfaction of employees of the ABC Kitchen Appliance Company. Suppose ABC has two plants located in the same state, each in a different region, but similar in geographical setting, socioeconomic status of employees, education level of employees, and just about everything else. In other words, for all intents and purposes, the two plants and the two groups of employees are very similar, if not identical, and even though employees are not randomly assigned to the plants, we will assume they are equivalent in all important demographic and subject characteristics. Now suppose, further, that we measure the satisfaction of

[9] See Ghiselli et al. (1981, Chaps. 8 and 9) for a full discussion of reliability.

the employees in both plants ($N = 50$ in each plant), then introduce a stress management program in one plant *but* not in the other, and finally, assess satisfaction in both plants 4 weeks later. This design is illustrated as follows:

	Pretest	Intervention	Posttest
Plant A	Yes	Yes	Yes
Plant B	Yes	No	Yes

Suppose we chose to use difference scores in our analysis of these data. Using MRC, we would code the two plants in some way and correlate the difference scores with the codes. But, as we pointed out, the use of difference scores does not control for differences in premeasures between the plants. Thus, we need to examine the influence of the intervention after we have controlled for the influence of the premeasure and removed it from the postmeasure; this is done by *hierarchical MRC*.

The analysis strategy we will describe is also called the **analysis of covariance (ANCOVA)**, which we will discuss in much greater detail in Chap. 22. We are considering ANCOVA here to complete our discussion of pre-post designs. We will describe the general outline of the analysis and refer you to the next chapter for the details and a numerical example. The hierarchical analysis may be described as consisting of the following steps:

1. First we correlate the postmeasure (Y) with the premeasure (X_1). Suppose we find that the correlation is $r_{Y1} = .55$ ($r_{Y1}^2 = .30$). This correlation tells us that, in general, and across all 100 employees in the study, those who are high in satisfaction at the outset are high in satisfaction 4 weeks later, and those who are low at the outset are low 4 weeks later. This correlation, however, does not take into account information about the plants in which the employees are located and that one plant is exposed to the intervention while the other is not.

2. In the second step, we enter the plant information into the analysis by means of an appropriate coded vector (X_2) and calculate a multiple correlation coefficient between Y and the two X variables. Suppose we found $R_{Y.1,2}^2 = .39$. The *increment* from r_{Y1}^2 (.30) to $R_{Y.1,2}^2$ (.39) indicates a 9 percentage point increase ($.39 - .30$) in explained variance for the intervention variable (X_2), after we have taken into account the correlation between the postmeasure (Y) and the premeasure (X_1); this increment

reflects the "unique" contribution of the stress management intervention. If the significance test of incremental variance is significant (and we will assume it is), it can be concluded that the stress management program has resulted in an increase in satisfaction. Ordinarily, we would stop our analysis here, but if we were interested in interaction, we would proceed to the next step.

3. In this step, we enter the interaction information (premeasure × plants) to study whether the pre-post relationship is different for the two plants. For our purpose, we will assume that the incremental variance for this step is not significant.[10]

In conclusion, since the second step in the analysis indicates that the intervention explains postmeasure variance after we have controlled for premeasure differences, we have some confidence that the intervention is effective. We have used the original raw scores, controlled for initial differences in satisfaction, and determined the unique contribution of the intervention to explaining satisfaction.

Comment

The hierarchical strategy should be used for pre- and posttest designs. This strategy assumes that initial differences between the two groups are only chance differences. If we are able to randomly assign the subjects to the two conditions, this condition is met and we then use this strategy to analyze the results of the study. On the other hand, if we must use intact groups, we attempt to verify that the groups are equivalent on all important dimensions and characteristics by using the hierarchical analysis to analyze the results, but remember that any inference we draw from the analysis must be qualified by the frank realization that differences between the two groups that are present before the start of the study will not be fully adjusted by the statistical procedure and may be responsible for the results. Perhaps the most responsible course of action is to view the outcome of the nonexperimental study as *suggestive* and any conclusions drawn from the analysis as *tentative* until corroborated by a new, more adequately controlled study. We will emphasize again in the next chapter the inability of the hierarchical strategy to compensate for differences between groups that have not been created by some form of random assignment.

---

[10] We will have more to say about this interaction in Chap. 22, where we will indicate that a significant interaction obtained with a set of *experimental* data may invalidate the statistical assumptions underlying the analysis. In many nonexperimental designs, the interaction is of interest in its own right.

21.6 SUMMARY

In this chapter we have extended the analytical strategies we introduced in Chap. 20, focusing on particular kinds of problems that are often investigated in non-experimental research. One particular concern in nonexperimental designs is the lack of control and, thus, the possibility that obtained relationships are influenced by other variables besides the variables of interest. To determine whether obtained relationships are spurious, we can resort to partial and semipartial correlation analyses. Partial correlation analyses examine the relationship between Y and X_1 by controlling for the influence of X_2 on both Y and X_1. Semipartial correlation analyses control for the influence of X_2 on X_1 only.

Another problem of interest is the study of interactions. Interactions can serve an explanatory purpose by contributing to our understanding of a phenomenon or behavior of interest; they can also serve a predictive purpose in the information they can provide regarding the use of tests or methods for different types of subjects (e.g. males or females). In either case, in nonexperimental research, where there is correlation among the various X variables, a hierarchical analysis is used to isolate particular components of the interaction to provide estimates of unique variance, and to assess test fairness.

Finally, designs in which the same instrument is used before ("pre") and after ("post") the introduction of an intervention were discussed. We looked at the influence that factors such as history, testing, and maturation might have on the interpretation of the results. We also discussed the inappropriateness of difference scores as a unit of analysis for this type of design. We recommended using ANCOVA, which we briefly introduced in this chapter but will discuss more fully in Chap. 22.

21.7 EXERCISES

1. Return to Problem 1 in Chap. 20 and add the additional information that subjects 1 through 10 are males and subjects 11 through 20 are females. We will call the gender variable X_4. (Disregard X_2 and X_3 for this problem.)

   a. Determine if the addition of gender increases the magnitude of the relationship between Y and scores on the bar examination (X_1).

   b. Conduct a hierarchical analysis to determine whether bar exam results are appropriate as predictors of success for men and women lawyers.

22

Analysis of Covariance

. . .

453

22.4 OTHER APPLICATIONS OF ANCOVA TO EXPERIMENTAL DESIGNS
Multiple Covariates
Within-Subjects Designs
Factorial Designs

22.5 ANCOVA AND NONEXPERIMENTAL DESIGNS

22.6 SUMMARY

22.7 EXERCISES

In Chap. 21, we considered two correlational methods commonly used to exercise statistical control over a set of data. The partial correlation technique provides a way to "remove," or control for, the influence of a variable or even a set of variables on a particular relationship between two other variables. The example we offered was a study of the correlation between scores on a job knowledge test administered to bankers and ratings of their job performance. It was hypothesized that a third variable, experience as a banker, might contaminate this correlation by affecting both the scores on the test and the ratings of job performance. With a partial correlation, then, we can remove the influence of this factor from the correlation of interest. On the other hand, a semipartial correlation analysis (or a hierarchical analysis in general) allows us to exercise control over the *predictor variables* (or *X* variables); it removes the effects of any intercorrelations between these variables and permits us to determine the *unique* influence of a variable (or set of variables) in explaining variability in *Y*.

In this chapter we are concerned with an extension of the second type of statistical control—hierarchical analysis—to the analysis of both experimental and nonexperimental designs. The procedure is called the **analysis of covariance (ANCOVA)** and is usually treated as a special topic in most textbooks that deal primarily with the analysis of experimental designs. As you will see, an analysis of covariance is much easier to conduct with MRC than with ANOVA-based procedures; in fact, we will reverse our usual procedure and consider the MRC approach first rather than second. Whichever approach is taken, however, the conclusions derived from the statistical outcomes are *identical*.

The purpose of ANCOVA in experimental designs is to correct for chance differences between groups that occur when subjects are assigned randomly to the treatment groups. The result of using ANCOVA is twofold: (1) the group means are adjusted for these preexisting differences and (2) the size of the error term used in the analytical process is reduced. We achieve both adjustments by obtaining before the experiment begins some information about the subjects that is presumed to be correlated with the response measure *Y*. Before we present the details of how this is accomplished, let us consider first the options an investigator has in designing an experiment. The simplest type of experiment is the completely randomized design, in which subjects are randomly assigned to receive one of the treatment conditions. As you know, any factors influencing the variability among the subjects will be reflected in the differences observed among the treatment means. The more uncontrolled variability there is, the more likely we will be to attribute the group differences to chance and the more difficult it will be to detect effects actually produced by the different treatment conditions. It is possible to minimize uncontrolled variability by attempting to hold constant all features surrounding an experiment except the differences associated with the independent variable, and by restricting the variation of other factors that might contribute to this variability. Even in the most refined purely randomized design, however, the variability is still sizable, and the only remaining method for increasing power is to increase sample size.

There are other solutions to this basic problem. Analysis of covariance is one. The use of matching designs is another. To illustrate the latter in our example of the effects of different lectures on the learning of vocabulary words, we could attempt to match subjects on some relevant variable before the experiment begins. For example, we could use scores from a general intelligence test to match subgroups of subjects and then assign equal numbers from each subgroup to the treatment conditions. This type of design, frequently called a **randomized-blocks design** or a **treatments-by-blocks design**, is discussed in a number of advanced books on experimental design (see, for example, Keppel, 1982, pp. 247–253; Kirk, 1982, pp. 293–298; Myers, 1979, pp. 146–155). An extreme but effective form of matching is to use the *same subject* in all the treatment conditions. This type of design, often referred to as a *within-subjects design* or a *repeated-measures design*, was considered in Chaps. 16 through 18. These two types of design provide a direct method for controlling unsystematic variability that would otherwise increase the size of the error term. In contrast, ANCOVA exerts its control of extraneous factors *indirectly* by purely statistical means. In our example, ANCOVA would remove the effect of intelligence from the vocabulary scores, and thus any differences found in such scores would be more directly attributable to exposure to the different lectures.

22.1 ANALYSIS OF COVARIANCE: THE MRC APPROACH

As mentioned, ANCOVA operates to remove the effects of a variable (or variables)—referred to as a **covariate** (or covariates)—from the dependent measure. Though the researcher assigns subjects randomly to treatment conditions, there is always the chance that a particular variable, a covariate, may influence the results, and this is a possibility the researcher wants to control for. The decision to consider examining a covariate at the outset of the experiment is based on the researcher's understanding of the theory or problem being studied. Even if there is only a slight possibility that a hypothesized covariate will have an effect, controlling for it will result in a more sensitive (powerful) test of the treatment conditions. Thus, to conduct the ANCOVA, as part of planning the experiment, we would identify a covariate—a variable that we hypothesize to be related to Y—and collect information on it for each of our subjects before the start of the experiment. We collect this information before the experiment begins in order to avoid contaminating the covariate with the independent variable, to avoid the possibility that exposure to the independent variable could influence responses to the covariate measure. Failing to guarantee this *independence* between the covariate and the independent variable will usually invalidate an analysis based on this information. Huitema (1980, pp. 133–135) discusses some of the problems encountered when the covariate is taken either after or during the course of an experiment.

The benefits of ANCOVA depend on the strength of the relationship between the covariate and Y. Generally, ANCOVA will increase the power of an experiment, provided that the correlation coefficient taken between the covariate and the dependent variable is greater than $r = .2$. For correlations less than .2, a standard ANOVA is actually more powerful than an ANCOVA based on the same data (Feldt, 1958, p. 347). For correlations greater than .2, however, there is some debate concerning the relative advantages of ANCOVA and the treatments-by-blocks design, which we described earlier. On the basis of the work reported by Feldt (1958), who studied the relative sensitivity of the two approaches, authorities have recommended the treatments-by-blocks design when the correlation coefficient ranges between .2 and .4, either approach when it ranges between .4 and .6, and ANCOVA when it is greater than .6. Later work by Maxwell, Delaney, and Dill (1984) suggests that the magnitude of the correlation coefficient is not a critical factor in deciding between these and other approaches. In any case, it is clear that ANCOVA will frequently increase the sensitivity of an experiment, provided that the correlation coefficient of the covariate and Y is greater than $r = .2$.

The MRC approach to ANCOVA involves a hierarchical strategy in which the covariate is the first variable (or set of variables) to be entered into the analysis and the vectors representing the independent variable are entered next. The initial inclusion of the covariate isolates the proportion of Y variability that is present (or predictable) before statistical consideration of the independent variable. The remaining Y variability represents that part which is *not* linearly related to the covariate; it is this "refined" variability that will now become the object of study. The first step is to divide this variability into two separate parts. The first part consists of the portion that is associated with the treatment conditions, *adjusted for any differences between groups that may exist before the experiment.* It is obtained by adding the A vectors to the analysis in a hierarchical fashion and using the increment in R^2 as an estimate of the treatment effects. The second part of the analysis concerns the *residual variation* that is not due either to the treatments or to differences present at the start of the experiment. As you will see, this second quantity will serve as the basis for evaluating the significance of the "refined" treatment effects.

A Numerical Example

Let us return to Chap. 10 and our continuing example of assessing the effects of three types of lectures (physical science, social science, and history) on vocabulary scores. Suppose we were able to obtain information on general intelligence (as measured by a standardized test, where the scores range from 50 to 150) for each of the subjects serving in our experiment. Our intent is to use this information as a covariate in the analysis of the experiment. The main reason for our choice of general intelligence as a covariate is that our research and a review of the literature suggest that intelligence has a relatively strong correlation with the dependent variable. Table 22-1 shows the scores and the layout for the design. The first column of data lists the scores on the dependent variable Y. The next column lists the measures of general intelligence, which we will refer to as X. The next two columns consist of vectors that represent the treatment effects. As you know by now, these two vectors represent the three conditions that constitute the A treatment effect. The vectors in Table 22-1, again, reflect two meaningful comparisons, namely, physical science versus social science (A1), and the two sciences combined versus history (A2). These comparisons happen to be orthogonal, but any type of coding that distinguishes between the three treatment conditions will suffice. The last two vectors in Table 22-1 are *interaction vectors*, which represent the interactions between the covariate and the treatment conditions. These interactions will be considered at a later point in this section.

The Hierarchical Analysis.   In our experimental procedure, the subjects available for study are given the standardized test of general intelligence and then randomly assigned to the treatment conditions, *without* consideration of the test scores. Once the assignments are made, we expose the groups to the treatments and obtain information on Y (the vocabulary score). We then undertake a hierarchical analysis of the data. As we have already indicated, the analysis begins with the correlation between Y and X, given by

$$r_{YX}^2 = .6531$$

which shows a sizable linear relationship between the dependent variable (vocabulary scores) and the covariate (intelligence). (For convenience, we will refer to this zero-order correlation as a multiple correlation.) This means that in general, subjects who have done better on the vocabulary test have also scored higher on the general intelligence test. Thus, the variability in Y can be explained, in part, by general intelligence.

But our concern is whether the *treatment conditions* can explain Y variability. ANCOVA functions by controlling for or removing the Y variability that is related

Table 22-1
Coding for the Analysis of Covariance: MRC Approach

Subject	Y	(1) X	(2) A1	(3) A2	(4) X × A1	(5) X × A2
a_1 1	53	115	1	1	115	115
2	49	120	1	1	120	120
3	47	118	1	1	118	118
4	42	119	1	1	119	119
5	51	105	1	1	105	105
6	34	90	1	1	90	90
7	44	118	1	1	118	118
8	48	106	1	1	106	106
9	35	110	1	1	110	110
10	18	84	1	1	84	84
11	32	75	1	1	75	75
12	27	85	1	1	85	85
a_2 13	47	110	−1	1	−110	110
14	42	105	−1	1	−105	105
15	39	106	−1	1	−106	106
16	37	118	−1	1	−118	118
17	42	119	−1	1	−119	119
18	33	118	−1	1	−118	118
19	13	88	−1	1	−88	88
20	16	92	−1	1	−92	92
21	16	95	−1	1	−95	95
22	10	85	−1	1	−85	85
23	11	78	−1	1	−78	78
24	6	75	−1	1	−75	75
a_3 25	45	112	0	−2	0	−224
26	41	110	0	−2	0	−220
27	38	102	0	−2	0	−204
28	36	110	0	−2	0	−220
29	35	105	0	−2	0	−210
30	33	90	0	−2	0	−180
31	46	119	0	−2	0	−238
32	40	110	0	−2	0	−220
33	29	99	0	−2	0	−198
34	21	88	0	−2	0	−176
35	30	98	0	−2	0	−196
36	20	85	0	−2	0	−170

to the covariate and then testing how much of the remaining Y variability can be explained by the treatment conditions. Thus, the next step is to add the two vectors representing the treatment effects ($A = A1$ and $A2$) to the analysis, which gives us

$$R^2_{Y.X,A} = .7717$$

By subtracting the squared correlation coefficient reflecting the relationship between Y and X ($R^2_{Y.X}$) from the squared multiple correlation coefficient reflecting the relationship between Y and the combination of the covariate and the two treatment vectors ($R^2_{Y.X,A}$), we obtain a more refined estimate of the effects of the three treatment conditions than we would have had we correlated Y with the two A vectors alone. We will refer to this difference, or incremental variability, as a squared *adjusted multiple correlation coefficient*, $R^2_{Y.A(adj.)}$.[1] (The reason why we adopt the term *adjusted* in this situation is that we will be concerned with Y means of the treatment groups that have been *adjusted* for the influence of the covariate. Adjusted means will be discussed shortly.) To illustrate this step with the two quantities we have already calculated, we find

$$R^2_{Y.A(adj.)} = R^2_{Y.X,A} - R^2_{Y.X} = .7717 - .6531 = .1186$$

These calculations reveal that almost 12 percent of the total variability in the dependent variable may be attributed to the introduction of the treatment conditions, after we have corrected for any differences among the groups in general intelligence (X) that may have existed before the start of the experiment.

The next step consists of the calculation of the residual variation—the variability remaining after we remove the influence of the covariate and the treatment effects—which will be used as the error term to test for the significance of the treatment effects. This error term, $R^2_{Y.S/A(adj.)}$, is obtained as follows:

$$R^2_{Y.S/A(adj.)} = 1 - R^2_{Y.X,A} = 1 - .7717 = .2283$$

Finally, we are able to calculate the F ratio, according to the formula originally given in Chap. 21 as Eq. (21-2). Adapting this formula to the present design, we have

$$F = \frac{(R^2_{Y.X,A} - R^2_{Y.X})/(k_l - k_s)}{(1 - R^2_{Y.X,A})/(N - k - 1)} \tag{22-1}$$

where $R^2_{Y.X,A} - R^2_{Y.X}$ = the adjusted treatment variability $R^2_{Y.A(adj.)}$

k_l, k_s = the number of vectors involved in the larger and smaller R^2's, respectively

---

[1] This difference, $R^2_{Y.A(adj.)}$, is actually a squared *semipartial multiple correlation coefficient* in which X is removed from Y before the treatment vectors are added to the analysis.

Table 22-2
Summary of the Analysis of Covariance: MRC Approach

Source	R^2	df	Mean R^2	F
A (adj.)	$R^2_{Y.X,A} - R^2_{Y.X} = .1186$	2	.0593	8.35*
S/A (adj.)	$1 - R^2_{Y.X,A} = .2283$	32	.0071	

* $p < .01.$

$1 - R^2_{Y.X,A} =$ the residual variability

$N =$ the total number of subjects

$k =$ the number of vectors involved in the calculation of $R^2_{Y.X,A}$

Substituting in Eq. (22-1), we have

$$F = \frac{(.7717 - .6531)/(3 - 1)}{(1 - .7717)/(36 - 3 - 1)}$$

$$= \frac{.1186/2}{.2283/32} = \frac{.0593}{.0071} = 8.35$$

which is significant. (The F is evaluated with $df_{num.} = 2$ and $df_{denom.} = 32$.) The analysis is summarized in Table 22-2.

A Comparison with the Unadjusted Analysis. It is informative to compare this ANCOVA analysis with the corresponding ANOVA analysis we conducted on the *unadjusted* Y scores in Chap. 10. We have duplicated the critical information from the two analyses in Table 22-3. Consider first the two F ratios. The one from

Table 22-3
A Comparison of ANOVA and ANCOVA

	ANOVA		ANCOVA	
	A	S/A	A	S/A
R^2	.2061	.7939	.1186	.2283
df	2	33	2	32
Mean R^2	.1031	.0241	.0593	.0071
F	$\dfrac{.1031}{.0241} = 4.28$		$\dfrac{.0593}{.0071} = 8.35$	

ANCOVA is nearly twice as large as the one from ANOVA. How does this difference come about? As you can see by comparing the mean R^2's from the two analyses, ANCOVA produces a considerably smaller residual variability (.0071 versus .0241) as well as a reduced treatment effect (.0593 versus .1031). The reduction in the error term is the expected result from ANCOVA, given the sizable relationship between Y and X that is removed in this analysis. The reduction in the size of the R^2 representing the *treatment effects* probably comes as a surprise to you. Earlier we indicated that ANCOVA results in two adjustments or corrections, the primary one being a reduction in residual variation, as you have seen in this example, and the other being an adjustment of the *treatment means* for differences among the treatment groups that are present before the start of the experiment. In this example, the three group means on the covariate are

$$\bar{X}_{A_1} = 103.75 \qquad \bar{X}_{A_2} = 99.08 \qquad \bar{X}_{A_3} = 102.33$$

and the corresponding means on the dependent variable are

$$\bar{Y}_{A_1} = 40.00 \qquad \bar{Y}_{A_2} = 26.00 \qquad \bar{Y}_{A_3} = 34.50$$

Note that the group with the highest average intelligence is level a_1 (physical science) and the group with the lowest average intelligence is level a_2 (social science); these are also the groups that showed the highest and lowest performance, respectively, on the vocabulary test. Consequently, an adjustment for group differences in intelligence will result in a somewhat lower vocabulary score for physical science and a somewhat higher vocabulary score for social science. (We will consider how these adjustments are made in a moment.) The necessary result of this adjustment, then, is to reduce the size of the treatment effects.

The adjustment of the treatment effects is undertaken to remove the chance differences present at the start of the experiment. In this example, we are using a test of general intelligence to serve in this capacity. Whether the adjusted treatment effects are increased or reduced depends in part on the pattern of the group differences on the covariate. Logically, the random assignment of subjects to conditions will produce a pattern of differences on the covariate that is *positively correlated* with that found on the dependent variable *half of the time*. This is what has happened here, of course, and it is the reason why the treatment effects are reduced in the adjustment process. For the *other half of the time*, however, the two patterns will be *negatively correlated*; if that had happened in this example, the treatment effects would be *increased* in the adjustment process.[2]

---

[2] The relationship between the pattern of differences on the covariate and that on the dependent variable is more complicated than we have described here. What is missing is the direction of the average relationship between Y and X observed within each of the treatment groups. Huitema (1980, pp. 31–38) provides a useful discussion of this complication.

Another way of looking at the benefits of ANCOVA is to note that we now express the magnitude of the treatment effects not as the proportion of *total* Y variability associated with the independent variable, which is the proportion we have used throughout this book, but as a different proportion based on the *adjusted* Y scores. That is, by entering the X variable into the MRC analysis *first*, we already explain a portion of the variation in the dependent variable. More specifically, $R_{Y.X}^2$ represents the Y variability that is predictable from a knowledge of the linear relationship between Y and X, while $1 - R_{Y.X}^2$ represents the Y variability that is *not* predictable from X, the covariate. The question now is how much of this latter, *residual* variability is explainable by the independent variable. This new proportion is given as follows:[3]

$$\frac{\text{Adjusted treatment effects}}{\text{Adjusted residual variability}} = \frac{R_{Y.X,A}^2 - R_{Y.X}^2}{1 - R_{Y.X}^2} \tag{22-2}$$

Entering the relevant values into Eq. (22-2), we find

$$\frac{.7717 - .6531}{1 - .6531} = \frac{.1186}{.3469} = .3419$$

which indicates that slightly over 34 percent of the total *adjusted* Y variability is attributed to the experimental manipulations. For comparison, the unadjusted $R_{Y.A}^2$ is .2061, or approximately 21 percent. Thus, even though the differences among the treatment means are reduced by the adjustment process, the actual magnitude of the treatment effects is *increased* by the analysis of covariance.

Adjusting the Treatment Means

Once we have established by the analysis of covariance that the omnibus F is significant, we need to correct or adjust the actual treatment means for any differences that exist before the start of the experiment. We base the adjustment on two factors, the nature of the differences on the covariate X and the size of the correlation between the covariate and the dependent variable Y. That is, group means that deviate the most from the grand mean of the covariate $\bar{X}_T$ will be adjusted more than group means that deviate the least from $\bar{X}_T$. Additionally, adjustments are greater when the correlation between X and Y is large than when it is small. In

---

[3] This proportion is actually a squared *partial* correlation coefficient, as shown in Eq. (21-1), in which an X variable is removed both from the Y variable and from the independent variable as well. To emphasize its nature as a partial R^2, we would designate the proportion as $R_{YA.X}^2$, which indicates that X is removed from both Y and A.

any case, we would expect these adjustments to be relatively minor for experiments, in which subjects are assigned randomly to the treatment conditions. Quasi-experiments, on the other hand, in which the treatments are administered to intact groups rather than to groups formed randomly, frequently produce relatively large adjustments because of the sizable differences among the groups on the covariate. Any such adjustment must always be viewed with caution, of course, since there is no guarantee that these *nonchance differences* on the covariate have been fully and appropriately taken into consideration in the adjustment process.

There are several ways to calculate the adjusted treatment means. The one we will present for the MRC analysis focuses on the regression equation based on the R^2 involving the covariate and the two treatment vectors ($R^2_{Y.X,A}$). Translated for use in calculating the adjusted means, the equation becomes

$$\bar{Y}'_{A_i} = b_1(\bar{X}_T) + b_2(A1_i) + b_3(A2_i) + a \tag{22-3}$$

where the three regression coefficients b_1, b_2, and b_3 are those associated with the three vectors used in the analysis, X, $A1$, and $A2$, respectively. The computer analysis reveals

$$\bar{Y}'_{A_i} = (.6941)(\bar{X}_T) + (5.3805)(A1_i) + (-.2879)(A2_i) - 37.1031$$

Substituting the appropriate code values for each treatment condition, we find

$$\bar{Y}'_{A_1} = (.6941)(101.72) + (5.3805)(1) + (-.2879)(1) - 37.1031 = 38.5934$$
$$\bar{Y}'_{A_2} = (.6941)(101.72) + (5.3805)(-1) + (-.2879)(1) - 37.1031 = 27.8324$$
$$\bar{Y}'_{A_3} = (.6941)(101.72) + (5.3805)(0) + (-.2879)(-2) - 37.1031 = 37.0766$$

Since we have conducted an analysis of covariance, we will be interested in the adjusted means rather than the unadjusted ones; we will base any comparisons we may wish to examine on the adjusted means. We will discuss the analysis of single-*df* comparisons in Sec. 22.3.

Homogeneity of Group Regression Coefficients

The two adjustments in ANCOVA are both based on the linear relationship between Y and X. The regression coefficient, which is central to the adjustment process, is essentially an average of the individual regression coefficients associated with the treatment groups considered separately. In any ANCOVA, it is necessary to determine whether these group coefficients are the same. If they are, we can safely proceed with the analysis we have already discussed. If they are not, we will probably have to drop the covariate from the analysis and return to an analysis based on the unadjusted Y data.[4] The assumption we are testing, which underlies the analysis of covariance, is referred to as the assumption of **homogeneity of regression.**

The test of this assumption is particularly easy with the MRC analysis; it is simply an extension of the preceding analysis. Consider the last two vectors in Table 22-1. These are *product* or *interaction vectors* formed by cross-multiplying the covariate X with each of the treatment vectors $A1$ and $A2$, namely, $XA1$ and $XA2$. Adding these two interaction vectors to the analysis, which gives us $R^2_{Y.X,A1,A2,XA1,XA2}$ or, more simply, $R^2_{Y.X,A,X \times A}$, allows us to determine the extent to which there is an *interaction* between the covariate and the independent variable A. More specifically, this interaction is represented by

$$R^2_{Y.X \times A} = R^2_{Y.X,A,X \times A} - R^2_{Y.X,A} \qquad (22\text{-}4)$$

The presence of a covariate × treatments interaction $(X \times A)$ indicates that the nature of the linear relationship between the covariate and the dependent variable depends on the levels of the independent variable (factor A). This test of the covariate × treatments interaction is equivalent to the analysis of interactions presented in Chap. 21, in Sec. 21.4. Stated differently, the interaction means that the individual group regression coefficients, which reflect the slopes of the lines relating X and Y for the different groups, are different. From analysis of the data, we find that $R^2_{Y.X,A,X \times A} = .8002$ and $R^2_{Y.X,A} = .7717$. Substituting in Eq. (22-4), we find

$$R^2_{Y.X \times A} = .8002 - .7717 = .0285$$

This R^2 is assessed by means of the F test appropriate for evaluating the significance of incremental variability,

$$F = \frac{(R^2_{Y.X,A,X \times A} - R^2_{Y.X,A})/(k_l - k_s)}{(1 - R^2_{Y.X,A,X \times A})/(N - k - 1)} \qquad (22\text{-}5)$$

Substituting the information we reported already, we have

$$F = \frac{(.8002 - .7717)/(5 - 3)}{(1 - .8002)/(36 - 5 - 1)} = \frac{.0285/2}{.1998/30} = \frac{.0143}{.0067} = 2.13$$

which, with $df_{num.} = 2$ and $df_{denom.} = 30$, is not significant. In short, the regression coefficients for the individual groups are not significantly different, and the ANCOVA is justified statistically.

---

[4] An alternative course of action is to undertake a procedure called the **Johnson-Neyman** technique, which is discussed in detail by Huitema (1980, pp. 270–297).

Logically, we should have presented the analysis differently. The first test that we should consider is the test for homogeneity of regression, which determines whether it is appropriate to continue with ANCOVA or not. To repeat, a non-significant F ratio at this point justifies a continuation of the analysis of covariance and an assessment of single-df comparisons involving the adjusted treatment means. A significant F, on the other hand, indicates that ANCOVA is not appropriate, since the group regression ceofficients are different and the average within-group regression coefficient $b_{S/A}$ cannot be used in the various adjustments. The result is that we essentially disregard the covariate information and turn to an analysis of *variance*, based on the unadjusted Y data, instead.

22.2   ANALYSIS OF COVARIANCE: THE ANOVA APPROACH

The analysis of covariance was developed for use with ANOVA in analyzing completely randomized experimental designs. We considered the MRC approach before the ANOVA approach because we feel that the logic of the analysis flows more directly from MRC than from ANOVA, although the underlying principles are the same.

The Preliminary Calculations

The first step in the analysis consists of making *three* calculations of the three basic sums of squares SS_A, $SS_{S/A}$, and SS_T required for the single-factor design: one for the scores on the covariate X, another for the scores on the dependent variable Y, and a third for the cross products of these two sets of scores. The data as they would be arranged for these preliminary calculations are presented in Table 22-4. For each of the three conditions, there are two columns of scores, one for X and the other for Y. From this information, we can easily calculate the required sums of squares. From the information provided in Table 22-4, then, we find the following basic ratios for the covariate:

$$[X] = \Sigma\, X^2 = 115^2 + 120^2 + \cdots + 98^2 + 85^2 = 379{,}446$$

$$[A_X] = \frac{\Sigma\, (A_X)^2}{s} = \frac{1245^2 + 1189^2 + 1228^2}{12} = \frac{4{,}471{,}730}{12} = 372{,}644.17$$

$$[T_X] = \frac{(T_X)^2}{(a)\,(s)} = \frac{3662^2}{(3)\,(12)} = \frac{13{,}410{,}244}{36} = 372{,}506.78$$

Table 22-4
Data and Preliminary Calculations for ANCOVA: The ANOVA Approach

	a_1		a_2		a_3	
	X	Y	X	Y	X	Y
	115	53	110	47	112	45
	120	49	105	42	110	41
	118	47	106	39	102	38
	119	42	118	37	110	36
	105	51	119	42	105	35
	90	34	118	33	90	33
	118	44	88	13	119	46
	106	48	92	16	110	40
	110	35	95	16	99	29
	84	18	85	10	88	21
	75	32	78	11	98	30
	85	27	75	6	85	20
Sum:	1245	480	1189	312	1228	414
Mean:	103.75	40.00	99.08	26.00	102.33	34.50
ΣX^2 or ΣY^2:	132,001	20,482	120,537	10,654	126,908	15,058
SS:	2832.25	1282.00	2726.92	2542.00	1242.67	775.00
ΣXY:	51,271		33,266		43,264	

The sums of squares based on these basic ratios are presented in Table 22-5. The same set of calculations are performed on the Y values:

$$[Y] = \Sigma Y^2 = 53^2 + 49^2 + \cdots + 30^2 + 20^2 = 46,194$$

$$[A_Y] = \frac{\Sigma (A_Y)^2}{s} = \frac{480^2 + 312^2 + 414^2}{12} = \frac{499,140}{12} = 41,595.00$$

$$[T_Y] = \frac{(T_Y)^2}{(a)(s)} = \frac{1206^2}{(3)(12)} = \frac{1,454,436}{36} = 40,401.00$$

The sums of squares derived from these values are also presented in the table. The final set of calculations involves analogous operations, except that they involve the *products* of pairs of numbers rather than the squares of numbers. For example, instead of squaring either X or Y, as was required in the previous calculations, we will multiply the corresponding pairs of values for the X and Y variables. To

Table 22-5
Sums of Squares and Sums of Products

Source	Covariate (X)	Dependent Variable (Y)	Cross Products (XY)
A	$[A_X] - [T_X] = 137.39$	$[A_Y] - [T_Y] = 1194.00$	$[A_{XY}] - [T_{XY}] = 403.00$
S/A	$[X] - [A_X] = 6801.83$	$[Y] - [A_Y] = 4599.00$	$[XY] - [A_{XY}] = 4721.00$
Total	$[X] - [T_X] = 6939.22$	$[Y] - [T_Y] = 5793.00$	$[XY] - [T_{XY}] = 5124.00$

illustrate,

$$[XY] = \Sigma\, XY = (115)(53) + (120)(49) + \cdots + (98)(30) + (85)(20)$$

$$= 127{,}801$$

$$[A_{XY}] = \frac{\Sigma\,(A_X)(A_Y)}{s} = \frac{(1245)(480) + (1189)(312) + (1228)(414)}{12}$$

$$= \frac{1{,}476{,}960}{12} = 123{,}080.00$$

$$[T_{XY}] = \frac{(T_X)(T_Y)}{(a)(s)} = \frac{(3662)(1206)}{(3)(12)} = \frac{4{,}416{,}372}{36} = 122{,}677.00$$

Combining these basic ratios in the same patterns as before creates quantities that are analogous to sums of squares but are more appropriately called *sums of products (SP)*, since they are based on XY cross products rather than on squared scores and sums. The three sets of sums of products are presented in Table 22-5.

Adjusting the Sums of Squares

The adjusted total sum of squares $SS_{T(adj.)}$ is calculated as follows:

$$SS_{T(adj.)} = SS_{T(Y)} - \frac{(SP_T)^2}{SS_{T(X)}} \tag{22-6}$$

where the first quantity to the right of the equal sign is the total sum of squares on the dependent variable and the other quantity on the right is a sum of squares representing the linear relationship between the covariate and the dependent variable. Substituting in Eq. (22-6), we obtain

$$SS_{T(adj.)} = 5793.00 - \frac{(5124.00)^2}{6939.22} = 5793.00 - 3783.62 = 2009.38$$

The next quantity we need is the adjusted within-groups sum of squares $SS_{S/A(adj.)}$, which we obtain in a similar fashion:

$$SS_{S/A(adj.)} = SS_{S/A(Y)} - \frac{(SP_{S/A})^2}{SS_{S/A(X)}} \tag{22-7}$$

Following through with the calculations, we find

$$SS_{S/A(adj.)} = 4599.00 - \frac{(4721.00)^2}{6801.83} = 4599.00 - 3276.74 = 1322.26$$

The adjusted between-groups sum of squares $SS_{A(adj.)}$ is obtained simply by sub-traction:[5]

$$SS_{A(adj.)} = SS_{T(adj.)} - SS_{S/A(adj.)} \tag{22-8}$$

Completing the calculations, we have

$$SS_{A(adj.)} = 2009.38 - 1322.26 = 687.12$$

The two adjusted SS's, $SS_{A(adj.)}$ and $SS_{S/A(adj.)}$, can easily be converted to the adjusted R^2's we obtained by MRC in Sec. 22.1. We can calculate these quantities by forming the following ratios:

$$R^2_{Y.A(adj.)} = \frac{SS_{A(adj.)}}{SS_{T(Y)}} = \frac{687.12}{5793.00} = .1186$$

$$R^2_{Y.S/A(adj.)} = \frac{SS_{S/A(adj.)}}{SS_{T(Y)}} = \frac{1322.26}{5793.00} = .2283$$

These values are identical to those presented in Table 22-2.

The final steps in the analysis are summarized in Table 22-6. The only new point to note is the number of degrees of freedom associated with the error term. Usually, this number is equal to

$$df_{S/A} = (a)(s - 1) = (3)(12 - 1) = (3)(11) = 33$$

In ANCOVA, we lose one degree of freedom by estimating the within-groups regression sum of squares, and so we have

$$df_{S/A(adj.)} = (a)(s - 1) - 1 = 33 - 1 = 32$$

The final F, 8.31, is equal within rounding error to the value of 8.35 obtained by MRC in Sec. 22.1.

---

[5] You might wonder why the treatment sum of squares is not adjusted in the same way as the other two sums of squares. The reason usually given is that this "indirect" method guarantees that the treatment effects do not enter into the adjustment process (see Kirk, 1982, p. 727).

Table 22-6
Summary of the Analysis of Covariance

Source	SS	df	MS	F
$A(adj.)$	687.12	2	343.56	8.31*
$S/A\ (adj.)$	1322.26	32	41.32	
Total $(adj.)$	2009.38	34		

*$p < .01$.

Adjusting the Treatment Means

In Sec. 22.1, we showed how the treatment means may be adjusted with the regression equation from the MRC analysis. With ANOVA, we also use a regression equation, though a different one, namely,

$$\bar{Y}'_{A_i} = \bar{Y}_{A_i} - (b_{S/A})(\bar{X}_{A_i} - \bar{X}_T) \tag{22-9}$$

where $\bar{Y}'_{A_i}$ = the adjusted treatment mean for level a_i

$\bar{Y}_{A_i}$ = the unadjusted treatment mean for level a_i

$b_{S/A}$ = the average within-group regression coefficient

$\bar{X}_{A_i}$ = the group mean on the covariate for level a_i

$\bar{X}_T$ = the grand mean on the covariate

The only quantity requiring explanation is $b_{S/A}$. This regression coefficient is an average of the regression coefficients between Y and X found separately for the treatment groups.[6] It is easily obtained from information already available; that is,

$$b_{S/A} = \frac{SP_{S/A}}{SS_{S/A(X)}} \tag{22-10}$$

Using the values from Table 22-5, we find

$$b_{S/A} = \frac{4721.00}{6801.83} = .6941$$

We are now ready to use Eq. (22-9) to calculate the adjusted treatment means. The group means on the dependent variable and the covariate are given in Table 22-4. The grand mean on the covariate is simply the mean of the three group means,

[6] The regression coefficient is actually a *weighted* average of the separate within-group regression coefficients (see Keppel, 1982, pp. 507–508).

101.72. Substituting in Eq. (22-9), we find

$$\bar{Y}'_{A_1} = 40.00 - (.6941)(103.75 - 101.72) = 40.00 - 1.4090 = 38.5910$$

$$\bar{Y}'_{A_2} = 26.00 - (.6941)(99.08 - 101.72) = 26.00 + 1.8324 = 27.8324$$

$$\bar{Y}'_{A_3} = 34.50 - (.6941)(102.33 - 101.72) = 34.50 - .4234 = 34.0766$$

Except for slight rounding errors, these values are the same as those calculated with Eq. (22-3) from the MRC analysis.

Testing for Homogeneity of Group Regression Coefficients

We indicated in Sec. 22.1 that the adjustment procedures in ANCOVA depend on the assumption of homogeneity of the regression coefficients representing the slopes of the regression lines for the different treatment groups. The ANOVA equivalent of this test is complicated—at least in comparison with MRC. It consists of dividing the adjusted within-groups sum of squares $SS_{S/A(adj.)}$ into two parts, one that represents the differences among the group regression coefficients, and another that represents deviations of the individual Y scores from their group regression lines. The first quantity is often called the *between regression* sum of squares, and the second quantity, the *within regression* sum of squares. In symbols,

$$SS_{S/A(adj.)} = SS_{bet.\ reg.} + SS_{w.\ reg.} \qquad (22\text{-}11)$$

We will present the formula for the first component, $SS_{bet.\ reg.}$, and then obtain the other component by subtraction.

The computational formula for $SS_{bet.\ reg.}$, which we will present in a moment, adds together the sums of squares associated with the individual group regression lines and then subtracts the sum of squares associated with the *average* regression line. We will consider this operation step by step. For any given treatment group, the sum of squares associated with the linear regression of X and Y, $SS_{lin.\ reg.}$, is given by the following formula:

$$SS_{lin.\ reg.} = \frac{(SP_{S/A_i})^2}{SS_{S/A_i(X)}} \qquad (22\text{-}12)$$

The numerator for Eq. (22-12) is given by

$$SP_{S/A_i} = \Sigma\ XY - \frac{(A_{i(X)})\,(A_{i(Y)})}{s}$$

where $\Sigma\ XY =$ the sum of the products of the X and Y scores for all the subjects in the treatment group

$\quad\ A_{i(X)} =$ the sum of the X scores for the group

$\quad\ A_{i(Y)} =$ the sum of the Y scores for the group

$\quad\quad\ s =$ the number of subjects in the group

The denominator for Eq. (22-12) is the within-group sum of squares for the treatment group on the covariate; that is,

$$SS_{S/A_i(X)} = \Sigma\,X^2 - \frac{(A_{i(X)})^2}{s}$$

Using the information from Table 22-4, we will illustrate the calculations for the first group, a_1:

$$SP_{S/A_1} = 51{,}271 - \frac{(1245)(480)}{12}$$

$$= 51{,}271 - \frac{597{,}600}{12} = 51{,}271 - 49{,}800 = 1{,}471.00$$

$$SS_{S/A_1(X)} = 132{,}001 - \frac{1245^2}{12}$$

$$= 132{,}001 - \frac{1{,}550{,}025}{12} = 132{,}001 - 129{,}168.75 = 2832.25$$

and from Eq. (22-12),

$$SS_{lin.\,reg.} = \frac{(1471.00)^2}{2832.25} = \frac{2{,}163{,}841}{2832.25} = 764.00$$

This final value of 764.00 represents the sum of squares associated with the regression line calculated for the first treatment group. The corresponding sums of squares for the other two groups are calculated in a similar fashion.

We are now ready for the formula for the between-regression sum of squares:

$$SS_{bet.\,reg.} = \Sigma\,\frac{(SP_{S/A_i})^2}{SS_{S/A_i(X)}} - \frac{(SP_{S/A})^2}{SS_{S/A(X)}} \tag{22-13}$$

The first term to the right of the equal sign is the sum of the regression sums of squares obtained separately for the different treatment groups, while the second term is the regression sum of squares based on an average of the separate regression coefficients. If the individual regression coefficients are homogeneous, the first term will approximately equal the second and $SS_{bet.\,reg.}$ will be close to zero. On the other hand, if they are not homogeneous, the first term will be larger than the second and $SS_{bet.\,reg.}$ will have a positive value. The size of the difference depends on the degree of heterogeneity present in the data. Using the information available in Table 22-4, we find

$$SS_{bet.\,reg.} = \left[\frac{(1471.00)^2}{2832.25} + \frac{(2352.00)^2}{2726.92} + \frac{(898.00)^2}{1242.67}\right] - \frac{(4721.00)^2}{6801.83}$$

$$= (764.00 + 2028.63 + 648.93) - 3276.74 = 3441.56 - 3276.74$$

$$= 164.82$$

You may recall from Eq. (22-11) that

$$SS_{S/A(adj.)} = SS_{bet.\,reg.} + SS_{w.\,reg.}$$

which we can use to calculate the other sum of squares needed for the analysis, namely,

$$SS_{w.\,reg.} = SS_{S/A(adj.)} - SS_{bet.\,reg.} \qquad (22\text{-}14)$$

Substituting in Eq. (22-14), we obtain

$$SS_{w.\,reg.} = 1322.26 - 162.82 = 1157.44$$

This last sum of squares represents the *residual* variation based on the deviation of each Y score from its group regression line. For this reason, $SS_{w.\,reg.}$ will be used to calculate the error term to evaluate the homogeneity assumption.

The final steps are summarized in Table 22-7. We convert the two component sums of squares to mean squares by dividing each sum of squares by the appropriate number of degrees of freedom. More specifically,

$$MS_{bet.\,reg.} = \frac{SS_{bet.\,reg.}}{a-1} \quad \text{and} \quad MS_{w.\,reg.} = \frac{SS_{w.\,reg.}}{(a)(s-2)}$$

The *df* for the between-regression sum of squares is 1 less than the number of groups $(a - 1)$. The *df* for the within-regression sum of squares reflects the fact that a sum of squares representing the variation around a group regression line, which would usually have 1 less degree of freedom than the number of subjects in the group (that is, $s - 1$), loses an additional *df* for estimating the group regression coefficient (that is, it becomes $s - 2$). Finally, we have the F test:

$$F = \frac{MS_{bet.\,reg.}}{MS_{w.\,reg.}}$$

Table 22-7
Summary of the Test for Homogeneity
of Regression

Source	SS	df	MS	F
Between regression	164.82	2	82.41	2.14
Within regression	1157.44	30	38.58	
S/A (adj.)	1322.26	32		

which is evaluated with $df_{num.} = a - 1$ and $df_{denom.} = (a)(s - 2)$. The F reported in Table 22-7, 2.14, is not significant. The value obtained from the MRC analysis was 2.13; the difference between the two values is due to rounding error. The homogeneity assumption is upheld.

Comment

You have seen again that MRC and ANOVA procedures may be used interchangeably in analyzing the results of an experiment. In this case, the procedure was the analysis of covariance. We mentioned earlier that in our opinion ANCOVA is easier to understand when it is conducted within the context of MRC. Since researchers will generally use a computer to conduct the ANCOVA analysis, neither approach has a distinct advantage from a practical point of view. The usefulness of ANCOVA is often overlooked by experimentalists, in part because of the computational complexities involved when the calculations are undertaken by hand. Often, covariates may be introduced into an experimental procedure at relatively little cost. Perhaps attitudes will change once researchers realize that the gain in sensitivity achieved through the use of ANCOVA comes at a considerable saving over other alternatives, such as increasing the sample size in an experiment or attempting to hold extraneous variables constant.

22.3 SINGLE-*df* COMPARISONS

As you know by now, our interest in the omnibus F test is usually only secondary. What most researchers wish to extract from an experiment is information about a number of planned comparisons involving the treatment means. This will also be true with the analysis of covariance, of course, except that the comparisons will be based on the *adjusted means* rather than the actual means observed in the experiment. Formulas for adjusting the treatment means were presented for both MRC and ANOVA in previous sections. From this point on, we will proceed identically with the analysis, regardless of how the adjusted treatment means were obtained. The only difference between MRC and ANOVA is in the calculation of error terms.

The Adjusted Comparison Sum of Squares

We start with the familiar formula from ANOVA for a sum of squares based on a single-*df* comparison, revised to reflect the use of adjusted rather than unadjusted treatment means. More specifically,

$$SS_{A_{comp.}(adj.)} = \frac{(s)(\hat{\psi}')^2}{\Sigma(c_i)^2} \tag{22-15}$$

where s = the sample size for each group

$\hat{\psi}'$ = the comparison calculated from the adjusted treatment means

c_i = the coefficients used to determine the adjusted comparison

To illustrate, we will calculate the adjusted sums of squares for the two comparisons we used to represent the treatment effects in the original MRC analysis in Sec. 22.1. The first $(c_i: +1, -1, 0)$ compares the two science conditions. For this comparison,

$$\hat{\psi}' = (+1)(38.59) + (-1)(27.83) + (0)(34.08) = 38.59 - 27.83 = 10.76$$

Substituting in Eq. (22-15), we find

$$SS_{A_{comp.}(adj.)} = \frac{(12)(10.76)^2}{(+1)^2 + (-1)^2 + (0)^2} = \frac{1389.33}{2} = 694.67$$

The second comparison contrasted the combined science conditions with the history condition. For this comparison we will use a fractional set $(c_i: +\frac{1}{2}, +\frac{1}{2}, -1)$ that will give a value for $\hat{\psi}'$ that will reflect the actual difference between the means rather than some multiple of it. (We would obtain the same adjusted sum of squares in either case, of course.) With these new coefficients, the comparison becomes

$$\hat{\psi}' = (+\tfrac{1}{2})(38.59) + (+\tfrac{1}{2})(27.83) + (-1)(34.08) = 33.21 - 34.08 = -.87$$

Completing the calculations, we get[7]

$$SS_{A_{comp.}(adj.)} = \frac{(12)(-.87)^2}{(+\tfrac{1}{2})^2 + (+\tfrac{1}{2})^2 + (-1)^2} = \frac{9.08}{1.5} = 6.05$$

---

[7] You may have noticed that the two adjusted comparison sums of squares do not add up to the adjusted treatment sum of squares even though the two comparisons are orthogonal. That is, $694.67 + 6.05 = 700.72$ does not equal the value of 687.12 for $SS_{A(adj.)}$ given in Table 22-6. In fact, the adjusted sum of squares for the first comparison (694.67) *exceeds* the adjusted treatment sum of squares. This discrepancy occurs because of the different ways in which the two sums of squares are calculated. In MRC, the adjusted treatment sum of squares is obtained as an *increment*, while the adjusted treatment means, upon which the adjusted comparison sums of squares are based, are obtained by means of a regression equation. In ANOVA, the adjusted treatment sum of squares is obtained by subtraction, while the adjusted treatment means are also obtained from a related regression equation. In spite of this confusion, the procedures we present here are correct.

The F Ratio

The final step is to calculate the F for each comparison. The error term for the two comparisons is not quite what you would expect from our earlier discussions dealing with the analysis of unadjusted Y scores. In brief, the error term starts with the adjusted error term we used to assess the omnibus F test, modified to take into consideration the magnitude of differences observed on the *covariate*. For convenience, and to be compatible with most other texts, we will express the F ratio in terms of mean squares. The formula for the F test is

$$F = \frac{MS_{A_{comp.}(adj.)}}{MS'_{error}} \tag{22-16}$$

where $MS_{A_{comp.}(adj.)}$ = the adjusted mean square for the comparison, which is equal to the adjusted comparison sum of squares (since the df for the comparison is 1)

MS'_{error} = the special error term that we will compute separately for ANOVA and MRC

We will consider the calculation of MS'_{error} next.

The ANOVA Approach.   This special error term MS'_{error} may be expressed as follows:

$$MS'_{error} = MS_{S/A(adj.)}\left(1 + \frac{MS_{A(X)}}{SS_{S/A(X)}}\right) \tag{22-17}$$

where $MS_{S/A(adj.)}$ = the adjusted error term from the ANCOVA analysis which we considered in Sec. 22.2

$MS_{A(X)}$ = the between-groups mean square based on the *covariate X*

$SS_{S/A(X)}$ = the within-groups sum of squares also based on the covariate

As you can see from Eq. (22-17), the adjusted error term $MS_{S/A(adj.)}$ is increased by an amount that reflects the degree to which the treatment groups differ on the *covariate* $(MS_{A(X)})$, relative to the pooled variability of subjects within the treatment groups $(SS_{S/A(X)})$. In most cases, this factor will be quite small and will have little effect on the final outcome of the analysis. The information needed for this formula may be found in Tables 22-5 and 22-6. From Table 22-5, then, we calculate first

$$MS_{A(X)} = \frac{SS_{A(X)}}{a - 1} = \frac{137.39}{3 - 1} = 68.70$$

Next we obtain $SS_{S/A(X)}$ from Table 22-5 and $MS_{S/A(adj.)}$ from Table 22-6. Substituting all three of these quantities in Eq. (22-17), we find

$$MS'_{error} = (41.32)\left(1 + \frac{68.70}{6801.83}\right) = (41.32)(1 + .01)$$

$$= (41.32)(1.01) = 41.73$$

We can now calculate the F ratios for the two comparisons. Substituting in Eq. (22-16), we have

$$F = \frac{MS_{Acomp.(adj.)}}{MS'_{error}} = \frac{694.67}{41.73} = 16.65$$

for the comparison between the two science conditions; and for the comparison between the two combined science conditions and the history condition,

$$F = \frac{6.05}{41.73} = .14$$

The first F is significant and the second is not.

The MRC Approach.   We may also find the special error term MS'_{error} by using information available from the MRC analysis. More specifically,

$$MS'_{error} = (\bar{R}^2_{Y.S/A(adj.)})(SS_Y)\left(1 + \frac{R^2_{X.A}/k}{1 - R^2_{X.A}}\right) \qquad (22\text{-}18)$$

where $\bar{R}^2_{Y.S/A(adj.)}$ = the error term from the overall MRC analysis of covariance, which we considered in Sec. 22.1

SS_Y = the total sum of squares based on the scores on the dependent variable Y

$R^2_{X.A}$ = a multiple correlation coefficient between the *covariate* X and the vectors representing the treatment conditions

k = the number of vectors required to represent the treatment conditions

We will now illustrate the calculations specified by Eq. (22-18). The first term in the formula, $\bar{R}^2_{Y.S/A(adj.)}$, is the error term from the overall analysis of covariance, which we calculated in Sec. 22.1; the value reported in Table 22-2 is .0071. The second term, SS_Y, is the total sum of squares on the dependent variable and is readily found in the computer summary of the analysis; in this case, the value is $SS_Y = 5793.00$. The final quantity needed for the calculations, $R^2_{X.A}$, would be obtained from an analysis in which the covariate X is correlated with the $k = 2$ treatment vectors; this analysis involves using X as if it were a Y or dependent variable and finding the multiple correlation between X and the two treatment vectors. The result of such an analysis reveals that $R^2_{X.A} = .0198$. Substituting in Eq. (22-18), then, we find

$$MS'_{error} = (.0071)(5793.00)\left(1 + \frac{.0198/2}{1 - .0198}\right)$$

$$= (41.1303)\left(1 + \frac{.0099}{.9802}\right) = (41.1303)(1 + .0101)$$

$$= (41.1303)(1.0101) = 41.5457$$

or 41.55 when rounded to two places. (The value obtained with ANOVA was 41.73; the discrepancy reflects rounding error.) From this point on, we proceed as we did with ANOVA, by substituting the necessary information in Eq. (22-16).

Comment

Again, it is instructive to see what we have accomplished by the analysis of covariance. A comparison of the error term used for the analysis of variance in Chap. 11 (139.36) with the error term used for the analysis of covariance (41.73 for ANOVA or 41.55 for MRC) shows a dramatic drop in favor of the analysis of covariance. This gain in precision is the primary reason for turning to the analysis of covariance. An examination of the mean squares for the two comparisons also shows fairly sizable drops (1176.00 versus 694.67 for the first comparison and 18.00 versus 6.05 for the second comparison). The reason for the reduction in the size of these single-df comparisons lies in the adjustment applied to the treatment means. You will recall that the physical science group scored higher on the intelligence test than did the social science group; the analysis of covariance reduced the difference between these two groups on the dependent variable to compensate for this initial advantage enjoyed by the physical science group. A similar explanation holds for the second comparison. The net result of these changes as reflected in the final F's, however, is that we achieve a marked gain in power by using the analysis of covariance.

22.4   OTHER APPLICATIONS OF ANCOVA TO EXPERIMENTAL DESIGNS

As we pointed out at the beginning of Sec. 22.2, ANCOVA was originally developed for use with between-subjects designs—designs in which subjects are assigned randomly to the treatment conditions. In fact, a central premise underlying the appropriate use of ANCOVA is that group differences existing before the experimental manipulation are the result of *chance differences only*. (As you will see in Sec. 22.5, many applications of ANCOVA to *non*experimental designs fail exactly at this point.) In this section, we will consider additional applications of ANCOVA to experimental designs.

Multiple Covariates

We are not restricted in the number of covariates we may use in the analysis of covariance. Although there may be a diminishing return as we continue to add covariates, since many relevant covariates will be highly intercorrelated, we still increase the sensitivity of an experiment whenever we include additional information in the analysis. For MRC, adding covariates creates no real problem—the covariates are simply added to the analysis as a *set* and are then treated as if the set were a single covariate. Several numerical examples of the use of multiple covariates are readily available in Cohen and Cohen (1983, pp. 387–402), Huitema (1980, Chap. 8), and Pedhazur (1982, pp. 513–519), among other sources. For ANOVA, the situation becomes quite complicated if the calculations are to be accomplished by hand. (There is no serious problem if a computer program is used, of course.) Examples with two multiple correlates may be found in Kirk (1982, pp. 737–740) and Winer (1971, pp. 809–812).

Within-Subjects Designs

"Pure" within-subjects designs, in which subjects serve in all the treatment conditions, do not benefit from a standard analysis of covariance. The reason is simple: there are no group differences to adjust, since each subject is present in all treatment conditions. Mixed factorial designs, in which between-subjects and within-subjects factors are incorporated into the same experiment, may be profitably subjected to ANCOVA procedures, however. In these cases, only the between-subjects sources of variability will be affected by the ANCOVA. On the other hand, the use of a covariate in a mixed factorial design is a creative way of taking advantage of two methods designed to increase power or sensitivity—having subjects serve as their own controls in the within-subjects portion of the analysis, and using the analysis of covariance for the between-subjects portion. For an example of such an analysis with the MRC approach, see Huitema (1980, pp. 223–230); and for an example with the ANOVA approach, see Winer (1971, pp. 796–805). There are ways to apply a covariance adjustment to within-subjects sources of variance, but these require the use of a covariate that can be administered just before the start of each of the different treatments the same subjects receive. For examples of this latter type of design that illustrate the ANOVA approach, see Myers (1979, pp. 424–428) and Winer (1971, pp. 805–808).

Factorial Designs

The analysis of covariance is easily adapted to factorial designs of any degree of complexity. Although space does not permit a detailed discussion of this topic, we will briefly describe the nature of the analysis. For MRC, the hierarchical strategy produces R^2's that represent the *unique* influences of the main effects and interactions. In a two-factor design, for example, we would have the covariate X and sets of vectors representing the two main effects and the interaction, which we will call A, B, and $A \times B$, respectively. The overall squared multiple correlation coefficient involving all four sets of information is $R^2_{Y.X,A,B,A \times B}$. We obtain the adjusted main effect of factor A by determining the unique contribution of the A vectors. More specifically,

$$R^2_{Y.A(adj.)} = R^2_{Y.X,A,B,A \times B} - R^2_{Y.X,B,A \times B}$$

where the difference between the two squared multiple correlation coefficients on the right of the equal sign clearly reflects the *increment* associated with the A vectors—that is, the A main effect. The other factorial effects are obtained in the same manner, by subtracting an R^2 for which the critical set of vectors has been deleted from the analysis. Examples of this analysis may be found in Huitema (1980, pp. 207–216). For ANOVA, the corresponding analysis involves analogous changes in procedure. We are unable to elaborate or describe these changes— again, for reasons of space. Fortunately, there are several readily available sources that you may consult when necessary (see, for example, Keppel, 1982, pp. 509– 511; Kirk, 1982, pp. 743–747; Myers, 1979, pp. 422–424; and Winer, 1971, pp. 787–792).

22.5 ANCOVA AND NONEXPERIMENTAL DESIGNS

The basic premise of ANCOVA, that differences existing before the start of an experiment can be taken into consideration during the statistical analysis, has been widely adopted by researchers who are working with nonexperimental designs. Unfortunately, most of these applications are *not supported* by the logic underlying the analysis of covariance. Consider, for example, the quasi-experimental designs we described in Chap. 21. Generally, these designs employ a number of intact or preexisting groups that can serve as treatment groups in the experiment. These may be different classes in a school system, different wards in a hospital, different assembly lines in a factory, and so on. Prior to the start of the experiment, each group is assigned, perhaps at random, to one of the treatment conditions. The experiment is then conducted and the data are analyzed. Contrast this situation with an actual experiment. In this case a pool of subjects is identified, and then groups are formed by random assignment from this pool. Finally, these groups are subjected to the different treatment conditions. How do these two scenarios differ? Superficially, they may appear to be the same, but fundamentally, they are not.

The experimental arrangement with intact groups is called a *quasi-experimental design* for good reason—it is not quite a true experimental design. The basic difference between an experiment and a quasi experiment lies in the assignment of subjects to treatments. In the quasi experiment, *intact groups* are assigned to the conditions, whereas in an experiment, *individual subjects* are assigned to the conditions. The logic underlying statistical hypothesis testing is that when the null hypothesis is true, the treatment groups will be equal, at least within the bounds of random error. This expectation is correct when subjects are assigned randomly to the treatments, but *not correct* when the *groups* are assigned to the treatments. The explanation is simple: for experiments, uncontrolled factors are *unsystematic* or random, while for quasi experiments, they are *systematic* or nonrandom.

We should elaborate this important distinction. Individual subjects will certainly differ among themselves in the experiment, but the differences are expected to "iron out" through the process of random assignment. That is, with larger and larger sample sizes, the chance differences existing among the groups are expected to become increasingly smaller. Additionally, we follow a procedure in which we take these chance differences into consideration when we evaluate the significance of a statistical test. These factors are not pertinent with quasi experiments. The groups of subjects are generally not constituted randomly, and so they will differ systematically on a number of characteristics relevant to the experiment. Moreover, increases in group size will have no systematic effect on preexisting differences, as they do when the individual assignment procedure is random. In addition, even if the groups were randomly created at one time, there is no guarantee that they would be treated equally following their random assignment. In short, then, the usual analysis procedures designed to interpret the results of experiments, in which subjects are randomly assigned to the treatment conditions, are simply inappropriate for designs in which intact groups of subjects are assigned to treatments.

What about ANCOVA? The method was devised to provide a statistical matching of groups of subjects that differ before the start of the experiment. But ANCOVA also depends on the assumption that individuals have been randomly assigned to the conditions. If this assumption is not met, any adjustment in treatment means cannot be defended or justified statistically. Therefore, most quasi experiments cannot be properly brought into statistical alignment by ANCOVA. Differences that are present at the beginning of the study must still be considered in the interpretation of the results at the end of the study. The example of a pretest-posttest design with intact groups, which we considered in Chap. 21 (pages

445–448), is a typical instance of what you will find in the literature. It is somewhat depressing to note that while all statistical methodology books continue to stress the conclusion that ANCOVA should not be used in quasi-experimental designs, misapplications of the procedure are still committed and reported in the literature. Pedhazur (1982, pp. 520–526), for example, describes a number of actual instances in which ANCOVA was incorrectly applied to nonexperimental designs. Huitema (1980, Chaps. 6 and 7) provides a detailed discussion of this and related problems. This does not mean that the situation is hopeless, but only that we cannot use statistical arguments to support the analysis of a quasi experiment as if it were a true experiment in which subjects were assigned randomly to the treatment conditions.

But as long as we keep in mind how our groups are formed and assigned to treatments, we can conduct *some* kind of appropriate analysis. If we cannot control for differences on a covariate in order to study differences between groups, we can conduct analyses of how the relationship between two variables differs for different groups. These latter analyses are possible through the study of interactions, which was presented in Chap. 21.

22.6   SUMMARY

In this chapter we considered a statistical procedure, the analysis of covariance (ANCOVA), that is used to increase the sensitivity of an experiment statistically. With ANCOVA, we use information about the subjects that is available before the start of an experiment to adjust for chance factors that are unrelated to the experimental manipulation. The analysis of covariance introduces two adjustments to the analysis, both of which are based on the relationship between the covariate and the dependent variable. One adjustment is a reduction in *error variance*, and the other is a correction for any bias among the treatment groups produced by the process of random assignment. In general, we expect the first adjustment to be the major one and the second to be secondary. Moreover, although the size of the error term will always be reduced by ANCOVA, the nature of the adjustment of systematic variance—the differences among the treatment groups—will depend on the relative patterns of differences observed on both the covariate and the dependent variable; because the discrepancies between groups are determined by chance factors, the adjustment will be an increase in the estimated treatment effects half of the time and a decrease in them the other half.

We introduced ANCOVA with the MRC approach. With MRC, analysis of covariance is accomplished through the use of a particular hierarchical strategy that isolates the variability associated with the dependent variable Y and its correlation with the prior information, or the covariate X. The R^2 reflecting the adjusted treatment effects is then represented as incremental variability, and the R^2 reflecting the adjusted error term is obtained as a residual variability. We also adjust the treatment means for chance differences that exist before the experiment, using information from the overall analysis. Single-df comparisons are based on the adjusted means and tested with a special error term. One of the assumptions underlying ANCOVA is that the regression coefficients relating X and Y are the same for all the treatment groups. This assumption of the homogeneity of regression must be met in order to justify the analysis statistically. To test for this homogeneity in the MRC analysis, we begin by adding interaction vectors to the analysis; the vectors are formed by cross-multiplying the covariate and the treatment vectors. We then use the interaction vectors to determine the extent to which individual regression coefficients differ among themselves.

In contrast with MRC, the ANOVA approach is relatively complicated and, to the novice, seemingly arbitrary and confusing. The adjustment procedures require the calculation of two sets of sums of squares—one set for the covariate and one for the dependent variable—and a set of sums of products which are based on the cross multiplication of subjects' X and Y scores. These quantities are then used to adjust the sums of squares for the actual analysis. The adjustment of treatment means and the analysis of single-df comparisons are essentially the same as in the MRC analysis. The test for homogeneity of regression is computationally complex in comparison with MRC, but it provides the same outcome nevertheless.

The analysis of covariance may be enhanced by the use of multiple covariates, and it may be extended to factorial designs, including mixed designs in which both within-subjects and between-subjects factors are present. The use of ANCOVA with nonexperimental designs to equate groups that were not created randomly at the time of the study represents a major misuse of the procedure. In most, if not all of the cases, ANCOVA is not statistically justified, since it depends critically on the assumption that individual subjects—not groups of subjects—have been assigned randomly to the treatment conditions.

22.7   EXERCISES

1. Let us return to the exercise in Chap. 10 in which we introduced an experiment concerned with the effect of verbal reinforcement on children's performance. Suppose we hypothesize that a measure of self-esteem (X) could explain differences observed in the experiment and thus collect scores on a self-esteem measure for

each of the children as follows:

Praise		Reproof		None	
X	Y	X	Y	X	Y
11	4	8	7	12	7
12	7	9	6	8	3
15	5	12	9	10	7
9	3	9	7	9	5
10	6	7	8	11	7
11	4	10	6	13	8
13	6	11	7	12	5

a. Perform an analysis of covariance on these data by MRC and ANOVA.
b. Determine the adjusted means in both cases.
c. Conduct two meaningful comparisons, one of "praise" with "reproof" and the other of the combination of "praise" and "reproof" with "none."

23

Analysis of Trend

. . .

485

In this chapter, we return to a topic that we could have presented initially in Chap. 11, when we considered the detailed analysis of a single-factor experiment. At that time, we indicated how an experiment with several treatment conditions could be divided profitably into smaller two-group "experiments," each representing a meaningful comparison between two treatment means or combinations of treatment means. In fact, we argued that these so-called single-df comparisons are ideally suited for the detailed analysis of experiments in which treatment conditions differ *qualitatively*, or in terms of the *type* or the *kind* of manupulation involved.

Not all experiments are profitably divided into these qualitatively different, miniature two-group experiments, however. Another major category consists of experiments in which the treatment conditions vary in the *degree* to which they reflect the independent variable. The independent variables in such experiments are called **quantitative independent variables**, to emphasize the fact that their levels represent discrete or continuous points on some ordered dimension. In such experiments we are interested not in the comparison of one group against another, as we were when we considered the analysis of qualitative independent variables in earlier chapters, but in determining the existence of a systematic relationship between variables, or a trend relating increases in the independent variable to changes in the dependent variable. For this reason, then, it is generally not profitable to analyze the results of such experiments as a set of differences between means; instead we undertake an analysis of mathematical relationships between the independent variable and the dependent variable.

Though in this chapter we will be discussing quantitative independent variables in experiments, the use of such variables in research should not be unfamiliar to you, since in Chaps. 20 and 21 we used quantitative variables in nonexperimental studies designed for prediction purposes. There, we were concerned with the degree to which a quantitative variable could predict a dependent variable; in this chapter, we will be concerned with a somewhat different question, namely, whether there is a *systematic* trend for the dependent variable to change as the level of the independent variable (or X variable) changes.

Initially, we will discuss the use of trend analysis in the single-factor design and show how such an analysis is conducted with ANOVA and with MRC. Next, we will extend the analysis to the two-factor design in which one of the independent variables is manipulated quantitatively and the other is manipulated qualitatively. Finally, we will briefly discuss the application of trend analysis to data from non-experimental designs.

23.1 A GENERAL OVERVIEW OF TREND ANALYSIS

When an independent variable is continuous, its levels are amounts or degrees that fall into a numerical order, and its effect on behavior is assumed to be a continuous process. For this reason, then, we generally analyze the results from experiments with a quantitative independent variable with all the treatment conditions contributing to the analysis. Suppose, for example, that we are studying the effect of background noise on reading comprehension and that five ordered treatment conditions varying in the loudness of the noise constitute the experimental manipulation. Most researchers would be interested in determining the *underlying trend* of the relationship between the independent and dependent variables, taking into consideration the means from all five treatment conditions. Unless there are theoretical or practical reasons for doing so, we would not want to compare one of the treatment means with another; instead, we will be interested in the nature of the changes in Y when the independent variable is systematically varied.

Types of Trend

In trend analysis, the goal is to search for the simplest way to represent the underlying relationship between X and Y. Relationships can be linear so that as we move, for example, from one level to another on the independent variable, the change in the dependent variable follows accordingly. Or we can have a relationship that is nonlinear, so that as we move, for example, from low to medium levels on the independent variable, the dependent variable also increases, but as the independent variable increases from medium to high levels, the dependent variable begins to decrease. The top half of Fig. 23-1 illustrates these two types of relationships.

Since the simplest way to describe a relationship mathematically is with a straight line, trend analysis usually starts with a determination of whether a significant **linear trend** is in evidence. It then proceeds with a search for progressively more complex trends. The first of these is a **parabolic**, or **quadratic trend**, in which curvature enters the picture either as a function that first increases and then decreases as X increases (a function shaped like an inverted U) or as one that shows the reverse (a U-shaped function).

Curves of greater complexity are distinguished by the number of times the function reverses direction. A linear function has no reversals, of course, whereas the quadratic function we just described has one. A curve with two reversals reflects **cubic trend**, and one with three reversals, **quartic trend**. Examples of both types of curves are presented in the bottom half of Fig. 23-1. Researchers in the behavioral sciences usually concentrate their attention on linear and quadratic trends, however, and are rarely interested in trends of greater complexity than the cubic. The pref-

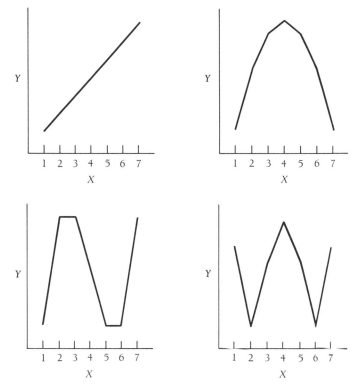

Figure 23-1   Examples of four types of trend.

erence for linear and quadratic trends is *simplicity*, both in the descriptive sense and in the theoretical sense. Imagine the difficulty one would have explaining why a relatively complex trend was significant! Fortunately, complex trends are quite rare and, if they do appear, are generally of minor influence, particularly when compared with linear and quadratic trends.

An Example of Trend Analysis

The classic example of trend analysis is found in a paper by Grant (1956), who is credited with introducing the procedure to experimental psychologists. The illustration, based on an actual study, was concerned with the tendency of a response conditioned to a particular stimulus to be elicited by other, similar stimuli. All subjects were first trained to respond to a circle 12 inches in diameter. Following training, the subjects were randomly assigned to seven different groups, each of which was tested with a different stimulus. One group was tested with the original training stimulus, while the others were tested with stimuli differing in size—three with stimuli smaller than the original stimulus (circles with diameter of 9, 10, and 11 inches) and three with stimuli larger than the original stimulus (circles with diameter of 13, 14, and 15 inches). The independent variable, size of the testing stimulus, was thus manipulated quantitatively.

Grant expected to find evidence for two trend components in the results of this experiment. The first expectation was that the response would become more consistent and intense as the size of the testing stimulus—the independent variable—increased from small to large. He hypothesized that this factor would be present because subjects have a general tendency to respond more vigorously (and more consistently) to larger stimuli than to smaller stimuli. He expected, therefore, an upward-sloping linear trend component. His second expectation, which was his main interest in the study, was that the response would be greatest among subjects for whom the testing stimulus was the *training* stimulus itself (the 12-inch circle) and would taper off gradually among subjects tested with stimuli increasingly different in size from the training stimulus. In this case, he was hypothesizing the presence of a *quadratic*, inverted U–shaped, function, showing a systematic decrease in responding as the testing stimulus deviated more and more from the training stimulus. He undertook a trend analysis that enabled him to test for the presence of both of these trends.

Grant's study is an excellent example of predicting the nature of a trend analysis on the basis of theory. That is, Grant based two planned comparisons on theoretical considerations. A great number of trend analyses are conducted without a specific theory to guide them, however. In these cases, researchers often undertake the analysis to detect the presence of significant lower-order trends, usually hoping to find relatively simple trend components that will assist them in *describing* the outcome of the experiment. Theoretical analysis in these cases often awaits the discovery of significant trends. In either situation—when trend components are hypothesized by theory or when trend components are used to simplify data description—the analysis of trend serves a useful purpose. Let us look now at the outcome of Grant's experiment.

The means from the experiment are presented in Fig. 23-2. Examine the seven means as a set and try to see whether a linear trend is present. That is, is there any general tendency for the means to increase steadily as stimulus size increases? Try drawing a "best-fitting" straight line through the seven data points. We assume that you "see" a general upward slope, which would suggest the possible presence of a linear trend. Deviations of the means from the line you have drawn reflect the success with which a straight line fits the actual data points. Large discrepancies would suggest that linear trend does not fully describe the relationship between

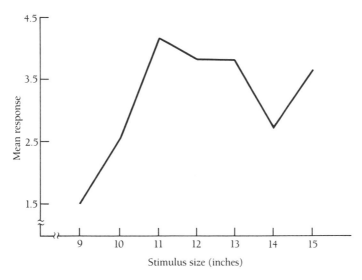

Figure 23-2   Mean response as a function of size of stimulus.

the independent and dependent variables. It should be clear that such is the case in Fig. 23-2, that linear trend alone is not sufficient to account for all (or even most) of the variation observed among the means.

As we have indicated, the general strategy of trend analysis at this point is to turn to more complex trends to see whether they capture or reflect any of the variability that is not accounted for by the linear function. Grant hypothesized a quadratic function. A closer examination of the means confirms his theoretical prediction, namely, that the response initially increases until it reaches a peak with the 11-inch circle and then drops off, without returning to this maximum level.[1]

Let us review what we have accomplished by looking at the outcome of the experiment in terms of linear and quadratic trends. The first two panels of Fig. 23-3 show how well the separate trend components describe the data points. The upper panel displays the best-fitting straight line, while the middle panel shows the plot of the best-fitting quadratic function. Although each trend component captures some aspects of the actual outcome, neither one does a fully adequate job by itself. (This is reflected in both cases by sizable deviations of the means from the respective best-fitting functions.) It is obvious that a *combination* of the two components, which is presented in the bottom panel, provides a much better fit.

[1] That the group exposed to the largest stimulus showed a relatively sizable rise rather than a continuing decline suggests the possibility of a cubic trend (two reversals), but this trend was not significant.

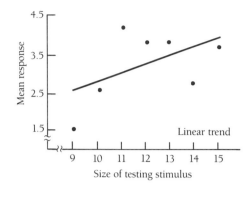

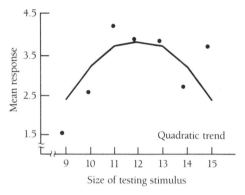

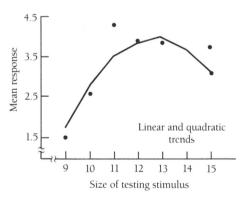

Figure 23-3   Mean response as a function of size of testing stimulus. The upper panel displays the linear component; the middle panel, the quadratic component; and the lower panel both components combined.

In summary, this example demonstrates that the analysis of quantitiative independent variables—like that of qualitative independent variables—is analytical. In contrast with the analysis of qualitative independent variables, where we tend to focus on differences between two means, trend analysis assesses the data for the presence of trend components, which are based on all the means, and offers a precise way of accounting for or explaining the overall variation among the treatment conditions.

Additional Considerations

An important point to add before we consider trend analysis in detail is that any conclusions concerning trend are limited to the levels included in the experiment. For example, we have no assurance that we can extend the findings beyond the two extremes of the independent variable, that is, to stimuli smaller than 9 inches or larger than 15 inches. Additional data will be necessary to settle this point. On the other hand, we might want to be able to apply the findings to values *between* any two consecutive levels—between 9 inches and 10 inches, 10 inches and 11 inches, and so on. (It is generally assumed that there are few abrupt or discontinuous changes in nature, and so it is usually "safe" to assume that changes in the function relating the independent variable to the response measure are continuous.)

The obvious solutions to these problems are to choose the two extremes wisely, so that the full extent of the independent variable is represented in the experiment, and to include a sufficient number of intermediate points as well to ensure reasonably safe interpolation between consecutive points on the independent variable.

23.2   STATISTICAL ANALYSIS OF TREND: THE SINGLE-FACTOR DESIGN

Trend analysis is accomplished quite easily with ANOVA and MRC through the use of special coefficients specifically designed to isolate variability associated with the different trend components. These coefficients are called **orthogonal polynomial coefficients**.They are designed to be "sensitive" to only one type of trend in its "pure" form—for example, a straight line or a U-shaped function; moreover, each set of polynomial coefficients is orthogonal to all others. For ANOVA, the coefficients are entered in the general formula for single-df comparisons that we used in Chap. 11 for qualitative comparisons, while for MRC, they are transformed into vectors and correlated with the dependent variable to indicate the trend that exists.

The number of trend components that can be isolated is limited—as you might suspect—by the degrees of freedom associated with the independent variable (that is, $df_A = a - 1$). Thus, an experiment with $a = 2$ treatments (which, again, represent different *amounts* of the variable) can yield information on linear trend only; one with $a = 3$ treatments yields information on linear and quadratic trends; one with $a = 4$ treatments yields information on linear, quadratic, and cubic trends; and so on.

The orthogonal polynomial coefficients for experiments ranging in size from $a = 3$ to 10 are presented in Table A-4 of the Appendix. Coefficients for trends up to quintic (i.e., for functions with up to four reversals) are provided in the table. More extensive tables may be found in Fisher and Yates (e.g., 1953) and Pearson and Hartley (e.g., 1970). In order to use Table A-4, you must first choose the correct collection of coefficients, of course; it is defined by the number of treatment levels. You can then use any or all of the sets of coefficients to extract information on orthogonal trend components.

There are two critical restrictions that apply to the use of this table: that the levels must represent intervals that are *equally spaced* on the dimension under study, and that *equal numbers of subjects* must be placed in each of the treatment conditions. Although violating either of the restrictions will not preclude trend analysis, it will prevent you from following exactly the procedures we will outline for using ANOVA and MRC to conduct the analysis. In Sec. 23.3 we will discuss solutions to the problem of unequal intervals, and we will consider the general problem of unequal sample sizes in Chap. 24.

Using ANOVA

We will now illustrate the procedures involved in conducting a trend analysis with ANOVA. For convenience, we will transform the experiment comparing three types of lectures, originally considered in Chap. 10, into an experiment in which the independent variable consists of three degrees of background noise present while the subjects are listening to the physical science lecture; that is, level a_1 now represents a low degree of noise, level a_2 a medium degree of noise, and level a_3 a high degree of noise. We will assume that the three levels are equally spaced on the loudness dimension. The information relevant for the trend analysis is presented in Table 23-1.

The means are based on the data appearing originally in Table 10-1 (page 121). The coefficients for the trend analysis have been obtained from Table A-4, from the sets designated for $a = 3$. With three data points, only two trend com-

Table 23-1

An Example of Trend Analysis

Means and Trend Coefficients

	Background Noise		
	Low (a_1)	Medium (a_2)	High (a_3)
Means	40.00	26.00	34.50
Linear coefficients	-1	0	1
Quadratic coefficients	-1	2	-1

Summary of the Analysis

Source	SS	df	MS	F
Linear	181.50	1	181.50	1.30
Quadratic	1012.50	1	1012.50	7.27*
S/A	4599.00	33	139.36	
Total	5793.00	35		

*$p < .01$.

ponents are possible, linear and quadratic. If we were to plot the coefficients on a graph, we would see that the linear coefficients $(-1, 0, +1)$ describe a straight line, while the quadratic coefficients $(-1, +2, -1)$ describe a curvilinear function (an inverted U). Both sets represent the two trends in their "pure" forms. That is, the linear function has no "bends," and the quadratic function has no "tilts." This property of orthogonal polynomial coefficients will be true with any set of coefficients selected from Table A-4.[2] In this regard, you should note that the two sets of coefficients are orthogonal; that is,

$$\Sigma\,(c_i)(c_i') = (-1)(-1) + (0)(+2) + (+1)(-1) = 0$$

[2] The "direction" of the trend exhibited by the coefficients—an upward rising linear function and an inverted U—is not important in detecting a trend component in a set of data. Because of the way sums of squares for trend components are calculated, you can change the direction of a set of coefficients by multiplying each coefficient by -1 without changing the final answer. In our example, we obtain the same sum of squares for the linear component by using the coefficients found in the table $(-1, 0, +1)$, which exhibit a positive linear slope, as we obtain if we multiply each coefficient by -1 and got $+1, 0, -1$, which exhibit a negative linear slope.

The formula for calculating a comparison sum of squares in given by Eq. (11-4),

$$SS_{comp.} = \frac{(s)(\hat{\psi})^2}{\Sigma (c_i)^2}$$

For the linear component,

$$\hat{\psi} = \Sigma (c_i)(\bar{Y}_{A_i})$$
$$= (-1)(40.00) + (0)(26.00) + (+1)(34.50) = -5.50$$

and

$$SS_{lin.} = \frac{(12)(-5.50)^2}{(-1)^2 + (0)^2 + (+1)^2} = \frac{363.00}{2} = 181.50$$

For the quadratic component,

$$\hat{\psi} = (-1)(40.00) + (+2)(26.00) + (-1)(34.50) = -22.50$$

and

$$SS_{quad.} = \frac{(12)(-22.50)^2}{(-1)^2 + (+2)^2 + (-1)^2} = \frac{6075.00}{6} = 1012.50$$

Since the two trend components are orthogonal,

$$SS_{lin.} + SS_{quad.} = 181.50 + 1012.50 = 1194.00$$

which is equal to the omnibus treatment sum of squares from the overall analysis (SS_A).

The remainder of the analysis is summarized in the bottom portion of Table 23-1. Each trend component is based on $df = 1$, and both mean squares are divided by the omnibus error term $MS_{S/A}$ calculated as it was in the earlier analysis (Table 10-2, page 121). Only the quadratic trend is significant. An examination of the means reveals a curvilinear, U-shaped function between background noise and vocabulary scores.

Using MRC

Conducting a trend analysis with MRC follows exactly the same steps we outlined in Sec. 11.3 for single-df comparisons involving qualitative independent variables. The key to the analysis is in the layout of the data; again, we use a listing of the Y scores and two vectors, chosen this time to reflect linear and quadratic trends. Whereas in previous analyses we set up a code matrix to reflect meaningful comparisons, in trend analysis, the code matrix contains the orthogonal coefficients from Table A-4:

	a_1	a_2	a_3
Linear	-1	0	$+1$
Quadratic	-1	$+2$	-1

Table 23-2 illustrates the format; the numbers for the two trend vectors are based on the sets of coefficients from Table A-4.

The standard MRC analysis will provide the omnibus R^2 ($R^2_{Y.max.}$) and the zero-order correlation coefficients. From these, we can complete the analysis: $R^2_{Y.max.}$ is used to calculate the error term, and the respective r^2's taken between Y and the two vectors are used as the numerator terms to assess the two trend components. From the correlation coefficients listed at the bottom of Table 23-2, we can calculate the $R^2_{Y.max.}$. Since the two trend vectors are orthogonal, we can use the simplified formula, Eq. (10-3),

$$R^2_{Y.max.} = r^2_{Y1} + r^2_{Y2}$$
$$= (-.1770)^2 + (-.4181)^2 = .0313 + .1748 = .2061$$

which provides one more demonstration that the omnibus $R^2_{Y.max.}$ is completely determined by the introduction of df_A vectors into the MRC analysis. The squared zero-order correlation coefficients are of primary interest, of course, since they reflect the proportion of Y variability attributable to the two trend components—$r^2_{Y1} = .0313$ for linear trend and $r^2_{Y2} = .1748$ for quadratic trend.

The F tests are specified by Eq. (11-9),

$$F = \frac{r^2_{comp.}}{(1 - R^2_{Y.max.})/(N - k - 1)}$$

For the linear component,

$$F = \frac{.0313}{(1 - .2061)/(36 - 2 - 1)}$$
$$= \frac{.0313}{.7939/33} = \frac{.0313}{.0241} = 1.30$$

and for the quadratic component,

$$F = \frac{.1748}{(1 - .2061)/(36 - 2 - 1)}$$
$$= \frac{.1748}{.0241} = 7.25$$

Table 23-2
Contrast Coding for Trend Analysis

Subject		Dependent Variable	Trend Vectors (1)	Trend Vectors (2)
a_1	1	53	−1	−1
	2	49	−1	−1
	3	47	−1	−1
	4	42	−1	−1
	5	51	−1	−1
	6	34	−1	−1
	7	44	−1	−1
	8	48	−1	−1
	9	35	−1	−1
	10	18	−1	−1
	11	32	−1	−1
	12	27	−1	−1
a_2	13	47	0	2
	14	42	0	2
	15	39	0	2
	16	37	0	2
	17	42	0	2
	18	33	0	2
	19	13	0	2
	20	16	0	2
	21	16	0	2
	22	10	0	2
	23	11	0	2
	24	6	0	2
a_3	25	45	1	−1
	26	41	1	−1
	27	38	1	−1
	28	36	1	−1
	29	35	1	−1
	30	33	1	−1
	31	46	1	−1
	32	40	1	−1
	33	29	1	−1
	34	21	1	−1
	35	30	1	−1
	36	20	1	−1

$$r_{lin.} = -.1770 \qquad r_{quad.} = -.4181$$
$$r_{12} = .0000$$

These two F ratios are identical, within rounding error, to those obtained with ANOVA and reported in Table 23-1.

The MRC analysis provides immediate information on the proportion of Y variability explained by each of the trends. The two proportions are given directly from the respective squared zero-order correlation coefficients, .0313 and .1748. We can obtain this same information from ANOVA simply by dividing each trend component sum of squares by the total sum of squares. To illustrate with the values presented in Table 23-1,

$$\frac{SS_{lin.}}{SS_T} = \frac{181.50}{5793.00} = .0313$$

and

$$\frac{SS_{quad.}}{SS_T} = \frac{1012.50}{5793.00} = .1748$$

which are identical to the proportions obtained with MRC.

23.3   TREND ANALYSIS WITH UNEQUAL INTERVALS

We have already noted that the orthogonal polynomial coefficients listed in Table A-4 may be used only when the treatment levels are evenly spaced. This poses a problem if a researcher wants a fine-grain examination of a certain portion of the independent variable—where dramatic or theoretically interesting changes are anticipated—and a coarser examination of the rest, since the researcher will then have to use unequal intervals, of course. We will consider two ways of analyzing trend with unequal intervals, one that involves the creation of a set of orthogonal polynomial coefficients, and another that involves a new way of coding the vectors in the MRC analysis.

Constructing Orthogonal Polynomial Coefficients

Anyone handy with algebra can construct orthogonal trend coefficients for any experiment, regardless of the number of treatment conditions or of the spacing between consecutive points on the independent variable. The method consists of solving equations that define a set of coefficients for each trend component in terms of the intervals included in the experiment and the basic shape of the trend component, whether linear, quadratic, or more complex. Equations with one or more unknowns are then established; these equations are based on two restrictions, namely, that the coefficients must sum to zero ($\Sigma\, c_i = 0$) and that all component sets of coefficients must be orthogonal ($\Sigma\, c_i c_i' = 0$).

The procedure is tedious, however, and highly prone to arithmetic errors and outright mistakes; in addition, rounding errors introduced during the solution of the simultaneous equations can seriously affect the calculation of the component sums of squares. If care is taken and calculations are carried out to a sufficient number of places, both problems can be eliminated or at least minimized. We will not illustrate this method, since it is treated in a number of readily available sources (e.g., Gaito, 1965; Keppel, 1982, pp. 629–633; Kirk, 1982, pp. 773–777; and Myers, 1979, pp. 441–445).

Using Powered Vectors

Power Coding. There is an alternative method for dealing with unequal intervals in which the intervals are represented by vectors based on the *actual values* of the independent variable, rather than on polynomial coefficients. The method uses what are called **powered vectors**, which are vectors coded in terms of integral powers of the values of the levels of the independent variable. To elaborate, the first vector uses the numbers representing the treatment conditions (X). In Grant's experiment, which we considered in Sec. 23.1, the numbers would correspond to the diameters in inches of the circles presented during the testing phase of the experiment, namely, 9, 10, 11, 12, 13, 14, and 15. The second vector is created by *squaring* the numbers in the first vector, i.e., raising them to the power of 2 (taking X^2). In this example, the respective codes would be

$$9^2 = 81, 10^2 = 100, \ldots, 14^2 = 196, \text{ and } 15^2 = 225$$

The third vector is constructed by raising the values of the first vector to the power of 3 (taking X^3). In the example, the respective codes would be

$$9^3 = 729, 10^3 = 1000, \ldots, 14^3 = 2744, \text{ and } 15^3 = 3375$$

The maximum number of vectors available for this analysis is equal to df_A; for this example, the number is 6.

Intercorrelation of Vectors. The first vector captures the *linear* trend component and will give the same $r_{lin.}^2$ as a vector based on the linear polynomial coefficients. The remaining vectors do not share this simplicity, unfortunately, but reflect more than one source of trend. More specifically, the second vector, which is based on the squared codes of the first vector, reflects the quadratic trend component *and* some portion of the linear component as well. You can see this if you plot the vector values for the Grant experiment: the progression of the numbers 81, 100, 121, 144, 169, 196, and 225 shows both a general upward slope (a linear trend) and a concave shape (a quadratic trend). This reflection of more than one source of trend in the second vector is indicated by the sizable correlation between the first two powered vectors ($r = .9974$).

The solution to this problem requires the use of MRC and a *hierarchical strategy* of the sort we discussed in Chap. 20 (page 410–413). Briefly, the strategy consists of evaluating the effects of the X variables (or vectors) in a particular order. We begin by correlating the first vector, the one based on the actual values of the independent variable, with the dependent variable; the correlation reflects the linear trend component directly. We obtain the quadratic trend component by adding to the analysis the next vector, which is based on the squared values of the levels of the independent variable. We determine the additional variability explained by the addition of the second vector by taking the difference between the second and first results. That is,

$$r^2_{quad.} = R^2_{Y.X,X^2} - r^2_{YX} \tag{23-1}$$

where $R^2_{Y.X,X^2}$ = the squared multiple correlation coefficient representing the combined linear and quadratic trend components

r^2_{YX} = the squared zero-order correlation coefficient representing the linear component alone.

We obtain each of the remaining components by systematically adding the next higher powered vector to the analysis. To illustrate, we obtain the cubic trend component by subtracting from the R^2 involving the *first three vectors*, $R^2_{Y.X,X^2,X^3}$, which contains information on all three trend components, the R^2 involving the *first two vectors*, $R^2_{Y.X,X^2}$, which contains information on the linear and quadratic trends combined. In symbols,

$$r^2_{cubic} = R^2_{Y.X,X^2,X^3} - R^2_{Y.X,X^2}$$

To test for significance of each trend component, we will use the formula for the F ratio in which the error term is based on the $R^2_{Y.max.}$ (or $1 - R^2_{Y.max.}$). In the Grant example, $R^2_{Y.max.}$ is $R^2_{Y.X,X^2,X^3,X^4,X^5,X^6}$.

An Example.   We will now see how the procedure works with the numerical example from Sec. 23.2. Table 23-3 shows the layout of the data for the analysis. Since the intervals in this example are equal, we have used the numbers 1, 2, and 3 as the code for vector 1 (the linear vector, X), although we would have entered the actual values of the independent variable if this were not a fictitious experiment.

Table 23-3
Powered Vectors for Trend Analysis

Subject		Dependent Variable	Powered Vectors	
			X	X^2
a_1	1	53	1	1
	2	49	1	1
	3	47	1	1
	4	42	1	1
	5	51	1	1
	6	34	1	1
	7	44	1	1
	8	48	1	1
	9	35	1	1
	10	18	1	1
	11	32	1	1
	12	27	1	1
a_2	13	47	2	4
	14	42	2	4
	15	39	2	4
	16	37	2	4
	17	42	2	4
	18	33	2	4
	19	13	2	4
	20	16	2	4
	21	16	2	4
	22	10	2	4
	23	11	2	4
	24	6	2	4
a_3	25	45	3	9
	26	41	3	9
	27	38	3	9
	28	36	3	9
	29	35	3	9
	30	33	3	9
	31	46	3	9
	32	40	3	9
	33	29	3	9
	34	21	3	9
	35	30	3	9
	36	20	3	9

$$r_{YX} = -.1770 \qquad r_{YX^2} = -.1155$$
$$r_{XX^2} = .9897$$

(The same information would be extracted, in any case.) We derive the second vector (X^2) from the first by taking the squares of the numbers defining vector 1, namely, $1^2 = 1, 2^2 = 4$, and $3^2 = 9$. The three zero-order correlation coefficients are given at the bottom of the table. As you can see, there is a substantial relationship between the two powered vectors ($r_{XX^2} = .9897$).

We have indicated that the zero-order correlation between Y and vector 1 (given by r_{Y1}^2) will provide unambiguous information concerning the degree to which a linear component is present. That is,

$$r_{lin.}^2 = r_{YX}^2 = (-.1770)^2 = .0313$$

This value is identical to the $r_{lin.}^2$ we obtained previously with the orthogonal polynomial coefficients.

The correlation coefficient taken between Y and vector 2, $r_{YX^2} = -.1155$, is quite different from the one we reported for orthogonal quadratic coefficients in Table 23-2 ($r_{quad.} = -.4181$). The reason for the discrepancy is the high intercorrelation between the two vectors with power coding ($r_{XX^2} = .9897$), the effect of which must be removed to reveal the pure quadratic component. We accomplished this by using Eq. (23-1) to isolate the proportion of Y variability *uniquely* due to vector 2 and quadratic trend. That is,

$$r_{quad.}^2 = R_{Y.X,X^2}^2 - r_{YX}^2$$

First, we will need to calculate $R_{Y.X,X^2}^2$. Using more precise values than those presented in Table 23-3 and applying Eq. (10-2), we find

$$R_{Y.X,X^2}^2 = \frac{r_{YX}^2 + r_{YX^2}^2 - 2r_{YX}r_{YX^2}r_{XX^2}}{1 - r_{XX^2}^2}$$

$$= \frac{(-.177005)^2 + (-.115466)^2 - (2)(-.177005)(-.115466)(.989743)}{1 - (.989743)^2}$$

$$= \frac{.031331 + .013332 - .040457}{1 - .979591} = \frac{.004206}{.020409} = .206086$$

which exactly equals the $R_{Y.1,2}^2$ rounded to four places, that we have reported on a number of occasions. Our reason for carrying out the calculations to six places is to reduce rounding error, which can become a serious problem with powered vectors, where the intercorrelations are extremely high. Most computer programs carry out the calculations to a sufficient number of significant places to minimize this sort of problem.

We can now calculate the proportion of Y variability associated exclusively with the quadratic component. This proportion is a squared semipartial correlation coefficient and is called *incremental variability*—the additional proportion of Y

Table 23-4
MRC Trend Analysis with Powered Vectors

Hierarchical Arrangement		Trend Component
$R^2_{Y.X}$	$=$	r^2_{linear}
$R^2_{Y.X,X^2} - R^2_{Y.X}$	$=$	$r^2_{quadratic}$
$R^2_{Y.X,X^2,X^3} - R^2_{Y.X,X^2}$	$=$	r^2_{cubic}
$R^2_{Y.X,X^2,X^3,X^4} - R^2_{Y.X,X^2,X^3}$	$=$	$r^2_{quartic}$
$R^2_{Y.X,X^2,X^3,X^4,X^5} - R^2_{Y.X,X^2,X^3,X^4}$	$=$	$r^2_{quintic}$
$R^2_{Y.X,X^2,X^3,X^5,X^6} - R^2_{Y.X,X^2,X^3,X^4,X^5}$	$=$	r^2_{sextic}

variability explained by the introduction of the second vector.[3] From Eq. (23-1),

$$r^2_{quad.} = R^2_{Y.X,X^2} - r^2_{YX}$$
$$= .2061 - .0313 = .1748$$

which is identical to the value obtained for the quadratic component with vectors based on orthogonal polynomial coefficients. With the values of the two components in hand, we can proceed with the last part of the analysis—that is, testing the significance of the two trend components—which is identical to that presented in the last section.

Higher-Order Trend Components.   As we suggested earlier, these computational procedures are easily generalized to designs with any number of treatment conditions. As an example, we will outline the analysis with Grant's study, in which $a = 7$ treatment conditions, although in real life we would probably use orthogonal polynomial coefficients because of the equal intervals. We have already indicated how the vectors are coded as increasing powers of X. We calculate a series of R^2's taken between Y and increasing numbers of vectors, starting with the linear vector X and then adding the next higher vectors one by one until all vectors are included in the final R^2. The R^2's needed to calculate the different trend components are given on the left side of Table 23-4. The determination of the r^2 trend is based on the hierarchical analysis where one R^2 is subtracted from another. In row 1, the single R^2 involves the correlation between Y and X. (We have used the notation

---

[3] The printouts of some computer programs also refer to incremental variability as the *change* in the proportion of explained variability ("R^2 Change") resulting from the addition of another vector into the multiple regression analysis.

for a multiple correlation rather than a zero-order correlation to emphasize the continuity in the steps of the analysis.) In row 2, the first R^2 on the left involves the correlation between Y and the two vectors, X and X^2; subtracting $R^2_{Y.X}$ from this yields the quadratic trend. In row 3, the first R^2 involves the correlation between Y and three vectors, X, X^2, and X^3; subtracting $R^2_{Y.X,X^2}$ from this quantity yields the cubic trend. We continue this systematic process until we reach the last row, where the R^2 on the left involves the correlation between Y and all six vectors ($R^2_{Y.X,X^2,X^3,X^4,X^5,X^6}$; this particular R^2 is also $R^2_{Y.max.}$ for this analysis); subtracting $R^2_{Y.X,X^2,X^3,X^4,X^5}$ yields the sextic trend.[4]

In summary, the use of powered vectors in trend analysis provides an example of the hierarchical strategy in MRC, which we discussed in Chap. 20. The main characteristic of this strategy is that the effects of the X variables (or vectors) are evaluated in a particular order. In the present situation, we began with the linear component X and determined the incremental variability obtained by adding X^2 to the analysis. Each of the remaining components is represented as incremental variability found by adding the next vector to those that have preceded it. The order in which the vectors are included is determined by the way in which they are derived (i.e., as powers of X) and the goal of parsimony: simpler explanations (lower-order trend components) are sought before more complex explanations (higher-order trends).

23.4 APPLICATION OF TREND ANALYSIS TO OTHER EXPERIMENTAL DESIGNS

Trend analyses may be applied to any experimental design in which one or more of the independent variables are manipulated quantitatively. We will consider first the analysis of trend in a factorial design in general and then discuss briefly the application of trend analysis to within-subjects designs in particular.

Factorial Designs

In Chap. 17, we introduced an experiment in which subjects received one of the three lectures (factor A) and then received three vocabulary tests, given immediately, 2 weeks later, and 4 weeks later (factor B). The results of this experiment are plotted in Fig. 23-4. An inspection of the figure suggests that while all

---

[4] Most multiple regression computer programs will calculate the incremental information directly, with little effort on your part beyond specifying the order in which the vectors (or sets of vectors) are introduced into the analysis. The "REGRESSION" program of SPSS, for example, lists the increments as "R SQUARE CHANGE" in the output from the analysis.

subjects seem to forget vocabulary words steadily over the 4 weeks, the amount of forgetting also seems to depend on the particular lecture they receive. Subjects given the social science lecture appear to forget more than the subjects given either the physical science lecture or the history lecture. The statistical analysis reported in Chap. 17, however, did not support these observations—the $A \times B$ interaction was *not* significant. Nevertheless, let us assume that the interaction was significant and see how a trend analysis may be applied to the analysis of interaction.

Consider again the performance of the three lecture groups. We already noted that all three groups exhibit a drop in recall over the testing interval. Suppose we try to simplify the outcome of the experiment by drawing a straight line through the three means for each lecture group. Each line would reflect the degree to which the amount of forgetting for a given group could be described (or expressed) by a straight line (or a linear function). Now let us compare the *slopes* of the three straight lines. If the three slopes are not the same, we would say that the $A \times B$ interaction has a *linear component*; if the slopes are roughly the same, we would say

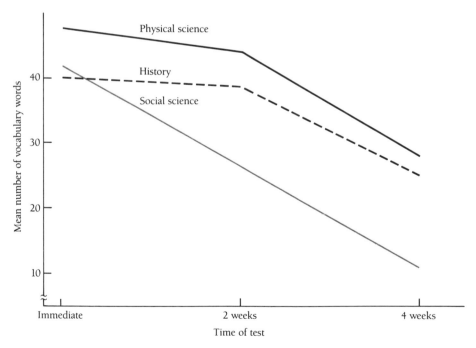

Figure 23-4   Mean number of vocabulary words as a function of type of lecture and time of test.

that the interaction has no linear component. Whether the slopes are the same or different would be assessed by an appropriate statistical test, of course.[5]

Since factor B (time of test) consists of three levels, it is also possible to examine the quadratic trend component of the interaction. In this case, the analysis would compare the individual quadratic functions for the three lecture groups—the function for each group being drawn through the three means for the group—to determine whether the degrees of curvature were the same or different. An inspection of Fig. 23-4 suggests that the physical science and history groups exhibit approximately the same modest bend, while the social science group displays only a linear trend and no quadratic trend at all. If these differences in quadratic trends for the three lecture groups proved to be significant, we would conclude that a *quadratic component* of the $A \times B$ interaction was present in the data.

Because of space limitations, we are unable to provide a formal presentation of the statistical procedures involved in assessing interaction trend components. Numerical examples illustrating the ANOVA approach may be found in a number of readily available sources (e.g., Kirk, 1982, pp. 379–387; Myers, 1979, pp. 445–456; and Winer, 1971, pp. 388–391 and 478–484). Pedhazur (1982, pp. 477–481) provides an illustration of interaction trend analysis using the MRC approach. The analyses introduce no new ideas or calculations. In fact, they are identical to the procedures we presented in Chaps. 14 and 15 for the detailed analysis of interaction. You can use the procedures directly, without modification. All that you need to do is to substitute the orthogonal polynomial trend coefficients for the coefficients (or vectors) representing qualitative comparisons. The only exception is when you have unequal intervals and must use powered vectors instead of calculating the appropriate orthogonal polynomial coefficients. We will discuss this exception in a moment.

Within-Subjects Designs

Although we introduced trend analysis in the context of a single-factor between subjects design, we could just as easily have used a within-subjects design as an illustration. The extraction of trend components is identical for all designs. The only complication associated with the within-subjects design is the need for separate error terms to evaluate the individual trend components. You may recall

---

[5] Interestingly, the statistical analysis, which we do not present, supports the conclusion that the slopes are not the same, even though the overall $A \times B$ interaction is not significant. This outcome is another example of the value of more focused analyses that examine specific aspects of a set of data that may be significant when evaluated as planned comparisons even if they are not of sufficient magnitude to influence the outcome of the omnibus test results.

Table 23-5
Words Recalled as a Function
of List Position

Subjects	a_1	a_2	a_3	a_4	a_5	a_6
s_1	7	3	2	2	1	1
s_2	4	8	3	8	1	2
s_3	7	6	3	1	5	4
s_4	8	6	1	0	2	0
s_5	7	2	3	0	1	3
s_6	6	3	3	1	1	1
s_7	4	2	0	0	0	0
s_8	6	7	5	1	3	2

our first discussion of this problem in Chap. 16 when we considered the evaluation of single-df comparisons in the $(A \times S)$ design (see pages 281–290). Briefly, each comparison required a unique error term based on the data specific to the comparison that actually enters into the analysis. The error term for a single-df comparison is the interaction of this comparison with subjects. That is, rather than use the error term from the overall analysis (the $A \times S$ interaction), we use instead the $A_{comp.} \times S$ interaction associated with this comparison. We will now apply this procedure to the analysis of trend.

Consider an actual experiment in which $s = 8$ subjects were given a series of learning-memory tests, each separated by 48 hours.[6] On the first day of the experiment, subjects learned a list of words. Two days later, they recalled the list and then learned a new one. Two days later, subjects recalled the second list and then learned a new one. Subjects went through six of these learning-testing cycles. The independent variable consisted of the ordinal position of the memory test—that is, level a_1 was the first memory test, level a_2 was the second memory test, and so on. Since each memory test followed at an interval of 48 hours, the $a = 6$ levels were equally spaced. Table 23-5 presents the results of this experiment, while Fig. 23-5 plots the means. As you can see from the figure, memory deteriorated rapidly at first and then began to level off on the later tests. These observations suggest the presence of two trend components, a linear component reflecting the systematic deterioration of memory over the six tests, and a quadratic component showing that the rapid drop was followed by a reduction in the decline.

[6] These data are based on part of a larger experiment reported by Keppel, Postman, and Zavortink (1968).

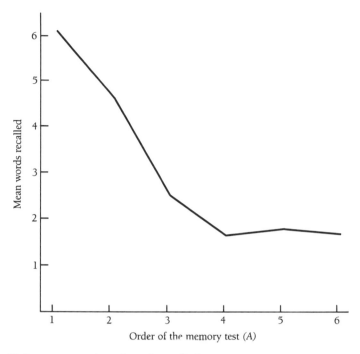

Figure 23-5   Mean number of words recalled on six memory tests.

Table 23-6 summarizes the results of the statistical analysis. With $a = 6$ levels, five trend components may be examined. Our interest is in the linear and quadratic components, but we have presented the entire set of trend components for the sake of completeness. The coefficients for the analysis were obtained from Table A-4. Following the procedure presented in Chap. 16 for single-df comparisons, we have calculated the sums of squares for the five trend components, each associated with 1 df. Since these components are orthogonal, the sum of squares for the complete set equals the overall treatment sum of squares ($SS_A = 143.92$). That is,

$$117.03 + 24.00 + .06 + 2.79 + .04 = 143.92$$

Separate error terms were calculated for each of the trend components. The error term for the linear component is a mean square based on the Linear X Subject interaction; the error term for the quadratic component is a mean square based on the Quadratic X Subject interaction; and so on. Except for rounding error, the sums of squares based on these interactions equal the $A \times S$ interaction sum of squares ($SS_{A \times S} = 97.75$). More specifically,

$$10.37 + 27.27 + 7.18 + 17.60 + 35.32 = 97.74$$

Table 23-6
Summary of the Analysis of Trend: ANOVA

Source	SS	df	MS	Error Term	F
A	(143.92)	(5)			
Linear	117.03	1	117.03	Linear $\times$ S	79.07**
Quadratic	24.00	1	24.00	Quadratic $\times$ S	6.17*
Cubic	.06	1	.06	Cubic $\times$ S	<1
Quartic	2.79	1	2.79	Quartic $\times$ S	1.11
Quintic	.04	1	.04	Quintic $\times$ S	<1
S	54.25	7	7.75		
A $\times$ S	(97.75)	(35)			
Linear $\times$ S	10.37	7	1.48		
Quadratic $\times$ S	27.27	7	3.90		
Cubic $\times$ S	7.18	7	1.03		
Quartic $\times$ S	17.60	7	2.51		
Quintic $\times$ S	35.32	7	5.05		
Total	295.92	47			

* $p < .05$.   ** $p < .01$.

You should note that the mean squares for the five error terms vary considerably in size—5.05 for the quintic component and 1.03 for the cubic component—and so you can see that it is important to use separate error terms to evaluate subsets of data from a within-subjects design. The analysis reveals significant linear and quadratic trends.

The MRC version of this analysis would use the polynomial coefficients to create five trend vectors. The correlation between Y and each trend vector would reflect the degree to which that trend was present in the data. The error terms for this analysis would be obtained from the five sets of interaction vectors formed by cross-multiplying separately each trend vector by the full set of subject vectors. The multiple correlation between Y and each set of interaction vectors would supply the information necessary to form the separate error terms. Table 23-7 shows the summary of the MRC analysis. As you can see, the F ratios are identical, within rounding error, to those in Table 23-6. You should realize that the form of this analysis is identical to the one illustrated in Chap. 16 for the evaluation of single-df comparisons (see pages 281–290).

Table 23-7
Summary of the Analysis of Trend: MRC

Source	R^2	df	Mean R^2	F
A	(.4863)	(5)		
Linear	.3955	1	.3955	79.10**
Quadratic	.0811	1	.0811	6.14*
Cubic	.0002	1	.0002	<1
Quartic	.0094	1	.0094	1.11
Quintic	.0001	1	.0001	<1
S	.1833	7	.0262	
A × S	(.3304)	(35)		
Linear × S	.0350	7	.0050	
Quadratic × S	.0922	7	.0132	
Cubic × S	.0243	7	.0035	
Quartic × S	.0595	7	.0085	
Quintic × S	.1194	7	.0171	
Total	1.0000	47		

* $p < .05$.   ** $p < .01$.

Trend Analysis with Powered Vectors

If the levels of a quantitative independent variable are not equally spaced, we cannot make use of the orthogonal polynomial trend coefficients found in Table A-4. As we pointed out in Sec. 23.3, we have two options. First, we can calculate the polynomial coefficients by means of some tedious algebra and then use these coefficients to proceed with the trend analysis with either ANOVA or MRC. Alternatively, we can use the actual levels of the independent variable to create powered vectors, except that we can employ *only* MRC to complete the analysis. We also discussed how this MRC analysis is conducted in Sec. 23.3 (see page 500–504). Unfortunately, one has to be careful in applying the technique to factorial designs and to within-subjects designs in general.

The problem has to do with the intercorrelations between the powered vectors. In the single-factor between-subjects design, this problem was overcome by using a hierarchical strategy and the systematic addition of powered vectors. In the factorial design, where a trend analysis extends to interactions, the intercorrelations spread to other sources of variability to complicate the statistical analysis. Suppose we wish to use powered vectors to analyze the trend components of an

$A \times B$ interaction in which factor B is a quantitative independent variable with unequal intervals between successive levels. For the analysis, we would create $a - 1$ vectors to represent the main effect of factor A, and $b - 1$ powered vectors to represent the main effect of factor B. The interaction vectors would be obtained by multiplying each A vector by all the B powered vectors. Suppose we wanted to conduct a standard analysis of this design, examining the two main effects and the interaction before turning to the trend analysis. Following the procedures developed in Chap. 13, we would use the set of A vectors to calculate $R^2_{Y.A}$, the set of B vectors to calculate $R^2_{Y.B}$, and the set of interaction vectors to calculate $R^2_{Y.A \times B}$. Unfortunately, this analysis would produce the *wrong* R^2 for the $A \times B$ interaction. Without going into detail, this occurs because the set of interaction vectors we constructed in the usual manner by cross-multiplying are *not orthogonal* to the set of vectors representing the A main effect as they are when coefficients are used rather than powered vectors.

Although these new intercorrelations pose no serious problem for the MRC analysis, as we will show in a moment, their presence does complicate it, for the MRC analysis is ordinarily relatively simple, focusing directly on orthogonal sets of vectors to represent a given treatment effect, whether it be a main effect or an interaction. The solution in the present case is to adopt a hierarchical strategy for the entire analysis. The effects of the new intercorrelations will be removed by an appropriate ordering of the vectors. The first set of vectors entered into the analysis is the set representing the *qualitative* independent variable, factor A. The R^2 taken between Y and these vectors gives the $R^2_{Y.A}$ directly. Next the B vectors are added to the analysis; the $R^2_{Y.B}$ is calculated by subtraction; that is,

$$R^2_{Y.B} = R^2_{Y.A,B} - R^2_{Y.A}$$

Finally, the interaction vectors are added, with the $R^2_{Y.A \times B}$ also calculated by subtraction as follows:

$$R^2_{Y.A \times B} = R^2_{Y.A,B,A \times B} - R^2_{Y.A,B}$$

The analysis after this point would proceed as usual.[7]

Let us return to our primary interest in this section, the anlaysis of interaction trend components. The hierarchical analysis is identical to the one we have just

---

[7] Strictly speaking, the hierarchical analysis need only be applied to the calculation of $R^2_{Y.A \times B}$ in this example. Given the nature of the intercorrelations, we need only to involve the A vectors and the interaction vectors in the hierarchical analysis. More specifically, we could calculate both $R^2_{Y.A}$ and $R^2_{Y.B}$ directly and then calculate the overall interaction as follows:

$$R^2_{Y.A \times B} = R^2_{Y.A,A \times B} - R^2_{Y.A}$$

We recommend the complete hierarchical analysis in order to minimize mistakes.

Table 23-8
MRC Factorial Trend Analysis

Hierarchical Arrangement	Trend Component
$R^2_{Y.A1}$	
$R^2_{Y.A1,B1} - R^2_{Y.A1}$	$= R^2_{Y.Linear}$
$R^2_{Y.A1,B1,B2} - R^2_{Y.A1,B1}$	$= R^2_{Y.Quadratic}$
$R^2_{Y.A1,B1,B2,B3} - R^2_{Y.A1,B1,B2}$	$= R^2_{Y.Cubic}$
$R^2_{Y.A1,B1,B2,B3,A1B1} - R^2_{Y.A1,B1,B2,B3}$	$= R^2_{Y.A \times Linear}$
$R^2_{Y.A1,B1,B2,B3,A1B1,A1B2} - R^2_{Y.A1,B1,B2,B3,A1B1}$	$= R^2_{Y.A \times Quadratic}$
$R^2_{Y.A1,B1,B2,B3,A1B1,A1B2,A1B3} - R^2_{Y.A1,B1,B2,B3,A1B1,A1B2}$	$= R^2_{Y.A \times Cubic}$

described except that now we must enter the powered vectors systematically. Table 23-8 summarizes the approach. For simplicity, we will assume that factor A has two levels and that factor B, the quantitative variable, has four levels, so that we can extract only three trend components, linear, quadratic, and cubic. We will refer to the A vector as $A1$ and the B vectors as $B1$, $B2$, and $B3$. (These latter vectors are actually the powered vectors X, X^2, and X^3, of course.) In order to isolate the individual trend components for the B main effect, the powered vectors are added to the analysis one at a time, as you can see if you examine the first R^2 in each successive row of Table 23-8. In each case, the difference between the two R^2's listed in the row is a different trend component expressed as a proportion of total variability. The analysis of the interaction proceeds in a similar fashion. The addition of the interaction vector $A1B1$ gives us the linear component of the interaction ($R^2_{Y.A \times Linear}$). Subsequent additions of the other two interaction vectors ($A1B2$ and $A1B3$) give us the quadratic ($R^2_{Y.A \times Quadratic}$) and cubic ($R^2_{Y.A \times Cubic}$) components of the interaction, respectively.

Summary

We have indicated how trend analysis may be extended to more complicated experimental designs. We have also indicated that you must plan your trend analysis carefully if you choose to use powered vectors. Solving the problems created by interaction vectors based on powered vectors is complicated, particularly in higher-order factorial designs and designs with repeated measures.

Table 23-9
Trend Analysis in a Nonexperimental Design

(1) Y	(2) X	(3) X^2	(4) X^3
3	17	289	4,913
4	22	484	10,648
4	12	144	1,728
3	9	81	729
2	4	16	64
5	10	100	1,000
4	14	196	2,744
7	13	169	2,197
5	19	361	6,859
7	14	196	2,744
1	3	9	27
3	3	9	27
2	8	64	512
6	15	225	3,375
6	18	324	5,832
4	17	289	4,913
3	22	484	10,648
4	20	400	8,000
2	6	36	216
3	6	36	216
1	4	16	64
2	5	25	125
3	12	144	1,728
5	15	225	3,375
4	8	64	512
4	6	36	216
2	3	9	27
6	19	361	6,859
3	7	49	343
5	20	400	8,000

$$r_{YX} = .6140 \qquad r_{YX^2} = .5157$$
$$r_{YX^3} = .4200$$

23.5   TREND ANALYSIS IN NONEXPERIMENTAL DESIGNS

Trend analyses in nonexperimental designs are always possible whenever an X variable represents a quantitative dimension of some sort. We will illustrate the procedure with the data appearing in Table 23-9. In this example, Y represents ratings of job performance and X scores on a clerical aptitude test. The correlation between these two variables is presented at the bottom of the table ($r_{YX} = .6140$). This correlation indicates that approximately 38 percent of the Y variability ($r_{YX}^2 = .3770$) is accounted for by the *linear relationship* between Y and X. Stated another way, the correlation represents the magnitude of the linear trend component, since $r_{lin.}^2 = r_{YX}^2$. Are any higher-order trends also present in the data? A scatterplot of the data (Fig. 23-6) suggests the possibility of a quadratic trend, with the job-rating scores tending to drop for the subjects with the higher clerical test scores.

The Hierarchical Analysis

Powered vectors can be easily used to assess this observation. Column 3 in Table 23-9 lists the powered vector based on the squared X scores (X^2). As indicated in Sec. 23.3, the correlation between Y and this powered vector reflects the presence

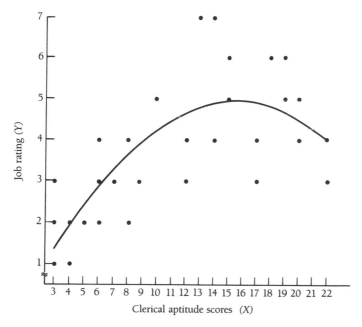

F i g u r e 23-6   Quadratic relationship between job ratings (Y) and clerical aptitude score (X).

of a quadratic trend as well as a major portion of the linear trend. That is, the fact that X and X^2 are highly correlated ($r_{XX^2} = .9794$) means that a major portion of the correlation between Y and X^2 ($r_{YX^2} = .5157$) is due to linear trend (predictable from X directly). A hierarchical analysis is used to disentangle the two trend components. More specifically,

$$r_{quad.}^2 = R_{Y.X,X^2}^2 - r_{YX}^2$$

where $r_{quad.}^2$ = the squared correlation coefficient representing the quadratic trend component

$R_{Y.X,X^2}^2$ = the squared multiple correlation coefficient between Y and vectors 2 and 3

r_{YX}^2 = the squared correlation coefficient representing the linear component $r_{lin.}^2$.

We can conduct this analysis with the information provided in Table 23-9. We start by calculating $R_{Y.X,X^2}^2$ as follows:

$$R_{Y.X,X^2}^2 = \frac{r_{YX}^2 + r_{YX^2}^2 - 2r_{YX}r_{YX^2}r_{XX^2}}{1 - r_{XX^2}^2}$$

$$= \frac{(.6140)^2 + (.5157)^2 - (2)(.6140)(.5157)(.9794)}{1 - (.9794)^2}$$

$$= \frac{.3770 + .2659 - .6202}{1 - .9592} = \frac{.0227}{.0408} = .5564$$

Performing the hierarchical analysis, we find

$$r_{quad.}^2 = R_{Y.X,X^2}^2 - r_{YX}^2$$

$$= .5564 - (.6140)^2 = .5564 - .3770 = .1794$$

The Preliminary F Tests

The statistical evaluation of these two trend components involves a slightly different procedure from the one we outlined and demonstrated for trend analysis in the single-factor between-subjects design. When the data are derived from an *experimental* design, the error term is based on the residual variability, $1 - R_{Y.max.}^2$, where $R_{Y.max.}^2$ is the squared multiple correlation coefficient taken between Y and the total set of $a - 1$ vectors. In the assessment of trend with data from a *nonexperimental design*, however, a preliminary analysis is conducted to identify significant trend components using a systematically changing residual term that depends on the number of vectors included at any given point in the analysis. Since the potential number of powered vectors that can be constructed is quite large, we have no reasonable way to specify $R^2_{Y.max.}$ before the data are analyzed, as we can in an experiment, where the number of vectors contributing to $R^2_{Y.max.}$ is determined by the degrees of freedom associated with the independent variable under analysis. After we have discovered which powered vectors (and trend components) should be included in the analysis, we will recalculate the F ratio for each trend component using a single error term ($R^2_{Y.max.}$) that is based on the components "surviving" the preliminary analysis.

To begin the preliminary analysis designed to identify significant trend components, we first calculate the error term for the *linear* trend:

$$1 - r^2_{YX} = 1 - (.6140)^2 = 1 - .3770 = .6230$$

where r^2_{YX} is the squared correlation coefficient (zero-order) between Y and the first vector (X). *Residual* at this point refers to all variability that is not explained by the linear relationship between Y and X. The F ratio becomes

$$F = \frac{r^2_{YX}}{(1 - r^2_{YX})/(N - k - 1)}$$

where N refers to the total number of subjects in the study and k to the number of vectors associated with the residual term. (The numerator, r^2_{YX}, is a squared zero-order correlation coefficient representing linear trend and thus is divided by 1, which we have not shown in the formula.) Completing the calculations, noting that $r^2_{YX} = (.6140)^2 = .3770$, we find

$$F = \frac{.3770}{(1 - .3770)/(30 - 1 - 1)} = \frac{.3770}{.6230/28} = \frac{.3770}{.0223} = 16.91$$

With $df_{num.} = 1$ and $df_{denom.} = 28$, the F is significant, and we can conclude that there is a linear relationship between Y and X.

The quadratic trend ($r^2_{quad.} = .1794$) is evaluated by means of a familiar formula, originally given in Chap. 21 as Eq. (21-2) for the assessment of incremental variance. Adapted to this analysis, Eq. (21-2) becomes

$$F = \frac{(R^2_{Y.X,X^2} - R^2_{Y.X})/(k_l - k_s)}{(1 - R^2_{Y.X,X^2})/(N - k - 1)}$$

Substituting the actual values, we find

$$F = \frac{(.5564 - .3770)/(2 - 1)}{(1 - .5564)/(30 - 2 - 1)} = \frac{.1794/1}{.4436/27} = \frac{.1794}{.0164} = 10.94$$

which, with $df_{num.} = 1$ and $df_{denom.} = 27$, is significant, indicating the presence of a quadratic trend component.

The analysis could continue with higher trends extracted in an analogous manner. The cubic component, for example, is found by determining the increase in predictability obtained by adding a third vector, which is based on the values of the first vector (X) raised to the third power (X^3). That is,

$$r^2_{cubic} = R^2_{Y.X,X^2,X^3} - R^2_{Y.X,X^2}$$

Using the data from Table 23-9, we discover that

$$r^2_{cubic} = .5866 - .5564 = .0302$$

which is considerably smaller than either the linear or the quadratic r^2. The error term for this component is based on the squared multiple correlation coefficient between Y and vectors 1 to 3 $(R^2_{Y.X,X^2,X^3})$. The F is given by

$$F = \frac{(R^2_{Y.X,X^2,X^3} - R^2_{Y.X,X^2})/(k_l - k_s)}{(1 - R^2_{Y.X,X^2,X^3})/(N - k - 1)}$$

where k again equals the number of vectors used to determine the residual term (that is, $k = 3$). Completing the calculations, we determine that

$$F = \frac{(.5866 - .5564)/(3 - 2)}{(1 - .5866)/(30 - 3 - 1)} = \frac{.0302/1}{.4134/26} = \frac{.0302}{.0159} = 1.90$$

which is not significant (in this case, $df_{num.} = 1$ and $df_{denom.} = 26$).

Evaluating the Final Regression Equation

When do we stop this process of extracting trends of greater and greater complexity? We suggest a strategy of testing one more trend beyond the first nonsignificant one, continuing with the process if it is significant and stopping the process if the trend is not significant. On the other hand, many researchers go no further than the quadratic trend unless they have good reason to expect higher-order trends to emerge.[8] In any case, the last significant trend determines the level of polynomial we would use to describe the relationship between Y and X. In our

---

[8] According to Pedhazur (1982, p. 424), higher-order trends are rarely found in nonexperimental research, are often unreliable, and are frequently difficult to interpret.

example, that function would be the *quadratic*, which has the form

$$Y_i' = a + b_1(X_i) + b_2(X_i^2)$$

where Y_i' = the value of Y predicted for a given subject from the best-fitting quadratic equation

b_1 = the regression coefficient associated with the linear component

X_i = the subject's score on the X variable

b_2 = the regression coefficient associated with the quadratic component

X_i^2 = the subject's squared X score

A computer analysis reveals that

$$Y_i' = -.4956 + (.6969)(X_i) - (.0223)(X_i^2)$$

Illustrating with the first subject in Table 23-9, for whom $X = 17$ and $X^2 = 289$, we find

$$Y_1' = -.4956 + (.6969)(17) - (.0223)(289)$$
$$= -.4956 + 11.8473 - 6.4447 = 4.9070$$

The quadratic function described by this function is presented in Fig. 23-6.

The final step in the analysis is to use a new error term to recalculate the F ratios for the trend components included in the final polynomial and discovered in the preliminary analysis. As we have already indicated, this error term is based on only those vectors included in this polynomial. In the present case, the residual would be based on $R_{Y.X,X^2}^2 = .5564$ The value of F for the linear component would now become

$$F = \frac{r_{lin.}^2}{(1 - R_{Y.X,X^2}^2)/(N - k - 1)}$$

$$= \frac{.3770}{(1 - .5564)/(30 - 2 - 1)} = \frac{.3770}{.0164} = 22.99$$

You should note that this F is *larger* than the one we originally calculated (16.91). The reason for the difference and for the recalculation is that the original error term (.0223) represented the variability in Y remaining after only the *linear trend* had been removed statistically. Since this residual variability still contained a significant trend component (quadratic) in addition to unexplained variability, the error term was too large. The new error term (.0164), which represents the variability in Y remaining after the linear *and* quadratic trends have been removed, reflects a more appropriate estimate of true residual variability. The F for the quadratic component does not need to be recalculated, since the correct error term was used. On the other hand, if a third-degree polynomial had been considered appropriate, both F's—linear and quadratic—would need to be recalculated.

Comment

There are several reasons why trend analyses are valuable and useful in the analysis of nonexperimental data. One of these we have mentioned already—the fact that a small zero-order correlation between Y and X does not necessarily mean that there is a weak relationship between these two variables. Instead, there may be a strong *curvilinear* trend that is simply not revealed by r_{YX}. The data in Table 23-9, for example, exhibit a strong linear relationship between Y and X ($r_{YX}^2 = .3770$), but there is an even stronger relationship when the quadratic trend is included ($R_{Y.X,X^2}^2 = .5564$). You should always examine a scatterplot of your data to guard against missing a curvilinear trend, as you may if you focus your attention only on r_{YX}. The trend analysis can follow to evaluate your interpretation of the scatterplot.

You should also not lose sight of the fact that the presence of curvilinear trend components increases your ability to predict Y from X. Again, in our example, the addition of the quadratic component increased the proportion of explained variance from .3770 to .5564. This gain in predictability was obtained at little "cost"—simply adding powered vectors, which is considerably cheaper than introducing a *new* X variable into the study. Also, from a theoretical perspective, we may hypothesize that some relationships are nonlinear. For example, in examining the relationship between ability and job performance, we could hypothesize that there is a linear relationship until we reach the higher scores on the test of ability, where, above a certain level, there is no further increase in performance. Or, in examining the relationship between job performance and turnover (the length of time a person stays in an organization before leaving), we may hypothesize that there is a U-shaped function: those who are poor performers could be expected to quit because of their performance, while those who are very good performers might quit to take other, better jobs in different organizations; those who stay in the organization are the ones with moderate performance levels.

Finally, we must point out that there is often a diminishing return when X variables are added to a nonexperimental design. If the variables that are chosen originally already represent major aspects of the behavior under study, it is unlikely that additional variables will increase R^2. The same could be said about adding higher-order trend components, particularly when there are more than two quantitative X variables. In any case, the use of trend analysis in nonexperimental designs adds an important analytical device to attempt to capture curvilinear relationships between Y and X, for both predictive and theoretical purposes.

23.6 SUMMARY

The analysis of trend components represents an ideal way to analyze and to inter-pret the results of experiments with quantitative independent variables. Trend analysis consists of the systematic analysis of individual trend components, each of which represents a function with a different degree of complexity. Most analyses begin with the simplest component—linear trend—and continue to examine func-tions exhibiting increasing numbers of reversals or bends. The goal is to find the simplest way to describe the nature of the relationship between the independent and dependent variables. Trend analysis can also be used to test theories that pre-dict the occurrence of a particular trend component (or components).

With experimental designs, the most common way to conduct trend analysis is through single-df comparisons, where the coefficients come from a table of orthogonal polynomial coefficients. For ANOVA, these coefficients and the general formula for single-df comparisons permit the relatively simple calculation of the sums of squares associated with any given trend component; for MRC, the same coefficients are used to define vectors which produce the analogous information in the form of zero-order correlation coefficients.

The procedures described above are applicable when the treatments them-selves represent equally spaced points on the dimension studied in the experiment. Two methods were presented for dealing with unequal intervals. One involved the calculation of a specialized set of orthogonal polynomial coefficients, and the other involved the use of vectors based on increasing powers of the first (or linear) vector. The latter method was presented in detail. Briefly, the method required the use of a hierarchical strategy in which we determine the incremental variability ob-tained as each vector of increasing power is added to the analysis. The increments in variability represent the different trends in the data.

Trend analysis can be extended to factorial designs and to designs with re-peated measures. Provided that the intervals between successive levels are equal, the analyses parallel those performed with qualitative independent variables. If the intervals are not equal and powered vectors are used, the analysis becomes com-plicated and care must be taken in specifying the order of introducing vectors into the MRC analysis.

The application of trend analysis to nonexperimental designs was also dis-cussed. Powered vectors can be used to assess nonlinear trend components for any quantitative X variables in the design. The MRC analysis follows a hierarchical strategy and a systematic evaluation of increasingly complex trends. A major value of trend analysis is that it helps you avoid the mistake of concluding on the basis of a zero-order correlation between Y and X that a small relationship (or no relationship) exists when in fact more complex relationships are present.

23.7   EXERCISES

1. Problem 1 in the exercises to Chap. 10 was concerned with the effects of verbal reinforcement on children's performance on a motor task. Suppose we change the qualitative independent variable we used to a quantitative one in which the three groups differ with regard to the *amount of reinforcement* they receive. The reinforcement in this case consists of the number of pieces of candy the children will receive for "doing well" on the task. Subjects in the first group receive 5 pieces; those in the second, 10 pieces; and those in the third, 15 pieces. A total of 21 subjects serve in the study, 7 in each condition. The data are presented below:

5 Pieces	10 Pieces	15 Pieces
4	7	7
7	6	3
5	9	7
3	7	5
6	8	7
4	6	8
6	7	5

a. Conduct a trend analysis using ANOVA procedures.
b. Conduct the trend analysis using MRC and using orthogonal polynomials as vectors.
c. Conduct the same analysis using MRC, but with powered vectors instead.

2. In Sec. 23.4 (pages 508–511), we considered a within-subjects single-factor design in which $s = 8$ subjects were given a series of $a = 6$ memory tests each separated by 48 hr. The data were presented in Table 23-5.

a. Conduct a complete trend analysis using the ANOVA procedure. Check your calculations with the values given in Table 23-6.
b. Conduct the same analysis using MRC and orthogonal polynomials. Check your calculations with the values given in Table 23-7.

3. Table 20-3 (page 400) presents four sets of information used to predict job performance on a clerical task. Conduct a trend analysis using the scores on the X_2 variable (spelling scores). Disregard the other predictor variables in Table 20-3 for this analysis. Extract only the linear and quadratic components for this problem.

24

Unequal Sample Sizes

. . .

Throughout most of this book, especially in the chapters on the design and analysis of experiments, we have emphasized and provided examples of situations in which equal numbers of subjects are placed in the different treatment conditions. Most experiments are designed with equal-sized samples, which are easy to create because the assignment of subjects to conditions is under the direct control of the researcher. The primary reason for designing experiments with equal sample sizes is the desire to give *equal weight* to the treatment conditions in the study. With the same number of subjects randomly assigned to each of the conditions, each treatment mean contributes equally in the determination of the various treatment effects extracted from the results of an experiment. To deliberately use unequal sample sizes, in most situations, makes little scientific sense. Nonexperimental designs, on the other hand, are usually planned with only the overall size of the sample (*N*) in mind. Thus, if an *X* variable consisted of a *classification variable*—such as religious beliefs, political affiliation, or socioeconomic status—little or no attention would be paid to the relative numbers of subjects falling into the different classifications. In fact, most researchers do not want to tamper with the naturally occurring numbers, since they want their studies to reflect the subdivisions actually present in the populations from which they are sampling.

   In this chapter, we consider how we can adjust the statistical analysis when unequal sample sizes occur in the context of either experimental or nonexperimental designs. For the experimental study, in which equal sample sizes *are* usually planned, the adjustments consist of a number of different approaches to the analysis, including the use of MRC procedures instead of the ANOVA procedures we have presented in the preceding chapters. For the nonexperimental study, in which unequal group sizes are the rule rather than the exception, the adjustments consist of the use of the *hierarchical strategy*, which we have already considered in the chapters beginning with Chap. 20. We will consider the problem of unequal sample sizes in experiments first.

24.1   UNEQUAL SAMPLE SIZES IN THE SINGLE-FACTOR DESIGN

Most experiments are designed with equal sample sizes. However, unequal sample sizes frequently result when there is an inadvertent loss of subjects during the course of the study. There are many reasons why subjects are "lost" in an experiment. Common reasons include illness, death, failure to complete a task or to reach a performance criterion, voluntary withdrawal, uncooperativeness, equipment breakdown, and experimenter error. Whatever the reason, the result of these occurrences is the same, namely, unequal numbers of subjects in the different treatment groups.

In some experiments, it is possible to restore the equal sample sizes. Suppose, for example, that a loud noise outside the laboratory has disturbed a subject participating in an experiment. Most researchers would simply replace this subject with the next person scheduled to serve in the experiment. Similarly, subjects are often replaced at the end of a study when it is discovered that an experimenter has made a mistake of some sort. Of course, when subjects must be replaced, the researcher's primary concern is to preserve the *random assignment of subjects to conditions*. A frequent alternative solution is to restore equal sample size by randomly discarding subjects from the various treatment conditions: the group with the largest number of "lost" subjects defines the new sample size, and subjects will be randomly excluded from groups with greater numbers of subjects. The objection to this latter procedure is the loss of potentially precious information, particularly if the number of subjects that need to be discarded is great. On the other hand, the numbers of subjects lost in actual experiments will generally not be large, and thus the loss of information may not present a practical problem.

A point we must stress is that the researcher must be certain that subjects' reasons for dropping out are totally unrelated to the particular treatments they receive. Loss of subjects due to equipment failure or experimenter error are examples of losses that can reasonably be tolerated. Situations that may cause problems are those in which the conditions themselves are responsible—in whole or in part—for the subject loss. Suppose, for example, that because of the nature of the experiment we have to drop subjects because they have failed to complete the task assigned to their treatment group. Is this particular cause for discarding a subject truly *random*, or is it *related to the treatment conditions*? The answer is that the cause is *not* random. Treatments that are more difficult will produce more subjects who are unable to reach a critical performance criterion or complete the experimental task than treatments that are less difficult. The "easy" conditions will eventually contain subjects who represent all ranges of ability, while the "difficult" conditions will contain only the better subjects. In short, loss of subjects under these circumstances destroys the results of random assignment and produces groups of subjects that are *not* reasonably equated before the start of the experiment. The result? An experiment in which the experimental manipulations are *confounded* by differences in subject ability, and a set of biased results.

The lesson to be learned from all this is that we must examine the *reasons* why subjects fail to complete an experiment. If the reasons are essentially *independent* of the experimental treatments, then the experiment is relatively free from systematic bias; if they are not, then the experiment is usually considered useless. Under the latter circumstances, adding subjects or dropping subjects randomly will simply not solve the problem. Neither will the more sophisticated procedures we will consider in this chapter. The first step, then, is to determine whether the loss of subjects is unrelated to the treatment conditions. If so, then we can consider certain specialized analysis techniques, but if not, then we must *redesign the experiment* so that no differential loss of subjects occur.

Using ANOVA: The Analysis of Unweighted Means

The first method we will consider is called the **analysis of unweighted means**. The essence of this approach is that an *average* sample size replaces the actual sample sizes, giving equal weight in the analysis to each treatment mean. This analysis has no direct counterpart in MRC.

The Overall Analysis.   To illustrate the analysis of unweighted means, let us return to an earlier example from Chap. 10, in which factor A consists of three types of lectures (physical science, social science, and history). The original data, which appeared in Table 10-1 (page 121), are presented again in Table 24-1 with one

Table 24-1
Vocabulary Scores Following Three Different Lectures

	Physical Science (a_1)	Social Science (a_2)	History (a_3)
	53	47	45
	49	42	41
	47	39	38
	42	37	36
	51	42	35
	34	33	33
	44	13	46
	48	16	40
	35	16	29
	18	10	21
	32	11	30
	27	6	—
Sum:	480	312	394
Sample Size:	12	12	11
Mean:	40.00	26.00	35.82
ΣY^2:	20,482	10,654	14,658
SS:	1282.00	2542.00	545.64

score missing—the score for subject 36 (the last subject in condition a_3), who has inadvertently been given the wrong instructions at the start of the experiment. Because the loss of subject 36 is unrelated to the experimental treatments, the data are not biased by subject selection and the means are assumed to reflect the treatment effects in the population.

The analysis of unweighted means, as its name implies, gives equal weight to the different treatment groups in the determination of treatment effects, regardless of the number of observations contributing to each treatment mean. One way this may be accomplished is to multiply each mean by an *average sample size* and to perform the calculations on the resulting transformed treatment *sums*. The first step is to calculate the average sample size. Rather than use the arithmetic mean of the three samples, we use, for theoretical reasons, the **harmonic mean** instead. The general formula for the harmonic mean (s_h) is as follows:

$$s_h = \frac{\text{number of treatment groups}}{\Sigma \ (1/\text{sample size})} \qquad (24\text{-}1)$$

For the single-factor design under consideration, Eq. (24-1) becomes

$$s_h = \frac{a}{1/s_1 + 1/s_2 + 1/s_3}$$

That is, we divide the total number of treatment groups a by the sum of the reciprocals of the sample sizes. For this case, the sample sizes are $s_1 = 12, s_2 = 12$, and $s_3 = 11$. The harmonic mean is

$$s_h = \frac{3}{\frac{1}{12} + \frac{1}{12} + \frac{1}{11}} = \frac{3}{.083 + .083 + .091} = \frac{3}{.257} = 11.673$$

or 11.67.

The next step is to multiply each treatment mean by 11.67 to obtain an adjusted treatment sum, which we will designate A^*. The three adjusted sums are calculated as follows:

$$A_1^* = (s_h)(\bar{Y}_{A_1}) = (11.67)(40.00) = 466.80$$
$$A_2^* = (s_h)(\bar{Y}_{A_2}) = (11.67)(26.00) = 303.42$$
$$A_3^* = (s_h)(\bar{Y}_{A_3}) = (11.67)(35.82) = 418.02$$

From this information we can obtain the adjusted grand sum T^*:

$$T^* = \Sigma \ A^* = 466.80 + 303.42 + 418.02 = 1188.24$$

From this point on, the calculation of the treatment sum of squares SS_A is identical to that outlined in Chap. 10, with the exception that we substitute s_h for s in the

formulas for the basic ratios involved in the calculations, which, in this case are
$[A*]$ and $[T*]$. (Again, the asterisk notation is used to indicate that these two quantities are adjusted basic ratios to be used in the analysis of unweighted means.)
For the two basic ratios, then, we find

$$[A*] = \frac{\Sigma (A*)^2}{s_h} = \frac{(466.80)^2 + (303.42)^2 + (418.02)^2}{11.67} = \frac{484{,}706.66}{11.67}$$

$$= 41{,}534.42$$

$$[T*] = \frac{(T*)^2}{(a)(s_h)} = \frac{(1188.24)^2}{(3)(11.67)} = \frac{1{,}411{,}914.30}{35.01} = 40{,}328.89.$$

The adjusted treatment sum of squares becomes

$$SS_A = [A*] - [T*] = 41{,}534.42 - 40{,}328.89 = 1205.53$$

The treatment mean square is obtained in the usual manner:

$$MS_A = \frac{SS_A}{df_A} = \frac{1205.53}{3 - 1} = \frac{1205.53}{2} = 602.77$$

    The final special step in the analysis of unweighted means is the calculation
of the sum of squares for the error term. Whereas the treatment sum of squares
uses the harmonic sample mean s_h and adjusted treatment sums, the within-
groups sum of squares $SS_{S/A}$ relies on the individual scores Y and the actual treatment sample sizes s_i. As you will recall, the $SS_{S/A}$ represents a pooling of the
within-group sums of squares from all the treatment groups. These three sums of
squares are given in the last row of Table 24-1. To illustrate, the sum of squares
for condition a_1, for example, is

$$SS_{S/A_1} = \Sigma (Y_{1j} - \bar{Y}_{A_1})^2$$
$$= (53 - 40.00)^2 + (49 - 40.00)^2 + \cdots + (32 - 40.00)^2$$
$$+ (27 - 40.00)^2$$
$$\doteq 1282.00$$

(The notation Y_{1j} indicates that the summation takes place over all j subjects in
condition a_1.) The same sum of squares may be calculated more simply as follows:

$$SS_{S/A_1} = \Sigma Y_{1j}^2 - \frac{(A_1)^2}{s_1}$$

$$= (53^2 + 49^2 + \cdots + 32^2 + 27^2) - \frac{480^2}{12} = 1282.00$$

Combining the three within-group sums of squares, we find

$$SS_{S/A} = 1282.00 + 2542.00 + 545.64 = 4369.64$$

The degrees of freedom for the error term may be obtained by pooling the df's for the individual within-group sums of squares:

$$df_{S/A} = (12 - 1) + (12 - 1) + (11 - 1) = 32$$

The error term becomes

$$MS_{S/A} = \frac{SS_{S/A}}{df_{S/A}} = \frac{4369.64}{32} = 136.55$$

We can now calculate the F ratio, and we find

$$F = \frac{MS_A}{MS_{S/A}} = \frac{602.77}{136.55} = 4.41$$

which is significant.

Single-df Comparisons. We have urged, on numerous occasions, that you plan your analysis around a small number of central comparisons. If you follow this advice, you will be more interested in the statistical evaluation of your *planned comparisons* than in the outcome of the omnibus F test we have just calculated. Single-df comparisons are easy to conduct in the context of an unweighted-means analysis. The only change we need to make in the basic formula for a single-df comparison is to substitute the harmonic sample size s_h for s. Thus, Eq. (11-4) becomes

$$SS_{A_{comp.}} = \frac{(s_h)\,(\hat{\psi})^2}{\Sigma\,(c_i)^2} \tag{24-2}$$

where $\hat{\psi}$ represents the comparison itself expressed as a difference between two means. As an example, let us look at the difference between the combined science conditions and the history condition. Using the information from Table 24-1, we find

$$\hat{\psi} = (c_1)\,(\bar{Y}_{A_1}) + (c_2)\,(\bar{Y}_{A_2}) + (c_3)\,(\bar{Y}_{A_3})$$
$$= (+\tfrac{1}{2})\,(40.00) + (+\tfrac{1}{2})\,(26.00) + (-1)\,(35.82)$$
$$= 20.00 + 13.00 - 35.82 = -2.82$$

We simply substitute this information in Eq. (24-2) and obtain

$$SS_{A_{comp.}} = \frac{(11.67)\,(-2.82)^2}{(+\tfrac{1}{2})^2 + (+\tfrac{1}{2})^2 + (-1)^2} = \frac{92.80}{1.50} = 61.87$$

Since there is one degree of freedom associated with $SS_{A_{comp.}}$, $MS_{A_{comp.}} = 61.87$. The resulting F ratio becomes

$$F = \frac{MS_{A_{comp.}}}{MS_{S/A}} = \frac{61.87}{136.55} = .45$$

which is not significant.

Comment.   The analysis of unweighted means represents an apparently straight-forward way of dealing with unequal sample sizes in a single-factor design. That is, the analysis focuses on the treatment *means* and treats them equally in the calculation of systematic sources of variability. In summary, we use the group means as estimates of what the outcome of the experiment would be if there were no loss of subjects. We calculate sums of squares based on these means, using standard computational formulas adjusted by the average (harmonic) number of subjects per treatment group. After this has been accomplished, the analysis parallels the usual analysis with equal sample sizes.

There is a problem with the analysis of unweighted means that we have not yet mentioned. Statisticians have shown that the F ratios produced by this procedure are not distributed according to the sampling distributions of F, which means that critical values of F you will obtain from Table A-1 in the Appendix are slightly *smaller* than the values they should be (Gosslee & Lucas, 1965). This means, therefore, that the critical value of F at the 5 percent level of significance may actually reflect the 6 percent or 7 percent level of significance when the analysis of unweighted means is employed. The presence of this bias is a major reason why many experts recommend using a different procedure to analyze experiments with unequal sample sizes, one that does not exhibit this problem. On the other hand, the bias will be relatively small provided that the subject loss is not great, and you can easily correct for it by working at a slightly more stringent significance level—for example, setting $\alpha = .025$ when operating at the 5 percent level of significance. In addition, procedures are available to reduce the bias by adjusting the $df_{denom.}$ used to select the critical value of F from the F table (see Gosslee & Lucas, 1965).

Using ANOVA: The Analysis of Weighted Means

An alternative ANOVA procedure for dealing with unequal sample sizes is a technique that weights a mean in accordance with its sample size—just the opposite of the approach represented by the analysis of *unweighted* means. The primary advantage of this approach is that the resulting F tests are not biased, and as you will see later in this section, the analysis is equivalent to the one we will present in the context of MRC.

The simplest way to understand this approach is to consider the defining formula for the between-groups sum of squares SS_A. The defining formula for SS_A may be expressed in a form we did not explicitly develop in Chapter 6:

$$SS_A = s[\Sigma \ (\bar{Y}_{A_i} - \bar{Y}_T)^2] \tag{24-3}$$

We may modify this formula without changing its value by moving s within the brackets as follows:

$$SS_A = \Sigma \ [(s) \ (\bar{Y}_{A_i} - \bar{Y}_T)^2] \tag{24-4}$$

With this modification, SS_A consists of the sum of the squared deviations of the treatment means (the $\bar{Y}_{A_i}$'s) from the grand mean $\bar{Y}_T$, where the squared deviations are weighted by the sample size s. It is a simple step to modify Eq. (24-4) to accommodate unequal sample sizes. More specifically,

$$SS_A = \Sigma \ [(s_i) \ (\bar{Y}_{A_i} - \bar{Y}_T)^2] \tag{24-5}$$

where each squared deviation is now weighted by the appropriate sample size s_i.

We will use the information in Table 24-1 to illustrate the operation of Eq. (24-5). The only new information we need is $\bar{Y}_T$, which is the grand mean of all the Y scores, namely,

$$\bar{Y}_T = \frac{\Sigma \ A}{N} = \frac{480 + 312 + 394}{12 + 12 + 11} = \frac{1186}{35} = 33.89$$

Substituting in the equation, we find

$$SS_A = (12) \ (40.00 - 33.89)^2 + (12) \ (26.00 - 33.89)^2 + (11) \ (35.82 - 33.89)^2$$
$$= (12) \ (37.33) + (12) \ (62.25) + (11) \ (3.72) = 447.96 + 747.00 + 40.92$$
$$= 1235.88$$

With $df_A = 2$, $MS_A = 1235.88/2 = 617.94$. The error term is the same as the one calculated for the unweighted-means analysis, $MS_{S/A} = 136.55$. The omnibus F then becomes

$$F = \frac{MS_A}{MS_{S/A}} = \frac{617.94}{136.55} = 4.53$$

which is significant. (For comparison, the F from the analysis of unweighted means was 4.41.)

Single-df comparisons may also be conducted by the method of weighted means. In this case, the formula for the comparison sum of squares is different from the one with which you became familiar in earlier chapters. That is,

$$SS_{A_{comp.}} = \frac{(\hat{\psi})^2}{\sum \frac{(c_i)^2}{s_i}} \tag{24-6}$$

As you can see from Eq. (24-6), the familiar formula for single-df comparisons is changed in that each coefficient c_i is divided by its corresponding sample size s_i. As an illustration, we will conduct the same comparison we examined with the analysis of unweighted means, namely, the comparison of the combined science conditions with the history condition. Substituting in Eq. (24-6), we have

$$SS_{A_{comp.}} = \frac{(-2.82)^2}{\frac{(+\frac{1}{2})^2}{12} + \frac{(+\frac{1}{2})^2}{12} + \frac{(-1)^2}{11}}$$

$$= \frac{7.95}{.02 + .02 + .09} = \frac{7.95}{.13} = 61.15$$

The F test reveals that

$$F = \frac{MS_{A_{comp.}}}{MS_{S/A}} = \frac{61.15}{136.55} = .45$$

This value is identical to the one we obtained for the analysis of unweighted means, but you should not be misled by this outcome. A difference does appear in the two sums of squares (61.87 versus 61.15). This relatively small difference is not the result of rounding error. In general, the size of the difference will depend on the comparison involved and the magnitude of the subject loss. Only when there are large variations in sample sizes do sizable discrepancies appear, and these situations rarely occur in carefully executed research.

Using MRC

Though it may not have been apparent, throughout our discussion of MRC and its use with nonexperimental designs (Chaps. 20 and 21), we were essentially applying MRC to data gathered from unequal sample sizes for points on the X variable. Yet we could proceed in the analysis under no statistical limitation, and we can do the same using MRC for unequal sample sizes in experimental research. As you will see, the results of the MRC analysis will be identical to those of the analysis of variance applied to the *weighted* means, which we have just discussed.

The data from Table 24-1 have been arranged in Table 24-2 for an MRC analysis. With three groups, two vectors are needed. As you can see, vector 1 ($A1$) represents a comparison between the two science conditions, and vector 2 ($A2$)

Table 24-2
Coding for Unequal Sample Sizes

Subject		Y	(1) A1	(2) A2
a_1	1	53	1	1
	2	49	1	1
	3	47	1	1
	4	42	1	1
	5	51	1	1
	6	34	1	1
	7	44	1	1
	8	48	1	1
	9	35	1	1
	10	18	1	1
	11	32	1	1
	12	27	1	1
a_2	13	47	−1	1
	14	42	−1	1
	15	39	−1	1
	16	37	−1	1
	17	42	−1	1
	18	33	−1	1
	19	13	−1	1
	20	16	−1	1
	21	16	−1	1
	22	10	−1	1
	23	11	−1	1
	24	6	−1	1
a_3	25	45	0	−2
	26	41	0	−2
	27	38	0	−2
	28	36	0	−2
	29	35	0	−2
	30	33	0	−2
	31	46	0	−2
	32	40	0	−2
	33	29	0	−2
	34	21	0	−2
	35	30	0	−2
	36	—	—	—

$$r_{Y1} = .4580 \qquad r_{Y2} = -.1034$$
$$r_{12} = .0000$$

represents a comparison between the combined science conditions and the history condition. The coding process is identical to that presented in Chap. 10 for equal sample sizes. The only difference here is that the vector codes will not necessarily sum to zero; whether they do depends on the nature of the vector code and the pattern of sample sizes. Vector 1, for example, sums to zero, while vector 2 does not (sum $= +2$). This causes no problem for MRC, however, as you will discover in a moment.

The zero-order correlation coefficients are presented at the bottom of the table. Since the correlation coefficient for the two vectors in this example is zero (that is, $r_{12} = .0000$), we can obtain $R^2_{Y.A}$ by summing the two r^2's that each involve Y and one of the vectors:[1]

$$R^2_{Y.A} = r^2_{Y1} + r^2_{Y2} = (.4580)^2 + (-.1034)^2 = .2098 + .0107 = .2205$$

(If there were a correlation between the two vectors, we could enter it into the computer or use Eq. (10-2), which takes this information into consideration.) The residual R^2 is obtained by subtracting $R^2_{Y.max.}$—in this case, $R^2_{Y.A}$—from 1; that is

$$R^2_{Y.S/A} = 1 - R^2_{Y.A} = 1 - .2205 = .7795$$

We can now use one of the familiar equations, for example, Eq. (10-8), for the overall F test. More specifically,

$$F = \frac{R^2_{Y.A}/k}{(1 - R^2_{Y.A})/(N - k - 1)}$$

$$= \frac{.2205/2}{.7795/(35 - 2 - 1)} = \frac{.1103}{.7795/32} = \frac{.1103}{.0244} = 4.52$$

which, with $df_{num.} = 2$ and $df_{denom.} = 32$, is significant. The corresponding value from the analysis of weighted means was 4.53, which is identical except for rounding error.

You can easily examine single-df comparisons of interest to you provided you have planned for them in choosing the coding system for the analysis. All you need to do is to divide the $r^2_{comp.}$ by the overall error term. For the comparison between history and the combined science groups, $r^2_{Y2} = .0107$. The F is

$$F = \frac{r^2_{comp.}}{(1 - R^2_{Y.A})/(N - k - 1)} = \frac{.0107}{.0244} = .44$$

[1] With unequal sample sizes, independent vectors usually lose their orthogonality. For example, suppose our two comparisons consisted of social science versus history $(0, +1, -1)$ and physical science versus social science and history combined $(+2, -1, -1)$. With equal numbers of subjects (assume 12 per group), the two vectors are orthogonal, while with the present pattern of unequal sample sizes, they are not $(r_{12} = -.0255)$.

which, except for rounding error, is identical to the F we found with the analysis of weighted means (.45).

Comment

With small differences in sample sizes, all three analysis procedures produce comparable results. As we mentioned before, the sampling distributions of the F ratios obtained by the analysis of unweighted means do not correspond exactly to the F distribution, while those obtained by the analysis of weighted means and the statistically equivalent MRC do. Even so, there is not much of a problem in using the analysis of unweighted means except when an observed F is just barely significant—that is, is slightly larger than the critical value obtained from the F table. An argument can be made that, approximate or not, the analysis of unweighted means is more faithful to the intent of the researcher. The analysis of weighted means and MRC are influenced by sample sizes in the sense that the groups with larger sample sizes contribute more to the treatment and comparison sums of squares than do the groups with smaller sample sizes. The analysis of unweighted means allows each mean to contribute equally to the calculations of these quantities.

24.2   UNBALANCED FACTORIAL DESIGNS: THE ANOVA APPROACH

Additional complications arise in factorial experiments from which subjects are lost or discarded. Such experiments are often called **unbalanced factorial designs**, for reasons we will consider in a moment. They are also called factorial designs with **disproportional sample sizes**. Both terms refer to the same situation.[2] You will also encounter the term **nonorthogonal designs**, which is applied to any experimental design that has unequal sample sizes (Appelbaum & Cramer, 1974). In this section, we will consider how the analysis of unweighted means may be

---

[2] There are designs in which *unequal* sample sizes are *planned* rather than forced upon the researcher by the unexpected loss of subjects. Frequently, these are designs that include a classification of subjects as an independent variable—for example, socioeconomic status— when researchers want the levels of the classification variable to reflect the distribution of the groups in the population. In such designs, sample sizes are generally *proportional* between cells within the rows or columns of the design matrix, with the same relative proportion maintained at all levels of the other independent variable. For a detailed description of the analysis of this type of experiment, see Kirk (1982, pp. 407–411).

used to analyze the results of an unbalanced factorial design; we will consider the MRC approach to this same type of design in Sec. 24.3.

One Consequence of Unbalanced Factorial Designs

With *balanced* factorial designs—that is, factorial designs with equal sample sizes—main effects and interactions are all mutually *orthogonal* or *independent*. In contrast, with unbalanced factorial designs, there will be a lack of independence among the independent variables. To illustrate, suppose we had the following 2×2 factorial experiment:

	a_1	a_2
b_1	$s = 4$	$s = 4$
b_2	$s = 4$	$s = 4$

Table 24-3 presents the arrangement of the data for a standard MRC analysis of this design. Vector 1 represents the main effect of factor A, vector 2 represents the main effect of factor B, and vector 3 represents the $A \times B$ interaction. As you have seen in earlier chapters, the intercorrelations between these three vectors will all be zero—the two main effects and the interaction are mutually independent.

Suppose, however, that we lost subject 16 in the a_2b_2 condition for some reason that had nothing to do with the experimental treatments. Now if we were to correlate each vector with the others, we would find that none of the intercorrelations is zero. The actual zero-order correlation coefficients are as follows:

$$r_{12} = -.0714 \qquad r_{13} = .0714 \qquad r_{23} = .0714$$

As you can see, the three vectors are no longer mutually independent. Since the three vectors represent supposedly orthogonal sources of variability—A, B, and $A \times B$—we need to turn to a different analysis procedure. A commonly suggested ANOVA procedure for dealing with unbalanced factorial designs is the *analysis of unweighted means*, which we considered in Sec. 24.1.

The Analysis of Unweighted Means

To illustrate the analysis of unweighted means in a factorial design, let us consider again the example from Chap. 13, in which factor A consists of three types of lectures (physical science, social science, and history) and factor B consists of two

Table 24-3
Coding in an Unbalanced Factorial Design

Subject		(1)	(2)	(3)
a_1b_1	1	1	1	1
	2	1	1	1
	3	1	1	1
	4	1	1	1
a_1b_2	5	1	-1	-1
	6	1	-1	-1
	7	1	-1	-1
	8	1	-1	-1
a_2b_1	9	-1	1	-1
	10	-1	1	-1
	11	-1	1	-1
	12	-1	1	-1
a_2b_2	13	-1	-1	1
	14	-1	-1	1
	15	-1	-1	1
	16	—	—	—

methods of presentation (computer and standard). The original data, which appeared in Table 13-2 (page 186), are presented again in the upper part of Table 24-4 with one score missing—the score for subject 36 (the last subject in condition a_3b_2), who was inadvertently given the wrong instructions at the start of the experiment. The treatment means for the data are found in the middle part of Table 24-4. Because the loss of subject 36 was unrelated to the experimental treatments, the data are not biased by subject selection and the means are assumed to reflect the treatment effects in the population.

By using the analysis of unweighted means, we determine the main effects and the interaction from the treatment means. One way we can accomplish this is to multiply each group mean by an *average sample size* and then to perform the calculations on the resulting transformed treatment *sums*, using the standard computational formulas for sums of squares. The first step is to calculate the average sample size, which consists of the harmonic mean of the six sample sizes. The general formula for the harmonic mean s_h was presented in Sec. 24.1 as Eq. (24-1).

Table 24-4
Numerical Example of an Unbalanced Factorial Design

	Vocabulary Scores					
	Physical Science		Social Science		History	
	Computer	Standard	Computer	Standard	Computer	Standard
	53	44	47	13	45	46
	49	48	42	16	41	40
	47	35	39	16	38	29
	42	18	37	10	36	21
	51	32	42	11	35	30
	34	27	33	6	33	—
Sum:	276	204	240	72	228	166
Sample Size:	6	6	6	6	6	5
Mean:	46.00	34.00	40.00	12.00	38.00	33.20
ΣY^2:	12,940	7542	9716	938	8760	5898
SS:	244.00	606.00	116.00	74.00	96.00	386.80

Treatment Means

	a_1	a_2	a_3
b_1	46.00	40.00	38.00
b_2	34.00	12.00	33.20

Adjusted Treatment Sums

	a_1	a_2	a_3	Sum
b_1	266.80	232.00	220.40	719.20
b_2	197.20	69.60	192.56	459.36
Sum	464.00	301.60	412.96	1178.56

Adapting this formula to the two-factor design under consideration, we have

$$s_h = \frac{(a)(b)}{\dfrac{1}{s_{1,1}} + \dfrac{1}{s_{1,2}} + \cdots + \dfrac{1}{s_{3,1}} + \dfrac{1}{s_{3,2}}}$$

That is, we divide the total number of treatment groups $(a)(b)$ by the sum of the reciprocals of the sample sizes. For this case, the sample sizes are 6 for all groups except a_3b_2, for which the sample size $(s_{3,2})$ is 5. The harmonic mean is

$$s_h = \frac{(3)(2)}{\frac{1}{6} + \frac{1}{6} + \frac{1}{6} + \frac{1}{6} + \frac{1}{6} + \frac{1}{5}}$$

$$= \frac{6}{.167 + .167 + .167 + .167 + .167 + .20} = \frac{6}{1.035}$$

$$= 5.797$$

or 5.80.

The next step is to multiply the treatment means by 5.80 to obtain adjusted treatment sums, which we will designate AB^*. The adjusted treatment sum for a_1b_1, for example, is

$$(s_h)(\bar{Y}_{A_1B_1}) = (5.80)(46.00) = 266.80$$

This and the remaining adjusted sums are entered in an AB^* matrix, as illustrated in the bottom part of Table 24-4. From this point on the calculations of the factorial effects are identical to those outlined in Chap. 13, except that we substitute s_h for s in the formulas. To illustrate with the adjusted treatment sums in Table 24-4, we find

$$[T^*] = \frac{(T^*)^2}{(a)(b)(s_h)} = \frac{(1178.56)^2}{(3)(2)(5.80)} = 39{,}913.90$$

$$[A^*] = \frac{\Sigma (A^*)^2}{(b)(s_h)} = \frac{(464.00)^2 + (301.60)^2 + (412.96)^2}{(2)(5.80)} = 41{,}102.98$$

$$[B^*] = \frac{\Sigma (B^*)^2}{(a)(s_h)} = \frac{(719.20)^2 + (459.36)^2}{(3)(5.80)} = 41{,}854.04$$

$$[AB^*] = \frac{\Sigma (AB^*)^2}{s_h} = \frac{(266.80)^2 + (232.00)^2 + \cdots + (69.60)^2 + (192.56)^2}{5.80}$$

$$= 43{,}860.99$$

The formulas for the sums of squares for the factorial effects are presented in Table 24-5. The SS_A, for example, is calculated as follows:

$$SS_A = [A^*] - [T^*] = 41{,}102.98 - 39{,}913.90 = 1189.08$$

The values for the three factorial effects—SS_A, SS_B, and $SS_{A \times B}$—are entered in the table.

The final special step in the analysis of unweighted means is the calculation of the sum of squares for the error term. As we said in Sec. 24.1, the sum of squares for the error term ($SS_{S/AB}$, in this case) represents a pooling of the within-group sums of squares. The sums of squares for the six treatment conditions and the

Table 24-5
Analysis of Unweighted Means

Source	SS	df	MS	F
A	$[A^*] - [T^*] = 1189.08$	2	594.54	11.32*
B	$[B^*] - [T^*] = 1940.14$	1	1940.14	36.95*
A × B	$[AB^*] - [A^*] - [B^*] + [T^*] = 817.87$	2	408.94	7.79*
S/AB	1522.80	29	52.51	

* $p < .01$.

information necessary to calculate them are given in the upper portion of Table 24-4. Combining these within-group sums of squares, we find

$$SS_{S/AB} = 244.00 + 606.00 + 116.00 + 74.00 + 96.00 + 386.80 = 1522.80$$

The degrees of freedom for the error term may be obtained by pooling the df's for the individual within-group sums of squares:

$$df_{S/AB} = (6 - 1) + (6 - 1) + (6 - 1) + (6 - 1) + (6 - 1) + (5 - 1) = 29$$

The remainder of the analysis proceeds on familiar ground. As you can see in Table 24-5, each of the factorial effects is significant.

All the analytical techniques we considered for the two-factor design can be used with the analysis of unweighted means. The formulas presented in Chap. 14 and 15 are easily modified for these analyses; we simply substitute s_h for s and adjusted treatment sums for treatment sums wherever they appear.

Comment

You will recall that we turned to the analysis of unweighted means for the study of unbalanced factorial designs to deal with the loss of independence among the vectors for the main effects and the interaction. Because of the correlations that exist between them—correlations that are normally absent in balanced factorial designs—the four sums of squares presented in Table 24-5 will not equal the total sum of squares. (This is why no SS_T appears in the table.) While the analysis is relatively simple and may be extended to higher-order factorial designs, the bias associated with these F tests that we discussed in Sec. 24.1 still exists. We also pointed out that this bias is relatively small provided that the loss of subjects is not great and that we can easily correct for it by working at a slightly more stringent significance level—for example, setting $\alpha = .025$ when operating at the 5 percent level of significance.

24.3 UNBALANCED FACTORIAL DESIGNS: THE MRC APPROACH

In Chaps. 20 and 21, we were essentially applying MRC procedures to data that exhibited unequal samples sizes on the X variable. To predict job performance (Y), as we did in Chap. 21, we used a test designed to measure clerical aptitude. We would certainly not expect to have equal numbers of subjects with the same X scores on the aptitude test. Yet in our example in Chap. 21, we continued with the analysis without a statistical limitation, and we can do the same using MRC in experimental research. The great attractiveness of MRC is its ability to isolate relationships within a particular set of variables from relationships between that set and another set of variables. As you will see, we can use this property of MRC to eliminate the intercorrelations between the main-effect and interaction vectors that result when subjects in a factorial experiment are unexpectedly discarded or lost.

The heart of the MRC analysis is the *hierarchical strategy* that we have encountered in the last several chapters. There is still considerable disagreement, however, concerning the *particular* hierarchical strategy to use—a debate that began with important papers by Appelbaum and Cramer (1974) and Overall and Spiegel (1969) and still has not been unambiguously resolved. We will adopt the strategy that most closely approximates the analysis we would conduct when the designs are balanced—that is, when there are equal sample sizes in the treatment groups. This approach assumes a statistical model that includes all the main effects and interactions normally extracted in a standard ANOVA. As we have suggested, other models have been proposed, but they seem more applicable to nonexperimental than to experimental designs.[3]

As with any MRC analysis, we begin by coding the two main effects. In this example, we will need two vectors to code the three levels of factor A and one

---

[3] There is strong agreement on the position we will present in this chapter. See, for example, the arguments offered by Carlson and Timm (1974); Edwards (1979, pp. 172–174); Kirk (1982, pp. 414–415); Myers (1979, p. 403); and Overall, Lee, and Hornick (1981). For an alternative point of view, see Appelbaum and Cramer (1974) and Cramer and Appelbaum (1980).

vector to code the two levels of factor B. Product vectors are then used to code the $A \times B$ interaction. Most experts recommend the use of *effect coding* of both independent variables, although any coding—dummy, effect, or contrast—will suffice, provided the system adopted represents each of the two independent variables appropriately.[4] We have chosen to use two comparisons that would be orthogonal in a balanced design to represent factor A, physical science versus social science $(1, -1, 0)$ and combined science versus history $(1, 1, -2)$. Only one comparison is required to represent factor B, of course: computer versus standard presentation $(1, -1)$. The assignment of vectors is indicated in Table 24-6. The $A \times B$ interaction is represented by two product vectors, which are each obtained by crossing one of the two A vectors with the single B vector. These vectors are also presented in the table.

The purpose of the analysis is to determine the *unique contribution* of the two main effects and the interaction in accounting for variation in the dependent variable. For the A main effect, this quantity is obtained by subtracting from the R^2 based on *all* vectors, $R^2_{Y.A,B,A \times B}$, the R^2 based on all the vectors *except* those representing the A main effect, $R^2_{Y.B,A \times B}$. That is,

$$R^2_{Y.A} = R^2_{Y.A,B,A \times B} - R^2_{Y.B,A \times B}$$

Similarly, the B main effect is defined as the unique contribution of the B vectors to the regression analysis. In symbols,

$$R^2_{Y.B} = R^2_{Y.A,B,A \times B} - R^2_{Y.A,A \times B}$$

Finally, the interaction is found by subtracting the R^2 representing the joint influence of the two main effects from the overall R^2; that is,

$$R^2_{Y.A \times B} = R^2_{Y.A,B,A \times B} - R^2_{Y.A,B}$$

In each case, the R^2 is obtained by isolating the unique contribution of the target source of variability from the other two sources of variability in this design.[5]

---

[4] The primary advantage of effect coding is that the regression coefficients from the overall regression equation can be shown to represent the actual treatment effects (see Edwards, 1979, pp. 164–167); that is, each coefficient represents the deviation of particular means in the experiment from the unweighted grand mean.

[5] Technically, these quantities are squared *semipartial multiple correlation coefficients* that could be symbolized as follows:

$$R^2_{Y.A} = R^2_{Y(A.B,A \times B)} \qquad R^2_{Y.B} = R^2_{Y(B.A,A \times B)} \qquad R^2_{Y.A \times B} = R^2_{Y(A \times B.A,B)}$$

In each case, we are representing the multiple correlation between Y and one of the factorial effects (A, B, or $A \times B$) with the other two effects "partialed out" or held constant.

Table 24-6
An Example of Coding in an Unbalanced Factorial Design

	Subject	(Y)	A1	A2	B1	A1B1	A2B1
							Vectors
a_1 — b_1	1	53	1	1	1	1	1
	2	49	1	1	1	1	1
	3	47	1	1	1	1	1
	4	42	1	1	1	1	1
	5	51	1	1	1	1	1
	6	34	1	1	1	1	1
a_1 — b_2	7	44	1	1	−1	−1	−1
	8	48	1	1	−1	−1	−1
	9	35	1	1	−1	−1	−1
	10	18	1	1	−1	−1	−1
	11	32	1	1	−1	−1	−1
	12	27	1	1	−1	−1	−1
a_2 — b_1	13	47	−1	1	1	−1	1
	14	42	−1	1	1	−1	1
	15	39	−1	1	1	−1	1
	16	37	−1	1	1	−1	1
	17	42	−1	1	1	−1	1
	18	33	−1	1	1	−1	1
a_2 — b_2	19	13	−1	1	−1	1	−1
	20	16	−1	1	−1	1	−1
	21	16	−1	1	−1	1	−1
	22	10	−1	1	−1	1	−1
	23	11	−1	1	−1	1	−1
	24	6	−1	1	−1	1	−1
a_3 — b_1	25	45	0	−2	1	0	−2
	26	41	0	−2	1	0	−2
	27	38	0	−2	1	0	−2
	28	36	0	−2	1	0	−2
	29	35	0	−2	1	0	−2
	30	33	0	−2	1	0	−2
a_3 — b_2	31	46	0	−2	−1	0	2
	32	40	0	−2	−1	0	2
	33	29	0	−2	−1	0	2
	34	21	0	−2	−1	0	2
	35	30	0	−2	−1	0	2
	36	—	—	—	—	—	—

The error term is calculated in the usual fashion, as a proportion of residual variability remaining after we subtract all systematic variability. We have represented this quantity as $1 - R^2_{Y.max.}$ in earlier chapters, which, in this case, will be

$$R^2_{Y.S/AB} = 1 - R^2_{Y.A,B,A \times B}$$

which has associated with it $N - k - 1$ degrees of freedom, where N is the total number of observations and k is the number of vectors defining $R^2_{Y.max.}$.

We can now continue with the analysis. A computer analysis reveals the following:

$$R^2_{Y.A} = R^2_{Y.A,B,A \times B} - R^2_{Y.B,A \times B} = .7283 - .5095 = .2188$$
$$R^2_{Y.B} = R^2_{Y.A,B,A \times B} - R^2_{Y.A,A \times B} = .7283 - .3818 = .3465$$
$$R^2_{Y.A \times B} = R^2_{Y.A,B,A \times B} - R^2_{Y.A,B} = .7283 - .5826 = .1457$$

The last quantity we need is the residual term, which is calculated as follows:

$$R^2_{Y.S/AB} = 1 - R^2_{Y.A,B,A \times B} = 1 - .7283 = .2717$$

The analysis is completed in Table 24-7. Here, again, we find all three effects to be significant. You should note that the sum of the four sources of variability does not equal 1.00, as is always the case with balanced designs. That is,

$$R^2_{Y.A} + R^2_{Y.B} + R^2_{Y.A \times B} + R^2_{Y.S/AB} = .2188 + .3465 + .1457 + .2717 = .9827$$

This is neither a mistake nor an example of rounding error. Although we have removed the effects of the unequal sample sizes from influencing the estimates of the separate sources of variability in the MRC analysis, the partitioning itself does not fully account for the total variability. We encountered the same phenomenon in the analysis of unweighted means.

You should compare the values of the F ratios in Table 24-7 with those from the analysis of unweighted means in Table 24-5. They are not *identical*, as they

Table 24-7
MRC Analysis of an Unbalanced Factorial Design

Source	R^2	df	Mean R^2	F
A	.2188	2	.1094	11.64*
B	.3465	1	.3465	36.86*
A × B	.1457	2	.0729	7.76*
S/AB	.2717	29	.0094	

*$p < .01$.

have been in our examples with equal sample sizes. On the other hand, they are not very far apart; they will be very close when the loss of subjects is minimal, as it was in this particular example. The divergence of the F's from the two approaches depends on the size of the subject loss and the pattern of the losses.

Comment

What procedure should you use, analysis of unweighted means or MRC? Not too long ago, most experts recommended the analysis of unweighted means. They did so with the full realization of the small bias associated with the F tests obtained with this procedure. With the increased availability of computers and sophisticated statistical programs, the tide has shifted and MRC analyses are the ones most recommended. In spite of opinions and recommendations, however, many experimentalists will continue to analyze unbalanced designs using unweighted means. One reason why experimentalists choose not to switch is that they do not want to give up the familiar procedures. And they can defend this position: they can point to the close correspondence between the two analyses when the subject loss is small, or they can adopt the simple strategy of using a slightly more stringent significance level when it is not. In addition, they can note that a potential problem occurs only when a particular F is of *borderline significance*. Why adopt a seemingly "foreign" procedure for the many circumstances when the F's do not fall in this range of ambiguity?

A complication to the use of MRC procedures is that experts do not agree on the *proper* course of action to follow when unbalanced designs are involved. If all researchers used the hierarchical strategy recommended here for the analysis of unbalanced factorial designs, there would be no ambiguity, but this is not the case. Some recommend a procedure of starting with a statistical model that includes all main effects and interaction—the usual model adopted by researchers analyzing a factorial experiment—and then revising the model, depending on the outcome of statistical tests (e.g., Appelbaum & Cramer, 1974). What this procedure does is to drop interactions from the model when they are not significant and to assign any variation associated with them to the residual variability and to some of the remaining factorial effects. What is disturbing about this approach is that it is *data-dependent* and is clearly not based on theory or on independent empirical information.

Finally, we should add that analytical comparisons, which lie at the heart of experimental design, are difficult to conduct with MRC when unequal sample sizes are present. In the first place, it will be difficult for researchers, who are not statistical experts, to know how to arrange a specialized analysis, consisting of some mixture of single-df comparisons, simple effects, and interaction comparisons, when the vectors representing these analyses are not orthogonal to other vectors and effects in the experiment. The analysis of the overall factorial design is straight-forward and relatively simple with unbalanced factorials, while the appropriate arrangement of an intricate, detailed analysis is not. How will a researcher know which vectors should be entered into an analysis first in order to provide statistical control over an analysis? In the second place, there remains the problem that single-*df* comparisons are affected by differences in sample sizes. The single-*df* comparisons supported by the MRC approach represent an analysis of *weighted means*, in which the statistical outcome is influenced not only by the difference between the two means, but by the differences in sample sizes. Most scientific questions asked by experimentalists are expressed in terms of the various treatment means. Consequently, these researchers will not want differences in sample sizes to influence the decision-making process. For this important reason, then, experimentalists might choose to conduct an analysis based on the unweighted means, which *does* give equal weight to the various means that are considered.

24.4   NONEXPERIMENTAL DESIGNS

Some nonexperimental studies outwardly resemble factorial designs. Suppose a researcher is interested in attitudes toward a proposed nuclear arms treaty between the United States and the Soviet Union. Two variables are selected that are expected to influence such attitudes: political affiliation and family income. The researcher identifies a random sample of individuals, who are then asked about their attitudes, their political affiliations, and their family incomes. For some researchers, the design would be conceptualized as a factorial created by crossing factor *A* (Democrat and Republican) with factor *B* (three different income levels). The immediate problem, of course, is that the design will be unbalanced, with unequal numbers of subjects appearing in the six different cells of the data matrix.

By now you should realize that this design is fundamentally different from a factorial experiment. There is no random assignment of subjects to the six cells of the matrix; the "independent" variables are neither independent nor manipulated by the experimenter; there is no temporal separation between the "independent" variables and the "dependent" variable; and so on. It makes no sense, therefore, to take steps to attempt to equate the cell sizes by such means as randomly dropping subjects from overpopulated cells or adding subjects to underpopulated cells, as we might in an experiment in which a few subjects are lost for reasons unrelated to the treatment manipulations. The differences in cell size are a vital part of the behavior under study in this particular design; if you remove the differences, then you necessarily change the outcome of the results and the meaning of the research.

How do we analyze data from this sort of nonexperimental design? The obvious answer is by turning to MRC and adopting a strategy that takes the differences in sample sizes into consideration. In this strategy, researchers might conceptualize the design as a factorial arrangement of the two variables, and they might then try to examine the same sources of variability they would extract in a factorial experiment, namely, two main effects and the interaction. You might be tempted to duplicate the type of MRC analysis we presented in Sec. 24.3 for the evaluation of an unbalanced factorial design, determining the *unique* contribution made to Y variability by each main effect and the interaction. This is only one possible solution, however, as we noted in Sec. 24.3 Yet not all experts agree that nonexperimental designs of this sort should be forced into what amounts to a factorial "mold." Pedhazur (1982, pp. 382–387), for example, argues that the main effects and interactions of the factorial experiment do not translate well to nonexperiment designs.[6]

It seems clear that researchers must give much more thought to the statistical model appropriate for their studies. If the purpose of a study is *prediction*, then a stepwise approach which adds variables according to the magnitude of added predictability is appropriate. As we indicated in Chap. 20, such an approach is atheoretical—the concern and interest is primarily in obtaining the best overall prediction with the smallest number of variables. If the purpose is *explanation*, however, a hierarchical strategy is usually adopted, in which variables are added in an order specified by theory. The most compelling examples of this approach are assessments of *causal theories* in which the ordering of variables is dictated by a consideration of causal mechanisms and the temporal point at which the influence of any given variable may be expected to occur.

24.5 SUMMARY

Though most experiments are designed with equal sample sizes for the treatment conditions, inadvertent loss of subjects due to equipment problems or voluntary termination may arise. If the loss of subjects is unrelated to the treatment condition, then the researcher can undertake specialized analysis techniques.

One option for the researcher is to undertake an analysis of unweighted means, an ANOVA approach that gives equal weight to the different treatment groups,

---

[6] In addition, we would question the wisdom of taking a continuous variable, such as family income, and dividing it into sets of arbitrary categories, simply to mimic a factorial arrangement. In our opinion, it is best to leave continuous variables intact so that their influence on Y may be most powerfully and faithfully assessed.

regardless of the number of subjects contributing to the treatment means. The analysis proceeds essentially as with equal sample sizes, except that the harmonic mean s_h of the sample sizes, given by Eq. (24-1), is substituted for s in the formulas for equal sample size. Likewise, the analysis of single-df comparisons is the same as the analysis with equal sample sizes, except that, again, the harmonic mean is used to determine the comparison sums of squares. A second option is to use another ANOVA approach, the analysis of weighted means, which weights the contribution of each treatment mean to the analysis in proportion to its sample size. The two options produce very similar results when the loss of data is not great.

The MRC analysis of experiments with unequal sample sizes is conducted in the same manner we have followed in the previous chapters. For the single-factor design, the MRC analysis and the analysis of weighted means are identical. The MRC analysis is widely recommended for the analysis of factorial designs, although many experimentalists will still prefer to conduct the analysis of unweighted means instead. For nonexperimental designs, MRC is *the* analysis procedure. The details of this approach were described in Chaps. 20 and 21.

24.6 EXERCISES

1. In Chap. 10, Problem 1, we introduced an experiment on the effects of verbal reinforcement on the performance of children on a simple motor-coordination task. Refer to the data in that experiment, but assume that the score for the last subject in the "praise" condition is missing.

    a. Analyze the data with an unweighted-means ANOVA.
    b. Analyze the data with a weighted-means ANOVA.
    c. Analyze the data with MRC.

2. In the problems at the end of Chap. 13, we introduced a two-factor experiment where factor A was the type of verbal reinforcement ("praise," "reproof," or "none") and factor B was the type of subject (child or adult). Refer to the data, but assume that the score for the seventh child in the "praise" condition is missing.

    a. Analyze the data with an unweighted-means ANOVA.
    b. Analyze the data with MRC, using contrast coding.

25

Epilogue

. . .

We have discussed the major research designs commonly employed in the behavioral sciences and indicated under what circumstances ANOVA and MRC can be used interchangeably. We have shown that in any situation where both analysis techniques can be used appropriately, the statistical results, and consequently the conclusions, are identical. In being able to use either technique you will have a greater understanding of research, design, and analysis. In this chapter, however, we examine the two procedures from a different viewpoint, considering what we assess to be their relative advantages and disadvantages. Which procedure you ultimately choose for the analysis of a given set of data is, of course, a personal decision. You should feel sufficiently comfortable with ANOVA and MRC to be able to switch from one to the other when the circumstances are appropriate. For example, suppose you were at home preparing an experiment for publication and needed to conduct an additional analysis or two but were unable to return to your office and your computer. Knowing how to conduct these analyses with a hand calculator, even though you completed your primary analysis on the computer, would clearly be convenient.

Historically, ANOVA and MRC were developed for use with different classes of designs—ANOVA for the analysis of experiments, and MRC for the analysis of nonexperimental designs and correlational data. The early histories of the two methods are discussed in articles by Lovie (1979) and Rucci and Tweney (1980). The fact that both are based on the same mathematical model was generally unknown. Moreover, we would rarely find a researcher who was reasonably well versed in the two procedures. In an influential paper, Cohen (1969) called attention to these common origins and to the special generality of MRC. That is, MRC could be applied to all situations for which ANOVA was used and to all other situations as well. Subsequent books by Cohen and Cohen (1975, 1983), Edwards (1979, 1985), Kerlinger and Pedhazur (1973), and Pedhazur (1982) discussed this overlap within the context of MRC, while books by others, for example, Kirk (1982) and Myers (1979), placed more stress on ANOVA. Our approach, which reflects that of Edwards (1979, 1985) and Stevens (1986), gives the two procedures relatively equal weight in our discussions of the analysis of experimental designs. We believe that the stage is set for a change in the statistical literacy of researchers in the social sciences. We hope that an increased familiarity with both procedures will be associated with the introduction of nonexperimental research, generally requiring the use of MRC, into areas of research in which *experiments* are the rule and with an increased use of sophisticated experimental designs and analyses in areas in which *nonexperimental designs* are more common.

Perhaps we do not need to remind you at this point that it is the nature of the research design itself that dictates the sorts of conclusions that may be drawn from a set of data, not the particular statistical procedure used to isolate various sources of variability and to test their significance. In fact, it is not even necessary to indicate whether ANOVA or MRC was used to produce a particular F ratio or to calculate a measure of treatment magnitude. As we have demonstrated on numerous occasions, the statistical outcomes are identical. Whether a researcher can conclude that a certain variable (X) was responsible for or caused differences in behavior (Y) depends on the nature of the design, not the statistical procedure. Thus, we can infer cause and effect with data from experiments, in which manipulation of the independent variable (or variables) is under the independent control of the researcher, whereas we can only make statements of association with data from nonexperimental or correlational studies, in which the variations in X reflect properties of individuals rather than differences controlled by the researcher.

Pedhazur (1982, p. 328) cites a number of factors that led him to conclude that MRC is the analysis technique of choice and, presumably, the method that all students should study and master in their training as social scientists. In general, Pedhazur believes that MRC is the preferred technique because (1) it is a more comprehensive and general approach on the conceptual as well as analytical level, (2) it requires fewer calculations of statistics (one need only calculate r and F), (3) it accommodates different types of variables (quantitative and categorical), (4) it accommodates unequal sample sizes without requiring adjustments in calculations, and (5) it is the logical choice when there are covariates and trends to be analyzed.

We believe that he has overstated the case. Although MRC can be applied to a wider range of situations than ANOVA can, its greater generality does not mean that the procedure *facilitates* the analysis of experiments. The relative simplicity of calculations in ANOVA allows us easier access to appropriate statistical analyses and in some cases a clearer understanding of what the analyses represent: a comparison of groups. Researchers tend to focus on the *differences between treatment means* when they are attempting to interpret the results of an experiment. For this reason, then, ANOVA seems to represent a more "natural" extension of our theoretical expectations, which we usually express as differences between treatment means, than does the equivalent analysis of correlations with MRC. In contrast, MRC requires the sometimes laborious task of establishing vectors to represent differences.

25.1 A COMPARISON OF ANOVA AND MRC: EXPERIMENTAL DESIGNS

For the remainder of this chapter, we will briefly compare the two procedures from the perspective of the statistics and calculations they entail.

General Considerations

We can easily transform statistical indices obtained from one approach into corresponding indices for the other. For example, we can express an MRC analysis in terms of ANOVA concepts simply by multiplying all relevant squared correlation coefficients (r^2 and R^2) by the total sum of squares (SS_Y) to produce corresponding sums of squares extracted in the analysis. For example,

$$(R^2_{Y.A})(SS_Y) = SS_A \qquad \text{and} \qquad (R^2_{Y.A \times B})(SS_Y) = SS_{A \times B}$$

In the other direction, we can express an analysis of variance in terms of MRC concepts by dividing all relevant sums of squares by SS_T to produce corresponding squared correlation coefficients. To illustrate,

$$\frac{SS_A}{SS_T} = R^2_{Y.A} \qquad \text{and} \qquad \frac{SS_{A \times B}}{SS_T} = R^2_{Y.A \times B}$$

These latter calculations from ANOVA easily provide us with estimates of treatment magnitude, although you may prefer to obtain alternative estimated measures such as estimated omega squared and estimated epsilon squared.

We will usually want to have available the means and standard deviations for the various treatment conditions in an experiment. This information is a natural byproduct of ANOVA whether the computations are conducted by hand or by computer. You can obtain this information with MRC, of course. You can calculate the means by using the regression equation based on a full set of treatment vectors ($R^2_{Y.max}$). Although you can obtain the standard deviations by using special sets of vectors designed to isolate the variation in a single treatment condition, which we did not discuss in this book, you will probably find it less complicated to calculate the treatment means and standard deviations by hand than to attempt to extract this information from the MRC computer analysis.

Assuming that you do conduct most of your analyses with a computer—regardless of your statistical preferences—you may very well find ANOVA programs easier to use than MRC programs simply because they have been specially designed for the analysis of experiments. In order to use an MRC program for the same analyses, you will have to program the analysis *yourself*, constructing appropriate vectors and specifying the exact details of the analysis. While such an exercise will test your understanding of the analyses themselves, you may find these steps excessively time-consuming.

Between-Subjects Designs

Single-Factor Design.   You can easily analyze the results of single-factor between-subjects designs with either procedure. For ANOVA, single-*df* comparisons require additional calculations if the analysis is being conducted by hand. Most ANOVA computer programs will allow you to include single-df comparisons as part of the analysis, although some statistical packages are easier to use than others. You can obtain measures of treatment magnitude directly from most computer programs, although you can calculate these indices using the information you already have available from the analysis.

For MRC, the exact nature of the analysis depends on the coding strategy you have adopted. Presumably you will use contrast coding and include in the analysis all single-df comparisons that will be of interest to you. The r^2's for these comparisons will be calculated along with the overall $R^2_{Y.max.}$. In order to calculate the error term, which requires $R^2_{Y.max.}$, you will need to include a sufficient number of comparison vectors to capture the total variability among the group means, namely, one less than the total number of treatment groups. Additional comparisons may be calculated by including the relevant vectors in the analysis and requesting a listing of the intercorrelation matrix in which the zero-order correlations for all variables are reported.

Factorial Designs.   The ANOVA approach is relatively easy to conduct by hand. The analysis of simple effects is modeled after designs of lesser complexity; interaction comparisons focus on an arrangement of the treatment means that reflects the relevant single-df comparisons involved in these analyses. Computer programs differ in the ease with which you may conduct these detailed analyses of interaction. Your choice of statistical package may be dictated by this particular consideration.

The MRC analysis requires specification of vectors that represent the separate main effects; interaction vectors are simply products of main-effect vectors. The analysis of simple effects will involve additional effort on your part, namely, creating specialized vectors that isolate relevant parts of the data analysis. The analysis of interaction comparisons is facilitated by the use of interaction vectors that reflect specific interaction contrasts that are of interest to you.

Within-Subjects Designs

The analysis of within-subjects designs, in which subjects receive at least two of the treatment conditions, involves a relatively simple extension of the analysis of between-subjects designs, in which subjects receive only one of the treatment conditions. The main complication in the analysis is in the frequent need for specialized error terms based on the subsets of data contributing to different comparisons or effects. Conducting an analysis of variance by hand usually represents a great deal of work. Each separate analysis—a single-df comparison, a simple effect, or an interaction contrast—represents about the same amount of work as does the overall analysis of main effects and interactions. Computer programs will certainly assist you in the analysis, but many fail to provide separate error terms, using instead error terms based on the overall analysis of variance. You must take great care in selecting ANOVA programs and determining how they deal with the issue of specialized error terms.

We can adapt the MRC approach to the analysis of within-subjects designs with little additional effort. The crucial step is in constructing the vectors needed for the different analyses. By constructing vectors that reflect single-*df* comparisons of interest to us, we can easily use this information to specify sets of vectors that represent these treatment effects and the error terms we need to test their significance. The basic flexibility of the MRC approach allows us to tailor our detailed analysis of an experiment exactly to our needs.

Analysis of Covariance

The analysis of covariance is a procedure that uses information on a subject variable—called a *covariate*—obtained before the start of an experiment, in order to reduce the variability of subjects treated alike and to adjust for chance differences occurring when subjects are assigned randomly to the different treatment conditions. Calculating an analysis of covariance by hand involves approximately 3 times the computational effort needed to conduct an ordinary ANOVA, which, of course, does not take advantage of the information provided by the covariate. Most comprehensive computer programs offer the analysis of covariance as an option, however, which means that computational effort should not be a critical concern in deciding between the ANOVA and MRC approaches. On the other hand, the MRC approach seems ideally suited to the analysis of covariance. You follow a simple hierarchical strategy in which you first enter the covariate scores and then the treatment effects of interest. The resulting *incremental variability* obtained when we add vectors reflecting treatment effects—main effects and interactions—provides the very corrections we need to complete the statistical analysis.

Unequal Sample Sizes

In most cases, you will design your experiments with equal numbers of subjects randomly assigned to the different treatment conditions. As discussed in Chap. 24, you may occasionally be forced to discard subjects from a study for reasons that are unrelated to the experimental treatments—for example, equipment failure, illness, and so on. When this happens you will usually not be able to use the ANOVA approach discussed throughout the book to analyze the results of your experiment. A common solution to this problem is an *unweighted means analysis*

(Chap. 24), in which you base the analysis on the *treatment means* and use an average sample size in the calculations; you can use this procedure with most types of experimental designs. (Alternatively, you could use the *weighted means analysis*, although this procedure is usually appropriate only for single-factor designs with unequal sample sizes.) Although unweighted means analysis has great intuitive appeal in that it focuses the analysis on the actual means, it suffers from a statistical bias which requires an adjustment of the significance levels to correct. (The weighted means analysis does not have this bias.)

The MRC approach to the analysis of experiments with unequal sample sizes is free from the problem of statistical bias. The analysis of a single-factor design with unequal numbers of subjects is identical to the analysis we described when equal numbers are involved; the resulting F ratios are equivalent to those obtained with the analysis of weighted means. For factorial designs, however, we use a different procedure—a hierarchical analysis—in which each of the treatment effects (main effects and interactions) is examined for its unique and independent contribution to the variability in the dependent variable Y. We prefer the MRC approach because it is free from the statistical bias that plagues ANOVA when unequal sample sizes occur.

25.2   THE ANALYSIS OF NONEXPERIMENTAL DESIGNS

The analysis of nonexperimental designs is essentially the exclusive domain of the MRC approach. Occasionally, quasi experiments may be analyzed by means of ANOVA, or, more typically, by analysis of covariance, but they may also be analyzed with MRC. We discussed the use of MRC in the analysis of nonexperimental designs in Chaps. 20 and 21. Most attempts to apply ANOVA to other nonexperimental designs either are incorrect or artificially distort the outcomes of these studies.

25.3   SUMMARY

We briefly considered the relative advantages of ANOVA and MRC in the analysis of the different sorts of designs we have discussed in this book. The two approaches give identical F ratios when they are applied to experimental designs with any number of independent variables. Which approach you choose is largely a matter of personal preference. It is our hope that future researchers will find ANOVA and MRC equally "comfortable." Whereas we showed that the statistics needed in

ANOVA are generally easily calculated by hand, we also suggested that the MRC approach has some advantages over ANOVA in the analysis of certain experimental designs. First, it is easier to use in analyzing data from within-subjects designs, particularly when special error terms are called for; not all ANOVA computer program provide the special error terms. Second, the analysis of covariance is a relatively simple analysis with MRC—simple to set up and simple to understand. Finally, MRC provides a statistically superior procedure for analyzing the data from factorial experiments in which subjects have been lost during the collection phase of the study; the ANOVA approach, consisting of an analysis of unweighted means, is more familiar to researchers but introduces a statistical bias in the evaluation process.

Under most circumstances, MRC is the only approach for analyzing the data from nonexperimental designs. Most attempts to apply ANOVA procedures to such data tend to distort the results of the study and limit the conclusions possible.

In conclusion, this book has provided you with multiple tools for analyzing research and with multiple perspectives for viewing research designs. Our final message is that there is no substitute for well thought out, meaningful research, ideas, and designs. Let your research ideas drive what you do and allow the statistical techniques to help you interpret your findings.

References

...

American Psychological Association. (1983). *Publication manual of the American Psychological Association* (3rd ed.). Washington, DC: American Psychological Association.

Appelbaum, M. I., & Cramer, E. M. (1974). Some problems in the nonorthogonal analysis of variance. *Psychological Bulletin, 81*, 335–343.

Asher, H. B. (1976). *Causal modeling.* Beverly Hills, CA: Sage Publications.

Barcikowski, R. S. (Ed.). (1983). *Computer packages and research design: Vol. 1. BMDP.* Lanham, MD: University Press of America.

Barcikowski, R. S. (Ed.). (1983). *Computer packages and research design: Vol. 2. SAS.* Lanham, MD: University Press of America.

Barcikowski, R. S. (Ed.). (1983). *Computer packages and research design: Vol. 3. SPSS and SPSSX.* Lanham, MD: University Press of America.

Berenson, M. L., Levine, D. M., & Goldstein, M. (1983). *Intermediate statistical methods and applications: A computer package approach.* Englewood Cliffs, NJ: Prentice-Hall.

Blalock, H. M., Jr. (1964). *Causal inferences in non-experimental research.* Chapel Hill, NC: University of North Carolina Press.

Boik, R. J. (1979). Interactions, partial interactions, and interaction contrasts in the analysis of variance. *Psychological Bulletin, 86*, 1084–1089.

Brewer, J. K. (1972). On the power of statistical tests in the *American Educational Research Journal. American Educational Research Journal, 9*, 391–401.

Campbell, D. T., & Stanley, J. C. (1966). *Experimental and quasi-experimental designs for research.* Chicago: Rand McNally.

Carlson, J. E., & Timm, N. H. (1974). Analysis of nonorthogonal fixed-effects designs. *Psychological Bulletin, 81,* 563–570.

Carmer, S. G., & Swanson, M. R. (1973). An evaluation of ten pairwise multiple comparison procedures by Monte Carlo methods. *Journal of the American Statistical Association, 68,* 66–74.

Cohen, J. (1962). The statistical power of abnormal-social psychological research: A review. *Journal of Abnormal and Social Psychology, 65,* 145–153.

Cohen, J. (1968). Multiple regression as a general data-analytic system. *Psychological Bulletin, 70,* 426–443.

Cohen, J. (1977). *Statistical power analysis for the behavioral sciences* (rev. ed.). New York: Academic.

Cohen, J., & Cohen, P. (1975). *Applied multiple regression/correlation analysis for the behavioral sciences.* Hillsdale, NJ: Lawrence Erlbaum Associates.

Cohen, J., & Cohen, P. (1983). *Applied multiple regression/correlation analysis for the behavioral sciences* (2nd ed.). Hillsdale, NJ: Lawrence Erlbaum Associates.

Cook, T. D., & Campbell, D. T. (1979). *Quasi-experimentation: Design and analysis issues in field settiings.* Chicago: Rand McNally.

Cozby, P. C. (1984). *Using computers in the behavioral sciences.* Palo Alto, CA: Mayfield Publishing Company.

Cramer, E. M., & Appelbaum, M. I. (1980). Nonorthogonal analysis of variance—once again. *Psychological Bulletin, 87,* 51–57.

Crano, W. D., & Brewer, M. B. (1973). *Principles of research in social psychology.* New York: McGraw-Hill.

Cronbach, L. J. (1957). The two disciplines of scientific psychology. *American Psychologist, 12,* 671–684.

Cronbach, L. J., & Snow, R. E. (1977). *Aptitude and instructional methods: A handbook for research on interactions.* New York: Irvington Publishers.

Dooling, D. J., & Danks, J. H. (1975). Going beyond tests of significance: Is psychology ready? *Bulletin of the Psychonomic Society, 5,* 15–17.

Dunnett, C. W. (1955). A multiple comparison procedure for comparing several treatments with a control. *Journal of the American Statistical Association, 50,* 1096–1121.

Dunnett, C. W. (1964). New tables for multiple comparisons with a control. *Biometrics, 20,* 482–491.

Dwyer, J. H. (1974). Analysis of variance and the magnitude of effects: A general approach. *Psychological Bulletin, 81,* 731–737.

Edwards, A. L. (1976). *An introduction to linear regression and correlation.* New York: Freeman.

Edwards, A. L. (1979). *Multiple regression and the analysis of variance and covariance.* New York: Freeman.

Edwards, A. L. (1985). *Multiple regression and the analysis of variance and covariance* (2nd ed.). New York: Freeman.

Feldt, L. S. (1958). A comparison of the precision of three experimental designs employing a concomitant variable. *Psychometrika, 23,* 335–353.

Fisher, R. A. (1949). *The design of experiments.* Edinburgh: Oliver & Boyd.

Fisher, R. A., & Yates, F. (1953). *Statistical tables for biological, agricultural and medical research* (4th ed.). Edinburgh: Oliver & Boyd.

Gaito, J. (1965). Unequal intervals and unequal *n* in trend analyses. *Psychological Bulletin, 63,* 125–127.

Geisser, S., & Greenhouse, S. W. (1958). An extension of Box's results on the use of the *F* distribution in multivariate analysis. *Annals of Mathematical Statistics, 29,* 885–891.

Ghiselli, E. E., Campbell, J. P., & Zedeck, S. (1981). *Measurement theory for the behavioral sciences.* New York: Freeman.

Gosslee, D. G., & Lucas, H. L. (1965). Analysis of variance of disproportionate data when interaction is present. *Biometrics, 21,* 115–133.

Grant, D. A. (1956). Analysis-of-variance tests in the analysis and the comparison of curves. *Psychological Bulletin, 53,* 141–154.

Greenwald, A. G. (1976). Within-subjects designs: To use or not to use? *Psychological Bulletin, 83,* 314–320.

Huitema, B. E. (1980). *The analysis of covariance and alternatives.* New York: Wiley.

Jöreskog, K. G. (1969). A general approach to confirmatory maximum likelihood factor analysis. *Psychometrika, 34,* 183–202.

Jöreskog, K. G., & Sorbom, D. (1984). *LISREL VI. Analysis of linear structural relationships by maximum likelihood, instrumental variables, and least squares methods.* Mooresville, IN: Scientific Software, Inc.

Kenny, D. A. (1979). *Correlation and causality.* New York: Wiley.

Keppel, G. (1982). *Design and analysis: A researcher's handbook* (2nd ed.). Englewood Cliffs, NJ. Prentice Hall.

Keppel, G., Postman, L., & Zavortink, B. (1968). Studies of learning to learn: VIII. The influence of massive amounts of training upon the learning and retention of paired-associate lists. *Journal of Verbal Learning and Verbal Behavior, 7,* 790–796.

Kerlinger, F. N., & Pedhazur, E. J. (1973). *Multiple regression in behavioral research.* New York: Holt, Rinehart & Winston.

Kirk, R. E. (1982). *Experimental design: Procedures for the behavioral sciences* (2nd. ed.). Monterey, CA: Brooks/Cole.

Lovie, A. D. (1979). The analysis of variance in experimental psychology: 1934–1945. *British Journal of Mathematical and Statistical Psychology, 32,* 151–178.

Maxwell, S. E., Camp, C. J., & Arvey, R. D. (1981). Measures of strength of association: A comparative examination. *Journal of Applied Psychology, 66,* 525–534.

Maxwell, S. E., Delaney, H. D., & Dill, C. A. (1984). Another look at ANCOVA versus blocking. *Psychological Bulletin, 95,* 136–147.

McNemar, Q. (1969). *Psychological statistics* (4th ed.). New York: Wiley.

Myers, J. L. (1979). *Fundamentals of experimental design* (3rd ed.). Boston: Allyn & Bacon.

Overall, J. E., Lee, D. M., & Hornick, C. W. (1981). Comparison of two strategies for analysis of variance in nonorthogonal designs. *Psychological Bulletin, 90,* 367–375.

Overall, J. E., & Spiegel, D. K. (1969). Concerning least squares analysis of experimental data. *Psychological Bulletin, 72*, 311–322.

Pearson, E. S., & Hartley, H. O. (Eds.). (1970). *Biometrika tables for statisticians* (3rd ed., Vol. 1). New York: Cambridge.

Pedhazur, E. J. (1977). Coding subjects in repeated measures designs. *Psychological Bulletin, 84*, 298–305.

Pedhazur, E. J. (1982), *Multiple regression in behavioral research: Explanation and prediction* (2nd ed.). New York: Holt, Rinehart & Winston.

Piaget, J. (1965). *The moral judgment of the child.* New York: Free Press.

Rosenthal, R., & Rosnow, R. L. (Eds.). (1969). *Artifacts in behavioral research.* New York: Academic.

Rucci, A. J., & Tweney, R. D. (1980). Analysis of variance and the "second discipline" of scientific psychology: A historical account. *Psychological Bulletin, 87*, 166–184.

Scheffé, H. A. (1953). A method for judging all possible contrasts in the analysis of variance. *Biometrika, 40*, 87–104.

Stevens, J. (1986). *Applied multivariate statistics for the social sciences.* Hillsdale, NJ: Lawrence Erlbaum Associates.

Tukey, J. W. (1953). *The problem of multiple comparisons.* Unpublished manuscript, Princeton University, Princeton, NJ.

Vaughan, G. M., & Corballis, M. C. (1969). Beyond tests of significance: Estimating strength of effects in selected ANOVA designs. *Psychological Bulletin, 72*, 204–213.

Winer, B. J. (1971). *Statistical principles in experimental design* (2nd. ed.). New York: McGraw-Hill.

Appendix

. . .

Table A-1
Critical Values of the F Distribution

df for Denominator	α	\multicolumn{18}{c}{df for Numerator}
		1	2	3	4	5	6	7	8	9	10	12	15	20	24	30	40	60	∞
1	.25	5.83	7.50	8.20	8.58	8.82	8.98	9.10	9.19	9.26	9.32	9.41	9.49	9.58	9.63	9.67	9.71	9.76	9.85
	.10	39.9	49.5	53.6	55.8	57.2	58.2	58.9	59.4	59.9	60.2	60.7	61.2	61.7	62.0	62.3	62.5	62.8	63.3
	.05	161	200	216	225	230	234	237	239	240	242	244	246	248	249	250	251	252	254
	.025	648	800	864	900	922	937	948	957	963	969	977	985	993	997	1001	1006	1010	1018
	.01	4052	5000	5403	5625	5764	5859	5928	5982	6022	6056	6106	6157	6209	6235	6261	6287	6313	6366
	.001	4053*	5000*	5404*	5625*	5764*	5859*	5929*	5981*	6023*	6056*	6107*	6158*	6209*	6235*	6261*	6287*	6313*	6366*
2	.25	2.57	3.00	3.15	3.23	3.28	3.31	3.34	3.35	3.37	3.38	3.39	3.41	3.43	3.43	3.44	3.45	3.46	3.48
	.10	8.53	9.00	9.16	9.24	9.29	9.33	9.35	9.37	9.38	9.39	9.41	9.42	9.44	9.45	9.46	9.47	9.47	9.49
	.05	18.5	19.0	19.2	19.3	19.3	19.3	19.4	19.4	19.4	19.4	19.4	19.4	19.5	19.5	19.5	19.5	19.5	19.5
	.025	38.5	39.0	39.2	39.3	39.3	39.3	39.4	39.4	39.4	39.4	39.4	39.4	39.5	39.5	39.5	39.5	39.5	39.5
	.01	98.5	99.0	99.2	99.3	99.3	99.3	99.4	99.4	99.4	99.4	99.4	99.4	99.5	99.5	99.5	99.5	99.5	99.5
	.001	999	999	999	999	999	999	999	999	999	999	999	999	999	1000	1000	1000	1000	1000
3	.25	2.02	2.28	2.36	2.39	2.41	2.42	2.43	2.44	2.44	2.44	2.45	2.46	2.46	2.46	2.47	2.47	2.47	2.47
	.10	5.54	5.46	5.39	5.34	5.31	5.28	5.27	5.25	5.24	5.23	5.22	5.20	5.18	5.18	5.17	5.16	5.15	5.13
	.05	10.1	9.55	9.28	9.12	9.01	8.94	8.89	8.85	8.81	8.79	8.74	8.70	8.66	8.64	8.62	8.59	8.57	8.53
	.025	17.4	16.0	15.4	15.1	14.9	14.7	14.6	14.5	14.5	14.4	14.3	14.2	14.2	14.1	14.1	14.0	14.0	13.9
	.01	34.1	30.8	29.5	28.7	28.2	27.9	27.7	27.5	27.4	27.2	27.0	26.9	26.7	26.6	26.5	26.4	26.3	26.1
	.001	167	148	141	137	135	133	132	131	130	129	128	127	126	126	125	125	124	124
4	.25	1.81	2.00	2.05	2.06	2.07	2.08	2.08	2.08	2.08	2.08	2.08	2.08	2.08	2.08	2.08	2.08	2.08	2.08
	.10	4.54	4.32	4.19	4.11	4.05	4.01	3.98	3.95	3.94	3.92	3.90	3.87	3.84	3.83	3.82	3.80	3.79	3.76
	.05	7.71	6.94	6.59	6.39	6.26	6.16	6.09	6.04	6.00	5.96	5.91	5.86	5.80	5.77	5.75	5.72	5.69	5.63
	.025	12.2	10.6	9.98	9.60	9.36	9.20	9.07	8.98	8.90	8.84	8.75	8.66	8.56	8.51	8.46	8.41	8.36	8.26
	.01	21.2	18.0	16.7	16.0	15.5	15.2	15.0	14.8	14.7	14.6	14.4	14.2	14.0	13.9	13.8	13.8	13.6	13.5
	.001	74.1	61.2	56.2	53.4	51.7	50.5	49.7	49.0	48.5	48.0	47.4	46.8	46.1	45.8	45.4	45.1	44.8	44.0

Percentage points of the F distribution (numerator degrees of freedom across; denominator degrees of freedom ν_2 and probability P at left).

ν_2	P	1	2	3	4	5	6	7	8	9	10	12	15	20	24	30	40	60	120	∞
5	.25	1.69	1.85	1.88	1.89	1.89	1.89	1.89	1.89	1.89	1.89	1.89	1.89	1.88	1.88	1.88	1.88	1.87	1.87	1.87
	.10	4.06	3.78	3.62	3.52	3.45	3.40	3.37	3.34	3.32	3.30	3.27	3.24	3.21	3.19	3.17	3.16	3.14	3.12	3.10
	.05	6.61	5.79	5.41	5.19	5.05	4.95	4.88	4.82	4.77	4.74	4.68	4.62	4.56	4.53	4.50	4.46	4.43	4.40	4.36
	.025	10.0	8.43	7.76	7.39	7.15	6.98	6.85	6.76	6.68	6.62	6.52	6.43	6.33	6.28	6.23	6.18	6.12	6.07	6.02
	.01	16.3	13.3	12.1	11.4	11.0	10.7	10.5	10.3	10.2	10.0	9.89	9.72	9.55	9.47	9.38	9.29	9.20	9.11	9.02
	.001	47.2	37.1	33.2	31.1	29.8	28.8	28.2	27.6	27.2	26.9	26.4	25.9	25.4	25.1	24.9	24.6	24.3	24.1	23.8
6	.25	1.62	1.76	1.78	1.79	1.79	1.78	1.78	1.78	1.77	1.77	1.77	1.76	1.76	1.75	1.75	1.75	1.74	1.74	1.74
	.10	3.78	3.46	3.29	3.18	3.11	3.05	3.01	2.98	2.96	2.94	2.90	2.87	2.84	2.82	2.80	2.78	2.76	2.74	2.72
	.05	5.99	5.14	4.76	4.53	4.39	4.28	4.21	4.15	4.10	4.06	4.00	3.94	3.87	3.84	3.81	3.77	3.74	3.70	3.67
	.025	8.81	7.26	6.60	6.23	5.99	5.82	5.70	5.60	5.52	5.46	5.37	5.27	5.17	5.12	5.07	5.01	4.96	4.90	4.85
	.01	13.8	10.9	9.78	9.15	8.75	8.47	8.26	8.10	7.98	7.87	7.72	7.56	7.40	7.31	7.23	7.14	7.06	6.97	6.88
	.001	35.5	27.0	23.7	21.9	20.8	20.0	19.5	19.0	18.7	18.4	18.0	17.6	17.1	16.9	16.7	16.4	16.2	16.0	15.8
7	.25	1.57	1.70	1.72	1.72	1.71	1.71	1.70	1.70	1.69	1.69	1.68	1.68	1.67	1.67	1.66	1.66	1.65	1.65	1.65
	.10	3.59	3.26	3.07	2.96	2.88	2.83	2.78	2.75	2.72	2.70	2.67	2.63	2.59	2.58	2.56	2.54	2.51	2.49	2.47
	.05	5.59	4.74	4.35	4.12	3.97	3.87	3.79	3.73	3.68	3.64	3.57	3.51	3.44	3.41	3.38	3.34	3.30	3.27	3.23
	.025	8.07	6.54	5.89	5.52	5.29	5.12	4.99	4.90	4.82	4.76	4.67	4.57	4.47	4.42	4.36	4.31	4.25	4.20	4.14
	.01	12.2	9.55	8.45	7.85	7.46	7.19	6.99	6.84	6.72	6.62	6.47	6.31	6.16	6.07	5.99	5.91	5.82	5.74	5.65
	.001	29.2	21.7	18.8	17.2	16.2	15.5	15.0	14.6	14.3	14.1	13.7	13.3	12.9	12.7	12.5	12.3	12.1	11.9	11.7
8	.25	1.54	1.66	1.67	1.66	1.66	1.65	1.64	1.64	1.63	1.63	1.62	1.62	1.61	1.60	1.60	1.59	1.59	1.58	1.58
	.10	3.46	3.11	2.92	2.81	2.73	2.67	2.62	2.59	2.56	2.54	2.50	2.46	2.42	2.40	2.38	2.36	2.34	2.32	2.29
	.05	5.32	4.46	4.07	3.84	3.69	3.58	3.50	3.44	3.39	3.35	3.28	3.22	3.15	3.12	3.08	3.04	3.01	2.97	2.93
	.025	7.57	6.06	5.42	5.05	4.82	4.65	4.53	4.43	4.36	4.30	4.20	4.10	4.00	3.95	3.89	3.84	3.78	3.73	3.67
	.01	11.3	8.65	7.59	7.01	6.63	6.37	6.18	6.03	5.91	5.81	5.67	5.52	5.36	5.28	5.20	5.12	5.03	4.95	4.86
	.001	25.4	18.5	15.8	14.4	13.5	12.9	12.4	12.0	11.8	11.5	11.2	10.8	10.5	10.3	10.1	9.92	9.73	9.53	9.33
9	.25	1.51	1.62	1.63	1.63	1.62	1.61	1.60	1.60	1.59	1.59	1.58	1.57	1.56	1.56	1.55	1.54	1.54	1.53	1.53
	.10	3.36	3.01	2.81	2.69	2.61	2.55	2.51	2.47	2.44	2.42	2.38	2.34	2.30	2.28	2.25	2.23	2.21	2.18	2.16
	.05	5.12	4.26	3.86	3.63	3.48	3.37	3.29	3.23	3.18	3.14	3.07	3.01	2.94	2.90	2.86	2.83	2.79	2.75	2.71
	.025	7.21	5.71	5.08	4.72	4.48	4.32	4.20	4.10	4.03	3.96	3.87	3.77	3.67	3.61	3.56	3.51	3.45	3.39	3.33
	.01	10.6	8.02	6.99	6.42	6.06	5.80	5.61	5.47	5.35	5.26	5.11	4.96	4.81	4.73	4.65	4.57	4.48	4.40	4.31
	.001	22.9	16.4	13.9	12.6	11.7	11.1	10.7	10.4	10.1	9.89	9.57	9.24	8.90	8.72	8.55	8.37	8.19	8.00	7.81

* Multiply these entries by 100.
This table is abridged from Table 18 in E. S. Pearson and H. O. Hartley (Eds.), *Biometrika tables for statisticians* (3rd ed., Vol. 1) Cambridge University Press, New York, 1970, by permission of the *Biometrika* Trustees.

Table A-1 (continued)
Critical Values of the F Distribution

df for Numerator

df for Denominator	α	1	2	3	4	5	6	7	8	9	10	12	15	20	24	30	40	60	∞
10	.25	1.49	1.60	1.60	1.59	1.59	1.58	1.57	1.56	1.56	1.55	1.54	1.53	1.52	1.52	1.51	1.51	1.50	1.48
	.10	3.29	2.92	2.73	2.61	2.52	2.46	2.41	2.38	2.35	2.32	2.28	2.24	2.20	2.18	2.16	2.13	2.11	2.06
	.05	4.96	4.10	3.71	3.48	3.33	3.22	3.14	3.07	3.02	2.98	2.91	2.85	2.77	2.74	2.70	2.66	2.62	2.54
	.025	6.94	5.46	4.83	4.47	4.24	4.07	3.95	3.85	3.78	3.72	3.62	3.52	3.42	3.37	3.31	3.26	3.20	3.08
	.01	10.0	7.56	6.55	5.99	5.64	5.39	5.20	5.06	4.94	4.85	4.71	4.56	4.41	4.33	4.25	4.17	4.08	3.91
	.001	21.0	14.9	12.6	11.3	10.5	9.92	9.52	9.20	8.96	8.75	8.45	8.13	7.80	7.64	7.47	7.30	7.12	6.76
11	.25	1.47	1.58	1.58	1.57	1.56	1.55	1.54	1.53	1.53	1.52	1.51	1.50	1.49	1.49	1.48	1.47	1.47	1.45
	.10	3.23	2.86	2.66	2.54	2.45	2.39	2.34	2.30	2.27	2.25	2.21	2.17	2.12	2.10	2.08	2.05	2.03	1.97
	.05	4.84	3.98	3.59	3.36	3.20	3.09	3.01	2.95	2.90	2.85	2.79	2.72	2.65	2.61	2.57	2.53	2.49	2.40
	.025	6.72	5.26	4.63	4.28	4.04	3.88	3.76	3.66	3.59	3.53	3.43	3.33	3.23	3.17	3.12	3.06	3.00	2.88
	.01	9.65	7.21	6.22	5.67	5.32	5.07	4.89	4.74	4.63	4.54	4.40	4.25	4.10	4.02	3.94	3.86	3.78	3.60
	.001	19.7	13.8	11.6	10.4	9.58	9.05	8.66	8.35	8.12	7.92	7.63	7.32	7.01	6.85	6.68	6.52	6.35	6.00
12	.25	1.46	1.56	1.56	1.55	1.54	1.53	1.52	1.51	1.51	1.50	1.49	1.48	1.47	1.46	1.45	1.45	1.44	1.42
	.10	3.18	2.81	2.61	2.48	2.39	2.33	2.28	2.24	2.21	2.19	2.15	2.10	2.06	2.04	2.01	1.99	1.96	1.90
	.05	4.75	3.89	3.49	3.26	3.11	3.00	2.91	2.85	2.80	2.75	2.69	2.62	2.54	2.51	2.47	2.43	2.38	2.30
	.025	6.55	5.10	4.47	4.12	3.89	3.73	3.61	3.51	3.44	3.37	3.28	3.18	3.07	3.02	2.96	2.91	2.85	2.72
	.01	9.33	6.93	5.95	5.41	5.06	4.82	4.64	4.50	4.39	4.30	4.16	4.01	3.86	3.78	3.70	3.62	3.54	3.36
	.001	18.6	13.0	10.8	9.63	8.89	8.38	8.00	7.71	7.48	7.29	7.00	6.71	6.40	6.25	6.09	5.93	5.76	5.42
13	.25	1.45	1.55	1.55	1.53	1.52	1.51	1.50	1.49	1.49	1.48	1.47	1.46	1.45	1.44	1.43	1.42	1.42	1.40
	.10	3.14	2.76	2.56	2.43	2.35	2.28	2.23	2.20	2.16	2.14	2.10	2.05	2.01	1.98	1.96	1.93	1.90	1.85
	.05	4.67	3.81	3.41	3.18	3.03	2.92	2.83	2.77	2.71	2.67	2.60	2.53	2.46	2.42	2.38	2.34	2.30	2.21
	.025	6.41	4.97	4.35	4.00	3.77	3.60	3.48	3.39	3.31	3.25	3.15	3.05	2.95	2.89	2.84	2.78	2.72	2.60
	.01	9.07	6.70	5.74	5.21	4.86	4.62	4.44	4.30	4.19	4.10	3.96	3.82	3.66	3.59	3.51	3.43	3.34	3.17
	.001	17.8	12.3	10.2	9.07	8.35	7.86	7.49	7.21	6.98	6.80	6.52	6.23	5.93	5.78	5.63	5.47	5.30	4.97

	α																		
14	.25	1.38	1.40	1.41	1.41	1.42	1.43	1.44	1.45	1.46	1.47	1.48	1.49	1.50	1.51	1.52	1.53	1.53	1.44
	.10	1.80	1.86	1.89	1.91	1.94	1.96	2.01	2.05	2.10	2.12	2.15	2.19	2.24	2.31	2.39	2.52	2.73	3.10
	.05	2.13	2.22	2.27	2.31	2.35	2.39	2.46	2.53	2.60	2.65	2.70	2.76	2.85	2.96	3.11	3.34	3.74	4.60
	.025	2.49	2.61	2.67	2.73	2.79	2.84	2.95	3.05	3.15	3.21	3.29	3.38	3.50	3.66	3.89	4.24	4.86	6.30
	.01	3.00	3.18	3.27	3.35	3.43	3.51	3.66	3.80	3.94	4.03	4.14	4.28	4.46	4.69	5.04	5.56	6.51	8.86
	.001	4.60	4.94	5.10	5.25	5.41	5.56	5.85	6.13	6.40	6.58	6.80	7.08	7.43	7.92	8.62	9.73	11.8	17.1
15	.25	1.36	1.38	1.39	1.40	1.41	1.41	1.43	1.44	1.45	1.46	1.46	1.47	1.48	1.49	1.51	1.52	1.52	1.43
	.10	1.76	1.82	1.85	1.87	1.90	1.92	1.97	2.02	2.06	2.09	2.12	2.16	2.21	2.27	2.36	2.49	2.70	3.07
	.05	2.07	2.16	2.20	2.25	2.29	2.33	2.40	2.48	2.54	2.59	2.64	2.71	2.79	2.90	3.06	3.29	3.68	4.54
	.025	2.40	2.52	2.59	2.64	2.70	2.76	2.86	2.96	3.06	3.12	3.20	3.29	3.41	3.58	3.80	4.15	4.77	6.20
	.01	2.87	3.05	3.13	3.21	3.29	3.37	3.52	3.67	3.80	3.89	4.00	4.14	4.32	4.56	4.89	5.42	6.36	8.68
	.001	4.31	4.64	4.80	4.95	5.10	5.25	5.54	5.81	6.08	6.26	6.47	6.74	7.09	7.57	8.25	9.34	11.3	16.6
16	.25	1.34	1.36	1.37	1.38	1.39	1.40	1.41	1.43	1.44	1.44	1.45	1.46	1.47	1.48	1.50	1.51	1.51	1.42
	.10	1.72	1.78	1.81	1.84	1.87	1.89	1.94	1.99	2.03	2.06	2.09	2.13	2.18	2.24	2.33	2.46	2.67	3.05
	.05	2.01	2.11	2.15	2.19	2.24	2.28	2.35	2.42	2.49	2.54	2.59	2.66	2.74	2.85	3.01	3.24	3.63	4.49
	.025	2.32	2.45	2.51	2.57	2.63	2.68	2.79	2.89	2.99	3.05	3.12	3.22	3.34	3.50	3.73	4.08	4.69	6.12
	.01	2.75	2.93	3.02	3.10	3.18	3.26	3.41	3.55	3.69	3.78	3.89	4.03	4.20	4.44	4.77	5.29	6.23	8.53
	.001	4.06	4.39	4.54	4.70	4.85	4.99	5.27	5.55	5.81	5.98	6.19	6.46	6.81	7.27	7.94	9.00	11.0	16.1
17	.25	1.33	1.35	1.36	1.37	1.38	1.39	1.40	1.41	1.43	1.43	1.44	1.45	1.46	1.47	1.49	1.50	1.51	1.42
	.10	1.69	1.75	1.78	1.81	1.84	1.86	1.91	1.96	2.00	2.03	2.06	2.10	2.15	2.22	2.31	2.44	2.64	3.03
	.05	1.96	2.06	2.10	2.15	2.19	2.23	2.31	2.38	2.45	2.49	2.55	2.61	2.70	2.81	2.96	3.20	3.59	4.45
	.025	2.25	2.38	2.44	2.50	2.56	2.62	2.72	2.82	2.92	2.98	3.06	3.16	3.28	3.44	3.65	4.01	4.62	6.04
	.01	2.65	2.83	2.92	3.00	3.08	3.16	3.31	3.46	3.59	3.68	3.79	3.93	4.10	4.34	4.67	5.18	6.11	8.40
	.001	3.85	4.18	4.33	4.48	4.63	4.78	5.05	5.32	5.58	5.75	5.96	6.22	6.56	7.02	7.68	8.73	10.7	15.7
18	.25	1.32	1.34	1.35	1.36	1.37	1.38	1.39	1.40	1.42	1.42	1.43	1.44	1.45	1.46	1.48	1.49	1.50	1.41
	.10	1.66	1.72	1.75	1.78	1.81	1.84	1.89	1.93	1.98	2.00	2.04	2.08	2.13	2.20	2.29	2.42	2.62	3.01
	.05	1.92	2.02	2.06	2.11	2.15	2.19	2.27	2.34	2.41	2.46	2.51	2.58	2.66	2.77	2.93	3.16	3.55	4.41
	.025	2.19	2.32	2.38	2.44	2.50	2.56	2.67	2.77	2.87	2.93	3.01	3.10	3.22	3.38	3.51	3.95	4.56	5.98
	.01	2.57	2.75	2.84	2.92	3.00	3.08	3.23	3.37	3.51	3.60	3.71	3.84	4.01	4.25	4.58	5.09	6.01	8.29
	.001	3.67	4.00	4.15	4.30	4.45	4.59	4.87	5.13	5.39	5.56	5.76	6.02	6.35	6.81	7.46	8.49	10.4	15.4
19	.25	1.30	1.33	1.34	1.35	1.36	1.37	1.38	1.40	1.41	1.41	1.42	1.43	1.44	1.46	1.47	1.49	1.49	1.41
	.10	1.63	1.70	1.73	1.76	1.79	1.81	1.86	1.91	1.96	1.98	2.02	2.06	2.11	2.18	2.27	2.40	2.61	2.99
	.05	1.88	1.98	2.03	2.07	2.11	2.16	2.23	2.31	2.38	2.42	2.48	2.54	2.63	2.74	2.90	3.13	3.52	4.38
	.025	2.13	2.27	2.33	2.39	2.45	2.51	2.62	2.72	2.82	2.88	2.96	3.05	3.17	3.33	3.56	3.90	4.51	5.92
	.01	2.49	2.67	2.76	2.84	2.92	3.00	3.15	3.30	3.43	3.52	3.63	3.77	3.94	4.17	4.50	5.01	5.93	8.18
	.001	3.51	3.84	3.99	4.14	4.29	4.43	4.70	4.97	5.22	5.39	5.59	5.85	6.18	6.62	7.26	8.28	10.2	15.1

df for Denominator	α	df for Numerator																	
		1	2	3	4	5	6	7	8	9	10	12	15	20	24	30	40	60	∞
20	.25	1.40	1.49	1.48	1.47	1.45	1.44	1.43	1.42	1.41	1.40	1.39	1.37	1.36	1.35	1.34	1.33	1.32	1.29
	.10	2.97	2.59	2.38	2.25	2.16	2.09	2.04	2.00	1.96	1.94	1.89	1.84	1.79	1.77	1.74	1.71	1.68	1.61
	.05	4.35	3.49	3.10	2.87	2.71	2.60	2.51	2.45	2.39	2.35	2.28	2.20	2.12	2.08	2.04	1.99	1.95	1.84
	.025	5.87	4.46	3.86	3.51	3.29	3.13	3.01	2.91	2.84	2.77	2.68	2.57	2.46	2.41	2.35	2.29	2.22	2.09
	.01	8.10	5.85	4.94	4.43	4.10	3.87	3.70	3.56	3.46	3.37	3.23	3.09	2.94	2.86	2.78	2.69	2.61	2.42
	.001	14.8	9.95	8.10	7.10	6.46	6.02	5.69	5.44	5.24	5.08	4.82	4.56	4.29	4.15	4.00	3.86	3.70	3.38
22	.25	1.40	1.48	1.47	1.45	1.44	1.42	1.41	1.40	1.39	1.39	1.37	1.36	1.34	1.33	1.32	1.31	1.30	1.28
	.10	2.95	2.56	2.35	2.22	2.13	2.06	2.01	1.97	1.93	1.90	1.86	1.81	1.76	1.73	1.70	1.67	1.64	1.57
	.05	4.30	3.44	3.05	2.82	2.66	2.55	2.46	2.40	2.34	2.30	2.23	2.15	2.07	2.03	1.98	1.94	1.89	1.78
	.025	5.79	4.38	3.78	3.44	3.22	3.05	2.93	2.84	2.76	2.70	2.60	2.50	2.39	2.33	2.27	2.21	2.14	2.00
	.01	7.95	5.72	4.82	4.31	3.99	3.76	3.59	3.45	3.35	3.26	3.12	2.98	2.83	2.75	2.67	2.58	2.50	2.31
	.001	14.4	9.61	7.80	6.81	6.19	5.76	5.44	5.19	4.99	4.83	4.58	4.33	4.06	3.92	3.78	3.63	3.48	3.15
24	.25	1.39	1.47	1.46	1.44	1.43	1.41	1.40	1.39	1.38	1.38	1.36	1.35	1.33	1.32	1.31	1.30	1.29	1.26
	.10	2.93	2.54	2.33	2.19	2.10	2.04	1.98	1.94	1.91	1.88	1.83	1.78	1.73	1.70	1.67	1.64	1.61	1.53
	.05	4.26	3.40	3.01	2.78	2.62	2.51	2.42	2.36	2.30	2.25	2.18	2.11	2.03	1.98	1.94	1.89	1.84	1.73
	.025	5.72	4.32	3.72	3.38	3.15	2.99	2.87	2.78	2.70	2.64	2.54	2.44	2.33	2.27	2.21	2.15	2.08	1.94
	.01	7.82	5.61	4.72	4.22	3.90	3.67	3.50	3.36	3.26	3.17	3.03	2.89	2.74	2.66	2.58	2.49	2.40	2.21
	.001	14.0	9.34	7.55	6.59	5.98	5.55	5.23	4.99	4.80	4.64	4.39	4.14	3.87	3.74	3.59	3.45	3.29	2.97
26	.25	1.38	1.46	1.45	1.44	1.42	1.41	1.39	1.38	1.37	1.37	1.35	1.34	1.32	1.31	1.30	1.29	1.28	1.25
	.10	2.91	2.52	2.31	2.17	2.08	2.01	1.96	1.92	1.88	1.86	1.81	1.76	1.71	1.68	1.65	1.61	1.58	1.50
	.05	4.23	3.37	2.98	2.74	2.59	2.47	2.39	2.32	2.27	2.22	2.15	2.07	1.99	1.95	1.90	1.85	1.80	1.69
	.025	5.66	4.27	3.67	3.33	3.10	2.94	2.82	2.73	2.65	2.59	2.49	2.39	2.28	2.22	2.16	2.09	2.03	1.88
	.01	7.72	5.53	4.64	4.14	3.82	3.59	3.42	3.29	3.18	3.09	2.96	2.81	2.66	2.58	2.50	2.42	2.33	2.13
	.001	13.7	9.12	7.36	6.41	5.80	5.38	5.07	4.83	4.64	4.48	4.24	3.99	3.72	3.59	3.44	3.30	3.15	2.82

28	.25	1.24	1.27	1.28	1.29	1.30	1.31	1.33	1.34	1.36	1.37	1.38	1.39	1.40	1.41	1.43	1.45	1.46	1.38
	.10	1.48	1.56	1.59	1.63	1.66	1.69	1.74	1.79	1.84	1.87	1.90	1.94	2.00	2.06	2.16	2.29	2.50	2.89
	.05	1.65	1.77	1.82	1.87	1.91	1.96	2.04	2.12	2.19	2.24	2.29	2.36	2.45	2.56	2.71	2.95	3.34	4.20
	.025	1.83	1.98	2.05	2.11	2.17	2.23	2.34	2.45	2.55	2.61	2.69	2.78	2.90	3.06	3.29	3.63	4.22	5.61
	.01	2.06	2.26	2.35	2.44	2.52	2.60	2.75	2.90	3.03	3.12	3.23	3.36	3.53	3.75	4.07	4.57	5.45	7.64
	.001	2.69	3.02	3.18	3.32	3.46	3.60	3.86	4.11	4.35	4.50	4.69	4.93	5.24	5.66	6.25	7.19	8.93	13.5
30	.25	1.23	1.26	1.27	1.28	1.29	1.30	1.32	1.34	1.35	1.36	1.37	1.38	1.39	1.41	1.42	1.44	1.45	1.38
	.10	1.46	1.54	1.57	1.61	1.64	1.67	1.72	1.77	1.82	1.85	1.88	1.93	1.98	2.05	2.14	2.28	2.49	2.88
	.05	1.62	1.74	1.79	1.84	1.89	1.93	2.01	2.09	2.16	2.21	2.27	2.33	2.42	2.53	2.69	2.92	3.32	4.17
	.025	1.79	1.94	2.01	2.07	2.14	2.20	2.31	2.41	2.51	2.57	2.65	2.75	2.87	3.03	3.25	3.59	4.18	5.57
	.01	2.01	2.21	2.30	2.39	2.47	2.55	2.70	2.84	2.98	3.07	3.17	3.30	3.47	3.70	4.02	4.51	5.39	7.56
	.001	2.59	2.92	3.07	3.22	3.36	3.49	3.75	4.00	4.24	4.39	4.58	4.82	5.12	5.53	6.12	7.05	8.77	13.3
40	.25	1.19	1.22	1.24	1.25	1.26	1.28	1.30	1.31	1.33	1.34	1.35	1.36	1.37	1.39	1.40	1.42	1.44	1.36
	.10	1.38	1.47	1.51	1.54	1.57	1.61	1.66	1.71	1.76	1.79	1.83	1.87	1.93	2.00	2.09	2.23	2.44	2.84
	.05	1.51	1.64	1.69	1.74	1.79	1.84	1.92	2.00	2.08	2.12	2.18	2.25	2.34	2.45	2.61	2.84	3.23	4.08
	.025	1.64	1.80	1.88	1.94	2.01	2.07	2.18	2.29	2.39	2.45	2.53	2.62	2.74	2.90	3.13	3.46	4.05	5.42
	.01	1.80	2.02	2.11	2.20	2.29	2.37	2.52	2.66	2.80	2.89	2.99	3.12	3.29	3.51	3.83	4.31	5.18	7.31
	.001	2.23	2.57	2.73	2.87	3.01	3.15	3.40	3.64	3.87	4.02	4.21	4.44	4.73	5.13	5.70	6.60	8.25	12.6
60	.25	1.15	1.19	1.21	1.22	1.24	1.25	1.27	1.29	1.30	1.31	1.32	1.33	1.35	1.37	1.38	1.41	1.42	1.35
	.10	1.29	1.40	1.44	1.48	1.51	1.54	1.60	1.66	1.71	1.74	1.77	1.82	1.87	1.95	2.04	2.18	2.39	2.79
	.05	1.39	1.53	1.59	1.65	1.70	1.75	1.84	1.92	1.99	2.04	2.10	2.17	2.25	2.37	2.53	2.76	3.15	4.00
	.025	1.48	1.67	1.74	1.82	1.88	1.94	2.06	2.17	2.27	2.33	2.41	2.51	2.63	2.79	3.01	3.34	3.93	5.29
	.01	1.60	1.84	1.94	2.03	2.12	2.20	2.35	2.50	2.63	2.72	2.82	2.95	3.12	3.34	3.65	4.13	4.98	7.08
	.001	1.89	2.25	2.41	2.55	2.69	2.83	3.08	3.31	3.54	3.69	3.87	4.09	4.37	4.76	5.31	6.17	7.76	12.0
120	.25	1.10	1.16	1.18	1.19	1.21	1.22	1.24	1.26	1.28	1.29	1.30	1.32	1.33	1.35	1.37	1.39	1.40	1.34
	.10	1.19	1.32	1.37	1.41	1.45	1.48	1.55	1.60	1.65	1.68	1.72	1.77	1.82	1.90	1.99	2.13	2.35	2.75
	.05	1.25	1.43	1.50	1.55	1.61	1.66	1.75	1.83	1.91	1.96	2.02	2.09	2.17	2.29	2.45	2.68	3.07	3.92
	.025	1.31	1.53	1.61	1.69	1.76	1.82	1.94	2.05	2.16	2.22	2.30	2.39	2.52	2.67	2.89	3.23	3.80	5.15
	.01	1.38	1.66	1.76	1.86	1.95	2.03	2.19	2.34	2.47	2.56	2.66	2.79	2.96	3.17	3.48	3.95	4.79	6.85
	.001	1.54	1.95	2.11	2.26	2.40	2.53	2.78	3.02	3.24	3.38	3.55	3.77	4.04	4.42	4.95	5.79	7.32	11.4
∞	.25	1.00	1.12	1.14	1.16	1.18	1.19	1.22	1.24	1.25	1.27	1.28	1.29	1.31	1.33	1.35	1.37	1.39	1.32
	.10	1.00	1.24	1.30	1.34	1.38	1.42	1.49	1.55	1.60	1.63	1.67	1.72	1.77	1.85	1.94	2.08	2.30	2.71
	.05	1.00	1.32	1.39	1.46	1.52	1.57	1.67	1.75	1.83	1.88	1.94	2.01	2.10	2.21	2.37	2.60	3.00	3.84
	.025	1.00	1.39	1.48	1.57	1.64	1.71	1.83	1.94	2.05	2.11	2.19	2.29	2.41	2.57	2.79	3.12	3.69	5.02
	.01	1.00	1.47	1.59	1.70	1.79	1.88	2.04	2.18	2.32	2.41	2.51	2.64	2.80	3.02	3.32	3.78	4.61	6.63
	.001	1.00	1.66	1.84	1.99	2.13	2.27	2.51	2.74	2.96	3.10	3.27	3.47	3.74	4.10	4.62	5.42	6.91	10.8

Table A-2
Critical Values of the Studentized Range Statistic

k = number of means

df_{error}	α_{FW}	2	3	4	5	6	7	8	9	10	11	12	13	14	15	16	17	18	19	20
5	.05	3.64	4.60	5.22	5.67	6.03	6.33	6.58	6.80	6.99	7.17	7.32	7.47	7.60	7.72	7.83	7.93	8.03	8.12	8.21
	.01	5.70	6.98	7.80	8.42	8.91	9.32	9.67	9.97	10.24	10.48	10.70	10.89	11.08	11.24	11.40	11.55	11.68	11.81	11.93
6	.05	3.46	4.34	4.90	5.30	5.63	5.90	6.12	6.32	6.49	6.65	6.79	6.92	7.03	7.14	7.24	7.34	7.43	7.51	7.59
	.01	5.24	6.33	7.03	7.56	7.97	8.32	8.61	8.87	9.10	9.30	9.48	9.65	9.81	9.95	10.08	10.21	10.32	10.43	10.54
7	.05	3.34	4.16	4.68	5.06	5.36	5.61	5.82	6.00	6.16	6.30	6.43	6.55	6.66	6.76	6.85	6.94	7.02	7.10	7.17
	.01	4.95	5.92	6.54	7.01	7.37	7.68	7.94	8.17	8.37	8.55	8.71	8.86	9.00	9.12	9.24	9.35	9.46	9.55	9.65
8	.05	3.26	4.04	4.53	4.89	5.17	5.40	5.60	5.77	5.92	6.05	6.18	6.29	6.39	6.48	6.57	6.65	6.73	6.80	6.87
	.01	4.75	5.64	6.20	6.62	6.96	7.24	7.47	7.68	7.86	8.03	8.18	8.31	8.44	8.55	8.66	8.76	8.85	8.94	9.03
9	.05	3.20	3.95	4.41	4.76	5.02	5.24	5.43	5.59	5.74	5.87	5.98	6.09	6.19	6.28	6.36	6.44	6.51	6.58	6.64
	.01	4.60	5.43	5.96	6.35	6.66	6.91	7.13	7.33	7.49	7.65	7.78	7.91	8.03	8.13	8.23	8.33	8.41	8.49	8.57
10	.05	3.15	3.88	4.33	4.65	4.91	5.12	5.30	5.46	5.60	5.72	5.83	5.93	6.03	6.11	6.19	6.27	6.34	6.40	6.47
	.01	4.48	5.27	5.77	6.14	6.43	6.67	6.87	7.05	7.21	7.36	7.49	7.60	7.71	7.81	7.91	7.99	8.08	8.15	8.23
11	.05	3.11	3.82	4.26	4.57	4.82	5.03	5.20	5.35	5.49	5.61	5.71	5.81	5.90	5.98	6.06	6.13	6.20	6.27	6.33
	.01	4.39	5.15	5.62	5.97	6.25	6.48	6.67	6.84	6.99	7.13	7.25	7.36	7.46	7.56	7.65	7.73	7.81	7.88	7.95
12	.05	3.08	3.77	4.20	4.51	4.75	4.95	5.12	5.27	5.39	5.51	5.61	5.71	5.80	5.88	5.95	6.02	6.09	6.15	6.21
	.01	4.32	5.05	5.50	5.84	6.10	6.32	6.51	6.67	6.81	6.94	7.06	7.17	7.26	7.36	7.44	7.52	7.59	7.66	7.73
13	.05	3.06	3.73	4.15	4.45	4.69	4.88	5.05	5.19	5.32	5.43	5.53	5.63	5.71	5.79	5.86	5.93	5.99	6.05	6.11
	.01	4.26	4.96	5.40	5.73	5.98	6.19	6.37	6.53	6.67	6.79	6.90	7.01	7.10	7.19	7.27	7.35	7.42	7.48	7.55
14	.05	3.03	3.70	4.11	4.41	4.64	4.83	4.99	5.13	5.25	5.36	5.46	5.55	5.64	5.71	5.79	5.85	5.91	5.97	6.03
	.01	4.21	4.89	5.32	5.63	5.88	6.08	6.26	6.41	6.54	6.66	6.77	6.87	6.96	7.05	7.13	7.20	7.27	7.33	7.39
15	.05	3.01	3.67	4.08	4.37	4.59	4.78	4.94	5.08	5.20	5.31	5.40	5.49	5.57	5.65	5.72	5.78	5.85	5.90	5.96
	.01	4.17	4.84	5.25	5.56	5.80	5.99	6.16	6.31	6.44	6.55	6.66	6.76	6.84	6.93	7.00	7.07	7.14	7.20	7.26

16	.05	3.00	3.65	4.05	4.33	4.56	4.74	4.90	5.03	5.15	5.26	5.35	5.44	5.52	5.59	5.66	5.73	5.79	5.84	5.90
	.01	4.13	4.79	5.19	5.49	5.72	5.92	6.08	6.22	6.35	6.46	6.56	6.66	6.74	6.82	6.90	6.97	7.03	7.09	7.15
17	.05	2.98	3.63	4.02	4.30	4.52	4.70	4.86	4.99	5.11	5.21	5.31	5.39	5.47	5.54	5.61	5.67	5.73	5.79	5.84
	.01	4.10	4.74	5.14	5.43	5.66	5.85	6.01	6.15	6.27	6.38	6.48	6.57	6.66	6.73	6.81	6.87	6.94	7.00	7.05
18	.05	2.97	3.61	4.00	4.28	4.49	4.67	4.82	4.96	5.07	5.17	5.27	5.35	5.43	5.50	5.57	5.63	5.69	5.74	5.79
	.01	4.07	4.70	5.09	5.38	5.60	5.79	5.94	6.08	6.20	6.31	6.41	6.50	6.58	6.65	6.73	6.79	6.85	6.91	6.97
19	.05	2.96	3.59	3.98	4.25	4.47	4.65	4.79	4.92	5.04	5.14	5.23	5.31	5.39	5.46	5.53	5.59	5.65	5.70	5.75
	.01	4.05	4.67	5.05	5.33	5.55	5.73	5.89	6.02	6.14	6.25	6.34	6.43	6.51	6.58	6.65	6.72	6.78	6.84	6.89
20	.05	2.95	3.58	3.96	4.23	4.45	4.62	4.77	4.90	5.01	5.11	5.20	5.28	5.36	5.43	5.49	5.55	5.61	5.66	5.71
	.01	4.02	4.64	5.02	5.29	5.51	5.69	5.84	5.97	6.09	6.19	6.28	6.37	6.45	6.52	6.59	6.65	6.71	6.77	6.82
24	.05	2.92	3.53	3.90	4.17	4.37	4.54	4.68	4.81	4.92	5.01	5.10	5.18	5.25	5.32	5.38	5.44	5.49	5.55	5.59
	.01	3.96	4.55	4.91	5.17	5.37	5.54	5.69	5.81	5.92	6.02	6.11	6.19	6.26	6.33	6.39	6.45	6.51	6.56	6.61
30	.05	2.89	3.49	3.85	4.10	4.30	4.46	4.60	4.72	4.82	4.92	5.00	5.08	5.15	5.21	5.27	5.33	5.38	5.43	5.47
	.01	3.89	4.45	4.80	5.05	5.24	5.40	5.54	5.65	5.76	5.85	5.93	6.01	6.08	6.14	6.20	6.26	6.31	6.36	6.41
40	.05	2.86	3.44	3.79	4.04	4.23	4.39	4.52	4.63	4.73	4.82	4.90	4.98	5.04	5.11	5.16	5.22	5.27	5.31	5.36
	.01	3.82	4.37	4.70	4.93	5.11	5.26	5.39	5.50	5.60	5.69	5.76	5.83	5.90	5.96	6.02	6.07	6.12	6.16	6.21
60	.05	2.83	3.40	3.74	3.98	4.16	4.31	4.44	4.55	4.65	4.73	4.81	4.88	4.94	5.00	5.06	5.11	5.15	5.20	5.24
	.01	3.76	4.28	4.59	4.82	4.99	5.13	5.25	5.36	5.45	5.53	5.60	5.67	5.73	5.78	5.84	5.89	5.93	5.97	6.01
120	.05	2.80	3.36	3.68	3.92	4.10	4.24	4.36	4.47	4.56	4.64	4.71	4.78	4.84	4.90	4.95	5.00	5.04	5.09	5.13
	.01	3.70	4.20	4.50	4.71	4.87	5.01	5.12	5.21	5.30	5.37	5.44	5.50	5.56	5.61	5.66	5.71	5.75	5.79	5.83
∞	.05	2.77	3.31	3.63	3.86	4.03	4.17	4.29	4.39	4.47	4.55	4.62	4.68	4.74	4.80	4.85	4.89	4.93	4.97	5.01
	.01	3.64	4.12	4.40	4.60	4.76	4.88	4.99	5.08	5.16	5.23	5.29	5.35	5.40	5.45	5.49	5.54	5.57	5.61	5.65

This table is abridged from Table 29 in E. S. Pearson and H. O. Hartley (Eds.), *Biometrika tables for statisticians* (3rd ed., Vol. 1), Cambridge University Press, New York, 1970, by permission of the *Biometrika* Trustees.

Table A-3
Critical Values of the Dunnett Test for Comparing Treatment Means with a Control

		Two-Tailed Comparisons								
		k = number of treatment means, including control								
df_{error}	α_{FW}	2	3	4	5	6	7	8	9	10
5	.05	2.57	3.03	3.29	3.48	3.62	3.73	3.82	3.90	3.97
	.01	4.03	4.63	4.98	5.22	5.41	5.56	5.69	5.80	5.89
6	.05	2.45	2.86	3.10	3.26	3.39	3.49	3.57	3.64	3.71
	.01	3.71	4.21	4.51	4.71	4.87	5.00	5.10	5.20	5.28
7	.05	2.36	2.75	2.97	3.12	3.24	3.33	3.41	3.47	3.53
	.01	3.50	3.95	4.21	4.39	4.53	4.64	4.74	4.82	4.89
8	.05	2.31	2.67	2.88	3.02	3.13	3.22	3.29	3.35	3.41
	.01	3.36	3.77	4.00	4.17	4.29	4.40	4.48	4.56	4.62
9	.05	2.26	2.61	2.81	2.95	3.05	3.14	3.20	3.26	3.32
	.01	3.25	3.63	3.85	4.01	4.12	4.22	4.30	4.37	4.43
10	.05	2.23	2.57	2.76	2.89	2.99	3.07	3.14	3.19	3.24
	.01	3.17	3.53	3.74	3.88	3.99	4.08	4.16	4.22	4.28
11	.05	2.20	2.53	2.72	2.84	2.94	3.02	3.08	3.14	3.19
	.01	3.11	3.45	3.65	3.79	3.89	3.98	4.05	4.11	4.16
12	.05	2.18	2.50	2.68	2.81	2.90	2.98	3.04	3.09	3.14
	.01	3.05	3.39	3.58	3.71	3.81	3.89	3.96	4.02	4.07
13	.05	2.16	2.48	2.65	2.78	2.87	2.94	3.00	3.06	3.10
	.01	3.01	3.33	3.52	3.65	3.74	3.82	3.89	3.94	3.99
14	.05	2.14	2.46	2.63	2.75	2.84	2.91	2.97	3.02	3.07
	.01	2.98	3.29	3.47	3.59	3.69	3.76	3.83	3.88	3.93
15	.05	2.13	2.44	2.61	2.73	2.82	2.89	2.95	3.00	3.04
	.01	2.95	3.25	3.43	3.55	3.64	3.71	3.78	3.83	3.88
16	.05	2.12	2.42	2.59	2.71	2.80	2.87	2.92	2.97	3.02
	.01	2.92	3.22	3.39	3.51	3.60	3.67	3.73	3.78	3.83
17	.05	2.11	2.41	2.58	2.69	2.78	2.85	2.90	2.95	3.00
	.01	2.90	3.19	3.36	3.47	3.56	3.63	3.69	3.74	3.79
18	.05	2.10	2.40	2.56	2.68	2.76	2.83	2.89	2.94	2.98
	.01	2.88	3.17	3.33	3.44	3.53	3.60	3.66	3.71	3.75
19	.05	2.09	2.39	2.55	2.66	2.75	2.81	2.87	2.92	2.96
	.01	2.86	3.15	3.31	3.42	3.50	3.57	3.63	3.68	3.72
20	.05	2.09	2.38	2.54	2.65	2.73	2.80	2.86	2.90	2.95
	.01	2.85	3.13	3.29	3.40	3.48	3.55	3.60	3.65	3.69
24	.05	2.06	2.35	2.51	2.61	2.70	2.76	2.81	2.86	2.90
	.01	2.80	3.07	3.22	3.32	3.40	3.47	3.52	3.57	3.61
30	.05	2.04	2.32	2.47	2.58	2.66	2.72	2.77	2.82	2.86
	.01	2.75	3.01	3.15	3.25	3.33	3.39	3.44	3.49	3.52
40	.05	2.02	2.29	2.44	2.54	2.62	2.68	2.73	2.77	2.81
	.01	2.70	2.95	3.09	3.19	3.26	3.32	3.37	3.41	3.44

Table A-3   (Continued)
Critical Values of the Dunnett Test for Comparing Treatment Means with a Control

Two-Tailed Comparisons

k = number of treatment means, including control

df_{error}	α_{FW}	2	3	4	5	6	7	8	9	10
60	.05	2.00	2.27	2.41	2.51	2.58	2.64	2.69	2.73	2.77
	.01	2.66	2.90	3.03	3.12	3.19	3.25	3.29	3.33	3.37
120	.05	1.98	2.24	2.38	2.47	2.55	2.60	2.65	2.69	2.73
	.01	2.62	2.85	2.97	3.06	3.12	3.18	3.22	3.26	3.29
∞	.05	1.96	2.21	2.35	2.44	2.51	2.57	2.61	2.65	2.69
	.01	2.58	2.79	2.92	3.00	3.06	3.11	3.15	3.19	3.22

This table is abridged from C. W. Dunnett, New tables for multiple comparisons with a control, *Biometrics*, 1964, *20*, 482–491. With permission of Biometric Society.

One-Tailed Comparisons.

k = number of treatment means, including control

df_{error}	α_{FW}	2	3	4	5	6	7	8	9	10
5	.05	2.02	2.44	2.68	2.85	2.98	3.08	3.16	3.24	3.30
	.01	3.37	3.90	4.21	4.43	4.60	4.73	4.85	4.94	5.03
6	.05	1.94	2.34	2.56	2.71	2.83	2.92	3.00	3.07	3.12
	.01	3.14	3.61	3.88	4.07	4.21	4.33	4.43	4.51	4.59
7	.05	1.89	2.27	2.48	2.62	2.73	2.82	2.89	2.95	3.01
	.01	3.00	3.42	3.66	3.83	3.96	4.07	4.15	4.23	4.30
8	.05	1.86	2.22	2.42	2.55	2.66	2.74	2.81	2.87	2.92
	.01	2.90	3.29	3.51	3.67	3.79	3.88	3.96	4.03	4.09
9	.05	1.83	2.18	2.37	2.50	2.60	2.68	2.75	2.81	2.86
	.01	2.82	3.19	3.40	3.55	3.66	3.75	3.82	3.89	3.94
10	.05	1.81	2.15	2.34	2.47	2.56	2.64	2.70	2.76	2.81
	.01	2.76	3.11	3.31	3.45	3.56	3.64	3.71	3.78	3.83
11	.05	1.80	2.13	2.31	2.44	2.53	2.60	2.67	2.72	2.77
	.01	2.72	3.06	3.25	3.38	3.48	3.56	3.63	3.69	3.74
12	.05	1.78	2.11	2.29	2.41	2.50	2.58	2.64	2.69	2.74
	.01	2.68	3.01	3.19	3.32	3.42	3.50	3.56	3.62	2.67
13	.05	1.77	2.09	2.27	2.39	2.48	2.55	2.61	2.66	2.71
	.01	2.65	2.97	3.15	3.27	3.37	3.44	3.51	3.56	3.61
14	.05	1.76	2.08	2.25	2.37	2.46	2.53	2.59	2.64	2.69
	.01	2.62	2.94	3.11	3.23	3.32	3.40	3.46	3.51	3.56
15	.05	1.75	2.07	2.24	2.36	2.44	2.51	2.57	2.62	2.67
	.01	2.60	2.91	3.08	3.20	3.29	3.36	3.42	3.47	3.52
16	.05	1.75	2.06	2.23	2.34	2.43	2.50	2.56	2.61	2.65
	.01	2.58	2.88	3.05	3.17	3.26	3.33	3.39	3.44	3.48

Table A-3   (Continued)
Critical Values of the Dunnett Test for Comparing Treatment Means with a Control

		One-Tailed Comparisons								
		k = number of treatment means, including control								
df_{error}	α_{FW}	2	3	4	5	6	7	8	9	10
17	.05	1.74	2.05	2.22	2.33	2.42	2.49	2.54	2.59	2.64
	.01	2.57	2.86	3.03	3.14	3.23	3.30	3.36	3.41	3.45
18	.05	1.73	2.04	2.21	2.32	2.41	2.48	2.53	2.58	2.62
	.01	2.55	2.84	3.01	3.12	3.21	3.27	3.33	3.38	3.42
19	.05	1.73	2.03	2.20	2.31	2.40	2.47	2.52	2.57	2.61
	.01	2.54	2.83	2.99	3.10	3.18	3.25	3.31	3.36	3.40
20	.05	1.72	2.03	2.19	2.30	2.39	2.46	2.51	2.56	2.60
	.01	2.53	2.81	2.97	3.08	3.17	3.23	3.29	3.34	3.38
24	.05	1.71	2.01	2.17	2.28	2.36	2.43	2.48	2.53	2.57
	.01	2.49	2.77	2.92	3.03	3.11	3.17	3.22	3.27	3.31
30	.05	1.70	1.99	2.15	2.25	2.33	2.40	2.45	2.50	2.54
	.01	2.46	2.72	2.87	2.97	3.05	3.11	3.16	3.21	3.24
40	.05	1.68	1.97	2.13	2.23	2.31	2.37	2.42	2.47	2.51
	.01	2.42	2.68	2.82	2.92	2.99	3.05	3.10	3.14	3.18
60	.05	1.67	1.95	2.10	2.21	2.28	2.35	2.39	2.44	2.48
	.01	2.39	2.64	2.78	2.87	2.94	3.00	3.04	3.08	3.12
120	.05	1.66	1.93	2.08	2.18	2.26	2.32	2.37	2.41	2.45
	.01	2.36	2.60	2.73	2.82	2.89	2.94	2.99	3.03	3.06
∞	.05	1.64	1.92	2.06	2.16	2.23	2.29	2.34	2.38	2.42
	.01	2.33	2.56	2.68	2.77	2.84	2.89	2.93	2.97	3.00

This table is reproduced from C. W. Dunnett, A multiple comparison procedure for comparing several treatments with a control, *Journal of the American Statistical Association*, 1955, *50*, 1096–1121, by permission of the author and the editor.

Table A-4 (Continued)
Coefficients of Orthogonal Polynomials

Number of Levels	Polynomial	Coefficients							$\Sigma\,(c_i)^2$
3	Linear	−1	0	1					2
	Quadratic	1	−2	1					6
4	Linear	−3	−1	1	3				20
	Quadratic	1	−1	−1	1				4
	Cubic	−1	3	−3	1				20
5	Linear	−2	−1	0	1	2			10
	Quadratic	2	−1	−2	−1	2			14
	Cubic	−1	2	0	−2	1			10
	Quartic	1	−4	6	−4	1			70
6	Linear	−5	−3	−1	1	3	5		70
	Quadratic	5	−1	−4	−4	−1	5		84
	Cubic	−5	7	4	−4	−7	5		180
	Quartic	1	−3	2	2	−3	1		28
	Quintic	−1	5	−10	10	−5	1		252
7	Linear	−3	−2	−1	0	1	2	3	28
	Quadratic	5	0	−3	−4	−3	0	5	84
	Cubic	−1	1	1	0	−1	−1	1	6
	Quartic	3	−7	1	6	1	−7	3	154
	Quintic	−1	4	−5	0	5	−4	1	84

Table A-4 (Continued)
Coefficients of Orthogonal Polynomials

Number of Levels	Polynomial	Coefficients										$\Sigma (c_i)^2$
8	Linear	−7	−5	−3	−1	1	3	5	7			168
	Quadratic	7	1	−3	−5	−5	−3	1	7			168
	Cubic	−7	5	7	3	−3	−7	−5	7			264
	Quartic	7	−13	−3	9	9	−3	−13	7			616
	Quintic	−7	23	−17	−15	15	17	−23	7			2184
9	Linear	−4	−3	−2	−1	0	1	2	3	4		60
	Quadratic	28	7	−8	−17	−20	−17	−8	7	28		2772
	Cubic	−14	7	13	9	0	−9	−13	−7	14		990
	Quartic	14	−21	−11	9	18	9	−11	−21	14		2002
	Quintic	−4	11	−4	−9	0	9	4	−11	4		468
10	Linear	−9	−7	−5	−3	−1	1	3	5	7	9	330
	Quadratic	6	2	−1	−3	−4	−4	−3	−1	2	6	132
	Cubic	−42	14	35	31	12	−12	−31	−35	−14	42	8580
	Quartic	18	−22	−17	3	18	18	3	−17	−22	18	2860
	Quintic	−6	14	−1	−11	−6	6	11	1	−14	6	780

This table is abridged from Table 47 in E. S. Pearson and H. O. Hartley (Eds.), *Biometrika tables for statisticians* (3rd ed., Vol. 1), Cambridge University Press, New York, 1970, by permission of the *Biometrika* Trustees.

Answers to the

Exercises

. . .

NOTE: We have rounded all calculations to two decimal places for ANOVA problems and to four decimal places for MRC problems. You may obtain slightly different final answers if you follow a different method of rounding.

Chapter 4

1a. Average height = 165.53 cm
Average weight = 61.13 kg
 b. The sum of the deviations from the mean is .05 for height and .05 for weight.
 c. $SS_{height} = 1749.73$ d. $\hat{\sigma}^2_{height} = 124.98$ $\hat{\sigma}_{height} = 11.18$
    $SS_{weight} = 1151.73$ $\hat{\sigma}^2_{weight} = 82.27$ $\hat{\sigma}_{weight} = 9.07$

Chapter 5

1a. $r^2_{XY} = .7643$
 b. With Eq. (5-4), $r = .7643$ (carrying the calculations to 4 places). With Eq. (5-5), $r^2 = .5841$ and $r = .7643$.
2a. $Y'_i = -41.50 + .62X_i$. The slope b indicates that a 1-cm increase in height is associated with a .62-kg increase in weight.
 b. 52.12 kg
 c. 61.13 kg. A student with an average height ($\bar{X} = 165.53$ cm) is predicted to have an average weight ($\bar{Y} = 61.13$ kg).

Chapter 6

2a. Average "drug" = 28.67 $\hat{\sigma} = 3.08$ b. $[Y] = 17{,}248$ c. $SS_A = 72.00$
    Average "no drug" = 32.67 $\hat{\sigma} = 4.64$ $[A] = 17{,}000$ $SS_{S/A} = 248.00$
                                                          $[T] = 16{,}928$ $SS_T = 320.00$

d. $MS_A = 72.00$ $df = 1$ e. Summary
   $MS_{S/A} = 15.50$ $df = 16$

Source	SS	df	MS	F
A	72.00	1	72.00	4.65
S/A	248.00	16	15.50	
Total	320.00	17		

Chapter 7

1a. NOTE: We used $+1$ to represent subjects in the drug group and -1 to represent subjects in the nondrug group. $r_{XY} = -.4743$. (If you reversed the code, -1 for the drug group and $+1$ for the nondrug group, $r_{XY} = .4743$.)

b. $Y'_i = 30.67 - 2.00X_i$. The negative slope (and r_{XY}) tells us that the group assigned $+1$ (drug) took *fewer* trials to learn the maze than the group assigned -1 (nondrug). The slope b can also be used to calculate the difference between the two group means.

Chapter 8

1a. Reject H_0 when $F_{observed} \geq 4.49$. The F of 4.65 is significant.
 b. Reject H_0 when $F_{observed} \geq 3.05$. The F is significant.

2a. $F = \dfrac{.2250}{(1 - .2250)/(18 - 2)} = 4.65$

 b. Reject H_0 when $F_{observed} \geq 4.49$. The F is significant.

Chapter 9

2a.

	a_1	a_2
Contrast	$+1$	-1
Dummy	1	0

b. $r^2 = .0883$ $(r = -.2972)$ c. $F = 1.74$

d. Contrast: $Y'_i = 32.85 - 2.25X_i$
   Dummy: $Y'_i = 35.10 - 4.50X_i$

e. For contrast coding, the intercept a (32.85) is the grand mean $\bar{Y}_T$ and the slope b (-2.25) indicates that "do your best" ($+1$) located fewer errors than "specific goal" (-1). For dummy coding, the intercept $(35.10) = \bar{Y}_{A_2}$ and the slope (-4.50) is the difference between the two group means.

Chapter 10

1a. Praise: $\bar{Y}_{A_1} = 5.00$ $\hat{\sigma} = 1.41$ b. ANOVA Summary
Reproof: $\bar{Y}_{A_2} = 7.14$ $\hat{\sigma} = 1.07$
None: $\bar{Y}_{A_3} = 6.00$ $\hat{\sigma} = 1.73$

Source	SS	df	MS	F
A	16.09	2	8.05	3.93*
S/A	36.86	18	2.05	
Total	52.95	20		

* $p < .05$

c. $\hat{\omega}_A^2 = .2180$ d. $R^2_{Y.max.} = \dfrac{SS_A}{SS_T} = \dfrac{16.09}{52.95} = .3039$

2a. $r_{Y1} = -.2571$ $r_{Y2} = .2938$ $r_{12} = .5000$
MRC Summary

Source	R^2	df	Mean R^2	F
A	.3039	2	.1520	3.93*
S/A	.6961	18	.0387	
Total	1.0000	20		

* $p < .05$

b. As an example, $\bar{Y}_{A_1} = 6.0476 - (1.0476)(+1) + (1.0952)(0) = 5.00$

3. $r_{Y1} = .3623$ $r_{Y2} = -.4181$ $r_{12} = -.5000$ $R^2_{Y.max.} = .2061$ $F = 4.28$

Chapter 11

1. For the three comparisons we have chosen:
   Praise vs. none $SS_{A_{comp.}} = 3.50$ $F = 1.71$
   Reproof vs. none $SS_{A_{comp.}} = 4.55$ $F = 2.22$
   Praise vs. reproof $SS_{A_{comp.}} = 16.03$ $F = 7.82*$
   *$p < .05$
2. Praise vs. none $r^2_{comp.} = .0661$ $F = 1.71$
   Reproof vs. none $r^2_{comp.} = .0863$ $F = 2.23$
   Praise vs. reproof $r^2_{comp.} = .3035$ $F = 7.84*$
   *$p < .05$

Chapter 12

1a. Tukey test (only pairwise differences are under consideration)
  b. Dunnett test (only comparisons between the verbal groups and the none group are under consideration)
  c. Scheffé test (a mixture of pairwise and complex comparisons is under consideration)
2a. $\bar{d}_T = \dfrac{(3.61)\sqrt{2.05}}{\sqrt{7}} = 1.95$. Any difference > 1.95 is significant.

b. $\bar{d}_D$ (two-tailed test) $= \dfrac{(2.40)\sqrt{2(2.05)}}{\sqrt{7}} = 1.83$. Any difference ≥ 1.83 is significant.

$\bar{d}_D$ (one-tailed test) $= \dfrac{(2.04)\sqrt{2(2.05)}}{\sqrt{7}} = 1.55$. Any difference ≥ 1.55 is significant.

c. $F_S = (3-1)(3.55) = 7.10$. Any $F_{comp.} \geq 7.10$ is significant.

Chapter 13

1a. ANOVA Summary

Source	SS	df	MS	F
A	.19	2	.10	<1
B	961.93	1	961.93	317.47*
A × B	36.57	2	18.29	6.04*
S/AB	109.14	36	3.03	
Total	1107.83	41		

* $p < .01$

c. MRC Summary

Source	R²	df	Mean R²	F
A	.0002	2	.0001	<1
B	.8683	1	.8683	321.59*
A × B	.0330	2	.0165	6.11*
S/AB	.0985	36	.0027	
Total	1.0000	41		

* $p < .01$

NOTE: The discrepancies between the F's for ANOVA and MRC are from rounding error; with sufficiently precise calculations, the corresponding F's will be identical.

Chapter 14

1a. ANOVA Summary

Source	SS	df	MS	F
A at b_1	16.09	2	8.05	2.66
A at b_2	20.66	2	10.33	3.41*
B at a_1	492.07	1	492.07	162.40**
B at a_2	185.79	1	185.79	61.32**
B at a_3	320.65	1	320.65	105.83**
S/AB	109.14	36	3.03	

* $p < .05$
** $p < .01$

b. MRC Summary

Source	R^2	df	Mean R^2	F
A at b_1	.0145	2	.0073	2.70
A at b_2	.0187	2	.0094	3.48*
B at a_1	.4442	1	.4442	164.52**
B at a_2	.1677	1	.1677	62.11**
B at a_3	.2894	1	.2894	107.19**
S/AB	.0985	36	.0027	

* $p < .05$
** $p < .01$

NOTE: The discrepancies between the F's for ANOVA and MRC are from rounding error; with sufficiently precise calculations, the corresponding F's will be identical.

Chapter 15

1a. ANOVA Summary

Source	SS	df	MS	F
Comp. 1	36.55	1	36.55	12.06*
Comp. 2	.00	1	.00	<1
S/AB	109.14	36	3.03	

* $p < .01$

b. MRC Summary

Source	R^2	df	Mean R^2	F
Comp. 1	.0330	1	.0330	12.22*
Comp. 2	.0000	1	.0000	<1
S/AB	.0985	36	.0027	

* $p < .01$

Chapter 16

1a. ANOVA Summary

Source	SS	df	MS	F
A	16.09	2	8.05	3.63
S	10.28	6	1.71	
$A \times S$	26.58	12	2.22	
Total	52.95	20		

b,c. ANOVA Summary

Source	SS	df	MS	F
Comp. 1	16.03	1	16.03	10.15*
$A_{comp.1} \times S$	9.47	6	1.58	
Comp. 2	.02	1	.02	<1
$A_{comp.2} \times S$	17.15	6	2.86	

* $p < .01$

2a. MRC Summary

Source	R^2	df	Mean R^2	F
A	.3040	2	.1520	3.64
S	.1942	6	.0324	
$A \times S$	.5018	12	.0418	
Total	1.0000	20		

b,c. MRC Summary

Source	R^2	df	Mean R^2	F
Comp. 1	.3035	1	.3035	10.22*
$A_{comp.1} \times S$	.1781	6	.0297	
Comp. 2	.0004	1	.0004	<1
$A_{comp.2} \times S$	.3237	6	.0540	

* $p < .01$

Chapter 17

1a. ANOVA Summary

Source	SS	df	MS	F
A	60.67	2	30.34	<1
S/A	359.75	9	39.97	
B	28.42	3	9.47	3.36*
A × B	106.83	6	17.81	6.32**
B × S/A	76.25	27	2.82	
Total	631.92	47		

* $p < .05$
** $p < 0.1$

b. MRC Summary

Source	R^2	df	Mean R^2	F
A	.0960	2	.0480	<1
S/A	.5693	9	.0633	
B	.0450	3	.0150	3.33*
A × B	.1691	6	.0282	6.27**
B × S/A	.1206	27	.0045	
Total	1.0000	47		

* $p < .05$
** $p < .01$

Chapter 18

1. ANOVA Summary

Source	SS	df	MS	F
B at a_1	86.75	3	28.92	22.08*
B × S at a_1	11.75	9	1.31	
B at a_2	37.25	3	12.42	21.41*
B × S at a_2	5.25	9	.58	
B at a_3	11.25	3	3.75	<1
B × S at a_3	59.25	9	6.58	

* $p < .01$

MRC Summary

Source	R^2	df	Mean R^2	F
B at a_1	.1373	3	.0458	21.81*
B × S at a_1	.0186	9	.0021	
B at a_2	.0589	3	.0196	21.78*
B × S at a_2	.0083	9	.0009	
B at a_3	.0178	3	.0059	<1
B × S at a_3	.0938	9	.0104	

* $p < .01$

2. ANOVA Summary

Source	SS	df	MS	F
A at b_1	3.50	2	1.75	<1
S/A at b_1	108.50	9	12.06	
A at b_2	4.17	2	2.09	<1
S/A at b_2	94.75	9	10.53	
A at b_3	12.67	2	6.34	<1
S/A at b_3	148.25	9	16.47	
A at b_4	147.17	2	73.59	7.84*
S/A at b_4	84.50	9	9.39	

* $p < .01$

MRC Summary

Source	R^2	df	Mean R^2	F
A at b_1	.0055	2	.0028	<1
S/A at b_1	.1717	9	.0191	
A at b_2	.0066	2	.0033	<1
S/A at b_2	.1499	9	.0167	
A at b_3	.0200	2	.0100	<1
S/A at b_3	.2346	9	.0261	
A at b_4	.2329	2	.1165	7.82*
S/A at b_4	.1337	9	.0149	

* $p < .01$

3a. Summary

Source	ANOVA				MRC			
	SS	df	MS	F	R^2	df	Mean R^2	F
$A_{comp.} \times B_{comp.}$	95.06	1	95.06	64.67*	.1504	1	.1504	65.39*
$B_{comp.} \times S/A$	13.24	9	1.47		.0210	9	.0023	

* $p < .01$

3b. Summary

Source	ANOVA				MRC			
	SS	df	MS	F	R^2	df	Mean R^2	F
$A_{comp.} \times B_{comp.}$	18.06	1	18.06	12.29*	.0286	1	.0286	12.43*
$B_{comp.} \times S/A$	13.24	9	1.47		.0210	9	.0023	

* $p < .01$

Chapter 19

1. Treatment Source	Error Term Source
A	$A \times S$
B	$B \times S$
C	$C \times S$
S	—
$A \times B$	$A \times B \times S$
$A \times C$	$A \times C \times S$
$B \times C$	$B \times C \times S$
$A \times B \times C$	$A \times B \times C \times S$

2b. Main effects: A, B, C, D
Two-way interactions: $A \times B, \quad A \times C, \quad A \times D, \quad B \times C, \quad B \times D, \quad C \times D$
Three-way interactions: $A \times B \times C, \quad A \times B \times D, \quad A \times C \times D, \quad B \times C \times D$
Four-way interaction: $A \times B \times C \times D$

3a,b. S/ABC for $A, B, C, A \times B, \quad A \times C, \quad B \times C, \quad A \times B \times C$
$D \times S/ABC$ for $D, A \times D, B \times D, C \times D, A \times B \times D, A \times C \times D, B \times C \times D, A \times B \times C \times D$

4a,b. S/AB for $A, B, A \times B$
$C \times S/AB$ for $C, A \times C, \quad B \times C, \quad A \times B \times C$
$D \times S/AB$ for $D, A \times D, \quad B \times D, \quad A \times B \times D$
$C \times D \times S/AB$ for $C \times D, \quad A \times C \times D, \quad B \times C \times D, \quad A \times B \times C \times D$

Chapter 20

1a. $R^2_{Y.max.} = .7314$; $F = \dfrac{.7314/3}{(1 - .7314)/(20 - 3 - 1)} = 14.51 \ (p < .01)$

b. Summary of the forward stepwise MRC analysis

Step	Variable Entered	R^2	Increment	F
1	X_3	.6543	—	38.95*
2	X_1	.7001	.0458	2.73
3	X_2	.7314	.0313	1.86

* $p < .01$

$$F_{step\,1} = \frac{.6543/1}{(1 - .7314)/(20 - 3 - 1)}$$

$$F_{step\,2} = \frac{.0458/(2 - 1)}{(1 - .7314)/(20 - 3 - 1)}$$

$$F_{step\,3} = \frac{.0313/(3 - 2)}{(1 - .7314)/(20 - 3 - 1)}$$

c. We entered the variables in a roughly temporal order: the bar examination was taken before the individuals practiced law, of course, and the winning of at least some cases would probably occur before any money was brought into the firm. (The validity of our "theory" is not important except that it illustrates the reasoning behind the choice of a particular ordering of the variables.)

Step	Variable Entered	R^2	Increment	F
1	X_1	.5921	—	35.24**
2	X_2	.6428	.0507	3.02
3	X_3	.7314	.0886	5.27*

* $p < .05$
** $p < .01$

$$F_{step\,1} = \frac{.5921/1}{(1 - .7314)/(20 - 3 - 1)}$$

$$F_{step\,2} = \frac{.0507/(2 - 1)}{(1 - .7314)/(20 - 3 - 1)}$$

$$F_{step\,3} = \frac{.0886/(3 - 2)}{(1 - .7314)/(20 - 3 - 1)}$$

Chapter 21

1a. Summary

Step	Variable Entered	R^2	Increment	F
1	X_1	.5921	—	24.88*
2	X_4	.5948	.0027	<1

* $p < .01$

$$F_{step\,1} = \frac{.5921/1}{(1 - .5948)/(20 - 2 - 1)}$$

$$F_{step\,2} = \frac{.0027/(2 - 1)}{(1 - .5948)/(20 - 2 - 1)}$$

Gender has no significant increment on the relationship between success (Y) and exam score (X_1).

b. Summary of the hierarchical MRC analysis

Step 1 Test of the interaction of bar examination and gender:

$$R^2_{Y.1,4,1\times4} - R^2_{Y.1,4} = .6025 - .5948 = .0077 \qquad F = \frac{.0077/(3 - 2)}{(1 - .6025)/(20 - 3 - 1)}$$
$$= .31$$

Step 2 Test of the difference between the intercepts for males and females:

$$R^2_{Y.1,4} - R^2_{Y.1} = .5948 - .5921 = .0027 \qquad F = \frac{.0027/(2 - 1)}{(1 - .6025)/(20 - 3 - 1)} = .11$$

Step 3 Test of the usefulness of the bar examination:

$$R^2_{Y.1,4} - R^2_{Y.4} = .5948 - .0163 = .5785 \qquad F = \frac{.5785/(2 - 1)}{(1 - .6025)/(20 - 3 - 1)}$$
$$= 23.33 (p < .01)$$

We can conclude from this analysis that the bar examination is not biased by gender and that it strongly predicts the success of the lawyers in this firm.

Chapter 22

1a. ANOVA and MRC Summaries

	ANOVA				MRC			
Source	SS	df	MS	F	R^2	df	Mean R^2	F
$A_{(adj.)}$	24.50	2	12.25	7.52*	.4629	2	.2315	7.52*
$S/A_{(adj.)}$	27.73	17	1.63		.5236	17	.0308	

* $p < .01$

b. ANOVA
$$\bar{Y}'_{A_i} = \bar{Y}_{A_i} - (.3873)(\bar{X}_{A_i} - \bar{X}_T)$$
$$\bar{Y}'_{A_1} = 5.00 - (.3873)(11.57 - 10.57) = 4.61$$
$$\bar{Y}'_{A_2} = 7.14 - (.3873)(9.43 - 10.57) = 7.58$$
$$\bar{Y}'_{A_3} = 6.00 - (.3873)(10.71 - 10.57) = 5.95$$

MRC
$$\bar{Y}'_{A_i} = .3873\,\bar{X}_T - 1.4864\,A1_i + .0515\,A2_i + 1.9531$$
$$\bar{Y}'_{A_1} = (.3873)(10.57) - (1.4864)(+1) + (.0515)(+1) + 1.9531 = 4.61$$
$$\bar{Y}'_{A_2} = (.3873)(10.57) - (1.4864)(-1) + (.0515)(+1) + 1.9531 = 7.58$$
$$\bar{Y}'_{A_3} = (.3873)(10.57) - (1.4864)(0) + (.0515)(-2) + 1.9531 = 5.94$$

c. ANOVA and MRC Summaries

Source	ANOVA				MRC			
	SS	df	MS	F	SS	df	MS	F
Comp. 1	30.87	1	30.87	16.69*	30.87	1	30.87	16.69*
Comp. 2	.11	1	.11	<1	.12	1	.12	<1
MS'_{error}		17	1.85			17	1.85	

* $p < .01$

$$MS'_{error}(\text{ANOVA}) = (1.63)\left(1 + \frac{8.14}{60.86}\right) \qquad MS'_{error}(\text{MRC}) = (.0308)(52.95)\left(1 + \frac{.2111/2^{\bullet}}{1 - .2111}\right)$$

Chapter 23

1a,b. ANOVA and MRC Summary

Source	ANOVA				MRC			
	SS	df	MS	F	R^2	df	Mean R^2	F
A	(16.09)	(2)			(.3039)	(2)		
Linear	3.50	1	3.50	1.71	.0661	1	.0661	1.71
Quadratic	12.55	1	12.55	6.12*	.2379	1	.2379	6.15*
S/A	36.86	18	2.05		.6961	18	.0387	
Total	52.95	20			1.0000	20		

* $p < .05$

c. MRC Summary (carried to 6 places to reduce rounding error)

Source	R^2	df	Mean R^2	F
A	(.303935)	(2)		
Linear	.066097	1	.066097	1.71
Quadratic	.237838	1	.237838	6.15*
S/A	.696065	18	.038670	

* $p < .05$

2a. See Table 23-6   b. See Table 23-7

3. $r_{YX} = .898579$ $r_{YX^2} = .873267$ $r_{XX^2} = .985254$ $R^2_{Y.XX^2} = .812400$
   $R^2_{Y.lin.} = .807444$ $R^2_{Y.quad.} = .812400 - .807444 = .004956$

Source	R^2	df	Mean R^2	F
Linear	.807444	1	.807444	116.21*
Quadratic	.004956	1	.004956	<1

* $p < .01$

$$F_{lin.} = \frac{.807444/1}{(1 - .812400)/(30 - 2 - 1)} \quad F_{quad.} = \frac{.004956/(2 - 1)}{(1 - .812400)/(30 - 2 - 1)}$$

Chapter 24

1a. ANOVA Summary (Unweighted Means Analysis)

Source	SS	df	MS	F
A	17.68	2	8.84	4.21*
S/A	35.69	17	2.10	

* $p < .05$

b. ANOVA Summary (Weighted Means Analysis)

Source	SS	df	MS	F
A	17.27	2	8.64	4.11*
S/A	35.69	17	2.10	

* $p < .05$

c. MRC Summary

Source	R^2	df	Mean R^2	F
A	.3259	2	.1630	4.11*
S/A	.6741	17	.0397	

* $p < .05$

2a. ANOVA Summary (Unweighted Means Analysis)

Source	SS	df	MS	F
A	.04	2	.02	<1
B	946.00	1	946.00	307.14*
A × B	38.22	2	19.11	6.20*
S/AB	107.97	35	3.08	

* $p < .01$

b. MRC Summary

Source	R^2	df	Mean R^2	F
A	.0000	2	.0000	<1
B	.8735	1	.8735	311.96*
A × B	.0348	2	.0174	6.21*
S/AB	.0996	35	.0028	

* $p < .01$

Author Index

· · ·

Subject Index

· · ·